EXAM ✓ PREP

MCSA/MCSE 70-290 Exam Prep:

Managing and Maintaining a Microsoft® Windows Server™ 2003 Environment

Lee Scales

MCSA/MCSE 70-290 Exam Prep: Managing and Maintaining a Microsoft® Windows Server™ 2003 Environment

Copyright © 2007 by Que Publishing

International Standard Book Number: 0-7897-3648-9

Printed in the United States of America

First Printing: November 2006

09 08 07 06   4 3 2 1

Trademarks

All terms mentioned in this book that are known to be trademarks or service marks have been appropriately capitalized. Que Publishing cannot attest to the accuracy of this information. Use of a term in this book should not be regarded as affecting the validity of any trademark or service mark.

Microsoft is a registered trademark of Microsoft Corporation.

Windows Server is a trademark of Microsoft Corporation.

Warning and Disclaimer

Every effort has been made to make this book as complete and as accurate as possible, but no warranty or fitness is implied. The information provided is on an "as is" basis. The author and the publisher shall have neither liability nor responsibility to any person or entity with respect to any loss or damages arising from the information contained in this book.

Bulk Sales

Que Publishing offers excellent discounts on this book when ordered in quantity for bulk purchases or special sales. For more information, please contact

U.S. Corporate and Government Sales

1-800-382-3419

corpsales@pearsontechgroup.com

For sales outside the United States, please contact

International Sales

international@pearsoned.com

Library of Congress Cataloging-in-Publication Data

Scales, Lee.

  MCSA/MCSE 70-290 exam prep : planning and maintaining a Microsoft Windows server 2003 network infrastructure / Lee Scales.

     p. cm.

  Includes index.

  ISBN 0-7897-3648-9 (pbk.)

  1. Electronic data processing personnel--Certification. 2. Microsoft software--Examinations--Study guides. 3. Microsoft Windows server. I. Title.

  QA76.3.S322 2006

  005.4'476--dc22

                        2006034410

PUBLISHER
Paul Boger

ACQUISITIONS EDITOR
Betsy Brown

DEVELOPMENT EDITOR
Deadline Driven Publishing

MANAGING EDITOR
Patrick Kanouse

PROJECT EDITOR
Tonya Simpson

COPY EDITOR
Barbara Hacha

INDEXER
Heather McNeill

PROOFREADER
Juli Cook

TECHNICAL EDITOR
Marc Savage

PUBLISHING COORDINATOR
Vanessa Evans

INTERIOR DESIGNER
Anne Jones

COVER DESIGNER
Gary Adair

PAGE LAYOUT
Mark Shirar

Contents at a Glance

Part III: Appendixes

Table of Contents

About the Author

Lee Scales holds the MCSE+I (NT4) as well as the MCSE (W2K/W2K3) certifications and has been working in the computer industry for more than 25 years, including employment and consulting engagements with several Fortune 100 companies. He is currently employed as a senior consultant with a Microsoft Gold Partner, where his duties include working with companies that are migrating to the Windows Server 2003 platform with Active Directory.

In addition to his consulting duties, he has been developing courseware for the Windows platform for several years and has been a contributing author and coauthor to titles in the original *Exam Cram*, *Exam Cram 2*, and *Windows Power Toolkit* series. When time allows, he also contributes articles to various technical magazines and websites.

When not buried neck deep in a networking project, Lee enjoys camping, hunting, and fishing, especially in places where you can't plug in a laptop and where the cell phone doesn't work.

Lee lives in Overland Park, Kansas with his son, Davin, and daughter, Alayanna. You can reach Lee at leescales@hotmail.com.

Dedication

To the true highlights of my life, Davin and Alayanna.

Acknowledgments

Many people have worked hard to make this book possible. It is my great pleasure to acknowledge the efforts of these people.

First, special thanks to Ed Tittel, for giving me my first writing job and always finding writing projects for me.

Thanks to my technical editor, Marc Savage, for sharing his technical expertise and reviewing the contents of this book for correctness. His constructive comments and suggestions also ensured that I did not miss anything that is of importance to the exam.

I would also thank the many individuals at Pearson who were working behind the scenes to take the final manuscript and put it between covers and on the shelf.

And last, but definitely not least, a very, very special thanks to my son, Davin, and daughter, Alayanna, who were both very understanding on those days when Daddy couldn't come out and play.

We Want to Hear from You!

As the reader of this book, *you* are our most important critic and commentator. We value your opinion and want to know what we're doing right, what we could do better, what areas you'd like to see us publish in, and any other words of wisdom you're willing to pass our way.

As a publisher for Que Publishing, I welcome your comments. You can email or write me directly to let me know what you did or didn't like about this book—as well as what we can do to make our books better.

Please note that I cannot help you with technical problems related to the topic of this book. We do have a User Services group, however, where I will forward specific technical questions related to the book.

When you write, please be sure to include this book's title and author as well as your name, email address, and phone number. I will carefully review your comments and share them with the author and editors who worked on the book.

Email: scorehigher@pearsoned.com

Mail: Paul Boger
          Publisher
          Que Publishing
          800 East 96th Street
          Indianapolis, IN 46240 USA

Reader Services

Visit our website and register this book at www.examcram.com/register for convenient access to any updates, downloads, or errata that might be available for this book.

Introduction

This book, *MCSA/MCSE 70-290 Exam Prep* (Exam 70-290), is for technicians, system administrators, and other technical professionals who are pursuing the goal of becoming a Microsoft Certified System Administrator (MCSA) or Microsoft Certified System Engineer (MCSE). This book covers the Managing and Maintaining a Windows Server 2003 Environment exam (70-290), which is a core exam for both of those certifications. The exam is designed to measure your skill in managing and maintaining servers in a Windows Server 2003 environment.

This book is designed to cover all the objectives Microsoft created for this exam. It doesn't offer end-to-end coverage of Windows 2003; rather, it helps you develop the specific core competencies that Microsoft says administrators who support Windows Server 2003 will need to master. You can pass the exam by learning the material in this book, without taking a class. Of course, depending on your own personal study habits and learning style, you might benefit from studying this book *and* taking a class.

Even if you are not planning to take the exam, you may find this book useful. The wide range of topics covered by the Microsoft exam objectives will certainly help you to accomplish the server-management tasks at your job. Experienced MCSA/MCSEs looking for a reference on the new features of Windows Server 2003 R2 in particular should appreciate the coverage of topics here. Also, this book has been updated to include coverage of service pack releases up to SP2.

How This Book Helps You

This book gives you a self-guided tour of all the areas of the product that are covered by the Managing and Maintaining a Windows Server 2003 Environment exam. The goal is to teach you the specific skills that you need to achieve your MCSA or MCSE certification. You will also find helpful hints, tips, examples, exercises, and references to additional study materials. Specifically, this book is set up to help you in the ways detailed in the following subsections.

Organization

This book is organized around the individual objectives from Microsoft's preparation guide for the Managing and Maintaining a Windows Server 2003 Environment exam. Every objective is covered in this book. These objectives are not covered in exactly the same order you will find them on the official preparation guide (which you can download from http://www.microsoft.com/learning/exams/70-290.asp) but are reorganized for more logical teaching. We have also tried to make the information more accessible in several ways:

▶ After this introduction is the full list of exam topics and objectives.

▶ After the introduction you will also encounter the "Study and Exam Tips" section. Read this section early on to help you develop study strategies. It also provides you with valuable exam-day tips and information.

▶ Each chapter starts with a list of objectives that are covered in that chapter.

▶ Each chapter also begins with an outline that provides an overview of the material for that chapter as well as the page numbers where specific topics can be found.

▶ We have also repeated each objective in the text where it is covered in detail.

Instructional Features

This book has been designed to provide you with multiple ways to learn and reinforce the exam material. Here are some of the instructional features you'll find inside:

▶ *Objective explanations*—As mentioned previously, each chapter begins with a list of the objectives covered in the chapter. In addition, immediately following each objective is a more detailed explanation that puts the objective in the context of the product.

▶ *Study strategies*—Each chapter also offers a selected list of study strategies—exercises to try or additional material to read that will help you learn and retain the material you'll find in the chapter.

▶ *Exam alerts*—Exam alerts appear in the margin to provide specific exam-related advice. Such tips might address what material is likely to be covered (or not covered) on the exam, how to remember it, or particular exam quirks.

▶ *Challenge exercises*—These exercises offer you additional opportunities to practice the material within a chapter and to learn additional facets of the topic at hand.

▶ *Key terms*—A list of key terms appears at the end of each chapter. You'll find definitions for these terms in the Glossary.

▶ *Notes*—These appear in the margin and contain various kinds of useful information, such as tips on technology, historical background, side commentary, or notes on where to go for more detailed coverage of a particular topic.

▶ *Cautions*—When using sophisticated computing technology, there is always the possibility of mistakes or even catastrophes. Cautions appear to alert you of such potential problems, whether they are in following along with the text or in implementing Windows Server 2003 in a production environment.

▶ *Step by Steps*—These are hands-on tutorial instructions that lead you through a particular task or function relevant to the exam objectives.

▶ *Exercises*—Found at the end of each chapter in the "Apply Your Knowledge" section, the exercises may include additional tutorial material and more chances to practice the skills you learned in the chapter.

Extensive Practice Test Options

The book provides numerous opportunities for you to assess your knowledge and practice for the exam. The practice options include the following:

▶ *Exam questions*—These questions also appear in the "Apply Your Knowledge" section. They reflect the kinds of multiple-choice questions that appear on the Microsoft exams. Use them to practice for the exam and to help you determine what you know and what you may need to review or study further. Answers and explanations are provided later in the section.

▶ *Practice Exam and Practice Exam Answers*—The "Final Review" section includes a complete practice exam and the answers to the practice exam. The "Final Review" section and the Practice Exam are discussed in more detail later in this chapter.

▶ *MeasureUp*—The MeasureUp software included on the CD-ROM provides additional practice questions.

Final Review

This part of the book provides you with the following valuable tools for preparing for the exam:

▶ *Fast Facts*—This condensed version of the information contained in the book will prove extremely useful for last-minute review.

▶ *Practice Exam*—A full practice test for the exam is included. Questions are written in the style and format used on the actual exams. Use it to assess your readiness for the real thing.

This book includes several valuable appendixes as well:

▶ Appendix A, "Accessing Your Free MeasureUp Practice Test—Including Networking Simulations!"

▶ Appendix B, "MeasureUp's Product Features"

▶ Appendix C, "Glossary"

These and all the other book features mentioned previously will provide you with thorough preparation for the exam.

For more information about the exam or the certification process, you should contact Microsoft directly:

- ▶ By email: `mailto:MCPHelp@microsoft.com`.

- ▶ By regular mail, telephone, or fax, contact the Microsoft Regional Education Service Center (RESC) nearest you. You can find lists of Regional Education Service Centers at www.microsoft.com/traincert/support/northamerica.asp (for North America) or www.microsoft.com/traincert/support/worldsites.asp (worldwide).

- ▶ On the Internet: www.microsoft.com/traincert/.

What You Should Know Before Reading This Book

The Microsoft Managing and Maintaining a Windows Server 2003 Environment exam assumes that you are familiar with Active Directory and networking in general, even though there are no objectives that pertain directly to this knowledge. We show you tasks that are directly related to the exam objectives, but this book does not include a tutorial in working with the finer points of Active Directory and networking. If you are just getting started with Microsoft Windows and networking, you should check out some of the references at the end of each chapter for the information you will need to get started. For beginners, we particularly recommend these references:

- ▶ *Mastering Windows Server 2003*, by Mark Minasi (Sybex, 2003). This is an excellent starting point for information on Windows Server 2003 and common tasks.

- ▶ *Windows XP Power Pack*, by Stu Sjouwerman, et al. (Que Publishing, 2003).

- ▶ *Microsoft Windows Server 2003 Delta Guide*, by Don Jones and Mark Rouse (Sams Publishing, 2003). This is a great book to have if you are already familiar with Windows 2000.

- ▶ *Microsoft Windows Server 2003 Unleashed R2 Edition*, by Rand Morimoto, et al. (Sams Publishing, 2006). This book covers the R2 features that we don't cover here.

Hardware and Software You'll Need

This volume is intended to be a self-paced study guide. As such, the concepts presented are intended to be reinforced by the reader through hands-on experience. To obtain the best results from your studies, you should have as much exposure to Windows Server 2003 as possible. The best way to do this is to combine your studies with as much lab time as possible. In this section, we will make some suggestions on setting up a test lab to provide you with a solid practice environment.

Microsoft Windows Server 2003 is available in the following versions:

▶ *Standard Edition*—Microsoft Windows Server 2003 Standard Edition is the entry-level product in the product line. This edition is designed for the small- to medium-sized environments and departmental servers.

▶ *Enterprise Edition*—Windows Server 2003 Enterprise Edition is designed for medium to large environments. It includes features for enterprise environments, such as clustering and support for up to eight processors and 32GB of memory.

▶ *Datacenter Edition*—Windows Server 2003 Datacenter Edition is designed for high availability and large environments. It includes support for up to 32 processors and 64GB of memory. This version is only available preinstalled on high-end hardware.

▶ *Web Edition*—Microsoft Windows Server 2003, Web Edition is positioned and priced as a lower-cost web platform. As such, it doesn't support features such as Terminal Services in Application mode, nor can it be used as a domain controller.

You should be able to complete all the exercises in this book with any of the first three editions of Windows Server 2003. (If you can afford to use a datacenter server as your lab machine, invite me over.) Your computer should meet the minimum criteria required for a Windows Server 2003 installation:

▶ Pentium or better CPU running at 133MHz or faster

▶ Minimum of 128MB RAM

▶ 2GB of disk space for a full installation

▶ CD-ROM or DVD drive

▶ Video card running at 800×600 with at least 256 colors

▶ Microsoft or compatible mouse

Of course, those are *minimum* requirements. I recommend the following, more realistic, requirements:

▶ Pentium III or better CPU running at 550MHz or faster

▶ At least 256 MB of RAM, and as much more as you can afford

▶ 5GB of disk space for a full installation

▶ CD-ROM or DVD drive

▶ Video card running at 1280×1024 or higher with at least 65,000 colors

▶ NIC

▶ Suitable switch or hub

▶ Microsoft or compatible mouse

In addition to a machine running Windows Server 2003, you might want one or more client workstations to test accessing shares over the network, Terminal Services, and other functions. For best results, Windows 2000 or Windows XP clients are recommended because they are required to support features such as Group Policy and the Software Update Service—items that will probably appear on the exam.

Two products that have proven invaluable to us in the writing field are VMWare (www.vmware.com) and Microsoft Virtual PC (www.microsoft.com). These products enable you to create and run multiple virtual client sessions on your PC.

Microsoft, of course, is highly motivated to spread the word about Windows Server 2003 to as many people as possible. So you can download trial versions of Windows Server 2003, along with other Microsoft products, at http://www.microsoft.com/windowsserver2003/evaluation/trial/default.mspx.

You might find it easier to obtain access to the necessary computer hardware and software in a corporate environment. It can be difficult, however, to allocate enough time within a busy workday to complete a self-study program. Most of your study time will probably need to occur outside normal working hours, away from the everyday interruptions and pressures of your job.

70-290 Exam Objectives Quick Reference

Managing and Maintaining a Microsoft Windows Server 2003 Environment

What Exam 70-290 Covers

The Managing and Maintaining a Windows Server 2003 Environment exam covers five major topic areas:

- ► Managing and maintaining physical and logical devices
- ► Managing users, computers, and groups
- ► Managing and maintaining access to resources
- ► Managing and maintaining a server environment
- ► Managing and implementing disaster recovery

The exam objectives are listed by topic area in the following sections.

Continues on Following Page

Study and Exam Preparation Tips

Those of us who have been in the business for a while have lived through the old days when after taking an exam we thoroughly understood the term "paper certified." These days it is far more difficult to pass a Microsoft exam without having a fair amount of experience with the product under your belt. The changes that Microsoft has made to the exams require you to know the material well, so when confronted with a problem or a simulated scenario, you can handle the challenge. With the newer exams, Microsoft has made it clear that as far as the MCSE or MCSA certifications are concerned, quality beats quantity.

This element of the book provides you with some general guidelines for preparing for any certification exam, including Exam 70-290, "Managing and Maintaining a Microsoft Windows Server 2003 Environment." It is organized into four sections. The first section addresses learning styles and how they affect preparation for the exam. The second section covers exam-preparation activities and general study tips. This is followed by an extended look at the Microsoft certification exams, including a number of specific tips that apply to the various Microsoft exam formats and question types. Finally, changes in Microsoft's testing policies and how they might affect you are discussed.

Learning Styles

To best understand the nature of preparation for the test, it is important to understand learning as a process. You are probably aware of how you best learn new material. You might find that outlining works best for you, or, as a visual learner, you might need to see things. You might need models or examples, or maybe you just like exploring the interface. Whatever your learning style, test preparation takes place over time. Obviously, you shouldn't start studying for a certification exam the night before you take it; it is very important to understand that learning is a developmental process. Understanding learning as a process helps you focus on what you know and what you have yet to learn.

Thinking about how you learn should help you recognize that learning takes place when you are able to match new information to old. You have some previous experience with computers and networking. Now you are preparing for this certification exam. Using this book, software, and supplementary materials will not just add incrementally to what you know; as you study, the organization of your knowledge actually restructures as you integrate new information into your existing knowledge base. This leads you to a more comprehensive understanding of the tasks and concepts outlined in the objectives and of computing in general. Again, this happens as a result of a repetitive process rather than a single event. If you keep this model of learning in mind as you prepare for the exam, you will make better decisions concerning what to study and how much more studying you need to do.

Study Tips

There are many ways to approach studying, just as there are many different types of material to study. However, the tips that follow should work well for the type of material covered on Microsoft certification exams.

Study Strategies

Although individuals vary in the ways they learn information, some basic principles of learning apply to everyone. You should adopt some study strategies that take advantage of these principles. One of these principles is that learning can be broken into various depths. Recognition (of terms, for example) exemplifies a rather surface level of learning in which you rely on a prompt of some sort to elicit recall. Comprehension or understanding (of the concepts behind the terms, for example) represents a deeper level of learning than recognition. The ability to analyze a concept and apply your understanding of it in a new way represents further depth of learning.

Your learning strategy should enable you to know the material at a level or two deeper than mere recognition. This will help you perform well on the exams. You will know the material so thoroughly that you can go beyond the recognition-level types of questions commonly used in fact-based multiple-choice testing. You will be able to apply your knowledge to solve new problems.

Macro and Micro Study Strategies

One strategy that can lead to deep learning includes preparing an outline that covers all the objectives and subobjectives for the particular exam you are working on. You should delve a bit further into the material and include a level or two of detail beyond the stated objectives and subobjectives for the exam. Then you should expand the outline by coming up with a statement of definition or a summary for each point in the outline.

An outline provides two approaches to studying. First, you can study the outline by focusing on the organization of the material. You can work your way through the points and subpoints of your outline, with the goal of learning how they relate to one another. For example, you should be sure you understand how each of the main objective areas for Exam 70-290 is similar to and different from another. Then you should do the same thing with the subobjectives; you should be sure you know which subobjectives pertain to each objective area and how they relate to one another.

Next, you can work through the outline, focusing on learning the details. You should memorize and understand terms and their definitions, facts, rules and tactics, advantages and disadvantages, and so on. In this pass through the outline, you should attempt to learn detail rather than the big picture (the organizational information that you worked on in the first pass through the outline).

Research has shown that attempting to assimilate both types of information at the same time interferes with the overall learning process. If you separate your studying into these two approaches, you will perform better on the exam.

Active Study Strategies

The process of writing down and defining objectives, subobjectives, terms, facts, and definitions promotes a more active learning strategy than merely reading the material does. In human information-processing terms, writing forces you to engage in more active encoding of the information. Simply reading over the information leads to more passive processing.

You need to determine whether you can apply the information you have learned by attempting to create examples and scenarios on your own. You should think about how or where you could apply the concepts you are learning. Again, you should write down this information to process the facts and concepts in an active fashion.

The hands-on nature of the exercises at the end of each chapter provides further active learning opportunities that will reinforce concepts as well.

Common-Sense Strategies

You should follow common-sense practices when studying: You should study when you are alert, reduce or eliminate distractions, and take breaks when you become fatigued.

Pretesting Yourself

Pretesting allows you to assess how well you are learning. One of the most important aspects of learning is what has been called *meta-learning*. Meta-learning has to do with realizing when you know something well or when you need to study some more. In other words, you recognize how well or how poorly you have learned the material you are studying.

For most people, this can be difficult to assess. Review questions, practice questions, and practice tests are useful in that they reveal objectively what you have learned and what you have not learned. You should use this information to guide review and further studying.

Developmental learning takes place as you cycle through studying, assessing how well you have learned, reviewing, and assessing again until you feel you are ready to take the exam.

You might have noticed the practice exam included in this book. You should use it as part of the learning process. The *MeasureUp Practice Exams, Preview Edition* test-simulation software included on this book's CD-ROM also provides you with an excellent opportunity to assess your knowledge.

You should set a goal for your pretesting. A reasonable goal would be to score consistently in the 90% range.

See Appendix A, "Accessing Your Free MeasureUp Practice Test—Including Networking Simulations!" and Appendix B, "MeasureUp's Product Features," for further explanation of the test-simulation software.

Exam Prep Tips

After you have mastered the subject matter, the final preparatory step is to understand how the exam will be presented. Make no mistake: A Microsoft Certified Professional (MCP) exam challenges both your knowledge and your test-taking skills. The following sections describe the basics of exam design and the exam formats, as well as provide hints targeted to each of the exam formats.

MCP Exam Design

Every MCP exam is released in two basic formats: *Fixed-Form* and Case Study. What's being called exam format here is really little more than a combination of the overall exam structure and the presentation method for exam questions.

Understanding the exam formats is key to good preparation because the exam format determines the number of questions presented, the difficulty of those questions, and the amount of time allowed to complete the exam.

All the exam formats use many of the same types of questions. These types or styles of questions include several types of traditional multiple-choice questions, multiple-rating (or scenario-based) questions, and simulation-based questions. Some exams include other types of questions that ask you to drag and drop objects onscreen, reorder a list, or categorize things. Still other exams ask you to answer various types of questions in response to case studies you have read. It's important that you understand the types of questions you will be asked and the actions required to properly answer them.

The following sections address the exam formats and the question types. Understanding the formats and question types will help you feel much more comfortable when you take the exam.

Exam Formats

As mentioned previously, there are two basic formats for the MCP exams: the traditional fixed-form exam and the case study exam. As its name implies, the fixed-form exam presents a fixed set of questions during the exam session. The case study exam includes case studies organized into testlets that serve as the basis for answering the questions. Most MCP exams these days utilize the fixed-form approach, with the case study approach running second.

Fixed-Form Exams

A fixed-form computerized exam is based on a fixed set of exam questions. The individual questions are presented in random order during a test session. If you take the same exam more than once, you won't necessarily see exactly the same questions. This is because two or three final forms are typically assembled for every fixed-form exam Microsoft releases. These are usually labeled Forms A, B, and C.

The final forms of a fixed-form exam are identical in terms of content coverage, number of questions, and allotted time, but the questions for each are different. However, some of the same questions are shared among different final forms. When questions are shared among multiple final forms of an exam, the percentage of sharing is generally small. Many final forms share no questions, but some older exams may have a 10%–15% duplication of exam questions on the final exam forms.

Fixed-form exams also have fixed time limits in which you must complete them.

The score you achieve on a fixed-form exam, which is always calculated for MCP exams on a scale of 0 to 1,000, is based on the number of questions you answer correctly. The passing score is the same for all final forms of a given fixed-form exam.

The typical design of a fixed-form exam is as follows:

- The exam contains 50–60 questions.

- You are allowed 75–90 minutes of testing time.

- Question review is allowed, including the opportunity to change your answers.

- Candidates must correctly answer 70% or more of the questions to pass.

- No points are deducted for incorrect answers—zero credit is given for those questions.

- Partial credit may be granted for some questions where multiple answers are expected for a complete solution and only a subset of the answers has been selected.

Case Study Exams

The case study–based format for Microsoft exams first appeared with the advent of the 70-100 exam (the original "Solution Architectures" exam) and then appeared in the MCSE sequence in the Design exams. The questions in the case study format are not the independent entities that they are in the fixed and adaptive formats. Instead, questions are tied to a case study, a long scenario-like description of an information technology situation. As the test taker, your job is to extract from the case study the information that needs to be integrated with your under-standing of Microsoft technology. The idea is that a case study will provide you with a situa-tion that is even more like a real-life problem than the other formats provide.

The case studies are presented as testlets. A *testlet* is a section within the exam in which you read the case study and then answer 10 to 20 questions that apply to the case study. When you finish that section, you move on to another testlet, with another case study and its associated questions. Typically, three to five of these testlets compose the overall exam. You are given more time to complete such an exam than to complete the other types because it takes time to read through the cases and analyze them. You might have as much as three hours to complete a case study exam—and you might need all of it. The case studies are always available through a linking button while you are in a testlet. However, when you leave a testlet, you cannot come back to it.

Figure 1 provides an illustration of part of such a case study.

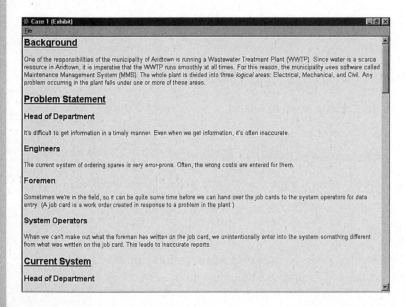

FIGURE 1 An example of a case study.

Question Types

A variety of question types can appear on MCP exams. We have attempted to cover all the types that are available at the time of this writing. Most of the question types discussed in the following sections can appear in each of the three exam formats.

A typical MCP exam question is based on the idea of measuring skills or the ability to complete tasks. Therefore, most of the questions are written so as to present you with a situation that includes a role (such as a system administrator or technician), a technology environment (for example, 100 computers running Windows XP Professional on a Windows Server 2003 network), and a problem to be solved (for example, the user can connect to services on the LAN but not on the intranet). The answers indicate actions you might take to solve the problem or create setups or environments that would function correctly from the start. You should keep this in mind as you read the questions on the exam. You might encounter some questions that just call for you to regurgitate facts, but these will be relatively few and far between.

The following sections look at the different question types.

Multiple-Choice Questions

Despite the variety of question types that now appear in various MCP exams, the multiple-choice question is still the basic building block of the exams. The multiple-choice question comes in three varieties:

▶ *Regular multiple-choice question*—Also referred to as an *alphabetic question*, a regular multiple-choice question asks you to choose one answer as correct.

▶ *Multiple-answer, multiple-choice question*—Also referred to as a *multi-alphabetic question*, this version of a multiple-choice question requires you to choose two or more answers as correct. Typically, you are told precisely the number of correct answers to choose.

▶ *Enhanced multiple-choice question*—This is a regular or multiple-answer question that includes a graphic or table to which you must refer to answer the question correctly.

Examples of multiple-choice questions appear at the end of each chapter in this book.

Simulation Questions

Simulation-based questions reproduce the look and feel of key Microsoft product features for the purpose of testing. The simulation software used in MCP exams has been designed to look and act, as much as possible, like the actual product. Consequently, answering simulation questions in an MCP exam entails completing one or more tasks the same as if you were using the product itself.

A typical Microsoft simulation question consists of a brief scenario or problem statement, along with one or more tasks that you must complete to solve the problem.

It sounds obvious, but your first step when you encounter a simulation question is to carefully read the question (see Figure 2). You should not go straight to the simulation application! You must assess the problem that's presented and identify the conditions that make up the problem scenario. You should note the tasks that must be performed or outcomes that must be achieved to answer the question, and then you should review any instructions you're given on how to proceed.

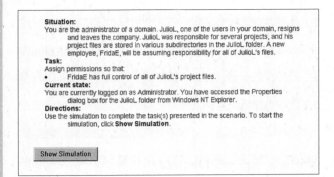

FIGURE 2   A typical MCP exam simulation with directions.

The next step is to launch the simulator by using the button provided. After you click the Show Simulation button, you see a feature of the product, as shown in the dialog box in Figure 3. The simulation application will partially obscure the question text on many test-center machines. You should feel free to reposition the simulator and to move between the question text screen and the simulator by using hotkeys or point-and-click navigation—or even by clicking the simulator's launch button again.

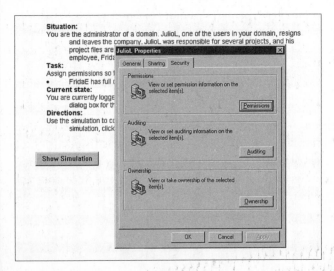

FIGURE 3   Launching the simulation application.

It is important for you to understand that your answer to the simulation question will not be recorded until you move on to the next exam question. This gives you the added capability of closing and reopening the simulation application (by using the launch button) on the same question without losing any partial answer you may have made.

The third step is to use the simulator as you would the actual product to solve the problem or perform the defined tasks. Again, the simulation software is designed to function—within reason—the same as the product does. But you shouldn't expect the simulator to reproduce product behavior perfectly. Most importantly, you should not allow yourself to become flustered if the simulator does not look or act exactly like the product.

Figure 4 shows the solution to the sample simulation problem.

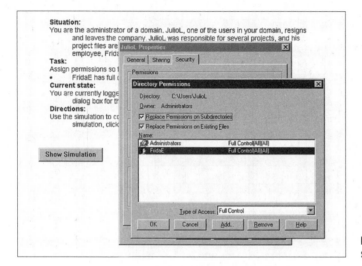

FIGURE 4   The solution to the simulation example.

Two final points will help you tackle simulation questions. First, you should respond only to what is being asked in the question; you should not solve problems that you are not asked to solve. Second, you should accept what is being asked of you. You might not entirely agree with conditions in the problem statement, the quality of the desired solution, or the sufficiency of defined tasks to adequately solve the problem. However, you should remember that you are being tested on your ability to solve the problem as it is presented.

The solution to the simulation problem shown in Figure 4 perfectly illustrates both of those points. As you'll recall from the question scenario (refer to Figure 2), you were asked to assign appropriate permissions to a new user, FridaE. You were not instructed to make any other changes in permissions. Therefore, if you were to modify or remove the administrator's permissions, this item would be scored wrong on an MCP exam.

Hot-Area Question

Hot-area questions call for you to click a graphic or diagram to complete some task. You are asked a question that is similar to any other, but rather than click an option button or check box next to an answer, you click the relevant item in a screenshot or on a part of a diagram. An example of such an item is shown in Figure 5.

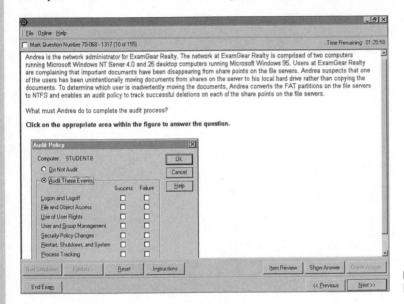

FIGURE 5 A typical hot-area question.

Drag-and-Drop Questions

Microsoft has utilized two types of drag-and-drop questions in exams: select-and-place questions and drop-and-connect questions. Both are covered in the following sections.

Select-and-Place Questions

Select-and-place questions typically require you to drag and drop labels on images in a diagram to correctly label or identify some portion of a network. Figure 6 shows you the actual question portion of a select-and-place item.

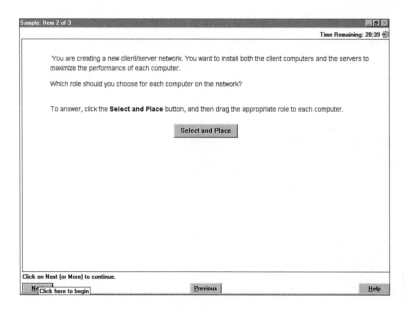

FIGURE 6 A select-and-place question.

Figure 7 shows the window you would see after you clicked Select and Place. It contains the actual diagram in which you would select and drag the various server roles and match them up with the appropriate computers.

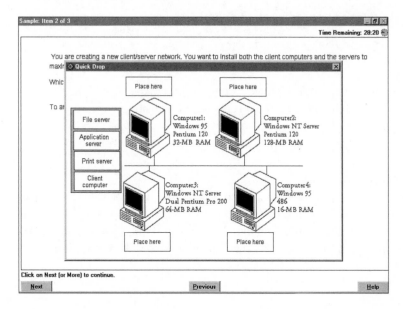

FIGURE 7 The window containing the select-and-place diagram.

Drop-and-Connect Questions

Drop-and-connect questions provide a different spin on drag-and-drop questions. This type of question provides you with the opportunity to create boxes that you can label, as well as connectors of various types with which to link them. In essence, you create a model or diagram to answer a drop-and-connect question. You might have to create a network diagram or a data model for a database system. Figure 8 illustrates the idea of a drop-and-connect question.

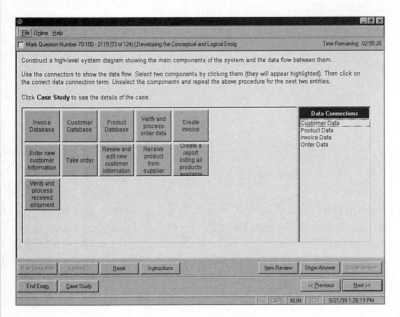

FIGURE 8   A drop-and-connect question.

Microsoft seems to be getting away from this type of question, perhaps because of the complexity involved. You might see the same sort of concepts tested with a more traditional question utilizing multiple exhibits, each of which shows a diagram; in this type of question, you must choose which exhibit correctly portrays the solution to the problem posed.

Ordered-List Questions

Ordered-list questions require you to consider a list of items and place them in the proper order. You select items and then use a button or drag and drop to add them to a new list in the correct order. You can use another button to remove the items in the new order in case you change your mind and want to reorder things. Figure 9 shows an ordered-list question.

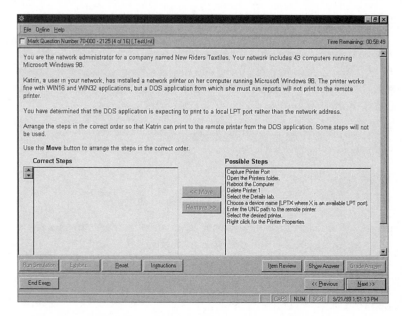

FIGURE 9 An ordered-list question.

Tree Questions

Tree questions require you to think hierarchically and categorically. You are asked to place items from a list into categories that are displayed as nodes in a tree structure. Such questions might ask you to identify parent-child relationships in processes or the structure of keys in a database. You might also be required to show order within the categories, much as you would in an ordered-list question. Figure 10 shows an example of a tree question.

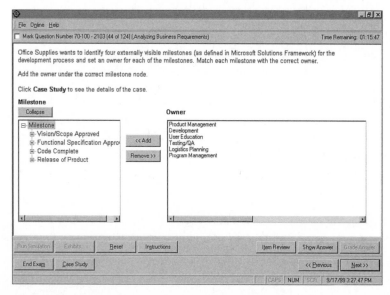

FIGURE 10 A tree question.

Putting It All Together

As you can see, Microsoft is making an effort to utilize question types that go beyond asking you to simply memorize facts. These question types force you to know how to accomplish tasks and understand concepts and relationships. You should study so that you can answer these types of questions rather than those that simply ask you to recall facts.

Given all the different pieces of information presented so far, the following sections present a set of tips that will help you successfully tackle the exam.

More Exam-Preparation Tips

Generic exam-preparation advice is always useful. Tips include the following:

▶ Become familiar with the product. Hands-on experience is one of the keys to success on any MCP exam. Review the exercises and the Step by Steps in the book.

▶ Review the current exam-preparation guide on the Microsoft Training & Certification website. The documentation Microsoft makes available on the Web identifies the skills every exam is intended to test.

▶ Memorize foundational technical detail, but remember that MCP exams are generally heavier on problem solving and application of knowledge than on questions that require only rote memorization.

▶ Take any of the available practice tests. We recommend the one included in this book and the ones you can create by using the MeasureUp software on this book's CD-ROM. As a supplement to the material bound with this book, try the free practice tests available on the Microsoft MCP website.

▶ Look on the Microsoft Training and Certification website for samples and demonstration items. (As of this writing, check www.microsoft.com/traincert/mcpexams/faq/innovations.asp, but you might have to look around for the samples because the URL may have changed.) These tend to be particularly valuable for one significant reason: They help you become familiar with new testing technologies before you encounter them on MCP exams.

Tips for Success During the Exam Session

The following generic exam-taking advice that you've heard for years applies when you're taking an MCP exam:

▶ To keep yourself sharp on the day of the exam, read over the items in the "Fast Facts" section of this book and get a good night's sleep the night before the exam.

▶ Take a deep breath and try to relax when you first sit down for your exam session. It is very important that you control the pressure you might (naturally) feel when taking exams.

▶ You will be provided scratch paper. Take a moment to write down any factual information and technical detail that you have committed to short-term memory.

▶ Carefully read all information and instruction screens. These displays have been put together to give you information relevant to the exam you are taking.

▶ Accept the nondisclosure agreement and preliminary survey as part of the examination process. Complete them accurately and quickly move on.

▶ Read the exam questions carefully. Reread each question to identify all relevant detail.

▶ In fixed-form exams, tackle the questions in the order in which they are presented. Skipping around won't build your confidence; the clock is always counting down.

▶ Don't rush, but also don't linger on difficult questions. The questions vary in degree of difficulty. Don't let yourself be flustered by a particularly difficult or wordy question.

Besides considering the basic preparation and test-taking advice presented so far, you also need to consider the challenges presented by the different exam designs, as described in the following sections.

Tips for Fixed-Form Exams

Because a fixed-form exam is composed of a fixed, finite set of questions, you should add these tips to your strategy for taking a fixed-form exam:

▶ Note the time allotted and the number of questions on the exam you are taking. Make a rough calculation of how many minutes you can spend on each question, and use this figure to pace yourself through the exam.

▶ Take advantage of the fact that you can return to and review skipped or previously answered questions. Record the questions you can't answer confidently on the scratch paper provided, noting the relative difficulty of each question. When you reach the end of the exam, return to the more difficult questions.

▶ If you have session time remaining after you complete all the questions (and if you aren't too fatigued!), review your answers. Pay particular attention to questions that seem to have a lot of detail or that require graphics.

▶ As for changing your answers, the general rule of thumb here is *don't*! If you read the question carefully and completely and you felt like you knew the right answer, you probably did. Don't second-guess yourself. However, if, as you check your answers, one clearly stands out as incorrect, of course you should change it. But if you are at all unsure, go with your first impression.

Tips for Case Study Exams

The case study exam format calls for unique study and exam-taking strategies:

▶ Remember that you have more time than in a typical exam. Take your time and read the case study thoroughly.

▶ Use the scrap paper or whatever medium is provided to you to take notes, diagram processes, and actively seek out the important information.

▶ Work through each testlet as if each were an independent exam. Remember that you cannot go back after you have left a testlet.

▶ Refer to the case study as often as you need to, but do not use that as a substitute for reading it carefully initially and for taking notes.

Final Considerations

Finally, a number of changes in the MCP program affect how frequently you can repeat an exam and what you will see when you do:

▶ Microsoft has an exam retake policy. The rule is "two and two, then one and two." That is, you can attempt any exam twice with no restrictions on the time between attempts. But after the second attempt, you must wait two weeks before you can attempt that exam again. After that, you are required to wait two weeks between subsequent attempts. Plan to pass the exam in two attempts or plan to increase your time horizon for receiving the MCP credential.

▶ New questions are always being seeded into the MCP exams. After performance data is gathered on new questions, the examiners replace older questions on all exam forms. This means that the questions appearing on exams change regularly.

These changes mean that the brute-force strategies for passing MCP exams have lost their viability. So if you don't pass an exam on the first or second attempt, it is likely that the exam's form could change significantly by the next time you take it. It could be updated from fixed-form to adaptive, or, even more likely, it could have a different set of questions or question types.

Microsoft's intention is not to make the exams more difficult by introducing unwanted change, but to create and maintain valid measures of the technical skills and knowledge associated with the different MCP credentials. Preparing for an MCP exam has always involved not only studying the subject matter but also planning for the testing experience itself. With the continuing changes, this is now truer than ever.

PART I

Exam Preparation

CHAPTER ONE

Windows Server 2003 Environment

Objectives

This chapter serves as an introduction to the Windows Server 2003 family and provides a brief overview of some the features that you can expect to see covered on the Managing and Maintaining a Microsoft Windows Server 2003 Environment exam.

Identify the members of the Windows Server 2003 family

▶ Windows Server 2003 is not a single product that can be used in any situation. Currently, Microsoft produces five separate versions of Windows Server 2003, each with features that are suitable for specific environments.

Install Windows Server 2003

▶ Before the operating system can be used, it must be installed and configured. It is important to know what hardware is supported and to understand the installation process.

Install and configure the Administrative Tools

▶ Microsoft Windows Server 2003 includes several utilities to aid system configuration and administration. These tools are accessed via the Administrative Tools folder in the Start Menu. This chapter takes a look at how to install and configure these tools.

Outline

Study Strategies

▶ In studying this section, be sure to practice all the activities described. Become very familiar with the different members of the Windows Server 2003 family, and which features are supported in each one. Also be sure to understand how to work with the Microsoft Management Console (MMC), and the requirements for password complexity.

▶ You will need access to a Windows Server 2003 member server. Many of the tools are new, or they differ from those available in Windows 2000, so don't try to get by with a Windows 2000 server.

▶ You don't have to buy Windows Server 2003 to try it out. You can download a free evaluation version (which expires in 180 days) from www.microsoft.com/windowsserver2003/evaluation/trial/default.mspx.

Introduction

Although most people are somewhat familiar with PCs and their uses and basic operations, that PC that is sitting on your desk, at home in your den, or collecting dust in your backpack is just a small part of the world of computing. The really down and dirty, heavy-duty computing tasks are performed by servers. A server is to a PC what an 18-wheeler is to a Toyota. For the light, quick work performed by individuals, a PC will do, but when you need heavy-duty tasks to service multiple users, you need a server!

In this chapter, we will take a look at the different members of the Windows Server 2003 family and perform a basic installation of our first server.

The Windows Server 2003 Family

Just like there are various sizes of trucks for different uses, various editions of Windows Server 2003 are each suited to a different use.

Windows Server 2003 Standard Edition

The standard edition of Windows Server 2003 is targeted for small businesses and departmental use. It supports the following hardware:

- ▶ Minimum CPU—133 MHz
- ▶ Minimum RAM—128 MB
- ▶ Up to 4 gigabytes of RAM
- ▶ Up to 4 processors
- ▶ Network load balancing

Unlike in Windows 2000, the standard edition of Windows Server 2003 includes support for load balancing. This feature allows you to set up a group of servers running identical applications, typically a web server. All the servers share a virtual address, so the user will be connected to any server that's available. If a server is removed from the load-balanced group, either for maintenance or because of a failure, the incoming connections are rebalanced over the remaining servers in the group.

Windows Server 2003 Enterprise Edition

The enterprise edition of Windows Server 2003 is targeted for medium to large businesses and departmental use. The enterprise edition adds support for fault-tolerant features such as clustering and load balancing. It supports the following hardware:

▶ Minimum CPU—133 MHz

▶ Minimum RAM—128 MB

▶ Up to 32 gigabytes of RAM in the 32-bit edition and 64 gigabytes of RAM in the 64-bit edition

▶ Up to 8 processors

▶ 8-way clustering

▶ Terminal services load balancing

▶ All features included in standard edition

Clustering is an advanced feature that allows the workload to be switched over from one server to another, either manually, or because of a hardware or software failure. This process is called *failover*. By configuring a set of servers to failover in case of an error, a high degree of application availability can be obtained. Each server in this type of configuration is referred to as a node.

However, for clustering to provide this fault tolerance, the applications must be cluster aware. This requires them to be specifically written to be able to temporarily suspend operation while being switched from one node to another, and then to pick up exactly where they left off after the transfer has been completed. Microsoft Exchange and SQL Server are two applications that are available in cluster-aware versions.

Note that the hardware requirements for a server to be approved for use in a cluster configuration are far more stringent than for a common Windows Server 2003 server. Hence, there are far fewer server models available, and the ones that meet the requirements are far more expensive.

> **NOTE**
>
> **Terminal Services Load Balancing**   Although similar in operation to the basic load-balancing feature included in Windows Server 2003 Standard Edition, a lot of added functionality is specifically included for Terminal Services. Terminal Services will be covered at length in Chapter 11, "Managing and Maintaining Terminal Services."

Windows Server 2003 Web Edition

The web edition of Windows Server 2003 is targeted specifically for use as a web server and does not support many of the functions of the other editions. For example, it cannot be used as a domain controller, an Internet Authentication Service (IAS) server, or a DHCP server. It supports the following hardware:

- ▶ Minimum CPU—133 MHz

- ▶ Minimum RAM—128 MB

- ▶ Up to 2 gigabytes of RAM

- ▶ Up to 2 processors

In addition, the web edition is available only from OEMs preinstalled on servers. It is not available at retail.

Windows Server 2003 Datacenter Edition

The datacenter edition of Windows Server 2003 is targeted for large businesses that require mission-critical high-availability applications. The datacenter edition adds support for larger amounts of memory and more processors than the other versions. It supports the following hardware:

- ▶ Up to 64 gigabytes of RAM in the 32-bit edition and 128 gigabytes of RAM in the 64-bit edition

- ▶ Minimum of 8 processors and up to 32 processors

- ▶ 8-way clustering

- ▶ All features included in standard and enterprise editions

The datacenter edition of Windows Server 2003 is only available preinstalled on specialized hardware available directly from and supported by the manufacturer. It is not available from retail channels.

Windows Server 2003 Enterprise Edition for 64-Bit Processors

This is another specialized version developed for the Intel Itanium and AMD 64-bit chipset. Although not very popular at the initial release of Windows Server 2003, it has become more relevant as the popularity of 64-bit servers has increased., The next release of Windows Server, currently code named Longhorn and several other upcoming Microsoft products are being developed with features that take advantage of the 64-bit processors.

Service Pack 1

From time to time, Microsoft rolls up the various hot fixes into a service pack. A service pack is an integrated and tested set of the fixes and security enhancements that have been released since the last official release of the product. Although Microsoft commonly states that service packs will not include any new functionality, usually a few new features are sneaked in.

For the purposes of the 70-290 exam, you will need to become familiar with the following new features in Windows Server 2003 SP1:

▶ *The Security Configuration Wizard*—The SCW automatically configures the file, services, auditing, and Registry settings for your server according to the server role to reduce the attack surface.

▶ *Windows Firewall*—The Internet Connection Firewall has been replaced with the Windows Firewall, first released in Windows XP Service Pack 2. Unlike in Windows XP, the firewall is turned off by default in Windows Server 2003. If needed, it must be manually enabled.

Windows Server 2003 R2

Starting with the initial release of Windows Server 2003, Microsoft committed to releasing a major version of its server product every four years, with an incremental version after two years. The first incremental version release under this philosophy is Windows Server 2003 R2. Unlike service packs, Microsoft will release new functionality in incremental versions. Some of the features will be totally new, whereas others will be add-ons that were released to the web after the initial release of the product.

For the purposes of the 70-290 exam, you will need to become familiar with the following new features in Windows Server 2003 R2:

▶ *The Print Management Console*—The Print Management Console enables you to manage all the printers on your network from a central console.

▶ *The File Server Resource Manager*—The File Server Resource Manager is a third-party add-on purchased from Veritas. It allows you more sophisticated quota management compared to the initial release of Windows Server 2003, and enables you to block the storage of undesirable files, such as MP3s, movies, and the like. This new tool is covered at length in Chapter 13, "Managing Data Storage."

Although many more features were added via Service Pack 1 and R2, we are including the ones most likely to appear on the exam. For a complete overview of the new features not discussed here, check out the Microsoft web site at http://www.microsoft.com/windowsserver2003/default.mspx.

For an overview of the Active Directory–specific features that have been added since the initial release of Windows Server 2003, reference the Microsoft article New Features for Active Directory at http://technet2.microsoft.com/WindowsServer/en/library/bb99fdd4-f8e0-490f-adae-6814cf081ff71033.mspx?mfr=true.

> **EXAM ALERT**
>
> **Be Familiar with Each Version**   Because there are several versions of Windows Server 2003, each with varying capabilities, know in what situations one version would be more appropriate than another. You must have a good understanding of this for the exam.

Installing Windows Server 2003

If you're going to learn how to work with an operating system, there's no substitute for some hands-on time. Realistically, that's the only way to truly start to understand the operation and some of the nuances of the operating system.

Hardware Requirements

Before you can get started, you will need to install the operating system. Before you install any operating system, the first thing that you should do is to examine the hardware requirements to make sure that your server hardware is adequate for use. The hardware requirements for the various editions of Windows Server 2003 are listed in Table 1.1.

TABLE 1.1   Minimum Hardware Requirements

Requirements	Standard Edition	Enterprise Edition
Minimum CPU	133MHz	133MHz
Recommended Minimum CPU Speed	550MHz	733MHz
Minimum Memory	128MB	128MB
Recommended Minimum Memory	256MB	256MB
Disk Space	1.5GB	1.5GB

Speaking Realistically

The table shows the Microsoft values that you will need to know for the exam. Realistically speaking, in the real world, you wouldn't want to run a production Windows Server 2003 server on anything less than 512MB of memory, with a 1GHz processor and a disk of at least 8 or 9GB.

As you can see, a server operating system requires far more advanced hardware than a typical desktop operating system such as Windows XP. However, remember our analogy from the beginning of this chapter? You wouldn't be able to ride around in your 18-wheeler on tires made for a Toyota, would you?

Hardware Compatibility

Now that we've determined what hardware is needed to run each version of Windows Server 2003, we need to determine what specific hardware is supported. Because you're running a server operating system, not just any hardware you might have lying around is supported. Because a server is targeted as a platform to run a business on, it is critical that the hardware that you are running on has been thoroughly tested for compatibility. For example, you wouldn't want to have problems with a device driver while running your payroll application, would you?

Fortunately, Microsoft has made it very easy for you to check your hardware for compatibility with Windows Server 2003. Microsoft has assembled a list of compatible hardware at http://www.microsoft.com/whdc/hcl/default.mspx. Note that the list is not all-inclusive, because new hardware is being produced every day. For the most up-to-date information, you should contact your hardware vendor.

NOTE

BIOS Is Important   Remember to check your hardware BIOS versions. Some older hardware is not compatible with Windows Server 2003 without a BIOS update.

The Real World

For the purposes of this book, and passing the exam, you won't require the mission-critical aspects of a quality server. For our purposes, a couple of workstations will allow you to make it through the hands on exercises, or better yet, a copy of virtualization software such as Virtual PC or VMWare will do just fine.

All the software that you will need is available in trial versions. Here are the links:

- ▸ *VMWare*—One of the oldest vendors of virtualization software. VMWare offers a 30-day evaluation version at http://www.vmware.com/download/ws/eval.html.

- ▸ *Microsoft Virtual PC*—The new kid on the block, sort of, since they purchased the code from Connectix. A 45-day evaluation is available at http://www.microsoft.com/windows/virtualpc/default.mspx.

- ▸ *Windows Server 2003*—Microsoft offers 180-day evaluation versions of Windows Server 2003 at http://www.microsoft.com/windowsserver2003/evaluation/trial/default.mspx.

Whichever method you choose, whether hardware based or virtual, the exercises in this book will be most easily accomplished using two machines or virtual images running any version of Windows Server 2003, except for the web edition.

Getting Started

Now that you've obtained the necessary hardware and software, let's get started!

> **NOTE**
>
> **Windows Server 2003 R2**   Windows Server 2003 R2 contains two product discs. Disc 1 contains Windows Server 2003 with the current Service Pack (SP1 or SP2). Disc 2 contains the installation files for the Windows Server 2003 R2 optional components.

To begin the installation procedure in Step by Step 1.1, boot directly from the Windows Server 2003 CD. Your CD-ROM must support bootable CDs.

> **NOTE**
>
> **Virtual CD-ROM**   If you're using a virtual solution, such as Virtual PC or VMWare, you will need to capture the CD-ROM drive. Because using these products is out of the scope of this book, we will assume that you have read the instructions supplied with the product.

STEP BY STEP

1.1 Installing Windows Server 2003

1. Insert the Windows Server 2003 CD in the CD-ROM drive.

2. Restart the computer; when prompted, press any key to boot from the CD.

3. If necessary press F6 to be prompted to install any special drivers.

4. On the Welcome to Setup screen, press Enter.

5. Review the licensing agreement; to agree to it, press F8.

6. If you had a previous version of Windows installed on the drive, you will see a message asking if you want to repair the installation. Press Esc to continue.

7. If present, delete all existing partitions until the only thing listed is unpartitioned space, as shown in Figure 1.1.

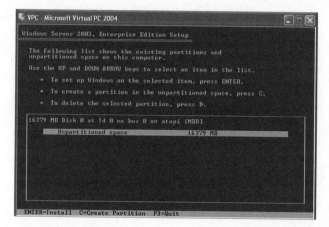

FIGURE 1.1 Set up a single partition for the operating system.

8. Press C to create a partition in the unpartitioned space on the disk drive.

9. After the New <Raw> partition is created, press Enter.

10. Select Format the Partition Using the NTFS File System <Quick>, and then press Enter.

11. Windows Server 2003 Setup formats the partition and then copies the files from the Windows Server 2003 Server CD to the hard drive. The computer restarts and the GUI portion of Windows Server 2003 Installation Program begins.

12. After the GUI is started, the Windows Server 2003 Setup Wizard will detect and install your devices. This can take several minutes. During the process your screen may flicker.

13. In the Regional and Language Options dialog box, make changes required for your locale (typically, none are required for the United States), and then click Next.

14. In the Personalize Your Software dialog box, enter your name in the Name box and type **70-290** into the Organization box. Click Next.

15. Type the Product Key (found on the back of your Windows Server 2003 CD case if you're installing a retail version) in the text boxes provided, and then click Next. If installing an evaluation or a Select or MSDN version, just click Next.

16. In the Licensing Modes dialog box, select Per Device, and then click Next.

17. In the Computer Name and Administrator Password dialog box shown in Figure 1.2, type the new computer name **70-290-DC** into the computer name box, and then click Next.

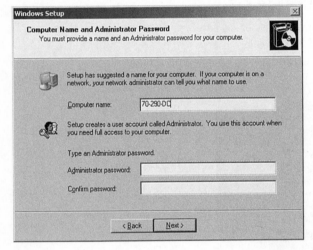

FIGURE 1.2   Give the server a relevant name.

18. When prompted by Windows Setup, click Yes to confirm a blank Administrator password.

19. In the Date and Time Settings dialog box, correct the current date and time if necessary, and then click Next.

20. In the Networking Settings dialog box, make sure Custom Settings is selected, and then click Next.

21. In the Network Components dialog box, select Internet Protocol (TCP/IP), and then click the Properties button.

22. On the General tab, select Use the Following Address, then key in an appropriate IP address and subnet mask. Example: 192.168.1.25 and 255.255.255.0. Enter the same IP address as the preferred DNS server. Enter **192.168.1.1** as the Default Gateway, as shown in Figure 1.3. Click OK when finished.

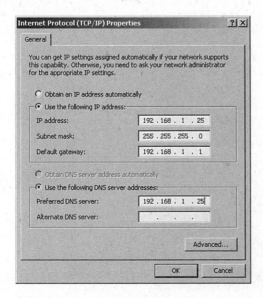

FIGURE 1.3 Enter the TCP/IP information.

23. When you are returned to the Networking Components dialog box, click Next to continue.

24. In the Workgroups or Computer Domain dialog box (No is selected by default), click Next.

25. The Windows Server 2003 Installation continues and configures the necessary components. This may take a few minutes.

26. The server restarts and the operating system loads from the hard drive.

27. When prompted, as shown in Figure 1.4, insert the Windows Server 2003 R2 Disk 2 CD-ROM.

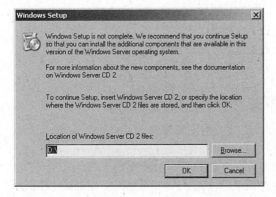

FIGURE 1.4 Windows Server 2003 R2 requires a second setup disk.

28. When the Welcome to the Microsoft Windows 2003 R2 screen appears, as shown in Figure 1.5, select Continue Windows Server 2003 R2 Setup.

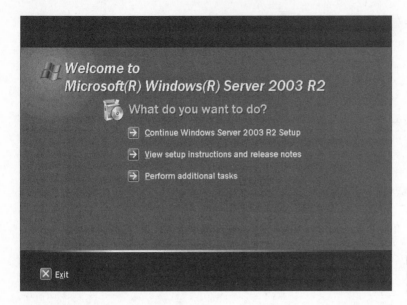

FIGURE 1.5 Select Continue Windows Server 2003 R2 Setup.

29. When the Windows Server 2003 R2 Setup Wizard appears, click Next to continue.

30. On the Setup Summary screen, click Next; the R2 files will be installed.

31. When the Completing Windows Server 2003 R2 Setup screen appears, read the instructions for installing the R2 components, and then click the Finish Button. Your server will reboot.

NOTE

Best Practice   To facilitate the steps in these guides, the Administrator password is left blank and there is no password. This is not an acceptable security practice. When installing a server for your production network, a password should always be set.

Logging On to Windows Server 2003

On the first boot after installation, you will be presented with the logon dialog box as shown in Figure 1.6. The User Name is a unique ID that is assigned to every user who needs to log on to the server. As shown in the figure, the username field is already filled in for you. This will typically be the username of the last person who logged on to the server, unless this field is set to blank by Group Policy. In our case, because we just completed loading Windows Server 2003, the only available username is Administrator, so it is displayed by default.

NOTE

First Timer   On the first boot after installation, the logon dialog box usually appears by default. However, on subsequent boots, you will need to press the Ctrl+Alt+Del keys together to make it appear so that you can log on.

FIGURE 1.6   User logon dialog box for a server in a workgroup.

The second field shown is Password. The password is a unique word or phrase that should be known only to the user who is logging on. By default, a Windows Server 2003 standalone server does not require a user to enter a complex password. However, for domain controllers and servers and PCs that are members of a network, the password complexity policy is enabled by default.

For a password to meet the complexity requirements, it must adhere to the following format:

▶ The password cannot contain all or part of the username.

▶ The password must be at least six characters in length.

▶ The password must contain characters from three of the following four categories:

  ▶ Uppercase characters (A through Z)

  ▶ Lowercase characters (a through z)

  ▶ Numeric characters (0 through 9)

  ▶ Nonalphabetic characters (for instance, !,@,#,$,%)

Because we didn't enter an administrator password during the installation, click the OK button to log on.

After the logon is completed, on Service Pack 1 and later servers, you will be presented with the Windows Server Post-Setup Security screen, as shown in Figure 1.7. As you can see, most incoming connections are blocked on your first boot of Windows Server 2003 and will remain blocked until you perform the steps shown on the screen, or click the Finish button at the bottom.

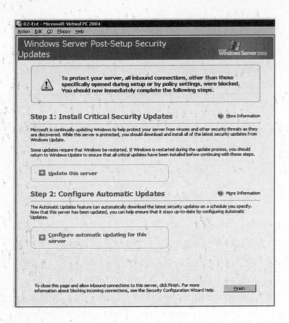

FIGURE 1.7 The Post-Setup Security Updates screen enables you to install updates before opening your server to the network. Service Pack 1 and later, only.

The main purpose of this screen is to ensure that all your security patches are up-to-date before you allow your server to be exposed to your network or the Internet. Because we are working in a lab environment, click the Finish button to continue.

> **NOTE**
>
> **One-Shot Deal** This screen appears only on the first boot. It will not be available upon another boot, or via the Start menu. However, these functions can be configured manually at a later time.

Servers and Their Roles

After you configure your update options, you will be presented with the screen shown in Figure 1.8. The Manage Your Server screen is a front end to the Configure Your Server Wizard. This wizard is an automated way to tune your server by letting you select a role from a list and then guiding you in the configuration of this role by prompting you for the desired configuration settings. The wizard can assist you in either adding or removing a role from your server. It will appear at every logon until you select the Don't Display This Page at Logon check box in the lower-left corner of the page. The Manage Your Server page can be opened at any time by clicking Start, All Programs, Administrative Tools, Manage Your Server.

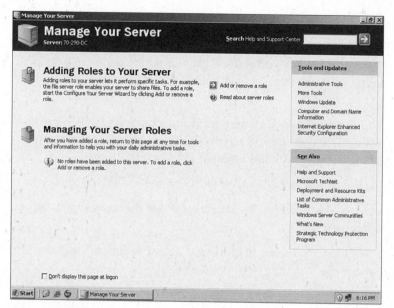

Manage Your Server

FIGURE 1.8 The Manage Your Server page enables you to start the Configure Your Server Wizard, which is used to configure your server for various roles.

NOTE

Run Separately After you become more familiar with the different options provided by Manage Your Server and the Configure Your Server Wizard, you can bypass the Manage Your Server page and directly select the Configure Your Server Wizard in the Administrative Tools folder.

Servers can host a variety of roles. If the server is large enough, it can support several roles. A server can supply the storage for those important files you need for your presentation; it can host a database of all the left-handed people in Bangladesh, or it can supply something as simple as email.

The following roles are available via the wizard:

▶ *File server*—A file server is used to provide centralized storage of files. This allows users to access them when needed and share them with other users, without having to pass them around on diskettes or CDs. A file server also allows files to be secured so that only certain users will have access to them.

▶ *Domain Controller*—Domain controllers are used to provide centralized storage and management of user accounts, process logons to the network, and authenticate user access to network resources.

▶ *DNS server*—A DNS server is used to register and resolve DNS domain names and provide name-to-IP address mapping for TCP/IP.

- ▶ *WINS server*—A Windows Internet Service (WINS) server is used to register and resolve NetBIOS names and provide name-to-IP address mapping.

- ▶ *Print server*—A print server is used as a centralized location where users can print to various printers. Printing will be covered at length in Chapter 6, "Implementing Printing."

- ▶ *Application server*—This is a new name for Internet Information Services (IIS) and refers to web servers, File Transfer Protocol servers (FTP), and their various components. IIS is covered in Chapter 5, "Administering Windows Server 2003."

- ▶ *Mail server*—This role provides a limited version of POP3 and SMTP functionality.

- ▶ *Remote Access/VPN server*—This role provides access to remote users, either via dial-up or via VPN over the Internet.

- ▶ *Streaming Media server*—This role is used to efficiently stream audio and video content over your local network or the Internet.

- ▶ *Terminal server*—Terminal Services provides an environment where users can run applications that are not installed on their PCs. Terminal Services will be covered in Chapter 11, "Managing and Maintaining Terminal Services."

It should be pointed out that these roles can be configured manually by an experienced network administrator who has done it many times before. For the novice, there are checklists generated either by your company or downloaded from Microsoft or third-party companies. However, to ensure consistency and avoid human error, the Configure Your Server Wizard offers a guided approach to ensure that you don't leave out any important steps.

Another descriptive term that we need to cover is the type of server. There are three types:

- ▶ *Standalone*—A standalone server is a server that is not a member of a domain. It can be the only machine used, or it can be part of a workgroup to provide distributed storage of files and printers. Although users can share resources in a workgroup, they might have to keep track of different passwords for each resource because there is no common source of security in a workgroup.

- ▶ *Domain Controller*—A domain controller is used to provide centralized storage of user accounts and provide authentication for users who need to access resources in the domain. A domain is a group of user accounts and network resources that share a common security database and common security policies. The domain controller is used to control access to these resources. We will cover domains and domain controllers in Chapter 2.

- ▶ *Member server*—A member server is any server that is a member of a domain that is not a domain controller. It can serve one or more of the roles that we discussed earlier.

Windows Server 2003 Administrative Tools

Keeping a Windows network functioning encompasses many activities. Such activities range from maintaining user accounts to configuring security, monitoring network traffic, correcting system problems, and enabling local and remote access. The size and complexity of a network is directly related to the number of tasks to be performed to keep it up and running.

The range of tasks required to sustain a network varies considerably from network to network. For example, all networks require managing user accounts, applying security controls, and backing up data. Some other networks may also require remote access management, performance monitoring, and error tracking.

All these duties are performed using the Administrative Tools. These tools are designed to manage servers remotely either from other Windows Server 2003 servers or from Windows XP Professional PCs with either hot fix QFE Q329357 or Service Pack 1 or later. Although these tools support both 32 and 64-bit servers, they currently can't be installed on 64-bit systems.

Just as a handyman needs the right tool for a particular job, you need to know which tools can perform which functions. In the following chapters, we walk through the administrative, management, monitoring, and related tools included with Windows Server 2003. In addition to reviewing the discussions in this book, you should take the time to work with the tools themselves. Hands-on experience is invaluable and cannot be substituted. You may want to review the online help documentation included in the tools, as well as materials from the Windows Server 2003 Resource Kit and TechNet.

Installing the Administrative Tools

The Administrative Tools are included on the Windows Server 2003 CD, and are not installed by default. To install the tools, you must be a member of the local administrator group on the server or PC where you want to install the tools.

To install the Administrative tools from the Windows Server 2003 R2 CD, follow the procedure in Step by Step 1.2.

STEP BY STEP

1.2 Installing the Administrative Tools

1. Insert the Windows Server 2003 R2 CD-ROM.

2. When the Welcome to the Microsoft Windows 2003 R2 screen appears, select Browse This CD, as shown in Figure 1.9.

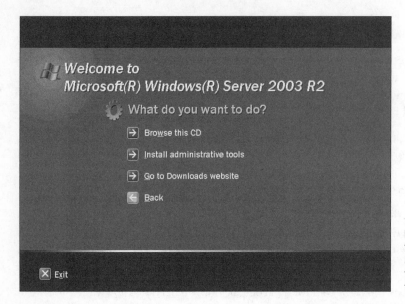

Welcome to
Microsoft(R) Windows(R) Server 2003 R2

What do you want to do?

→ Browse this CD

→ Install administrative tools

→ Go to Downloads website

← Back

☒ Exit

FIGURE 1.9 After the initial installation of Windows Server 2003, additional features can be installed from the CD.

3. Double-click the I386 folder.

4. Scroll down and double-click the Adminpak.msi file.

5. Accept the defaults and let the installation continue. This will take a minute or two.

EXAM ALERT

Adminpak.msi **Although the** Adminpak.msi **file is present on every Windows Server 2003 server in the** \Windows\System32 **folder, the exam always refers to loading it from the CD. Although either way will work fine, the version in System32 will always be the current version because it is upgraded with each service pack installation**

The Microsoft Management Console: Where Management Begins

Back when Microsoft introduced the Windows NT Option Pack in version 4.0, it introduced the Microsoft Management Console (MMC). The Microsoft vision at that time was that the MMC would become the de facto tool for administration in future versions of Windows. This vision has since become reality.

What makes the MMC different from previous tools is that the MMC itself doesn't perform any management duties. Instead, it is simply a shell into which administrative tools, called snap-ins, can be added, modified, or removed. As you can see in Figure 1.10, when the MMC is started (by issuing the `mmc.exe` command), a blank window is opened.

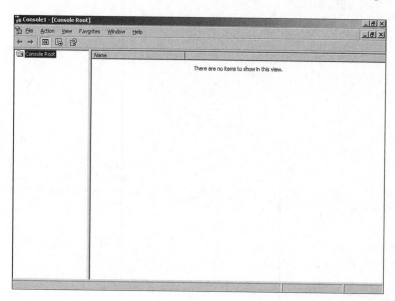

FIGURE 1.10 The MMC allows you to start with a blank slate and add only the administrative snap-ins that you need.

The capability to pick and choose which administrative tools a console is to have makes MMC extremely flexible, especially in an environment in which several administrators perform different tasks. The administrators can create (or have created for them by the system administrator) an MMC that has only the tools that they require. For example, Sue may be responsible for monitoring server performance, the event logs, and the Domain Name Service, whereas Joe's job is to create users and groups and set security policies for each user.

For example, to create Joe's MMC, follow the steps shown in Step by Step 1.3.

STEP BY STEP

1.3 Creating a Custom Management Console

1. Select Start, Run, type MMC.exe into the field, and click OK.

2. Choose the Add/Remove Snap-In option from the Console menu and click the Add button.

3. Select the Group Policy Snap-In and click Add.

4. Select the Local Users and Groups Snap-In and click Add.

5. Click the Close button.

6. Click OK. The MMC as shown in Figure 1.11 should appear.

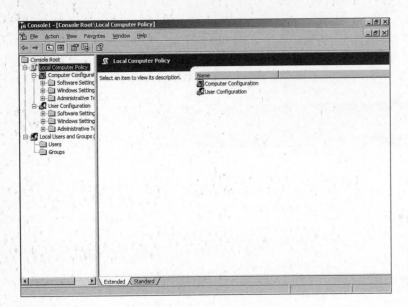

FIGURE 1.11 The completed MMC showing the custom snap-ins that were selected.

With the release of Windows Server 2003 R2, Microsoft has updated the MMC to version 3.0. In this version, an additional Action pane is added, as shown in Figure 1.12.

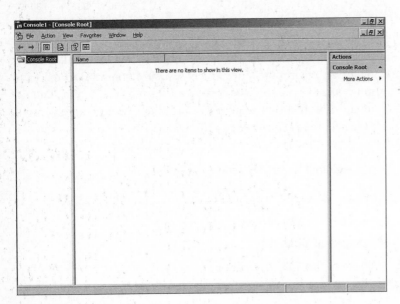

FIGURE 1.12 MMC version 3.0 showing the Action pane.

The MMC now accepts snap-ins based on the .Net Framework, which allows additional functionality to be added to the Management Console. As of service Pack 2, most of the older snap-ins, such as Computer Management and Active Directory Users and Computers, have not been rewritten to take advantage of the new functionality. However, the newer snap-ins, such as the Disk Quota management console, are written for MMC version 3.0.

To download a copy of MMC 3.0 to use on pre-R2 versions of Windows Server 2003 and Windows XP, go to http://support.microsoft.com/?kbid=907265.

Chapter Summary

In this chapter, you learned about the various versions of Windows Server 2003 and what features it supports. In addition, you learned the hardware requirements, both the minimum and the recommended minimums.

You also learned how to log on to a Windows Server 2003 server for the first time and what screens you are presented with. A server can host various roles, and Microsoft has made it easier to configure these roles for you by supplying the Configure Your Server Wizard. This tool can be used to either add or remove roles from your server, and can be run at any time from the Administrative Tools folder.

Next, you learned about the Microsoft Management Console and how to add snap-ins to customize it for your needs.

Key Terms

- ▶ Administrative tools
- ▶ Clustering server
- ▶ Load balancing
- ▶ Member server
- ▶ MMC
- ▶ Node
- ▶ Password
- ▶ Server roles
- ▶ Snap-in
- ▶ Standalone server
- ▶ Username

Apply Your Knowledge

You have seen the roles that a Windows Server 2003 server can support on a network. Although these roles can be configured manually using checklists either generated by your company or downloaded from Microsoft, the Configure Your Server Wizard offers a guided approach to ensure that you don't leave out any important steps.

In this exercise you're going to use the wizard to configure your server for the File Server role, probably the most common role you will encounter in the real world. To perform this exercise, you use the test server that you built earlier in this chapter.

Exercises

1.1 Preparing a Windows Server 2003 server to be a file server

The Configure Your Server Wizard guides you in configuring your Windows Server 2003 server for a specific role.

Estimated Time: 20 minutes.

1. Start the Wizard by clicking Start, All Programs, Administrative Tools, Configure Your Server Wizard.

2. On the Welcome to the Configure Your Server Wizard screen, click Next.

3. On the next screen, review the preliminary steps, then click Next.

4. On the Server Role screen shown in Figure 1.13, highlight the entry for File Server, and then click Next.

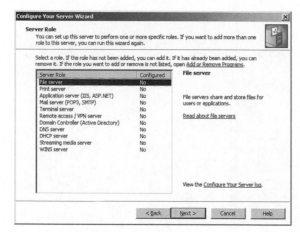

FIGURE 1.13 Select the File Server role. Only one role can be selected at a time, but you can run the wizard multiple times.

5. On the File Server Disk Quotas screen, click Next.

6. On the File Server Indexing Service screen, select the option to turn the Indexing service on. Click Next.

7. On the Summary screen, review your selections. If they are correct, click Next. If not, click the Back button to change them.

8. This starts the Share a Folder Wizard. Click Next.

9. On the Folder Path screen, enter **C:\Test**. Click Next. You will be prompted to create the folder if it doesn't already exist. Click Yes.

10. On the Name, Description and Settings screen, accept the defaults as shown in Figure 1.14, and then click Next.

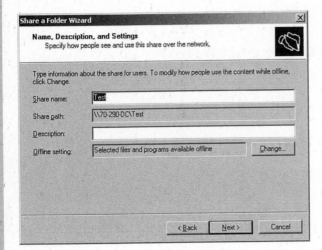

FIGURE 1.14 If the share name isn't descriptive, type in a description so that end users can identify the share.

11. On the Permissions screen, as shown in Figure 1.15, select the second option: Administrators Have Full Access; Others Have Read-only Access. Click Finish.

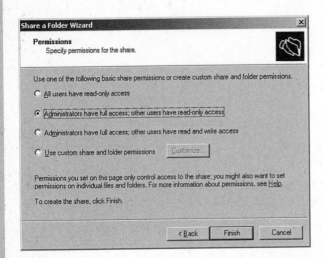

FIGURE 1.15 The Permissions screen configures the access that users have to the share over the network.

12. As shown in Figure 1.16, the wizard should indicate that the sharing was successful. If not, review the messages and repair the problem. Click the Close button to end the wizard.

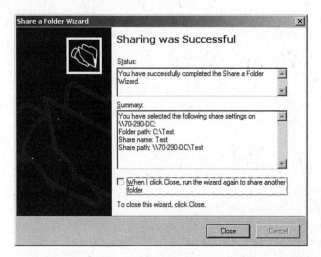

FIGURE 1.16 If the share process wasn't successful, follow the instructions to fix it. You also have the option to run it again to share more folders.

13. This returns you to the Configure Your Server Wizard. Click Finish.

Exam Questions

1. Joe wants to create a password for his newly installed Windows Server 2003 server. His server is a member of a workgroup, not a domain. Which of the following passwords would meet the complexity requirements? (Choose all that apply.)

   ○ **A.** password

   ○ **B.** P@ssw0rd

   ○ **C.** Joe

   ○ **D.** blank password

   ○ **E.** All of the above

   ○ **F.** None of the above

2. Joe wants to create a password for his newly installed Windows Server 2003 server. His server was installed as a domain controller for his test domain. Which of the following passwords would meet the complexity requirements? (Choose all that apply.)

   ○ **A.** password

   ○ **B.** P@ssw0rd

   ○ **C.** Joe

   ○ **D.** A blank password

   ○ **E.** All of the above

   ○ **F.** None of the above

3. Jack wants to use an old server that he has lying around as a Windows Server 2003 file server. What steps should he take to make sure that the server is compatible with Windows Server 2003? (Choose all that apply.)

   ○ **A.** Check the hardware requirements

   ○ **B.** Check the hardware compatibility list

   ○ **C.** Upgrade his BIOS to the latest level

   ○ **D.** All of the above

   ○ **E.** None of the above

4. Frank needs to replace a couple of his older domain controllers with new ones running Windows Server 2003. He is buying them directly from a vendor with the operating system preinstalled, but he needs to specify which version of Windows Server 2003 that he wants. Which of the following versions of Windows Server 2003 would be most suitable for a single-CPU server with 512MB of RAM? (Choose the best answer.)

   ○ **A.** Windows Server 2003 Enterprise Edition

   ○ **B.** Windows Server 2003 Standard Edition

   ○ **C.** Windows Server 2003 Web Edition

   ○ **D.** All of the above

   ○ **E.** None of the above

5. Gary has received a request from his boss to put together a hardware specification to support a mission-critical web application. This application is somewhat finicky, so the server must be rebooted frequently, and updates to the software must be performed frequently. However, it is required to be available 24/7. What edition and feature of Windows Server 2003 would provide Gary with the best cost-effective solution to support this application?

   ○ **A.** Windows Server 2003 Web Edition with clustering

   ○ **B.** Windows Server 2003 Enterprise Edition with clustering

   ○ **C.** Windows Server 2003 Standard Edition with clustering

   ○ **D.** Windows Server 2003 Web Edition with load balancing

   ○ **E.** None of the above

Answers to Exam Questions

1. **E.** When a Windows Server 2003 server is not part of a domain, password complexity is not enabled, so any password is allowed, even a blank one. See "Logging on to Windows Server 2003."

2. **B.** The only valid answer is B. When a Windows Server 2003 server is installed as a domain controller, the password complexity rules are enabled by default. For a password to be acceptable, it must not contain all or part of the username, which makes C wrong. In addition, it must be six characters or greater, which invalidates both C and D. It also must contain characters from three of the following four groups: capital letters, lower case letters, numbers, or special characters. This makes B the only logical choice. See "Logging on to Windows Server 2003."

3. **A and B.** First, Jack needs to make sure that his hardware meets the minimum specifications for RAM, CPU speed, and disk space. Then he needs to check the Hardware Compatibility List to make sure that his hardware is supported on Windows Server 2003. See "Hardware Requirements" and "Hardware Compatibility."

4. **B.** The Enterprise Edition of Windows Server 2003 is meant for a multiple-CPU, fault-tolerant environment, and would be wasted on a single CPU server with a modest amount of memory. The web edition of Windows Server 2003 cannot be used as a domain controller. See "The Windows Server 2003 Family."

5. **D.** A and C are incorrect because neither of those two versions support clustering. In addition, it wasn't specified that the application was cluster-aware, so that eliminates B, and clusters are also usually expensive. Because it's required to host a web application, the most cost-effective way to support it is using a load-balanced configuration of Windows Server 2003 Web Edition servers. In this configuration, one or more servers can be taken offline for repairs or software maintenance while the other servers are still processing connections. See "The Windows Server 2003 Family."

Suggested Readings and Resources

1. Boswell, William. *Inside Windows Server 2003*. New Riders, 2003. ISBN 0735711585.

2. Matthews, Marty. *Windows Server 2003: A Beginners Guide*. McGraw-Hill, 2003. ISBN 0072193093.

3. Minasi, Mark, et al. *Mark Minasi's Windows XP and Server 2003 Resource Kit*. Sybex, 2003. ISBN 0782140807.

4. Minasi, Mark, et al. *Mastering Windows Server 2003*. Sybex, 2003. ISBN 0782141307.

5. Shapiro, Jeffrey, et al. *Windows Server 2003 Bible*. John Wiley & Sons, 2003. ISBN 0764549375.

6. Windows Server 2003 Deployment Guide. http://technet2.microsoft.com/WindowsServer/en/Library/c283b699-6124-4c3a-87ef-865443d7ea4b1033.mspx?mfr=true Microsoft Corporation.

7. *Windows Server 2003 Resource Kit*. Microsoft Press, 2005. ISBN 0735614717.

CHAPTER TWO

Managing User and Computer Accounts

Objectives

This chapter covers the following Microsoft-specified objectives for the "Managing Users, Computers, and Groups" section of the Managing and Maintaining a Microsoft Windows Server 2003 Environment exam:

Create and manage user accounts.

▶ **Create and modify user accounts by using the Active Directory Users and Computers console**

▶ **Create and modify user accounts by using automation**

▶ **Import user accounts**

▶ A primary function of a network administrator is to create and manage user accounts because user accounts are needed for users to authenticate to the network and to determine what resources the user can access.

▶ For a small network, creating and modifying the user accounts one at a time with a management tool is not too time consuming. But on a network with hundreds or thousands of users, it makes sense to use tools that automate the process. If the data about the users exists in some other form, such as a new-hire database, you can create the user accounts by importing them from a compatible file.

Manage local, roaming, and mandatory user profiles

▶ The settings for a user's work environment are stored in the user's profile. Any changes the user makes to the environment (Favorites, Start menu items, icons, colors, My Documents, Desktop, local settings, application-specific settings) are saved when the user logs off. The profile is reloaded when the user logs on again.

▶ It is important for administrators to know how to manage user profiles so that the users' settings are saved from session to session. If managed properly, this also ensures that the users see the same desktop no matter where they log on.

Create and manage computer accounts in an Active Directory environment

▶ Every computer running Windows NT, Windows 2000/2003, or Windows XP that is a member of a domain has a computer account in that domain. The computer account is a security principal, and it can be authenticated and granted permissions to access resources. A computer account is automatically created for each computer running these operating systems when the computer joins the domain.

Troubleshoot user accounts

▶ **Troubleshoot account lockouts.**

▶ **Troubleshoot issues related to user account properties.**

▶ With a large group of users, there are sure to be trouble calls every day from users having difficulties with their accounts. One system setting that often results in trouble calls is Account Lockout—a user cannot log in because the account has been disabled after too many incorrect passwords were entered. Other problems can arise because of inappropriate settings in the user accounts.

Troubleshoot user-authentication issues

▶ Sometimes a user will not be able to log on to the network. This can be caused by simple factors, such as a user error when entering a user ID and password, or by more complex issues such as the computer account being unusable. The network administrator must be able to determine what is causing the problem and to promptly correct the situation.

Troubleshoot computer accounts

▶ **Diagnose and resolve issues related to computer accounts by using the Active Directory Users and Computers MMC snap-in.**

▶ **Reset computer accounts.**

▶ When a computer account is operating incorrectly, it may be impossible to log on to the domain from the computer. In this case it is necessary to reset the computer's account and rejoin the computer to the domain. This process reestablishes the secure relationship between the computer and the domain it is a member of.

Outline

Study Strategies

▶ In studying this section, be sure to practice all the activities described. Become very familiar with Active Directory Users and Computers, creating user and computer accounts, resetting user and computer accounts, and defining roaming profiles and mandatory profiles. Microsoft is proud of the new command-line directory-management tools—dsquery, dsadd, dsmod, and dsget—so be sure you know what each one is for as well as how to use it. Also be sure you understand piping—sending the output from one command as the input to another.

▶ Use both `ldifde` and `csvde`, but don't spend hours making them work. Understand what they are for, and get to know the command structure. Work through the exercises until you can explain authoritatively `ldifde` and `csvde` to a colleague.

▶ You will need access to a Windows Server 2003 domain controller. Many of the tools are new, or they differ from those available in Windows 2000, so don't try to get by with a Windows 2000 domain controller.

▶ You don't have to buy Windows Server 2003 to try it out. You can download a free evaluation version (which expires in 180 days) from www.microsoft.com/windowsserver2003/evaluation/trial/default.mspx.

Introduction

Starting with this chapter, you're going to learn about some of the common daily duties of a Windows Server 2003 administrator. It is likely that you will perform the tasks you learn in this chapter in the near future. This chapter discusses creating and managing user accounts, computer accounts, and setting up roaming profiles.

Troubleshooting is a big part of the job, too. Troubleshooting entails helping users understand why they cannot connect to the network—whether it's because of locked-out user accounts, inoperative computer accounts, or other reasons. We'll start with user accounts. Let's get to it!

Creating and Managing User Accounts

Objective:
Create and manage user accounts

User accounts are created so that people can identify themselves and receive access to the local and network resources they need. In Windows Server 2003 with Active Directory enabled, user accounts (often called *user IDs*) are assigned using the Active Directory Users and Computers management console. On standalone Windows Server 2003 computers, user accounts are created using the Local Users and Groups snap-in in the Computer Management Microsoft Management Console (MMC).

A *user account* is a record stored in a database—either the Security Accounts Manager (SAM) database stored on a workstation or server, or the Active Directory database stored on your domain controllers. The user account contains the user ID, password, Security Identifier, and other information pertaining to that user. A user account is similar to the electronic door cards that some of us use for access to our offices. Like the door cards, our user account contains information on who we are, what we do, and what doors (network resources) we have access to. Also, like the door cards, the system administrator has a record of what doors (network resources) you accessed and when.

When users log on to a PC or server, they are identified by their Security Identifier (SID). This SID is a unique number that is used to identify the user. Although we use a name to identify a user, Windows uses the SID. The user name (a.k.a. User ID) can be changed, but the SID stays the same. If you delete a user account and create a new one with the same name, it will receive a different SID. SIDs are never reused.

NOTE

Smart Cards Because we're using door cards as an analogy, it should be pointed out that Windows Server 2003 supports the use of Smart Cards. These cards have the user identity information encoded on them and allow the user to log on by swiping the card in a reader and entering a personal identification number.

Having a unique user account for each user allows the system administrator to selectively grant access to the resources on the server or network. If, for example, you store salary information on a server, you wouldn't want all the users to have access to that information!

Every user should have a separate account. If there are problems with system usage or a security breach, it's necessary that the administrator be able to tell who was acting incorrectly. If all the engineers in a department logged on using a single account called "Engineer," it would be impossible to tell which one of the engineers was accessing the resources. Allocating separate accounts also allows each user to have access to exactly the resources needed and no more. Also, each user account can have its own private home directory—multiple users sharing a single account would have no such private storage.

The following subsections discuss the methods of creating and managing user accounts:

▶ Creating and modifying local user accounts

▶ Creating and managing accounts with the Active Directory Users and Computers management console

▶ Creating a user account template

▶ Creating and managing accounts with automated processes

▶ Creating and managing accounts using bulk Import/Export tools

Creating and Modifying Local User Accounts

Each Windows Server 2003 server that is a member server or a standalone server can have local accounts. Local accounts are accounts that are stored in the SAM database on that server. Local accounts can be used to access resources only on that server; they cannot be used to access resources on other servers or on the network, if present.

NOTE

Log on Locally   We should clarify that typically a local account is used to grant access *over the network* to users located at other PCs in a workgroup situation. For example, if a shared folder or printer is attached to a workgroup server, users at their PCs would access this resource over the network. Although a local user can log on locally to a workgroup server, that is not recommended. After a server is added to a domain, the log on locally permission for anything other than administrators is restricted.

Each Windows Server 2003 server contains the following built-in user accounts:

▶ *Administrator*—The local Administrator account has complete authority over the resources on the server. It can be used to grant or deny access to other users. You cannot delete the Administrators account, but you can rename it or disable it. This account was used for the first logon to the server.

▶ *Guest*—The Guest account does not require a password and is used for users who do not have a user account. However, by default it has limited access to resources and is disabled. You can enable it and grant it access to resources, if needed, but this is not recommended.

▶ *Support_388945a0*—This account is used to allow ordinary users to run scripts from within the Help and Support Service. This capability must be delegated by the administrator.

▶ *HelpAssistant*—This account will not be created until you start a Remote Assistance session.

You will need to create user accounts for users other than the Administrator so they have access to resources on the server. Local user accounts are created using the Local Users and Groups snap-in, in the Computer Management MMC.

Usernames must be unique; they cannot be identical to any other user or group name on the computer. The name can contain up to 20 characters, except for the following: " / \ [ ] : ; | = , + * ? < >. The username cannot consist solely of periods or spaces. The password cannot be longer than 127 characters.

To create a local user account, follow Step by Step 2.1:

STEP BY STEP

2.1 Creating a local user account

1. Open the Computer Management MMC by selecting Start, All Programs, Administrative Tools, and then click Computer Management.

2. In the left pane of the Computer Management MMC, expand System Tools, and then select Local Users and Groups.

3. Right-click the Users folder and select New Users from the action menu.

4. In the New User dialog box, as shown in Figure 2.1, enter the User Name and Password. If desired, you can enter a Full Name and Description.

FIGURE 2.1   The username must be unique.

5. Click the Create button to save the user account.

6. Click the Close button to quit.

In the New User dialog box, there are four options that we didn't discuss. Three of the four relate to password management.

They are the following:

▶ *User Must Change Password at Next Logon*—This option is useful when creating user accounts for new users or resetting the password of a user account. This allows the administrator to initially set the password to a known value, and the next time the user logs on, that user is prompted to create a new password. This way, only the users know what their password is.

▶ *User Cannot Change Password*—This option is useful for shared accounts, where if a user changes the password, the other people using the account will be locked out. (Remember, account sharing is not a good practice).

▶ *Password Never Expires*—This option is typically used for service accounts, where the password should be changed only by the application that is using it, or where an expired password would keep the application from running.

▶ *Account Is Disabled*—This option disables the account, which prevents the user from logging on.

Challenge

You are a system administrator who is responsible for managing the security for a Windows Server 2003 server that contains all the information used to run your company.

Because of an upswing in business, management has purchased a new application and has hired four new people. Two of these people are going to be receptionists. They are both part-timers and will be sharing a PC. They both need access to a calendar and printer on the server, but won't need any other access.

The other two new hires are engineers. They are working in two different departments, so their server access needs will be different. In addition, the new application must run as a background application, so it will need a dedicated service account.

Your task is to create the necessary user accounts for both the new users and the new application. Make sure that everything is configured so that the end user has the correct access while maintaining a comfortable level of security. Draw up a plan for creating these accounts while adhering to these specifications.

Try to complete this exercise on your own, listing your conclusions on a sheet of paper. After you have completed the exercise, compare your results to those given here.

1. The two receptionists can share a user account because they won't have any access to secure resources. Configure their account with a password that doesn't expire, so that one user won't change the password and lock the other out.

2. Because the engineers are working in different departments, give each of them a unique account. Set the account to require the users to change the password when they first log on.

3. Configure the service account password for the new application to never expire.

Creating and Modifying User Accounts Using Active Directory Users and Computers

Objective:

Create and modify user accounts by using the Active Directory Users and Computers MMC

In the previous section, you learned how to create local accounts; however, when a server is located in a domain, it is more practical to use domain accounts. A domain account allows a user to sign on with a single account and access resources on any machine in the domain that the user has been granted access to. As your network gets larger, you will see that domain accounts are a good thing, because you will no longer have to maintain a local account on each server.

Before you can use and create domain accounts, you need to create a domain controller. A *domain controller* is used to store the user accounts, computer accounts and other objects contained in a Windows domain. Similar to the SAM that is contained on each server, a domain controller has a database called the Active Directory. Because this database is designed for use in larger environments, it is far more robust that the simple server SAM, and the changes to the Active Directory on one domain controller are automatically replicated to all the other domain controllers in the domain.

> **EXAM ALERT**
>
> **Have a Very Basic Understanding of Active Directory**   Understand when, how, and why you would use a domain controller versus a standalone server in a workgroup. However, the intricacies of Active Directory and replication are reserved for the 70-294 exam.

Before you can work with Active Directory, you must install it. An Active Directory domain controller is created by promoting a member server to a domain controller using the DCPromo utility.

> **EXAM ALERT**
>
> **Multiple Methods**   Recall from Chapter 1, "Windows Server 2003 Environment," that you can also use the Manage Your Server Wizard to change the role of your server to a domain controller. You should understand how to do it both ways for the exam.

In Step by Step 2.2, we will take the Windows Server 2003 member server that we created in the previous chapter and promote it to a domain controller.

STEP BY STEP

2.2 Promoting a member server to a domain controller

1. Log on to your Windows Server 2003 server as an administrator.

2. Load your Windows Server 2003 CD, click Start, Run, and enter **dcpromo** in the dialog box. Click the OK button to start the process.

3. On the Welcome to the Active Directory Installation Wizard screen, click the Next button.

4. On the Operating System Compatibility screen shown in Figure 2.2, make sure that you read about the new security settings in Windows Server 2003 and how they affect older operating systems. After you have reviewed the screen, click the Next button.

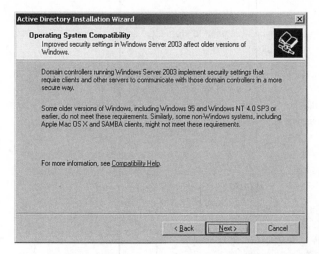

FIGURE 2.2 Most of the older operating systems are not supported in a Windows Server 2003 domain.

5. On the domain controller Type screen, select Domain Controller for a New Domain because this is going to be the first domain controller in our new domain. Click the Next button.

6. On the Create New Domain screen, select Domain in a New Forest. Click the Next button.

7. On the New Domain Name screen, you are prompted to enter the name of the new domain. Type in **70-290.int**. Click the Next button.

8. On the NetBIOS Domain Name screen, you are prompted to enter the NetBIOS name for the domain. Accept the default and click the Next button.

9. On the Database and Logs folders shown in Figure 2.3, you are prompted for the location where you want to store the Active Directory database and its transaction log. For our lab, the default locations are fine. Click the Next button to continue.

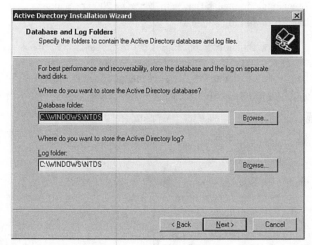

FIGURE 2.3 Like any other database, Active Directory requires storage space for both the database and the transaction log.

10. On the Shared System Volume screen, you are prompted for the location of the SYSVOL, a folder that is replicated to each domain controller in your domain. It is used to store login scripts and Group Policies. Accept the default. Click the Next button to continue.

11. If your server fails to contact a DNS server, you will be presented with the DNS Registration Diagnostics screen, as shown in Figure 2.4. Here you have the choice of reconfiguring your TCP/IP setting to use an existing DNS server, then running the diagnostics again, ignoring the error and moving on, or letting Windows install a DNS server on your server. Select the option to install and configure DNS on your server, and then click the Next button.

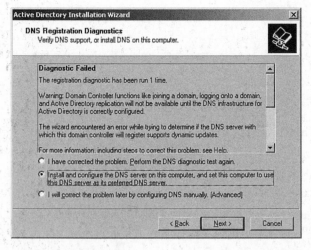

FIGURE 2.4 In most cases, it's best to host your DNS server on your domain controller.

12. On the Permissions screen, you have the option of loosening your security so that certain functions of older servers will operate. Unless you are running a Windows NT 4.0 Remote Access Server, you would normally select the default setting of Permissions Compatible Only with Windows 2000 or Windows Server 2003 Operating Systems. Click the Next button to continue.

13. On the next screen, you are prompted to enter the Directory Services Restore mode password. This is not the same as the Administrator password. This password is used only during disaster recovery of the Active Directory database. This will be covered in Chapter 16, "Implementing Administrative Templates and Audit Policy." For now, enter a password, and then click the Next button.

14. On the Summary screen, review your selections, and then click the Next button.

15. The Active Directory Installation Wizard will run for the next 10 to 15 minutes. When it is completed, click the Finish button.

16. When prompted, select the option to reboot. Active Directory is installed.

Choosing a Domain Name

In the previous exercise, you might have noticed that we used the suffix .int when naming the Active Directory domain. This is to ensure the uniqueness of our domain name, since a domain name with the .int extension cannot be registered and used as a valid domain on the Internet. You should avoid using a domain name with any registerable extensions such as .com, .net., or .org because the domain name might already be in use. More information on how and why to choose domain names will be covered on the 70-294 exam.

Logging On to a Windows Server 2003 Domain Controller

Now that you've promoted your member server to a domain controller, you need to log on. Like you did before, press Ctrl+Alt+Del to present the logon dialog box. Do you notice anything different? Note: You might have to click the Options button. Take a close look at Figure 2.5.

FIGURE 2.5 The name of the domain is displayed on the logon dialog box.

There is now an additional field on the logon dialog box, the Log On To field. The name of the domain is now displayed when you log on to your domain controller. Before, you were logging on to a standalone server, and the only method of authentication was from the local SAM. In our case, now that our server is a domain controller, the only method of authentication is via the Active Directory (AD) database. When AD is installed, the SAM is removed. However, if this was a member server or a workstation, the Log On To field would let you select from logging on via the local SAM or to the domain. If you log on via the SAM, you have access to resources only on that machine, versus logging on to a domain where you could potentially have access to resources throughout the domain!

Using the Active Directory Users and Computers Console

Now that we've logged on to our freshly built domain controller, let's talk about another difference between it and the standalone server we worked with earlier in the chapter. We've already pointed out that when Active Directory is installed, the local SAM is removed. This also means that we can no longer create user accounts using the Local Users and Groups snap-in, because there are no longer any local users or groups!

Each Windows Server 2003 domain controller contains the following built-in user accounts:

▶ *Administrator*—The domain Administrator account has complete authority over the resources in the domain. It can be used to create and modify user accounts or to grant or deny access to other users. You cannot delete the Administrators account, but you can rename it or disable it. This account was used for the first logon to the server.

▶ *Guest*—The Guest account is used for users who do not have a user account, and it doesn't require a password. However, by default it has limited access to resources and is disabled. You can enable it and grant it access to resources, if needed, but this is not recommended.

▶ *Support_388945a0*—This account is used to allow ordinary users to run scripts from within the Help and Support Service. This capability must be delegated by the administrator.

▶ *HelpAssistant*—This account will not be created until you start a Remote Assistance session.

> **EXAM ALERT**
>
> **Log on Locally** Unlike a standalone server, by default, only the Administrator has log on locally rights on a domain controller. This will probably come up in a question on the exam.

Creating Domain Accounts

Now that we're in a domain, we have to create domain accounts to give users access to the resources in our domain. The Active Directory Users and Computers (ADUC) console is the most straightforward way to create and modify domain user accounts. It is accessible from Start, Administrative Tools, Active Directory Users and Computers; from the Manage Your Server Wizard; or by using Start, Run and typing `dsa.msc` into the Run dialog box.

When you start Active Directory Users and Computers, as shown in Figure 2.6, you will see a familiar Explorer-like display. In the left pane is a folder containing saved queries (we'll talk about queries later in the chapter) and an icon showing the name of the domain the managing computer is attached to (70-290-int, in this case). The right pane shows the contents of the container selected in the left pane. Because we have the Builtin container selected in the figure, we see the contents of that container in the right pane.

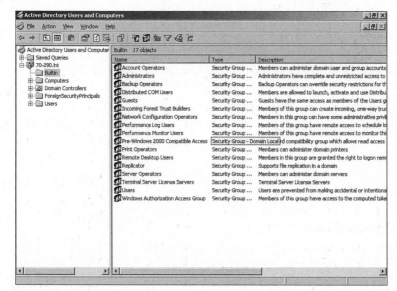

FIGURE 2.6 Selecting a container on the left pane displays its contents in the right pane.

NOTE

Containers?? If you look closely in the left pane of the Active Directory Users and Computers MMC, you will notice that all the folder icons are not the same. Some icons are plain—these are containers. The other icons have an open folder label on them—these are OUs. Most of the containers are automatically created by the operating system, and control of some of them cannot be delegated.

Let's assume we're the network administrators for the Kansas City location of our organization, and we need to create some user accounts. Because the Kansas City Organizational Unit (OU) hasn't yet been created, we will need to do that. OUs are used in Active Directory to store users, groups, and resources. We'll create that OU and two more subordinate OUs below it in Step by Step 2.3.

EXAM ALERT

Be Familiar with OUs OUs are containers that the administrator creates to contain users, groups, and resources, such as computers and file shares. The administrator can then delegate authority over or assign a Group Policy to the items contained in the OU. You must have a good understanding of this for the exam. OUs will be covered at length in Chapter 8, "Managing Access to Objects in Organizational Units."

STEP BY STEP

2.3 Creating OUs

1. In the left pane of the Active Directory Users and Computers console, select the top-level container in which you want to create the OU. In our example, the top-level container is `70-290.int`.

2. Right-click the container and choose New, Organizational Unit. Type the name **Kansas City** for the OU into the Name box.

3. Right-click the Kansas City OU and choose New, Organizational Unit. Type **Users**.

4. Repeat step 3, calling this OU **Workstations**.

We now have the organizational structure we want. This basic structure will be used in the exercises in this chapter, and later in the book.

Creating Domain User Accounts

Now that we have our organizational structure in place, we can create a user account. Follow the procedure in Step by Step 2.4 to create a user account.

STEP BY STEP

2.4 Creating a User Account

1. In the left pane of the Active Directory Users and Computers console, select the top-level container in which you want to create the users. In our example, the top-level container is `70-290.int`.

2. Right-click the Kansas City\Users container and select New, User.

3. Type the first and last names and the user logon name, as in Figure 2.7. In this organization, the default rule for creating the user logon name is the initial letter of the first (given) name, followed by the full last name (surname).

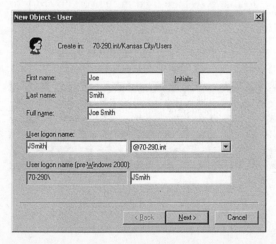

FIGURE 2.7 Fill in the name of the person for whom you are creating the user account.

4. Type the initial password for the user and repeat it in the confirmation field (see Figure 2.8). Accept the default password options.

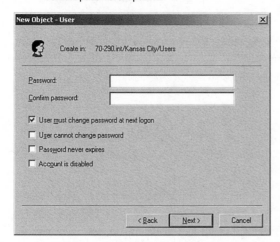

FIGURE 2.8 In most organizations, the default password settings for a new user are acceptable.

5. Review the information in the confirmation dialog box and select Finish to create the user object.

NOTE

User Account Settings In the New User Creation Wizard, the default password settings (shown in Figure 2.8) force the new user to change the password at the first successful logon. This ensures that the administrator does not know the user's credentials and therefore cannot impersonate the user. Also, forcing the user to change his password immediately makes him aware of any password complexity rules the organization has chosen, because if the password is too short or not complex enough, Windows Server 2003 will reject it and force the user's new password to comply with the complexity rules.

The second password setting is User Cannot Change Password. Typically, an organization wants users to be able to change their own passwords, but occasionally (as for a visitor account) the password should not be changed.

Next is a setting that allows the administrator to exempt this account from the password-expiration rule. Most organizations want their users to change their passwords regularly (every 60 days, for example), so that if a password has been compromised, its useful period to gain access to the network is limited. The exception to this rule is for service accounts. A service account is used so that applications, such as Microsoft Exchange and Microsoft SQL Server, have access to network resources. These applications expect the password to never be changed, or if it is changed, the change must be performed using the management tool for the application and not through the ADUC.

Finally, the account can be disabled with the last check box, Account Is Disabled. This feature is generally used in one of two cases: when the account is created before the user is physically onsite or when the user is temporarily or permanently gone from the organization. In both cases, no one should be able to use the account, so disabling it is an appropriate security precaution.

The account has now been created, and at this point the user could log in. However, there are many properties of the account that we have not yet set, so let's look at how to modify a user account with Active Directory Users and Computers.

After the user object has been created, you can select it and review or set its properties. Double-clicking the object in the right panel of ADUC opens a Properties dialog box, as shown in Figure 2.9.

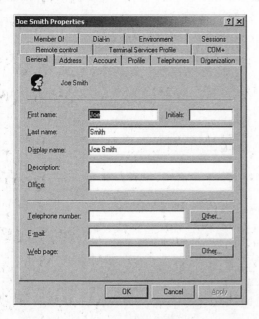

FIGURE 2.9 Change any of the properties on the General tab of the user account dialog box.

Larger organizations generally have a list of the required information that must be entered for each user account. For example, it might be mandatory to fill in the Office Location field, and there might be a fixed list of allowable entries. Like all fields in a user object, it is possible to search on the contents of the Office Location field. However, if one administrator enters Salt Lake, another enters SLC, and a third enters Salt Lake City, how are users to search for that location? Requiring administrators to use office location names from a published list will resolve that problem.

More About Directories

The Active Directory is, in effect, a directory for the company, so rather than relying on a printed booklet, the users can pull all organization and contact information right from AD. Also, entry of organizational info (but not account creation) is often given to the Human Resources department because it often has the rights to update certain properties because of changes that are happening. (For example, Bob just got promoted; he will be moving to a new office.) There are also some companies that leave it to the users to update themselves. (For example, if their extension changes, they can update that info in AD.) Microsoft is hoping that this will do away with some other internal directories that are in use (for example, printed books, email systems, databases used for printing, departmental phone lists, and so on).

The Address tab is available so that Active Directory can hold personal and business address information about the user. Most large organizations have personnel systems that carry this information, however, and these systems can use Active Directory or other database systems to store the data. Even if Active Directory is the directory system used to hold this employee data, the personnel system would update the directory programmatically, not via the Active Directory Users and Computers console.

The Account tab contains several useful entry areas. The Logon Hours button allows you to specify which hours during the week the user is permitted to log on to the system. The Log On To button lets you specify the NetBIOS or the fully qualified domain name (FQDN) of the computers the user is permitted to log on to. Among the Account options is the setting Smart Card Is Required for Interactive Logon, which, if activated, requires the user to present a smart card to log on directly to a server or workstation. For this to work, this smart card must be encoded with a certificate issued to the user, and a smart card reader must be installed on the computer. The smart card eliminates the need for a username and password; the user just needs the smart card and a personal identification number (PIN).

NOTE

Beware of Interactive Logons An *interactive logon* is a logon performed at the console of the server or via a Terminal Services session. A user who can log on directly to a server is more of a risk than a user who is logged on across the network, because when someone has physical access to the server, there is very little the OS can do to protect itself.

Account Expiration Date is the final entry area on the Account tab. Although we would expect most accounts to be valid indefinitely, for temporary employees, such as summer students, interns, or contractors, it is wise to specify the last date an account can be used (see Figure 2.10).

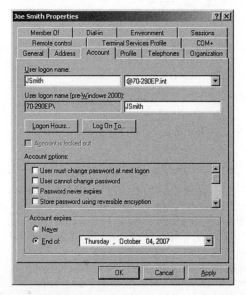

FIGURE 2.10 Use the End Of option button to select a date after which the account will no longer be valid.

NOTE

Managing Your Server Remotely   Remember from Chapter 1 that you can install the Administrative Tools for Windows Server 2003 on a Windows XP workstation so that you don't have to be logged on to the server console to manage it.

If you want to manage a computer running Windows Server 2003 from a workstation that is not running Windows XP, the only available method is to start a Terminal Services session. Fortunately, Terminal Services clients are available for all Windows operating systems from Windows 95 on.

On the Profile tab, shown in Figure 2.11, in the User Profile section you can specify where the user's profile data will be stored. We'll discuss profiles in depth later in this chapter, in the "Managing Local, Roaming, and Mandatory User Profiles" section. Also on the Profile tab, you can specify the name of the logon script (the scripted commands that will run on the user's behalf) when the user logs on.

In the Home Folder section of the Profile tab, you can specify the path where the user's home folder will be located. This can either be a path on the local computer or a network drive mapped to a shared folder on a server.

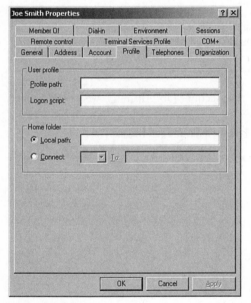

FIGURE 2.11   Enter values for profile path, logon script, and home directory location on this tab.

NOTE

Group Policy Is Preferred   These methods of specifying profile, logon script, and home folder information have generally been superseded by Group Policies in Windows 2000 and Windows Server 2003. They were retained for consistency with previous versions of the operating system.

The Help and Support Center for Windows Server 2003 describes managing user profiles with Group Policies as a best practice. See "Managing Terminal Services Users with Group Policy" in Help and Support.

The next tabs all concern how the user interacts with *Terminal Services*—a method for having multiple users run programs in sessions that actually operate on a network server. The user can work at a low-function workstation (even one running Windows 95) and run programs that need the power and resources of a computer running Windows Server 2003.

The Remote Control tab allows the administrator to control whether a user's session can be controlled remotely. If Remote Control is enabled, the administrator can choose whether the user's permission is needed before the administrator can see the user's session. The administrator can also choose whether a session being controlled remotely can be operated by the administrator or merely viewed. Terminal Services is covered in Chapter 11, "Managing and Maintaining Terminal Services."

Remote Control can be a very helpful facility for help desk staff. With the appropriate authorization, a help desk analyst can connect to a user's Terminal Services session and see what the user is seeing or is having difficulties with. If needed, the analyst can take control of the session to demonstrate how a task is to be performed or to investigate program settings. This is much more efficient than having the user describe to the analyst what is on the screen, and it's much faster than having the analyst go to the user's desk to see the problem.

NOTE

Remote Assistance   Remote Assistance is a similar facility that allows an analyst to control a user's session remotely. Available only for Windows XP and Windows Server 2003 computers, this facility lets a user request help from a helper (typically a help desk analyst or a friend). The helper can then see the user's session and take control of it if necessary (if allowed to do so). Remote Assistance is covered in Chapter 11.

The Terminal Services Profile tab allows the administrator to configure the user profile applied to the user's Terminal Services session. The administrator can specify the path of the profile to be used and the home folder location. These items can be different from the profile path and home folder location specified on the Profile tab. There is also a check box on which the administrator can determine whether the user is allowed to log on to the terminal server (see Figure 2.12).

NOTE

Terminal Services   These Terminal Services settings should be changed only at the individual user-configuration level if specific functions are to be added or denied to a specific user.

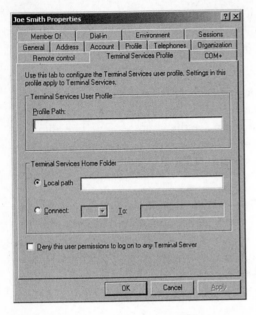

FIGURE 2.12 Use the Terminal Services Profile tab to specify the profile path and home folder location for the user's Terminal Services sessions.

On the Environment tab, the administrator can configure the startup environment a Terminal Services user sees. Any setting specified here will override the setting specified by the Terminal Services client. The administrator can require that a program start automatically at logon— when the user exits the program, the session will be logged off. This is a way of limiting users to a specific application instead of presenting them with a Windows Server 2003 desktop, which is the default. In addition, the administrator can control whether drives and printers on the client computer are available from the session, as well as whether print jobs are automatically sent to the default printer of the client computer.

EXAM ALERT

Be Familiar with the Added Features Administrators who have used previous versions of Windows Terminal Services might unwittingly ignore the options for device mapping. However, these options are now fully supported in Windows Server 2003 Terminal Services without requiring the Citrix add-on. Expect to see questions on these added features on the exam.

On the Sessions tab, shown in Figure 2.13, the administrator can specify what to do with Terminal Services sessions that are disconnected or left idle. A session is disconnected when the user disconnects rather than logging off or when the communication between the client computer and the Terminal Services server is broken. The administrator can choose to leave the disconnected session running forever, or only for a fixed period (such as 3 hours). The administrator can also specify how long an active session can continue, and how long an idle session can be left connected. When either of these limits is met, the session can be disconnected or ended. Finally, when the session has been disconnected, the administrator can specify whether reconnection is allowed from any client computer, or only from the client computer with which the disconnected session was initiated.

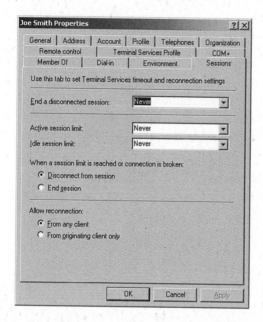

FIGURE 2.13 Specify how idle and disconnected sessions are handled on the Sessions tab.

On the Dial-In tab, the administrator can determine whether a user can connect to a Windows Server 2003 machine remotely, either by a dial-in or a virtual private network (VPN) connection. When the domain is at the Windows 2000 native or Windows Server 2003 functionality level, remote access can be controlled through Remote Access Policy, which is substantially more sophisticated than a simple Allow Access or Deny Access setting. For example, a remote access policy can specify that only members of specific groups can access the network by dial-in, and then only from specific IP addresses and during stated periods in the day or week.

Also on the Dial-In tab, the administrator can choose to verify caller ID on the dial-in connection. The administrator can also require, for additional certainty, that only authorized locations are dialing in. By the administrator configuring the callback options, the server can break the connection as soon as authentication is complete, and then call the user back at a preset telephone number.

Saving Time with User Templates

In most organizations, many people have the same resource access needs. Perhaps all Kansas City engineers need print and management access to a particular printer, and read and write access to two shared folders. Also, staff in a particular location may have the same logon hours or other information, which is the same from person to person.

Rather than laboriously entering the same information for each user account, it's easier to create one account as a template and then copy that account whenever you need to create another user account with the same characteristics.

To do this, create a new user account and give it a display name that will cause it to be shown at the start of the username list in the container in Active Directory Users and Computers. Because special characters sort first, a name such as _Engineer or _Engineer Template would work well. Assign the account to the groups the users will be in, specify logon hours and logon computer restrictions, and enter the information on the Address, Account, Profile, and Organization tabs that you want to apply to all users. It's a good idea to disable the template account so that when new accounts are created from the template, they will be disabled also. This ensures new accounts won't be automatically available to anyone with malicious intent.

As an example of a user template, note the Organization page of the _Engineer account shown in Figure 2.14. This is the template account used to create the Test Engineer account.

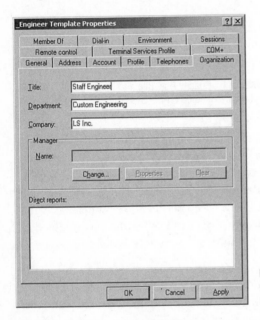

FIGURE 2.14 The template account should have commonly needed information in the fields of the Organization tab.

After the template has been created, all you have to do to create a new user with the same characteristics is right-click the template account and choose Copy. You enter the username, user ID, and password of the specific user, and the resulting account has both the specific information for an actual user and the necessary ancillary information applicable to all users in the group because most of it was already entered into fields in the template account.

When a new account for Test Engineer was created by copying the _Engineer account, most of the information on the Organization tab was carried over, as you can see in Figure 2.15.

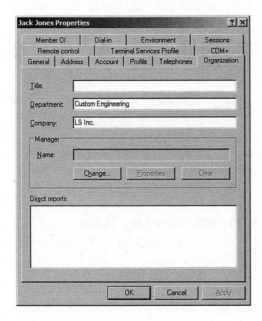

FIGURE 2.15 The Title field was not copied to the new account.

You might be wondering which attributes are copied to a new account created by copying a template. The values included in any attributes marked "Attribute Is Copied when Duplicating User" in the Active Directory Schema snap-in will be included in the copied account. With the necessary privileges, you can change which attributes are copied and which are not.

CAUTION

Schema Changes Are Not Reversible You should exercise extreme caution when making changes to the Active Directory schema. Additions made to the schema are not reversible; they can only be disabled.

When creating template accounts, consider making separate templates for temporary employees. If your organization is planning to hire several summer students, set up a template with the account-expiration dates set to the end of the summer. This way, all the users created using the _Summer Intern template will have the correct expiration already set when the accounts are created.

A good rule when creating template accounts is that you want to have a new template account for every set of new user types that might have unique information prepopulated. For example, in the case of the summer interns, their accounts are unique because of the expiration date. Using the _Summer Intern template would not be appropriate for a new employee whose account will not expire, and vice versa. You might decide to create template accounts for the different departments in your company or for those who have different work hours or managers. The key thing to remember is that the template you use must match the characteristics of the user you are creating. Otherwise, information will be automatically placed in the user account properties (via the template copy) that is not relevant for that user.

Creating Accounts Using Automation

Objective:

Create and modify user accounts by using automation

When you have only a few accounts to create or change, it's reasonable to use Active Directory Users and Computers. But for large numbers, you would want to automate the process. This section discusses using the command-line tools in conjunction with batch files to create many accounts, and we'll discuss importing user accounts as well.

Creating and Modifying User Accounts with Command-Line Tools

New in Windows Server 2003 are several command-line tools that can help in automating the creation and modification of user accounts:

- ▶ dsadd—Used to create Active Directory objects

- ▶ dsget—Used to retrieve specific properties of a user account

- ▶ dsmod—Used to change a property in a user account

- ▶ dsmove—Used to move or rename an Active Directory object

- ▶ dsrm—Used to delete Active Directory objects

The first one we'll discuss is dsadd, which adds accounts to the Active Directory service.

Creating Accounts with dsadd

The dsadd command can be used to create several types of objects in Active Directory. You can consider these to be subcommands of the dsadd command:

- ▶ dsadd computer—Adds a computer to the directory

- ▶ dsadd contact—Adds a contact to the directory

- ▶ dsadd group—Adds a group to the directory

- ▶ dsadd ou—Adds an OU to the directory

- ▶ dsadd user—Adds a user to the directory

- ▶ dsadd quota—Adds a quota specification to a directory partition

To learn how to use the `dsadd` command, open a command prompt and enter the following:

```
dsadd /?
```

To learn about the use of the subcommands, at the command prompt enter the following:

```
dsadd user /?
```

The `dsadd user` command can take several parameters, but the only required one is DN (distinguished name).

What's a distinguished name? It is the name assigned to an object in Active Directory, and it's made up of the object name (for example, Bill Bailey), the container it resides in, and the list of all the parent containers of that container, right up to the domain. Here's the distinguished name for Bill Bailey:

```
"CN=Bill Bailey,OU=Users,OU=Kansas City,DC=70-290,DC=int"
```

The following list examines the parts of this name:

▶ `CN=Bill Bailey`—CN stands for common name. It can be used for users, groups, computers, and containers.

▶ `OU=Users,OU=Kansas City`—This string lists all the containers in order, from the one the object resides in, up to the first container below the domain object.

▶ `DC=70-290,DC=int`—DC stands for domain component, and we need a DC for each part of the fully qualified domain name (FQDN) of the domain, `70-290.int`.

EXAM ALERT

Know the Difference The default Active Directory folders shown in the root of the Active Directory Users and Computers MMC—Users, Builtin, and Computers—are actually containers and not OUs. When referencing these containers, you have to use the `CN=` attribute and not `OU=`.

Windows Server 2003 will not permit you to create more than one object with the same distinguished name, so that you can be sure a distinguished name refers to a unique object. A good example of this is the Users OU we created earlier. Although its name is the same as the Users container that is created by default, the distinguished name is unique. With that knowledge in mind, you now know that we can create a new user in the same container as Bill Bailey's with the following command:

```
dsadd user "CN=Tom Thomson,OU=Users,OU=Kansas City,DC=70-290,
➡DC=int"
```

Having run this command, we return to Active Directory Users and Computers, and after refreshing the contents of the Users container under Kansas City, we see the new user object, as shown in Figure 2.16.

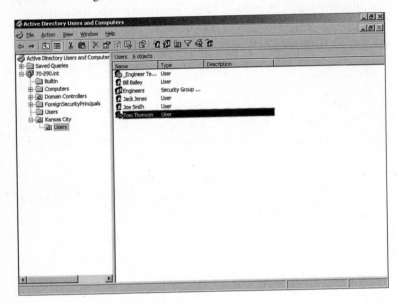

FIGURE 2.16 The user object for Tom Thomson now exists.

If you look at the properties of the object, you will see that none of the user-defined fields have been filled in. Note that, by default, the account is shown as disabled.

Obviously, using `dsadd` in this way doesn't save us much time if we later have to go into the properties of the object manually to add the user's details. However, all the usually defined properties can be included in the `dsadd` command, along with the distinguished name, so the whole object-creation process, including the user details, can be automated.

The following is a partial list of the properties that can be included with the `dsadd` command (from `dsadd user /?`):

▶ `-samid`—The user ID in a form that is usable with non–Active Directory accounts management.

▶ `-upn`—The user principal name is an alternative name that can be used for logon. In place of the usual `domain\user`, you can enter `name@domain`. For example, Bill Bailey could log on as `bbailey@70-290.int`.

▶ `-fn`—The user's first name.

▶ `-mi`—The user's middle initial.

▶ `-ln`—The user's last name.

▶ -display—The name that denotes the account in listings, such as in Active Directory Users and Computers.

▶ -empid—An EmployeeID field.

▶ -pwd—This field can contain the password to be assigned to the account. If you want to be prompted for a password when creating the account, enter *. This wildcard is probably not appropriate for mass creating users because the script will stop each time a user is created, asking for a password.

▶ -desc—A description of the user.

▶ -memberof—A list of distinguished names of the groups the user should be made a member of.

▶ -office—The name of the user's office.

▶ -tel—The user's main phone number.

▶ -email—The user's email address.

▶ -webpg—The user's web page address.

▶ -title—The user's title.

▶ -dept—Department.

▶ -company—Company.

▶ -mgr—The manager of this user.

▶ -hmdir—The path to the user's home directory.

▶ -hmdrv—The drive letter assigned to the user's home directory.

▶ -mustchpwd—The user must change the password at next logon: {yes | no}.

▶ -canchpwd—The user is able to change the password: {yes | no}.

▶ -reversiblepwd—The password is stored with reversible encryption (used with Macintosh systems and digest authentication): {yes | no}.

▶ -pwdneverexpires—The password does not expire: {yes | no}.

▶ -acctexpires—The number of days until the account expires.

▶ -disabled—The account is disabled: {yes | no}.

▶ -q—The command should run with no output to the console.

Using as many of these parameters as necessary to define the user account, the administrator can create the account with a single command, like this:

```
dsadd user "CN=Arthur Lismer,OU=Users,OU=Kansas City,DC=70-290,
➥DC=int" -samid ALismer -upn alismer@70-290.int -fn Arthur
➥-ln Lismer -pwd Passw0rd -memberof "CN=Kansas City Users,
➥DC=70-290,DC=int" -office Kansas City -disabled no
➥-mustchpwd yes
```

"But wait," you say, "that's more effort than working my way through Active Directory Users and Computers to create a user." That's true, for one user. However, if you're creating a thousand of them, and you have their names in a spreadsheet, it takes very little work to create a batch file where each line in the file creates another user.

After you have invested the time to master dsadd, you can save huge amounts of time in creating large numbers of user accounts.

NOTE

Using Net User Another way to create users from the command line is with the Net User command. It works with a limited set of parameters compared to dsadd, but its biggest drawback is that any user account created using Net User is placed in the Users container. If you have any structure in your Active Directory tree (and you should, to allow administrative flexibility), you would be much better off with dsadd than with Net User.

It is possible to change the default containers for newly created accounts. The command redirusr.exe changes the default container for users, and redircmp.exe changes the default container for computers. But even with these specific commands to enhance the Net User command, it is clear that dsadd is much more flexible.

Listing the Properties of User Accounts with dsget

If you want to get the value of some properties of a user account with a command-line tool, you use dsget user. The syntax of the command is as follows:

```
dsget user <dn> <list of properties>
```

The properties you can use are shown in the following list, from Windows Server 2003 Help and Support:

- ▶ -dn—Shows the DN of the user.

- ▶ -samid—Shows the SAM account name of the user.

- ▶ -sid—Shows the user's Security ID.

- ▶ -upn—Shows the user principal name of the user.

- ▶ -fn—Shows the first name of the user.

▶ `-mi`—Shows the middle initial of the user.

▶ `-ln`—Shows the last name of the user.

▶ `-display`—Shows the display name of the user.

▶ `-empid`—Shows the user employee ID.

▶ `-desc`—Shows the description of the user.

▶ `-office`—Shows the office location of the user.

▶ `-tel`—Shows the telephone number of the user.

▶ `-email`—Shows the email address of the user.

▶ `-hometel`—Shows the home telephone number of the user.

▶ `-pager`—Shows the pager number of the user.

▶ `-mobile`—Shows the mobile phone number of the user.

▶ `-fax`—Shows the fax number of the user.

▶ `-iptel`—Shows the user IP phone number.

▶ `-webpg`—Shows the user's web page URL.

▶ `-title`—Shows the title of the user.

▶ `-dept`—Shows the department of the user.

▶ `-company`—Shows the company info of the user.

▶ `-mgr`—Shows the user's manager.

▶ `-hmdir`—Shows the user's home directory. It also displays the drive letter to which the home directory of the user is mapped (if the home directory path is a Universal Naming Convention [UNC] path).

▶ `-hmdrv`—Shows the user's home drive letter (if home directory is a UNC path).

▶ `-profile`—Shows the user's profile path.

▶ `-loscr`—Shows the user's logon script path.

▶ `-mustchpwd`—Shows whether the user must change his or her password at the time of next logon. Displays yes or no.

▶ `-canchpwd`—Shows whether the user can change his or her password. Displays yes or no.

▶ `-pwdneverexpires`—Shows whether the user's password never expires. Displays yes or no.

▶ -disabled—Shows whether the user account is disabled for logon. Displays yes or no.

▶ -acctexpires—Shows when the user account expires. Displays a value (a date when the account expires or the string never if the account never expires).

▶ -reversiblepwd—Shows whether the user password is allowed to be stored using reversible encryption. Displays yes or no.

For example, the command

```
dsget user "CN=Najma Lakhani,OU=Users,OU=Kansas City,DC=70-290,
➥DC=int" -fn -ln -desc -office
```

returns the following information:

```
desc                fn      ln        office
Senior Engineer     Najma   Lakhani    Kansas City
```

This command can be very useful in determining the values of the properties of one or several user accounts.

Modifying User Accounts with dsmod

You've probably been wondering what you would do if you had to make a change to hundreds or thousands of users. Well, just as dsadd allows you to automate the creation of users, dsmod allows you to change them.

dsmod uses the same parameters as dsadd, so you indicate the account you want to change with its distinguished name and then specify the parameter and the value it should have. For example, the following would change the value of the office parameter to Burnaby, while leaving all the other parameters unchanged:

```
dsmod user "CN=Arthur Lismer,OU=Users,OU=Kansas City,DC=70-290,
➥DC=int"-office Burnaby
```

Using Piping Commands

If you're like some administrators, you took one look at the dsmod command in the previous paragraph and said, "There's too much work in typing distinguished names! I'm sticking with Active Directory Users and Computers!"

This is where *piping* comes in. Piping allows you to use the output of one command as the input for a second command. If you can issue a dsquery command that finds the Arthur Lismer user object, you can pipe (using the | symbol on the keyboard) the output from the dsquery command into the dsmod command. Let's walk through this:

```
C:\>dsquery user -name arthur*
"CN=Arthur Lismer,OU=Users,OU=Kansas City,DC=70-290,DC=int"
"CN=Arthur Adams,OU=Users,OU=Kansas City,DC=70-290,DC=int"
```

No, that produced too many Arthurs. Let's try this:

```
C:\>dsquery user -name *lismer
"CN=Arthur Lismer,OU=Users,OU=Kansas City,DC=70-290,DC=int"
```

There we go, just the user we wanted. Now let's pipe the output of dsquery into dsget to find the current value of the office parameter:

```
C:\>dsquery user -name *lismer | dsget user -office
  Office
  Vancouver
dsget succeeded
```

Good. Now we change the value of the office parameter with a dsmod command:

```
C:\>dsquery user -name *lismer | dsmod user -office Burnaby
dsmod succeeded:CN=Arthur Lismer,OU=Users,OU=Kansas City,
➥DC=70-290,DC=int
```

And now we can confirm that the change was made:

```
C:\>dsquery user -name *lismer | dsget user -office
  Office
  Burnaby
dsget succeeded
```

This is much more efficient than typing long distinguished names! And if you use a dsquery that returns several user accounts, the dsmod command can modify the same field in all the returned accounts, all at once.

For example, as in the preceding example when we changed the office location, typing the following command changes the user's telephone number without typing the DN:

```
C:\>dsquery user -name *lismer | dsmod user -tel 803-734-1122
```

You can use similar logic to change any other piece of information in the directory by searching for the user's name, UPN, location in the directory, or even several other parameters you can see when using dsquery user /?. Hopefully, you are starting to see that the power of these commands is far greater than what it first appears.

Moving or Renaming Objects with dsmove

If you need to move an object to another location within a domain, or you want to rename the object, you can do so with dsmove. The syntax of dsmove is as follows:

```
dsmove <ObjectDN> [-newparent <ParentDN>] [-newname <NewName>]
```

So if Najma Lakhani moves from Vancouver to Phoenix, and she changes her name to Najma Larson, we could accomplish the change with the following command:

```
C:\>dsquery user -name "Najma*" |dsmove -newparent
"OU=Users,OU=Phoenix,DC=70-290,DC=int"
➥ -newname "Najma Larson"
```

Checking in Active Directory Users and Computers shows Najma Larson in the new OU. Note that only the object name has changed. To complete the user's name change, properties of the object such as display name, last name, and email address will still have to be modified with dsmod or Active Directory Users and Computers.

Removing Objects with dsrm

The final command-line tool for Active Directory is dsrm. It is used to delete Active Directory objects. If the object being referenced is a container, it's possible to delete the objects in the container but retain the object itself.

The syntax for dsrm is as follows:

```
dsrm <ObjectDN ...> [-noprompt] [-subtree [-exclude]]
```

- ▶ -noprompt—Do not prompt for confirmation before deleting object.

- ▶ -subtree—Delete the object and all objects included in it.

- ▶ -exclude—Used with subtree. Do not delete the object, just its contents.

For example, assume the Phoenix office has just completed a Systems Analysis course and wants to delete the accounts that were created for students in the course. The accounts were in the OU called AnalysisStudents under the "OU=Phoenix,DC=70-290,DC=int" OU. The AnalysisStudents OU should be retained for future classes. The following command will delete all the objects in the AnalysisStudents OU but retain the OU:

```
C:\>dsrm "OU=AnalysisStudents,OU=Phoenix,DC=70-290,DC=int"
➥ -subtree -exclude
Are you sure you wish to delete all children of
OU=AnalysisStudents,OU=Phoenix,DC=70-290,DC=int (Y/N)? y
dsrm succeeded:OU=AnalysisStudents,OU=Phoenix,
➥DC=70-290,DC=int
```

Importing and Exporting User Accounts

Objective:

Import user accounts

Some organizations occasionally have a need to create, modify, or delete thousands of user accounts at a time. Think of a large university with an incoming class of several thousand students at the start of each term. You certainly wouldn't want to create each of those accounts with Active Directory Users and Computers!

What saves the day here is two facts: Almost certainly there is a database somewhere in the organization that has all the information needed to define the needed accounts, and Microsoft has provided two programs with Windows Server 2003, `ldifde` and `csvde`, that can be used to import accounts into Active Directory.

To create the thousands of user accounts, you would export the necessary information from the database system, manipulate the data so that it is in the format the import program needs, and then run the import program. It may take some time to go through these steps, but that's better than many days of tedious and error-prone work with Active Directory Users and Computers.

Why are there two import utilities, and how do they differ? The next sections answer those questions. `csvde` is simpler, so we'll discuss it first.

More About Importing/Exporting

Although the utilities we discuss here are fine for small- to medium-sized organizations, large enterprises need tools that are built to handle a large volume of changes. HP offers a tool called LDAP Directory Synchronization Utility (LDSU) that can easily handle the import and export changes described here, and it's robust enough for large enterprises to rely on.

LDSU was used to synch the Digital and Compaq directories during that merger (105,000 users and mailboxes), as well as the Compaq and HP directories (165,000 user accounts and mailboxes). Both of them were completely in synch within hours after the merger was finalized.

The beauty of LDSU is that it is simple to use, and it can "map" fields and formatting from one side to the other and keep the directories in sync as changes occur in the future.

Some basic information on LDSU is provided at `http://h18008.www1.hp.com/services/messaging/mg_ldap_fact.html`.

The csvde Utility

The csvde (Comma Separated Value Directory Exchange) utility exports data from Active Directory, or imports data into Active Directory, in Comma Separated Value (CSV) format. In this format, each line of data represents one record, and each field is separated from the next by a comma. If any field has commas as part of the data, the whole field is enclosed by quotation marks. So that the import utility can properly allocate each value to the appropriate field, the first line of the data file lists the names of the fields in the order they will appear in the data records.

As an example, here is the output from csvde of the Arthur Lismer record in our sample company:

```
DN,objectClass,ou,distinguishedName,instanceType,whenCreated,whenChanged,
⮞uSNCreated,uSNChanged,name,objectCategory,dSCorePropagationData,
⮞cn,sn,physicalDeliveryOfficeName,givenName,displayName,
⮞userAccountControl,codePage,countryCode,accountExpires,
⮞sAMAccountName,userPrincipalName,description,mail,c,l,st,
⮞title,postalCode,co,department,company,streetAddress,
⮞userWorkstations,manager"CN=ArthurLismer,OU=Users,OU=Vancouver,
⮞DC=70-290,DC=int",user,,"CN=ArthurLismer,OU=Users,
⮞OU=Phoenix,DC=70-290,DC=int",4,20030421210344.
⮞0Z,20030421210345.0Z,33732,33738,ArthurLismer,"CN=Person,
⮞CN=Schema,CN=Configuration,DC=70-290,DC=int",
⮞,ArthurLismer,Lismer,Phoenix,Arthur,
⮞,512,0,0,9223372036854775807,ALismer,alismer@t70-290.int
⮞,,,,,,,,,,,,,
```

The first line (starting DN,objectClass... is the header line, listing the fields in the data. The second line is the data for the Arthur Lismer record. It's hard to read, but if you load it into a spreadsheet program, each field will be in a separate column, and it's easy to work with then.

This output was created with the following command:

```
csvde -f c:\lismer.csv -r "(name=*lismer)"
```

The parameter -f c:\lismer.csv sends the output of the command to the file c:\lismer.csv, and the parameter -r "(name=*lismer)" tells the utility to select just those records whose name field ends in lismer.

To make the output of csvde easier to use, you can specify the fields you want to have exported. For example, the command

```
C:\>csvde -f c:\lismer.csv -r "(name=*lismer)" -l
l,company,objectclass,name,title,company,l,telephoneNumber,
⮞userAccountControl,samaccountname
```

results in the simpler output file

```
DN,objectClass,title,telephoneNumber,company,name,
➥userAccountControl,sAMAccountName "CN=Arthur
➥Lismer,OU=Users,OU=Phoenix,DC=70-290,
➥DC=int",user,Network Architect,555-5678,Thomson Associates,
➥Arthur Lismer,512,Alismer
```

It is useful to run csvde in output mode first, to list the names of the attributes.

Now, to import a user, we make a text file in the same format as the output files and then run csvde in import mode. For example, let's run the command

```
csvde -i -f c:\adams-in.csv -j c:\
```

with the following input file:

```
DN,objectClass,title,telephoneNumber,company,name,userAccountControl,
➥sAMAccountName"CN=ArthurAdams,OU=Users,OU=Phoenix,
➥DC=70-290,DC=int",user,Network Architect,555-5678,
➥Thomson Associates,Arthur Adams,514,Aadams
```

This creates a user account for Arthur Adams, with the attributes listed. Note that we have used the userAccountControl value of 514, which means the account is disabled when it is first created. This is because our work is not yet done; we haven't assigned the user to any groups and we haven't set the user's password (csvde cannot import or export passwords). We can complete these tasks with the dsmod utility and then enable the account.

The ldifde Utility

The name of this utility, ldifde, means LDIF Directory Exchange. *LDIF (LDAP Data Interchange Format)* is a definition of how data can be exchanged between LDAP-based directories. *LDAP (Lightweight Directory Access Protocol)* is an industry-standard protocol for accessing directories. For complete information about LDAP, see RFCs 2251–2256, and for information on LDIF, see RFC 2849, which can be read at www.ietf.org/rfc/rfc2849.txt.

There are two primary differences between ldifde and csvde. First, whereas csvde can only import and export records, ldifde can also modify records and delete records, making it a much more powerful utility. Second, the data format is very different. Instead of a file with a header record and one record per entry, the file contains many lines per entry, with the field name as the first part of each line.

Here is what the ldifde output looks like for the Arthur Lismer user account. Note that an entry starts with the distinguished name (dn) of the entry, then a changetype line (the changetype command can be add, modify, or delete), and then the attributes of the entry, in alphabetical order by attribute name:

```
dn: CN=Arthur Lismer,OU=Users,OU=Phoenix,DC=70-290,DC=int
changetype: add
accountExpires: 9223372036854775807
cn: Arthur Lismer
codePage: 0
countryCode: 0
distinguishedName:  CN=Arthur Lismer,OU=Users,OU=Phoenix,
➥DC=70-290,DC=int
givenName: Arthur
instanceType: 4
name: Arthur Lismer
objectCategory: CN=Person,CN=Schema,CN=Configuration,DC=70-290,
➥DC=int
objectClass: top
objectClass: person
objectClass: organizationalPerson
objectClass: user
physicalDeliveryOfficeName: Phoenix
sAMAccountName: ALismer
sn: Lismer
userAccountControl: 512
userPrincipalName: alismer@t70-290.int
uSNChanged: 33738
uSNCreated: 33732
whenChanged: 20030421210345.0Z
whenCreated: 20030421210344.0Z
```

To use ldifde to create a series of user accounts, we'll need to build an input file of records in the format shown.

The following input file was used with the command

```
Ldifde -i -f c:\ldif-in1.txt
```

to create a new user account for Frank Carmichael:

```
dn: CN=Frank Carmichael,OU=Users,OU=Phoenix,DC=70-290,
➥DC=int
changetype: add
cn: Frank Carmichael
codePage: 0
countryCode: 0
distinguishedName:  CN=Frank Carmichael,OU=Users,OU=Phoenix,
➥DC=70-290,DC=int
givenName: Frank
instanceType: 4
name: Frank Carmichael
```

```
objectCategory: CN=Person,CN=Schema,CN=Configuration,DC=70-290,
➥DC=int
objectClass: top
objectClass: person
objectClass: organizationalPerson
objectClass: user
physicalDeliveryOfficeName: Phoenix
sAMAccountName: FCarmichael
sn: Carmichael
userAccountControl: 514
userPrincipalName: fCarmichael@t70-290.int
```

Using dsmod as described earlier, we can add three users' accounts to the Phoenix Users group with this command (entered as a batch file):

```
dsmod group  "CN=Phoenix Users,DC=70-290,DC=int" -addmbr
➥ "CN=Tom Thomson,OU=Users,OU=Phoenix,DC=70-290,DC=int"
➥ "CN=Arthur Adams,OU=Users,OU=Phoenix,DC=70-290,DC=int"
➥ "CN=Frank Carmichael,OU=Users,OU=Phoenix,DC=70-290,
➥DC=int" -c
```

A second dsmod command sets all these users' passwords to Secur1ty and requires them to change their passwords at the next logon:

```
dsmod user "CN=Tom Thomson,OU=Users,OU=Phoenix,DC=70-290,
➥DC=int" "CN=Arthur Adams,OU=Users,OU=Phoenix,DC=70-290,
➥DC=int" "CN=Frank Carmichael,OU=Users,OU=Phoenix,
➥DC=70-290,DC=int" -pwd Secur1ty -mustchpwd yes
```

And a final dsmod command enables the three accounts:

```
dsmod user "CN=Tom Thomson,OU=Users,OU=Phoenix,DC=70-290,
➥DC=int" "CN=Arthur Adams,OU=Users,OU=Phoenix,DC=70-290,
➥DC=int" "CN=Frank Carmichael,OU=Users,OU=Phoenix,
➥DC=70-290,DC=int" -disabled no
```

A common use for ldifde is to create a set of objects in a new directory from an existing one. For example, you might be creating a set of user accounts in a new test directory from the user accounts in a production directory.

It's a fairly simple process to use ldifde in export mode to create a file containing information about the existing user accounts. Then running ldifde in import mode will load the accounts into the new location. However, the distinguished names will all have to be changed because they will refer to the source directory.

For example, imagine that we are setting up a test domain called 70-290.com. We want to populate the new directory with information exported from our 70-290.int domain. All the information about the accounts will be the same, but the Active Directory paths will be different in all the distinguished names.

This is where the -c parameter is used. Using ldifde with -c <old string> <new string> causes the replacement of any occurrences of <old string> by <new string> before the data is acted on by ldifde.

Troubleshooting User Accounts

Objective:
Troubleshoot user accounts

There are several reasons why users may find that they cannot use their user accounts. In this section, we will look at account lockouts and at reasons why an account might not be usable.

Troubleshooting Account Lockouts

Objective:
Diagnose and resolve account lockouts

Account lockout is a Windows Server 2003 security feature designed to protect accounts from repeated attempts to guess the account's password. A policy can be set that causes a user account to be disabled if a specific number of invalid login attempts are made within the specified time frame. The account is disabled for a specific number of minutes; if the specified time frame passes without another invalid attempt, the count of invalid attempts is reset to zero.

The term *invalid logon attempt* includes attempts to guess a password that is protecting a workstation's session, whether with a password-protected screensaver, a Ctrl+Alt+Del Lock Workstation command, the initial login dialog box, or from across the network.

Table 2.1 shows the default values and the ranges of possible values for the account lockout feature.

TABLE 2.1   Default Values for Account Lockouts

Setting	Default Value	Range of Values
Account lockout duration	30 minutes	From 0–99,999 minutes. A setting of 0 means the account is locked out until an administrator unlocks it.
Account lockout threshold	Five invalid attempts	From 0–999. A setting of 0 means account lockout will not be used.
Reset lockout counter after	30 minutes	From 1–99,999 minutes.

Many administrators initially set the account lockout duration to 0 so that they will always know if an attempt was made, and this is certainly the most secure approach. However, a few irate calls from locked-out users usually results in a setting of 30 or 60 minutes!

Indefinite Lockouts

Why is an indefinite lockout the most secure approach? If the default settings are in effect, and an intruder tries all weekend to guess an account's password, he could try dozens of times, but nobody would know about the attempts if the intruder stops 30 minutes before the actual user comes to log on.

If a user account is locked out, you can allow it to be used again with Active Directory Users and Computers. Figure 2.17 shows the location.

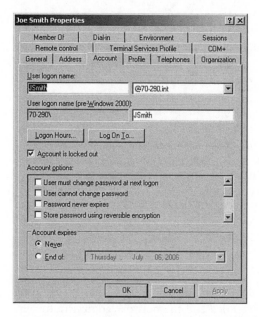

FIGURE 2.17 Allow the account to be used by clearing the Account Is Locked Out check box.

To implement account lockout, modify the Default Domain Policy (in the Group Policy tab of the domain object of Active Directory Users and Computers). The account lockout settings are found under Computer Configuration, Windows Settings, Security Setting, Account Policies, Account Lockout Policy.

Like password policies, account lockout can be defined only at the domain level. So be careful—all password policy settings will affect every user account in your domain.

Account lockout is a security feature that must be put in place for any production network to be considered secure. Be sure you have management agreement with any new account password settings, and give your user community several days' warning before you implement it.

Troubleshooting Issues Related to User Account Properties

Objective:

Diagnose and resolve issues related to user account properties

Many help desk analysts will tell you that a large portion of the calls they receive have to do with settings on the user account. Here are several situations that arise because of settings on user account properties.

Account Disabled

It is common practice to disable the account of any user who is either on leave for an extended period or no longer with the organization. Of course, when the user returns and attempts to use the account, she will be unable to log on.

A disabled account can easily be enabled using the Active Directory Users and Computers MMC. Either open the properties of the user account and clear the Account Is Disabled check box on the Accounts tab, or just right click the account and select Enable from the popup menu. Alternatively, you can use `dsmod` and enter the following:

```
dsmod user <distinguished name> -disabled no
```

> **NOTE**
>
> **Disable, Don't Delete!**   Why not just delete the account of a user who leaves an organization? One reason is that the user account probably has access to files on the network that may be useful to the organization. If you delete the account, retrieving those files can be difficult. It's best to disable the account and then change the password and reenable the account when a person has been designated to review the files to which the account has access.

Account Expired

We know that an account can have an expiration date—the date after which the account cannot be used. If a temporary worker's contract is extended and the network administrator has not been asked to adjust or remove the account expiration date, the worker will not be able to log in until the expiration date is reset.

This setting can be modified in Active Directory Users and Computers: Open the properties of the user account; then on the Account tab, in the Account Expires section, select either Never or a new date. Alternatively, with `dsmod`, you can enter

```
dsmod user <distinguished name> -acctexpires never
```

or

```
dsmod user <distinguished name> -acctexpires <number of days>
```

Dial-in Disallowed

A user might complain of being unable to connect by dial-in connection or through a virtual private network (VPN) connection. In this case, check the Dial-In tab of the user account's properties, as shown in Figure 2.18.

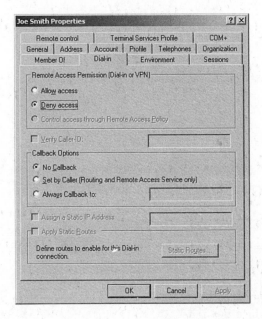

FIGURE 2.18 If the Remote Access Permission setting is Deny Access, no dial-in or VPN connections will be allowed.

To permit dial-in or VPN connections, select Allow Access or, in domains where the functional level is at least Windows 2000 native, Control Access Through Remote Access Policy.

Cannot Change Password

In some cases, users call the help desk because the operating system does not allow them to change their password. There are two possible reasons for this situation.

First, the account may have been set up with the User Cannot Change Password option. This situation is easily rectified, if appropriate, by going to the Account tab of the user account Properties dialog box and clearing the check box.

Second, a user may be unable to change the user account's password because the password entered does not meet the complexity requirements determined by the domain account policies. If enabled, this policy requires that passwords meet the following minimum requirements:

▶ Not contain all or part of the user's account name

▶ Be at least six characters in length

> ▶ Contain characters from three of the following four categories:

>> ▶ English uppercase characters (A through Z)

>> ▶ English lowercase characters (a through z)

>> ▶ Base 10 digits (0 through 9)

>> ▶ Nonalphabetic characters (for example, !, $, #, %)

If the user's password change is being denied due to password complexity requirements, minimum password age, or other restrictions, you must explain the requirements to the user.

Using Saved Queries

A very useful tool in Windows Server 2003 is Saved Queries, a new function under Active Directory Users and Computers. With this facility, a user can define a query that is frequently used and return to it easily whenever it is needed.

Microsoft has supplied several predefined queries to support common administrative tasks such as user management. This includes queries for disabled user accounts, non-expiring passwords, and days since last logon. However, the query function allows you to query for common attributes for user, computer or group accounts. For example, assume that the administrator wants to list all the user accounts in the Engineering department. Follow the procedure in Step by Step 2.5 to create a query that will list all Engineering users.

STEP BY STEP

2.5 Creating a saved query

1. Open Active Directory Users and Computers and right-click the Saved Queries folder, as shown in Figure 2.19.

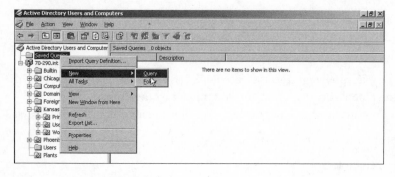

FIGURE 2.19 Select New, Query from the pop-up menu.

2. Select New, Query from the pop-up menu.

3. On the New Query dialog box, shown in Figure 2.20, enter the name of the query and a description. When finished, click the Define Query button.

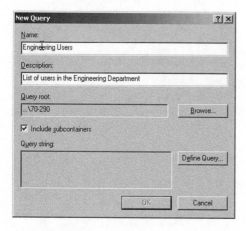

FIGURE 2.20   Enter a descriptive name for your query.

4. When the dialog box opens, select Users, Contacts and Groups from the Find drop-down, and then select the Advanced tab.

5. As shown in Figure 2.21, click the Field button, and then select Users, Department from the pop-up menus.

FIGURE 2.21   You can query on most fields of Active Directory objects.

6. Next, click the drop-down for the Condition filed and select IS(Exactly). Enter Engineering in the Value field.

7. Click the Add button, and then click OK twice to save.

8. To see the results of the saved query, select it in the left pane and the results will be displayed in the right pane. (See Figure 2.22.)

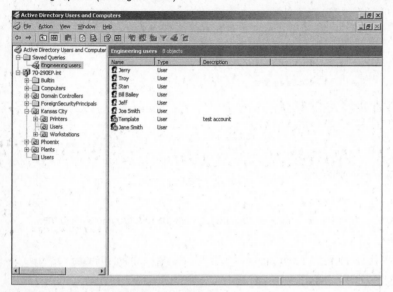

FIGURE 2.22   The results of the saved query.

The resulting query is available for use anytime the administrator returns to the Saved Queries function.

You can define quite complex queries, using the fields of any Active Directory object, and save it to be run in the future.

Challenge

You are the administrator of a network for a manufacturing company that has multiple Windows Server 2003 servers used for file and print services.

Common to most manufacturing entities is the need to protect sensitive design data from industrial espionage. The products that your company manufactures are for very price-conscious consumers—not only the design of the products, but also the manufacturing techniques, must be protected.

You need to find a way to minimize the exposure of external users hacking in to your servers.

(continues)

(continued)

Using the things that you have learned so far in this chapter, what is the best way to solve this issue in Windows Server 2003? On your own, try to develop a solution that would involve the least amount of downtime and expense.

If you would like to see a possible solution, follow these steps:

This is a fairly straightforward decision, mainly because the only security features we have discussed so far are user accounts and passwords. To increase security in your domain, you can modify the default domain policy to adjust the account-lockout settings so that hackers can't repeatedly try different passwords to access your servers. In addition, you can require complex passwords so that dictionary attacks won't be effective.

1. From the Start menu, select All Programs, Administrative Tools, Active Directory Users and Computers.

2. Right-click the domain name entry and select Properties from the pop-up menu.

3. From the Properties dialog box, click the Group Policy tab.

4. On the Group Policy tab, double-click the Default Domain Policy entry.

5. From the Group Policy MMC, navigate to Default Domain Policy, Computer Configuration, Windows Settings, Security Settings, Account Policy, Password Policy. Ensure that the following settings are applied:

   ▶ Account Lockout Threshold—3

   ▶ Account Lockout Duration—60

   ▶ Passwords Must Meet Complexity Requirements—Enabled

6. Close the MMC and then click OK in the Properties dialog box to save.

With the lockout threshold set, the account will be locked after three failed logon attempts, and it will be reenabled automatically after 1 hour. Passwords will be required to meet the complexity requirements discussed earlier in this chapter.

Managing Local, Roaming, and Mandatory User Profiles

Objective:

Manage local, roaming, and mandatory user profiles

The settings for a user's work environment are stored in a set of files and folders known as the *user profile*. The profile is automatically created the first time a user logs on to a computer running any version of Windows, and any changes to the environment (Favorites, Start menu items, icons, colors, My Documents, local settings) are saved when the user logs off. The profile is reloaded when the user logs on again. Table 2.2 lists the components of a user profile (from Windows Server 2003 Help and Support).

TABLE 2.2   User Profile Folders and Their Contents

User Profile Folder	Contents
Application Data	Program-specific data (for example, a custom dictionary). Program vendors decide what data to store in this user profile folder.
Cookies	Website user information and preferences.
Desktop	Desktop items, including files, shortcuts, and folders.
Favorites	Shortcuts to favorite Internet locations.
Local Settings	History and temporary files.
My Documents	User documents and subfolders.
My Recent Documents	Shortcuts to the most recently used documents and accessed folders.
NetHood	Shortcuts to My Network Places items.
PrintHood	Shortcuts to printer folder items.
SendTo	Shortcuts to document-handling utilities.
Start Menu	Shortcuts to program items.
Templates	User template items.

The user profiles facility allows several people to use the same computer running Windows, yet each can see his or her own private desktop, and the settings will be remembered each time the user logs on.

User profiles are stored under C:\Documents and Settings. By default, all servers will have two profiles: All Users and Default Users. The contents of the Default Users profile are used to create a user profile for a new user who logs on to the server. The All Users folder contains files and folders and icons that are common to all users.

Initially, the profile exists only on the computer where it was created: For this reason, it is called a *local user profile*. However, the profile can also be stored on a server, allowing the user to see the same desktop no matter what machine he or she is logged on to. This server-based profile is known as a *roaming user profile*. For some groups of users, we can also create mandatory user profiles, which cannot be changed by the users.

Creating and Modifying Local User Profiles

The first time a user logs on to a computer running Windows Server 2003, the folder structure shown in Figure 2.23 is created. This structure used the data and shortcuts contained in the DefaultUser profile as a template. In Figure 2.23 you see the Administrator profile.

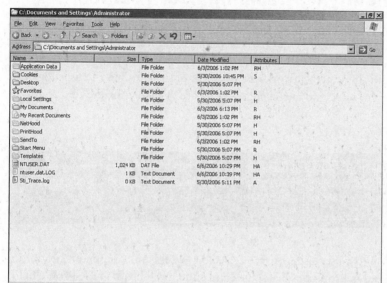

FIGURE 2.23   The folder structure of a user profile.

The folders of interest in the structure are Application Data, where software vendors store data for particular users, Cookies, where data about website preferences are stored, Desktop, which contains the desktop items, including any files stored there, My Documents, which is the default location for the storage of user data, and Start Menu, from which programs can be accessed that were installed for this user, but not all users of this computer.

> **NOTE**
>
> **For More Information**   For a full description of the folders, search Help and Support for "Contents of a User Profile." As you can imagine, the contents of the user profile structure can become quite large, especially because My Documents is one of the folders.

Within the root folder of the profile, you will see a file called `NTuser.dat`. This file contains the contents of the current user-specific section of the Registry (`HKEY_CURRENT_USER`). This file is updated each time the user logs off.

Another profile structure that is used to create the user work environment is the All Users folder. Profile items that all users will see, such as program links that are on all users' All Programs menu, are stored in the All Users folder.

The contents and settings of the user profile are modified by working with the environment—using Control Panel applets, such as Display, installing programs, and creating shortcuts on the desktop.

Creating and Modifying Roaming User Profiles

Because many users move from computer to computer and would like to see the same work environment each time, the Roaming User Profiles facility has been created. This facility allows the profile to be stored on a network server. When the user logs on, the profile is downloaded from the server, and the expected work environment is seen. When the user logs off, the profile is uploaded to the server, so any changes made are available for the next logon at that or any other computer.

> **EXAM ALERT**
>
> **Expect a Roaming Profile Question**   Expect at least one exam question that deals with the topic of roaming profiles. Remember that although Windows 9x/Me and Windows NT support roaming profiles, they aren't compatible, and they cannot be maintained via Group Policy the way that Windows 2000/XP/2003 can.

To assign a roaming profile to a user using Active Directory Users and Computers, go to the Profile tab on the user accounts Properties dialog box and enter a valid path in the Profile field, as shown in Figure 2.24.

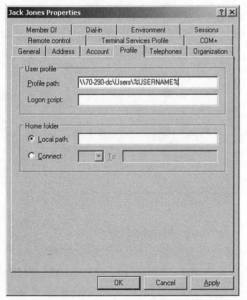

FIGURE 2.24   Use the %username% variable to substitute for the username.

EXAM ALERT

Know Your UNC Paths! Be very familiar with the use of Universal Naming Convention (UNC) paths for the exam. For example, in the path \\mars\profiles\%username%, MARS is the NetBIOS name of the server that the PROFILES shared folder resides on. The replaceable parameter %username% refers to the name of the folder that will be created.

The next time the user logs on, the profile type will be changed to "Roaming," and after logoff the server-based profile will be updated.

Note that Active Directory Users and Computers will allow you to change some properties of multiple user accounts at once. That is, you can select multiple users and then choose Action, Properties, and set the values for those properties. See Figure 2.25 for the Profile tab of the Properties on Multiple Objects dialog box.

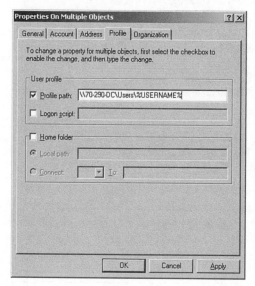

FIGURE 2.25 Changing the home folder and profile path on multiple user accounts at once.

You can also use dsmod to set the home folders and profile paths for multiple users. The following command entered as a batch file, for convenience, sets the profile path and the home folder path simultaneously:

```
dsmod user "CN=Tom Thomson,OU=Users,OU=Phoenix,DC=70-290,
➡DC=int" "CN=Arthur Lismer,OU=Users,OU=Phoenix,
➡DC=70-290,DC=int" "CN=Arthur Adams,OU=Users,OU=Phoenix,
➡OU=LTI,DC=70-290,DC=int" -profile "\\mars\users\
➡$username$\profile" -hmdrv x: -hmdir \\mars\users\$username$
```

> **NOTE**
>
> **Encrypted Files Are Not Allowed**   You cannot include encrypted files in roaming user profiles.

Creating and Enforcing Mandatory User Profiles

You might want to ensure that the profiles for a specific group of users are the same for all the users and unchangeable. A preconfigured profile that is not allowed to be changed by the user is called a *mandatory user profile*. In addition, you probably want to set up a mandatory user profile for a group of user accounts, all of whom do the same limited set of tasks, such as an inside sales group.

To set up a mandatory user profile, first create a temporary user account and assign a profile path (such as `\\mars\profiles\Adams`) in Active Directory Users and Computers. Ensure that the user has permissions to update files in the profile path. After the profile path is defined, the user has a roaming profile. Log on as that user, make the changes to the work environment (appearance of the desktop, icons available, programs installed, and so on) that are appropriate for the group of users, and then log off.

Log on again as an administrator, navigate to the user's profile folder, and rename the `NTuser.dat` file to `NTuser.man`.

To test that the mandatory profile is working, log on as the temporary user, change some settings, and log off. Log on again as the same user, and you should see that the changes you made in the previous session were discarded.

> **NOTE**
>
> **Use Group Policy**   This method of controlling the user's profile works the same as it has since the early days of Windows NT. However, it is now considered preferable to use Group Policies to control most user environment settings. See "How to Create a Mandatory User Profile" under User Profiles in the Client Computers section of the Help and Support Center.

The template user account now has a mandatory user profile assigned. You can assign the same mandatory user profile to any number of user accounts by adding the profile path to the Profile tab of ADUC. In addition, all users or groups who will be assigned the mandatory profile must be granted Write permissions for the folder.

Creating and Managing Computer Accounts in an Active Directory Environment

Objective:

Create and manage computer accounts in an active directory environment

For every computer running Windows NT, Windows 2000 Professional, or Windows XP and every server running Windows Server 2003 that is a member of a domain, a computer account must be created in the domain. The computer account is a security principal, and it can be authenticated and granted permissions to access resources. A computer account is automatically created for each computer running the listed operating systems when the computer joins the domain.

> **NOTE**
>
> **No Account** No computer accounts are created for computers running any version of Windows 95, Windows 98, or Windows Me. They lack the advanced security features that make the computer accounts worthwhile. This is an important fact—most network administrators prefer to have no computers running these operating systems in their networks because it is difficult to manage and secure these computers.

Although it is true that computer accounts are created automatically when a computer joins a domain, sometimes it is worthwhile to create computer accounts manually. Doing so allows a user to install a new computer in the appropriate location in the domain, even if that user doesn't have the necessary administrative privileges, using the name of the computer account that already exists.

Note that even if the computer object has been precreated, the user installing the computer must have been delegated the right to join a computer to the domain.

Creating Computer Accounts Using the Active Directory Users and Computers Console

To create a computer account using Active Directory Users and Computers, right-click the container you want the account to appear in and then choose New, Computer from the context menu. Assign the necessary values to the parameters available and click OK. Figure 2.26 shows the New Object dialog box in which you type the computer name and give a pre–Windows 2000 computer name (limited to 15 characters). You may also designate the computer as a pre–Windows 2000 computer, and you may state that the computer is to be a Windows NT 4 backup domain controller.

FIGURE 2.26 Type the name of the computer. Windows Server 2003 will automatically create a pre–Windows 2000 computer name.

Creating Computer Accounts by Joining the Domain

The easiest way to add a computer account to a domain is from the computer that you want to add. To create a computer account by joining a domain, follow the procedure in Step by Step 2.6.

STEP BY STEP

2.6 Creating a computer account by joining the domain

1. Log on to the computer you want to join to the domain with the credentials of a user with administrative privileges on that computer.

2. Open the Control Panel, and select the System applet.

3. From the System Properties dialog box, select the Computer Name tab. To join a domain, click the Change button, as shown in Figure 2.27.

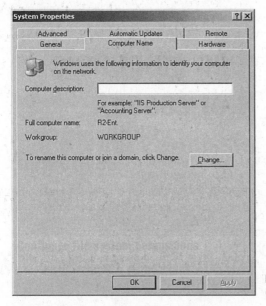

FIGURE 2.27 Click the Change button to join a domain or rename your server.

4. When the Computer Name Changes dialog box opens, select the Domain radio button and enter the name of the domain that you want to join, as shown in Figure 2.28.

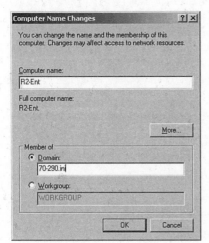

FIGURE 2.28 Enter the name of the domain you want to join.

5. Click OK. The system will ask you for the credentials of a user object that has the necessary rights to add a computer to the domain. Enter the requested credentials, and click OK.

After a short pause, a dialog box will appear to welcome the computer to the domain. The computer must be rebooted so that it can come up as a member of the domain.

After the computer is a member of the domain, a user logging on to the domain has the logon request passed by the workstation through a secure channel to the domain controller. The computer must have a domain computer account for the secure channel to be created.

Challenge

You are the administrator of a network for a manufacturing company that has multiple Windows Server 2003 servers used for applications and file and print services. The Research and Development Department has received a massive increase in funding this fiscal year, and it is purchasing all new desktop computers.

You plan to delegate the desktop replacements to the desktop support group. However, because Windows XP Professional computers are being installed, a computer account will need to be added for each computer. You do not want to grant the desktop support group the necessary access to add the computer accounts, but you cringe at the idea of adding 500 computer accounts manually.

You must find a way to automate this process.

What is the best way to solve this issue in Windows Server 2003? On your own, try to develop a solution that would involve the least amount of downtime and expense.

If you would like to see a possible solution, follow these steps:

This is a fairly easy solution. You can use the `dsadd` utility with the computer option to add a computer account to the domain. The `dsadd` utility allows you to accept the computer account name from standard input (stdin) so that you can redirect the contents of a text file that contains a list of the computer names to be used in creating the accounts.

1. From the Start menu, select Run.

2. From the Run dialog box, enter **CMD** to open a command window.

3. On the command line, enter the following command, where *names.txt* is a text file that contains a listing of the computer names:

   ```
   dsadd computer <names.txt>
   ```

By default, `dsadd computer` uses the user context of the currently logged on user to connect a domain controller in the logon domain. Administrative access is required.

Troubleshooting Computer Accounts

Because computers need to authenticate to one another, they need accounts and passwords. In addition to the two methods described previously, a computer account is also created when a Windows Server 2003 server is promoted to a domain controller with `dcpromo`.

Like user accounts, each computer account has a password. Passwords are created by the process that creates a computer account. On a defined interval, a process running on the local computer changes the password automatically, and the new password is communicated securely to a domain controller in the computer's domain.

What happens if, at the time a server running Windows Server 2003 changes its password, there is no domain controller available for the new password to be written to? The next time the two computers are able to communicate, the server with the changed password, on finding that the new password is not accepted, uses the previous one instead. After authentication is complete with the old password, the new password is stored on the domain controller and is subsequently replicated to all domain controllers in the domain.

Troubleshooting Issues Related to Computer Accounts by Using the Active Directory Users and Computers Console

Objective:

Diagnose and resolve issues related to computer accounts by using the Active Directory Users and Computers Console

Reset accounts

When a computer account is operating incorrectly, it may be impossible to log on to the domain from the computer. You can see how, if the computer cannot authenticate to the domain controller, it will be impossible for the user to log on. In this case it is necessary to reset the computer's account and rejoin the computer to the domain. This process reestablishes the secure relationship between the computer and the domain it is a member of.

To reset a computer's account using Active Directory Users and Computers, select the folder containing the computer account and right-click the computer object. Choose Reset Account from the context menu, and click Yes from the confirmation dialog box. Reboot the workstation and then rejoin the domain as described earlier.

To reset a computer's account from the command line, you use the `dsmod` command with the `-reset` switch:

```
dsmod computer <dn of computer> -reset
```

As in the case where the computer account was reset using Active Directory Users and Computers, you will have to rejoin the computer to the domain.

Challenge

T Foster is a wholesaler for farm equipment based in the Midwest. T Foster has decided to merge with Harshaw, Inc., one of its biggest rivals, located in the Upper Midwest. The mission of this newly formed conglomerate is to dominate the wholesale farm implement business in the plains states.

T Foster now wants to merge the information technology systems of the two companies as quickly as possible. Fortunately, the two companies run the same order-entry and inventory software, so there won't be any end-user training required.

T Foster has decided to give the former Harshaw employees access to resources on the T Foster network, while slowly migrating the Harshaw data over.

Here are the essential elements:

▶ Export the Harshaw user accounts.

▶ Change the Harshaw accounts to reflect that they are now T Foster employees.

▶ Import the Harshaw data into the T Foster AD.

Try to complete this exercise on your own, listing your conclusions on a sheet of paper. After you have completed the exercise, compare your results to those given here.

The features in Windows Server 2003 enable T Foster to merge the two companies with the least amount of difficulty. The first step is to export the user list from the Harshaw Active Directory using `ldifde`. This extracts the existing user accounts to a file.

The next step is to change the distinguished name in all the user records because the users are now part of T Foster. All the information about the accounts will be the same, but the Active Directory paths will be different in all the distinguished names. This can be accomplished by using `ldifde` with `-c` `<old string>` `<new string>` to cause the replacement of any occurrences of `<old string>` with `<new string>`.

Here's an overview of the requirements and solutions in this case study:

Requirement	Solution Provided By
Export the Harshaw user accounts. Active Directory using ldifde.	Exporting the user list from the Harshaw
Change the Harshaw accounts to reflect that they are now T Foster employees.	Using ldifde with the **-c** switch to change the distinguished names.
Import the Harshaw data into the T Foster AD.	Importing the user list from the Harshaw AD into the T Foster AD using ldifde.

Chapter Summary

This chapter discussed many important skills—skills that you will use every day as a network administrator.

You started with creating and modifying user accounts. You used Active Directory Users and Computers first, learning how to create user accounts in the graphical user interface (GUI). You then progressed to using the command-line tools: dsadd to create a user account, dsget to inquire into an object's properties, dsmod to change properties, dsquery to find objects of any type, and dsrm to remove objects from Active Directory. Then you moved on to using csvde and ldifde to create user accounts automatically, by importing information about the new user accounts from data created from other sources, such as enrollment databases or other directories.

You also covered computer accounts. There is much less that a network administrator needs to do with computer accounts compared to user accounts because computer accounts are typically created automatically when the computer joins the domain and are managed automatically thereafter by the operating system. The network administrator gets involved only if a computer account needs to be reset.

Key Terms

- ▶ Active Directory Users and Computers
- ▶ Organizational Unit (OU)
- ▶ User accounts—domain and local
- ▶ Password
- ▶ User templates
- ▶ Command-line tools for Active Directory tasks
- ▶ dsadd
- ▶ dsquery
- ▶ dsget
- ▶ dsmod
- ▶ dsmove
- ▶ dsrm
- ▶ csvde
- ▶ CSV (Comma Separated Value)

- ▶ ldifde
- ▶ LDAP Data Interchange Format
- ▶ Account lockout
- ▶ Disabled account
- ▶ Expired account
- ▶ User profiles—local, roaming, and mandatory
- ▶ Properties on multiple objects
- ▶ Computer accounts
- ▶ Local accounts
- ▶ Security Identifier (SID)
- ▶ Remote installation services (RIS)

Apply Your Knowledge

Exercises

2.1 Creating user accounts via automation

Imagine that our fictional company, CompTrainers, has a class starting next week, and the students registered for the class will need user accounts. Each account will need to be a member of the Students group, and we'll need the student's title, company name, and business phone number in the user account information.

We will use dsadd, csvde, and dsmod to make an OU called LAN Students, create user accounts, set passwords, and make the user accounts members of the Students global group.

Here is the data we'll be using:

Amell	Bernie	Trainer	555-7179	Prairie Sky Consulting
Blanchard	Verna	Systems Analyst	555-4296	Housing Associates
Bond	Dorothy	Trainer	555-7096	Prairie Sky Consulting
Clark	Cathie	Trainer	555-7028	Prairie Sky Consulting
Ducharme	Lydia	Network Administrator	555-7220	Goldenrod Developments

Emmett	Matt	Network Administrator	555-6057	Goldenrod Developments
Guyn	Karen	Network Administrator	555-1544	Goldenrod Developments
Guyn	Pat	Systems Analyst	555-6669	Goldenrod Developments
James	Robert	Systems Analyst	555-8729	Housing Associates
Jensen	Nicole	Systems Analyst	555-8849	Goldenrod Developments
Kyle	Ann	Trainer	555-8849	Prairie Sky Consulting
Magnus	Holly	Trainer	555-5295	Prairie Sky Consulting
Michell	Christine	Network Administrator	555-4755	Prairie Sky Consulting
Myers	Leslie	Network Administrator	555-1479	Goldenrod Developments
Nowlin	Patty	Systems Analyst	555-4296	Housing Associates
Poulin	Paule	Systems Analyst	555-8606	Housing Associates
Rutherford	Donna	Trainer	555-7612	Prairie Sky Consulting
Ryan	Kathleen	Network Administrator	555-5467	Goldenrod Developments
Sept	Rick	Systems Analyst	555-6057	Housing Associates
Stratton	Susan	Systems Analyst	555-6669	Housing Associates
Swenson	Kathi	Network Administrator	555-5487	Goldenrod Developments

Estimated Time: 45 minutes

1. Open a command prompt and change to the root directory of the C: drive.

2. Use dsadd to create an OU called "OU=LanStudents,OU=Phoenix,DC=70-290,DC=int".

3. Type a csvde command to create a list of the user accounts in the OU=Users, OU= Phoenix,DC=70-290,DC=int OU. Use the parameter -l l,company,objectclass,name,title,company,l,telephoneNumber, userAccountControl,samaccountname to limit the number of fields displayed. Send the output to csvde-out.txt. Copy the file to csvde-in.txt.

4. Use a spreadsheet program, a database program, or Notepad to modify csvde-in.txt. Retain the first record (it has the field names we'll need), but replace the data lines with data from the preceding table. Ensure that the fields are in the proper columns.

5. Use `csvde` to input the data in `csvde-in.txt` into Active Directory. Confirm that the records were created with Active Directory Users and Computers (`csvde -i -f csvde-in.csv -j c:\`).

6. Use `dsquery` to display all the users in the LanTrainers OU, and pipe the result as input to a `dsmod` command that sets the password for all users to Secur1ty and enables the account (`dsquery user "OU=LanStudents,OU= Phoenix,DC=70-290,DC=int" | dsmod user -pwd Secur1ty -mustchpwd yes -disabled no`).

7. Open Active Directory Users and Computers and navigate to the LanStudents OU to see the user accounts.

Exam Questions

1. You want to create a user account for Joan Myles using a command from the command prompt. The account is to be a member of the Engineers group in the Vancouver container, disabled when created, have Secur1ty as its password, and be placed in the `"ou=Users,ou=Vancouver, ou=LTI,dc=Lantrainers, dc=int"` container. Which of the following tools or combination of tools can do the job?

   ○ **A.** `Net User` followed by `dsmove`

   ○ **B.** `ldifde` followed by `dsmod`

   ○ **C.** `dsadd`

   ○ **D.** `csvde` followed by `dsmove`

   ○ **E.** `dsquery` followed by `dsmod`

2. A manager tells you one of his staff has taken a job in another company. The manager wants to ensure that the user cannot access his computer or his files on the network file server. What is your best course of action?

   ○ **A.** Delete the user account.

   ○ **B.** Rename the user account to "Departed User."

   ○ **C.** Select the Account Is Disabled check box.

   ○ **D.** Change the value in the Account Expires field.

3. A manager tells you that his administrative assistant has left the company. The manager wants to ensure that her replacement has access to her computer and her files on the network file server. What is your best course of action?

   ○ **A.** Create a new user account for the replacement and grant the replacement access to the necessary files.

   ○ **B.** Rename the old user account for the new user.

   ○ **C.** Create a new user account for the replacement and copy the necessary files to her home directory.

   ○ **D.** Give the new user the user ID and password of the departed administrative assistant.

4. You need to explain profiles to your management, and you realize that you need to start your presentation with definitions of the three profile types. Choose the three profile types.

　○　**A.** Active Directory user profile

　○　**B.** Local user profile

　○　**C.** Group profile

　○　**D.** Group policy user profile

　○　**E.** Roaming user profile

　○　**F.** Mandatory user profile

5. You are the network administrator for a small company that provides customer service operators for other companies. One of your users calls to complain that the photograph of her grandson that she added to her desktop yesterday wasn't there when she logged on this morning. What is the most likely cause of her problem?

　○　**A.** Her user profile is corrupted.

　○　**B.** She logged in to a different computer.

　○　**C.** She is logged on locally.

　○　**D.** She was assigned a mandatory profile.

6. Due to economic circumstances, your company had to lay off 200 people. The Human Resources Department has provided you with a list of names in a text file. Which command can be used to delete these user accounts?

　○　**A.** dsmod

　○　**B.** dsadd delete

　○　**C.** csvde

　○　**D.** dsrm

7. Your company has recently purchased a small company. The other company runs Unix with an LDAP-compatible directory. Your job is to create user accounts in Active Directory for the employees from this company. What is the best tool to use for this task?

　○　**A.** dsadd

　○　**B.** ldifde

　○　**C.** csvde

　○　**D.** dsrm

8. You are the administrator for a small university. As usual for this type of environment, bored students try to hack into the university billing system every night between 10 p.m. and 2 a.m. What two steps can you take to ensure that a dictionary attack will fail, while still allowing your user to log on at 8 a.m.?

   ○ **A.** Set Account Lockout Threshold to 0.

   ○ **B.** Set Account Lockout Duration to 60.

   ○ **C.** Set Account Lockout Duration to 0.

   ○ **D.** Set Account Lockout Threshold to 3.

9. You are the network administrator for a small company that provides customer service operators for other companies. One of your users calls to complain that she can't see any files in her My Documents folder. She was able to get to them with no problem yesterday. Group Policy is not in use. What is the most likely cause of her problem?

   ○ **A.** Her user profile is corrupted.

   ○ **B.** She logged in to a different computer.

   ○ **C.** She is logged on locally.

   ○ **D.** She was assigned a mandatory profile.

10. You are the administrator for a small, family-owned firm. Because of the firm's size and informality, it has been tough to get users to understand the need for security. You want to change the password policy so that the users will be required to change their passwords every 30 days and can't reuse a password more than every two years. Which of the following choices will accomplish this?

   ○ **A.** Set the password history to 730 and the maximum password age to 30.

   ○ **B.** Set the password history to 365 and the maximum password age to 30.

   ○ **C.** Set the password history to 25 and the maximum password age to 28.

   ○ **D.** Set the password history to 24 and the maximum password age to 30.

Answers to Exam Questions

1. **B, C.** ldifde (with the appropriate data file as input) followed by dsmod (to change the password) does the job, as does dsadd by itself. Net User cannot create a group membership. csvde cannot create group memberships, and dsmove is unnecessary because csvde can create the user account in any container. dsquery cannot create a user account. See the "Creating Accounts Using Automation" section for more information.

2. **C.** It is best to disable the account immediately and then reset the password and enable the account again when someone is ready to review the files held by the account. Deleting the user account makes the review of files very difficult. Renaming the account without changing the logon name or password does not stop the user from accessing the account. Changing the value in the Account Expires field would work, but it is inappropriate to the situation and hence would confuse other administrators. See the "Creating and Modifying User Accounts Using Active Directory Users and Computers" section for more information.

3. **B.** The easiest way to give the new user the proper access is to just rename the old account with the new user's name because they will be performing the same duties and need access to the same files. See the "Creating and Modifying User Accounts Using Active Directory Users and Computers" section for more information.

4. **B, E, F.** These are the profile types. Local, Roaming and Mandatory are the only valid types of profiles listed in Windows Server 2003; the other types listed don't exist. See the "Managing Local, Roaming and Mandatory User Profiles" section for more information.

5. **D.** Although all the other choices are possibilities, in a customer service environment, it's most likely that mandatory profiles are in use. A mandatory profile allows you to make changes; however, those changes are not saved when you log off. See the "Creating and Enforcing Mandatory User Profiles" section for more information.

6. **D.** The dsrm command can be used to delete Active Directory objects, using a text file as input. The csvde command can be used only to import or export accounts, the dsmod command can be used only to change the properties of accounts, and the dsadd command doesn't have a delete option. See the "Creating Accounts Using Automation" section for more information.

7. **B.** ldifde is the best tool to use for this task. It allows you to extract the user list from the LDAP-compatible directory on the Unix server. Next, it allows you to change the distinguished name in the exported file to match your AD structure. Then it imports the new users into AD. See the "Creating Accounts Using Automation" section for more information.

8. **B, D.** Setting the lockout threshold to 3 locks the account after three failed attempts to log on. Setting the lockout duration to 60 reenables the account after 60 minutes. Setting the lockout threshold to 0 allows an indefinite number of logon attempts— definitely not what you want. Setting the lockout duration to 0 will keep the account locked until the administrator manually reenables it. See the "Creating and Modifying User Accounts Using Active Directory Users and Computers" section for more information.

9. B. The most likely problem is that she logged on to a different computer, and roaming profiles are not in use. See the "Managing Local, Roaming and Mandatory User Profiles" section for more information.

10. D. With the maximum age set to 30 days, users are prompted to change their passwords every 30 days. The history setting will retain 24 passwords, approximately two years' worth. See the "Creating and Modifying User Accounts Using Active Directory Users and Computers" section for more information.

Suggested Readings and Resources

1. Boswell, William. *Inside Windows Server 2003*. New Riders, 2003. ISBN 0735711585.

2. For information about LDAP, see RFCs 2251–2256. For information on LDIF, see RFC 2849.

3. Matthews, Marty. *Windows Server 2003: A Beginners Guide*. McGraw-Hill, 2003. ISBN 0072193093.

4. Minasi, Mark, et al. *Mark Minasi's Windows XP and Server 2003 Resource Kit*. Sybex, 2003. ISBN 0782140807.

5. Minasi, Mark, et al. *Mastering Windows Server 2003*. Sybex, 2003. ISBN 0782141307.

6. Shapiro, Jeffrey, et al. *Windows Server 2003 Bible*. John Wiley & Sons, 2006. ISBN 0764549375.

7. Windows Server 2003 Deployment Guide. http://technet2.microsoft.com/WindowsServer/en/Library/c283b699-6124-4c3a-87ef-865443d7ea4b1033.mspx?mfr=true Microsoft Corporation.

8. Windows Server 2003 Resource Kit. Microsoft Press, 2005. ISBN 0735614717.

CHAPTER THREE

Managing Groups

Objectives

This chapter covers the following Microsoft-specified objectives for the "Managing Users, Computers, and Groups" section of the Managing and Maintaining a Microsoft Windows Server 2003 Environment exam:

Create and manage groups

▶ **Create and modify groups by using the Active Directory Users and Computers console.**

▶ **Identify and modify the scope of a group.**

▶ **Manage group membership.**

▶ **Find domain groups in which a user is a member.**

▶ **Create and modify groups by using automation.**

▶ For simplicity of network administration, we can create group objects and allocate resource access rights to these objects. Then by making user accounts members of the group, we can grant them the access that the group objects have been assigned.

Outline

Study Strategies

▶ In studying this section, be sure to practice all the activities described. Become very familiar with Active Directory Users and Computers and creating groups.

▶ Examine the use of the default groups. Know their capabilities and limitations.

▶ You will need access to a Windows Server 2003 domain controller. Many of the tools are new, or they differ from those available in Windows 2000, so don't try to get by with a Windows 2000 domain controller.

▶ Memorize the AGDLP acronym and what it means. It is a best practice that will serve you well, both on the exam and on the job.

Introduction

This chapter continues your study of some of the common daily duties of a Windows Server 2003 administrator. You can rest assured that you will perform the tasks you learn in this chapter very often. This chapter discusses creating and managing group accounts, including what type of group to use for particular situations. An especially important topic is group scope, as well as how it is affected by domain functional level. We'll be starting with creating and managing groups. Let's get to it!

Creating and Managing Groups

Objective:

Create and manage groups

It's much easier to administer a network when you can manage several users at once. We can expect that all members of a given section of an organization will have the same needs in accessing data or using printers, and it's also likely that they should be subject to the same security restrictions. Rather than granting individual users the rights to print to a particular printer or to update files in a given folder, we can allocate those rights to a group object.

With users belonging to groups, you can allocate resource access permissions to the group one time rather than individually to each user in that group. For example, you might have 50 members of a human resource group. You can individually grant access to human resource files and folders to the 50 members, but that obviously could take a long time and leave you open to committing an error that potentially could breach the security of highly sensitive human resource data. Now, if you create a human resource group and add the 50 human resource members to the group, you can configure the necessary access levels to all 50 human resource users at one time by configuring the proper access permissions to the group. It's a one-time action that takes care of 50 individuals!

Making user accounts members of the group automatically grants them any rights that group object has. Therefore, it is useful to create groups, allocate members to those groups, and grant resource access permissions to the groups.

Windows Server 2003 has a number of ways of defining groups of user accounts. We'll describe the different methods a little later, but first you have to understand that Windows Server 2003 domains can be in four different functional levels, and those levels impact what types of groups are possible and what nesting of those groups can be done. (The functional levels have implications related to other capabilities as well, such as Active Directory replication efficiencies, but we're interested only in group behavior here.)

The Four Domain Functional Levels

When the Windows Server 2003 version of Active Directory is installed, a basic set of features is enabled that allows the new domain controller to retain backward compatibility with older domain controllers running Windows NT 4.0 or Windows 2000. As these older domain controllers are removed from the network, the administrator can enable the additional features by raising the domain functional level. The domain functional level determines what features are available and whether older domain controllers are supported. Here are the four domain functional levels:

> **NOTE**
>
> **Active Directory Functional Levels** In fact, several capabilities are available only in the Windows Server 2003 functional level, including improved Active Directory replication and schema handling. For the exam, we're interested only in the effect the domain functionality level has on groups.

- ▶ *Windows 2000 mixed*—The default level in Windows Server 2003, this level is equivalent to mixed mode in Windows 2000. At this level, a domain can contain domain controllers on computers running Windows NT, Windows 2000, or Windows Server 2003. This flexibility comes with a price, as you'll see, because at this level you cannot use the enhanced group features available in either Windows 2000 or Windows Server 2003.

- ▶ *Windows 2000 native*—After you have removed all Windows NT domain controllers from the domain, you can increase the domain functionality level to Windows 2000 native. At the Windows 2000 native level, you get the improved group capabilities of Active Directory as delivered in Windows 2000, such as the capability to "nest" groups and the availability of groups of Universal scope.

- ▶ *Windows Server 2003 interim*—Both Windows NT and Windows Server 2003 domain controllers can exist in a domain at this level. As with the Windows 2000 mixed level, enhanced group functionality cannot be used.

- ▶ *Windows Server 2003*—Only domains that have no Windows 2000 or Windows NT domain controllers can be raised to this level of domain functionality. This is the most advanced level of domain functionality. Although important enhancements are achieved in upgrading from Windows 2000 to Windows Server 2003 Active Directory, there are no significant differences in group functionality between the two levels.

Figure 3.1 shows raising the domain functional level using the Active Directory Users and Computers Microsoft Management Console (MMC).

CAUTION

Raising Functional Levels This step is not reversible, so it should be initiated on a production network only by an experienced network administrator.

EXAM ALERT

Expect Functional Level Questions Expect several exam questions that deal with the topic of the different features enabled at different functional levels.

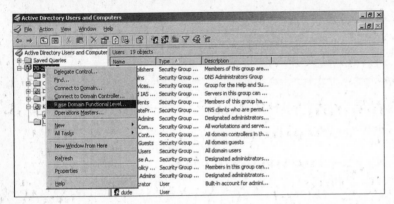

FIGURE 3.1 Raising the domain functional level.

The Three Forest Functional Levels

If you remember when we were promoting our member server to a domain controller, we were prompted as to whether to create a new Forest. A Forest is a logical construct within Active Directory. Logical in that you really can't see or manage it. The forest encompasses all the objects, domains, organizational units (OUs), and so on within it. By default, all domains created in a forest are linked together via transitive trusts so that the administrator has the option of granting access to resources in his or her domain to users and groups in other domains.

Although you can expect forests to be covered at length in other exams, for this one, you will only need to know the following:

▶ *Windows 2000 forest*—The default level in Windows Server 2003, this level is equivalent to mixed mode in Windows 2000. At this level, a domain can contain domain controllers on computers running Windows NT, Windows 2000, or Windows Server 2003. At this level, each group can contain no more than 5,000 accounts. This level is the default with a new installation.

▶ *Windows Server 2003 interim forest*—Only Windows NT and Windows Server 2003 domain controllers can exist in a forest at this level. As with the Windows 2000 level, enhanced group functionality cannot be used. This level is the default when upgrading from Windows NT 4.0.

▶ *Windows Server 2003 forest*—Only forests that have no Windows 2000 or Windows NT domain controllers can be raised to this level of forest functionality. This level enables support for groups containing more than 5,000 members.

Figure 3.2 shows raising the forest functional level using the Active Directory Domains and Trusts MMC.

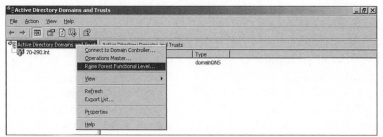

FIGURE 3.2 Raising the forest functional level.

Group Type

The two types of groups are *distribution groups*, which are used only for email lists, and *security groups*, which can be used both for email distribution and resource access. You choose the type depending on the reason you are creating the group:

▶ *Distribution Groups*—Used for email distribution lists only. Cannot be assigned permissions to use resources.

▶ *Security Groups*—Used both for assignment of permissions to use resources and for email distribution.

Group Scope

Objective:

Identify and modify the scope of a group

The second way of classifying a group is by defining its *scope*. Group scope means determining where the group members and the resources that the group can be granted access permissions to reside. Table 3.1 lists the scope of the group object in the first column (domain local, Global, and Universal); in the second column, the object types that can be members of this kind of group; in the third column, the locations of the resources that a group can be given access to.

Note that in several cases, the characteristics of the group object differ depending on the functionality of the domain.

TABLE 3.1 Group Scopes and Applicable Members and Rights

Scope	Can Include	Can Be Granted Access to Resources In
domain local	Accounts, global groups, and universal groups from any domain, and, in Windows 2000 native or Windows Server 2003 functional level domains, other domain local groups from the same domain as the group object.	The local domain
Global	In domains at the Windows 2000 mixed level or at the Windows Server 2003 interim level, only accounts from the same domain as the group object. In Windows 2000 native or Windows Server 2003 functional level domains, accounts and other global groups from the same domain as the group object.	Any domain in the forest and any domain in any other forest that trusts the local domain
Universal	(Not available in domains at the Windows 2000 mixed level or the Windows Server 2003 interim level.) Accounts, global groups, and universal groups from any domain.	Any domain in the forest and any domain in any other forest that trusts the local domain

How would you choose the scope of a group you need to create? Let's talk about each scope in turn.

EXAM ALERT

Understand Groups and Scope   Expect at least one exam question that deals with the scope of groups in Windows Server 2003. Microsoft has always tested heavily on the different types of groups and their scope. This exam will probably not be any different.

Domain Local Groups

Groups of the domain local scope are typically used for resource access. When creating a group of this scope, you think of the resource that we're granting access to, rather than the users who might use the resource. You also name the group object after the resource. You might create a domain local group with the name DL-PhoenixEngineeringResources, for example. You would grant this group Read and Write access to the folders and printers that are used by engineers in Phoenix. The members of the group can be (refer back to Table 3.1) user accounts, global groups, and universal groups from any domain trusted by this domain.

> **NOTE**
>
> **Scope of Trusts**   A domain trusts all other domains in its forest and any other domains that the administrator has explicitly set the domain to trust. Trusts are covered on the 70-294 exam.

If the domain is at the Windows 2000 native functional level or the Windows Server 2003 functional level, the new group can also have other domain local group accounts among its members. The capability to make a group a member of another group of the same type is called *nesting*.

> **NOTE**
>
> **Nesting Groups**   The capability to nest groups is very useful in administration. With nesting, you could define a DL-PhoenixUsers group, whose members are groups called DL-PhoenixPersonnel, DL-PhoenixEngineers, and DL-PhoenixHR. You would make the user accounts members of the departmental groups, with no need to also make them members of the city group.

We have just listed the types of objects that can be members of our new domain local group, but what types are we likely to use? Typically, the member list of a domain local group includes an administrator account and one or more global group accounts. More rarely, you may also see universal group accounts in the domain local group member list.

> **NOTE**
>
> **Local Versus Domain Local**   It's easy to confuse domain local groups with local groups. Local groups are the groups that are resident on a server and have no visibility in the domain. Although they can be used to grant access to resources on that server, you will have to log on or connect to that server to work with them. Domain local groups are stored and managed by Active Directory; therefore, they are visible throughout the domain. However, they are not visible in other domains. We discuss local groups in the upcoming section, "Default Groups."

Global Groups

A *global group* is used to collect user accounts, typically according to the function the members perform in their work. Therefore, their names reference the accounts that are on the group member list—typical global group names are G-PhoenixEngineers and G-KansasCityHR. Only accounts in the same domain as the group object can be members of the global group. The reason the group is called "global" is that the group can be assigned access to any resource or made a member of any domain local group in the entire forest.

Identifying Groups

You've probably noticed that we've been prefixing group names with "DL-" or "G-." This is a shorthand way of identifying the group type, so that we know what the scope of the group is at a glance. For the short scenarios we cover in this book, it's probably not necessary, but in the real world, it can save a lot of time, especially when troubleshooting a permissions problem. Will you remember the type of a group you or your co-workers created six months ago?

If the domain is at the Windows 2000 native functional level or the Windows Server 2003 functional level, the new group can also have other global group accounts from its domain among its members.

A good example of the use of global groups is when users are disbursed and resources exist in few domains. For example, an engineering company has engineers in its Kansas City, Phoenix, and Chicago offices. Each location hosts its own domain in a Windows Server 2003 Active Directory forest. All engineering resources are located in the Phoenix domain. Each domain administrator places his engineers in an "engineers" Global group for his domain. The Phoenix domain administrator creates the EngRes domain local group and assigns the selected permissions to that group. He then places each Engineers Global group from each domain into the EngRes group. The Phoenix administrator relies on the other administrators to determine who in their respective domains is allowed access to the resources.

Universal Groups

A *universal group*, as its name implies, has no limitations as to where its members are located, or in what domains it can be granted resource access. Its members can come from any trusted domain, and it can be a member of any group or be granted access to resources in any trusted domain. These qualities make the group type seem ideal: no worrying about whether the source of members is all right or whether the group can be assigned access in another domain.

There is a cost to this universality, however: The list of members of a universal group is kept in the Global Catalog (GC) and therefore is replicated to all domain controllers designated as Global Catalog servers in the forest. However, the new link-value replication feature in Windows Server 2003 reduces the amount of replication traffic significantly, compared to Windows 2000, where the entire universal group membership list was replicated whenever a change was made.

Global Catalog   The Global Catalog of a forest is a directory that contains a subset of each of the objects in every domain of the forest, though only some of the properties of each object. Although the main purpose of the Global Catalog is to provide an index for forestwide searches, it is also used during authentication (the process of ensuring that an object has the right to access the resources it is requesting) to get the list of all the groups a user object is a member of.

You create a universal group when both these conditions apply:

▸ The members of the group come from more than one domain.

▸ The group needs resource access in more than one domain.

Universal groups are useful when users and resources are disbursed in all domains. For example, when every domain has EngRes and Engineer Global groups, this might not be bad during the initial setup, but it becomes a nightmare as new domains are added. The Universal groups make it easier, in that each domain's Engineers Global group gets added to the Engineers Universal group, and the Engineers Universal group is added to each domain's EngRes domain local group. As new domains come online, they only have to add their Engineers Global group to the Engineers Universal group, and the Engineers Universal group to the domain local group that they have assigned permissions for the shared resources to.

Recommended Sequence of Groups

The recommended usage of groups is as follows:

▸ Make accounts members of global groups.

▸ Make global groups members of domain local groups.

▸ Assign resource access permissions to the domain local groups.

In some cases it is helpful to make global groups members of universal groups and then to make the universal groups members of domain local groups. This is necessary only when a universal group is needed—that is, when a group will have members from multiple domains and will need access to resources in multiple domains.

This sequence is known as *AGUDLP*, which stands for Accounts, Global, Universal, domain local, and Permissions. This is the sequence that you will use when you have multiple domains or are planning to have multiple domains in the future. If you are going to have only a single domain, the recommended sequence is AGDLP, which stands for Accounts, Global, Domain Local, and Permissions.

Here's the hierarchy, then: Suppose we have three domains (Trainers, Writers, and Consultants), and there is a global group in each domain that holds all the finance mangers in that domain (Trainers/G-FinanceManagers, Writers/G-FinanceManagers, and Consultants/ G-FinanceManagers). We could make the U-FinanceManagers universal group with these three global groups as members, and then place the universal group on the member list of a domain local group in each of the domains to give the finance managers access to the resources the domain local group provides. Finally, we could add U-FinanceManagers to the member list of the DL-FinanceResources domain local group in each domain.

You might wonder why we don't grant access to the resources directly to the universal group. We could, of course, but our assumption is that the domain local groups would exist already, to give access to the resource to groups within the local domain.

This hierarchy of groups allows very simple handling of new employees. When a new finance manager joins any of the companies, the local administrator needs only to make the finance manager's user account a member of the G-FinanceManagers global group in the new user's local domain, and that user will immediately be able to access the resources needed.

Default Groups

In the previous chapter we discussed the various default users that are created on a Windows Server 2003 server. In addition to these user accounts, a number of default groups are created. There are different groups created, depending on whether the server is a member server or a domain controller.

These groups are preconfigured with a specific set of permissions that determine what access the users they contain are granted for a variety of resources.

Default Groups on Member Servers

A number of default groups are created on Windows Server 2003 member servers. They are managed via the Local users and Groups snap-in that was discussed in the previous chapter. They are listed here:

▶ *Administrators*—Members of this group have full control over the server. They can access all resources, create users and groups, and assign permissions for the resources to other users. If in a domain, the Domain Admins group is automatically made a member of this group, allowing all administrators in the domain full control access to this server.

▶ *Backup Operators*—Members of this group can perform backups and restores of the files on the server, even if they have not been specifically granted access to those files. However, they cannot change the security settings on the files.

▶ *DHCP Administrators*—Members of this group have full control over the DHCP service. They cannot access any resources not associated with DHCP without being granted additional rights. This group is present only if the DHCP role has been added to the server.

▶ *DHCP Users*—Members of this group can view the configuration of the DHCP server service. However, they cannot change the configuration. This group is present only if the DHCP role has been added to the server.

▶ *Guests*—Members of this group have limited access to the server. The Guest account is a member of this group.

▶ *HelpServicesGroup*—This group can be used to grant permissions to application support accounts. The default member of this group is the account used for the Remote Assistance feature.

▶ *Network Configuration Operators*—Members of this group have full control over the TCP/IP configuration.

▶ *Performance Monitor Users*—Members of this group can monitor the Performance Counters on the server, either locally or remotely. They cannot configure the performance counters.

▶ *Performance Log Users*—Members of this group can manage the configuration of the performance Counters on the server, either locally or remotely.

▶ *Power Users*—This group can be used to create and modify users and groups. They can also delete users and groups, but only those that they created. In addition, they can add users to the Power Users, Users and Guests groups, but can remove only those that they have added. They can also share resources, but can manage only those that they have created.

▶ *Print Operators*—Members of this group can manage printers and print queues.

▶ *Remote Desktop Users*—Members of this group can remotely log on to the server.

▶ *Replicator*—Members of this group are used to logon to the replicator service. This is more of a service account and not a user account.

▶ *Terminal Server Users*—This group contains the accounts of users who are currently logged on to the server remotely via Terminal Services. The default permissions assigned to this group should be sufficient for most applications.

▶ *Users*—Members of this group can perform common tasks on the server. If in a domain, the Domain Users group is automatically made a member of this group, allowing all users in the domain access to this server.

▶ *WINS Users*—Members of this group can view the configuration of the WINS server service. However, they cannot change the configuration. This group is present only if the WINS role has been added to the server.

Default Groups in Active Directory

There are several default groups created in Windows Server 2003 Active Directory. Because these are domainwide groups, they are managed via the Active Directory Users and Computers MMC, in the Builtin and the Users containers. The groups are listed here:

▶ *Enterprise Admins*—This group is present only in the root domain in the forest. Members of this group have full control over the forest. They can access all resources, create users and groups, and assign permissions for the resources to other users. This account is added to the membership of the local Administrators group of every workstation or member server that joins any domain in the forest.

▶ *Schema Admins*—This group is present only in the root domain in the forest. Members of this group have full control over the Active Directory schema.

▶ *Domain Admins*—Members of this group have full control over the domain. They can access all resources, create users and groups, and assign permissions for the resources to other users. This account is added to the membership of the local Administrators group of every workstation or member server that joins the domain.

▶ *Domain Users*—This group contains every user in the domain. This account is added to the membership of the local Users group of every workstation or member server that joins the domain.

▶ *Domain Guests*—Members of this group have limited access to the server. The Guest account is a member of this group.

▶ *Domain Controllers*—This group contains the computer accounts of all domain controllers in the domain.

▶ *Domain Computers*—This group contains the computer accounts of all workstations and servers added to the domain.

▶ *DNSAdmins*—Members of this group have full control over the DNS service. They cannot access any resources not associated with DNS without being granted additional rights.

▶ *DNSUpdateProxy Users*—Members of this group can perform DNS updates for other clients. Typically the DHCP servers are members of this group.

▶ *Account Operators*—This group can be used to create, modify, and delete users, groups, and computer accounts, except for those in the domain controllers OU. They also cannot add or remove members to the Domain Admins group.

▶ *Backup Operators*—Members of this group can perform backups and restores of the files in the domain, even if they have not been specifically granted access to those files. However, they cannot change the security settings on the files.

▶ *Cert Publishers*—Members of this group have the capability to publish security certificates in Active Directory.

▶ *Group Policy Creators*—Members of this group can modify Group Policy.

▶ *HelpServicesGroup*—This group can be used to grant permissions to application support accounts. The default member of this group is the account used for the Remote Assistance feature.

▶ *Incoming Forest Trust Builders*—This group is present only in the root domain in the forest. Members of this group can create one-way incoming forest trusts, but only in the forest root domain.

▶ *Pre–Windows 2000 Compatible Access*—This group has read access to all users and groups in the domain. The Everyone group is automatically added to this group. This group is to provide backward compatibility for computers running Windows NT 4.0.

▶ *Print Operators*—Members of this group can manage printers and print queues.

▶ *RAS and IAS Servers*—Members of this group are permitted access to the remote access properties of users in the Active Directory.

▶ *Server Operators*—This group can be used to manage domain controllers.

▶ *Terminal Service License Servers*—Members of this group distribute licenses to Terminal Services users.

EXAM ALERT

Be Sure You Know What Groups Are Built in and Their Capabilities   Expect to see a few questions relating to membership of the built-in groups, especially those at the domain level.

When assigning users to the default groups, make sure that you understand exactly what access they are being given. It is usually not a good idea to assign or remove specific rights to or from a default group. It is better to create a new group and add the custom rights to it.

System Groups

The last set of default groups are System Groups. System Groups are automatically created by the operating system, but unlike the other default groups, you cannot change or manage them. In most cases, the membership of a system group is changed dynamically by the operating system. They are listed here:

▶ *Anonymous Logon*—This group is used to represent any users or services that access a computer over the network without a username or password. Unlike in Windows NT, the Anonymous Logon group is not a member of the Everyone group.

▶ *Everyone*—This group is used to represent all users or services, including those from other domains. You can grant permissions to the Everyone group, but it's not a good idea for anything other than read-only, because the Anonymous Logon group can become a member of the everyone group.

▶ *Network*—This group is used to represent all users accessing a specific resource over the network. The user is added to this group automatically.

▶ *Interactive*—This group is used to represent all users logged on locally to a computer. The user is added to this group automatically.

Creating and Modifying Groups by Using the Active Directory Users and Computers Console

Objective:

Create and modify groups by using the Active Directory Users and Computers console

To create a group with Active Directory Users and Computers, first select the domain or OU where you want the group object to reside. Generally you should place the group objects inside OUs because you will most likely delegate responsibility for all the objects in an OU to a subadministrator. In our sample company, it has been agreed that any global group that has members from outside the domain will be created at the users' level. Also, global groups will be created at the level in the hierarchy above all the objects in the groups' member list. So the DL-FinanceResources domain local group is created at the users' level, as is G-FinanceManagers. The G-PhoenixEngineers group would be created at the Phoenix OU level.

In Step by Step 3.1 we'll create groups with domain local, Global, and Universal scope.

STEP BY STEP

3.1 Creating groups with domain local, global, and universal scope

1. Open Active Directory Users and Computers and select the Phoenix OU.

2. Right-click the User OU, under the Phoenix OU.

3. Select New, Group from the context menu.

4. When the dialog box opens, ensure that the domain local and Security option buttons are selected, and then type the name **DL-FinanceResources** (see Figure 3.3).

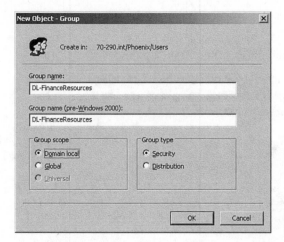

FIGURE 3.3 Give the group a name and specify its type and scope.

5. Click OK, and the group object is created.

6. Right-click the Users OU again and select New, Group from the context menu.

7. This time, ensure the Global and Security option buttons are selected, and then type the name **G-FinanceManagers** and click OK.

8. Right-click the LTI OU a third time and select New, Group from the context menu.

9. This time, ensure that the Universal and Security option buttons are selected and then type the name **U-FinanceManagers** and click OK. Now we have our three groups—and in production we would create several others (see Figure 3.4).

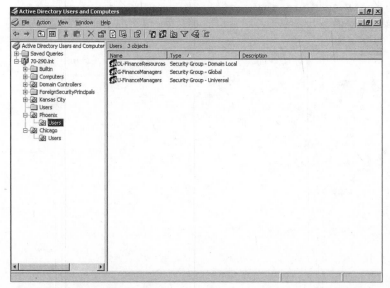

FIGURE 3.4 The group objects are shown in the details pane for the OU in which they were created.

10. Now we want to make G-FinanceManagers a member of U-FinanceManagers, and we want to make U-FinanceManagers a member of DL-FinanceResources.

11. Right-click the U-FinanceManagers object and choose Properties. Select the Members tab.

12. Click Add. In the Select Users, Contacts, Computers or Groups dialog box (in the Enter the Object Names to Select area), type **G** and click Check Names. A dialog box appears listing all the users, contacts, computers, or groups whose names start with *G* (see Figure 3.5).

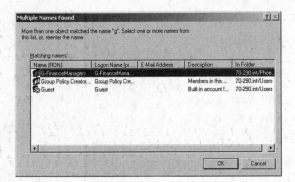

FIGURE 3.5 Select the group you want and click OK.

13. Select G-FinanceManagers and click OK twice. G-FinanceManagers is now a member of U-FinanceManagers. In production we would add the G-FinanceManagers global groups from the other domains as well.

14. Now click the Member Of tab. Select Add, type **DL** into the Enter Object Names to Select area, and click Check Names. Select DL-FinanceResources and click OK twice.

15. We now want to create the \\MARS\Finance share and give DL-FinanceResources access rights to it. To do this, start the Share a Folder Wizard by clicking Add Shared Folder from the Manage Your Server application, as shown in Figure 3.6.

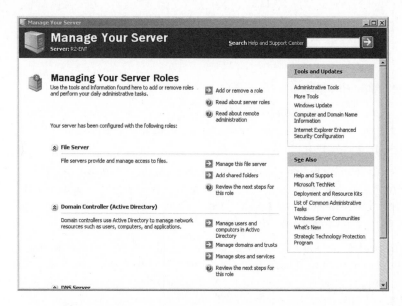

FIGURE 3.6 Select the Add Shared Folders option from the File Server category.

16. After selecting the folder to be shared, naming the share Finance, and assigning a share name, choose Use Custom Share and Folder Permissions, and in the dialog box click Add and browse to the DL-FinanceResources group. Assign the group Full Control rights, remove the Everyone group from the list, and click OK.

NOTE

Add Shared Folders   The Add Shared Folders option will appear on the main screen of the Manage Your Server application only if you have added the File Server role to your server, as we did in Chapter 1, "Windows Server 2003 Environment."

We have accomplished our task. Any member of the G-FinanceManagers global group will have the correct access to the \\MARS\Finance share.

Identifying and Modifying the Scope of a Group

Objective:

Identify and modify the scope of a group

Now you know that the scope of a group object in a domain can be domain local, Global, or Universal. (On a member server, standalone server, or workstation, local groups can also exist.) So how can you tell the scope of a group object?

The first thing to know is that it won't help you to look at the icons in the details pane of Active Directory Users and Computers. The icons used to denote group objects of all scopes are the same. However, the Type column in the details pane does indicate both the group scope and the group type. Refer to Figure 3.4 to confirm this.

Perhaps you have a global group, and you have realized that it would be useful to add accounts from another domain to the member list. That's not possible with a global group, but it is with a universal group. If you change the scope to universal, you can add members from domains in different parts of the enterprise and retain the domain local memberships the existing group has.

If the domain functionality level of your domain is Windows 2000 mixed or Windows Server 2003 interim, you cannot change a group's scope. Universal groups are not available at that domain functionality level, and you cannot change a group's scope from domain local to global, or vice versa.

If the domain functionality level is Windows 2000 native or Windows Server 2003, you can change a group's scope, but only if the group is not a member of another group and has no group members that would be illegal for groups of the new scope.

Here are some examples:

▶ *You want to change the scope of a group from Global to Universal*—This is not allowed if the group is a member of another global group.

▶ *You want to change the scope of a group from domain local to Universal*—This is not allowed if the group has another domain local group as one of its members.

▶ *You want to change the scope of a group from Universal to Global*—This is not allowed if the group has another universal group as one of its members.

▶ *You want to change the scope of a group from Universal to domain local*—This is allowed under all conditions.

NOTE

Changing Group Scope Note that it is not possible to *directly* change a domain local group to a global group, or vice versa. However, you can change a global group to a universal group and then change it to a domain local group.

To change a group's scope with Active Directory Users and Computers, first you have to select the group and look at its properties. Click the option button beside the new scope and click OK to change the scope. If you have followed group naming conventions that indicate the scope of the group, you will probably want to rename the group to show the new scope.

To determine the scope of a group object from the command line, you can use `dsget`. This command shows the description of a group, whether its type is security, and its scope:

```
dsget group <dn> [-desc] [-secgrp] [-scope]
```

To change a group's scope from the command line, you can use `dsmod`. Its syntax in this case is very simple; you just type the following:

```
dsmod group <dn> -scope <L, G, or U>
```

You must be a member of Domain Admins, Enterprise Admins, or Account Operators, or you have to have been delegated the appropriate authority to change the scope of a group by either method.

Challenge

You are a system administrator who is responsible for managing all the computer resources for your company. Your company has decided, for security reasons, to separate the Human Resources users and resources into a separate domain. However, there is a color printer in the original domain that the Human Resources department will need to use occasionally. The users in the current domain have been granted access to the printer by being members of a global group contained in a domain local group that has print permission. Both domains are running at the Windows Server 2003 functional level.

Your task is to configure the permissions for this printer so that everyone who needs access to it can print.

Try to complete this exercise on your own, listing your conclusions on a sheet of paper. After you have completed the exercise, compare your results to those given here.

1. Because there are now two separate domains, you will need to assign permissions to groups from both domains to this printer. Create a global group in the Human Resources domain who need access to this printer. Then place the Human Resources global group in the domain local group.

2. You could place all the users from both domains in a universal group and make the universal group a member of the domain local group.

3. You could create a global group in the Human Resources domain containing the users in that domain who need access to this printer. Place both global groups in a universal group, and make the universal group a member of the domain local group. This method adheres to the AGUDLP strategy.

You could also assign print permissions to a universal group and add members from both domains to it. Basically, there is no right answer to this challenge, as there are a multiple of ways to accomplish this goal.

Managing Group Membership

Objective:

Manage group membership

You can make an account a member of a group in two ways:

▶ Start with the properties of the account and change the list of groups of which the account is a member.

▶ Start with the properties of the group object and change the member list of the group.

There are several methods for changing the group membership, both from Active Directory Users and Computers and from the command line.

In Active Directory Users and Computers, you can use the Member Of tab of the account to see the list of groups the account belongs to, or you can use the Members tab of the group to see the list of members.

Let's look at the Member Of method first. Choose the properties of a user, group, or computer object in Active Directory Users and Computers, and then click the Member Of tab. A list of group objects is displayed. Click Add and use the Object Picker to locate the group or groups you want the account to be a member of. Click OK, and the Member Of list is updated, as shown in Figure 3.7.

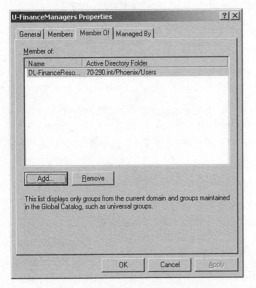

FIGURE 3.7 Click Add to make the group a member of another group.

Another way to use Active Directory Users and Computers to add accounts to a group is to select multiple accounts and then choose File, Properties, and click the Member Of tab. With the Object Picker, find the group whose member list you want to add the accounts to, select it, and select OK. Alternatively, you can right-click the objects and choose Add to a Group from the shortcut menu.

Now let's try starting from the group object. Display its properties and choose Members. Use the Object Picker again, but this time the goal is to find the accounts that should be added to the member list of the group. Select the objects and click Add.

A third method (but not recommended) is to select the accounts you want to add to a group's member list and then drag them to the group object. Dropping the accounts on the group object adds them to the member list. This method is not recommended because it is too easy to drop the accounts on the wrong group object.

There are two ways to allocate users to groups. You can either open the Membership property of a group and add users to it, or you can open the Member Of property of a user and select the groups to which that user will belong. Step by Step 3.2 shows you how to make a user a member of a group.

STEP BY STEP

3.2 Adding a member to a group

1. In Active Directory Users and Computers, navigate to a user account object and open its properties.

2. Select the Member Of tab and view the existing memberships. By default, new users created in a domain are only members of the Domain Users group, as shown in Figure 3.8.

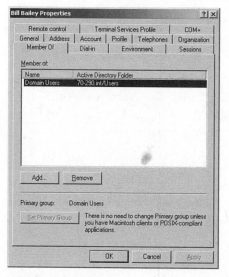

FIGURE 3.8 A new user by default is only a member of the Domain Users group.

3. Click the Add button to bring up the Select Groups dialog box. Type the name of the group and then click the Check Names button. Figure 3.9 shows the results of typing **Engineers** and then selecting Check Names.

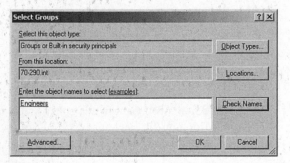

FIGURE 3.9 Adding a user to the Engineers group.

4. Click OK to complete the addition of the Engineers group to the user account and to see the new list of groups to which the user belongs.

5. Click OK to close the user's properties.

NOTE

New and Improved   This is the first time we've used the new-and-improved Object Picker. In Figure 3.9, we could have typed **Eng** and clicked the Check Names button to find the Engineers group. We could have also selected the Advanced button and typed **Art** into the Name Starts With field and found both Arthur Lismer and Arthur Adams. Take a few minutes to play with the new Object Picker.

Adding Accounts to Groups with Command-Line Tools

Objective:

Create and modify groups by using automation

Naturally, a command-line tool is also available for this purpose—you can change the member list of a group with the dsmod group command. This command adds the accounts whose distinguished names follow -addmbr to the member list of the group specified:

```
dsmod group <groupdn> -addmbr <dn's of accounts to be added>
```

Note that dsmod group has two similar-looking parameters that can be used to alter the membership list of a group. As you can see from Table 3.2, -chmbr and -addmbr both change the membership list, but with quite different results.

TABLE 3.2 The chmbr and addmbr Commands

Parameter	Member List Before	Member List After
-addmbr John	Jack, Barbara, Gill, Catherine	Jack, Barbara, Gill, Catherine, John
-chmbr John	Jack, Barbara, Gill, Catherine	John

dsmod with the -addmbr parameter adds the account to the member list of the group, whereas the -chmbr parameter replaces the current member list with the accounts following -chmbr. And dsmod group with the -rmmbr parameter removes the accounts listed from the group's member list.

You're probably expecting to find that there is a command-line method for adding a member to a group using dsmod user. There isn't! In the Active Directory Users and Computers interface you cannot tell whether the group membership information is a property of the user object or the group object. But because dsmod allows only group membership changes with dsmod group, it is clear that the membership information belongs to the group object.

NOTE

Group Membership Changes   As in all previous versions of the Windows server products, the group membership information is rebuilt when the user logs on. After you have changed group membership for users, be sure to tell them to log off and on again to see the effect of the group membership change.

Users on the Local Computer

Although we have been talking about domain users and domain groups in this section, you may find you need to create users and groups at the local computer level, too. Here are some examples:

▶ A member server in a domain may need a group account to provide access to the resources on that computer.

▶ You might need to share a printer installed on a standalone server, and you want to create a local group account to permit this.

▶ You have a computer running Windows Server 2003 that is not part of a domain, and you want to define users and groups to allow access to its resources.

These tasks are performed using Local Users and Groups in Computer Management or with the net localgroup command. After the users and groups have been created, you can grant them rights to access resources on the computer.

Finding Domain Groups in Which a User Is a Member

Objective:

Find domain groups in which a user is a member

If you want to know what groups a user belongs to, you can easily find out with Active Directory Users and Computers by looking at the properties of the user object and then selecting the Member Of tab. There you will see the groups the user belongs to.

There is a problem, however. What if the user is a member of group A, and group A is a member of group B? In that case, the user is effectively a member of group B, but that fact is not shown on the Member Of tab of the properties of the user object. In fact, there is no way within Active Directory Users and Computers to show the expanded member list. However, we can use `dsget user` to show this information.

To find all the groups the user belongs to, *not counting* those due to group nesting, use the following `dsget` command:

```
dsget user <dn> -memberof
```

To find all the groups the user belongs to, including those due to group nesting, use the following `dsget` command:

```
dsget user <dn> -memberof -expand
```

In Figure 3.10, you can see the output of these two commands for the same user.

FIGURE 3.10 The first command shows the direct group memberships of the user, whereas the second shows the nested memberships as well.

Do you remember the discussion of piping earlier in this chapter? We can pipe the output of one command to another command, which will allow us to avoid having to know the distinguished name of an account in `memberof` queries. Look at Figure 3.11.

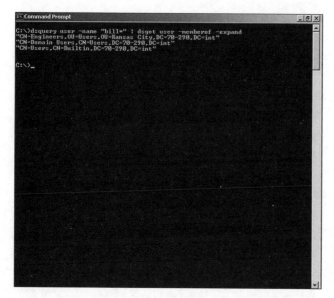

FIGURE 3.11 We need to know only enough of the user's name to make the `-name` parameter unique.

As you can see from the figure, it was sufficient to enter **Bill*** to select the one user whose group memberships are wanted.

Creating and Modifying Groups by Using Automation

Objective:

Create and modify groups by using automation

In Chapter 2, "Managing User and Computer Accounts," we described using `ldifde` to create and modify user accounts. `ldifde` can also be used to create and modify group accounts.

In Step by Step 3.3, we will list the group accounts in the KansasCity OU, modify the names to create new group accounts, and add user accounts to the group accounts.

STEP BY STEP

3.3 Creating group accounts

1. Open a command prompt and change to the root of the C: drive.

2. Type the following command:

   ```
   ldifde -f ldifgroupout.txt -d "OU=KansasCity,DC=70-290,
   ➥DC=int" -l objectclass,cn,distinguishedname,name,
   ➥samaccountname -r "(objectclass=group)"
   ```

   This command will change the OU's distinguished name appropriately, if necessary, and list the group names in the `ldifgroupout.txt` file.

3. Type notepad ldifgroupout.txt to open the file in Notepad.

4. Change the names of the groups to new ones—for example, `Marketing` and `Production` in place of `Sales` and `Engineering`.

5. Remove the entry for `KansasCityUsers`.

6. Save the file as `ldifgroupin1.txt`.

7. Type the following command:

   ```
   ldifde -i -f ldifgroupin1.txt -j c:\ -k
   ```

   `-j c:\` puts a log file called `ldif.log` on `c:\`, and `-k` tells `ldifde` to continue in case of errors. You should see the message 2 entries modified successfully.

8. In Notepad, create a file called `ldifgroupin2.txt` to change the member list of the KansasCity Users group, with the following content (note that `ldifde` can replace only the complete member list of a group, so you have to include all members in this file):

   ```
   dn: CN=KansasCity Users,OU=KansasCity,DC=70-290,DC=int
   changetype: modify
   replace: member
   member: CN=Sales,OU=KansasCity,DC=70-290,
   ➥DC=intmember: CN=Engineers,OU=KansasCity,
   ➥DC=70-290,DC=intmember:CN=Marketing,OU=KansasCity,
   ➥DC=70-290,DC=int
   ➥member: CN=Production,OU=KansasCity,DC=70-290,DC=int
   -
   ```

9. At the command prompt, type the following command:

   ```
   ldifde -i -f ldifgroupin2.txt -j c:\ -k
   ```

   You should see the message 1 entry modified successfully.

10. In Active Directory Users and Computers, view the group objects in the KansasCity OU to see that the Marketing and Production groups have been created and that the four groups listed in `ldifgroupin2.txt` are shown as members of the KansasCity OU.

A second method of creating groups via the command line is by using the `dsadd` command. We used `dsadd` in the previous chapter to create users, and the operation is very similar.

To learn about the use of the `group` subcommands for `dsadd`, enter the following at the command prompt:

```
dsadd group /?
```

```
dsadd group <GroupDN> [-secgrp {yes | no}] [-scope {l | g | u}]
        [-samid <SAMName>] [-desc <Description>] [-memberof <Group ...>]
        [-members <Member ...>] [{-s <Server> | -d <Domain>}] [-u <UserName>]
        [-p {<Password> | *}] [-q] [{-uc | -uco | -uci}]
```

The `dsadd group` command can take several parameters, including group scope, group type, members, and member of, but the only required parameter is the DN (distinguished name).

For example, to create a domain local security group named DL-Engineers in the Kansas City OU, you would enter the following command:

```
Dsadd group "CN=DL-Engineers,OU=Kansas City,DC=70-290,DC=local"
  ➥-secgrp yes -scope l
```

NOTE

dsadd   For a quick review of some of the other capabilities of the `dsadd` command, refer to the section "Creating Accounts with `dsadd`" in Chapter 2.

Assigning Groups

In Windows Server 2003, you have the capability to assign a domain user as the manager of the group. This has the following advantages:

▶ *Assigns a contact for the group*—This gives the administrator a designated person to contact if there are any questions about the group membership.

▶ *Delegation*—This allows the administrator to designate a domain user to manage the additions and deletions to the group.

Delegating the management of a group allows the administrator to assign the process of maintaining the membership of a group to someone who will probably be more familiar with the changes needed to be made to the group. Usually someone like a department manager or a human resources person is responsible for managing certain groups. In Step by Step 3.4, we look at how to delegate the management of a group.

STEP BY STEP

3.4 Delegating management of a group

1. In Active Directory Users and Computers, navigate to the Users OU located under the KansasCity OU in the hierarchy.

2. In the right pane, right-click the entry for the Engineers group and select Properties.

3. Select the Managed By tab and click the Change button.

4. In the Select User, Contact or Group dialog box, enter Bill Bailey, and then click OK.

5. This returns you to the Properties dialog box as shown in Figure 3.12. Select the Manager Can Update Membership List check box.

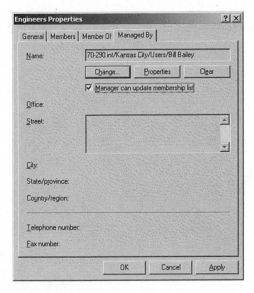

FIGURE 3.12 Grant the manager the capability to manage the membership.

6. Click OK to save.

After the administrator has created a group and assigned permissions to it, it can then be handed off to someone else to maintain the membership list. This can greatly cut down on the administrator's workload in larger companies where there are a lot of groups to maintain.

Chapter Summary

This chapter was a continuation of Chapter 2 because we discussed more of the important skills that you will use every day as a network administrator.

Here you learned about Windows Server 2003 group accounts. You discovered the two types of groups—security and distribution—and the three possible scopes a group account in a domain can have: domain local, Global, and Universal. Again, you started with Active Directory Users and Computers and progressed to the command-line tools. Then you learned about using `ldifde` to create groups.

In addition, you learned about the default groups in Windows Server 2003, and how and when they are used. Finally, you learned how to delegate some of the management of groups to an end user.

Key Terms

▶ AGDLP

▶ AGUDLP

▶ Domain functionality level

▶ Group accounts

▶ Group scope—domain local, Global, Universal

▶ Group types—distribution and security

▶ Nesting groups

Apply Your Knowledge

Exercises

3.1 Creating users and groups

In this exercise we will create three groups and add members to them. Then we will make the three groups members of a universal group. Because there aren't many groups to work with, we'll use Active Directory Users and Computers.

Estimated Time: 5 minutes

1. Open Active Directory Users and Computers and navigate to the LanStudents OU.

2. Create a global security group object called AdminStudents. Add the user accounts for those users whose title is Network Administrator to the member list of the group.

3. Create a global security group object called AnalystStudents. Add the user accounts for those users whose title is Systems Analyst to the member list of the group.

4. Create a global security group object called TrainerStudents. Add the user accounts for those users whose title is Trainer to the member list of the group.

5. Create a universal security group object called AllStudents. Add the three group accounts we just created to the member list of the group.

Exam Questions

1. You want to create a user account for Joan Myles using a command from the command prompt. The account is to be a member of the Engineers group in the KansasCity container, disabled when created, have Secur1ty as its password, and be placed in the `"ou=Users,ou=KansasCity,DC=70-290,DC=int"` container. Which of the following tools or combination of tools can do the job?

   ○ **A.** `Net User` followed by `dsmove`

   ○ **B.** `ldifde` followed by `dsmod`

   ○ **C.** `dsadd`

   ○ **D.** `csvde` followed by `dsmove`

   ○ **E.** `dsquery` followed by `dsmod`

2. You are the junior administrator for a large engineering firm with several locations. You read in a magazine that the best way to assign resources in a multidomain environment is to assign permissions to a domain local group, then add the Global groups to the domain local group, and then add the Global groups to a Universal group. However, the server won't let you create a Universal group. What is the most likely problem?

   ○ **A.** You don't have the proper authority.

   ○ **B.** The domain functional level is at Windows 2000 mixed.

   ○ **C.** The domain functional level is at Windows 2000 native.

   ○ **D.** The domain functional level is *not* at Windows 2003 native.

3. You are planning for resource access in a multidomain forest. Some users from all domains will need access to three continental headquarters domains. What is the recommended strategy for providing access to these resources?

- ○ **A.** Users→universal groups→global groups→domain local groups→permissions to resources

- ○ **B.** Users→global groups→universal groups→domain local groups→permissions to resources

- ○ **C.** Users→domain local groups→universal groups→global groups→permissions to resources

- ○ **D.** Users→universal groups→permissions to resources

4. You are the network administrator for JJamis Inc. The network consists of a single Active Directory domain named jjamis.com. The functional level of the domain is Windows 2000 native. Some network servers run Windows 2000 Server, and others run Windows Server 2003. All users in your accounting department are members of an existing global distribution group named G-Acct. You create a new network share for the accounting users. You need to enable the members of G-Acct to access the file share. What should you do?

- ○ **A.** Raise the functional level of the domain to Windows Server 2003.

- ○ **B.** Change the group type of G-Acct to security.

- ○ **C.** Change the group scope of G-Acct to universal.

- ○ **D.** Raise the functional level of the forest to Windows Server 2003.

5. You are the network administrator for JJamis Inc. The network consists of two Active Directory domains. The functional level of both of the domains is Windows 2000 mixed. Some domain controllers run Windows 2000 Server, and others run Windows Server 2003. You are trying to create a Universal group to allow you to share a printer between the two domains, but when you try to create a group, the option to create it as a Universal group is grayed out. What should you do?

- ○ **A.** Raise the functional level of the domain to Windows Server 2003.

- ○ **B.** Assign permissions for the printer to a domain local group. Create a global group in each domain. Add the desired users to the global group in each domain. Add both global groups to the domain local group.

- ○ **C.** Create a global group in each domain. Add the desired users to the global group in each domain. Assign permissions for the printer to a global group. Add both user global groups to the printer global group.

- ○ **D.** Raise the functional level of the forest to Windows Server 2003.

6. You are the network administrator for JJamis Inc. The network consists of a single Active Directory domain named jjamis.com. The functional level of the domain is Windows 2000 mixed. Some domain controllers run Windows 2000 Server, and others run Windows Server 2003. All users in your accounting department are members of an existing global distribution group named G-Acct. You create a new network share for the accounting users. You need to enable the members of G-Acct to access the file share. What should you do?

   ○ **A.** Raise the functional level of the domain to Windows Server 2003.

   ○ **B.** Change the group type of G-Acct to security.

   ○ **C.** Change the group type of G-Acct to universal.

   ○ **D.** Raise the functional level of the forest to Windows Server 2003.

   ○ **E.** None of the above.

7. You are the network administrator for LS Inc. The network consists of a single Active Directory domain named lsinc.com. The functional level of the domain is Windows 2000 native. You're getting ready to go to an offsite meeting, but you need to create 20 accounts for new users that are starting tomorrow morning. Your secretary is willing to enter the new accounts for you, but she has only domain user access. What should you do? Choose the best answer.

   ○ **A.** Add her to the Domain Administrators group and have her create the user accounts.

   ○ **B.** Add her to the Domain Admins group and have her create the user accounts.

   ○ **C.** Add her to the Account Operators group and have her create the user accounts.

   ○ **D.** Add her to the Power Users group and have her create the user accounts.

8. You are the network administrator for LS Inc. The network consists of a single Active Directory domain named lsinc.com. The functional level of the domain is Windows 2000 native. You're in an offsite meeting, and you get a call from your secretary. The new system administrator started today. She created his account, he can log on, but he still can't access some domain resources. You gave her the permissions listed in the last question, and she successfully created his account. What is the problem? Choose the best answer.

   ○ **A.** Have her add his account to the Domain Administrators group.

   ○ **B.** Have her add his account to the Domain Admins group.

   ○ **C.** Have her add his account to the Account Operators group.

   ○ **D.** Have her add his account to the Power Users group.

   ○ **E.** None of the above.

Answers to Exam Questions

1. **B, C.** `ldifde` (with the appropriate data file as input) followed by `dsmod` (to change the password) does the job, as does `dsadd` by itself. `Net User` cannot create a group membership. `csvde` cannot create group memberships, and `dsmove` is unnecessary because `csvde` can create the user account in any container. `dsquery` cannot create a user account. See "Adding Accounts to Groups with Command-Line Tools."

2. **B.** Universal groups are available only at the Windows 2000 native and Windows Server 2003 functional levels. The Windows 2000 mixed and Windows Server 2003 interim levels are used to support Windows NT 4.0 domain controllers, so Global group nesting and Universal groups cannot be used. See "The Four Domain Functional Levels."

3. **B.** This is the recommended method for providing access to resources through group membership. See "Recommended Sequence of Groups."

4. **B.** Changing the group type to security is the only correct answer. Distribution groups cannot be used to assign permissions. Because this is a single domain environment, a universal group is not necessary. Changing the functional level by itself will not accomplish anything. See "Group Type."

5. **B.** The only correct answer is B. You can't nest global groups in Windows 2000 mixed mode. You still have Windows 2000 domain controllers, so you can't enable either Windows Server 2003 domain or Windows Server 2003 Forest functional levels. See "The Four Domain Functional Levels," "The Three Forest Functional Levels," and "Group Scope."

6. **E.** Distribution groups cannot be used to assign permissions. Unfortunately in Windows 2000 Mixed mode, you cannot convert a distribution group to a security group of any kind, domain local, global or universal. Because we still have Windows 2000 domain controllers, we can't change the forest or the domain functional level to Windows Server 2003. The only solution would be to change the domain functional level to Windows 2000 native, but because it's not listed, there is no good answer listed. See "The Four Domain Functional Levels," "The Three Forest Functional Levels," and "Group Scope."

7. **C.** There is not a Domain Administrators group, and the Power Users group is a local group. Adding a user to the Domain Admins group, even temporarily, is not a good idea because it gives them access to everything in the domain. The Account Operators group will allow your secretary to create and edit accounts without opening up too many resources on your domain. See "Default Groups."

8. **E.** There is not a Domain Administrators group, and the Power Users group is a local group. It is assumed from the previous question that the secretary was added to the Account Operators group. The Account Operators group cannot add or remove users from the Domain Admins group, so the only relevant answer is E. See "Default Groups."

Suggested Readings and Resources

1. Boswell, William. *Inside Windows Server 2003*. New Riders, 2003. ISBN 0735711585.

2. For information about LDAP, see RFCs 2251–2256. For information on LDIF, see RFC 2849.

3. Matthews, Marty. *Windows Server 2003: A Beginners Guide*. McGraw-Hill, 2003. ISBN 0072193093.

4. Minasi, Mark, et al. *Mark Minasi's Windows XP and Server 2003 Resource Kit*. Sybex, 2003. ISBN 0782140807.

5. Minasi, Mark, et al. *Mastering Windows Server 2003*. Sybex, 2003. ISBN 0782141307.

6. Shapiro, Jeffrey, et al. *Windows Server 2003 Bible*. John Wiley & Sons, 2006. ISBN 0764549375.

7. Windows Server 2003 Deployment Guide. Microsoft Corporation.

8. Windows Server 2003 Resource Kit. Microsoft Corporation.

CHAPTER FOUR

Managing and Maintaining Access to Resources

Objectives

This chapter covers the following Microsoft-specified objectives for the "Managing and Maintaining Access to Resources" section of the Managing and Maintaining a Microsoft Windows Server 2003 Environment exam:

Configure file system permissions

▶ **Verify effective permissions when granting permissions**

▶ **Change ownership of files and folders**

▶ The purpose of this objective is to teach you how to control the access and the type of access allowed to files and folders in the Windows Server 2003 environment. You need to know not only how to grant permissions, but also what the cumulative effect is when combining file and folder permissions.

Configure access to shared folders

▶ **Manage shared folder permissions**

▶ The purpose of this objective is to teach you how to configure and manage user access to the shared folders created in Windows Server 2003.

Troubleshoot access to files and shared folders

▶ The purpose of this objective is to teach you how to troubleshoot problems related to file and folder access in the Windows Server 2003 environment.

Manage a web server

▶ **Manage Internet Information Services (IIS)**

▶ Now more than ever, it is very important that you properly install and manage Internet Information Services (IIS) in the Windows Server 2003 environment. With all the exploits targeted at IIS, it is essential that you keep your IIS 6.0 server locked down so that it doesn't become an easy target for hackers or viruses.

Outline

Study Strategies

▶ The sections in this chapter outline features that are basic to using and managing a Windows Server 2003 server. A server is basically useless unless you have an easily manageable mechanism to share resources.

▶ A key part of this chapter is the configuration and management of shared folders. You need to know how to configure access to shared folders and how to troubleshoot shared folder access problems.

▶ The process of working with share and NTFS permissions has always been a major focus on Microsoft exams. Make sure you have a complete understanding of how the different permissions are applied when you access a folder over the network versus accessing it from the server console.

▶ This chapter covers the management and configuration of Offline Folders Services. In addition to knowing how to properly configure Offline Folders to access your server, you need to be able to configure Synchronization Manager to keep the all copies of the files current.

▶ Know how to configure IIS and its various features. A lot of options and scenarios are available in IIS 6.0. The best strategy is to install it, set up several test websites to get a feel for how IIS works, and try some of the various configuration options.

Introduction

As mentioned in previous chapters, one of the primary roles of a Windows Server 2003 server is that of a data repository or file server. The main administrative task of a file server is the management and maintenance of folder and file system permissions. This can range from deciding which users can access the files and folders on the server to deciding exactly what type of access they will have. In addition, the system administrator should be able to troubleshoot problems with file and folder access, not only when users are unable to access a necessary file or folder, but more importantly, when they have a higher level of access than they should.

This chapter covers the tasks and procedures required to maintain data in Windows Server 2003. This type of information is not only crucial for a job as a system administrator, it is also very important for the exam.

Configuring File System Permissions

Objective:

Configure file system permissions

In today's security-conscious environment, few items are as important as basic file system security. There are several levels and methods of protection for files and folders in Windows Server 2003. The two levels of file system security you must be familiar with for the exam are Local Security (also known as NTFS security) and Share security.

Local security applies to a user who is either logged on to the server console or connected via Terminal Services. By default, the following groups have the right to log on locally on a domain controller:

- ▶ Administrators
- ▶ Account Operators
- ▶ Backup Operators
- ▶ Print Operators
- ▶ Server Operators

The following groups have logon locally rights on a workstation or member server:

- ▶ Administrators (Domain Administrators)
- ▶ Backup Operators
- ▶ Power Users

▶ Users

▶ Guest (if not disabled)

Because the members of these groups can log on to the server or workstation directly, it is always recommended that you format your volumes with the New Technology File System (NTFS). This is because you can use local security to block access for various users and groups to files and folders on an NTFS volume. On the other hand, File Allocation Table (FAT) volumes have no local security whatsoever. A user who has the necessary rights to log on to a server or workstation has unrestricted access to all the files and folders contained on a FAT volume.

NOTE

Domain Controllers   The partition of a domain controller that contains SYSVOL and the Active Directory database is required to be formatted with NTFS.

For a more detailed explanation of the various types of FAT volumes and how they differ from NTFS volumes, refer to the "Working with Basic Disks" section in Chapter 12, "Managing Server Storage Devices."

Configuring and Managing Shared Folders

Objective:
Configure access to shared folders

Now that we have examined the properties of local security, let's take a look at share security. As previously discussed, one of the main roles of a computer running Windows Server 2003 is that of a file server. The role of a file server is to provide centralized access to files over a network. Regardless of whether the server is serving files to a workgroup or a domain, this is an important role.

Unfortunately, without the proper security in place, just having physical access to the network allows any user to access any file on the file server. In this section, we examine not only how to share files and folders over a network, but also how to assign permissions to restrict access to the appropriate users.

Creating and Managing Shared Folders

Users on other computers can connect to a file server via shares. The term *share* is shorthand for *shared folder*. Sharing a folder allows the contents of the folder to be available to multiple concurrent users on a network. When a folder is shared, any user with the proper permissions can access it.

A shared folder can contain applications, data, or a user's personal data. Using shares allows an administrator to centralize the management, security, and backup of applications and data. Shared folders can be implemented on either workstations or servers.

When a folder is shared, the Everyone group is granted Read access by default. As additional users or groups are added to the share, they are also given Read permission initially. Unless there is a good reason not to do so, you should always remove the permissions from the Everyone group and assign the proper permissions directly to other groups.

EXAM ALERT

Better Security in Windows Server 2003   In previous versions of Windows, when a folder was shared, the Everyone group was granted Full Control permissions.

NOTE

Be Careful with Deny   If you want to remove the permissions for the Everyone group for an object, remove the Everyone entry from the Permissions dialog box. Do not assign the Deny permission to the Everyone group because the Everyone group includes all users, including administrators.

Only members of the Administrators, Server Operators, or Power Users (member servers only) groups are permitted to share folders. To share a folder on a local volume, follow the procedure outlined in Step by Step 4.1.

STEP BY STEP

4.1 Creating a shared folder on a local volume

1. Open either My Computer or Windows Explorer. Navigate to the folder that you want to share.

2. Right-click the folder and select Sharing and Security from the pop-up menu. The Documents Properties dialog box appears, as shown in Figure 4.1. Click the Share This Folder option button.

3. Enter a share name. This is the name that users will use to access this folder over the network. It does not have to be the same as the folder name. The description is optional; some user interfaces display this field, whereas others do not. The User Limit field allows you to specify the maximum number of users that can concurrently access the share.

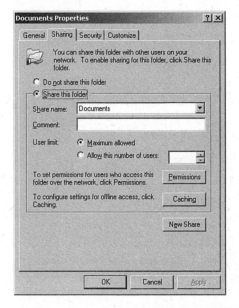

FIGURE 4.1 The Documents Properties dialog box, showing the Sharing tab.

4. Select the desired options and then click OK to save.

5. The shared folder appears in Windows Explorer or My Computer as an icon of a hand holding a folder, as shown in Figure 4.2.

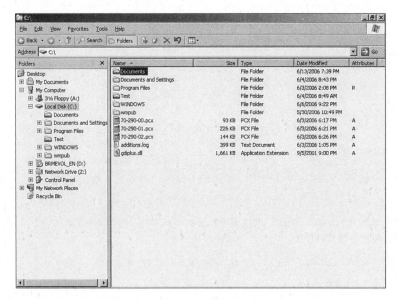

FIGURE 4.2 Windows Explorer, showing the shared folder icon.

A share can also be created on a remote computer. This is accomplished using the Shared Folders snap-in of the Computer Management Microsoft Management Console (MMC).

To share a folder on a remote volume, follow the procedure outlined in Step by Step 4.2.

STEP BY STEP

4.2 Creating a shared folder on a remote volume

1. Click Start, All Programs, Administrative Tools, Computer Management.

2. From the Computer Management MMC, in the left pane right-click the Computer Management (Local) entry. From the pop-up menu, select Connect to Another Computer.

3. From the Select Computer dialog box, enter the name of the remote computer and then click the OK button.

4. From the Computer Management MMC, shown in Figure 4.3, click the System Tools entry in the left pane.

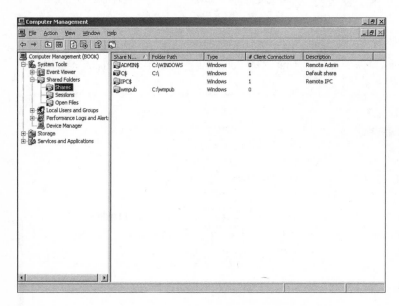

FIGURE 4.3 The Computer Management MMC, showing the Shared Folders snap-in, pointing to a remote server.

5. From the expanded tree, click the Shared Folders entry. Under Shared Folders, right-click Shares and select New Share from the pop-up menu.

6. This starts the Share a Folder Wizard. Click Next on the opening screen of the wizard.

7. From the Folder Path screen of the Share a Folder Wizard, shown in Figure 4.4, enter the path of the folder to be shared. If desired, you can click the Browse button to search for it. Click Next to continue.

8. On the Name, Description, and Settings screen, enter a share name. This is the name users will use to access this folder over the network. It does not have to be the same as the folder name. The description is optional; some user interfaces display this field, whereas others do not. Click Next to continue.

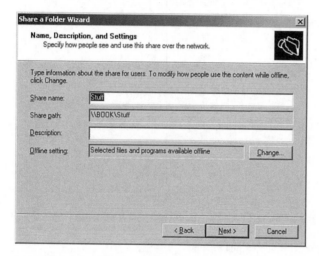

FIGURE 4.4 Enter a share name and description.

9. From the Permissions screen, select one of the following permissions depending on the desired level of access, and then click the Finish button.

   ▶ All users have read-only access

   ▶ Administrators have full access; other users have read-only access

   ▶ Administrators have full access; other users have read and write access

   ▶ Use custom share and folder permissions

10. If the operation was successful, click the Close button to end the wizard.

11. As shown in Figure 4.5, the shared folder appears in the right pane of the Shared Folders snap-in as an icon of a hand holding a folder.

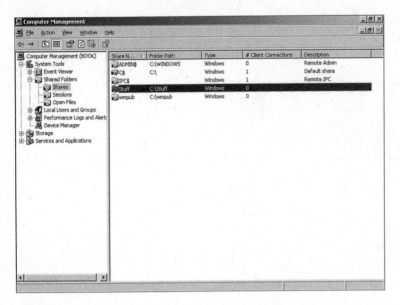

FIGURE 4.5 The Shared Folders snap-in, showing the shared folder icon.

Administrative Shares

As you might have noticed in Figure 4.5, when the new share was created, several shares were already present—most of which have a dollar sign ($) after their name. These shares are Administrative Shared folders. These folders are shared during the default installation of Windows Server 2003. They are used for the convenience of administrators and the operating system to administer files and folders on remote computers.

The permissions for Administrative Shared folders cannot be changed. By default, members of the Administrators group are granted Full Control access. The names and purposes of the folders are as follows:

▶ *C$, D$, E$, and so on*—The root of every volume is automatically shared. Connecting to this share gives you access to the entire volume. Typically, you will use the administrative share to remotely connect to the computer to perform administrative tasks.

▶ *Admin$*—This is a shortcut to the `%systemroot%` folder. This is handy because the systemroot folder can be on any volume, and depending on whether your installation of Windows Server 2003 is an upgrade or a clean installation, the systemroot could be either in a `\winnt` or `\windows` folder. This folder is shared for administrative purposes.

▶ *IPC$*—This is a system folder that is used for interprocess communications (IPC). It is used by most of the Windows Server 2003 administrative tools.

▶ *Print$*—This folder contains the installed print drivers. In addition to the Administrators group, the Server Operators and Print Operators groups have Full Control permissions to this folder. The Everyone group has Read permission.

▶ *FAX$*—This shared folder is used as temporary storage for the Windows Server 2003 Fax application.

The dollar sign after the name tells Windows Server 2003 not to display the folder in My Network Places or when the server is being browsed. You can create your own hidden shares

NOTE

Some Administrative Shares Are Optional   As you probably noticed in Figure 4.5, the Print$ and FAX$ shares weren't present. These shares are optional and appear only if print drivers and the fax service have been installed.

by adding the trailing dollar sign at the end of the share name.

Publishing a Shared Folder in Active Directory

In Windows Server 2003, you can publish a shared folder as a shared folder object in Active Directory using the Active Directory Users and Computers snap-in. This allows users to query Active Directory for the shared folder instead of browsing to locate it. Just creating a shared folder is not enough; it must also be published to be visible in Active Directory.

To publish a shared folder in Active Directory, use the procedure outlined in Step by Step 4.3.

STEP BY STEP

4.3 Publishing a shared folder in Active Directory

1. Click Start, All Programs, Administrative Tools, Active Directory Users and Computers.

2. From the Active Directory Users and Computers MMC, in the left pane click the domain entry to expand the tree. Then navigate to the container of the organizational unit (OU) in which you want to publish the folder.

3. Right-click the desired container. From the pop-up menu, select New, Shared Folder.

4. The New Object—Shared Folder dialog box appears.

5. In the New Object—Shared Folder dialog box, type in the Fully Qualified Domain Name (FQDN) path of the shared folder that you would like to publish (*servername.domainname*.com*sharename*).

6. Type in the name you want to use to refer to the shared folder within Active Directory.

7. Click OK to save.

> **NOTE**
>
> **Use the Fully Qualified Domain Name**   Notice in the previous Step by Step that the fully qualified domain name was used to refer to the network path for the shared folder. If you use the NetBIOS name, only users within your domain can access the share

Any shared folder accessible via a Universal Naming Convention (UNC) name (that is, \\server\share) or FQDN can be published in Active Directory. This includes both shares on servers and workstations. An additional advantage of publishing a share in Active Directory is that if the share is moved to another server, only the reference in Active Directory has to be updated—the users do not have to change their configuration.

Managing Shared Folder Permissions

Objective:
Manage shared folder permissions

Shared folder permissions are important, especially when the share is hosted on a FAT volume. Because the objects on FAT volumes can't be assigned permissions at the file or folder level, share permissions are the only type of file security available.

Share permissions, as you might have guessed from the name, apply only when a file or folder is accessed over the network through a shared folder. Permissions assigned to a share have no effect on a user logged on to the server console or logged on to a Terminal Services session on that server.

When a share is created, the Everyone group is granted Read access by default. Obviously, this isn't appropriate for many circumstances, so you should make adjustments. Only three types of access permissions can be configured on a share. The default permission is Read, and it allows you to perform the following:

▶ View file and subfolder names.

▶ View the contents of files.

▶ Execute applications.

The second permission is Change. It allows you to do everything that the Read permission allows as well as the following:

▶ Add files and subfolders.

▶ Change the contents of files.

▶ Delete files and subfolders.

The last permission is Full Control. It allows you to perform all the Read and Change tasks in addition to allowing you to change the permissions on NTFS files and subfolders in the share.

To share a folder on a local volume, follow the procedure outlined in Step by Step 4.4.

STEP BY STEP

4.4 Configuring shared folder permissions

1. Open either My Computer or Windows Explorer and navigate to the shared folder that you want to configure.

2. Right-click the folder and select Sharing and Security from the pop-up menu. The Folder Properties dialog box appears. Click the Permissions button.

3. The Share Permissions dialog box appears, as shown in Figure 4.6. By default, the Everyone group is granted Read permission. Click the Remove button; this deletes the entry for the Everyone group. Click the Add button; this opens the Select Users or Groups dialog box. Add a user or group and then click the OK button to save.

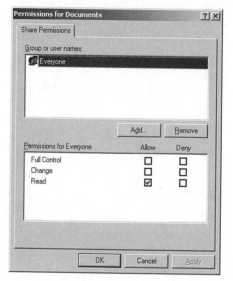

FIGURE 4.6 The Share Permissions tab, showing the default settings.

4. This returns you to the Share Permissions dialog box. Select the desired permissions for the user or group that was added. Then click OK here and in the Folder Properties dialog box to save.

Connecting to Shared Folders

After the share folders are configured on your server or workstation, they can be accessed over the network. Users can access shared folders using either My Network Places, Map Network Drives, or the Run command.

Using the Run command is the easiest and quickest way to access a remote share, as long as you know the server and share name. All you have to do is type it in, as shown in the Run dialog box in Figure 4.7, and then click OK.

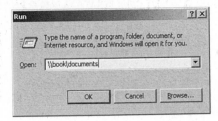

FIGURE 4.7   The Run dialog box, showing how to access a shared folder using a UNC path.

You can also map a network drive using the Map Network Drive option. When you map a drive, you assign the share to a drive letter, which you can use to reference the share. This makes it easier to reference your files. The procedure for mapping a drive is shown in Step by Step 4.5.

STEP BY STEP

4.5 Mapping a drive

1. Click the Start button, then right-click the My Computer icon and select Map Network Drive from the pop-up menu.

2. The Map Network Drive dialog box appears, as shown in Figure 4.8.

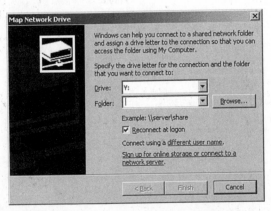

FIGURE 4.8   The Map Network Drive dialog box.

3. From the Map Network Drive dialog box, you can either enter the UNC name for the shared folder that you want to map to, or click the Browse button and search for it. You can also use the drive field to specify any drive designation that's not already in use on your workstation.

4. When you're done, click the Finish button to connect to the drive.

In Figure 4.8, there is a check box labeled Reconnect at Logon. This creates a *persistent* drive mapping—that is, it will remain mapped until you manually disconnect it, even if you reboot your machine. The other option is Connect Using a Different User Name. This option allows you to connect to a share using a different username from what you used when logging on to your machine.

The final method to access a shared folder is via My Network Places. My Network Places is available in the left pane of My Computer (unless you selected Classic Folders).

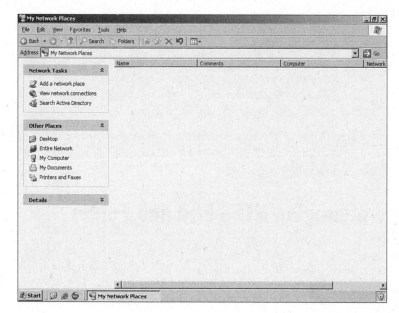

FIGURE 4.9 My Network Places is available in the My Computer MMC.

There are two ways you can access a folder via My Network Places. The first method is to browse to it by clicking My Network Places, Entire Network, Microsoft Windows Network. This allows you to browse the servers in the domains and workgroups on your network, and click on the shares to connect. As shown in Figure 4.10, all the available shares on the \\Book server are shown in the list, except for those that are hidden.

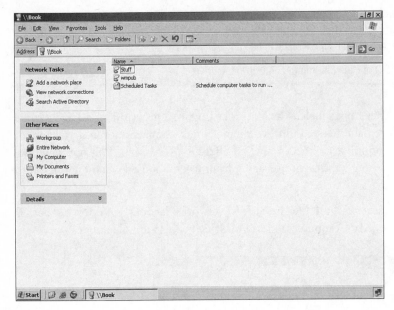

FIGURE 4.10 Browsing shares using My Network Places.

The second method is to click the Add a Network Place entry, listed under the Network Tasks section in the left pane of My Network Places, as shown earlier in Figure 4.10.

This starts the Add Network Place Wizard. It guides you through adding a share via a UNC name, a web share, or a File Transfer Protocol (FTP) address. This allows you to add a network place on your local network or on the Internet.

Configuring and Managing NTFS File and Folder Permissions

Although the various versions of FAT provide no local security, NTFS was created with the capability to control access to every file and folder on an NTFS volume. When a file or folder is created on an NTFS volume, an Access Control List (ACL) is created. The ACL contains a list of every user, group, or computer that has been granted access to the file or folder and what type of access was granted. Each user, group, or computer that has been allowed access to the resource has its own Access Control Entry (ACE) in the ACL. Whenever a file or folder is accessed on an NTFS volume, the operating system reads the ACE to determine whether the user, group, or computer has the necessary permissions for the type of access it is requesting.

Permissions define the type of access that is granted to a user or group for an object, such as a file or folder. Permissions can be assigned to local users or groups, or if the server is a member of a domain, permissions can be assigned to any user or group that is trusted by that domain.

The type of permission varies by object. Folders are used as containers to store files or other folders. Files are executed or written, so the permissions assigned to them apply to the amount of manipulation a user or group can perform against them.

NTFS permissions can be granted to either users or groups. By default, the Administrators group can assign permissions to all files and folders on a server.

The following permissions apply to a file:

▶ *Read*—This permission allows you to read the contents of a file and its attributes, including file ownership and assigned permissions.

▶ *Read and Execute*—This permission includes all the Read permissions, in addition to the ability to run applications.

▶ *Write*—This permission includes all the Read permissions, in addition to the ability to overwrite the file and change its attributes.

▶ *Modify*—This permission includes all the Read and Execute and the Write permissions, in addition to the ability to modify and delete the file.

▶ *Full Control*—This permission includes all the Modify permissions, in addition to allowing you to take ownership of a file and configure the permissions for it.

The following permissions apply to a folder and to the files and subfolders contained in that folder:

▶ *Read*—This permission allows you to read the contents of a folder and its attributes, including ownership and assigned permissions.

▶ *Read and Execute*—This permission includes all the Read permissions, in addition to the ability to run applications.

▶ *Write*—This permission includes all the Read permissions, in addition to the ability to create new files and subfolders and change the folder's attributes.

▶ *List Folder Contents*—This permission includes all the Read permissions, but for the folder only.

▶ *Modify*—This permission includes all the Read and Execute and the Write permissions, in addition to the ability to modify and delete the folder.

▶ *Full Control*—This permission includes all the Modify permissions, in addition to allowing you to take ownership of a folder and configure the permissions to it.

> **NOTE**
>
> Notice that while under the normal permissions, when granting Write access, the Read access permissions are included. However when using special permissions, only the explicit Write functionality selected is granted.

The creator or owner of a file or folder is able to control how permissions are set and to whom permissions are granted on that object. To configure the permissions on a file or folder, use the procedure outlined in Step by Step 4.6.

STEP BY STEP

4.6 Configuring NTFS file and folder permissions

1. Open either My Computer or Windows Explorer. Navigate to the object for which you want to configure permissions.

2. Right-click the object and select Properties from the pop-up menu. Click the Security tab in the resulting dialog box.

3. From the Security tab, shown in Figure 4.11, click the Add button.

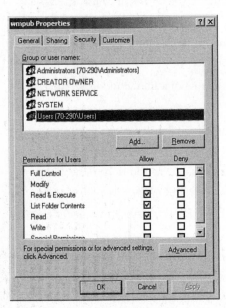

FIGURE 4.11 The folder Properties dialog box, showing the Security tab. This dialog box allows you to see and change the permissions applied to each user or group.

4. The Select Users or Groups dialog box appears. This dialog box allows you to select either a local or domain user or group to assign permissions to. Enter the user or group and then click OK.

5. This returns you to the folder Properties dialog box. Note that, by default, the user or group just added has been granted Read and Execute, List Folder Contents, and Read permissions for the folder.

6. In the Permissions section of the folder Properties dialog box, select the check box for Write and then click the OK button to save.

This Properties dialog box allows you to add or delete users or groups that have access to a file or folder. In addition, you can explicitly select to either allow or deny the basic permissions that apply to that object.

Special Permissions

In addition to the basic permissions, NTFS also allows you to assign more granular, special permissions. Special permissions are generally a subset of the basic NTFS permissions and allow you to limit access to a file or folder to specific tasks. These special permissions apply to both files and folders and are detailed in the following list:

▶ *Traverse Folder/Execute File*—This permission enables users to pass through a folder they do not have access to in order to access a file or folder to which they do have access. This permission may initially have no effect because, for it to apply, the user privilege Bypass Traverse Checking must be enabled. In the default system policy, Bypass Traverse Checking is disabled.

▶ *List Folder/Read Data*—This permission allows a user to list the contents of a folder. When it's applied to a file, this permission allows the file to be opened for Read access.

▶ *Read Attributes*—This permission allows a user to see the file or folder attributes.

▶ *Read Extended Attributes*—This permission allows a user to see special file or folder attributes that are created by applications. This is not commonly used.

▶ *Create Files/Write Data*—When applied to a folder, this permission allows a user to create new files. When applied to a file, it allows the user to edit a file.

▶ *Create Folders/Append Data*—When applied to a folder, this permission grants the user the ability to create new folders. When applied to a file, it allows the user to append data to the file (but not the ability to change existing data).

▶ *Write Attributes*—This permission allows a user to change the file or folder attributes.

▶ *Write Extended Attributes*—This permission allows a user to change special file or folder attributes that are created by applications. This is not commonly used.

▶ *Delete Subfolders and Files*—This permission allows a user to delete subfolders and files, even when the Delete permission is denied at the file and subfolder levels.

▶ *Delete*—This permission allows a user to delete the subfolder or file to which the permission is applied. This permission can be overruled by the Delete Subfolders and File permission.

▶ *Read Permissions*—This permission allows a user to see the permissions applied to a file or folder.

▶ *Change Permissions*—This permission allows a user to change the permissions applied to a file or folder.

▶ *Take Ownership*—This permission allows a user to seize ownership of a file or folder. After a user has ownership of a file or folder, the user will have Full Control.

▶ *Synchronize*—This permission applies to multithreaded, multiprocess programs and is typically used only by developers.

To configure the special permissions on a file or folder, use the procedure outlined in Step by Step 4.7.

STEP BY STEP

4.7 Configuring special permissions

1. Open either My Computer or Windows Explorer. Navigate to the object for which you want to configure permissions.

2. Right-click the object and select Properties from the pop-up menu. Click the Security tab on the resulting dialog box.

3. From the Security tab, click the Advanced button.

4. The Advanced Security Settings dialog box appears (see Figure 4.12). This dialog box allows you to select or add a user or group to assign permissions to by clicking the Add button. Alternatively, you can modify the permissions that are assigned to an existing user or group by highlighting the appropriate entry and then clicking the Edit button. Highlight a user or group and then click Edit.

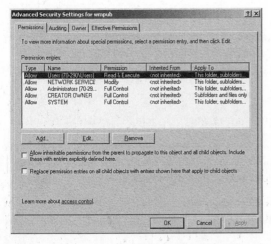

FIGURE 4.12 The Advanced Security Settings dialog box allows you to add or edit the special permissions applied to each user or group.

5. The Permission Entry dialog box appears (see Figure 4.13). This dialog box allows you to allow or deny special permissions for the user or group selected in the Advanced Security Settings dialog box. Select the desired permissions, and then click the Apply Onto drop-down list.

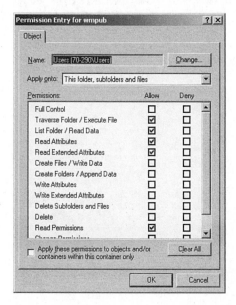

FIGURE 4.13 The Permission Entry dialog box allows you to select the special permissions to be applied.

6. As you can see in Figure 4.13, the Apply Onto drop-down list allows you to specify where to apply the newly selected special permissions. This allows you to select various combinations of files, folders, and subfolders. At the bottom of the dialog box is a check box that prevents the permissions from being inherited by subfolders. Click OK when finished.

7. This returns you to the Advanced Security Settings dialog box. Click OK here and on the Folder Properties dialog box to save.

Special permissions are subsets of the basic permissions discussed earlier. To see which basic permissions the special permissions are included in, see Table 4.1.

TABLE 4.1   Relating Basic Permissions to Special Permissions

Special Permissions	Full Control	Modify	Read & Execute	List Folder Contents	Read	Write
Traverse Folder/ Execute File	X	X	X	X		
List Folder/ Read Data	X	X	X	X	X	
Read Attributes	X	X	X	X	X	
Read Extended Attributes	X	X	X	X	X	
Create Files/ Write Data	X	X				X
Create Folders/ Append Data	X	X				X
Write Attributes	X	X				X
Write Extended Attributes	X	X				X
Delete Subfolders and Files	X					
Delete	X	X				
Read Permissions	X	X	X	X	X	X
Change Permissions	X					
Take Ownership	X					
Synchronize	X	X	X	X	X	X

As you can see, the special permissions allow you to grant permission for just a specific task. This allows you to avoid giving a user Full Control access when all you want the user to be able to do is delete files. In some cases, the basic permissions allow users to perform more tasks than you want them to have access to.

Managing Permissions Inheritance

So far we have covered *explicit* permissions—the permissions explicitly assigned on a file or folder. However, NTFS supports *inherited* permissions; these are the permissions inherited from the parent folder.

NTFS can be thought of as an upside-down tree, with the root at the top. By default, when you assign file and folder permissions, these permissions are automatically applied to the files and folders underneath them in the hierarchy. This means that any permissions applied at the root of an NTFS drive flow down to files and folders at the lowest level, unless the inheritance has been removed. In addition, if you create a file or folder in an existing folder, the permissions in effect for that folder apply to the new objects.

Unless you remove inheritance from the parent, you cannot configure the existing permissions on an object; however, you can still add new ones. As shown in Figure 4.14, the permissions are grayed out. When removing inheritance, you have the option to set the initial permissions by copying the existing inherited permissions or removing them completely. Any explicitly configured permissions remain unchanged.

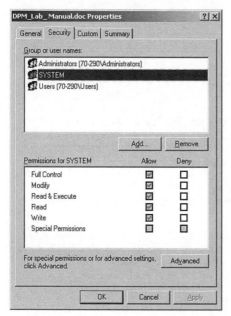

FIGURE 4.14 The file Properties dialog box, showing the inherited permissions. The grayed-out check boxes indicate that the permissions were inherited and cannot be changed.

Here are two key points to remember about inherited permissions:

▶ Inherited Deny permissions are overridden by an explicit Allow permission.

▶ Explicit permissions always take precedence over inherited permissions.

To block inheritance on a file, use the procedure outlined in Step by Step 4.8.

STEP BY STEP

4.8 Removing inheritance from a file

1. Open either My Computer or Windows Explorer and navigate to the file for which you want to configure permissions.

2. Right-click the file, select Properties from the pop-up menu, and click the Security tab in the resulting dialog box.

3. From the Security tab, click the Advanced button.

4. The Advanced Security Settings dialog box appears (see Figure 4.15). Note that the Permission Entries area of the dialog box displays the permissions and where they were inherited from. Deselect the check box Allow Inheritable Permissions from the Parent to Propagate to This Object and All Child Objects.

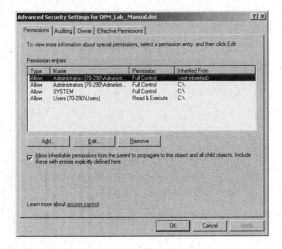

FIGURE 4.15 The Advanced Security Settings dialog box. The check box can be deselected to prevent the object from inheriting permissions from the parent containers.

5. The Security prompt appears (see Figure 4.16). This prompt allows you to either copy or remove the inherited permissions for the object. Select Copy.

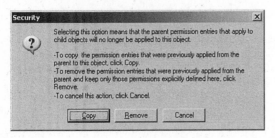

FIGURE 4.16 The Security prompt, which allows you to select whether to copy or remove the inherited permissions.

6. This returns you to the Advanced Security Settings dialog box. The existing permissions were retained; however, the Inherited From field is now empty. Click OK.

7. The file Properties dialog box appears, as shown in Figure 4.17. Click OK to save.

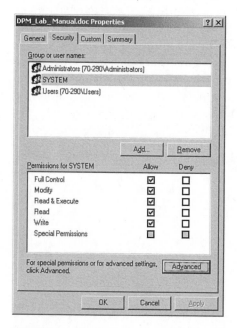

FIGURE 4.17 The file Properties dialog box. Notice that the permissions entries are no longer grayed out and can be changed.

> **NOTE**
>
> **Be Careful with Remove** If you choose to remove the inherited permissions, the only permissions that remain are those that were explicitly added. If there are no added permissions, no one can access the object. The administrator must either assign permissions to it or turn propagation of permissions back on.

Changing Ownership of Files and Folders

Objective:

Change ownership of files and folders

What happens when the owner of a file or folder leaves the company? How do you regain access to the data she controls? As an administrator, you have the option of resetting the password and logging on using her user account. However, this is not a viable option in many cases because security restrictions may not allow the administrator to be the owner of secure user files. Instead, to ensure the audit trail is intact and not interrupted by the administrator accessing the files, the administrator must transfer the ownership to the new user responsible for the files.

As mentioned earlier, when a file or folder is created, by default the creator is granted ownership of the object. In the case of someone leaving the organization, the administrator can assign the Take Ownership permission to another user or group so that it can take control of the former user's files and folders. In this case, the user or group must then take ownership of the files to complete the process. In Windows Server 2003, however, the administrator also has the option to assign ownership to the new user or group. Either method of transferring ownership allows the administrator to pass control to the new user or group responsible for the files without the administrator having ownership and disrupting the auditing trail.

The Take Ownership setting is configured on the Permission Entry dialog box for the object, as shown in Figure 4.18.

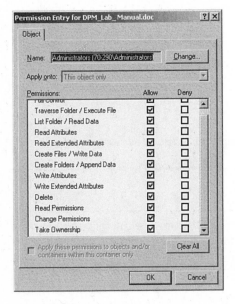

FIGURE 4.18 The Permission Entry dialog box, showing the Take Ownership permission.

EXAM ALERT

You Can Assign Ownership Unlike in previous versions of Windows, where the administrator could take ownership, in Windows Server 2003, you can assign ownership of a file or folder to another user.

Ownership of an object can be taken by the following users and groups:

- ▶ Administrators
- ▶ A user or group that has been assigned the Take Ownership permission
- ▶ A user or group that has the Restore Files and Directories privilege

To assign ownership of a file or folder, use the procedure outlined in Step by Step 4.9.

STEP BY STEP

4.9 Assigning ownership of a file or folder

1. Log on as an administrator.

2. Open either My Computer or Windows Explorer. Navigate to the object for which you want to configure permissions.

3. Right-click the object, select Properties from the pop-up menu, and click the Security tab in the resulting dialog box.

4. From the Security tab, click the Advanced button.

5. The Advanced Security Settings dialog box appears. Select the Owner tab.

6. The Owner tab, shown in Figure 4.19, allows you to assign ownership of the object to a user or group. Click the Other Users or Groups button.

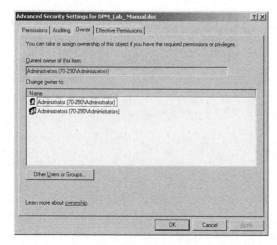

FIGURE 4.19 The Advanced Security Settings dialog box, showing the Owner tab.

7. The Select User or Group dialog box appears. Enter the desired user or group and then click the OK button.

8. This returns you to the Advanced Security Settings dialog box. Click OK here and in the Object Properties dialog box to save.

Verifying Effective Permissions When Granting Permissions

Objective:

Verify effective permissions when granting permissions.

NTFS file and folder permissions are cumulative. This means that the effective permissions are a combination of the permissions granted to the user and those permissions granted to any group to which the user belongs. For example, Dave is a member of the Accounting group, and the Accounting group has Read access to the ACCT folder. However, Dave is also a member of the Managers group. The Managers group has Write access to the ACCT folder. In this case, Dave would have Read and Write access to the ACCT folder.

Let's look at another example. Joe has been granted Full Control access to the EOY folder. Joe is a member of the Managers group, which has Read access to the EOY folder. Joe is also a member of the Planning group, which has Deny Full Control permission on the EOY folder. Joe's effective permission is Deny Full Control.

Another important point to remember is that the least-restrictive permissions apply. For example, if Mary is a member of the HR group, which has Read access to a folder, and she's also a member of the Managers group, which has Full Control access, her effective permission for the folder is Full Control.

All NTFS permissions are cumulative, except in the case of Deny, which overrules everything else. Even if the user has been granted Full Control in several groups, being a member of one group that has been assigned the Deny permission negates everything else.

Windows Server 2003 includes the Effective Permissions tool. This tool automatically looks at a user's permissions and the permissions of the groups of which the user is a member to calculate the effective permissions for an object on an NTFS volume.

To view the effective permissions for an object, follow the procedure outlined in Step by Step 4.10.

STEP BY STEP

4.10 Viewing the effective permissions of a file or folder

1. Open either My Computer or Windows Explorer and navigate to the object for which you want to view permissions.

2. Right-click the object, select Properties from the pop-up menu, and click the Security tab in the resulting dialog box.

3. From the Security tab, click the Advanced button.

4. The Advanced Security Settings dialog box appears. Select the Effective Permissions tab.

5. The Effective Permissions tab appears. This page allows you to display the effective permissions of the object for a user or group. Click the Select button.

6. The Select User or Group dialog box appears. Enter the desired user or group and then click the OK button.

7. This returns you to the Advanced Security Settings dialog box. The effective permissions for the user are shown in Figure 4.20. Click OK here and in the Object Properties dialog box to quit.

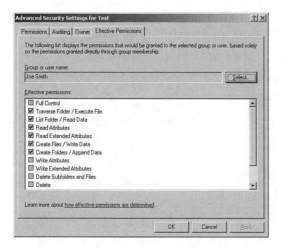

FIGURE 4.20   The Advanced Security Settings dialog box, showing the Effective Permissions tab.

NOTE

Share Permissions   Share permissions are not included in the effective permissions calculations.

Copying and Moving Files and Folders

When files and folders are copied or moved on an NTFS partition, the configured permissions may change. This depends on whether the file or folder was copied or moved, and where it was moved to. Several rules apply when you move or copy NTFS files and folders. The possible outcomes of moving or copying NTFS files and folders are as follows:

▶ Moving a file or folder to another folder on the same NTFS volume results in the file or folder retaining its permissions, regardless of the permissions configured on the target folder.

▶ Moving a file or folder to a different NTFS volume results in the file or folder assuming the permissions of the target folder.

▶ Moving a file or folder from a FAT volume to an NTFS volume results in the file or folder assuming the permissions of the target folder.

▶ Moving a file or folder from an NTFS volume to a FAT volume results in all NTFS-specific properties (including permissions) being lost.

▶ Copying a file to another folder on the same NTFS volume results in the file assuming the permissions of the target folder.

▶ Copying a file or folder to a different NTFS volume results in the file or folder assuming the permissions of the target folder.

▶ Copying a file or folder from a FAT volume to an NTFS volume results in the file or folder assuming the permissions of the target folder.

▶ Copying a file or folder from an NTFS volume to a FAT volume results in all NTFS-specific properties being lost.

It's important to note that if you configure permissions on a folder, you can choose whether to propagate the permissions to the existing files and subfolders contained within that folder. However, any new files or subfolders created within that folder automatically inherit the permissions of the container.

Combining Share and NTFS Permissions

When you're accessing the contents of a shared folder on an NTFS volume, the effective permissions for the object that you are trying to access is a combination of the share and the NTFS permissions applied to the object. The effective permission is always the more restrictive of the two.

For a real-world example, think about it in this way: John has just been named Employee of the Month. As part of this award, he gets a party in his department's break room. Sitting around a table in the break room are several employees from John's department. Sitting on the table is a cake and in John's pocket is the bonus check John received with the award. Think of the people sitting around the table as users sitting at the console of a workstation or server. The check in John's pocket has his name on it, so effectively he has Full Control permissions on the check. Because the check was explicitly made out to John, no other users have access to it, even if they are sitting at the console, or in our example, the table in the break room.

On the other hand, the cake is for everybody in the department, so imagine that the Everyone group has Full Control permissions to the cake. This means that anyone sitting at the table has full access to the cake.

Being a good friend of John, you of course wouldn't miss his celebration, even though you work in another department. However, as usual, you're running late. You approach the door of the break room and discover that you need a card key or access code to get in, which you do not have. Even though you are a member of the Everyone group, and you have permissions to access the cake, you can't get to it because you don't have the proper level of access to get through the door.

A shared folder is similar to the door in our example. If you don't have the necessary access rights for a folder, you can't get to its contents, even if you have been granted the necessary rights at the object level.

To carry the example a little further, say that the door to the break room is made of glass. In this case, because you can see through the door, you have permission to look around (Read), but you can't eat any of the cake (Change). Although the cake still has the permission of Everyone Full Control, because you can only see through the door, you have only the rights that were granted through it.

In a nutshell, this is how combined file and share permissions work. If you are sitting at the server or workstation console, only the NTFS file and folder access permissions apply to you. However, if you are trying to access the files across the network via a shared folder, both the file and the share permissions apply. And the most restrictive permission applies.

Let's use our previous example again. Say that Mary, a member of John's department, is also late for the party. She is able to enter the break room because she has full access rights as a member of John's department (that is, she has the necessary card key or access code to get in). However, she still does not have access to John's bonus check because she doesn't have the proper permissions.

As you can see, when you combine file and share permissions, the most restrictive permissions apply.

Troubleshooting Access to Files and Shared Folders

Objective:

Troubleshoot access to files and shared folders

As you saw in the previous section, share permissions, not just NTFS permissions, can prevent access to a file or folder. However, the problem of a user having too much access to data can be an even more severe problem. For example, how many people in your organization need to know the salaries of the IT staff?

Most access problems are caused by simple things, such as bad passwords or incorrectly con-figured permissions. For example, does the user who is having problems accessing the file or shared folder have the necessary permissions for proper access? Is the user a member of a group that has been denied access to the file or shared folder? Remember that Deny has prece-dence over a granted permission.

When you're tracking down permissions problems, sometimes creating a new user account can be a good troubleshooting aid. Does the new user account fail in the same way as the existing ones? The Effective Permissions tool can be helpful—up to a point. Because share permissions are not included in effective permissions calculations, the Effective Permissions tool can be used to verify that you are obtaining the desired results from the NTFS permissions, but you will still need to analyze the combination of share and NTFS permissions.

Challenge

You are the administrator of a network that includes multiple servers running Windows Server 2003 for file and print services. The Human Resources Department wants to have its files stored on one of your servers, but it doesn't want anyone outside the group to have access to them. The users in the HR department will not be logging on to the server, but they need to access the files over the network. They want you to set this up for them.

What is the best way to solve this issue in Windows Server 2003? On your own, try to develop a solution that would involve the least amount of downtime.

If you would like to see a possible solution, follow these steps:

1. Open either My Computer or Windows Explorer. Navigate to the volume where you want to create a folder.

2. Create a folder and name it HR.

3. Right-click the folder and select Sharing and Security from the pop-up menu.

4. On the Sharing tab of the HR Properties dialog box, select the Share This Folder option, and accept the default share name of HR.

5. Click the Permissions button. The Permissions for HR dialog box appears.

6. Click the Add button. From the Select Users, Computers, or Groups dialog box, enter the HR group. Click the OK button to save.

7. Back at the Permissions for HR dialog box, make sure the HR group entry is highlighted and then click the Full Control check box.

8. Highlight the Everyone entry and then click the Remove button.

9. Click OK. Then click OK again on the HR Properties dialog box to save.

One of the key things to remember when creating a shared folder is that the Everyone group is given Read permission by default. For greater security, you should always remove this group as you add per-missions for specific groups.

Managing Access to Shared Files Using Offline Caching

So far we've talked about sharing files over the network. But what happens when you need to take some files with you? How about that long coast-to-coast flight you have next week—couldn't you use the time to work on your budget for the next fiscal year?

Obviously, servers aren't portable, but you conceivably will be setting up your file server so that portable users—for instance, those users with laptops—will be able to take work home with them, or on the road. Although end users could always manually copy the desired files directly to their laptops, save them to diskette, or burn them on a CD, it can be tough to remember to make these copies. And what happens when users have worked on the files on their laptops and reconnect to the server? Which files have changed, and which have not?

This is where the Offline Files feature of Windows Server 2003 comes in handy. This feature allows the user to specify either single files or a complete folder to be copied to a PC. The Windows Server 2003 operating system manages these files and folders and synchronizes them in the background so that the user will always have the most current version available.

The Offline Files feature works by reserving space on the client machine to store the offline files. By default, this local cache will not exceed more than 10% of the space on the disk. The files are not stored in a recognizable format, so you can't work with them directly.

The following caching options are available:

▶ *Only the Files and Programs That Users Specify Will Be Available Offline*—The user must manually select the items that they want stored in the local cache. This is the default.

▶ *All Files and Programs That Users Open from the Share Will Be Automatically Available Offline*—When this option is selected, as the user uses a file or program contained in the share, it will be added to the user's local cache.

▶ *Optimize for Performance*—This option will automatically cache all of the program files in the share so that they will be run locally.

▶ *Files and Programs from the Share Will Not Be Available Offline*—This option disables all offline caching for the file share.

When using the automatic option, to keep the percentage of disk space used for the cache at or under 10%, the system will automatically delete the oldest files. When you're using the manual option, the cache will take as much space as it needs, potentially filling your hard drive.

However, after the Offline Files feature is enabled, the end user will notice no difference in accessing the files. Even when they are offline, if they had originally accessed the file share via drive mappings or My Network Neighborhood, the same methods will seem to work. The users' view of the file location will not change. They can continue to work with the files as if they were still connected to the server. When users are working with the files, they have no idea, nor should they care whether they are working on the files locally or across the network.

Using Offline Files is a two-step process. First the system administrator must verify that caching is enabled on each shared folder that she wants to allow users to use with the offline files feature (it should be enabled by default). Then the user needs to select the files and/or folders that he wants to have available to him offline. In Step by Step 4.11, we will enable caching on a file share on our Windows Server 2003 server.

STEP BY STEP

4.11 Enabling caching on a file share

1. On the test server, open the Computer Management MMC by clicking Start, All Programs, Administrative Tools, and then Computer Management.

2. In the left pane of the Computer Management MMC, select Shared Folders, and then click Shares.

3. In the right pane, right-click the share that you want to enable, and then click Properties from the pop-up menu.

4. In the Properties dialog box, click the Offline Settings button.

5. From the Offline Settings dialog box, as shown in Figure 4.21, select one of the options to cache the files in the folder.

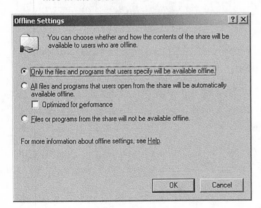

FIGURE 4.21   The Offline Settings dialog box, showing the available configuration settings. Select Optimized for performance to cache all programs in the folder.

6. Click OK twice to save your selections.

Note that the preceding steps, like most file management functions in Windows Server 2003, can be performed on local shares via My Computer, Windows Explorer, or the Shared Folders snap-in, or on remote shares via the Shared Folders snap-in.

The second step of this process is to select the files that you want cached. This step is automatically performed for you if you selected the All Files and Programs That Users Open from the Share Will Be Automatically Available Offline option—whatever files you work with will be downloaded to your cache. However, if you need to select files or folders individually, open My Computer or Windows Explorer on your workstation, right-click the files or folders, and select Make Available Offline, as shown in Figure 4.22.

FIGURE 4.22 To manually select the file or folders that you want to have available offline, select Make Available Offline.

After you select a file(s) the Offline Files Wizard appears and asks you whether you want to automatically synchronize your files as you log on and off the network, as shown in Figure 4.23.

You can tell which files are marked as Offline Files by looking in the folder where they are stored. They will be marked with the offline symbol as shown in Figure 4.24.

FIGURE 4.23 The Offline Files Wizard assists you in setting up your files and synchronizing.

FIGURE 4.24 Offline Files will be shown with a special icon.

When the user is reconnected to the network, any changes made to the files while the user was offline will be automatically synchronized with the files on the network. If for some reason, the files on the network are newer than the files in the cache (if other users were working on them, for example), the user will be prompted as to which version of the file to save, or both, if you prefer.

The files are kept in sync by the Synchronization Manager. The Synchronization Manager is responsible for comparing the items on the network to the items in your local cache and making sure that the most current version is available both places. Synchronization Manager can be configured to synchronize your files and folders at the following times:

- ▶ At configured intervals while your computer is idle
- ▶ At logon and logoff
- ▶ At configured intervals

You can configure Synchronization Manager separately for each resource.

> **NOTE**
>
> **Synchronize Anytime**   You can also synchronize your files anytime by selecting Tools, Synchronize from the menu of My computer or Windows Explorer.

Synchronization Manager can be started by selecting Start, All Programs, Accessories, Synchronize. The Synchronization Manager and the various options available via the different tabs is shown in Figure 4.25.

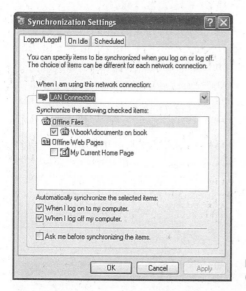

FIGURE 4.25   Synchronization Manager offers a variety of configuration settings.

> **NOTE**
>
> **Secure Your Files**   The Offline Files feature is enabled on the server by default. Important files and folders will need to be secured.

Managing Internet Information Services (IIS) 6.0

Objective:

Manage Internet Information Services (IIS)

Of all the components in Windows Server 2003, Internet Information Services 6.0 has received the most attention. It has been completely reworked so that it retains very little of the basic architecture from previous versions. The majority of the improvements have been in the following areas:

▶ Security

▶ Reliability

▶ Management

Installing Internet Information Services (IIS)

In previous versions of Windows, IIS was installed and enabled by default. This vulnerability was displayed multiple times over the past few years as various viruses and exploits targeting IIS were distributed, and administrators who had applied only IIS patches to their "web servers" were presented with a rude awakening. Countless servers that were not intended to perform any web-serving role were brought to their knees, mainly because a lot of administrators did not realize that they had installed IIS on their servers.

As part of the overall Microsoft Security Initiative, in Windows Server 2003, Microsoft has made IIS an optional component. It is no longer installed as a default component. In addition, even after it is installed, it presents only static pages. If your website requires the use of Active Server Pages (ASP) or other dynamic content, you must manually enable the support for each feature.

> **EXAM ALERT**
>
> **Active Server Pages**   Active Server Pages are web pages with the .ASP extension that utilize ActiveX scripting, typically VBScript or Jscript. When an ASP page is loaded, IIS uses the code in the ASP file to dynamically create an HTML page that is sent to the browser. ASP is similar to CGI scripting, except it enables programmers trained in Microsoft languages to create web pages. You will not need to know the workings of ASP pages for the exam.

In addition, during an upgrade from a previous version of Windows, IIS is installed; however, the service is disabled, and you must start it manually. This prevents administrators from carrying over vulnerabilities from previous versions of Windows. Microsoft's intention is for administrators to run only IIS on those servers that require it, and only with the bare minimum of features, thereby reducing the overall vulnerability to attack.

To install IIS, follow the procedure outlined in Step by Step 4.12.

STEP BY STEP

4.12 Installing Internet Information Services (IIS) 6.0

1. Click Start, All Programs, Control Panel, Add or Remove Programs.

2. Click the Add/Remove Windows Components button in the left pane of the Add or Remove Programs dialog box.

3. The Windows Components Wizard appears. Select the Application Server check box, as shown in Figure 4.26. Click the Next button to continue.

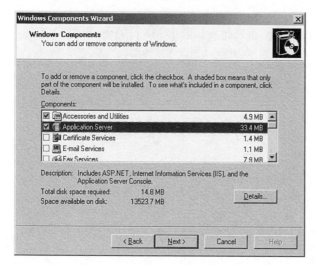

FIGURE 4.26 The Windows Components Wizard.

4. The Configuring Components screen appears. When prompted, insert the Windows Server 2003 CD-ROM and then click the OK button to continue.

5. When the Completing the Windows Component Wizard screen appears, click the Finish button.

The previous steps install the default components of IIS 6.0. As we discussed earlier, the default installation for IIS 6.0 is in "locked down" mode. In locked down mode, only pages containing static content are displayed. All other pages return a 404 error when they are accessed.

Default Installation of IIS 6.0

In the previous Step by Step, we covered a basic installation of IIS 6.0. If you click the Details button, as shown in Figure 4.26, you can select or deselect the various components of IIS, including the IIS Services Manager, FrontPage Server Extensions, and the FTP server.

The following features can be enabled using the Web Service Extensions node in the IIS Manager snap-in:

▶ *ASP*—Active Server Pages; dynamically created web pages based on ActiveX.

▶ *ASP.NET*—The update of ASP built on the Microsoft .NET Framework.

▶ *Server-Side Includes*—Typically used to paste the contents of one file inside another.

▶ *WebDAV Publishing*—Web-based Distributed Authoring and Versioning is a set of extensions that enables users to edit and manage files remotely on web servers.

▶ *FrontPage Server Extensions*—Additional code that enables IIS to support additional features provided by the Microsoft FrontPage website design package.

▶ *ISAPI Extensions*—Internet Server Application Programming Interface is an API used to extend the functionality of the web server.

▶ *CGI Extensions*—Common Gateway Interface is a protocol used to provide an interface between application software and the web server.

Using IIS Manager, you can allow, prohibit, or add additional web service extensions to allow different types of dynamic content to be used on your websites.

To enable the Web Service Extensions in IIS, follow the procedure outlined in Step by Step 4.13.

STEP BY STEP

4.13 Enabling Web Service Extensions in IIS 6.0

1. Click Start, Administrative Tools, Internet Information Services Manager.

2. The IIS Manager MMC opens with the default status of the Web Service Extensions, as shown in Figure 4.27.

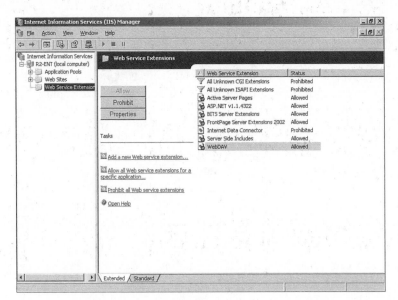

FIGURE 4.27 The IIS Manager MMC, showing the default status of the Web Service Extensions. The list varies, depending on what extensions are installed.

3. Highlight the desired extensions in the right pane of the MMC and then click the Allow button. The setting listed in the Status column for the extension is changed from Prohibited to Allowed.

Web Service Extensions are just a group of EXE and DLL files that are required for the specific function being enabled. For example, for Active Server Pages to be used, the `asp.dll` file must be enabled. To get a list of the files required for each Web Service Extension, in the IIS Manager MMC, highlight the desired extension and click the Properties button. The files are displayed on the Required Files tab of the Properties page.

If you need to add a custom extension, you can click the Add a New Web Service Extension link, which opens the New Web Service Extension dialog box. This dialog box allows you to enter a name for the extension, add the required files, and set the status of the extension to Allowed.

Reliability

IIS 6.0 allows you to run your web applications in either of two modes:

▶ IIS 5.0 Isolation mode

▶ Worker Process Isolation mode

IIS 5.0 Isolation mode is used to run older IIS 5.0–compatible applications that do not run natively in IIS 6.0. By default, a web server that is upgraded from a previous version of IIS is enabled in IIS 5.0 Isolation mode, to ensure that the application installed continues to run. IIS 5.0 Isolation mode manages applications in a similar manner to the way that they were managed in IIS 5.0: All in-process applications are run inside a single instance of `inetinfo.exe`, whereas all out-of-process applications are run in separate DLL hosts. Unfortunately, this mode brings along all the problems that were inherent in IIS 5.0, such as a single application bringing the entire web service down, and memory leaks that require the server to be restarted.

These problems are fixed in the native mode of IIS 6.0, Worker Process Isolation mode. In this mode, applications and processes can be separated into *application pools*. An application pool is a set of one or more applications that are assigned to a set of one or more worker processes. An application pool can contain websites, applications, and virtual directories. Each application pool is isolated from the others. Because of this, a failure or memory leak affects only the processes running in that application pool and has no effect on any of the other functions in other application pools.

In Windows Server 2003, you can run in either IIS 5.0 Isolation mode or Worker Process Isolation mode, but not both simultaneously on the same server.

To change the application mode in IIS, follow the procedure outlined in Step by Step 4.14.

STEP BY STEP

4.14 Changing the application mode in IIS 6.0

1. Click Start, Administrative Tools, Internet Information Services Manager.

2. The IIS Manager MMC opens with the current isolation mode indicated by the presence or absence of the Application Pools folder, as shown in Figure 4.28.

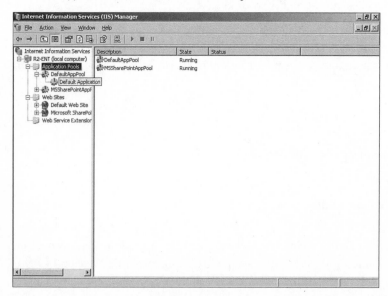

FIGURE 4.28 The IIS Manager MMC, showing the current isolation mode. The server must be in Worker Process Isolation mode because the Application Pools folder is displayed.

3. In the left pane of the MMC, right-click the Web Sites entry and then select Properties from the pop-up menu.

4. From the Web Sites Properties dialog box, click the Service tab. From the Service tab, click the Run WWW Service in IIS 5.0 Isolation Mode check box.

5. Click OK to save this setting.

When IIS is running in the default Worker Process Isolation mode, all processes are assigned to the default pool, named DefaultAppPool. To take advantage of Worker Process Isolation mode, you should create multiple pools and separate your applications.

To add application pools in IIS, follow the procedure outlined in Step by Step 4.15.

STEP BY STEP

4.15 Adding application pools in IIS 6.0

1. Click Start, Administrative Tools, Internet Information Services Manager.

2. The IIS Manager MMC opens with the Worker Process Isolation mode indicated by the presence of the Application Pools folder. If the folder is not present, use the previous procedure to enable Worker Process Isolation mode.

3. In the left pane of the MMC, expand the Application Pools entry and then right-click the DefaultAppPool entry. Select New, Application Pool from the pop-up menu.

4. The Add New Application Pool dialog box appears, as shown in Figure 4.29. Select the configuration settings to use and then click the OK button to save them.

FIGURE 4.29 The Add New Application Pool dialog box. You can use the system defaults or an existing application pool as a template for the configuration.

5. The new application pool entry appears in the MMC.

Management

IIS 6.0 can be managed via the following four methods:

- ▶ IIS Manager MMC
- ▶ Administration scripting
- ▶ Manually editing the configuration file
- ▶ Remote Administration website

These management options give you greater flexibility in that you can use whatever method of administration makes sense for a particular environment. For example, if you are managing only one or two web servers, it might not be worth the trouble to write administrative scripts to make configuration changes. In this situation, either making a couple quick changes using the IIS Manager MMC or manually editing the configuration file might be the most efficient way to accomplish the changes. However, in a larger environment, possibly hosting 10 or more web servers, automating changes via scripting is the only way to go!

IIS Management Using Administrative Scripting

IIS 6.0 installs with a selection of Visual Basic–based scripts that allow you to perform the following functions:

- ▶ Starting and stopping web services
- ▶ Creating default websites
- ▶ Backing up and restoring websites
- ▶ Configuring web extensions
- ▶ Managing FTP sites
- ▶ Managing IIS configuration

These scripts allow you to automate common tasks from the command line, and to even generate a new website from a backup so that a failed server can be replaced. These scripts are stored in the `%systemroot%\System32` folder. All the scripts are ready to be used; just enter the name of the script on the command line to see the required parameters. For additional details on scripting, refer to the IIS online help.

EXAM ALERT

Administrative Scripting   Although the ability to perform administrative scripting is becoming more essential in most environments, you probably will not see it covered at length on the exam.

IIS Management Through Manually Editing the Metabase

In previous versions of IIS, the configuration information was stored in a binary file called the Metabase. Starting in IIS 6.0, this file is no longer stored in a binary format. It is now stored as an XML file that can be directly edited via Notepad or a similar text-editing program. This allows you to quickly make changes to the configuration of IIS, even when it is running. You no longer have to start and stop the WWW service to apply configuration changes. The `Metabase.xml` file is stored in the `%systemroot%\System32\inetsrv` folder.

To edit the `Metabase.xml` file without stopping the IIS service, you must ensure that two items are enabled:

▶ *The Metabase History feature*—This feature saves the last 10 changes to the Metabase file. It is enabled by default.

▶ *The Enable Direct Metabase Edit feature*—This item is turned on via the Local Computer Properties dialog box in the IIS Manager.

To make configuration changes in IIS by editing the `Metabase.xml` file, follow the procedure outlined in Step by Step 4.16.

STEP BY STEP

4.16 Configuring IIS 6.0 by editing the metabase file

1. Click Start, Administrative Tools, Internet Information Services Manager.

2. From the IIS Manager MMC, right-click the Local Computer entry and then select Properties from the pop-up menu.

3. On the Local Computer Properties dialog box, select the Enable Direct Metabase Edit check box.

4. Click OK to save this setting.

5. Click Start, All Programs, Accessories, Notepad.

6. Click File, Open and then navigate to the %systemroot%\System32\inetsrv folder and select the Metabase.xml file.

NOTE

Manually Editing the Metabase Although Microsoft has made it easier to manually edit the Metabase, and even allows you to do it while your website is up and running, you should always use extreme caution when doing so.

IIS Management Using the IIS Manager MMC

The IIS Manager MMC, first introduced with the Windows NT 4.0 Option Pack, is still with us, and although the basic operations haven't really changed that much, additional options have been added to support the new features in IIS 6.0. The IIS snap-in can be added to other MMCs using the methods covered in the beginning of this chapter.

> **EXAM ALERT**
>
> **Know IIS Manager** All the configuration options available in IIS 6.0 can be configured via the IIS Manager MMC, so it is important to become very familiar with its operation, both for your day-to-day administration tasks and for the exam.

You should already be somewhat familiar with the IIS Manager MMC because we have used it in previous examples in this chapter. In the field, the IIS Manager is the most commonly used administrative tool for IIS. It is still the quickest and easiest method of creating and configuring IIS in small-to-medium-sized environments.

The IIS Manager MMC is just like the other MMCs covered in this chapter in that it can be used to configure either the local computer or a remote computer by right-clicking the Local Computer entry and selecting Connect from the pop-up menu.

Managing the Default Website

Unlike previous versions of IIS, which were installed with multiple virtual directories and lots of sample pages that could be exploited by hackers, the default installation of IIS 6.0 is set up with a minimum of files. Basically only enough content is installed to present an Under Construction page, which you can see by entering **http://localhost** on your test server.

From the IIS Manager MMC, you can set the properties for each website, or you can set the defaults for all websites hosted on the server. To view and set the defaults for all websites, right-click the Web Sites entry in the IIS Manager MMC, and then select Properties from the pop-up menu.

> **NOTE**
>
> **Scope of Settings** Unless otherwise indicated, the settings shown on the Properties pages can be applied either globally to all websites or uniquely to each individual website.

From the Web Site tab, shown in Figure 4.30, you can select the timeout settings, whether to log website activity, and the format and the location for the log files. Notice that certain settings, such as the IP Address field, are grayed out. This is because those settings are unique to each individual website.

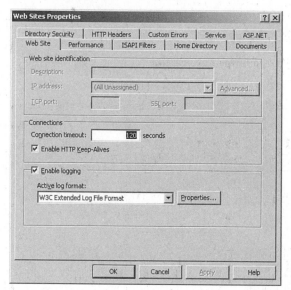

FIGURE 4.30 The Web Site tab.

Click the Performance tab (see Figure 4.31). From here you can adjust the settings that determine the overall performance of your web server. The Bandwidth Throttling setting, along with the Web Site Connections setting, is used to control the amount of bandwidth that is consumed by the web server, and it also limits the amount of memory that is preallocated to caching. This allows you to prioritize the amount of bandwidth consumed by each web server over a shared connection. This can be used to ensure that a higher availability website is granted more bandwidth than a less significant site.

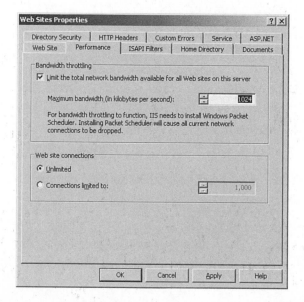

FIGURE 4.31 The Performance tab.

The ISAPI Filters tab allows you to add custom-written filters that respond to specific events during an HTTP request.

The Home Directory tab, shown in Figure 4.32, allows you to specify the location of the files used for your websites. This tab is used for individual sites.

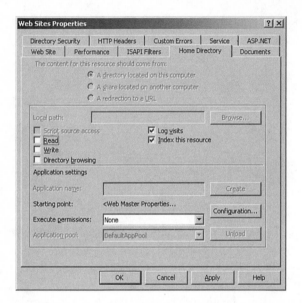

FIGURE 4.32 The Home Directory tab.

The Home Directory tab allows you to assign content for your website from the following locations:

▶ *A Directory Located on This Computer*—This is the default. Enter a local path, or select one by clicking the Browse button and navigating to it.

▶ *A Share Located on Another Computer*—This option allows you to specify a server and share name where the necessary resources are stored. After entering the share name, you have the option of entering a specific user ID and password if needed to access the share by clicking the Connect As button.

▶ *A Redirection to a URL*—This option allows you to specify a website or virtual directory that will provide content.

In addition to controlling access via NTFS or share permissions, the Home Directory tab allows you to specify what visitors to the site can do.

The options are as follows:

▶ *Script Source Access*—If either Read or Write access is selected, this option allows visitors to see the source code of the pages that they are viewing. This option should be selected only for development sites.

▶ *Read*—This option allows visitors to view the web pages and to download files. If this option is not selected, the website cannot be viewed.

▶ *Write*—This option allows visitors to upload files to the website and to edit the content of a file that they have the necessary permissions for. This option requires a browser that supports HTTP 1.1 or later.

▶ *Directory Browsing*—This option allows users to see a listing of the files and sub-directories.

▶ *Log Visits*—This option allows you to select to log all user interaction with the site. This option requires logging to be enabled on the Web Site tab.

▶ *Index This Resource*—If the Indexing service was installed, this option allows the site to be indexed for faster searching.

The Execute Permissions field allows you to select what type of scripts or executable files can be invoked by a browser:

▶ *None*—With this option, only static HTML pages or image files will be displayed.

▶ *Scripts Only*—This option allows ASP scripts to run; however, executables such as ASAPI DLLs and CGIBIN applications cannot be run.

▶ *Scripts and Executables*—This option allows any file type to be run.

NOTE

Invitation to Disaster   Allowing both Execute and Write access allows visitors to upload and execute any code that they want on your site.

The Application Pool drop-down list allows you to specify the application pool the website is to be a member of.

The Documents tab, as shown in Figure 4.33, is used to specify the default document that is sent to the browser when no specific document is requested. This can be either a home page or an index page. The Enable Document Footer option allows you to attach a footer to every document that is displayed.

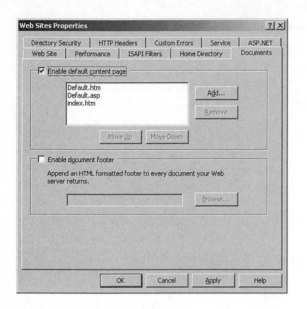

FIGURE 4.33   The Documents tab.

The Directory Security tab allows you to control the access to your website. This tab is covered at length later in this chapter.

The HTTP Headers tab, shown in Figure 4.34, enables you to configure the values returned to the browser via the header included in the HTML page. These values include Content Expiration, which tells the browser when to refresh cached pages, Content Rating, which identifies the type of content provided by the site, and the Mime Types setting, which maps a file extension to a file type.

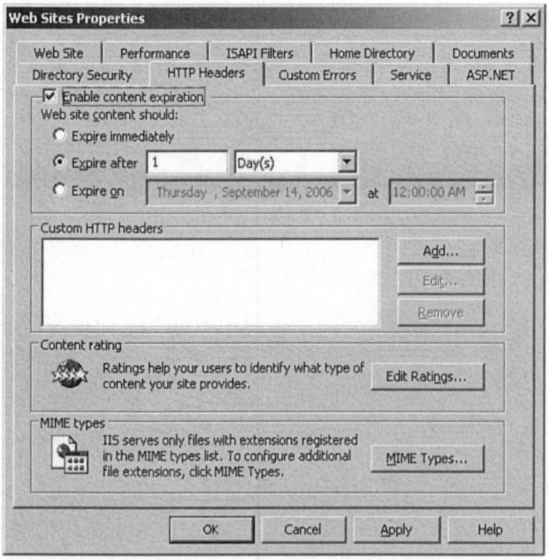

FIGURE 4.34   The HTTP Headers tab.

The Custom HTTP Headers option allows you to send custom HTTP headers to a client browser. These can be used to support browser features that the website does not yet officially support.

The Custom Errors tab allows you to define replacement error messages. Instead of the default numerical messages, you can define something more informative.

The Service tab (see Figure 4.35) allows you to set the mode in which the web server is run— either IIS 5.0 Isolation mode or Worker Process Isolation mode. There are also settings for HTTP Compression. HTTP Compression mode allows you to compress static files or dynamic content, or both, to be sent to the browser. Sending compressed files consumes less bandwidth, and this feature can be very useful in limited-bandwidth situations.

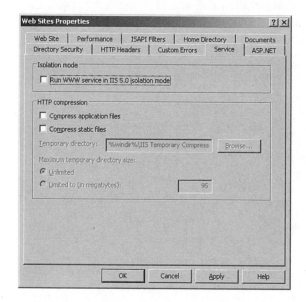

FIGURE 4.35 The Service tab.

However, compressing and uncompressing the files consumes additional processing cycles, both on the web server and the client, so the HTTP Compression options should not be enabled if the web server is already processor starved.

Creating a Website

Like most other functions in Windows Server 2003, a wizard is supplied to make creating a website easier. To create a new website, follow the procedure outlined in Step by Step 4.17.

STEP BY STEP

4.17 Creating a new website

1. Click Start, Administrative Tools, Internet Information Services Manager.

2. From the IIS Manager MMC, right-click the Web Sites entry and then select New, Web Site from the pop-up menu.

3. On the Welcome to the Web Site Creation Wizard screen, click the Next button to continue.

4. On the Web Site Description screen, type in a descriptive name for the website. Click the Next button to continue.

5. The IP Address and Port Settings screen appears, as shown in Figure 4.36. From this screen, you can select the IP address, TCP port, or host header to which this website will respond. Make the appropriate choices, and then click the Next button to continue.

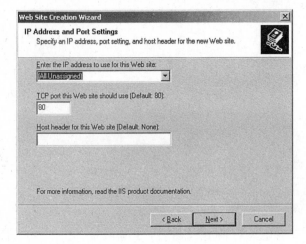

FIGURE 4.36 Specify the IP or port settings for the new website.

6. The Web Site Home Directory screen appears. From this screen, you can select the folder that contains the files for your website. You can also specify that you want to allow anonymous access to your site. Make the appropriate choices and then click the Next button to continue.

7. The Web Site Access Permissions screen appears. From this screen, you can specify the permissions you are granting visitors to your website. You should always specify the minimum permissions needed. Make the appropriate choices and then click the Next button to continue.

8. When the Finishing the Web Site Creation Wizard screen appears, click the Finish button to save your settings. The new website appears in the IIS Manager console, listed under the Default Web Site entry.

Hosting Multiple Websites

In the previous Step by Step, you learned how to add an additional website to a web server, but we left out one small detail. If a web server is hosting multiple websites, how do you determine which website is presented to the browser?

When you're hosting multiple websites on a single server, each website must have a unique identity. This is accomplished by using the following identifiers:

- ▶ *Unique IP address*—Unique IP addresses are used for each website hosted on the server. This method is commonly used for websites accessed over the Internet. Unique IP addresses are required when Secure Sockets Layer (SSL) is used.

- ▶ *Host header name*—Host header names are used to differentiate websites when a single IP address is used.

- ▶ *Nonstandard port number*—Nonstandard port numbers, such as TCP port numbers, are rarely used on production web servers.

By configuring one or more of these identifiers, you can uniquely identify each website on your server. When using multiple IP addresses to identify the websites on your server, you can either install multiple network interface cards (NICs), each with a unique IP address, or just assign multiple IP addresses to a single NIC.

To identify a new website by IP address, use the procedure outlined in Step by Step 4.18.

STEP BY STEP

4.18 Identifying a new website by IP address

1. Click Start, Control Panel, Network Connections, Local Area Connection.

2. From the Local Area Connection Status dialog box, click the Properties button.

3. From the Local Area Connection Properties dialog box, highlight the Internet Protocol (TCP/IP) entry and then click the Properties button.

4. When the Internet Protocol (TCP/IP) Properties dialog box appears, click the Advanced button.

5. From the Advanced TCP/IP Settings dialog box, click the Add button.

6. From the Advanced TCP/IP Address dialog box, enter the new IP address and subnet mask. When you're finished, click the Add button. Repeat this process for additional addresses.

7. Click OK twice and then click the Close button on the Local Area Connection Properties dialog box and the Local Area Connection Status dialog box to save your settings.

8. Click Start, Administrative Tools, Internet Information Services Manager.

9. From the IIS Manager MMC, right-click the Web Sites entry and then select New, Web Site from the pop-up menu.

10. On the Welcome to the Web Site Creation Wizard screen, click the Next button to continue.

11. On the Web Site Description screen, type in a descriptive name for the website. Click the Next button to continue.

12. The IP Address and Port Settings screen appears, as shown in Figure 4.37. Notice that if you click the drop-down list for the IP Address field, the new IP address you entered in the previous steps is available. Select the new IP address for your website and then refer to the information in Step by Step 4.17 to complete the website configuration.

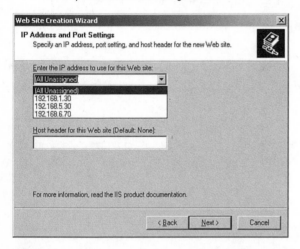

FIGURE 4.37 Specify the IP address for the new website.

With the explosion in popularity of the Internet and the slow adoption of IPv6, the number of available IP addresses is dwindling rapidly. This means that it's not always possible or feasible to lease multiple IP addresses from an ISP to host multiple websites. Fortunately, websites can also be configured to respond to a unique host header.

A *host header* is nothing more than a unique DNS name that is used to identify one of the additional websites. The site that is using the host header shares the same port and IP address, but when the browser connects to the default website, it asks for the site using the host header entry. The server reads the request from the browser and directs it to the requested site. This allows you to host multiple sites at the same IP address; they just have to have unique header names, such as www.abc.com, www.xyz.com, and so on.

Host headers require that you use a browser that supports HTTP 1.1 or later. If your browser does not support HTTP 1.1, you will be connected to the default website.

To identify a website by host header, use the procedure outlined in Step by Step 4.19.

STEP BY STEP

4.19 Identifying a website by host header

1. Click Start, Administrative Tools, Internet Information Services Manager.

2. From the IIS Manager MMC, right-click a website entry and then select Properties from the pop-up menu.

3. From the Web Site tab of the Properties dialog box, click the Advanced button.

4. This opens the Advanced Web Site Identification dialog box. To add an additional host header to the existing IP address, highlight the IP address entry and then click the Add button.

5. This opens the Add/Edit Web Site Identification dialog box, shown in Figure 4.38. Enter the desired host header name and assign it to port 80. Then click the OK button to save your settings. Repeat this for any additional host headers.

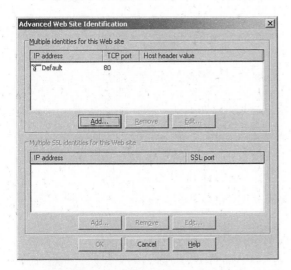

FIGURE 4.38 The Advanced Web Site Identification dialog box. Note that you can enter unique port numbers using this dialog box.

NOTE

Additional Security Because all the sites now have host headers, you will not be able to connect to the website by IP address, giving an additional layer of security.

As noted in the previous procedure, the port number can be changed as well. When you're using a unique port number, it has to be entered in the URL as follows:

```
www.abc.com:60
```

A port number can be any number from 1 to 65535. Port numbers are rarely used, except for testing purposes.

NOTE

Port Numbers   Although it is technically true that any port to 65K can be used, it is not the best idea to use any well-known ports for this purpose. Ports such as 25 (SMTP), 110 (POP), 3268 (LDAP), and 443 (SSL), among many others, would not make sense to serve web pages from.

EXAM ALERT

SSL and Host Headers Don't Mix   Host headers cannot be used with SSL because the domain name is encoded in the certificate, and the browser is able to see only the IP address. When using SSL, you must use a unique IP addresses.

Challenge

When new websites and applications are added to a web server, by default they are placed in the DefaultAppPool application pool. To obtain the maximum benefit from running IIS 6.0, you should assign your applications to separate application pools.

In this scenario, you are required to create a new website and then assign it to a new application pool. You should do this using as few steps as possible.

How would you set this up?

You should try working through this problem on your own first. If you get stuck, or if you'd like to see one possible solution, follow these steps:

1. Click Start, Administrative Tools, Internet Information Services Manager.

2. From the IIS Manager MMC, right-click the Web Sites entry and then select New, Web Site from the pop-up menu.

3. On the Welcome to the Web Site Creation Wizard screen, click the Next button to continue.

4. On the Web Site Description screen, type in a descriptive name for the website. Click the Next button to continue.

5. The IP Address and Port Settings screen appears. From this screen, you can select the IP address, TCP port, or host header to which this website will respond. Make the appropriate choices and then click the Next button to continue.

6. The Web Site Home Directory screen appears. From this screen, you can select the folder that contains the files for your website. You can also specify that you want to allow anonymous access to your site. Make the appropriate choices and then click the Next button to continue.

(continues)

(continued)

7. The Web Site Access Permissions screen appears. From this screen, you can specify the permissions you are granting visitors to your website. You should always specify the minimum permissions needed. Make the appropriate choices and then click the Next button to continue.

8. When the Finishing the Web Site Creation Wizard screen appears, click the Finish button to save your settings.

9. From the IIS Manager MMC, expand the Web Sites entry, right-click the name of the website you just created, and then select Properties from the pop-up menu.

10. This opens the Web Sites Properties dialog box. Click the Home Directory tab.

11. From the Home Directory tab, shown in Figure 4.39, select the application pool you want to assign the website to. Click the OK button to save this setting.

12. The website is listed in the assigned application pool.

FIGURE 4.39 The Home Directory tab, where you select the application pool for your website.

Managing Security for IIS

Objective:

Manage Security for IIS

As mentioned earlier in the chapter, IIS is probably the subsystem of Windows Server 2003 that has received the most attention, especially related to security. In IIS 6.0, the worker processes and most of the ASP functions run in the Network Service security context, which is a low-privileged context. In addition, each of these worker processes can exist in separate application pools, thereby isolating them from other processes. This lessens the exposure to poorly written code or of hackers inserting malicious code that would crash the entire web server.

In addition, when a buffer overflow occurs, previously a favorite exploit, the worker processes automatically terminate. With these low-level changes and the refusal to accept requests for files with unknown extensions, in addition to preventing the execution of command-line tools, IIS 6.0 is far more secure than any previous version.

We partially covered the contents of the Directory Security tab when configuring restrictions for access to the Remote Administration Console. We have already examined how to restrict access to a website by IP address and domain name. However, several other settings are important to IIS security.

If you select the Edit button in the Authentication and Access Control section of the Directory Security tab, you open the Authentication Methods dialog box, shown in Figure 4.40.

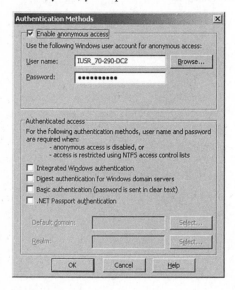

FIGURE 4.40 Multiple authentication methods are available from this dialog box.

When IIS is installed, two accounts are created: IUSR_*servername* and IWAM_*servername*. IWAM_*servername* is run in the Network Service security context and is used to start and run most applications. The IUSR_*servername* account is a member of the GUEST local group and is used to control anonymous access to published resources on IIS. For example, if you have a website that you want to publish so that anyone on the Internet can access it without authentication, you would use the IUSR_*servername* account to assign read access to the necessary resources. You have the ability to change the account used for anonymous access, or you can disable anonymous access completely.

The second half of the dialog box controls authenticated access. Authenticated access is used to integrate the web server with Windows security. The user is required to present a user ID and password to access website resources. These user IDs and passwords are stored either as a local account on the web server or in the Active Directory domain database. When anonymous access is disabled, all users who attempt to access the website are prompted for a user ID and password. Authentication is also required when the website resources are protected via NTFS permissions.

Four types of authenticated access are available:

▶ *Integrated Windows Authentication*—If the web server and the client are members of trusted domains, the browser passes the user ID and password to the web server automatically and the user is not prompted for a password. This method does not work through some firewalls, but it's fine for intranets. The password is transmitted as a hash value.

▶ *Digest Authentication*—This method is supported only if the client is using Internet Explorer 5 or later, in an Active Directory domain, and the password is stored in clear text. However, this method works through most firewalls. The password is transmitted as an MD5 hash value.

▶ *Basic Authentication*—This is the least secure method because it transmits the password as clear text. However, it is supported by just about any browser available. Basic Authentication is usually used in combination with SSL so that the passwords are encrypted.

▶ *.NET Passport Authentication*—This is a new feature in Windows Server 2003. This method uses the Passport Authentication system that Microsoft is marketing to e-commerce websites. It allows a user to create a single sign-on that is honored across various Passport-enabled sites. Authentication is performed by a central Passport Authentication server. When Passport Authentication is selected, a default domain must be specified.

The final two options available from the Authentication Methods dialog box are as follows:

▶ *Default Domain*—By entering the name of the default domain, users who are members of that domain will not need to enter the domain name when logging on to the website.

▶ *Realm*—This field allows you to specify the name of an alternative authentication service, such as a Remote Authentication Dial-Up User Service (RADIUS) server or Microsoft's Internet Authentication Server (IAS).

As mentioned briefly in the previous paragraphs, NTFS can be used to control access to resources on the web server. For example, if anonymous access is enabled but there are sensitive areas on your web server, you can control access to those areas using NTFS security. You can simply exclude or deny access for those resources to the Anonymous user account. The user is prompted for a user ID and password when she attempts to access those resources.

Another method of securing access to a web server is via Secure Sockets Layer (SSL). We mentioned SSL briefly in this chapter, but we haven't taken the time to explain it yet. SSL is used with HTTP to encrypt all traffic between the browser and the web server. This is especially critical for e-commerce sites because the last thing you want to do is to transmit your credit card number in clear text over the Internet!

SSL works by using encryption keys—in this case, certificates that are distributed by a trusted source. These certificates are used to encrypt the data that passes between the client and the web server. Certificates are issued by Certificate Authorities (CAs), of which VeriSign is the most prominent. Website administrators apply to the CA for a certificate, and they must provide the proper credentials to prove their identity. After the CA is satisfied that they are who they say they are, the CA issues the certificates and the website administrators install them on their web servers.

This same process can be used by enterprises using their own CAs to issue certificates to employees or contractors wishing to access web content from outside the boundaries of these organizations' LANs. In this case, the CA issuing the certificates is not a public CA (like VeriSign) but rather a private one controlled internally. In many cases, organizations choose to run Microsoft Certificate Services to issue and manage these certificates. Other CA software vendors also exist, but Microsoft's CA is the most common because the software is included as part of Windows Server 2003 for no additional charge.

When clients try to access the website, they might be presented with a prompt asking whether they trust the source of the certificate. This normally does not occur if the web server is using a certificate issued by VeriSign or one of the other common CAs. The client and the web server then negotiate a connection, and all traffic between them is encrypted.

In addition to server certificates, clients can be issued certificates also. This enables a password-free logon because the certificate serves as both the user ID and the password. Three steps are involved in setting up SSL on a Web server:

1. Generate a certificate request.

2. Install the certificate.

3. Configure the server to use certificates.

To generate a certificate request, use the procedure in Step by Step 4.20.

STEP BY STEP

4.20 Generating a certificate request

1. Click Start, Administrative Tools, Internet Information Services Manager.

2. From the IIS Manager MMC, right-click the website entry, and then select Properties from the pop-up menu.

3. From the Directory Security tab of the Properties dialog box, click the Server Certificate button.

4. This opens the IIS Certificate Wizard. Click the Next button to continue.

5. The Server Certificate screen appears, as shown in Figure 4.41. Select the Create a New Certificate radio button, and then click the Next button.

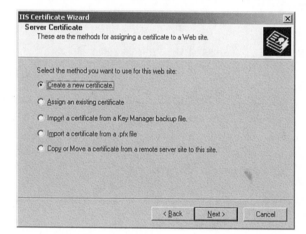

FIGURE 4.41 The Server Certificate screen presents various options to use with certificates.

6. The Delayed or Immediate Request screen appears. Select Prepare the Request Now, but Send It Later radio button. Click Next to continue.

7. The Name and Security Settings screen appears. Enter a descriptive name for the website, and provide the length of the key. A long key is more secure. Click Next to continue.

8. The Organization Information screen appears. Enter a descriptive name for your organization. Click Next to continue.

9. The Site Common Name screen appears. Enter the DNS name for your website. Click Next to continue.

10. The Geographical Information screen appears. Enter the appropriate information for your organization, and click Next to continue.

11. The Certificate Request File Name screen appears. Enter the location where you want to save the certificate request file. Click Next to continue.

12. The Request File Summary screen appears, as shown in Figure 4.42. Confirm that the settings are correct, and then click Next to continue.

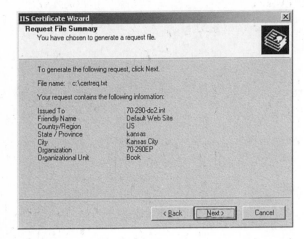

FIGURE 4.42 Verify the settings.

13. Click Finish to save the request file.

After the request file has been created, it must be sent to the Certificate Authority for approval. After the CA has processed your request, you receive a certificate from the CA. To install the received certificate, follow the procedure outlined in Step by Step 4.21.

STEP BY STEP

4.21 Installing a certificate

1. Click Start, Administrative Tools, Internet Information Services Manager.

2. From the IIS Manager MMC, right-click the website entry, and then select Properties from the pop-up menu.

3. From the Directory Security tab of the Properties dialog box, click the Server Certificate button.

4. This opens the IIS Certificate Wizard. Click Next to continue.

5. The Pending Certificate Request screen appears, as shown in Figure 4.43. Select the Process the Pending Request and Install the Certificate radio button, and then click the Next button.

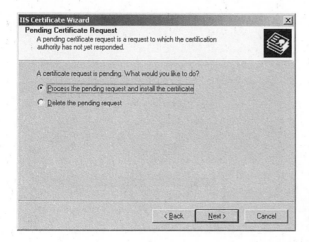

FIGURE 4.43 The Pending Certificate Request screen enables you to process the request or delete it.

6. The Process a Pending Request screen appears. Select the path and filename of the certificate, and click Next to continue.

7. The certificate is loaded, and you are presented with the Certification Summary screen. If the displayed configuration is correct, click Next to continue.

8. Click the Finish button.

After the certificate is installed, the final step is to configure the settings on the website to use SSL. To configure the website to support SSL, follow the procedure outlined in Step by Step 4.22.

STEP BY STEP

4.22 Configuring the website to support SSL

1. Click Start, Administrative Tools, Internet Information Services Manager.

2. From the IIS Manager MMC, right-click the website entry, and then select Properties from the pop-up menu.

3. From the Directory Security tab of the Properties dialog box, click the Edit button in the Secure Communications area.

4. This opens the Secure Communications dialog box, shown in Figure 4.44. Select the Require Secure Channel (SSL) check box. Then click OK.

FIGURE 4.44 SSL can be used with 40-bit encryption (the default) or 128-bit encryption.

Managing security for IIS 6.0 is an important topic, especially in light of all the attention IIS has received as a favored target for hackers. It is important to understand that one of the best strategies to secure IIS is to enable only the minimal features required to support the applications being run on IIS. Also, never grant more authority to any users than they will ever possibly require.

Chapter Summary

This chapter has covered a lot of ground. We started by covering the main features in Windows Server 2003 used for sharing and protecting data. To summarize, we looked at the following main points relating to files and folder:

▶ *Securing files*—This includes planning for and implementing both local and remote security.

▶ *Publishing resources*—This includes creating and maintaining network shares.

▶ *Using Offline Caching*—This includes configuring both servers and workstations so that important files and programs are available offline.

That was followed by a discussion of the new features in IIS 6.0. It is important to remember that, unlike previous versions of Windows, in Windows Server 2003 IIS is not installed by default. In addition, when IIS 6.0 is installed, it is installed in "lockdown mode." In this mode, only static pages can be served, and the support for dynamic content such as ASP or CGI has to be manually configured. These default settings present a far smaller "attack surface" for viruses and hackers.

Managing security for IIS 6.0 is an important topic, especially in light of all the attention that IIS has received as a favorite target for hackers. It is important to understand that the best way to secure IIS is to enable only the minimal features required to support the applications being run on IIS. Also, you should never grant more authority to any users than they can ever possibly require.

Key Terms

▶ Application pool

▶ ASP

▶ ASP.NET

▶ File share

▶ FrontPage Server Extensions

▶ Internet Information Services (IIS)

▶ Offline Caching

▶ Permissions

▶ Secure Sockets Layer (SSL)

▶ Server-Side Includes

▶ Synchronization Manager

Apply Your Knowledge

Exercises

4.1 Securing a local folder

Because all users accessing a Windows Server 2003 member server at the console will have been granted the Log On Locally right, you will need to use local security to prevent them from accessing certain folders. In this exercise, you will secure a local folder so that only selected users can access its contents.

Estimated Time: 40 minutes

1. Verify that the volume the desired folder is on is an NTFS volume. If it is not, use the CONVERT command to change it to NTFS.

2. Open either My Computer or Windows Explorer. Navigate to the folder on which you want to configure security.

3. Right-click the object and select Properties from the pop-up menu. Click the Security tab on the resulting dialog box.

4. From the Security tab, click the Add button.

5. The Select Users or Groups dialog box appears. This dialog box allows you to select either a local or domain user or group to assign permissions to. Enter the user or group and then click OK.

6. This returns you to the Folder Properties dialog box. Note that by default, the user or group just added has been granted Read and Execute, List Folder Contents, and Read permissions for the folder.

7. In the Permissions section of the Folder Properties dialog box, select the desired permissions and then click the OK button to save.

4.2 Creating a website

In this exercise, you use the Web Site Creation Wizard to create a website to serve some Active Server Pages. Because only static content is allowed with the default installation of IIS 6.0, you must configure IIS to use Active Server Pages manually.

Estimated Time: 20 minutes

Additional Requirements: A folder containing a sample website.

1. Click Start, Administrative Tools, Internet Information Services Manager.

2. From the IIS Manager MMC, right-click the Web Sites entry and then select New, Web Site from the pop-up menu.

3. On the Welcome to the Web Site Creation Wizard screen, click the Next button to continue.

4. On the Web Site Description screen, type in a descriptive name for the website. Click the Next button to continue.

5. The IP Address and Port Settings screen appears. From this screen, you can select the IP address, TCP port, or host header to which this website will respond. Make the appropriate choices and then click the Next button to continue.

6. The Web Site Home Directory screen appears. From this screen, you can select the folder that contains the files for your website. You can also specify that you want to allow anonymous access to your site. Make the appropriate choices and then click the Next button to continue.

7. The Web Site Access Permissions screen appears. From this screen, you can specify the permissions you are granting visitors to your website. You should always specify the minimum permissions needed. Make the appropriate choices and then click the Next button to continue.

8. When the Finishing the Web Site Creation Wizard screen appears, click the Finish button to save.

9. The new website appears in the IIS Manager console, listed under the Default Web Site entry.

10. In the left pane of the IIS Manager, click the Web Service Extensions folder.

11. Highlight the Active Server Pages entry in the right pane of the MMC and then click the Allow button. The status of the extension is changed to Allowed.

12. Close IIS Manager.

Exam Questions

1. You are the administrator for a small sporting goods company. The Human Resources manager of your company creates several files in a shared folder called HR-Data on a Windows Server 2003 server. The share and the files have the permissions shown.

   HR-Data Share Permissions:

   Users: Read

   Administrators: Read

   HR Managers: Full Control

   HR-Data NTFS Permissions:

   Users: Read

   Administrators: Read

   HR Managers: Full Control

   While the HR manager is on vacation, you receive a call from one of your users. It seems that one of the files in the HR-Data folder contains some very sensitive information, and it should be removed. How can you accomplish this without disrupting normal operations, using the minimum amount of authority necessary to delete the file?

   ○ **A.** Grant yourself Full Control permission for the HR-Data folder. Delete the file. Remove Full Control permission for the HR-Data folder.

   ○ **B.** Take ownership of the HR-Data folder. When prompted, take ownership of existing files. Grant yourself Full Control permission for the file. Delete the file.

   ○ **C.** Take ownership of the file. Delete the file.

   ○ **D.** Grant yourself Modify permission for the HR-Data folder and its contents. Delete the file. Remove Modify permission for the HR-Data folder.

2. As part of a server consolidation, you are moving a group of shared folders to a new Windows Server 2003 server. After moving the folders and their contents using XCOPY, you turn the server back over to the users. Soon, your telephone rings with users complaining that they can't see the file shares. What steps will you need to perform to fix the problem?

   ○ **A.** You need to reconfigure the NTFS permissions.

   ○ **B.** You need to reconfigure the share permissions.

   ○ **C.** You need to restart the Server service on the new server.

   ○ **D.** You need to reshare the shares.

   ○ **E.** You need to give the shares unique names.

3. The administrative assistant for the CIO of your company resigns without warning. The assistant's personal folders contain several files that the CIO needs access to. The folders have the following permission:

Admin Assistant: Full Control

All the user folders are located on a server formatted with NTFS. What's the quickest way to give the CIO access to these files?

○ **A.** Reset the password on the administrative assistant's account and give the CIO the user ID and the new password.

○ **B.** Assign ownership of the files to the CIO.

○ **C.** Take ownership of the files and give the CIO Full Control permission.

○ **D.** Move the files to the CIO's folders.

4. The Contracts folder is configured with the following permissions:

Share Permissions:

Managers: Full Control

Legal department: Change

HR: Read

NTFS Permissions:

Managers: Full Control

Legal department: Modify

HR: Read

If Bill is a member of the legal department and the HR group, what is his effective permission over the network?

○ **A.** Change

○ **B.** Modify

○ **C.** Read

○ **D.** Full Control

5. As part of a server consolidation, you are moving several websites on your intranet from Windows 2000 Servers to a new Windows Server 2003 server. After moving the websites, you turn the server back over to the users. Soon, your telephone rings with users complaining that they are receiving 404 errors when they try to access any of the websites. What steps will you need to perform to fix the problem?

- ○ **A.** You need to reconfigure the NTFS permissions.

- ○ **B.** You need to reconfigure the share permissions.

- ○ **C.** You need to restart the Server service on the new server.

- ○ **D.** You need to enable the Web Service Extensions.

6. After reading about how much improved IIS 6.0 is over IIS 5.0, you decide to perform an in-place upgrade of one of the Windows 2000 servers for your intranet. After the upgrade has completed, you check all the install logs and the Event Viewer and don't see any problems. After you turn the web server back over to the users, your telephone rings with users complaining that they cannot access the website. What step must you perform to fix the problem?

- ○ **A.** Replace the network interface card.

- ○ **B.** Start the web service.

- ○ **C.** Rewrite the web apps to be compatible with IIS 6.0.

- ○ **D.** Reconfigure the web service in IIS 5.0 Isolation mode.

- ○ **E.** Reconfigure the web service in Worker Process Isolation mode.

7. You are the administrator for a Windows Server 2003 server running IIS 6.0. The CIO is extremely security conscious. She wants you to set up an intranet site in such a way that only authorized users can access it. All users on your network are running Windows XP. What is the easiest way to accomplish this?

- ○ **A.** Turn off anonymous access for the site and configure it for Digest Authentication.

- ○ **B.** Turn off anonymous access for the site and configure it for Basic Authentication in combination with SSL.

- ○ **C.** Turn off anonymous access for the site and configure it for Integrated Authentication.

- ○ **D.** Turn off anonymous access for the site and configure it for Basic Authentication.

8. You are the administrator for a Windows Server 2003 server running IIS 6.0. The CIO is extremely security conscious. She wants you to set up a site on the Internet in such a way that only authorized users can access it. The website should support all types of browsers. What is the easiest way to accomplish this?

○ **A.** Turn off anonymous access for the site and configure it for Digest Authentication.

○ **B.** Turn off anonymous access for the site and configure it for Basic Authentication in combination with SSL.

○ **C.** Turn off anonymous access for the site and configure it for Integrated Authentication.

○ **D.** Turn off anonymous access for the site and configure it for Basic Authentication.

Answers to Exam Questions

1. **C.** You must take ownership of the file and then you can delete the file. See "Configuring and Managing NTFS File and Folder Permissions."

2. **A, B, D.** When a shared folder is moved, it is no longer shared. When it is moved to a different server, it will assume the NTFS permissions of the target folder, which probably won't be the same as the original folder. See "Copying and Moving Files and Folders."

3. **B.** Unlike in previous versions of Windows, in Windows Server 2003, the administrator can assign the ownership of files and folders. Moving the files would not work because files moved to a different folder on an NTFS partition will retain their existing permissions. The other options would work, but they involve more steps. See "Changing Ownership of Files and Folders."

4. **A.** Because Bill is accessing the folder through a share, his permissions will be the more restrictive of the combined share and NTFS permissions. See "Combining Share and NTFS Permissions."

5. **D.** In Windows Server 2003, the default for IIS 6.0 is to install in "locked down" mode. In locked down mode, only pages containing static content are displayed. All other pages return a 404 error when they are accessed. Enabling the Web Service Extensions allows you to use pages containing dynamic content. See "Installing Internet Information Services (IIS)."

6. **B.** During an upgrade from a previous version of Windows, IIS is installed; however, the service is disabled, and you must start it manually. This prevents administrators from carrying over vulnerabilities from previous versions of Windows. A web server that is upgraded from a previous version of IIS is enabled in IIS 5.0 Isolation mode, by default, to ensure that the application installed continues to run. See "Installing Internet Information Services (IIS)."

7. **C.** Integrated Authentication is the best answer. Although the other options would work, they all have limitations. Basic Authentication would work, but it transmits the password in clear text. Anyone with a Sniffer utility could discover the passwords. Adding SSL would be fine, but you would either have to purchase a certificate or set up your own CA. Digest Authentication requires the passwords to be stored unencrypted in the Active Directory. See "Managing Security for IIS."

8. **B.** The only correct answer for this situation is Basic Authentication in combination with SSL. Basic Authentication is the only option that supports all browsers, and SSL is required to encrypt the traffic between the browser and the website. See "Managing Security for IIS."

Suggested Readings and Resources

1. Boswell, William. *Inside Windows Server 2003*. New Riders, 2003. ISBN 0735711585.

2. Hassell, Jonathan. *Learning Windows Server 2003*. O'Reilly, 2006. ISBN 0596101236.

3. Jones, Don. *Windows Server 2003 Crash Course*. Wiley, 2003. ISBN 0764549251.

4. Matthews, Marty. *Windows Server 2003: A Beginners Guide*. McGraw-Hill, 2003. ISBN 0072193093.

5. Microsoft Windows 2003 File Server Best Practices: http://www.microsoft.com/technet/treeview/default.asp?url=/technet/prodtechnol/windowsserver2003/proddocs/entserver/file_srv_bestpractice.asp?frame=true.

6. Minasi, Mark, et al. *Mark Minasi's Windows XP and Server 2003 Resource Kit*. Sybex, 2003. ISBN 0782140807.

7. Minasi, Mark, et al. *Mastering Windows Server 2003 Server*. Sybex, 2003. ISBN 0782141307.

8. Shapiro, Jeffrey, et al. *Windows Server 2003 Bible 2nd edition*. John Wiley & Sons, 2006. ISBN 0764549375.

9. *Windows Server 2003 Deployment Guide*. Microsoft Corporation. http://www.microsoft.com/windowsserver2003/techinfo/reskit/deploykit.mspx.

10. *Windows Server 2003 Resource Kit*. Microsoft Corporation. Look for a link to it on the Technical Resources for Windows Server 2003 page. http://www.microsoft.com/windowsserver2003/techinfo/default.mspx.

CHAPTER FIVE

Administering Windows Server 2003

Objectives

This chapter covers the following Microsoft-specified objectives for the "Managing and Maintaining a Server Environment" section of the Managing and Maintaining a Microsoft Windows Server 2003 Environment exam:

Manage servers remotely.

▶ **Manage a server by using Remote Assistance**

▶ **Manage a server by using Terminal Services Remote Desktop for Administration mode**

▶ **Manage a server by using available support tools**

▶ The purpose of this objective is to teach you how to use the various tools available in Windows Server 2003 to remotely manage your servers.

Manage software site licensing

▶ Each Microsoft server and workstation must have an appropriate software license. It's important to understand the different licensing modes so that you don't purchase licenses that you don't need.

Outline

Study Strategies

▶ The sections in this chapter outline features that are essential to managing a Windows Server 2003 environment.

▶ Expect to see a number of questions on an area that is being heavily emphasized in Windows Server 2003: the various types of remote server management. Know how these features work, under what circumstances they should be used, and how to implement them.

▶ If possible, add another Windows Server 2003 server or a workstation to your lab environment. Practice using the tools covered in this chapter, especially the remote features.

▶ Know and understand the different licensing modes, and understand which one is more advantageous in specific environments.

Introduction

Windows Server 2003 system administration is a task-based responsibility that requires you to rely on the tools and utilities at your disposal. If you are unfamiliar with your tools, you cannot perform the required tasks.

Just as a handyman needs the right tool for a particular job, you need to know which tools can perform which functions. In the following sections, we walk through some of the management tools included with Windows Server 2003. In addition to reviewing the discussion in this chapter, you should take the time to work with the tools themselves. Hands-on experience is invaluable and cannot be substituted. You also may want to review the online help documentation included in the tools, as well as the following material:

▶ *Microsoft Technical Information Network (TechNet)*—A monthly CD-based publication that delivers numerous electronic titles on Windows products. Its offerings include all the Microsoft Resource Kits (see next bullet), product facts, technical notes, tools, utilities, the entire Microsoft Knowledge Base, as well as service packs, drivers, and patches. A single-user license to TechNet costs $299 per year (TechNet Plus, which includes Beta and Evaluation versions of Microsoft products, costs $499), but it is well worth the price. For more details, visit www.microsoft.com/technet/ and check out the information under the TechNet Subscription heading in the About TechNet menu entry.

▶ *Microsoft Press Resource* Kits—Available on nearly all major products from Microsoft. The Microsoft Windows Server 2003 Resource Kit and the Microsoft Windows XP Professional Resource Kit are essential references for Windows information. Both book sets come with CD-ROMs that contain useful tools. Visit http://mspress.microsoft.com for additional information on the resource kits.

Additional resources that provide information about Windows Server 2003 are also available. For instance, a quick search at www.amazon.com using the phrase "Windows Server 2003" turns up a list of additional references on this subject.

Managing Servers Remotely

Objective:
Manage servers remotely

There are always situations in which the system administrator must perform a task on a Windows Server 2003 server but is currently not physically located near the server console. In some cases, the system administrator is not located in the same part of the building as the server room or may even be located in a different country!

Microsoft has included several tools for remotely managing servers with Windows Server 2003. These tools allow the system administrator to perform system management tasks as though he or she were physically sitting in front of the console of each server in the organization. Knowing which tool to use in specific situations allows you to be more effective as a system administrator.

The Microsoft Management Console: Where Management Begins

Objective:
Manage a server by using available support tools

In Chapter 1, "Windows Server 2003 Environment," we introduced the Microsoft Management Console (MMC) and showed you how to add additional snap-ins to create a custom console.

However, the real beauty of the MMC snap-in administrative tools is that they don't limit you to managing only the local machine you are working on. As you saw when working with the Shared Folders snap-in in Chapter 4, "Managing and Maintaining Access to Resources," by selecting Connect to Another Computer, you can connect the tool to a remote computer and perform the administrative tasks as though you were sitting at the system console. This allows you not only to manage all your servers from one server but to manage either servers or workstations from any Windows 2000 or later computer by starting the appropriate MMC and snap-ins.

In the following challenge exercise, we review some of the things we have looked at in the previous chapters to refresh your memory and prepare you for the rest of the chapter.

Challenge

In this scenario, you must connect to a remote server and check to see what local user accounts are configured. You should do this using as few steps as possible.

How would you accomplish this task?

You should try working through this problem on your own first. If you get stuck, or if you'd like to see one possible solution, follow these steps:

1. From the Start menu, select All Programs, Administrative Tools, Computer Management.

2. In the left pane of the Computer Management MMC, right-click the Computer Management (Local) entry and then select Connect to Another Computer from the pop-up menu. This opens the Select Computer dialog box.

(continues)

(continued)

3. From the Select Computer dialog box, you can either browse for or enter the name of the remote computer to manage. Enter the name of the computer and then click the OK button.

4. The Computer Management MMC opens with the focus assigned to the remote computer.

5. Select System Tools, and then Local users and Groups. Next, click the Users folder and observe the configured user accounts in the right pane of the Computer Management MMC.

If the user has the proper permissions, she can use any computer in the Windows 2000/2003/XP family to manage other family members via the Computer Management MMC. For example, a Windows 2000 Professional computer can be used to manage a Windows Server 2003 or Windows XP Professional computer. Only the features supported on the remote computer are available in the Computer Management MMC. For example, if you are using a Windows Server 2003 computer to manage a Windows XP Professional computer, the selection for RAID-5 within the Disk Management snap-in is not available because it is not supported on the remote computer, which in this case is Windows XP Professional.

You can access the rest of the tools that appear in this book either through their own administrative tools or by creating a custom MMC and adding their respective snap-ins. A good example of an MMC with a variety of snap-ins included is the Computer Management MMC. The purpose of the Computer Management MMC is to group together a selection of Windows utilities in a single MMC that can be connected to either the local computer or a remote computer. We have used the Computer Management MMC to access various snap-ins in the previous chapters, but we haven't taken the time to examine it yet.

The Computer Management MMC comes prepopulated with the most commonly used administrative tools:

- ▶ *Event Viewer*—Used to view the events that are recorded in the Application, System, and Security logs. These logs are used to identify possible hardware, software, or security issues.

- ▶ *Shared Folders*—Use to view and manage shared folders.

- ▶ *Local Users and Groups*—Used to create and manage local computers and groups.

- ▶ *Performance Logs and Alerts*—Used to monitor and collect performance data.

- ▶ *Device Manager*—Used to view, manage, and troubleshoot the hardware devices installed on your servers.

- ▶ *Removable Storage*—Used to manage your removable storage media and manage the libraries that they are members of.

- ▶ *Disk Defragmenter*—Used to analyze and defragment your hard disks.

▶ *Disk Management*—Used to manage your hard disk volumes and partitions.

▶ *Services*—Used to stop, start, pause, resume, or disable a service.

▶ *WMI Control*—Used to manage the Windows Management Service.

▶ *Indexing Service*—Used to configure and manage the Indexing service that speeds up searches for files on your server.

As you can see, using the Computer Management MMC, you can perform tasks such as adding and managing disks, adding shared folders, and stopping and starting services on local or remote computers.

NOTE

Administrative Tools By running adminpak.msi, you can add additional MMC-based tools to manage your domain. For a Step by Step on how to accomplish this, see Chapter 1.

In addition to the capabilities mentioned previously, the MMC can be used to manage tasks simultaneously on multiple remote computers. That is the scenario used in the Challenge Exercise.

Challenge

In this scenario, you must log the performance of four Windows Server 2003 servers from a remote computer. You should do this using as few steps as possible.

How would you set this up?

You should try working through this problem on your own first. If you get stuck, or if you'd like to see one possible solution, follow these steps:

1. From the Start menu, select Start, Run. Type **MMC** into the field and click OK.

2. The MMC appears. Select File, Add/Remove Snap-In from the Console menu.

3. The Add/Remove Snap-In dialog box appears. Click the Add button.

4. The Add Standalone Snap-In dialog box appears. Select the Performance Logs and Alerts snap-in and then click the Add button.

5. Repeat the previous step three more times to add additional instances of the Performance Logs and Alerts snap-in.

6. At the Add Standalone Snap-In dialog box, click the Close button. This returns you to the Add/Remove Snap-In dialog box. If the selections are correct, click the OK button.

7. From the custom MMC, you can right-click each instance of Performance Logs and Alerts and add objects and counters from different servers on the General tab of the Properties dialog box.

There are many advantages to using the MMC for server management. For example, as you have seen in this Challenge Exercise, you can manage multiple instances of the same or different tools connected to multiple servers, all within a single MMC. Moving from server to server or tool to tool is as simple as clicking the mouse.

Administrative Groups

However, not every user can manage a server. For security (and common sense) reasons, it is best to limit the number and scope of users who have management access to the servers on your network. As was covered briefly in Chapter 3, "Managing Groups," the following domain local groups can be used to delegate various management tasks on your network:

▶ *Administrators*—Can perform all tasks on any client or server on the network.

▶ *Account Operators*—Can create, modify, and delete user accounts and groups, except for members of the Administrators group or any of the Operators groups.

▶ *Backup Operators*—Can back up and restore files and folders on any client or server on the network, even if the user has not been granted access to them.

▶ *Print Operators*—Can set up and configure local or network printers.

▶ *Server Operators*—Can back up and restore files and folders, share folders, manage services, format the hard drive, and shut down and reboot the server. Members of the Server Operators group are the only group besides the Administrators that can log on locally on a domain controller.

Users should always be assigned to the group that gives them the minimum of permissions and rights necessary to perform their duties. This will improve the security of the domain and prevent users from performing unauthorized functions.

Remote Desktop for Administration

Objective:

Manage a server by using Terminal Services remote administration mode

The basic functionality of the Remote Desktop for Administration feature has been available for some time from other vendors, such as Citrix, and even from Microsoft, as Windows Terminal Services.

Terminal Services is available in two modes: Remote Desktop for Administration (formerly called Remote Administration mode) and Application Server mode. Application Server mode configures the Windows Server 2003 machine to operate similar to the previous version of

Windows NT Terminal Server 4.0. Remote Desktop for Administration mode is used to provide remote server management. Unlike in Windows 2000, where the Remote Administration mode was an option, the Remote Desktop for Administration mode is automatically installed in Windows Server 2003. However, incoming connections are disabled by default.

> **NOTE**
>
> **More Info on Terminal Services Modes** For a detailed discussion of Windows Server 2003 Terminal Services in Application Server mode, see Chapter 11, "Managing and Maintaining Terminal Services."

Terminal Services in Remote Desktop for Administration Mode

As mentioned previously, the Terminal Services (TS) Remote Administration mode was first available in Windows 2000. The previous versions of Windows Server and Windows Terminal Services did not have this feature.

With Windows 2003 Terminal Services in Remote Desktop for Administration mode, you are allowed two concurrent sessions, plus a console session to the Windows server. These sessions can be used to remotely access any programs or data on the server. The console session takes over the physical console of the server. In the past, a lot of tools and applications could not be run via a Terminal Services session because they were written to interact directly with "session 0," the physical server console. Also, most system messages are automatically routed to the console, so if you are trying to manage the server remotely and receive a pop-up error message, you won't be able to see it.

Using the Terminal Services client is just like working on the server console. The Remote Desktop for Administration mode allows you to have two concurrent TS sessions without any additional Client Access Licenses required. The beauty of the Remote Desktop for Administration mode is that it allows you to manage your server from just about anywhere and from just about any computer. Because the TS client is supported on a variety of Windows clients, including Windows CE, you can load the client on any Windows box that you have available and manage your server. Imagine managing your server from your Pocket PC!

Like the tools discussed in the previous section, Remote Desktop enables you to open a session on a remote Windows Server 2003 machine and run applications as though you were physically sitting at the console of the remote machine. In addition, because the Remote Desktop Protocol (RDP) connection between the server and the client requires a minimum of bandwidth, you are not limited to having a high-speed LAN connection. The Terminal Services client can access the servers via a dial-up connection, the Internet, or even a wireless connection. With this feature, you can connect to your Windows Server 2003 servers from home or a hotel room and have full access to all your applications, files, and other network resources.

EXAM ALERT

Required Port   If the RDP client is connecting to a server through a firewall, port 3389 must be open. This is important to know in the field, and for the exam.

To use Remote Desktop, you must enable it on your server and grant access to the appropriate users and groups by following the procedure in Step by Step 5.1.

STEP BY STEP

5.1 Enabling the Remote Desktop for Administration feature

1. Log on to the Windows Server 2003 server as a member of the local Administrators group.

2. Open Control Panel and select the System applet.

3. In the System Properties dialog box, select the Remote tab.

4. From the Remote tab, shown in Figure 5.1, select the Enable Remote Desktop on This Computer check box.

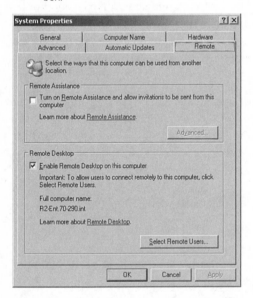

FIGURE 5.1   Remote Desktop must be manually enabled on Windows Server 2003.

5. When the Remote Sessions information prompt appears, read the information, and then click the OK button to continue.

6. Click the Select Remote Users button. By default, members of the local Administrators group have been granted access.

7. The Remote Desktop Users dialog box appears.

8. Click the Add button. The Select Users dialog box appears.

9. In the Select Users dialog box, you are given the opportunity to select the users and/or groups that are granted access to your machine via Remote Desktop for Administration. The terminology can be somewhat confusing. Just remember that users and groups are objects, and the location is either the individual server or a domain. Table 5.1 defines the terms used in this interface.

10. After making your other selections, if you click the Advanced button, a search dialog box opens, and you can search for the users or groups you want to add.

11. When you're finished, click OK three times to save your settings.

TABLE 5.1 Object Type Definitions

Prompt	Meaning
Object Types	Users or groups.
Locations	This can show users or groups from an individual machine. If you're connected to a domain, you can select the domain directory.
Object Names	User or group names.

These steps configure Windows Server 2003 to accept incoming connections. The Windows 2003 Remote Desktop Connection (RDC) client can be installed on any version of Windows from Windows 95 and later. To install the client, insert the Windows Server 2003 CD-ROM into the client machine's CD-ROM drive. When the Welcome page appears, click Perform Additional Tasks and then click Set Up Remote Desktop Connection.

NOTE

Using Older Clients   Windows Server 2003 also supports connections from the older Windows Terminal Services clients, so you can use the 16-bit client from a Windows 3.1 machine, if you still have one. However, some of the newer features, such as device redirection, are not available. Citrix clients are not supported because they use the Independent Computing Architecture (ICA) protocol instead of the RDP used with the RDC client. The Windows XP version of the client, which is supported on Windows 95 and later, is available at http://www.microsoft.com/downloads/details.aspx?FamilyID=80111f21-d48d-426e-96c2-08aa2bd23a49&DisplayLang=en.

To connect to your Windows Server 2003 server remotely, start the RDP client on the remote computer. This computer must have a connection of some kind to the other computer—LAN, WAN, VPN, or dial-up. Enter the IP address or the name of the remote computer and then click the Connect button. Enter the username and password, and you're in!

NOTE

Connecting to the Console   To specifically connect to the console session of a Windows Server 2003 server, type `mstsc /console` on the command line.

Remote Desktops Snap-In

The Remote Desktops snap-in is useful for those situations when you need to remotely manage or monitor several Windows Server 2003 servers. This snap-in allows you to be connected concurrently to the RDC sessions of multiple servers. Each session can be given focus by selecting it via a navigable tree interface.

Step by Step 5.2 walks you through connecting to multiple remote computers using the Remote Desktops snap-in.

STEP BY STEP

5.2 Connecting to multiple remote computers to perform management tasks

1. From the Start menu, select All Programs, Administrative Tools, Remote Desktop.

2. If this is the first time that Remote Desktop has been selected, the MSI file is loaded. In the left pane of the Remote Desktops MMC, right-click the Remote Desktops entry and then select Add New Connection from the pop-up menu.

3. This opens the Add New Connection dialog box, which allows you to either browse for or enter the name or IP address of a remote computer to manage. Notice that you are given the option to connect to the console session.

4. Enter the name or the IP address of the remote server and then click the OK button.

5. As shown in Figure 5.2, the Remote Desktops MMC lists all configured connections.

6. To connect to a remote server, right-click the appropriate entry in the left pane of the Remote Desktops MMC and select Connect from the pop-up menu.

7. The remote session now appears in the right pane of the MMC.

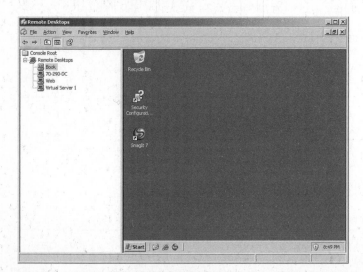

FIGURE 5.2 The Remote Desktops MMC allows you to connect to multiple servers simultaneously.

You can switch between multiple remote sessions by clicking the entry in the left pane of the MMC. By creating multiple custom MMCs, you can have several Remote Desktops MMCs that are preconfigured to connect to different groups of servers.

Remote Assistance

Objective:
Manage a server by using Remote Assistance

Diagnosing a computer problem can be difficult if you are not sitting in front of the computer. The Windows Server 2003 Remote Assistance feature enables you to grant a friend or a help desk operator permission to connect to your computer and assist you with a problem. Your computer must have a connection of some kind to the other computer, such as a LAN, WAN, VPN, or dial-up connection.

The Remote Assistance function is similar to the Remote Desktop function in that it allows a remote user to connect to your Windows Server 2003 machine. Remote Desktop, however, is designed to allow you to run applications remotely on your computer, whereas the Remote Assistance function is designed to allow a remote user to log in to your running session and assist you in determining a problem with a currently running session. Remote Assistance is more of a remote-control tool, similar to PCAnywhere.

Remote Assistance allows you to exchange messages via a chat session, or you can talk to another user if you both have the required sound cards and microphones. You can even grant a remote user the ability to take over your desktop to make changes and run programs.

The Remote Assistance feature was first available on Windows XP Professional and XP Home Edition. Unlike in the versions of Windows XP, it is disabled by default in Windows Server 2003.

To use Remote Assistance, you must enable it on your server by following the procedure in Step by Step 5.3.

STEP BY STEP

5.3 Enabling the Remote Assistance feature

1. Log on to the Windows Server 2003 server as a member of the local Administrators group.

2. Open Control Panel and select the System applet.

3. In the System Properties dialog box, select the Remote tab.

4. From the Remote tab, select the Turn On Remote Assistance and Allow Invitations to Be Sent from This Computer check box.

5. Click the OK button to save this setting.

After enabling Remote Assistance, you must issue an invitation before another user can connect to your machine. This invitation can be sent to the other user via one of the following methods:

- ▶ Windows Messenger (the preferred method)
- ▶ Email
- ▶ Disk

The invitation is an encrypted ticket used to grant the remote user access to the Windows Server 2003 server. The remote user must have the ticket and a password to be permitted access. You can send the password separately by email (not recommended), instant messaging, or telephone.

By default, the invitation is good for 30 days, but you should probably change it to 24 hours or less.

Challenge

You are a system administrator who is responsible for managing all Windows Server 2003 servers for your company. The security officer for your company has decided that the default invitation duration for the Remote Assistance feature is too long and makes your servers vulnerable to attack. He has assigned you to change the default invitation time to 24 hours.

How will you accomplish this?

Try to complete this exercise on your own, listing your conclusions on a sheet of paper. After you have completed the exercise, compare your results to those given here.

1. Log on to the Windows Server 2003 server as a member of the local Administrators group.

2. Open Control Panel and select the System applet.

3. In the System Properties dialog box, select the Remote tab.

4. From the Remote tab, click the Advanced button.

5. From the Remote Assistance Settings dialog box, set the invitation time to 24 hours. The default setting is 30 days, as shown in Figure 5.3.

(continues)

(continued)

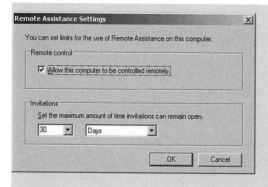

Figure 5.3 The Remote Assistance Settings dialog box allows you to control whether the server can be remote controlled and how long an invitation is valid.

6. Click the OK button twice to save your settings.

An example of when the Remote Assistance feature comes in handy is if you are having a problem on a Windows Server 2003 server and you require assistance from a support person. You can allow the support person to view your activities on the server console. The first step in this process is to create an invitation for the support person.

To create an invitation, perform the procedure outlined in Step by Step 5.4.

STEP BY STEP

5.4 Creating an invitation

1. Click Start, All Programs, Remote Assistance.

2. Click the Invite Someone to Help You button, shown in Figure 5.4.

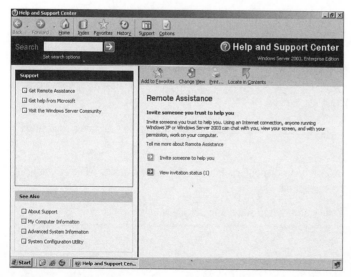

FIGURE 5.4 The Remote Assistance page in the Help and Support Center allows you to generate invitations or check on the status of existing invitations.

3. In the next window, you can elect to send the invitation via Windows Messenger or email, or you can save it as a file. Click the Save Invitation as a File button.

4. The Remote Assistance—Save Invitation window appears. Enter your name. Note that the default invitation duration for a file is 1 hour.

5. The next window allows you to specify a password for the support person to use to connect to your server. Enter a password and then click the Save Invitation button to continue.

6. From the Save As dialog box, save the invitation file to an appropriate location. You are returned to the opening Remote Assistance page.

The invitation has been saved to a file. This file can be emailed, saved to a disk and carried to a remote user, or copied to a network share. The user from whom you have requested assistance must be running a version of Windows XP or Windows Server 2003.

To respond to an invitation, perform the procedure outlined in Step by Step 5.5.

STEP BY STEP

5.5 Responding to an invitation

1. On the remote machine, the assisting user must locate the invitation and double-click it.

2. The Remote Assistance dialog box opens, and the assisting user will see this message: Do you want to connect to user's computer now? (see Figure 5.5). The assisting user will need to enter the password and then click the Yes button.

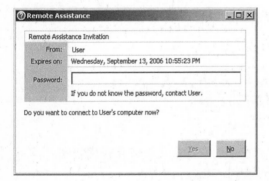

FIGURE 5.5 Enter the Remote Assistance password.

3. On the computer requesting assistance (your computer), a dialog box appears asking whether you want to accept the connection. Click the Yes button.

4. The assisting user is now able to see your desktop and communicate with you via chat.

If the assisting user needs to take over your machine, he can click the Take Control icon on his toolbar. You are prompted as to whether you want this to happen. You can both share control of the desktop until you press the Esc key. When you're finished, click the Disconnect button on the Remote Assistance dialog box (see Figure 5.6).

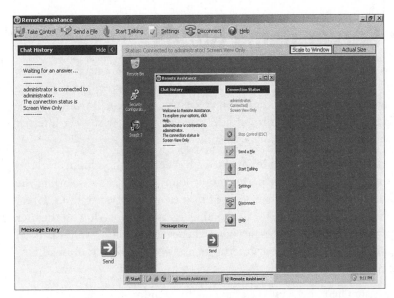

FIGURE 5.6 Remote Assistance, showing the view from the assisted desktop.

Of course, allowing someone to take over your machine requires a great amount of trust. Don't open this feature to anyone you don't know! Make sure your invitations always require a password, which should *not* be sent with the invitations, and keep your invitation durations as short as possible.

Problems with Remote Assistance

If you are accessing a Remote Assistance computer that is behind a firewall, port 3389 must be open. Table 5.2 lists some common connection scenarios.

TABLE 5.2 Remote Assistance Connection Scenarios

Assistant	Client	Result
Behind NAT device	Behind NAT device	Doesn't work.
Behind NAT device	Normal	Works.
Normal	Behind NAT device	Works with Windows Messenger, but not with file or email invitations.
Behind proxy server	Behind proxy server	Doesn't work.
Behind proxy server	Normal	Must install proxy software on Assistant.
Normal	Behind proxy server	Doesn't work.

For more information on the Remote Assistance feature, consult Microsoft Knowledge Base Article Q301529, "Supported Connection Scenarios for Remote Assistance," or Article Q306298, "Description of the Windows Messenger Reverse Connection Process Used by Remote Assistance."

Managing a Server Using RunAs

When an Administrator is logged on to a server using an account with administrative rights, the server is vulnerable to attacks by malicious software because the software will be run in the administrator's security context. Even though most people do not check email from a server console, which typically is the most common form of infection, just visiting a suspect Internet site could initiate the download of a malicious piece of code.

For years, one of the best practices for system administration has been for the administrator to have two accounts: a common user account for performing common tasks such as surfing the Internet and reading email, and an administrative account for performing system tasks. Great in theory, but in practice, it was quite unwieldy for the administrator to have to log off the user account, then log back on with the administrative account whenever the administrator needed to perform a system task such as creating a user or resetting a password. In reality, most administrators never used their common user account.

Fortunately, Microsoft has supplied the RunAs command in Windows Server 2003. The RunAs command, also known as secondary logon, allows the administrator to log on using a common user account. This prevents any malicious software from running in the administrative context. Then when administrative credentials are required to run a task, the administrator can use the RunAs command to run the task, using the credentials of his administrative account.

> **NOTE**
>
> **Log on Locally** Sharp readers will wonder how an administrator can take advantage of the RunAs command when a common user account cannot be used to log on to the console of a domain controller. The answer is to manage your domain controllers from your workstation, where you are logged on as common user, and then use the RunAs command when using the administrative tools.

You can use the RunAs command to perform most common administrative tasks, such as using the Active Directory users and Computers snap-in for working with user accounts, or any of the tasks in the Computer Management snap-in.

The RunAs command can be used in three ways:

▶ *From the command line*—The RunAs command can be used to start a program or process from the command line using the following syntax: `RunAs /user:domain\administrator "mmc %windir%\System32\Dsa.msc"`. This is handy for use in scripts.

▶ *By right-clicking in the Start menu*—From the pop-up menu, select Run As.

▶ *By right-clicking in Windows Explorer*—Select a program file, right-click, and then select Run As from the pop-up menu (see Figure 5.7).

FIGURE 5.7 In Windows Explorer or My Computer, right-click a program file, then select Run As from the pop-up menu.

In Step by Step 5.6, we will open the Computer Management MMC using the RunAs command.

STEP BY STEP

5.6 Opening computer management using RunAs

1. Log on to a workstation or member server as a common user.

2. Select Start, Administrative Tools, and then right-click the Computer Management shortcut, as shown in Figure 5.8.

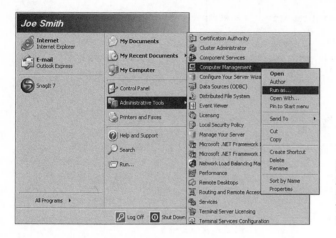

FIGURE 5.8 From the Start Menu, select Administrative Tools, right-click the Computer Management shortcut, and then select Run As from the pop-up menu.

3. Select Run As from the pop-up menu.

4. The Run As dialog box appears, as shown in Figure 5.9. Enter an account and password with administrative rights, and then click the OK button.

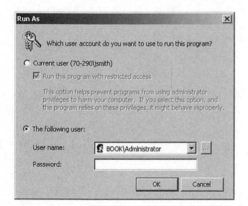

FIGURE 5.9 From the Run As dialog box, enter a user account and password with administrative rights.

5. The Computer Management MMC is opened under the context of the administrator account.

NOTE

Run As If you right-click a program and Run As does not appear, hold down the Shift key, and then right-click the shortcut. Run As will appear on the pop-up menu.

Challenge

You're a junior system administrator at FlyByNight Airlines. One of the senior administrators has a batch job that needs to be run ASAP from the command prompt with administrative privileges. How can you do this quickly?

Try to complete this exercise on your own, listing your conclusions on a sheet of paper. After you have completed the exercise, compare your results to those given here.

1. On the Start menu, click Run.

2. In the Run dialog box, type in the following command: `RunAs /user:domain\ administrator cmd`.

3. When the command window opens, run the batch job from the command line.

Managing and Administering Software Site Licensing

Objective:

Manage software site licensing

One of the lesser-known, but extremely important, responsibilities of a network administrator is software licensing. It is important to ensure that your company has the correct number of licenses for the software in use in your organization. Not only does this save your company money by purchasing only the number of licenses needed, but more importantly, you avoid lawsuits by software publishers that discover you are using their software illegally.

Microsoft requires that every Windows client computer have a client license. This is obtained automatically when you buy a copy of the client operating system over the counter, or when you make a volume purchase via one of Microsoft's volume licensing programs, such as Open or Select Licensing. In a similar manner, a license is required for each copy of Windows Server 2003 that you use.

In addition to the client and server licenses, Microsoft also requires that every user or device that connects to a Microsoft server obtain a Client Access License (CAL).

There are two methods of licensing for Windows Server 2003 servers:

▶ Per seat

▶ Per server

In the *per-server* licensing method, the server is licensed for a specific amount of concurrent connections. The connections are allowed on a first-come-first-served basis. For example, if your server is licensed for 100 CALs, the 101st client that attempts to connect to your server would be refused.

In the *per-seat* licensing method, each user or device is required to obtain a CAL. This CAL allows the user or device to connect to multiple servers. The default licensing mode in Windows Server 2003 is per server.

Typically, per-server licensing is used in environments where there is only one server. The per-seat licensing mode is more economical for enterprise environments where each client needs to access multiple servers.

For example, if you have 100 clients and a single server, you would be required to purchase 100 CALs under the per-server licensing. In this case, you are licensing the number of connections to the server.

However, if you have two servers, and your clients need to access both servers, under the per-server licensing mode, you would have to purchase 200 CALs. This is because each server would need to be licensed for 100 connections each.

Using the per-seat licensing mode, you would have to purchase only 100 CALs because the licensing is by the number of clients, not by the number of connections to the server.

> **NOTE**
>
> **Additional CALs**   In addition to the CALs required for connecting to a Windows Server 2003 server, you might be required to purchase CALs for applications such as Microsoft Exchange Server or SQL Server.

Two tools are used to administer Microsoft licenses, depending on the scope of your enterprise:

▶ *Licensing applet*—This applet is found in the Control Panel and is used to manage per-server licensing on the server that the applet is run on.

▶ *Licensing utility*—This utility is found in the Administrative Tools folder and is used to manage per-seat licensing for the enterprise.

By default, licensing is enforced; however, it is not tracked or monitored. Before you can manage and track licensing, you must enable the License Logging service. The service is disabled by default in Windows Server 2003. To enable the License Logging service, change the Startup type to Automatic using the Services utility in the Administrative Tools folder, as shown in Figure 5.10. After the Startup type is set, click the Start button to start the service.

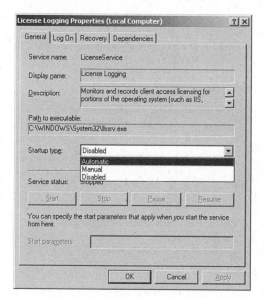

FIGURE 5.10 The Services tool, showing how to change the Startup type of the License Logging service to Automatic.

After the Licensing service is started, you can use either of the two licensing tools to manage your licenses.

Licensing Applet

The Licensing applet in Control Panel can be used to do the following:

- ▶ Add or remove client licenses for the per-server mode.

- ▶ Change the licensing mode from per server to per seat.

- ▶ Configure the replication of the server's licensing information to the Site License Server.

To add per-server licenses, follow the procedure in Step by Step 5.7.

STEP BY STEP

5.7 Adding per-server licenses

1. Click Start, Control Panel, Licensing.

2. The Choose Licensing Mode dialog box appears. If this is the first time you have run the Licensing applet, you will need to select a licensing mode and then click the OK button. If this is not the first time that you have run the Licensing applet, go to step 6.

3. Select the Per Server option button and then click the OK button.

4. From the License Violation dialog box, select the No. On the Server Licensing dialog box, select the I Agree check box to accept the terms and conditions. Then click the OK button.

5. Click Start, Control Panel, Licensing.

6. The Choose Licensing Mode dialog box appears, as shown in Figure 5.11. Click the Add Licenses button.

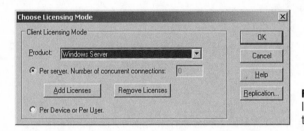

FIGURE 5.11 The Choose Licensing Mode dialog box allows you to add or remove licenses or to change the licensing mode.

7. The New Client Access License dialog box appears. This dialog box allows you to enter the number of Client Access Licenses to add. After entering the desired number of licenses, click the OK button.

8. The Per Server Licensing Terms and Conditions dialog box appears. Read the text and click the I Agree check box. Then click the OK button twice to save.

9. Close the Group Policy MMC.

Removing licenses can be accomplished by following the procedure in the previous Step by Step and selecting the Remove Licenses button.

Changing Licensing Modes

The licensing mode can be changed from per server to per seat using the Licensing applet. This is a one-time change, so you should always confirm that this is what you really want to do. This can be accomplished by clicking the Per Device or Per User option button on the Choose Licensing Mode dialog box, as shown in Figure 5.11. When the License Violation dialog box appears, read the warning and then click the No button to change the mode.

Configuring License Replication

In an enterprise environment, you will configure a Site License Server to collect all the licensing data for that site. The Licensing applet allows you to configure the replication time and frequency to send the licensing data to the Site License Server. This can be configured by starting the Licensing applet and clicking the Replication button on the Choose Licensing Mode dialog box, as shown in Figure 5.11. When the Replication Configuration dialog box appears, as shown in Figure 5.12, enter appropriate values for the start time or the replication frequency.

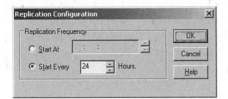

Figure 5.12 The Licensing applet, showing how to change the replication frequency of the license information to the Site License Server.

Licensing Utility

The Licensing utility, available in the Administrative Tools folder, allows you to manage licensing at the site or the enterprise level.

The Licensing utility can be used to perform the following:

▶ Add or remove client licenses for the servers in the site or enterprise.

▶ View all per-server, per-device, and per-user licenses for the site or enterprise.

▶ Manage the replication of the server licensing information on the network.

▶ View user usage statistics.

Before you can administer the Site License Server, you must determine what server is currently holding that role. By default, the Site License Server is the first domain controller installed in a site. Although the Site License Server is not required to be a domain controller, it should reside within the site that is being managed.

To display or change the server used as the Site License Server, follow the procedure in Step by Step 5.8.

STEP BY STEP

5.8 Displaying or changing the server used as the site licensing server

1. Click Start, All Programs, Administrative Tools, Active Directory Sites and Services.

2. In the left pane, click the site that you want to display. The Licensing Site Settings icon will be displayed in the right pane, as shown in Figure 5.13.

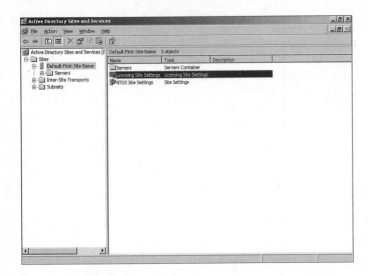

FIGURE 5.13 The Active Directory Sites and Service MMC, showing the location of the Licensing Site Settings icon.

3. In the right pane, double-click the Licensing Site Settings entry. In the Licensing Site Settings Properties dialog box, the licensing server is displayed in the Computer field.

4. If desired, click the Change button to assign the Site Licensing Server role to another server. Select a server, and then click OK twice to save.

5. Close the Group Policy MMC.

After you determine which server is the Site Licensing Server, you can open the Licensing utility by clicking Start, Administrative Tools, Licensing on that server. The Licensing utility defaults to the Purchase History tab, as shown in Figure 5.14. The Purchase History tab shows you when, how many, and what type of licenses were added or deleted.

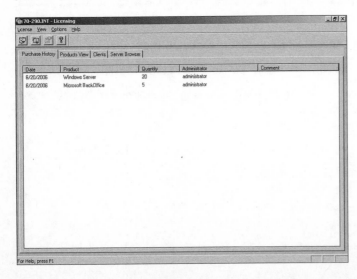

FIGURE 5.14 The Licensing utility, showing the Purchase History tab.

The Products View tab displays the following information for each product on the server:

- ▶ The number of per-device or per-user licenses purchased

- ▶ The number of per-device or per-user licenses allocated

- ▶ The number of per-server licenses purchased

- ▶ The number of connections for per-server mode that have been reached

The Clients tab displays the following information for each client that has accessed the server:

- ▶ The username

- ▶ The licensed usage to the server

- ▶ The unlicensed usage to the server

- ▶ The product that was accessed by the user (for example, Microsoft BackOffice or Windows Server)

The Server Browser tab, displays the servers, sites, and domains in Active Directory.

License Groups

License groups are created in special circumstances in which the basic per-seat or per-server licensing may not be the best fit. A good example of this is a situation where several users share a computer. The License Logging service tracks licenses by username. So even though the server is accessed only from a single computer, several licenses are consumed because every user will need a license, even though they will never all be connected to the server concurrently.

To create a license group, follow the procedure in Step by Step 5.9.

STEP BY STEP

5.9 Creating a license group

1. Click Start, All Programs, Administrative Tools, Licensing.

2. From the system menu of the Licensing utility, select Options, Advanced, New License Group.

3. From the New License Group dialog box, shown in Figure 5.15, enter a group name.

FIGURE 5.15   The New License Group dialog box.

4. Enter the number of licenses to be assigned to the group. Click the Add button.

5. The Add Users dialog box appears. Click the Add button to add the desired users. When you're finished, click OK twice to save.

When you create a license group and add users to it, the Licensing service will treat the members of the group as a single entity, so all the users will consume only one license.

Chapter Summary

In this chapter we discussed the administration features of Windows Server 2003. We started with a discussion of the remote management capabilities of Windows Server 2003, using the Computer Management MMC, which we have used briefly in previous chapters.

Next we discussed the Remote Desktop for Administration feature. This feature, first introduced as an optional feature in Windows 2000 Server, has been improved and made a default feature in Windows Server 2003.

An additional, but not commonly used feature for administration is the Remote Assistance feature. This allows you to selectively grant access to your server console, typically in tech support situations.

That was followed by an overview of software licensing, a commonly overlooked but very important topic.

Key Terms

- ▶ License group
- ▶ Remote Assistance
- ▶ Remote Desktop Protocol (RDP)
- ▶ Remote Desktop for Administration
- ▶ RunAs Command

Apply Your Knowledge

Exercises

Exercise 5.1 Creating a custom MMC

In this exercise, you create a custom MMC. This MMC is for an enterprise administrator responsible for managing the configuration of sites, domains, and trusts.

Estimated Time: 20 minutes

1. From the Start menu, select Start, Run. Type **MMC** into the field and click OK.

2. The MMC appears. Select File and then Add/Remove Snap-In from the Console menu.

3. The Add/Remove Snap-in dialog box appears. Click the Add button.

4. The Add Standalone Snap-In dialog box appears. Select the Active Directory Sites and Services snap-in and then click the Add button.

5. Select the Active Directory Domain and Trusts snap-in and then click the Add button.

6. Back at the Add Standalone Snap-In dialog box, click the Close button. This returns you to the Add/Remove Snap-In dialog box. If the selections are correct, click the OK button.

7. This returns you to the custom MMC. To save it, select File, Save As from the system menu. Enter an appropriate name and location and then click the Save button.

Exercise 5.2 Creating a RunAs shortcut

In this exercise, you will create a desktop shortcut that will start the Computer Management MMC and prompt you for your administrative credentials. This shortcut is used so that you can log on to your system with your domain user account and quickly access your administrative tools without logging off.

Estimated Time: 10 minutes

1. Right-click the desktop and select New, Shortcut from the pop-up.

2. The Create Shortcut dialog box appears. Type in the following command: `Runas /user:domain\administrator "mmc %windir%\system32\ compmgmt.msc"`. Click Next.

3. On the Select a Title dialog box, enter Computer Management. Click Finish.

4. Double-click the shortcut you just created. On the command line that appears, enter your administrative password.

5. The Computer Management MMC is opened with administrative permissions.

Exam Questions

1. You are the administrator of a small network. You have configured a Windows Server 2003 server to run in Remote Desktop for Administration mode. What is the maximum number of users that can be supported?

   ○ **A.** The same amount as the number of Terminal Server licenses that were purchased.

   ○ **B.** Two, plus one for the console.

   ○ **C.** About 100 on Windows Server 2003 Standard Edition and 200 on Windows Server 2003 Enterprise Edition.

   ○ **D.** As many as the performance of the server supports.

2. You have just finished building a new Windows Server 2003 server. Your plan is to manage it remotely using Remote Desktop for Administration mode, just like you've been doing with your Windows 2000 servers. However, when you open the RDP client and try to connect to the new server, you can't seem to get connected. What is the most likely cause of the problem?

   ○ **A.** A bad network interface card.

   ○ **B.** The personal firewall is blocking the ports for the browse list.

   ○ **C.** Remote Desktop for Administration mode has not been enabled.

   ○ **D.** Remote Desktop for Administration mode has not been installed.

3. Bill is the lead administrator for BigCO, Inc. An associate administrator in one of the branch offices calls Bill and requests his help on a server problem. Bill attempts to assist the associate administrator, but the associate is fairly green, and he is having trouble describing what he is seeing on his screen. What technology in Windows Server 2003 can Bill use to show the associate how to fix his problem?

   ○ **A.** Remote Desktop for Administration

   ○ **B.** Terminal Services

   ○ **C.** Remote Assistance

   ○ **D.** Remote Administrator

4. You are the network administrator for FlyByNight Airlines. The network consists of a single Active Directory domain. The functional level of the domain is Windows 2000 native. All network servers run Windows Server 2003, and all client computers run Windows XP Professional.

The network includes a shared folder named FlightSchedules1. Some of your users report that they are often unable to access this folder. You discover that the problem occurs whenever more than 10 users try to connect to the folder.

You need to ensure that all appropriate users can access FlightSchedules1. What should you do?

   ○ **A.** Decrease the length of the folder name.

   ○ **B.** Raise the functional level of the domain to Windows Server 2003.

   ○ **C.** Purchase additional client access licenses.

   ○ **D.** Move FlightSchedules1 to one of the servers.

5. You are the network administrator for FlyByNight Airlines. The network consists of a single Active Directory domain. All network servers run Windows Server 2003, and all client computers run Windows XP Professional.

XML web services for the internal network run on a member server named Web1, which is configured with default settings. You are a member of the local Administrators group on Web1. You need the ability to remotely manage Web1. You have no budget to purchase any additional licensing for your network until the next fiscal year. How should you reconfigure Web1?

○ **A.** In the System Properties dialog box, enable Remote Desktop.

○ **B.** Add your user account to the Remote Desktop Users local group.

○ **C.** In the System Properties dialog box, enable Remote Assistance.

○ **D.** Install Terminal Services by using Add or Remove Programs.

6. You are the lead network administrator for FlyByNight Airlines. The network consists of a single Active Directory domain. All network servers run Windows Server 2003, and all client computers run Windows XP Professional. Site License Logging is enabled in the domain. The junior administrators report that they cannot manage Client Access Licenses. When they attempt to open the Licensing utility, they receive the following error: "RPC Server too busy."

You suspect there is a problem on the domain controller that functions as the site license server. However, you do not know which domain controller is the site license server. You need to locate the site license server. What should you do?

○ **A.** Open Licensing, click the Server Browser tab, and expand your domain. Inspect the properties of each server.

○ **B.** Open Active Directory Sites and Services, and open the properties for the site name. Inspect the contents of the Location tab.

○ **C.** Open the Active Directory Users and Computers, click your domain name, click Action, and select Operations Masters. Inspect the contents of the Infrastructure tab.

○ **D.** Open Active Directory Sites and Services and click your site name. Inspect the properties of the Licensing Site Settings.

7. You are the file server administrator for Skelly, Inc. The company network consists of a single Active Directory domain. The domain contains 10 Windows Server 2003 computers and 7,500 Windows XP Professional computers. You manage three servers named Skelly1, Skelly2, and Skelly3. You need to update the driver for the network adapter that is installed in Skelly1.

You log on to Skelly1 by using a domain user account. You open the Computer Management console. When you select Device Manager, you receive the following error message: You do not have sufficient security privileges to uninstall devices or to change device properties or device drivers.

You need to be able to run the Device Manager to update the driver. What should you do?

○ **A.** In Control Panel, open System Tools. Then right-click the Computer Management shortcut and click Run As on the shortcut menu.

○ **B.** In Control Panel, open Administrative Tools. Then right-click the Computer Management shortcut and click Run As on the shortcut menu.

○ **C.** In Control Panel, open Administrative Tools. Then right-click the Computer Management shortcut and click Run with Administrative rights on the shortcut menu.

○ **D.** In Control Panel, open System Tools. Then right-click the Device Manager and click Run As on the shortcut menu.

8. You are the administrator of a Windows Server 2003 computer named Skelly1. Backups of the System State data of Skelly1 occur each day by using the local Administrator account. A new company requirement restricts you from running services by using the Administrator account. To meet the requirement, you create a new service account named BackupSkelly1 to be used for backups. You want this account to have the minimum permissions necessary to perform backups.

You need to grant the appropriate permissions to the BackupSkelly1 account and to configure the backup job to use the BackupSkelly1 account. What should you do?

○ **A.** Add the BackupSkelly1 account to the Server Operators global group.

○ **B.** Add the BackupSkelly1 account to the Backup Operators domain local group.

○ **C.** Add the BackupSkelly1 account to the Server Operators domain local group.

○ **D.** Add the BackupSkelly1 account to the Backup Operators global group.

9. You are the lead network administrator for FlyByNight Airlines. The network consists of a single Active Directory domain. All network servers run Windows Server 2003, and all client computers run Windows XP Professional. One of the junior administrators reports that when she attempts to create a new volume on one of the servers, she receives the message `Access Denied`. What should you do?

   ○ **A.** Add the junior administrator's user account to the Server Operators domain group.

   ○ **B.** Add the junior administrator's user account to the local Administrators group on the server.

   ○ **C.** Configure the junior administrator's client computer to enable the IPSec Server (Request Security) policy.

   ○ **D.** Assign the junior administrator's user account the Allow logon through Terminal Services user right for the server.

10. You are the lead network administrator for FlyByNight Airlines. The network consists of a single Active Directory domain, spread across 20 locations. You are trying to install a new application on one of your severs in a remote office using the Remote Desktop for Administration feature, but the installation procedure seems to have hung. One of the junior administrators at the remote location reports that there is some kind of message displayed on the console of the server. This is a critical application, and it must be installed immediately. What should you do?

   ○ **A.** FedEx the installation disks to the remote location and have the junior administrator install it for you.

   ○ **B.** Log off your session, log back on, then restart the application install using RunAs.

   ○ **C.** Log off your session, enter **mstsc /install** on the command line, then restart the application installation.

   ○ **D.** Log off your session, enter **mstsc /console** on the command line, then restart the application installation.

Answers to Exam Questions

1. **B.** The number of concurrent Remote Desktop for Administration sessions on Windows Server 2003 is two RDP sessions, plus the console. Terminal Services connections on all versions of Windows Server 2003 are unlimited. See "Terminal Services in Remote Desktop for Administration Mode."

2. **C.** Unlike in Windows 2000 Server, Windows Server 2003 Remote Desktop for Administration mode is installed by default; however, it is not enabled. See "Remote Desktop for Administration."

3. **C.** The Remote Assistance feature allows both Bill and the associate administrator to see and control the console on the server. See "Remote Assistance."

4. **D**. Since the magic number is 10, it is most likely that the share exists on a Windows XP client. That would lead to a situation where the Windows XP client computer allows only up to 10 connections at the same time, resulting in users being unable to access FlightSchedules1 when the 10 connections are full. Moving the shared folder to a server computer will allow more concurrent connections. Because the domain doesn't have any Windows 9x clients, the length of the share name isn't a problem. This is obviously a connectivity issue; the functional level of the domain is not the cause of the problem. Because the licensing service doesn't block connections, this is not a CAL problem. See "Managing and Administering Software Site Licensing."

5. **A**. The solution is to enable the Remote Desktop feature, which will allow you to remotely manage the server while not requiring any additional licenses. B is not necessary because the administrator is a member of the group by default. Remote Assistance is useful only if someone is sitting at the console of the server and is able to grant you permission to connect to it. Installing Terminal Services would incur additional license expense, which is not in the budget. See "Remote Desktop for Administration."

6. **D**. The Site License server is identified in the AD Sites and Settings MMC under Licensing Site Settings properties. See "Managing and Administering Software Site Licensing."

7. **B**. The RunAs command is used to enable an administrator to run programs and processes with a different logon from the one the administrator used to log on to the system. The Computer Management MMC is available in the Administrative Tools folder in the Control Panel. There is not a System Tools folder in Control Panel. See "Managing a Server Using RunAs."

8. **B**. By adding the account to the Backup Operators domain local group, the backups can be performed without granting an excessive amount of rights that using the Server operators would. All the Administrative groups are domain local groups, not global groups. See "Administrative Groups."

9. **B**. Only members of the Administrators group have the necessary permissions to format a volume or partition. See "Administrative Groups."

10. **D**. Some applications will display messages and prompts only to the system console. When using Remote Desktop for administration, you will be connected to one of the other sessions by default. You can connect to the system console on a remote server by entering `mstsc /console` on the command line. See "Remote Desktop for Administration."

Suggested Readings and Resources

1. Boswell, William. *Inside Windows Server 2003*. New Riders, 2003. ISBN 0735711585.

2. Matthews, Marty. *Windows Server 2003: A Beginners Guide*. McGraw-Hill, 2003. ISBN 0072193093.

3. Minasi, Mark, et al. *Mark Minasi's Windows XP and Server 2003 Resource Kit*. Sybex, 2003. ISBN 0782140807.

4. Minasi, Mark, et al. *Mastering Windows Server 2003 Server*. Sybex, 2003. ISBN 0782141307.

5. Morimoto, Rand, et. al. *Microsoft Windows Server 2003 Unleashed (R2 Edition)*. Sams, 2006. ISBN 0672328984.

6. Shapiro, Jeffrey, et al. *Windows Server 2003 Bible*. John Wiley & Sons, 2003. ISBN 0764549375.

7. Stanek, William. *Microsoft Windows Server 2003 Administrator's Pocket Consultant*. Microsoft Press, 2003. ISBN 0735613540.

8. *Windows Server 2003 Deployment Guide*. Microsoft Corporation. http://www.microsoft.com/windowsserver2003/techinfo/reskit/deploykit.mspx.

9. *Windows Server 2003 Resource Kit*. Microsoft Corporation. Look for a link to it on the Technical Resources for Windows Server 2003 page. http://www.microsoft.com/windowsserver2003/techinfo/default.mspx.

CHAPTER SIX

Implementing Printing

Objectives

This chapter covers the following Microsoft-specified objectives for the "Managing and Maintaining a Server Environment" section of the Managing and Maintaining a Microsoft Windows Server 2003 Environment exam:

Troubleshoot print queues

▶ The purpose of this objective is to teach you how to control the access and the type of access allowed printing devices in the Windows Server 2003 environment. You need to know not only how to add and configure print devices, but also how to manage and troubleshoot problems in a networked environment.

Outline

Study Strategies

▶ In studying this section, be sure to practice all the activities described. Become very familiar with the terminology associated with printers in Windows Server 2003 because Microsoft's definitions are not necessarily what you would expect. For example, you need to be able to identify the different components that are involved in the printing process and know how to determine which component is failing when you can't print.

▶ To perform the exercises in this chapter, it's not essential that you have a physical printer attached to your server. Most of the exercises will work fine because they're tied to the logical printer configuration. Just remember not to attempt to print any test pages!

▶ As mentioned in previous chapters, you must become familiar with the Windows Server 2003 interface. Working with a Windows 2000 server will not be sufficient. Microsoft has made a large number of changes to the printer interface in Windows Server 2003. Using a Windows Server 2003 test server will be essential.

▶ Although it would seem that because Microsoft dedicated only a single objective to the print process, it might be lightly covered on the exam. This is far from the case. Historically, printing has been heavily emphasized on the Microsoft exams, and it is an essential part of your duties as a system administrator.

Introduction

For years, we have heard about how the paperless office is the wave of the future. Even after the adoption of online documents, intranets, and the exploding use of email, the love affair with paper documents has not faded.

To this day, file and print services remain the bread and butter of the networking world. Printing is one of the key capabilities around which networks and computers are designed. Most computer operators cannot function without being able to transfer data onto paper. Accessing a shared printer is one of the most frequently used network capabilities. This chapter examines the Windows Server 2003 printing system and covers printer installation, management, configuration, and troubleshooting.

Printing with Windows Server 2003

The Windows Server 2003 printing subsystem has an advanced architecture capable of supporting a large user base, managing a variety of printer types and capabilities, and offering several layouts and access controls. As long as the printer host is a member of a network, any type of network client(s) can use printers hosted by a Windows Server 2003 system, including Windows 2000 Server and Windows XP, Windows 2000 Professional, Windows NT, Windows 95/98, Windows for Workgroups, Windows 3.x, DOS, NetWare servers, Macintosh, Unix, and other TCP/IP clients.

The Windows Server 2003 Print Architecture

The Windows Server 2003 print architecture design is comprehensible, but many of the terms and concepts it uses must be defined because they are used in ways contrary to common sense or common usage. The following list explains most of Microsoft's printing-related terms. You should become familiar with these terms before working with the Windows Server 2003 printing system:

▶ *Logical printer*—This term is used by Microsoft to refer to the software construct that redirects print jobs from a client to the print server. Logical printers appear in the Printers folder, and you can create them using the Add Printer Wizard from that folder. The logical printer is where you define configuration settings for the physical print devices. Logical printers also are used to control and manage access to physical printers. The term logical printer often is synonymous with printer in Microsoft documentation.

▶ *Print device*—This is the actual physical device that creates the printed document. In some cases, this term is synonymous with physical printer.

▶ *Client*—A client is either a computer hosting a specific operating system or an application submitting a print job. The terms client, client system, client computer, and client application are used interchangeably in most cases. The client can be a true network client that submits a print job to a print server on the network, or the client can be the same computer system that serves as the print server. The term client refers to the relationship between the object submitting the print job and the object hosting the printer spool.

▶ *Connecting to a printer*—This action creates a logical printer that redirects print jobs to a network printer share. Use the Add Printer Wizard in the Printers folder to create a logical printer.

▶ *Creating a printer*—This term is similar to connecting to a printer, but it is most commonly used in reference to a locally attached physical printer—that is, a printer connected directly to the computer via a parallel cable. In creating a printer, you also use the Add Printer Wizard from the Printers folder. Creating a printer involves installing the device-specific driver, setting any configuration options, and possibly sharing the printer with the network.

▶ *Dynamic print clients*—Dynamic print clients do not have print drivers installed locally for network printer shares. Each time a print job is sent to a logical printer, the print server sends a print driver for the appropriate client operating system to the client. The client uses the driver to format and submit the print job. This system enables print drivers to be stored in a single location, simplifying maintenance and upgrades.

▶ *Network-attached printer*—A network-attached printer is a print device that has a built-in or specially attached network interface connected to the network media instead of to a computer. Such printers still require that you define a computer as the print server where the spool file(s) reside, but they are independent network devices. Network-attached printers typically employ TCP/IP for communications.

▶ *Print client*—This term is used interchangeably with client, client system, client computer, and client application. A print client is any object that submits a print job to a printer.

▶ *Print job*—The object transmitted from a client to a print server that contains not only the document or content to be printed, but also control and processing instructions. The client creates print jobs and sends them to a print server via a logical printer redirector. The print server stores the print job to a spool, and when the printer is available, the print job is pulled from the spool and sent to the physical print device.

▶ *Print server*—This is the actual computer that controls and manages a printer. It accepts print jobs from clients, stores them in a spool, supervises the physical printer, and sends print jobs from the spool to the physical printer when it is available. A print server can manage either a locally attached or a network-attached printer. The print server also is the storage location for print drivers used by dynamic print clients. On Windows Server 2003 networks, print servers can be Windows Server 2003, Windows XP Professional, Windows 2000 Server or Professional, Windows NT Server or Workstation, or Windows 98 systems. Print drivers are stored on these servers in the `\\printserver\print$` directory.

▶ *Print resolution*—Print resolution is a measurement of pixel density in dots per inch (dpi). It determines how sharp and clear the printed document appears. In most cases, a higher dpi results in a better printed document. The base dpi for most laser and ink-jet printers is around 300 dpi; however, several printer models can print up to 2,400 dpi. Higher-DPI resolutions are obtainable on professional printing systems.

▶ *Print server services*—You can expand the Windows Server 2003 print system's printing capabilities through the use of print server services. These add-on modules are used to broaden the client base from which print jobs can be submitted. Print server services include Services for Macintosh, File and Print Services for NetWare, and TCP/IP Print Services. Print server services not only add support for additional client types, they expand the range of protocols that can be used to submit print jobs.

▶ *Print spooler or spooler*—The spool is the temporary storage area hosted by the print server for submitted print jobs. The software component of the print server that manages the spool is the spooler. The spooler is responsible for saving new print jobs to a file and for sending print jobs from the spool to the physical printer. In most cases, the print job is retained in the spool until it has successfully printed. The spooler can be bypassed with a change to the logical printer configuration, causing print jobs to be sent directly to the printer instead of being stored in the spool. Doing this suspends the client sending the print job; the print job is communicated only as fast as the printer can create the printed output.

▶ *Print users*—A print user is any user on the local system or network who has been granted the privilege of printing. Print users can be given Print, Manage Documents, or Manage Printers access privileges. Print access enables users to submit print jobs and to manage their own print jobs (pause, resume, restart, and delete). Manage Documents access enables a user to submit print jobs and to manage any print job in the queue (pause, resume, restart, and delete). Manage Printers access enables a user to submit print jobs, to manage any print job in the queue (pause, resume, restart, delete), to make changes to the settings and configuration of the logical printer, and to alter the security settings and access privileges for the logical printer.

▶ *Printer*—Also called the logical printer, this refers to the logical printer software construct that redirects print jobs from a client to the print server rather than to the physical print device. The type of device used as the physical printer does not affect the rest of the print model as long as the correct device driver is installed.

▶ *Printer ports*—The software interfaces (such as LPT1) between the computer and the print device.

▶ *Print driver*—A print driver is a software element used to inform the print server or print client about the capabilities and limitations of a printer. It informs the print server how to communicate with the physical printer, and it informs print clients how to format print jobs.

▶ *Print$*—This share contains the installed print drivers. In addition to the Administrators group, the Server Operators and Print Operators groups have Full Control permissions to this folder. The Everyone group has Read permission.

▶ *Queue or print queue*—The print server maintains a queue (or list) of print jobs for each physical print device. These jobs are automatically managed by the print server. Each logical printer has its own print queue. Each physical printer can have multiple logical printers defined for it, so it can have multiple print queues. Multiple queues allow for priority processing of print jobs. Print users can manipulate only those print jobs they have submitted. Print users with Manage Documents access can manipulate any print job in a queue. Print users with Manage Printers access can manipulate any print job in a queue, and can change the settings and configuration of the queue and the logical printer. You can view a print queue by opening the logical printer from the Printers folder. Individual print queues operate in first in, first out (FIFO) mode.

▶ *Rendering*—Rendering is the process of transforming video display images from video system-specific instructions to printer model-specific language codes that reproduce the image on paper. The Windows Server 2003 print system renders images using the print driver installed for a particular logical printer/physical printer.

From this list, you can see that the Microsoft print system is not focused on the physical print device, but on the software redirecting mechanisms that direct print jobs from the client to the physical printer's connection point to the print system (a print server). After you attach the physical print device either directly to a computer or to the network and then install the proper drivers, the Windows print system pays little attention to the physical device. You'll interact with the physical printer only to retrieve documents, add paper, and troubleshoot hardware-specific problems.

The print system design is modular, just like that of every other part of Windows Server 2003. This enables you to interchange, tweak, control, and replace individual components of the overall system based on the needs of the system and the types of hardware present.

Each element of the print architecture is designed to manage or perform a single task. A print job traverses the system one step at a time, providing a seamless procession from print client to printed document. Each module of the system can communicate with its immediate neighbors, but not with other components located elsewhere in the system. The following list presents the key elements of the print architecture in the order in which a print job encounters them (see Figure 6.1):

1. A Windows-based print client uses an application to create a document or other printable element and then initiates a print job.

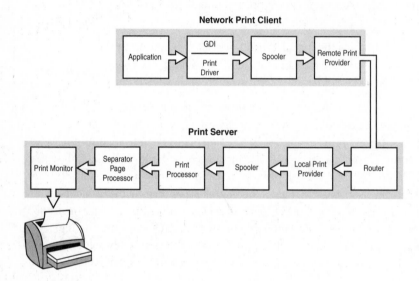

FIGURE 6.1 High-level overview of the printing process in Windows Server 2003.

2. The print client application interacts with the graphics device interface (GDI) and print driver to create a valid print job for the specified logical printer. GDI is a software element that interacts with both the video and printer systems to enable images to be rendered for display or print. GDI is what makes the Windows What You See Is What You Get (WYSIWYG) capability possible. The interaction of the GDI with the actual print driver helps create a print job that accurately reproduces the displayed image.

3. The print job is sent to the local print spooler. The print job is held there until it can be transmitted to the print server by the remote print provider.

4. Non-Microsoft print clients perform similar functions that result in a formatted print job being sent to the appropriate print server service hosted by the print server.

5. The spooler is a multipart element that consists of the router, the local print provider, the print processor, and the separator page processor. The spooler is responsible for accepting print jobs from clients and holding them until they are passed on to the print monitor.

6. The router is responsible for directing print jobs to either local or remote printers. The router passes print jobs for a local printer to the local print provider. It passes print jobs for a remote printer to the remote network print server such as a NetWare print server.

7. The local print provider writes the print job to a spool file (`.spl`).

8. The print processor despools print jobs and performs any additional processing before sending the print job on to the print monitor.

9. The separator page processor adds any logical printer-specific separate pages to the beginning of each document as it is sent to the print monitor.

10. The print monitor is the print system component that communicates directly with the printer. It manages the connection port and the language used by bidirectional print devices.

11. The print device receives the print job and prints the data.

As you can see, the Windows Server 2003 print system architecture is fairly extensive. As a system manager or a print user, you do not need to know all the architectural details. All that is required to adequately support printing under Windows Server 2003 is that you understand how to add, configure, and troubleshoot printing. Discussion of the architecture is included here, so you will have a clearer understanding of what is going on under the hood when a print job is submitted by a client.

If you need more details or additional information about the structure, elements, and architecture of the Windows Server 2003 print system, consult the Windows Server 2003 Server Resource Kit and the TechNet website at http://technet.microsoft.com/en-us/default.aspx.

Print Clients in Windows Server 2003

Printing within the Windows Server 2003 environment is much easier than the complex architecture suggests. After a logical printer is defined on a client, any application can send print jobs to that printer. Logical printers are a design element of the Microsoft print system that most of the Microsoft operating systems support. As mentioned earlier, the Windows Server 2003 print system is not limited to Microsoft clients. In fact, support for non-Microsoft clients is included on the Windows Server 2003 distribution CD. To encourage Windows Server 2003 deployment, Microsoft includes print services for Macintosh and TCP/IP clients, thus broadening the range of networks to which Windows Server 2003 can bring new services and resources.

Print Services for Macintosh (PSFM) is a Windows Server 2003 Server-only installable service. This service adds capabilities to the Windows Server 2003 network so that Macintosh clients can participate. Basically, this service enables Macintosh clients to share and access printers. Macintosh clients are able to submit print jobs to Windows Server 2003 Server-hosted printers by sending them to a print device redirector created by SFM within the AppleTalk network. Likewise, PSFM can capture Macintosh shared printers and enable Windows Server 2003 to connect to them. For more details about installing and configuring PSFM, see the Windows Server 2003 Server manuals, the Windows Server 2003 Server Resource Kit, and the TechNet website.

TCP/IP clients can host printers for Windows Server 2003 network clients, or they can print to Windows Server 2003 network print servers. The Microsoft Print Services for Unix Printing service (formerly know as the TCP/IP Printing Service) adds Line Printer Daemon (LPD) and Line Printer Remote (LPR) functionality to the existing Windows Server 2003 print system. LPD is used to enable Unix or other TCP/IP clients to print documents on Windows Server 2003 network-hosted print server printers. LPD accepts print jobs from LPR utilities hosted by TCP/IP clients. Likewise, Windows Server 2003 clients can use LPR to send print jobs out to LPDs hosted on TCP/IP clients, allowing Windows Server 2003 clients to print to Unix or other TCP/IP print servers.

The Microsoft Print Services for Unix is installed from the Windows Server 2003 CD. It requires that the TCP/IP protocol be present on the Windows Server 2003 host print server. After the service is installed, you can use the Add Printer Wizard to create logical printers that use the LPR port. The LPR port can be directed to a Windows Server 2003 Print share or to a Unix or other TCP/IP operating system LPD print queue. To make this link, you need to know the IP identifier of the print server or the print device itself (typically, the DNS name or the IP address) and the name that the LPD print server uses to reference the print device. For more details about TCP/IP printing, see the Windows Server 2003 manuals, the Windows Server 2003 Server Resource Kit, and TechNet.

Not to be confused with the Microsoft Print Services for Unix Service is the Internet Printing Protocol (IPP). IPP allows any supported client (Windows 95 and later) to print to a Windows Server 2003 server via their Internet browser. Internet Information Services (IIS) must be installed on the Windows Server 2003 server.

NetWare clients also can enjoy access to Windows Server 2003 resources; however, this requires an additional software component. The File and Print Service for NetWare (FPNW) grants NetWare clients access to printers and file shares hosted by Windows Server 2003 systems without requiring additional software on each client. FPNW is an extra-cost option from Microsoft that makes Windows Server 2003 systems look and act like NetWare 3.11 servers to NetWare clients.

Adding Printers in Windows Server 2003

Whether you are installing a printer for local use only, configuring a network print server, or even defining a print server for a network-attached printer, Windows Server 2003 makes adding new printers easy. The following sections discuss each of these printer installation issues.

Locally Attached Printers

Local printers are attached directly to the computer. The type of attachment you use doesn't matter as long as the operating system recognizes the bus type and the print driver corresponds. Local printers usually are attached using parallel or USB cables, but serial ports and other technologies can be used.

Before beginning the installation of a local printer, you need to have a few key pieces of information on hand:

▶ The exact make and model of the printer

▶ The port to which the physical print device is connected

▶ The location of print drivers, if they are not included on the Windows Server 2003 distribution CD

▶ A name for the logical printer (if you are using a naming convention, be sure to comply with its rules)

▶ Whether you will be sharing the printer with the network

The basic steps for adding a local printer are listed in Step by Step 6.1.

STEP BY STEP

6.1 Adding a local printer

1. Physically set up and attach the printer to the computer.

2. Power up the printer.

3. Open the Printers folder (Start, Printers and Faxes).

4. Launch the Add Printer Wizard by double-clicking the Add A Printer icon in the Printers folder. This brings up the Add Print Wizard's first page. Click Next.

5. Select Local Printer and click Next. This reveals the port selection page of the Add Printer Wizard.

6. Select the port to which the printer is connected and click Next. This brings up the Printer Model Selection page. This is a list of print drivers included on the Windows Server 2003 distribution CD.

7. Select the manufacturer in the left column, and select the printer model in the right column, as shown in Figure 6.2.

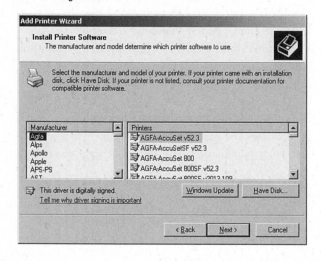

FIGURE 6.2 The Install Printer Software dialog box allows you to select the printer drivers shipped with Windows Server 2003, or click the Have Disk button to supply your own.

8. If your printer is not listed, click the Have Disk button. You'll need to point the dialog box to the location of the manufacturer-supplied drivers. You can also click the Windows Update button to download drivers from Microsoft.

9. Click Next. This brings up the Printer Name page. This is the name that will appear below the logical printer icon in the Printers folder on your local machine.

10. Enter a name, or accept the offered default name. Remember that if you want MS-DOS applications to print to this printer, the printer name must be no more than eight characters long and must have no spaces. In addition, some newer applications will not recognize names of more than 31 characters. Click Next.

11. Unlike some previous versions of Windows, the default in Windows Server 2003 is for local printers to be shared. If this printer is to be used by the local system only, select Do Not Share This Printer. (See "Network-Attached Printers" later in this chapter for more information about this page of the Add Printer Wizard.)

12. Click Next. This brings up the Location and Comment page. By filling in these optional fields, users who are searching in Active Directory will be able to read or search on these fields.

13. Click Next. This brings up the Print a Test Page screen. The default is to print a test document to the newly installed printer to verify that setup was successful. If you do not want to print a test page, select No and click Next.

14. Click Finish.

This final step of the Add Printer Wizard initiates the printer installation routine. The wizard might prompt you for the path to the print driver and associated print system files. After the required drivers are installed, the newly installed printer icon appears in the Printers folder. You might need to refresh the display (by selecting View, Refresh, or F5) to see the new icon. If you selected to print a test page, a dialog box appears asking whether the page printed successfully. If the page printed, click Yes. If the page failed to print, click No. The hardware troubleshooter for printers appears and walks you through several options for remedying the printing problem. Most of these options are discussed in the "Troubleshooting Printing Problems" section in Chapter 7.

If you've installed a printer on this system before, you will see an additional question on the Printer Name page asking whether to make the printer you currently are installing the default printer. The default selection is No. If you want the new printer to be the printer to which all applications print by default, select Yes.

If you already have a printer of the same type or a printer that uses the same print driver installed on this system, you will see an additional page (after the Printer Model Selection page) asking whether to keep the existing driver or to replace the existing driver. In most cases, you can accept the default and recommended option of retaining the existing driver. If you want to reinstall the driver or install a new driver from a new source, select Replace the Existing Driver.

Plug and Play Printers

Plug and Play is a feature that has now been included in Microsoft's server operating systems, starting with Windows Server 2003. This feature was previously implemented in Windows 95/98/2000/XP. With Plug and Play, a printer that is connected via USB or an IEEE 1394 (FireWire)-compatible port is automatically detected and identified. After the printer is identified, the drivers are automatically loaded, and the printer is configured for you. Some older printers that are connected to the parallel port will be detected only when the computer is restarted. It is also possible to start the detection process by starting the Add Hardware applet from the Control Panel. After the printer is installed, you can make any desired configuration changes, just as you would with a manually installed printer. Network and serial port attached printers are not Plug and Play compatible and must be installed and configured manually.

For a detailed description of the Windows Server 2003 Plug and Play feature, see Chapter 15, "Managing and Troubleshooting Hardware Devices."

Shared Printers

You can create shared printers through a simple procedure of installing a locally attached printer, sharing that logical printer, and connecting to that printer from each client. The simplest way to share a local printer is to select the Shared option during the Add Printer Wizard installation process. If you want to share an existing logical printer, however, you need to modify only the Sharing tab of the printer's properties.

Creating a new printer to be shared with the network requires the same preparation and installation steps as a local-only printer, with a few additions. You need to have the following additional pieces of information on hand:

▶ The name of the printer share (if you are using a naming convention, be sure to comply with its rules)

▶ The operating-system-specific print drivers you want to host from the print server

The installation process for a shared printer is shown in Step by Step 6.2.

STEP BY STEP

6.2 Adding a shared local printer

1. Follow steps 1 through 10 for local-only printer installation, as shown in Step by Step 6.1.

2. In the Printer Sharing dialog box, as shown in Figure 6.3, select the Share Name option button.

3. In the Share Name field, enter the name to be used on the network for this printer share. Remember that if you want MS-DOS, Windows 3.x, Windows for Workgroups, and other operating system clients that don't support long filenames to use this print share, the share name must be no more than eight characters long.

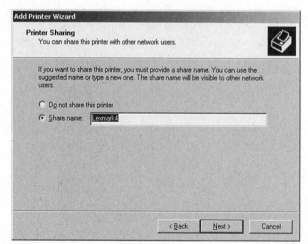

FIGURE 6.3 The Printer Sharing dialog box allows you to specify that the printer will be shared and to enter an appropriate share name.

4. Click Next. This brings up the Location and Comment page. By filling in these optional fields, users who are searching in Active Directory will be able to read or search on these fields.

5. Click Next. This brings up the Print a Test Page screen. The default is to print a test document to the newly installed printer to verify that setup was successful. If you do not want to print a test page, select No and click Next.

6. Click Finish.

At this point, you have installed a local printer that is shared with the network. The next step is to connect the client to the network printer share. This is performed from each client. The actual process varies somewhat, depending on the operating system. If you need additional information about connecting other clients to network printer shares, consult TechNet or the manufacturer of the client operating system.

On any Windows 95/98/NT/200x/XP system, follow the steps in Step by Step 6.3 to connect to a network printer share.

STEP BY STEP

6.3 Connecting to a shared printer

1. Open the Printers folder by clicking Start, then Printers and Faxes.

2. Launch the Add Printer Wizard by double-clicking the Add Printer icon in the Printers folder. This brings up the Add Printer Wizard's first page. Click Next.

3. Select the A Network Printer, or a Printer Attached to Another Computer option button.

4. Click Next. This brings up the Specify a Printer dialog box (see Figure 6.4).

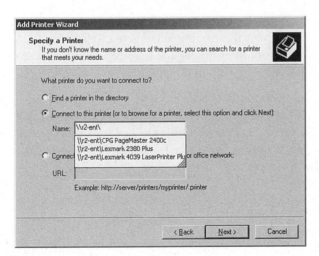

FIGURE 6.4 The Specify a Printer dialog box allows you to specify what shared printer you want to connect to. Notice that you can browse the printers on a server by entering the server name.

5. Here, you can choose to connect to a printer on your intranet or the Internet just by entering the appropriate URL. You also have the option of typing in the printer name if you know it, or searching in Active Directory. Or, you can select the option button next to the Connect to This Printer field and then click Next.

6. This opens the Browse for Printer dialog box, as shown in Figure 6.5. Traverse the network resource browser tree to locate the print server and the share name of the printer share. Select the desired printer share.

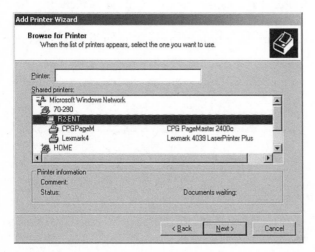

FIGURE 6.5 The Browse for Printer dialog box allows you to locate the shared printer you want to connect to. Notice that you have the ability to browse for printers on multiple domains.

7. Click OK, and then click Finish.

If the print server hosts the print drivers for your client operating system, the Add Printer Wizard requires no additional files. If print drivers must be installed on your client PC, you are prompted to provide the path to their location. After the required drivers are installed, the newly installed printer icon appears in the Printers folder. You might need to refresh the display (View, Refresh) to see the new icon.

If you selected to print a test page, a dialog box appears asking whether the page printed successfully. If the page printed, click Yes. If the page failed to print, click No. The hardware troubleshooter for printers appears and walks you through several options for remedying the printing problem. Most of these options will be discussed in the "Troubleshooting Printing Problems" section in Chapter 7.

Challenge

You are a system administrator who is responsible for installing a new print server and two locally attached Hewlett Packard LaserJet 5MP printers. You will need to share these printers as KC1 and KC2. You will also need to specify their locations; KC1 will be on the first floor of the main building, and KC2 will be on the second floor.

Try to complete this exercise on your own, listing your conclusions on a sheet of paper. After you have completed the exercise, compare your results to those given here.

1. Physically set up and attach the printers to the server.

2. Power up the printers.

3. Open the Printers folder (Start, Printers and Faxes).

4. Launch the Add Printer Wizard by double-clicking the Add a Printer icon in the Printers folder. This brings up the Add Print Wizard's first page. Click Next.

5. Select Local Printer for a locally attached printer and click Next. This reveals the port selection page of the Add Printer Wizard.

6. Select the port to which the printer is connected and click Next. This brings up the Printer Model Selection page. This is a list of print drivers included on the Windows Server 2003 distribution CD.

7. Select the HP in the left column, and select LaserJet 5MP in the right column.

8. If your printer is not listed, click the Have Disk button and point the dialog box to the location of the manufacturer-supplied drivers. Click Next.

9. Enter the KC1 as the printer name. Click Next.

10. Accept the default to share the printer; click Next.

11. Add the floor that the printer is located on. Click Next.

12. Print a test page, and click Next.

13. Click Finish.

14. Repeat for the second printer.

Make sure that you complete the challenge exercise as shown. The results will be used in several upcoming exercises.

Network-Attached Printers

A network-attached printer is a printer equipped with its own network interface, making the printer a network device. Use network-attached printers when communication speed is important (such as when printing large or complex documents) or when no suitable system has an available communication port. Network-attached printers require a print server—that is, a printer attached directly to the network relies on a computer to manage print jobs, process the spool, and control user access.

By default, Windows Server 2003 uses the TCP/IP protocol to communicate print data from a print server to a network-attached printer, but NWLink also can be employed. In addition, some printer vendors have proprietary protocols. Ultimately, the protocol used to support printing on network-attached printers is not important as long as the printer and the supporting software function properly.

Configuring a network-attached printer can involve a variety of steps, configurations, and driver installations. You need to read the installation instructions included with the printer to learn exactly what must be done for that particular device. In general, the steps are as shown in Step by Step 6.4.

STEP BY STEP

6.4 Installing a Network-Attached Printer

1. If not already present, install the network interface into the printer.

2. Attach the printer to the network.

3. Perform any necessary hardware-specific routines to prepare the device for network communications. These might include switching print modes, defining protocol-specific parameters, or enabling the network interface. The printer/NIC manual should detail the required steps.

4. Install the communication protocol on the system destined to be the print server for the network-attached printer: TCP/IP(installed by default on Windows Server 2003), NWLink, or a vendor-supplied protocol.

5. Open the Printers folder by selecting Start, then Printers and Faxes.

6. Launch the Add Printer Wizard by double-clicking the Add Printer icon in the Printers folder. This brings up the Add Printer Wizard's first page. Click Next.

7. Select Local Printer Attached to This Computer.

8. Deselect the Automatically Detect and Install My Plug and Play Printer check box, and then click Next.

9. The Select a Printer Port dialog box appears (see Figure 6.6). Select Standard TCP/IP form the drop-down list, and then click Next.

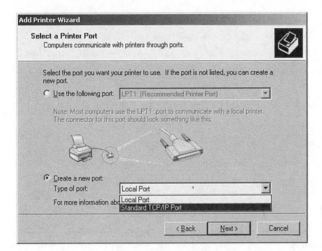

FIGURE 6.6 The Select a Printer Port dialog box allows you to specify what port you will use to connect to your printer.

10. The Add Standard TCP/IP Printer Port wizard is started. Click Next.

11. The Add Port dialog box appears, as shown in Figure 6.7. Enter the IP address or NetBIOS name of the network printer. Notice that the port name by default is IP_ and the IP address, or just the NetBIOS name if you decide not to use an IP address. You can change the port name to whatever makes it recognizable to you for identification purposes.

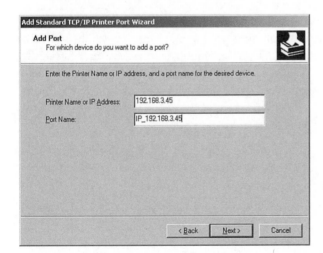

FIGURE 6.7 Enter either the NetBIOS name or the IP address of your network printer.

12. When prompted, click the Finish button.

13. In the remaining steps, select the print driver and share name as you have done in previous exercises.

During this process we added a virtual port to the machine we were using as a print server. This is a process in which a new port that is used to redirect print jobs from the print server to the actual print device is defined to the system. A port usually is created on the Port Selection Page of the Add Printer Wizard by selecting Create a New Port. Some vendors, however, have their own installation routine. The Windows Server 2003 distribution CD includes several ports that can be installed, including the Hewlett-Packard and Digital network ports.

Network-attached printers are managed and controlled in the same manner as locally attached printers. In some cases, vendors provide additional control or interface software that can enhance the foundational controls offered through the Windows Server 2003 print system.

NOTE

Name Resolution   If you configure your network-attached printer with a static IP address, make sure that you create an A record for it in your DNS zone. If the IP address is assigned manually, it will not be automatically registered in DNS, as it would if it were assigned via DHCP. An A record maps a hostname to an IP address and is required for your clients to resolve the printer name.

Print Servers

A print server is the computer that controls and manages a printer. It accepts print jobs from clients, stores them in a spool, supervises the physical printer, and sends print jobs from the spool to the physical printer when it is available. Every computer that has a printer physically attached to it is in effect a print server. A print server can manage both locally attached and network-attached printers. Although in large environments a print server might be a dedicated server with a fast processor, ample memory, and a fast disk subsystem, typically the print server role is implemented on a server that is performing other duties.

A print server can be a server with multiple printers physically attached, but it is more likely to be used to manage network-attached printers. When using a network-attached printer, it can be managed using either of two methods:

- ▶ By adding a printer (remember, this is a logical device) to each computer that needs to print to it.

- ▶ By adding the printer to a print server, sharing the printer, and connecting each computer to the print share.

Although either method would work, there are certain advantages to managing your printers via a print server:

▶ *Central management*—All the configuration options for the printer are managed in a central location. This makes it easier to manage, and also easier to delegate and track permissions.

▶ *Single print queue*—All users see the same print queue. This allows them to see the progress of their print job in relation to any other print jobs currently running on the printer. When a printer is connected directly to a computer, users can see only their print jobs.

▶ *Shared notification*—All users receive any error messages. This allows everyone to know the actual state of the printer. For example, if an out-of-paper error is posted, a user who has submitted a job to the printer will know to go add paper to it, instead of wondering why it's taking so long to print the document.

▶ *Central logging*—Only one log for the administrators to monitor.

▶ *Delegated processing*—Some of the print job processing overhead is passed off to the server. For most brief reports, this is usually not noticeable. However, for large graphic-intensive print jobs, it can be more efficient to pass the processing off to a server and allow the end user to proceed with other duties.

▶ *Centralized driver distribution*—Most modern operating systems (Windows NT 4.0 and later) will automatically update their print drivers when they connect to the print server. This means that the administrator has to install the drivers only once.

Although any Windows operating system can be used as a print server, the client operating systems have the limitation of allowing only 10 concurrent connections. For best results, you should use a Windows Server 2003 server computer as your print server. In addition, you will need to make sure that it has additional memory over the minimums stated by Microsoft (See "Windows Server 2003 Environment" in Chapter 1) and lots of disk space, because the print jobs will be spooled to the disk while they are waiting to print.

Publishing a Printer in Active Directory

In Windows Server 2003, any printer attached to a machine that is logged in to the domain or any network-attached printer can be shared and published. By publishing a printer in Active Directory, users can locate it by searching on various attributes such as features or location. This is advantageous because in a pure Windows Server 2003 TCP/IP-only environment, there is no browser service (NetBIOS) available to find shared resources. However, if your network hosts printers that need to be restricted to a small group of users, such as a check printer or a color plotter, you might prefer not to publish it in AD. While the users can be prevented from using a printer via permissions, if they see it in AD, they still might attempt to connect to it, and call the help desk to complain that they don't have access.

All resources that are to be shared must be published in Active Directory. For a printer to be published in Active Directory, it must first be shared. However, a printer can still be shared without being published. You can still connect to it using the net use command.

By default, when you use the Add Printer Wizard to add a printer on a Windows Server 2003 Server, it is shared and published. On Windows XP Professional, the default is to not share the printer. It must be manually configured to be shared.

To share and publish a printer in Windows Server 2003, follow the procedure in Step by Step 6.5.

STEP BY STEP

6.5 Publishing a printer in Active Directory

1. Click Start, and then select the Printers and Faxes folder.

2. Right-click the icon of the desired printer and select Sharing.

3. From the Sharing tab of the Properties window as shown in Figure 6.8, go to the Share This Printer field and type in the name that you want to appear in the Active Directory database.

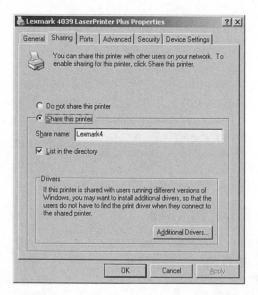

FIGURE 6.8 The Sharing tab allows you to specify the share name of the printer and control whether it appears in Active Directory.

4. Select the List In the Directory check box, and then click OK to save.

NOTE

Make Publishing Mandatory When a printer is installed, it may or may not be shared and published in the Active Directory, depending on what operating system you are using. The default behavior can be changed to make publishing mandatory via Group Policy. For information on Group Policies, see Chapter 10, "Managing the User Environment by Using Group Policy."

Publishing a Non-Windows Server 2003 Printer in Active Directory

In Windows Server 2003, printers attached to machines running Windows NT and also Unix printers can be published. For these printers to be published in Active Directory, they must first be properly installed and shared on their respective platforms.

To publish a non-Windows Server 2003 printer in Active Directory, follow the procedure in Step by Step 6.6.

STEP BY STEP

6.6 Publishing a non-Windows Server 2003 printer in Active Directory

1. Click Start, Programs, Administrative Tools, and then select Active Directory Users and Computers.

2. Click the desired domain; then right-click the container of the organizational unit (OU) that you want to publish the printer in.

3. From the pop-up menu, select New, Printer. The New Object—Printer window appears (see Figure 6.9).

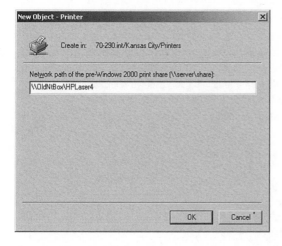

FIGURE 6.9 The New Object—Printer dialog box allows you to publish printers on pre-Windows 2000 or non-Windows servers.

4. In the New Object—Printer window, type in the Universal Naming Convention (UNC) path of the printer that you want to publish—that is, \\servername\printername.

5. Click OK to save.

Searching for Printers in Active Directory

If NetBIOS is enabled on your network, you can still browse for printers using My Network Places. However, one of the nice things about Active Directory in general is that it uses DNS for its location mechanism, so NetBIOS is slowly going away. Starting with Windows 2000, Active Directory client users can locate printers that are published in Active Directory and configure them for use with their computers.

To find and install a printer using Active Directory in Windows Server 2003, perform the procedure in Step by Step 6.7.

STEP BY STEP

6.7 Finding and installing a printer published in Active Directory

1. Click Start, and then select the Printers and Faxes folder.

2. In the Printers and Faxes folder, double-click Add a Printer to start the Add Printer Wizard. Click Next to continue.

3. On the Local or Network Printer window, select the Network Printer option button. Click Next to continue.

4. The Specify a Printer window appears. In this window, you have the choice of entering the printer name, browsing the network for a printer, or entering a Universal Resource Locator (URL) to connect to a printer on the Internet or your intranet. Select the Find a Printer in the Directory option button, and then click Next to continue.

5. The Find Printers window appears (see Figure 6.10). There are many search options available here to base a search on. The user can search for the printer by name, location, or model. Or by selecting the Features tab, you can search for specific features such as paper type, paper size, print resolution, and print speed; or whether the printer supports color. For an even more detailed search, select the Advanced tab and then click Field. This has additional options such as Asset Number, Input Trays, Supports Collation, and many others. The In field in the Find Printers window allows you to limit your search in Active Directory to either a specific domain or the entire Directory.

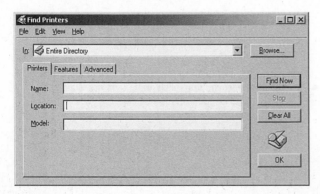

FIGURE 6.10 Find Printers, showing some of the features that a search command can locate.

6. Type "**Second Floor**" into the location and click Find Now to continue.

7. A list of printers that match the search criteria is returned. To examine the individual properties of the returned printers to make sure that they are suitable, right-click the printer name in the returned objects field and then select Properties from the pop-up menu.

8. The Printer Properties window appears. Verify that it is the correct printer and then click OK to close the window.

9. Make sure that the desired printer is highlighted and then click OK.

10. The Default Printer window appears. If you want this printer to be your default printer, click the Yes option button. Click Next to continue.

11. The Completing the Add Printer Wizard window appears. Check the options listed. If anything needs to be changed, click Back; otherwise, click Finish to end.

NOTE

Printer Location Tracking   A better method of searching for printers is via printer location tracking. Printer location tracking allows users to locate printers that are in close proximity to them. Enabling and configuring printer location tracking requires the creation and configuration of site and subnet objects, two topics that aren't covered on the 70-290 exam or in this book. For more information on printer location tracking, search for "Enabling printer location tracking" in the Windows Server 2003 online help, or see the Microsoft website at http://technet2.microsoft.com/WindowsServer/en/library/f33624bc-7518-4c2d-8f73-8a3d4571dae91033.mspx?mfr=true.

Printer Settings and Configurations

After you've installed a printer using the Add Printer Wizard, you can modify and change its settings to meet your specific needs. You can change a printer's configuration either from the print server itself or from any logical printer on any client connected to a printer share. In both cases, you must have sufficient access (Manage Printers) to manipulate the configuration of a printer.

You can make configuration changes using the multitabbed printer Properties dialog box. You can access this dialog box by opening the Printers folder, selecting a printer, and then issuing the File, Properties command from the menu bar (or by right-clicking the printer and selecting Properties from the pop-up menu). This brings up the Properties dialog box specific to this printer. Keep in mind that changing the settings on a client also changes the settings on the print server for that printer, so all clients using that printer share will have the same configuration settings applied to them.

The actual fields available on each tab of the printer Properties window vary by device.

General Tab

The General tab of the printer Properties dialog box (see Figure 6.11) enables you to do the following:

▶ Provide comments about the printer.

▶ Describe the physical location of the printer.

▶ Print a test document to investigate the current printer settings.

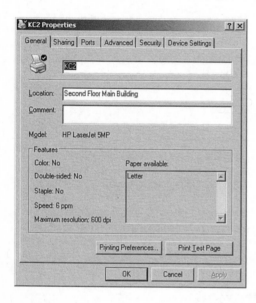

FIGURE 6.11 The General tab of the printer Properties dialog box showing the options that can be configured.

In Windows NT, the Comments and Locations fields were commonly ignored. However, in Windows Server 2003, it is essential to fill in these fields so that they can be used to locate the printer in the Active Directory. For more information, see the sections "Publishing a Printer in Active Directory" section earlier in this chapter.

Sharing Tab

The Sharing tab of the printer Properties dialog box (see Figure 6.12) enables you to do the following:

▶ Enable sharing of this printer.

▶ List in the Directory. This option publishes the printer in the Active Directory.

▶ Define the share name for the printer. Remember that if you want MS-DOS, Windows 3.x, Windows for Workgroups, and other non-LFN operating system clients to use this print share, the share name must be no longer than eight characters.

▶ Select the operating system type and version-specific print drivers to maintain on the print server for Point and Print capabilities support.

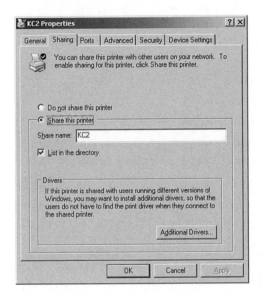

FIGURE 6.12   The Sharing tab of the printer Properties dialog box showing where to select the option to add additional drivers.

Ports Tab

The Ports tab of the printer Properties dialog box (see Figure 6.13) enables you to do the following:

▶ Define the communication port(s) used to send print jobs to the physical print device

▶ Add or remove specialty ports

▶ Configure ports

▶ Enable bidirectional communication support

▶ Enable printer pooling (see the "Printer Pooling" section in Chapter 7)

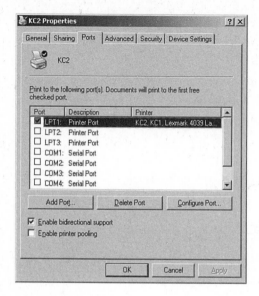

FIGURE 6.13 The Ports tab of the printer Properties dialog box showing where to add additional ports.

Advanced Tab

The Advanced tab of the printer Properties dialog box (see Figure 6.14) enables you to do the following:

▶ Set printer availability to Always available, or to a specific time range. Print jobs sent to the printer while it is unavailable are stored by the spooler and are printed when the printer becomes available.

▶ Set the processing priority for this logical printer from 1 (lowest) to 99 (highest). This feature is useful only when multiple logical printers serve a single printer. Granting high priority to one logical printer instructs the print server to print its documents before those of the lower-priority logical printers.

▶ Enable or disable spooling. When spooling is enabled, print jobs are stored to disk. This frees up the client quickly so it can perform other tasks while the print job is processing. When disabled, print jobs are sent directly to the printer. This situation suspends the client while it waits for the print job to complete.

▶ Set whether to begin printing only after the entire print job is spooled or as soon as possible.

▶ Hold mismatched documents. The print server can inspect each print job before it is sent to the print monitor to verify that the job has valid credentials, such as origin, printer destination, and data type. Invalid documents are not printed. Mismatched documents can cause printer errors that take a printer offline, requiring human intervention at the physical print device.

▶ Instruct the print server to give print priority to spooled documents over direct-to-printer documents. This feature is useful only when multiple logical printers serve a single printer.

▶ Retain print jobs in the spool after they have successfully printed. If your organization needs to keep track of all printed materials, this provides an electronic means to maintain a paper trail of print jobs.

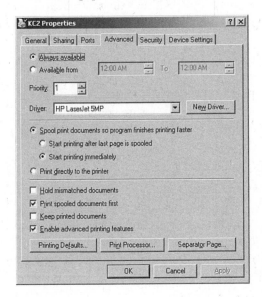

FIGURE 6.14 The Advanced tab of the printer Properties dialog box.

Security Tab

The Security tab of the printer Properties dialog box enables you to access permission, auditing, and ownership controls. Clicking the appropriate button on this tab reveals a topic-specific dialog box.

The Permissions section of the Security tab is where users and groups are granted access to use this logical printer. The types of access that can be assigned are as follows:

▶ *Print*—Users can send print jobs to the printer and can manage (pause, resume, restart, delete) their own print jobs in the print queue.

▶ *Manage Documents*—Users can send print jobs to the printer and can manage (pause, resume, restart, delete) any print job in the print queue.

▶ *Manage Printers*—Users can send print jobs to the printer, manage (pause, resume, restart, delete) any print job in the print queue, change printer settings, and alter access permissions.

▶ *Special Permissions*—Administrators can create custom permissions.

Device Settings Tab

Use the printer Properties dialog box Device Settings tab to configure device-specific settings, options, and features. This GUI interface grants you a Windows Server 2003–based control mechanism to all the printer capabilities usually accessed through a clunky LCD/LED multi-button control interface on the physical print device itself. You'll see common features such as memory settings, paper sizes, tray capabilities, support for envelope feeders, hardware-based fonts, graphical controls, and print density. Consult the printer's documentation for specifics about how to properly configure your printer using this GUI interface.

Managing Print Drivers

A print driver is a software element used to inform the print server or print client about the capabilities and limitations of a printer. It informs the print server how to communicate with the physical printer, and print clients how to format print jobs. It also serves as the interface between your programs and the print device.

The print driver is responsible for converting the commands from your computer into a format that the print device understands. Print drivers are usually unique to each device because printers vary widely in capabilities and features, such as different numbers of paper trays, duplex capabilities, fonts, and colors supported. A properly written print driver will display only those options that are present on the print device it was written for and will fully utilize those capabilities. In addition, when a printer is shared from a print server, you can select additional operating system version-specific and platform-specific print drivers to install on the server.

Point and Print is a term created by Microsoft to describe a collection of print features. Not all of these features require a print driver to be installed on the client; some allow the print server to host the print drivers. Windows Server 2000/2003, Windows XP, Windows 95, Windows 98, and Windows NT (3.1, 3.5, 3.51, and 4.0) all support Point and Print.

This technology allows the user to browse for printers either through Active directory or My Network Places. When the printer is located, the user right-clicks the printer entry and selects Connect from the pop-up menu, as shown in Figure 6.15. When a client that supports Point and Print uses the printer, the print server sends the appropriate print driver to the client. This enables the client to properly process the print job before actually submitting it to the print server.

Another benefit of this scheme is drag-and-drop printing. Even if a client does not have a logical printer defined for a printer share, a document can be dropped onto the printer share (as listed in a browse list from Network Neighborhood or Windows Explorer). This initiates the print driver exchange, and the document is printed.

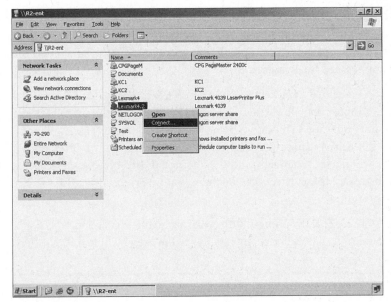

FIGURE 6.15 Connecting to a printer via My Network Places

Installing New or Upgraded Drivers

Installing new or upgraded drivers for existing printers is a snap. The Advanced tab (refer back to Figure 6.14) of the printer's Properties dialog box contains a New Driver button. The procedure to install new or upgraded drivers is listed in Step by Step 6.8.

STEP BY STEP

6.8 Installing new or upgraded printer drivers

1. Click Start, and then select the Printers and Faxes folder.

2. In the Printers and Faxes folder, right-click the printer that you want to update, and select Properties from the pop-up menu.

3. On the Properties dialog box, select the Advanced tab, and then click the New Driver button. This starts the Add Printer Driver Wizard. Click Next to continue.

4. The Printer Driver Selection window appears. Because these are new drivers, you'll need to point the dialog box to the location of the manufacturer-supplied drivers.

5. After selecting the new drivers, click OK, and then click the Next button.

6. When the Completing the Add Printer Driver Wizard dialog box appears, review your selection and then click the Finish button.

Adding Drivers for Other Operating Systems

By default, most of the printer drivers installed with Windows Server 2003 only are installed with support for Windows 2000 and later platforms. In some cases, support is included for older platforms, but it is not enabled by default.

In addition, not all the drivers included with Windows Server 2003, or those that are supplied with your printer, provide support for all clients. For example, most of the later Hewlett Packard drivers install support only for Windows XP and Windows Server 2003. By default, there is no support code in these drivers for older platforms such as Windows NT or Windows 9x. In these situations, you will need to manually add the additional drivers necessary to support these platforms. In most cases, these drivers can be found on the printer driver CD or can be downloaded from the Internet.

The Sharing tab (refer to Figure 6.12) of the printer's Properties dialog box contains an Additional Drivers button. The procedure to install additional drivers is listed in Step by Step 6.9.

STEP BY STEP

6.9 Adding drivers for other operating systems

1. Click Start, and then select the Printers and Faxes folder.

2. In the Printers and Faxes folder, right-click the printer that you want to update, and select Properties from the pop-up menu.

3. On the Properties dialog box, select the Sharing tab, and then click the Additional Drivers button.

4. The Additional Drivers window appears, as shown in Figure 6.16. This window shows which platforms the currently installed drivers support. Select the entry for Windows NT 4.0.

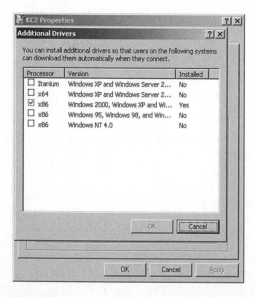

FIGURE 6.16 The Additional Drivers window allows you to select drivers for other platforms

5. After selecting the new drivers, click OK. You are returned to the printer Properties dialog box.

In this Step by Step, we selected a printer where the drivers for the older platform were already included in Windows Server 2003; they just weren't installed. In most cases, you will have to click the Have Disk button and browse to the location of the new drivers.

No matter whether you have upgraded drivers or added new ones, the Windows NT, 2000 and XP clients will automatically receive the new driver the next time that they connect to the print server. However, you will need to manually refresh the print drivers on Windows 95 and 98 clients. As a rule, print a test page to verify that everything worked out the way you planned after you switch drivers.

This print driver management scheme allows for a single repository of print drivers so that upgrading is quick and easy. This also reduces the complexity of connecting to network printer shares from a client perspective.

NOTE

Other Platforms   Print drivers must be manually installed and maintained on the client system for any Microsoft operating system that is pre-Windows NT and all non-Microsoft operating systems.

Chapter Summary

This chapter was devoted to a very important topic, both on the exam and in the field—printing. As a system administrator, you will spend a lot of your time planning for, configuring, and troubleshooting printers, and the exam reflects this.

In this chapter you learned the Microsoft terminology for printing and how the process flows. You also learned how to install printers, both local and network, and how to share printers so that others can use them.

We also looked at installing an updated driver, and briefly covered working with print clients from non-Windows environments.

Key Terms

▶ Logical printer

▶ Network-attached printer

▶ Print device

▶ Print driver

▶ Print share

Apply Your Knowledge

Exercises

6.1 Connecting to a shared printer

In this exercise, you will search Active directory and then use the Connect option to make a temporary connection to a shared printer. You can perform this exercise from your second Windows Server 2003 server or from a workstation computer.

Estimated Time: 10 minutes

1. Log on to your computer; then select Start, My Computer.

2. In the left pane of My Computer, double-click My Network Places.

3. In the left pane under Network Tasks, double-click Search Active Directory.

4. This opens the Find users, Contacts and Groups dialog box. Click the Find drop-down list and select Printers.

5. Enter **First Floor** in the location field, and then click the Find Now button.

6. The KC1 printer that you configured in a previous exercise should appear in the search results.

7. Right-click the entry for the KC1 printer and select Connect.

8. Open the Printers and Faxes folder by clicking Start, Printers and Faxes, and verify that an icon for the KC1 printer is present. If you have a physical printer connected, print a test page.

Exam Questions

1. You are the network administrator for FlyByNight Airlines. The network consists of a single Active Directory domain. The functional level of the domain is Windows 2000 native. All network servers run Windows Server 2003, and all client computers run Windows XP Professional.

   The network includes a printer named FlightPrinter123. Some of your users report that they are often unable to access this printer. You discover that the problem occurs whenever more than 10 users try to connect to it.

   You need to ensure that all appropriate users can access FlightPrinter123. What should you do?

   ○ **A.** Decrease the length of the printer name.

   ○ **B.** Raise the functional level of the domain to Windows Server 2003.

   ○ **C.** Purchase additional client access licenses.

   ○ **D.** Move FlightPrinter123 to one of the servers.

2. You are the network administrator for FlyByNight Airlines. The network consists of a single Active Directory domain. All network servers run Windows Server 2003, and all client computers run Windows 2000 Professional. You install Windows Server 2003 with default settings on a new computer named FBNSrv1. You install and share several printers on FBNSrv1. You instruct all users to connect to these printers by using the address http://FBNSrv1/Printers. However, users report that they cannot connect to this address. You need to ensure that all users can connect to the printers by using HTTP.

   Which two actions should you perform? (Each correct answer presents part of the solution. Choose two.)

   ○ **A.** Publish all shared printers that are installed on FBNSrv1.

   ○ **B.** Create a virtual directory named Printers on FBNSrv1.

   ○ **C.** Install IIS with default settings on FBNSrv1.

   ○ **D.** Reinstall all printers on FBNSrv1.

   ○ **E.** Install the Internet Printing component of IIS.

3. You are the network administrator for Troy, Inc. The network consists of a single Active Directory domain. All network servers run Windows Server 2003, and the client computers run a mix of Windows 2000 and Windows XP Professional.

   You set up a network-attached printer TroyPrnt1 and give it a static IP address. For some reason, users cannot attach to it. What should you do?

   ○ **A.** On your DNS server, add an alias (CNAME) record that references TroyPrnt1.

   ○ **B.** In the Hosts file on your DNS server, add a line that references TroyPrnt1.

   ○ **C.** On your DNS server, add a service locator (SRV) record that references TroyPrnt1.

   ○ **D.** On your DNS server, add a host (A) record that references TroyPrnt1.

4. You are the network administrator for Hasty, Inc. You just bought a couple of parallel-port connected Plug and Play computers for your office. You connect one of the printers to your Windows Server 2003 server and wait for the wizard to appear, but nothing happens. What should you do?

   ○ **A.** Reboot your server.

   ○ **B.** Try the other printer; this one isn't working.

   ○ **C.** Start the Add/Remove Hardware applet in the Control Panel.

   ○ **D.** Restart the printer.

5. You are the system administrator for a small company. Because it is a small company, you are hosting both the file and print roles on your only server.

   Your server is currently low on free space on the hard drive. Your boss needs to print a large print job, but you estimate the size of the job, and it could possibly fill up your hard drive. What should you do?

   ○ **A.** Set up a quota on the boss's account.

   ○ **B.** Disable print spooling.

   ○ **C.** Have your boss print after the other users have left for the day.

   ○ **D.** Enable printer pooling.

6. You are the network administrator for FlyByNight Airlines. The network consists of a single Active Directory domain. The functional level of the domain is Windows 2000 native. All network servers run Windows Server 2003, and all client computers run Windows XP Professional.

   The network includes a printer named FlightPrinter123. Some of your users report that when graphics-intensive print jobs are submitted to FlightPrinter123, the documents print slowly, pausing for several seconds after each page. What can you do to correct this problem using the least amount of administrative effort?

   ○ **A.** Add a second printer that prints to the same print device as FlightPrinter123.

   ○ **B.** Configure FlightPrinter123 to start printing after the last page is spooled.

   ○ **C.** Create a printer pool

   ○ **D.** Increase the priority of FlightPrinter123.

Answers to Exam Questions

1. **D.** Because the magic number is 10, it is most likely that the printer is shared on a Windows XP client. That would lead to a situation where the Windows XP client computer allows only up to 10 connections at the same time, resulting in users being unable to access FlightPrinter123 when the 10 connections are full. Moving the printer to a server computer will allow more concurrent connections. Because the domain doesn't have any Windows 9x clients, the length of the printer name isn't a problem. Because this is obviously a connectivity issue, the functional level of the domain is not the cause of the problem. Because the licensing service doesn't block connections, this is not a CAL problem. See "Print Servers."

2. **C and E.** The Internet Printing Protocol (IPP) allows any supported client (Windows 95 and later) to print to a Windows Server 2003 server via the Internet browser. Internet Information Services (IIS) and IPP must be installed on the Windows Server 2003 server, neither of which is installed by default. See "Print Clients in Windows Server 2003."

3. **D.** The clients' printer software needs to know the IP address of the printer. Because the IP address was assigned manually, it was not automatically registered in DNS, as it would be if it were assigned via DHCP. To correct the problem, you can enter a host (A) record in the DNS zone. An A record maps a hostname to an IP address. An alias (CNAME) can only point to an A record. Best practice states that you should always use DNS, not a host's file. SRV records are used for computers providing a service, such as a domain controller, for example. See "Network-Attached Printers."

4. **A.** Reboot your server. Unlike USB- or FireWire-connected devices, the server must be rebooted for a parallel port–connected Plug and Play device to be recognized by Windows Server 2003. It's doubtful that the printer is broken; restarting it won't change anything, and there is not an Add/Remove Hardware applet in the Control Panel in Windows Server 2003. It is now named Add Hardware. See "Plug and Play Printers."

5. **B.** Because you are low on hard drive space, the only reasonable answer is to disable spooling. When spooling is enabled, print jobs are stored to disk. See "Advanced Tab."

6. **B.** If the printer is pausing between pages, it's most likely because the job isn't being spooled to disk. The print job is running directly from the computer, and the pause is the printer waiting for the next page to be generated. It's usually more efficient for the print job to be run from the spooler; this prevents having the printer wait for the pages to be rendered. Adding another printer, setting up a printer pool, or increasing the priority of the printer wouldn't solve the problem because the problem is the slow flow of data to the printer. See "The Windows Server 2003 Print Architecture."

Suggested Readings and Resources

1. Boswell, William. *Inside Windows Server 2003*. New Riders, 2003. ISBN 0735711585.

2. Canon: http://www.usa.canon.com

3. Hewlett Packard: http://www.hp.com

4. Lexmark: http://lexmark.com

5. Minasi, Mark, et al. *Mastering Windows Server 2003*. Sybex, 2003. ISBN 0782141307.

6. Windows Server 2003 Deployment Guide. Microsoft Corporation. http://technet2.microsoft.com/WindowsServer/en/Library/c283b699-6124-4c3a-87ef-865443d7ea4b1033.mspx?mfr=true.

7. *Windows Server 2003 Resource Kit*. Microsoft Press, 2005. ISBN 0735614717.

CHAPTER SEVEN

Managing Printing

Objectives

This chapter covers the following Microsoft-specified objectives for the "Managing and Maintaining a Server Environment" section of the Managing and Maintaining a Microsoft Windows Server 2003 Environment exam:

Troubleshoot print queues

▶ When working in a Windows Server 2003 environment, it is important that you have a thorough understanding of troubleshooting print problems. Printing is one of the major roles of a Windows Server 2003 server.

Monitor file and print servers. Tools might include Task Manager, Event Viewer, and System Monitor.

▶ **Monitor print queues**

▶ The purpose of this objective is to teach you how to monitor print usage using the various tools available in Windows Server 2003.

Outline

Study Strategies

▶ In studying this section, be sure to practice all the activities described. Become very familiar with the Print Management Console, how it is installed, and its capabilities and limitations.

▶ To perform the exercises in this chapter, it's not essential that you have a physical printer attached to your server. Most of the exercises will work fine because they're tied to the logical printer configuration. Just remember not to attempt to print any test pages!

▶ Pay particular attention to managing access to printers through the use of permissions and groups.

▶ It would seem that because Microsoft dedicated only two objectives to the print process, it might be lightly covered on the exam. However, this is far from the case. Historically, printing has been heavily emphasized on the Microsoft exams, and it is an essential part of your duties as a system administrator.

Introduction

In the previous chapter, we discussed how printing is accomplished in Windows Server 2003. We also looked at the terminology involved and how to implement printing in the Windows environment.

However, implementation is just part of the job. After printers are set up on the network they need to be managed. Users need to be assigned permissions, special printers and printing procedures need to be worked out, and the administrator needs to be able to figure out what's going on when printing doesn't work.

Printing with Windows Server 2003

This chapter continues our examination of the Windows Server 2003 printing system and covers printer management, permissions, advanced configuration, and troubleshooting.

Working with the Print Spooler

In the previous chapter, we defined and discussed most of the different parts of the printing process. In addition, we worked with installing and configuring print drivers and print devices.

The intermediate link between the print driver and the print device is the *print spool*, which is also known as the *spool file*. It's a file on the print server that contains the data to be printed. This file contains the print data and the print device–specific commands needed to format the printed output. Most print jobs do not go directly to the print device, especially on a print device that is heavily used. Because a print device usually prints slower than the print job can be processed, the file is stored in the spool file so that the user can continue on with his or her work while the print server manages the print job. This has additional benefits. Printers, being mechanical devices, tend to jam and run out of paper. Because the print job is stored in a file, it can be resumed when the print device is repaired. In addition, the print job can be restarted, if some of the pages were damaged or lost.

The content of the spool file is referred to as the *print queue*. Users have the ability to view the print queue, using the Print Manager applet. Users can hold or cancel their own print jobs, or the print jobs of other users if they are granted the appropriate permissions. After the print device finishes printing the job, the print job is deleted.

> **NOTE**
>
> **Save Print jobs**   Windows Server 2003 has an option to save all print jobs on the hard drive of the print server. Use this option only if required by your company, because it can fill a hard drive very quickly.

The print spooler is part of the operating system and runs as the Print Spooler service. The print spooler manages the print queues for all local or network printers that are managed by the server. By default, the spool file is located at `%systemroot%\System32\Spool\Printers`.

As you might have noticed, this is on the system drive. In environments where a large number of printers are hosted on the server, this may impact performance because there will be a large number of files written to and read from the spool file, in addition to the constant accessing of the operating system files.

In this situation, it's best to move the spool file to another volume, preferably one that's attached to a different controller. To move the spool file, use the procedure in Step by Step 7.1.

STEP BY STEP

7.1 Relocating the spool file

1. From the Start menu, click Start, Printers and Faxes.

2. In the left pane of the Printers and Faxes window, under Printer Tasks, click Server Properties. This opens the Print Server Properties dialog box, as shown in Figure 7.1.

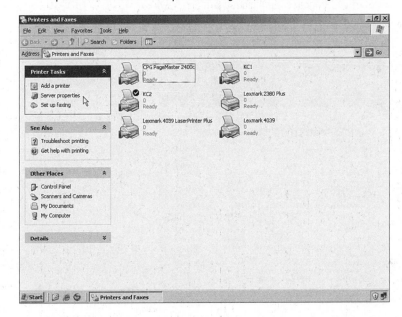

FIGURE 7.1 Click Server Properties, where you can choose settings for the print server.

3. On the Print Server Properties dialog box, select the Advanced tab, as shown in Figure 7.2.

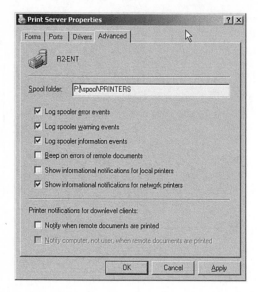

FIGURE 7.2   Enter the new location for the spool folder.

4. In the Spool Folder field, enter the new destination for the spool files. Click OK when finished.

5. From the Start Menu, click Start, All Programs, Administrative Tools, Services.

6. In the Services MMC, as shown in Figure 7.3, highlight the Print Spooler entry, and then click Restart.

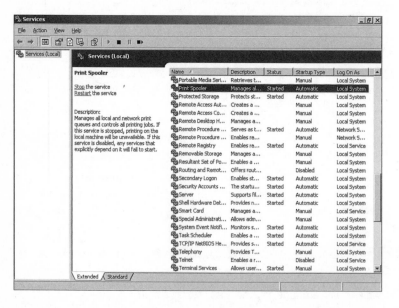

FIGURE 7.3   Restart the Print Spooler service to complete the spooler relocation process.

7. After the service is restarted, close the MMC.

On servers that have been assigned to be print servers, you will want to relocate the spool file for the following reasons:

▶ *Performance*—As mentioned earlier, isolating the spool file from the disk where the operating system files are located will increase performance because both functions are disk intensive. In addition, because the spool file is constantly being created and delet-ed, the disk will become fragmented pretty quickly. This can negatively affect the oper-ation of both the operating system and the print process.

▶ *Disk space issues*—Print jobs can get quite large, especially those with lots of graphics. This can cause a problem if the spool file fills up the free space on the operating sys-tem drive, because the page file needs write space. If the page file is unable to write to the disk, the operating system may become unstable.

▶ *Disk quotas*—By setting a disk quota at the user group or folder (R2 and later) level, you can limit the amount of space to be used so that no single user or group can fill up all the space on the server. When this happens, other users are prevented from printing until some of the print jobs have finished, releasing some space on the server.

▶ *Security*—If the print jobs are to be saved, it is easier and more secure to configure security on a drive where you don't have to worry about inherited permissions.

A separate set of spool files are generated for each print job. After the job has completed suc-cessfully, the spool files will be deleted from the spool folder. Each print job consists of two files:

▶ *Spool file*—This is the file that contains the information to be printed, such as text, graphics, and formatting information.

▶ *Shadow file*—The shadow file has the extension .shd and is used to store administration information about the print job, such as position in the print queue, job owner, docu-ment name, and so on.

Large print jobs can generate a significant impact on the network and print server loads. The print spooler files on a Windows Server 2003 print server can be relocated to a dedicated hard disk if these loads are going to be high. For more information about how to do this, see KB article 314105, "How to Move the Windows Default Paging File and Print Spooler to a Different Hard Disk," at http://support.microsoft.com/?kbid=314105. If network perform-ance is an issue, consider directly connecting the print device to the server, because this will reduce the impact on the server from printing to approximately half; the print job from the server will be passed over the parallel or USB bus rather than the network.

Assigning Print Permissions

Like any Windows resource, the printing environment in Windows Server 2003 is highly secure and configurable. Access to printer objects is controlled in the same manner as access to objects such as files and folders—they are defined on a user and group basis. For printer objects, three basic roles are granted the permissions shown in Table 7.1. These permissions allow users who are assigned these predefined roles to print, manage documents, or manage printers.

TABLE 7.1   Printer-Specific Permissions

Permission	Print	Manage Documents	Manage Printer
Print documents	X	X	X
Pause, restart, and cancel own documents	X	X	X
Connect to a printer	X	X	X
Control job settings for all documents		X	X
Pause, restart, and cancel all documents		X	X
Share a printer			X
Change printer properties			X
Delete printers			X
Change printer permissions			X

The permissions are broken down by the default groups that are granted the predefined roles, as shown in Table 7.2.

TABLE 7.2 Group-Specific Roles

Group	Print	Manage Documents	Manage Printer
Administrators	X	X	X
Creator Owner		X	
Everyone	X		
Power Users	X	X	X
Print Operators	X	X	X
Server Operators	X	X	X

The previous two tables outline the default permissions and roles. However, these can be changed to provide more granularity. While you will find that in most situations, the standard permissions will suffice, there will be specific circumstances where limiting access to printers is necessary.

For example, access to printers that print payroll checks, or to specialized photo or high-resolution color printers, should be limited to a select group of users both for security reasons and because of the cost per page compared to other printers.

As you can see in Table 7.1, when a shared printer is installed, by default all users are able to print to it. In Step by Step 7.2, we will change the permissions of a shared printer to remove the default access and grant access to a specific group.

STEP BY STEP

7.2 Changing shared printer permissions

1. From the Start menu, click Start, Printers and Faxes.

2. On the Printer Properties dialog box, select the Security tab, as shown in Figure 7.4.

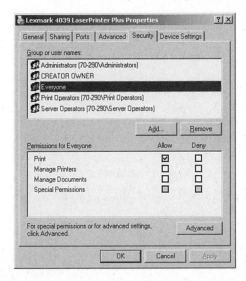

FIGURE 7.4 Permissions for shared printers can be managed on the Security tab.

3. Highlight the Everyone entry, and click the Remove Button.

4. Click the Add button. From the Select Users, Computers, or Groups dialog box shown in Figure 7.5, enter the Engineers group. (This group was created in a previous chapter.)

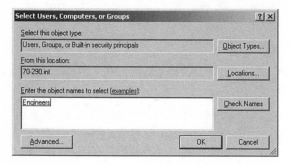

FIGURE 7.5 Enter the user and/or group to grant print permissions to.

5. Click OK to return to the printer Properties dialog box. By default, the Engineers group is granted the Print permission. Click OK again to save.

Print Job Management

You can manage print jobs through the Print Queue window. Each logical printer has its own print queue that can be accessed by double-clicking its icon in the Printers folder.

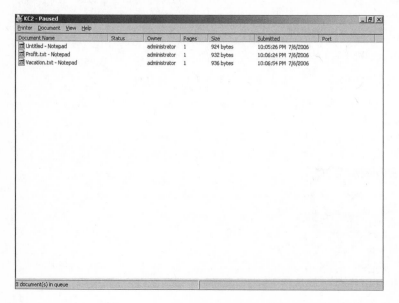

FIGURE 7.6 The Print Queue window, showing paused print jobs.

You can manage documents by selecting one or more documents in the queue and then issuing one of the following commands from the Document menu:

▶ *Pause*—This command prevents the selected document(s) from being printed; the document(s) is retained in the queue.

▶ *Resume*—This command releases the selected document(s) so it prints normally.

▶ *Restart*—This command stops the current print processing of the selected document(s) and starts the process over.

▶ *Cancel*—This command removes the selected document(s) from the print queue.

▶ *Properties*—This command displays the properties for the selected document(s).

Keep in mind that the documents you can manage depend on your access level. If you have only Print access to the printer, you can manage only your own documents. If you have Manage Documents or Manage Printers access to the printer, you can manage any print job in the queue.

If you have Manage Documents or Manage Printers access to a printer, you also can use the commands from the Printer menu of the Print Queue window. These commands include the following:

▶ *Pause Printing*—This halts the printing process for all print jobs in the queue. Any data in the physical printer's buffer continues to print, but no new data is sent from the print server.

▶ *Set as Default Printer*—This sets the current logical printer as the default printer for all print applications on this client.

▶ *Document Defaults*—This opens the Default Document Properties dialog box. The Page Setup tab of this dialog box is used to define the association of paper type to trays, the number of copies to print, and whether to print in portrait or landscape mode. The Advanced tab displays the same controls discussed previously for the Device Settings tab of the printer Properties dialog box.

▶ *Sharing*—This accesses the Sharing tab of the printer Properties dialog box, as previously discussed.

▶ *Purge Print Documents*—This removes all documents in the print queue.

▶ *Properties*—This opens the printer Properties dialog box (previously discussed and accessed directly from the Printers folder).

As we saw earlier in this section, you can also use printer permissions to delegate management of the printers and the print jobs to other users, without having to add them to other groups that would grant them more permissions than you want them to have. This will free you as the system administrator for other tasks.

Printer Pooling

Printer pooling is a form of load balancing in that two or more print devices are represented by a single printer. The users send their print jobs to what looks like a single printer. The print server then queues the print jobs in the order they were submitted. When a print device finishes a print job, it receives the next job in the queue.

For example, suppose that the accountant is printing a year-end summary report. Typically, these types of reports can be very detailed and take a long time to print. Unfortunately, several other users also have print jobs that need to be completed, and they have already submitted these jobs to the same printer as the year-end summary report. Normally, if the other users needed to get their print jobs completed in a reasonable amount of time, they would have to cancel the jobs they sent to the first printer, then resubmit them to another printer. However, with printer pooling, while one printer is tied up with the year-end summary report, the other print jobs are automatically routed to other available printers in the pool.

Printer pooling is a very efficient way to print because it balances the load. You never have multiple jobs waiting for a specific printer while another printer is idle.

For printer pooling to work successfully, the following conditions must be met:

▶ The printers must use the same print driver. They don't all have to be the same exact model, as long as they give the same results using a common printer driver.

▶ They must all be configured on the same print server because they have to share the same driver and print queue. They can be either locally or network attached.

▶ They should be located in close proximity to each other. The user has no way of knowing which printer the print job ended up on, so it's best to have them all in the same room.

To configure a printer pool, use the procedure outlined in Step by Step 7.3.

STEP BY STEP

7.3 Configuring a printer pool

1. From the Start menu, click Start, Printers and Faxes.

2. In the left pane of the Printers and Faxes window, under Printer Tasks, click Add a Printer. This starts the Add Printer Wizard. Follow the procedure in the previous chapter to install the appropriate printer device, if it's not already present.

3. In the Printers and Faxes window, right-click the printer you want to set up in a pool and select Properties from the pop-up menu.

4. In the Printer Properties dialog box, select the Ports tab, as shown in Figure 7.7

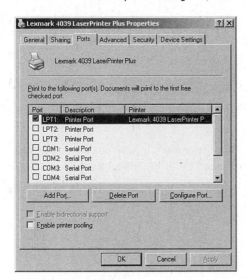

FIGURE 7.7 The Ports tab allows you to select the ports that the printers for your pool are connected to.

5. Select the Enable Printer Pooling check box and then select the desired ports. Click OK when you're finished.

After the procedure has been completed, if you look at the Ports tab, you will see that several ports have the identical printer name assigned to them, as shown in Figure 7.8.

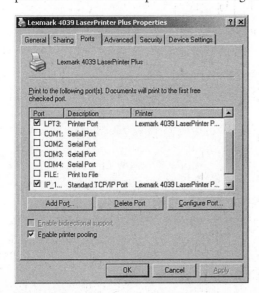

FIGURE 7.8 The Ports tab showing the completed configuration.

As you can see in Figure 7.8, the ports can be of different types; the only limitation is that the same driver must be used for all printers.

The advantage of printer pooling is that users don't have to figure out which printer is available, so they can get their print job out quickly. This is all handled automatically by the server.

Scheduling Printer Availability

In the previous section, we examined how to use one logical printer to represent several physical print devices. However, we can do just the opposite—we can set up several logical printers to represent one physical print device.

You can set up several logical printers, each with slightly different configurations (but using the same print driver). For example, take a look at the Advanced tab of the printer Properties dialog box shown in Figure 7.9.

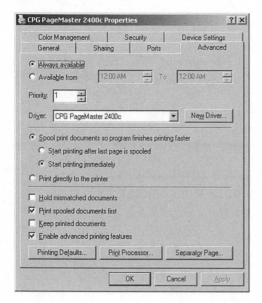

FIGURE 7.9 The printer Properties dialog box's Advanced tab.

The first area is the Always Available and Available From option buttons. The default is for the printer to always be available. However, suppose the Accounting department has a weekly job that prints a 500-page report. Unless you have a very fast printer, you wouldn't want to print that during normal business hours because no one else would be able to print. Although you could pause this large job and enable it after the other jobs have finished, that isn't easy, and can become tiresome when there are lots of print jobs to manage. There's a much easier way to accomplish this.

For example, you could create an additional logical printer and name it After Hours. The Advanced tab of the Printer Properties dialog box for the After Hours printer might say that it is available only from 6:00 p.m. to 6:00 a.m. Then, whenever users need to print a huge print job, they would print to the After Hours logical print device. The job would sit in the print queue for that logical device until 6:00 p.m., and then start printing when everyone has gone home.

To schedule printer availability, use the procedure outlined in Step by Step 7.4.

STEP BY STEP

7.4 Scheduling printer availability

1. From the Start menu, click Start, Printers and Faxes.

2. On the Printer Properties dialog box, select the Security tab, as shown in Figure 7.9.

3. Click the Available From option button and configure the time fields to reflect a 6:00PM to 6:00AM time window.

4. Click the OK button when you're finished.

Although this sounds great in theory, as the system administrator you must use a combination of user education and printer permissions to make it work. You will need to educate users about which printers are available 24 hours, which ones are not, and why. After instructing them to use the after hours printers for all large print jobs, make it a habit to cancel any large jobs that are sent to other printers. In addition, starting with Windows Server 2003 version R2, you have the ability to set disk quotas at the folder level. This allows you to limit the size of jobs that a user or group can send to a logical printer by setting a quota for these users on the folder that the spool file is located in.

Another idea is to make the scheduled printers easily identifiable by giving them recognizable names such as After Hours, Big Jobs, and so on. In addition, make liberal use of comments in the comments field for the printers. You can also use printer permissions to deny access to printers for users who should always print their jobs after hours. Conversely, those users who never print large jobs should be denied access to the after hours printers so that they inadvertently don't send a print job to them.

NOTE

Disk Space Make sure that the server that holds the print queue for the After Hours printer has a lot of free space, because several large print jobs could possibly remain on the disk until after hours.

Setting Printer Priority

Another way of controlling the precedence of print jobs is via Printer Priority. Priority is used to set the default importance of the print jobs in the queue. Priority can be set from 1 to 99. The job assigned the higher numerical number is printed first. For example, suppose you have a department with 30 employees and 2 managers. The managers believe that their print jobs should be printed before the employee print jobs. In this case, you would create two logical printers, one for the managers and one for the employees. The managers' printer would have a priority of 99, whereas the employees' printer could be left at 1.

With this configuration, any job sent to the managers' logical printer would be placed in the queue and print before any job sent to the employees' logical printer. The employees' print jobs would be processed only after the managers' jobs are completed.

To configure a second logical printer with a different priority, follow the procedure in Step by Step 7.5.

STEP BY STEP

7.5 Setting printer priority

1. From the Start menu, click Start, Printers and Faxes.

2. In the Printers and Faxes window, click Add a Printer and use the Add Printer Wizard to install a second instance of one of the printers that you already have installed. Name it Managers.

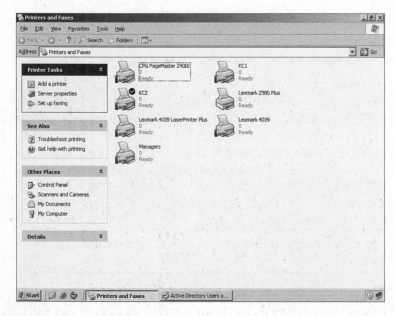

FIGURE 7.10 Name the new logical printer Managers.

3. Right-click the printer you just created and select Properties from the pop-up menu.

4. In the Printer Properties dialog box, select the Advanced tab. Change the Priority setting to 99, as shown in Figure 7.11.

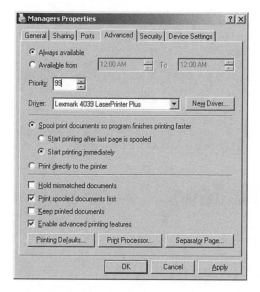

FIGURE 7.11   Set the Priority to 99.

5. Click the OK button to save.

In the previous section, we outlined the default permissions and roles. However, these can be changed to provide more granularity. For example, let's configure a logical printer for the managers group referred to in the previous example.

Challenge

On the surface, setting different print priorities for different logical devices sounds like a great idea. However, what's to stop some devious employee from trying to print using the managers' logical printer?

What steps would you take to configure a logical printer that grants a higher priority to print jobs submitted by managers, but also prevents common users from printing to it?

Try to complete this exercise on your own, listing your conclusions on a sheet of paper. After you have completed the exercise, compare your results to those given here.

1. From the Start menu, click Start, Printers and Faxes.

2. In the Printers and Faxes window, right-click the printer you want to configure and select Properties from the pop-up menu.

(continues)

(continued)

3. In the Printer Properties dialog box, select the Advanced tab. Change the Priority setting to 99.

4. Select the Security tab. Click the Add button to open the Select Users or Groups dialog box. Enter the Managers and Employees groups. Click OK.

5. From the Security tab of the Managers print object's Properties dialog box, highlight the Employees group and select Deny for all entries. If desired, you can add the Manage Printers and Documents roles to the Managers group.

6. Click OK when you're finished.

This works unless the managers are also members of the Employees group. Review the rules on Deny Access from Chapter 4, "Managing and Maintaining Access to Resources."

Managing Printing in Windows Server 2003 R2

As we've previously mentioned, printing is a function that doesn't seem to ever go away. The concept of the paperless office seems even further away now than it did 10 years ago! If anything, the printers have become more full-featured, and more complicated for the system administrator to manage.

For those who have worked with printing in the previous versions of Windows, not much has changed over the years, until recently.

As we mentioned in the overview in Chapter 1, "Windows Server 2003 Environment," the R2 release of Windows Server 2003 includes the Print Management Console (PMC). The PMC allows the system administrator to manage all the printers on the network from a single console. This includes printers in the local office or on the other side of the world!

Installing the Print Management Console

The Print Management Console is an updated Microsoft Management Console (MMC) snap-in that you can use to view and manage printers and print servers in your organization. You can use Print Management from any computer running Windows Server 2003 R2 or later, and you can manage all network printers on print servers running Windows 2000 Server, Windows Server 2003, or Windows Server 2003 R2.

The Print Management Console is not installed by default. It must be manually installed after your initial installation of Windows Server 2003 R2. In addition, the schema additions for R2 must be installed to support the new "Fast Query" lookup via LDAP in Active Directory.

> **NOTE**
>
> **Updating the Schema** The procedure to update the schema for R2 is covered on the Microsoft TechNet website in the article "Steps for Extending the Schema" at http://technet2.microsoft.com/WindowsServer/ en/library/509ada1a-9fdc-45c1-8739-20085b20797b1033.mspx?mfr=true.

After the schema is updated, you can install the PMC in either of two ways, depending on what role you want your server to have:

▶ *Print server*—Install from the Manage Your Server screen. This sets up your server to not only include the PMC, but optimizes it for the print server role.

▶ *Management console*—If you want to manage the print servers only from your server, open Add/Remove Programs in Control Panel and insert the Windows Server 2003 R2 CD2 and select Add/Remove Windows Components. You can also insert the Windows Server 2003 R2, and select Install Optional Windows Components from the opening splash screen.

> **NOTE**
>
> **R2 Only** Although the domain can still be Windows 2000 or Windows Server 2003 without R2, the server the PMC is installed on must be R2 or later.

To install the Print Management console on a Windows Server 2003 server, follow the procedure in Step by Step 7.6.

STEP BY STEP

7.6 Installing the Print Management Console

1. From the Start menu, click Start, Control Panel, Add or Remove Programs.

2. In the Add or Remove Programs window, as shown in Figure 7.12, click Add/Remove Windows Components.

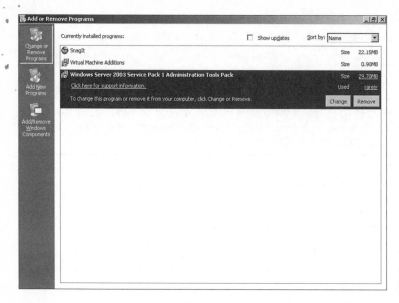

FIGURE 7.12 Installing Windows components.

3. This starts the Windows Components Wizard, as shown in Figure 7.13. From the Windows Components dialog box, select the check box for Management and Monitoring tools, and then click the Details button.

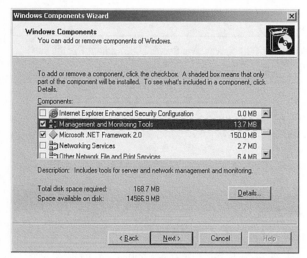

FIGURE 7.13 Select the Management and Monitoring Tools component.

4. In the Management and Monitoring Tools dialog box, select the Print Management Component subcomponent, as shown in Figure 7.14. Click OK to return to the wizard.

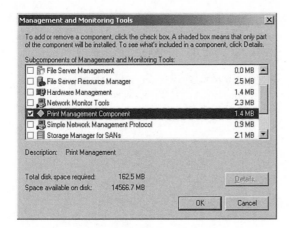

FIGURE 7.14 Select the Print Management Component.

5. On the Windows Components dialog box, click the Next button to continue.

6. When prompted, insert the requested Windows Server 2003 R2 CDs. (You will need both CD1 and CD2.)

7. The necessary files are loaded. When completed, click the Finish button.

After the PMC is installed, it can be opened by selecting the Printer Management icon in the Administrative Tools folder, as shown in Figure 7.15.

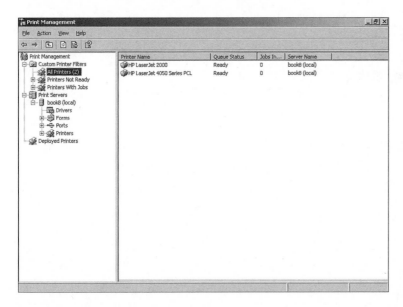

FIGURE 7.15 The Print Management console.

As you can see in the figure, the printers that were already installed on the local server (Book8) were automatically added to the console. Now that we have the PMC installed, we can add any printers found on your local subnet, or import an existing print server.

To scan the local subnet for shared printers, follow the procedure in Step by Step 7.7.

STEP BY STEP

7.7 Scanning the local subnet for printers

1. From the Start menu, click Start, Control Panel, Administrative Tools, Print Management.

2. In the Print Management MMC, right-click the local server and select Automatically Add Network Printers from the pop-up menu.

3. This opens the Automatically Add Network Printers dialog box, as shown in Figure 7.16. Click the Start button to begin the scan.

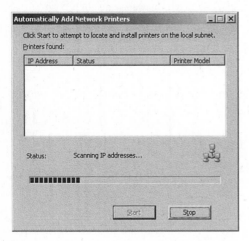

FIGURE 7.16 The PMC allows you to scan the local subnet for printers and automatically add them to the console.

4. When the Process is Complete status is displayed, click the Close button.

5. Any additional printers found will be displayed in the Print Management console.

As you saw in the Step by Step, when the subnet is scanned, the information gathered will be used to automatically install the necessary printer drivers, create the print queues, and share the printers. In those cases where the required driver wasn't included with Windows Server 2003, you will be prompted for the location of the driver.

If you have existing print servers in your organization, the printers connected to them can be centrally managed from the PMC. This includes not only printers on your local subnet, but printers anywhere in your organization, even in remote locations.

These printers are added to the PMC by importing the printer configuration information from the existing print servers on your network.

To import your existing print servers, follow the procedure in Step by Step 7.8.

STEP BY STEP

7.8 Importing print servers

1. From the Start menu, click Start, Control Panel, Administrative Tools, Print Management.

2. In the Print Management MMC, right-click the Print Servers entry in the left pane and select Add/Remove Servers from the pop-up menu.

3. This opens the Automatically Add/Remove Servers dialog box, as shown in Figure 7.17.

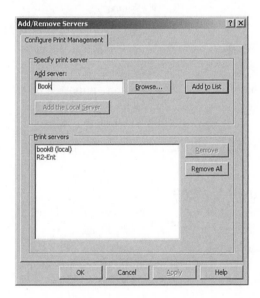

FIGURE 7.17 The Add/Remove Servers dialog box allows you to enter existing print servers by name, IP address, or by browsing the network.

4. Enter the print server that you want to add, and then click the Add to List button to add it to the list of print servers.

5. Repeat for any additional print servers, and then click the OK button to save.

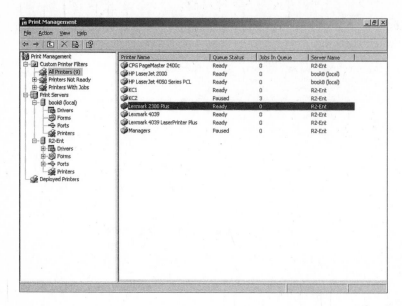

FIGURE 7.18 All the printers in your organization can be managed from a central console.

As you can see in Figure 7.18, all printers from the local print server and any imported print servers are shown in the console. From here their print queues can be monitored and managed, their drivers updated, and their default forms specified. Basically any task that you could do from each individual print server, you can now do from one console for all printers in your organization.

Adding Drivers via the Printer Management Console

Other than managing print queues, one of the most common tasks a system administrator has to perform in the printing arena is updating and/or adding print drivers. Drivers are commonly updated to add new functionality or to correct problems in the driver code. The PMC makes this easy because the drivers can be updated from a central location. To see how easy it is to add additional print drivers, follow the procedure in Step by Step 7.9.

STEP BY STEP

7.9 Adding print drivers

1. From the Start menu, click Start, Control Panel, Administrative Tools, Print Management.

2. In the Print Management MMC, click the Print Servers entry in the left pane, and then select the print server that you want to install the new drivers on.

3. Right-click the Drivers entry and select Add Driver from the pop-up menu.

4. From the Processor and Operating System Selection dialog box shown in Figure 7.19, select the operating systems of all computers that will be using the printer. Click Next.

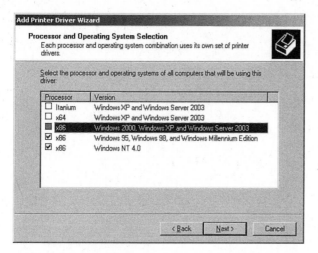

FIGURE 7.19 Select the Operating Systems that the clients will be using.

5. The Printer Driver Selection dialog box appears, as shown in Figure 7.20. Click the Have Disk button.

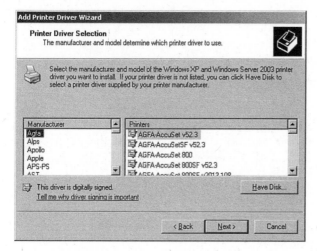

FIGURE 7.20 Click the Have Disk button to install updated drivers.

6. When the Install from Disk dialog box appears, browse to the location of the updated drivers, and then click OK.

7. When the Completing the Add Printer Driver Wizard screen appears, click the Finish button. The new drivers will be installed, as shown in Figure 7.21.

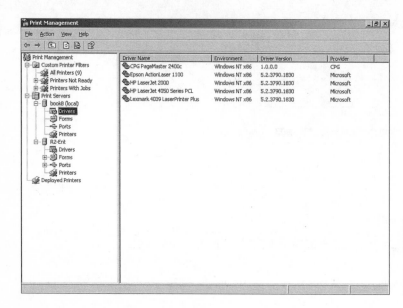

FIGURE 7.21 The Print Management Console, showing the installed drivers, the operating systems supported, and the version numbers.

Using Printer Filters

Although the Print Management console provides a centralized view of all the printers in your organization, if your organization is very large, this might be too much of a good thing. For example, if you need to check on the status of a printer in Cleveland, it might be difficult to find it if there's 2,000 printers listed in the console.

Fortunately, Microsoft has taken situations such as this into consideration in the design of the PMC and provided the Printer Filters feature. As you can see in Figure 7.22, there are three preconfigured printer filters:

- ▶ *All Printers*—This list contains all printers in your organization.

- ▶ *Printers Not Ready*—This list shows any printer with a not ready condition because of error, being paused, out of paper, and so on.

- ▶ *Printers with Jobs*—This list shows all printers with print jobs currently in their print queues.

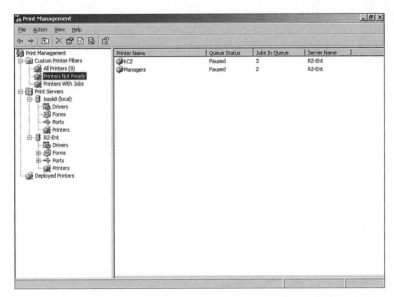

FIGURE 7.22 The Print Management Console, showing the standard custom printer filters.

Printer Filters can be used to group your printers according to various criteria, so that they can be found and managed easily. You can create a filter using the following properties:

- ▶ Printer Name
- ▶ Queue Status
- ▶ Jobs in Queue
- ▶ Server Name
- ▶ Comments
- ▶ Driver Name
- ▶ Is Shared
- ▶ Location
- ▶ Share Name

In the situation that we mentioned previously, we want to identify a printer by location. Follow the procedure in Step by Step 7.10 to add a custom filter to identify the printers in Cleveland.

STEP BY STEP

7.10 Adding a custom printer filter

1. From the Start menu, click Start, Control Panel, Administrative Tools, Print Management.

2. In the Print Management MMC, right-click the Custom Printer Filters entry in the left pane, and select Add New Printer Filter from the pop-up menu.

3. This starts the New Printer Filter Wizard. On the first screen, shown in Figure 7.23, enter the name of the filter, and select the option to display the number of printers. Click Next.

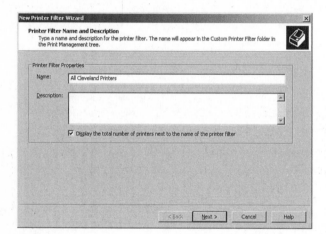

FIGURE 7.23   Enter a name and description for the custom filter.

4. From the Define a Printer Filter dialog box shown in Figure 7.24, select the conditions for the filter. Click Next.

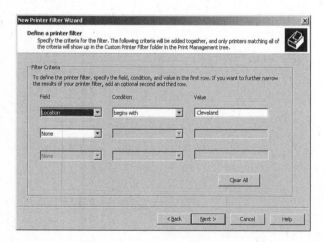

FIGURE 7.24   Select the filter conditions from the drop-down lists. You can select multiple conditions to narrow your results.

5. On the Set Notifications screen, you have the option to send and email or run a script when your condition is satisfied. This isn't necessary in our situation, so click the Finish button.

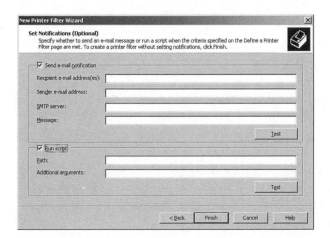

FIGURE 7.25 You can optionally send a notification email or run a script.

After the rule is in place, right-click it and select Refresh from the pop-up menu. The filtered printers will be listed, as shown in Figure 7.26.

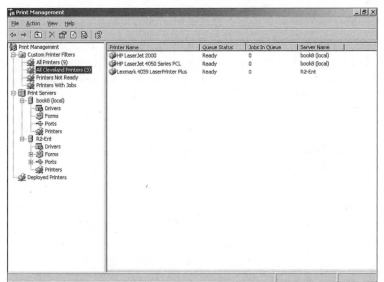

FIGURE 7.26 Filtered View showing printers by location.

The nice thing about filters is that they are dynamic—whenever a printer satisfies the configured conditions, it is automatically added, or removed when the condition is no longer satisfied. This means that the system administrator has to create the filters only once, and they will be automatically updated.

NOTE

Deploying Printers Using Group Policy Sharp observers will notice that the bottom node in the PMC is titled "Deployed Printers." One of the features in the PMC is the capability to deploy printers via Group Policy. We will discuss various GPO scenarios in Chapter 10, "Managing the User Environment by Using Group Policy."

With the new Print Management console, administrators have a single interface for managing all the printers connected to all the print servers within an organization. Through PMC, administrators can monitor printer errors, deploy printer connections to clients, and automatically find and install printers on a local branch office subnet.

Troubleshooting Printing Problems

Objective:

Troubleshoot print queues

Troubleshooting problems with the Windows Server 2003 print system is a straightforward endeavor. Problems can occur in one or more of the following six areas:

▶ *The physical print device*—The printer itself can experience problems including paper jams, paper feed problems, ink depletion, toner cartridge malfunction, power surges, or failed memory/control chips. In most cases, clearing out the paper, replacing print cartridges, and cycling the power restores the printer to operation. If not, consult the printer's manual for additional troubleshooting steps before calling a repair technician.

One of the most common problems is a simple oversight of making sure the printer is online. Some printers must be manually enabled to receive print jobs; others automatically switch into online mode after their power-on self-test. If you've changed or manipulated the default settings of the printer, you might want to issue a memory/setting reset to return the printer to its factory defaults.

▶ *The print driver*—The most common driver-failure problem occurs when a disk becomes highly fragmented or a virus infection causes a corruption in a driver file. In most cases, reinstalling or replacing the driver resolves the issue. In rarer cases, updating Windows Server 2003 might change print driver–dependent DLL files. In these cases, you need to obtain newer driver files that have been tested with the new service pack from the manufacturer. In some cases, the problem can be found in the logical printer itself. If replacing the driver fails to resolve the problem, try deleting the logical printer and re-creating it from scratch. Keep in mind that if the logical printer is shared with the network, you need to re-create the logical printers connecting to that share on every client. (The name might be the same, but to Windows Server 2003, it is a completely different object with a new SID.)

▶ *Access permissions*—Resolving print-related access permission problems involves the same steps as resolving them for any other type of security object. First, try accessing the object from another account with the same or similar privileges. Next, test the problem account from different clients. Then test a Manage Document, a Manage Printers, and an Administrator account from the original fault client. These tests should tell you whether the problem is specific to a user account, a computer, or the object. In any case, you should check the permission settings at the print server to make sure you've set the access correctly. You might want to review the group memberships through the User Manager.

▶ *Network shares*—Network share–related problems revolve around failed network connections, unshared printers, offline servers, or congested traffic pathways. To determine whether the problem is printing related, try accessing other shared objects from the suspect client and server. If these succeed, check to see that the printer is actually shared. If they fail, inspect the network for a point of failure and make sure the server is online.

▶ *Communications and connections*—Communications between the print server and the physical print device are essential to the printing process. If they are disrupted, printing will cease. Resolution of these problems often centers around disconnected cables. Release and reconnect all connections between the print server and the printer (whether locally attached or network attached). Next, verify that the protocol required by network-attached printers is installed on the print server and is properly configured on both the print server and the print device.

▶ *Spooler*—The spooler is the final place to check for problems. It is possible for the spooler to be interrupted so that it hangs in the middle of an operation. This can happen when the Windows Server 2003 Kernel grants more processing time to tasks other than the print system. Hung spoolers might continue to accept new print jobs or might reject them. (This means either the client receives an error or the print job is dropped with no error.) Usually, spooler problems can be corrected by stopping and restarting the Spooler service through the Services applet. If this fails to resolve the problem, check to make sure the spooler's host drive has at least 50MB of free space. If it doesn't, change the spool host drive and reboot the system. In some cases, a simple reboot corrects the spooler problem. In addition, sometimes it's necessary to delete the `.spl` files from the spooler and restart.

If these suggestions fail to resolve your printer problems, you might want to contact the vendor or a licensed printer repair center for further help. In rare cases, reinstalling Windows Server 2003 might solve the problem. It is recommended, however, that you exhaust all other options before attempting this final solution.

Chapter Summary

In this chapter, we looked at printer management. The various printer management tasks range from changing print server configurations to manipulating active print jobs in a queue.

Large print jobs can generate a significant impact on the network and print-server loads. The print spooler files on a Windows Server 2003 print server can be relocated to a dedicated hard disk if these loads are going to be high. You can perform this procedure for all printers on the server or on a printer-by-printer basis.

As you know, the Windows Server 2003 print system allows multiple logical printers to serve a single printer. Likewise, multiple logical printers can serve a printer pool. This enables you to create logical printers with different printing priorities, varied availability time frames, or different paper trays.

Printer pooling is a Windows Server 2003 print system function that enables a single logical printer to serve multiple physical printers. Print pooling is often used in offices in which many documents are printed on a continuous basis and a single printer is inadequate. As print jobs are sent to the logical printer, the print server sends each print job to the next available printer. This results in an overall faster time and more efficient use of multiple printers.

It is important to note that all the printers in a print pool must be operated by the same print driver. In most cases, it is best to use identical printers, but this is not strictly necessary. Working with printers from the same manufacturer within a generation or so of each other provides adequate similarity for printer pooling.

Last, but certainly not least, the Print Management console allows you to manage all printers and print servers in your organization from a single console. This allows faster, more efficient management of all your print devices.

Key Terms

- ▶ Printer Priority
- ▶ Spool file
- ▶ Print Management Console (PMC)
- ▶ Printer pooling
- ▶ Print queue
- ▶ Printer filters

Apply Your Knowledge

Exercises

7.1 Installing shared printers

In this exercise, you will install a new printer using the Print Management Console.

Estimated Time: 10 minutes

1. From the Start menu, click Start, Control Panel, Administrative Tools, Print Management.

2. In the Print Management MMC, click the Print Servers entry in the left pane, and then select the Print Server that you want to use.

3. Right-click the print server and select Add Printer from the pop-up menu.

4. This opens the Add Printer Wizard. Click Next.

5. Select Local Printer and click Next. This reveals the port selection page of the Add Printer Wizard.

6. Select the port to which the printer is connected and click Next. This brings up the Printer Model Selection page. This is a list of print drivers included on the Windows Server 2003 distribution CD.

7. Select the HP as the manufacturer in the left column, and select the HP LaserJet 4050 as printer model in the right column.

8. Click Next. This brings up the Printer Name page. This is the name that will appear below the logical printer icon in the Printers folder on your local machine.

9. Enter a name, or accept the offered default name. Click Next.

10. On the Printer Sharing dialog box, click Next.

11. Click Next. This brings up the Location and Comment page. By filling in these optional fields, you can control where they appear in the PMC using custom filters. Click Next.

12. Click Next. This brings up the Print a Test Page screen. If you do not want to print a test page, select No and click Next.

13. Click Finish.

7.2 Managing the print queue

In this exercise, you will manage the print queue of the new printer that you installed in the previous exercise, using the Print Management Console. Make sure that you observe what happens with each command.

Estimated Time: 20 minutes

1. From the Start menu, click Start, Control Panel, Administrative Tools, Print Management.

2. In the Print Management MMC, click the All Printers entry in the left pane.

3. In the right pane of the MMC, right-click the printer that you just added and select Pause Printing from the pop-up menu.

4. Next, right-click the printer that you just added and select Print Test Page from the pop-up menu.

5. Repeat the previous step three or four times and observe the Jobs in Queue entry in the PMC.

6. Next, right-click the printer that you just added and select Open Printer Queue from the pop-up menu.

7. Right-click one of the jobs in the queue and select Cancel from the pop-up menu. Notice what happens.

8. Right-click one of the jobs in the queue and select Restart from the pop-up menu. Notice what happens.

9. Right-click one of the jobs in the queue and select Pause from the pop-up menu. Notice what happens.

10. Select Printer from the menu bar of the Print Queue, and deselect Pause Printing from the pop-up menu. Notice what happens.

11. Right-click the paused job in the queue and select Resume from the pop-up menu. Notice what happens.

Exam Questions

1. You are the network administrator for FlyByNight Airlines. The network consists of a single Active Directory domain. The functional level of the domain is Windows 2000 native. All network servers run Windows Server 2003, and all client computers run Windows XP Professional.

   The network includes a printer named FlightSchedules1. Some of your users report that they are often unable to access this printer. You discover that the problem occurs whenever more than 10 users try to connect to the printer.

   You need to ensure that all appropriate users can access FlightSchedules1. What should you do?

   ○ **A.** Decrease the length of the printer name.

   ○ **B.** Raise the functional level of the domain to Windows Server 2003.

   ○ **C.** Purchase additional client access licenses.

   ○ **D.** Move FlightSchedules1 to one of the servers.

2. Dave is the system administrator for a large law firm. He has to manage 20 servers and 10 print servers in addition to 400 desktops. To streamline the printing of large documents, Dave has set up an empty office as a print center and installed four Behemoth 2000 printers. All four printers are similarly configured. Unfortunately, one of the printers is heavily used while the other three see little usage.

Because the contract from Behemoth has a rider that charges Dave extra for exceeding a certain amount of use, he wants to balance the usage across the four printers as closely as possible.

What can Dave do to more efficiently use his printers?

- ○ **A.** Create multiple logical printers.

- ○ **B.** Create a single logical printer with four drivers.

- ○ **C.** Create a single logical printer with four ports.

- ○ **D.** Set the priority on all printers to 25.

3. You work in a mid-sized advertising agency. You have a color printer that is lightly used, but it should always be available for the account managers to use because they sometimes need brochures in a hurry. What's the best way to accomplish this?

- ○ **A.** Configure two logical printers that are assigned to the same printing device. Assign different priorities and groups to each printer.

- ○ **B.** Buy another identical printer. Set up a printer pool that contains both printers.

- ○ **C.** Configure the printer so that only the account managers have access to it.

- ○ **D.** Instruct the other users on how to kill their print jobs when an account manager needs the printer.

4. Don is the system administrator for a mid-sized company. He needs to delegate some of his trivial duties so that he can get more of his important work done. He decides to delegate some of the document-management duties to some of the administration assistants. What default group can he make them a member of so that they can manage print documents, without giving them too much authority?

- ○ **A.** Server Operators

- ○ **B.** Power Users

- ○ **C.** Print Operators

- ○ **D.** Printer Operators

5. The legal department of your company has a monthly print job that details the company's efforts to correct past human rights violations in third-world countries. This monthly print job is more than 1,000 pages, so it needs to be printed outside of normal business hours. What is the best way to accomplish this?

○ **A.** Create two logical printers for a print device. Assign one with a priority of 99 and name it Overnight. Leave the other with the default settings. Use the Overnight printer for the monthly report.

○ **B.** Create two logical printers for a print device. Assign one with a priority of 1 and name it Overnight. Configure the other with a priority of 99. Use the Overnight printer for the monthly report.

○ **C.** Create two logical printers for a print device. Assign one with a priority of 1 and name it Overnight. Set the hours available on the Overnight Printer to 6:00 p.m. to 6:00 a.m. Configure the other with a priority of 99. Use the Overnight printer for the monthly report.

○ **D.** Buy another printer and dedicate it to the monthly print job.

6. Frank works for a manufacturing company that has 30 servers running Windows Server 2003, 600 Windows NT workstations, 700 Windows XP Professional workstations, and 200 Windows 98 computers. The main print server is running Windows Server 2003 and is used to support several color printers. The printers are shared from the print server, with drivers loaded for all the client machines.

The manufacturer of the color printers releases new drivers with more features. Frank installs the updated drivers on the print server. After getting everything set up, Frank tests printing from the clients and notices that whereas the Windows NT and XP clients seem to support the new features, the Windows 98 clients do not. What is the most likely cause of the problem?

○ **A.** Frank installed the wrong drivers on the print server.

○ **B.** Frank did not install the Windows 98 drivers on the print server.

○ **C.** Frank needs to install the drivers on the Windows 98 clients.

○ **D.** Frank needs to restart the Spooler service so that the Windows 98 clients are recognized.

7. You are the network administrator for FlyByNight Airlines. The network consists of a single Active Directory domain. You have one print server with the following configuration:

Windows Server 2003 Standard Edition

Dual 3.6GHZ CPUs

2GB RAM

Single 3GB Hard Drive 15K

2 teamed 1GB NICs

During periods of heavy use, the print server becomes unresponsive, and the documents are slow to print. You need to increase the performance of the print server. What should you do?

- ○ **A.** Create two logical printers for a print device. Assign one with a priority of 99 and name it Large Jobs. Leave the other with the default settings. Use the Large Jobs printer for the large reports.

- ○ **B.** Buy another printer and dedicate it to the larger print jobs.

- ○ **C.** Install another hard drive and move the spool folder to it.

- ○ **D.** Buy another printer and dedicate it to the monthly print job.

8. Don is the system administrator for a mid-sized company. He needs to delegate some of his trivial duties so that he can get more of his important work done. He decides to delegate some of the document-management duties to some of the administration assistants. What steps must he take to give them the power to pause documents, but not pause a printer? Choose two:

- ○ **A.** Assign them the Allow—Manage Documents permissions

- ○ **B.** Assign them the Allow—Manage Printers permissions

- ○ **C.** Remove the Allow—Manage Documents permissions

- ○ **D.** Remove the Allow—Manage Printers permissions

9. You are the network administrator for FlyByNight Airlines. The network consists of a single Active Directory domain. You have one print server with one printer attached. The HR Manager complains that she has documents that need to be printed right away, but she has to wait for everyone else's print jobs to complete. What can you do to make sure her jobs print quicker?

- ○ **A.** Assign her the Allow—Manage Documents permissions

- ○ **B.** Assign her the Allow—Manage Printers permissions

- ○ **C.** Configure a new logical printer and point it to the existing device. Set the priority to 1. Configure the permissions so that only the HR manager can print to it.

- ○ **D.** Configure a new logical printer and point it to the existing device. Set the priority to 99. Configure the permissions so that only the HR manager can print to it.

10. You are the network administrator for Skelly Inc. The network consists of a single Active Directory domain, with 32 separate locations. All servers are running Windows Server 2003 SP1. You are having trouble locating the printers when the help desk calls with a printer problem. What technology can you use to alleviate this problem?

   ○ **A.** Use a custom filter in the Print Management Console.

   ○ **B.** Use a custom filter in the Active Directory Users and Computers.

   ○ **C.** Use a custom filter in the GPO that contains the printers.

   ○ **D.** None of the above.

Answers to Exam Questions

1. **D.** Because the magic number is 10, it is most likely that the printer is shared on a Windows XP client. That would lead to a situation where the Windows XP client computer allows only up to 10 connections at the same time resulting in users being unable to access FlightSchedules1 when the 10 connections are full. Moving the printer to a server computer will allow more concurrent connections. Because the domain doesn't have any Windows 9x clients, the length of the printer name isn't a problem. Because this is obviously a connectivity issue, the functional level of the domain is not the cause of the problem. Because the licensing service doesn't block connections, this is not a CAL problem. See "Managing Software Site Licensing" in Chapter 5.

2. **C.** To use a printer pool, all the printers must be capable of using the same printer driver, must be connected to the same print server, and should (for the convenience of the users) be located in close proximity to each other. See the "Printer Pooling" section for more information.

3. **A.** You should configure two logical printers assigned to the same printing device and then assign the Account Managers group a priority of 99 on one logical printer and leave the defaults on the other. See the "Setting Printer Priority" section for more information

4. **C.** Print Operators is the best choice. It gives them the ability to manage both documents and printers without giving them any additional administrative rights. The Server Operators and Power Users groups would give them more authority than they need. The Printer Operators group does not exist. See the "Assigning Print Permissions" section for more information.

5. **C.** Windows Server 2003 allows you to create multiple logical printers that point to a single print device. Each of these logical printers can be configured differently and assigned to different users via permissions. In this case, when you print to the Overnight printer, it will hold the print job in its queue until its time window begins. See the "Scheduling Printer Availability" section for more information.

6. **C.** Frank has to manually update the appropriate drivers on the Windows 98 clients. Unlike Windows NT and later, which automatically download new and updated drivers when they connect to the print server, Windows 98 clients must have the print drivers updated manually. See the "Scheduling Printer Availability" section for more information

7. **C.** After looking at the hardware configuration of the server, you see that the weak link is the hard drive space. The print server is performing poorly because the spool files are filling up the hard drive. To improve performance, the spool folder needs to be moved to another hard drive. The other solutions listed would just make the problem worse by requiring even more space on the hard drive. See the "Working with the Print Spooler" section for more information.

8. **A, D.** The Manage Documents permission allows them to pause, resume, start, delete and configure any document related settings. The Manage Printers permission would, among other things, give them the ability to pause the printer, which is not desirable. See the "Assigning Print Permissions" section for more information.

9. **D.** Allowing the HR manager the ability to manage documents and printers would allow her to pause or cancel other people's print jobs so that she could print, but that's not a good solution. The best solution is to set up another logical printer with a higher priority so that her print jobs are printed before others. The default priority is 1, the highest is 99. See the "Setting Printer Priority" section for more information.

10. **D.** Although a custom print filter in the PMC would solve the problem, the PMC wasn't available in SP1; it is part of the R2 release. The other MMCs mentioned, don't have a custom filter for printers. See the "Using Printer Filters" section for more information.

Suggested Readings and Resources

1. Boswell, William. *Inside Windows Server 2003*. New Riders, 2003. ISBN 0735711585.

2. Print Management Feature Overview. Microsoft Corporation.
   http://technet2.microsoft.com/WindowsServer/en/Library/8a497ff6-feca-4626-883a-f110bf28c6901033.mspx?mfr=true.

3. Print Management Step-by-Step Guide. Microsoft Corporation.
   http://www.microsoft.com/downloads/details.aspx?FamilyID=83066ddc-bc96-4418-a629-48c8abd2c7a0&displaylang=en.

4. Windows Server 2003 Deployment Guide
   http://technet2.microsoft.com/WindowsServer/en/Library/c283b699-6124-4c3a-87ef-865443d7ea4b1033.mspx?mfr=true Microsoft Corporation.

5. Windows Server 2003 Resource Kit. Microsoft Press, 2005. ISBN 0735614717.

For more information about network-attached printers, visit the manufacturers' websites, such as the following:

► Canon: http://www.usa.canon.com

► Hewlett Packard: http://www.hp.com

► Lexmark: http://lexmark.com

CHAPTER EIGHT

Managing Access to Objects in Organizational Units

Objectives

This chapter doesn't cover any specific objectives on the Microsoft Managing and Maintaining a Microsoft Windows Server 2003 Environment exam. However, it does cover information that you will most likely see on the test—and on the job.

Outline

Study Strategies

▶ In studying this section, be sure to practice all the activities described. Become very familiar with the Delegation of Control Wizard, what standard tasks can be delegated, and how to create a custom task.

▶ The exercises in this chapter are built on the users, groups, and OUs that you created in the exercises in Chapter 3, "Managing Groups," and Chapter 4, "Managing and Maintaining Access to Resources." If you have not yet completed those exercises, now would be a good time to do it!

▶ Pay particular attention to managing access to OUs through the use of permissions.

▶ Know the differences between standard and special permissions, and when each should be used.

Introduction

In previous chapters, we have briefly worked with and discussed Organization Units (OUs), including how to create them and how to add objects to them. In this chapter, we discuss how to manage objects in OU. This includes setting permissions, moving objects between OUs, and delegating control to OUs.

Organizational Unit Overview

Objects in Active Directory are the building blocks of the network. Typical objects used in Active Directory are users, computers, groups, shared folders, and printers.

An OU is a container used to organize the Active Directory objects within a domain into logical administrative groups for purposes such as delegating specific administrative tasks or applying Group Policy. In general, OUs

- Are independent of the OU structure in other domains—each domain has its own hierarchy.

- Allow for logically organizing and storing objects within the domain.

- Are containers within a domain that can house user accounts, groups, computers, printers, applications, file shares, and other OUs from the same domain.

- Can provide a means for delegating administrative authority.

- Cannot be made members of security groups—you cannot grant access because a user belongs to an OU, but must assign a group policy to the OU.

There are three primary reasons to have OUs:

- To allow delegation of administration—To designate groups of users who have control over users, computers, or other objects in an OU.

- For application of Group Policies.

- To restrict visibility—Users can view only resources to which they have been granted access

OUs have the following advantages:

- Flexibility

- Users can move between OUs easily, using the move user command in Active Directory Users and Computers.

- ▶ Creating/deleting OUs is easy and straightforward.

- ▶ Administrators can delegate control over network resources and tasks while maintaining the ability to manage them.

- ▶ Similar objects can be grouped for the application of security policies.

Modifying Permissions for Objects in an OU

When a user logs in to a Windows Server 2003 domain, the user account is *authenticated*; it is checked to make sure that the user has an account in the domain, and that the user is actually who he or she claims to be. This initial authentication process results only in the user gaining access to the network; there still has to be a mechanism in place to determine what access the user has to objects in Active Directory.

Security Descriptors

Every Active Directory object has a *security descriptor* attached to it that describes the type of access allowed by specific entities. The security descriptor is automatically created with the object. These security descriptors are what Windows Server 2003 uses to control access to Active Directory objects. This method of access control is an example of an object-based security model.

Security descriptors are structures that are made up of four components:

- ▶ *Owner SID*—Windows Server 2003 uses the owner Security Identifier (SID) to identify users, groups, and other objects. Although we refer to a user as jsmith@70-290.com, Windows Server 2003 uses a string of alphanumeric characters to uniquely identify the same object. SIDs are unique and are never reused. Even if the object is deleted and re-created with the same name, it will receive a new SID.

- ▶ *Group SID*—This is required for POSIX and the Services for Macintosh, but is not used by Active Directory.

- ▶ *DACL*—In Active Directory, every object has an owner. Typically, the owner will be the user or the process that created the object. The owner of the object can control who has access to the object through the use of an Access Control List (ACL). An Access Control List is the list of users who can access the object and the specific actions that the user can perform on the object. Each entry in the list is known as an Access Control entry (ACE)

- ▶ *SACL*—The System Access Control List (SACL) stores the system security policies such as logging and auditing.

Some Active Directory objects will have an ACL that controls the entire object and will also have individual ACLs that control access to individual attributes of the object. This allows an administrator to control not only which users can see an object, but also what attributes of that object each individual user can see.

An example of this is an employee list. All users would have read access to the standard fields, such as name, location, telephone numbers, and so on, but the owner of the object would have full control for all the attributes in the listing, including some attributes that ordinary users would not know exist, such as salary history, employee rating, and the like. Access control could also be configured so that individual users could also update the common attributes of their own object.

Permissions

As you can see, access control in Active Directory can be controlled at a granular level. The access to objects is controlled by *permissions*. Permissions are what define the type of access that is granted to a user for an object or attribute. The owner of an object can grant any user or security group permission to do to the object whatever the owner is authorized to do with it.

Different types of objects will have different permissions, depending on the function of the object. For example, you wouldn't assign read permission to a printer.

The basic security model in Windows Server 2003 is similar to the one used in previous versions of Windows. In Windows Server 2003, you are allowed to allow or deny various levels of permissions for objects. All permissions are cumulative. This means that if a user is a member of two groups, one with read permission to an object and the other group with write permission, that user would have both read and write permission for the object.

Permissions can be allowed or denied. Similar to previous versions of Windows where No Access always overrides any other permissions, in Windows Server 2003 the Deny permission overrides any other permission that is granted to the object. An example is the situation where a user is a member of three groups, all of which have read access to a folder. If that user becomes a member of another group that has been denied any access to that folder, the single denied permission will override several allowed permissions, so the user will no longer have any access to the folder.

Although Active Directory permissions seem to be the same as the New Technology File System (NTFS) permissions that we discussed in previous chapters, there are some differences, especially in the area of implicit and explicit permissions. For example, if you deny a user access to an object, you have *explicitly denied* access to that object. However if you neither grant nor deny a user access to an object, by default, access is implicitly denied. In Active Directory, a user will have access to an object only if it is explicitly permitted.

Active Directory objects in Windows Server 2003 use two types of permissions: Standard and Special. The Standard permissions are the same as in previous versions of Windows:

▶ Read

▶ Write

▶ Create All Child Objects

▶ Delete All Child Objects

▶ Full Control

Special permissions are the components of the standard permissions. All the individual permissions that make up the write permission, such as list, read, write all properties, and so on are available separately as Special permissions. This permits a very granular level of access to an object.

Assigning Permissions to Active Directory Objects

In Windows Server 2003, the permissions for objects and their attributes are configured using the Active Directory Users and Computers snap-in. All permissions for objects are configured from the Properties window of the object, via the Security tab. However, the default in Windows Server 2003 is for the Security tab to not be displayed.

To be able to see the Security tab, follow the procedure in Step by Step 8.1.

STEP BY STEP

8.1 Enabling the Security tab in Active Directory Users and Computers

1. Click Start, Programs, Administrative Tools, and select Active Directory Users and Computers.

2. From the system menu select View, and then select Advanced Features.

3. Right-click the Computers container and select Properties from the pop-up menu. Notice in Figure 8.1 that the Security tab is now present.

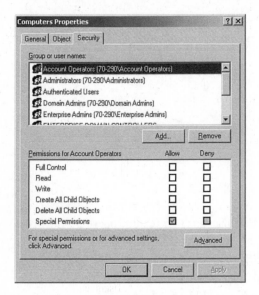

FIGURE 8.1 Enabling Advanced Features in the Active Directory Users and Computers MMC allows you to view additional options.

After you do this, notice that it also causes several new containers to appear: ForeignSecurityPrincipals, Lost and Found, and System and NTDS Quotas.

Now that you have selected Advanced Features and turned on access to the Security tab, let's look at some of the settings that allow you to control access to Active Directory objects. We will start by going to one of the OU containers and selecting a user, and then changing the access that has been granted to the user.

In Step by Step 8.2, we will modify the permissions on one of the objects that we created in the exercises in Chapter 2.

STEP BY STEP

8.2 Modifying permissions for an Active Directory object

1. Open the Active Directory Users and Computers MMC.

2. From the main window of Active Directory Users and Computers, click to open the Kansas City container, and then open the Users container underneath it.

3. Right-click one of the user objects in the right pane, and then select Properties from the pop-up menu.

4. Click the Security tab. From the Security tab, we can see what permissions have been granted for this user object. By selecting an entry in the top window, the permissions granted to that user or group will be displayed in the bottom window.

5. Select the SELF entry in the top window. In Figure 8.2 you can see that the user has read access to most properties, but will be allowed to change personal information. Click the Advanced button.

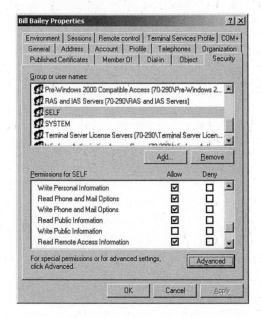

FIGURE 8.2 The Active Directory Users and Computers MMC showing the permissions for the user.

6. This opens the Access Control Settings window. Click the entry SELF, and then select Edit.

7. This opens the Permission Entry window, shown in Figure 8.3. It opens on the Object tab. This window shows the permissions that apply to this object only. In other words, any changes here will apply only to the selected user object.

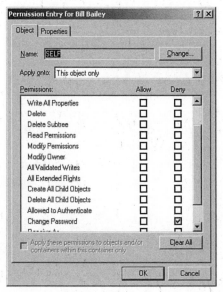

FIGURE 8.3 The Active Directory Users and Computers MMC showing the permissions for the user object.

8. Select the Properties tab. This window shows the individual attributes that make up the user object. In other words, each individual field in the record in Active Directory for the user is displayed here, and you can control what the user can do to his object, or even whether the user can see these fields.

9. Select the Allow check box for the Read All Properties entry. Notice that the one selection automatically selects the read permission for all the other fields for the object, as shown in Figure 8.4.

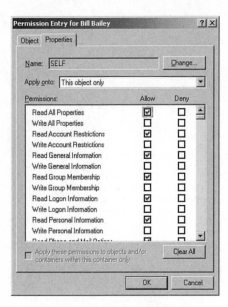

FIGURE 8.4 The Active Directory Users and Computers MMC showing the effect of selecting the Read All Properties check box.

10. Click OK to close the Permission Entry window. Then click OK twice to get back to Active Directory Users and Computers.

In most cases, the standard permissions will be sufficient for most object access. However, in some situations, granting one of the standard access permissions will give users more access than you think they should have. In that situation, you can assign a user Special Permissions. Special permissions are the component parts of standard permissions. They are far more granular than standard permissions. In Step by Step 8.3, we will grant a user the ability to read the Department field of user objects instead of granting the full standard permission to read most fields of the object.

STEP BY STEP

8.3 Granting Special Permissions for an Active Directory object

1. Open the Active Directory Users and Computers MMC.

2. From the main window of Active Directory Users and Computers, click to open the Kansas City container, and then open the Users container underneath it.

3. Right-click one of the user objects in the right pane, and then select Properties from the pop-up menu.

4. Click the Security tab.

5. Click the Add button. In the Select Users dialog box, select one of the other domain user accounts, and then click OK. Back at the user Properties dialog box, you can see in Figure 8.5 that the user you just added was automatically granted read access to most properties. Click the Advanced button.

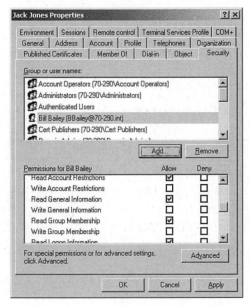

FIGURE 8.5 The added user is automatically granted read permissions for the user account.

6. This opens the Access Control Settings Window. Click the entry for the added user, and then select Edit.

7. This opens the Permission Entry window; from there select the Properties tab. Notice in Figure 8.6 that Read All Properties is selected.

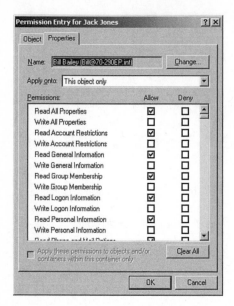

FIGURE 8.6 The Read All Properties selection is the default.

8. Click the Clear All button. Scroll down in the window and select Read Department.

9. Click OK to close the Permission Entry window. Then click OK twice to get back to Active Directory Users and Computers.

As mentioned earlier, the network administrator has granular control over Active Directory objects. However, it can easily become a management nightmare trying to keep up with and document the changes to specific attributes of unique objects. To help manage these types of changes, the network administrator should turn on auditing of permissions changes. We cover auditing in Chapter 16.

Permissions Inheritance

To help simplify the management of permissions in Active Directory, Microsoft has used a method called *Permissions Inheritance*. This allows you to set access permissions on a parent object, and then allow the permissions to be automatically propagated to the child objects. In Windows Server 2003, when the access permissions on a container are changed, the changes are inherited by both existing objects and any newly created objects within that container.

The default for Windows Server 2003 is for Permissions Inheritance to be turned on, but it can be turned off at the object or container level by de-selecting a check box on the Properties window of the object or container (see Figure 8.7).

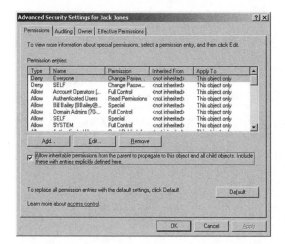

FIGURE 8.7 Permissions Inheritance can be turned on or off via the check box.

When you deselect the check box, you will be presented with the following options:

▶ *Copy Inherited Permissions*—This will leave any inherited permissions in place. However, no new permissions set at the parent level will be inherited.

▶ *Remove Inherited Permissions*—This will remove any existing permissions that were inherited from the parent. You will need to explicitly grant any permissions desired.

Moving AD Objects

Objects can be easily moved between OUs in Active Directory. This type of task is commonly performed when a user gets transferred to a new department or location or when two departments merge and their resources such as computers and printers have to be combined into one OU.

To move a user or other object to another OU, follow the procedure in Step by Step 8.4.

STEP BY STEP

8.4 Moving an Active Directory object

1. Click Start, Programs, Administrative Tools, and select Active Directory Users and Computers.

2. Click the desired domain, and then click the container of the OU in which the user you want to move is located.

3. In the right pane of the window, right-click the name of the user to be moved, and then select Move from the pop-up menu.

4. In the Move dialog box, select the folder to which you want to move the user, and then click OK.

> **NOTE**
>
> **Drag and Drop**   Starting in Windows Server 2003, you can use drag and drop to move objects in Active Directory.

This procedure is identical for users, groups, computers, and shared folders.

There are a couple of conditions relating to permissions that you need to be aware of when moving Active Directory objects:

▶ Permissions that were inherited from the previous OU will no longer apply. All the permissions applicable in the new OU will apply.

▶ Any permissions that were granted specifically to the object will remain the same.

> **NOTE**
>
> **Dsmove**   To move or rename objects from the command line, use the `dsmove` utility. This utility is discussed in Chapter 2 in the section "Moving or Renaming Objects with `dsmove`."

The Active Directory Users and Computers snap-in cannot be used to move users between domains. For interdomain moves, use the Active Directory Migration Tool (ADMT). The ADMT is used to move objects from one domain to another. The ADMT is located in the `\I386\ADMT` folder of the Windows Server 2003 Server CD-ROM.

Effective Permissions

With all the permissions and special permissions in Active directory, it can get confusing trying to figure out who has access to what, and exactly what access they have.

Windows Server 2003 includes the *Effective Permissions* tool. This tool automatically looks at a user's permissions and the permissions of the groups of which the user is a member to calculate the effective permissions for an object in Active Directory.

To determine the Effective Permission on an object, the user using the tool must have the Read Membership permission on all objects in Active Directory. In a Windows Server 2003 domain running in pre-Windows 2000 access compatibility mode, all domain users have this permission by default. If the domain is running in Windows Server 2003 mode, only the domain administrators will have the necessary permissions.

To view the effective permissions for an object, follow the procedure outlined in Step by Step 8.5.

STEP BY STEP

8.5 Viewing the Effective Permissions of an Active Directory object

1. Open Active Directory Users and Computers and navigate to the object for which you want to view permissions.

2. Right-click the object, select Properties from the pop-up menu, and click the Security tab in the resulting dialog box.

3. From the Security tab, click the Advanced button.

4. The Advanced Security Settings dialog box appears. Select the Effective Permissions tab.

5. The Effective Permissions tab appears, as shown in Figure 8.8. This page allows you to display the effective permissions of the object for a user or group. Click the Select button.

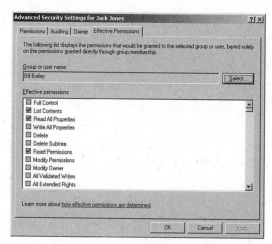

FIGURE 8.8   The Advanced Security Settings dialog box, showing the Effective Permissions tab.

6. The Select User or Group dialog box appears. Enter the desired user or group and then click the OK button.

7. This returns you to the Advanced Security Settings dialog box. The Effective Permissions for the user are shown. Click OK here and in the Object Properties dialog box to quit.

NOTE

More Info For more information on Effective Permissions (also know as the TGGAU attribute), consult the Microsoft Knowledge Base at http://support.microsoft.com/kb/331951.

Remember: When assigning permissions, even though Windows Server 2003 gives you the capability to configure permissions at a granular level, use this capability only when absolutely necessary. As we discussed previously, when you're working with users and groups, it is far easier to manage permissions when they are assigned at a group level. This allows you to add or remove members of the group, instead of having to try to configure each user the same way. The same philosophy applies to configuring permissions on individual attributes of objects. Whenever possible, control access to the individual attributes of objects at the container level so that you have to perform the configuration only once.

Another advantage of configuring permissions changes at the group or container level is that it can be done using the Delegation of Control Wizard. This wizard makes it very easy to make permissions changes to Active Directory objects and containers. We will be looking at this wizard in the next section.

Challenge

You are a system administrator who is responsible for managing all Active Directory resources for your company. One of the department heads has stopped by your office and expressed concerns that a secretary in his department has too much access to user accounts in the Active Directory. He feels that she should not have access to the home telephone number field in the user account.

While you don't recall granting this individual access to that specific attribute, she was granted access to some fields for updating purposes. You need to verify what access she does have.

How would you accomplish this in Windows Server 2003? On your own, try to develop a solution that would involve the least amount of downtime and expense.

For a possible solution, follow the procedure outlined here.

1. Open Active Directory Users and Computers and navigate to the user for which you want to view permissions.

2. Right-click the object, select Properties from the pop-up menu, and click the Security tab in the resulting dialog box.

(continues)

(continued)

3. From the Security tab, click the Advanced button.

4. The Advanced Security Settings dialog box appears. Select the Effective Permissions tab.

5. The Effective Permissions tab appears. Click the Select button.

6. The Select User or Group dialog box appears. Enter the name of the user you think has too much access, and then click the OK button.

7. This returns you to the Advanced Security Settings dialog box. The Effective Permissions for the user are shown. Scroll down in the window to see if the user has been granted access to the Home Phone Number attribute.

Delegating Control of an OU

Inheritance and delegation are probably two of the most important features of Active Directory management. We already discussed how inheritance is used to allow the permissions set on a parent object to be automatically propagated to the child objects. This simplifies the administrative tasks of the directory because the network administrator does not have to manually assign permissions on each object.

Through the use of delegation, the network administrator can grant specific administrative rights for containers and objects to users or groups. This allows selected users to perform some of the management and administrative tasks that would normally be the responsibility of the network administrator. Properly used, this has the potential to lighten the administrator's workload and push specific administrative duties down the hierarchy closer to the end user, where they can usually be performed more efficiently.

For example, if you have a department that prefers to manage itself, either for security or political reasons, you can create an OU that contains all the users, computers, and resources for that department. Then you can assign full control for that OU to an administrators group that consists of the users who are the designated administrators of that department.

In Windows NT, the domain was the administrative and security boundary. Starting with the Windows 2000 versions of Active Directory, although the domain can be used in the same way, it is advantageous to use the OU in this role because OUs are easier to create, delete, move, and modify than domains are.

Windows Server 2003 allows the administrator to delegate the ability to create, delete, or modify objects at the container, OU, object, or property level. In most cases, it will be best to not assign administrative control at lower than the container or OU level.

> **NOTE**
>
> **Containers?** If you look closely in the left pane of the Active Directory Users and Computers MMC, you will notice that all the folder icons are not the same. Some icons are plain—these are containers. The other icons have an open folder label on them—these are OUs. Most of the containers are automatically created by the operating system, and control of some of them cannot be delegated.

The Delegation of Control Wizard should be used to delegate administrative control of OUs and containers. The wizard allows you to select the OUs and objects to be controlled, the user or group to which you want to delegate control, and the permissions to access and modify objects. To grant permissions at the property level, you must manually configure the properties of the objects.

The Delegation of Control Wizard is available in the Active Directory Users and Computers snap-in. It will lead you step by step through the process of delegating control at the OU or container level.

To see how the wizard accomplishes these types of tasks, follow the procedure outlined in Step by Step 8.6 to delegate control of the Kansas City\Users OU to members of the Managers Group.

STEP BY STEP

8.6 Using the Delegation of Control Wizard

1. Select Start, Programs, Administrative Tools, and then select Active Directory Users and Computers.

2. Select the desired domain, select the Kansas City OU, and then right-click the Users OU.

3. From the pop-up menu, select Delegate Control. The Delegate Control Wizard starts.

4. The Welcome to the Delegation of Control Wizard window appears. Click Next to continue.

5. The Users or Groups window appears; click Add. The Select Users, Computers, or Groups window appears.

6. Enter the Managers group. Click OK to continue. You are returned to the Users or Groups window, as shown in Figure 8.9. Click Next to continue.

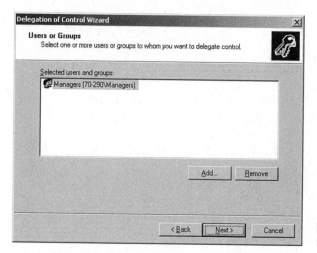

FIGURE 8.9 The Users or Groups dialog box, showing the selected group.

7. The Tasks to Delegate window appears, as shown in Figure 8.10. This window displays tasks that will typically be delegated, such as creating and modifying user accounts or groups and resetting passwords. This is where you would configure access for a help desk group that would normally need to work with user accounts, reset passwords, and so on. Because we are delegating complete control over the OU, we will select the Create a Custom Task to Delegate option button. Click Next to continue.

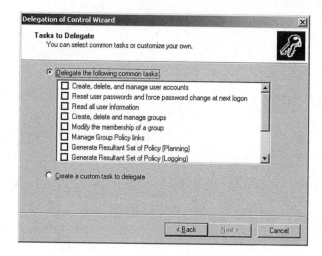

FIGURE 8.10 The Tasks to Delegate dialog box, showing some of the delegatable tasks.

8. The Active Directory Object Type window appears (see Figure 8.11). This window allows you to specify individual object types to delegate control of. Because we are delegating control of the entire OU, we will select the This Folder, Existing Objects in This Folder, and Creation of New Objects in This Folder option button. Click Next to continue.

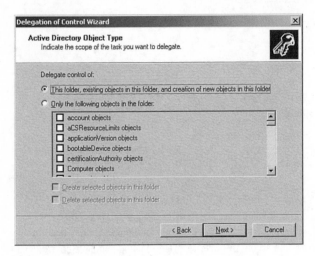

FIGURE 8.11 Showing the object types that can be delegated.

9. The Permissions dialog box appears, as shown in Figure 8.12. In this window, you can choose from three levels of permissions:

- ▶ General

- ▶ Property-specific

- ▶ Creation/Deletion of Specific Child Objects

Because we are delegating full control of the OU, we will select General, and then select the Full Control check box. Click Next to continue.

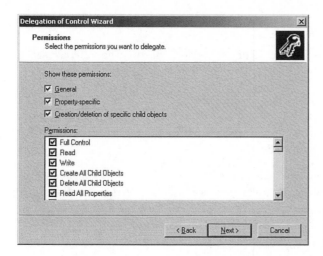

FIGURE 8.12 The Permissions dialog box; selecting General and Full Control automatically selects all the other options.

10. The Summary window appears. Review the items to make sure they are correct. If not, click the Back button and make the necessary corrections, and then click Finish.

The proper use of delegation can also enhance network security. In Windows NT, few of the administrative tasks could be assigned to other users. Because of this, it was necessary to give more people user accounts with administrative access than it was probably wise to do. By being able to delegate specific tasks and control the level of access at a granular level, you can limit the number of accounts that are members of the Domain Admins group to a highly trusted few.

EXAM ALERT

Limitations of the Delegation of Control Wizard The Delegation of Control Wizard can only apply permissions, not remove them. In addition, if you run the wizard multiple times, the permissions assigned are cumulative, and cannot be viewed using the wizard. To view and remove the permissions, you will have to view the Security tab for the object that you assigned permissions on using the wizard. Watch for Delegation of Control Wizard questions on the exam.

Chapter Summary

Objects in Active Directory are the building blocks of the network. In this chapter, you learned how to manage access to these objects by using both standard permissions and special permissions.

You also learned how to verify the effects of these permissions by using the Effective Permissions tool. We also briefly touched on how to move objects between OUs and what happens to the effective permissions when we do.

In the last part of the chapter, we worked with the delegation of control of objects in an OU. Although this can be done by assigning individual permissions, the Delegation of Control Wizard makes this task quick and efficient.

Key Terms

- ▶ Security Descriptor
- ▶ Access Control Entry (ACE)
- ▶ Access Control List (ACL)
- ▶ Discretionary Access Control List (DACL)
- ▶ Effective Permissions
- ▶ Delegation of Control Wizard

Apply Your Knowledge

Exercises

8.1 Delegating administrative control

In this exercise, you will use the Delegation of Control Wizard to assign the reset password permissions for the Kansas City\Users OU to a domain user.

Estimated Time: 20 minutes

1. Select Start, Programs, Administrative Tools, and then select Active Directory Users and Computers.

2. Select the desired domain, select the Kansas City OU, and then right-click the Users OU.

3. From the pop-up menu, select Delegate Control. The Delegate Control Wizard starts.

4. The Welcome to the Delegation of Control Wizard window appears; click Next to continue.

5. The Users or Groups window appears; click Add. The Select Users, Computers, or Groups window appears.

6. Enter one of the users that you created in previous exercises. Make sure that this user is *not* a member of the Managers group. Click OK to continue. You are returned to the Users or Groups window. Click Next to continue.

7. The Tasks to Delegate window appears. Select the Reset Users Passwords and Force Password Changes at Next Logon check box. Click Next to continue.

8. The Summary window appears. Review the items to make sure they are correct. If not, click the Back button and make the necessary corrections, or click Finish to end.

9. Log on as the user on a member server or workstation in your test domain (not the domain controller).

10. Open the Active Directory Users and Computers MMC.

11. Navigate to the Kansas City\Users OU, and reset the password of one of the users.

12. Log off when you are finished.

8.2 Checking effective permissions

In this exercise, you will continue the previous exercise by verifying that the reset password permissions for the Kansas City\Users OU was assigned by checking the effective permissions on a user object in the OU.

Estimated Time: 10 minutes

1. Select Start, Programs, Administrative Tools, and then select Active Directory Users and Computers.

2. Select the desired domain, select the Kansas City OU, and then right-click the Users OU.

3. Select a user object in the Users OU, right-click the object, select Properties from the pop-up menu, and click the Security tab in the resulting dialog box.

4. From the Security tab, click the Advanced button.

5. The Advanced Security Settings dialog box appears. Select the Effective Permissions tab.

6. The Effective Permissions tab appears. Click the Select button.

7. The Select User or Group dialog box appears. Enter the user who was granted reset password permissions, and then click the OK button.

8. This returns you to the Advanced Security Settings dialog box. The Effective Permissions for the user are shown. Scroll down to verify the Reset Password entry. Click OK here and in the Object Properties dialog box to quit.

Exam Questions

1. You are the network administrator for FlyByNight Airlines. The network consists of a single Active Directory domain. The functional level of the domain is Windows Server 2003 native. All network servers run Windows Server 2003, and all client computers run Windows XP Professional.

   You decide to assign the Reset Password permission for the Cessna OU to the SmallPlaneManagers Group. However, when you open the Properties page for the OU object, you don't see the Security tab. What should you do?

   ○ **A.** Log off and then log on again with an account with Domain Administrators rights.

   ○ **B.** Use the RunAs command.

   ○ **C.** Select Tools from the system menu and select Advanced Features.

   ○ **D.** Select View from the system menu and select Advanced Features.

2. You are the system administrator for a small manufacturing company. Your company just bought another company of about the same size, and you have just finished adding their users to your domain. Unfortunately, all the IT personnel from the other company quit, leaving you to manage everything.

   You have spoken to several of the department managers, and they have agreed to take over some of the low-level administrative tasks such as creating users and resetting passwords.

   What is the best way to grant them the proper authority?

   ○ **A.** Add the department managers to the Domain Administrators group.

   ○ **B.** Add the department managers to the Account Operators group.

   ○ **C.** Use the Delegation of Control Wizard.

   ○ **D.** Create a separate domain.

3. You are the system administrator for a small manufacturing company. Your company has decided to split off the research and development department into a wholly owned subsidiary. Unfortunately, this new subsidiary is undercapitalized, so it will still use the same office space and will need to continue to use your network.

   However, their general manager wants to manage all the computers and users himself. What is the best way to grant him the proper authority? (Choose two.)

   ○ **A.** Add his user account to the Domain Administrators group.

   ○ **B.** Add his user account to the Account Operators group.

   ○ **C.** Use the Delegation of Control Wizard.

   ○ **D.** Create a separate domain, and move the subsidiary's resources into the domain.

   ○ **E.** Create a separate OU, and move the subsidiary's resources into the OU.

4. You are the system administrator for a small chemical company. One of your department managers just called, and she wants you to give Joe, one of the employees, read access to an object in Active Directory.

The objects have the current assignments

Read—Managers group

Read—Supervisors group

Deny—Employees group

Joe is currently a member of the Employees group. What must you do to give him access to only this object?

- ○ **A.** Add his user account to the Managers group.

- ○ **B.** Add his user account to the Supervisors group.

- ○ **C.** Remove his user account from the Employees group.

- ○ **D.** None of the above.

5. You are the system administrator for a mid-sized research firm. You assigned one of your junior administrators to block inheritance of the permissions on all objects in your test OU so that only you will be able to manage them. The permissions are as follows:

BEFORE

Full Control—Domain Admins group

Read—Junior Admins

Deny—Employees group

AFTER

Full Control—Domain Admins group

Read—Junior Admins

Deny—Employees group

You verified that inheritance was disabled. What did the junior administrator do wrong?

- ○ **A.** Nothing, this is the default.

- ○ **B.** He selected Copy permissions.

- ○ **C.** He selected Remove permissions.

- ○ **D.** He selected Cancel permissions.

6. You are the system administrator for Rite-Built, Inc. Your company has decided to split off the research and development department into a wholly owned subsidiary. You are going to create a new domain and move all the research ad development's resources into the new domain. What is the best tool to use to accomplish this task?

   ○ **A.** Active Directory User and Computers

   ○ **B.** Dsmove.

   ○ **C.** The Delegation of Control Wizard

   ○ **D.** Active Directory Migration Tool

7. You are the system administrator for a small manufacturing company. Your company has decided to split off the research and development department into a wholly owned subsidiary. All their resources are currently stored in the RD OU.

   Although they don't have a problem with you, the system administrator, having access to their resources, they no longer want the Plant Managers group to have any access to their OU. The Plant Managers group was previously given administrative rights to all resources in the OU via the Delegation of Control wizard.

   What is the best way to remove the administrative rights on the RD OU that were previously granted to the Plant Managers group?

   ○ **A.** Use the Delegation of Control Wizard to remove the administrative rights previously granted to the Plant Managers group.

   ○ **B.** Use the OUEdit command-line tool to remove the administrative rights previously granted to the Plant Managers group.

   ○ **C.** Use the Effective Permissions tool to remove the administrative rights previously granted to the Plant Managers group.

   ○ **D.** Use the Security tab on the RD OU object to assign the Deny permission to the Plant Managers group.

8. You are the system administrator for a small company. Your network consists of a single Windows Server 2003 domain running in Windows Server 2003 mode. This domain was created from scratch, so you decided not to include any pre-Windows Server 2003 functionality.

One of your junior administrators responded to a help desk call for a user who was having trouble accessing the resources in an OU in Active Directory. The junior administrator attempted to investigate the problem using the Effective Permissions tool, but received a message that she didn't have the proper authority. Junior administrators are not members of the Domain Administrators group.

What is the best way to allow the junior administrator to use the Effective Permissions tool?

- ○ **A.** Add her user account to the Domain Admins group.
- ○ **B.** Add her user account to the Pre-Windows 2000 Compatibility Access group.
- ○ **C.** Use the Delegation of Control Wizard to grant her access to the Effective Permissions tool.
- ○ **D.** Add her user account to the local Administrators group on the file server containing the shared folder she is investigating.

Answers to Exam Questions

1. **D.** In Windows Server 2003, the permissions for objects and their attributes are configured using the Active Directory Users and Computers snap-in. All permissions for objects are configured from the Properties window of the object, via the Security tab. However, the default in Windows Server 2003 is for the Security tab to not be displayed. It must be enabled by selecting Advanced Features from the system menu. See "Assigning Permissions to Active Directory Objects."

2. **C.** While adding the department managers user accounts to the domain Admins or Account Operators groups will give them the necessary permissions, it will also give them some permissions that you might not want them to have. Creating a separate domain is a solution left over from Windows NT. The best solution is to group the user accounts in an appropriate OU, and then use the Delegation of Control Wizard to assign the department managers accounts only the permissions they need in that OU. See "Delegating Control of an Organizational Unit."

3. **C and E.** Creating a separate domain is a solution left over from Windows NT. Also, because the new subsidiary is short on funds, it might not have the budget for the new hardware that a new domain would require. The best solution is to move the resources for the subsidiary to a separate OU, and then use the Delegation of Control Wizard to assign the general managers accounts full control over that OU. See "Delegating Control of an OU."

4. **D.** Adding Joe's user account to either of the two groups mentioned won't give him access, because he's a member of the Employees group, which has the Deny permission, which overrides any other permission. Removing his account from the Employees group will not give him access to the object because if you are not explicitly granted permissions to objects in AD, by default you are implicitly denied access. See "Modifying Permissions for Objects in an OU."

5. **B.** When the junior administrator turned off permissions inheritance, he elected to copy permissions. This will leave any existing inherited permissions in place. What he should have done was select the option to remove inherited permissions. This would have removed any existing permissions that were inherited from the parent. If he had selected Cancel, the permissions would still be in place, but so would inheritance. See "Permissions Inheritance."

6. **D.** Neither the Active Directory Users and Computers snap-in nor the dsmove utility can be used to move users or resources between domains. For interdomain moves, use the Active Directory Migration Tool (ADMT), which is used to move objects from one domain to another. The Delegation of Control Wizard can be used only to grant access to objects. See "Moving AD Objects."

7. **D.** The Delegation of Control Wizard can only apply permissions, not remove them. To view and remove the permissions, you will have to view the Security tab for the object on which you assigned permissions using the wizard. The Effective Permissions tool can be used only to view permissions, not to edit them. The OUEdit tool doesn't exist. See "Delegating Control of an OU."

8. **B.** During the Dcpromo process, you are prompted as to whether you want to set permissions compatible with pre-Windows 2000 server operating systems. This selection adds the Everyone group to the Pre-Windows 2000 Compatible Access group, and thereby grants the Everyone group read access to most Active Directory objects. If you do not select this option, the Pre-Windows 2000 Compatible Access group is created, but it is empty. In this case, only domain administrators can use the Effective Permissions tool for Active Directory objects. Adding a junior administrator to the Domain Admins group just so she can use the Effective Permissions tools is not a good idea. The Delegation of Control Wizard cannot be used to grant access to the Effective Permissions tool. Because this is an Active Directory object she is investigating, she would need her account added to a domain controller, which doesn't have a local administrators group. See "Effective Permissions."

Suggested Readings and Resources

1. *Best Practices for Delegating Active Directory Administration*. Microsoft Corporation. http://www.microsoft.com/technet/prodtechnol/windowsserver2003/technologies/directory/activedirectory/actdid3.mspx.

2. *Step-by-Step Guide to Using the Delegation of Control Wizard*. Microsoft Corporation. http://www.microsoft.com/technet/prodtechnol/windowsserver2003/technologies/directory/activedirectory/stepbystep/ctrlwiz.mspx.

3. *The Effective Permissions Tool*. Microsoft Corporation. http://technet2.microsoft.com/WindowsServer/en/Library/155c4905-6660-4c4c-9a0a-5a668907e83c1033.mspx?mfr=true.

4. *Windows Server 2003 Deployment Guide*. Microsoft Corporation. http://technet2.microsoft.com/WindowsServer /en/Library/c283b699-6124-4c3a-87ef-865443d7ea4b1033.mspx?mfr=true.

5. *Windows Server 2003 Resource Kit*. Microsoft Press, 2005. ISBN 0735614717.

6. *Working with Active Directory Permissions in Exchange Server 2003*. Microsoft Corporation. http://www.microsoft.com/technet/prodtechnol/exchange/2003/library/ex2k3ad.mspx.

CHAPTER NINE

Implementing Group Policy

Objective

This chapter covers information that you will most likely see on the test—and on the job; however, it doesn't cover any specific objectives on the Microsoft Managing and Maintaining a Microsoft Windows Server 2003 Environment exam.

Outline

Study Strategies

▶ In studying this section, be sure to practice all the activities described. Become very familiar with the Group Policy Management Console, how it is installed, its capabilities, and its limitations.

▶ To perform the exercises in this chapter, you should have the domain controller that you built in previous chapters, and at least one other machine, either a workstation or a server.

▶ The exercises in this chapter use the users and Organizational Unit (OU) structure that we first created in Chapter 2, "Managing User and Computer Accounts." If you do not already have them in place, review the exercises in that chapter and re-create them.

▶ Make sure that you nest your OUs to test the effects of inheritance and blocking inheritance. These two concepts will be important for the exam.

▶ Some of the exercises in this chapter have been written to reflect the use of the Group Policy Management Console. Most of them can still be performed from the Group Policy tab of the OU or domain object in the Active Directory Users and Computers Microsoft Management Console (MMC).

▶ Although it would seem that because Microsoft didn't devote any bullet points for Group Policy on the Skills Measured by Exam 70-290 listing on its website, it might not be covered on the exam. This is far from the case. Historically, Group Policy has been featured on the 70-290 exams, and it is an essential part of your duties as a system administrator.

Introduction

In the previous chapters, we looked at how to manage and configure servers, folders, files and printers—one at a time. In the next few chapters, we examine a method of managing multiple objects at the same time and ensuring that they have similar configurations. This makes managing your servers a lot easier, whether you have 5 or 5,000.

Group Policy Overview

Starting in Windows 2000, Microsoft introduced the IntelliMirror technology. Although not really a technology per se, IntelliMirror is more of a technology umbrella that encompasses the following technologies:

▶ Remote Installation Services (RIS)

▶ Folder Redirection

▶ Software Installation

▶ Group Policy

Group Policy allows you to define a standard collection of settings and apply them to some or all of the computers and/or users in your enterprise. Group Policy has the capability to provide centralized control of a variety of components of a Windows network, such as security, application deployment and management, communications, and the overall user experience.

Group Policy is applied by creating an object that contains the settings that control the users' and computers' access to network and machine resources. This Group Policy Object (GPO) is created from templates that are stored on the workstation or server.

These GPOs are linked to a container that holds Active Directory objects such as users, groups, workstations servers, and printers. The settings in these GPOs will be applied to the objects in the container. The container can be an OU, a domain, or a site. GPOs can also be applied to a single computer through the use of Local Policy. You can apply multiple GPOs to a container. In this case, the settings will be merged. If there is a conflict in the settings between GPOs, the last setting applied wins.

Group Policy works by manipulating Registry and security settings on the workstation or server. Unlike the System Policies used in Windows NT, Group policy does not permanently (tattoo) change the Registry. After Group Policy is removed, the Registry settings return to their defaults.

Each Group Policy object has two separate sections: User and Computer configuration.

Group Policy for users includes settings for

- ► Operating System Behavior

- ► Desktop Settings

- ► Security Settings

- ► Application Settings

- ► Application Installation

- ► Folder Redirection Settings

- ► Logon and Logoff Scripts

User settings are applied at user logon, and during the periodic Group Policy refresh cycle. When these settings are applied to a user, they apply to that user at whatever computer the user logs on to.

Group Policy for computers includes settings for

- ► Operating System Behavior

- ► Desktop Settings

- ► Security Settings

- ► Application Settings

- ► Application Installation

- ► Folder Redirection Settings

- ► Computer Startup and Shutdown Scripts

You will probably notice that a lot of the same settings are available via both User and Computer settings. This allows you to specify settings that will apply to a particular user, or to all users who log on to a computer. When the settings between user and computer conflict, user settings generally take precedence.

NOTE

Loopback Processing   This behavior can be changed so that the computer policy settings take precedence, no matter what user logs on. Check the Windows Server 2003 online help for the section on loopback processing, or the Microsoft Knowledgebase article "Loopback Processing of Group Policy" at http://support.microsoft.com/?id=231287.

In addition, because the GPO is divided into two somewhat separate sections, you can specify that you want to disable one of the sections. For example, if you're planning to use a GPO only to configure settings for a user, you can disable the Computer section of the GPO. By disabling the section that is not being used, you can cut down on the time that it takes to process the GPO, because the system doesn't have to compare its settings against any other GPOs.

Figure 9.1 shows the Group Policy Object Editor MMC, which is used to configure Group Policy settings. If you look in the left pane of the MMC, you can see the various categories of settings that make up both the User and Computer configuration.

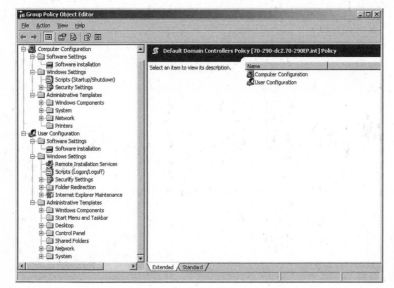

FIGURE 9.1 The Group Policy Editor MMC showing the various Group Policy setting categories.

The categories of note and their uses are the following:

▶ *Software Settings*—These settings are used to control the automated installation of software packages. They can be assigned to either users or computers.

▶ *Scripts*—This category controls the logon/logoff scripts for users, and the startup/shutdown scripts for computers.

▶ *Security Settings*—The category is used to configure the permissions, user rights, and restrictions.

▶ *Folder Redirection*—Used to redirect certain folders, such as My Documents, from the user's computer to a server.

▶ *Administrative Templates*—Used to configure Registry-based policies. These configurations are stored as .adm files on the server or workstation.

These components are stored in a Group policy object. GPOs are stored in two parts—as part of a Group Policy Template (GPT) and as objects inside a container in Active Directory called a Group Policy Container (GPC).

GPTs contain settings related to software installation policies and deployments, scripts, and security information for each GPO. They are stored in the `%SystemRoot%\`
`SYSVOL\`*`domain`*`\Policies` directory on every domain controller. The GPTs usually contain subfolders called Adm, USER, and MACHINE (see Figure 9.2) to separate the data to be applied to different portions of the Registry.

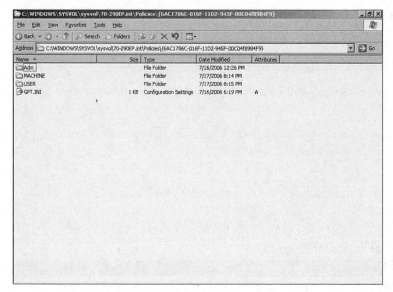

FIGURE 9.2 There are separate policy folders for each branch of the Registry.

As you might guess, the USER portion is applied to keys in HKEY_CURRENT_USER, and the MACHINE portion is applied to keys in HKEY_LOCAL_MACHINE. The Adm portion can contain settings for either branch of the Registry.

GPCs contain information, such as version, status, or extensions for the policy itself, regarding the GPO's link to Active Directory containers. Each GPC is referred to by a 128-bit string called a globally unique identifier, or GUID. The GUID is used as the name of the folder under POLICIES, as shown in the figure. Data stored in the GPC is used to indicate whether a specific policy object is enabled, as well as to control the proper version of the GPT to apply.

GPOs can be used to control only Windows 2000 or later servers and workstations.

Refreshing Group Policy

Computer settings are applied at operating system initialization and user settings at logon. Both settings are refreshed during the periodic Group Policy refresh cycle of 90 minutes, plus or minus a stagger interval of 30 minutes. The stagger interval is in place so that all the computers on the network aren't trying to update their policies at the same time, possibly flooding the network with traffic. The default group policy refresh cycle of 90 minutes can be changed via Group Policy.

Changes made to existing GPOs and new GPOs will be applied during the refresh cycle. The exceptions are the following:

- ▶ Software installation settings will be updated only at reboot or logon.

- ▶ Folder redirection settings will be updated only at reboot or logon.

- ▶ Computer configuration changes will be refreshed every 16 hours whether they have been changed or not.

- ▶ Domain controllers refresh Group Policy every 5 minutes, so that critical settings, such as security settings, are not delayed.

Changes can be implemented immediately using the gpupdate tool. Table 9.1 shows available command line options for the tool.

TABLE 9.1   Command-Line Options for Gpupdate

Value	Description
`/Target:{Computer	User}`	Specifies that only user or only computer policy settings are refreshed. By default, both user and computer policy settings are refreshed.
`/Force`	Reapplies all policy settings. By default, only policy settings that have changed are reapplied.
`/Wait:{value}`	Sets the number of seconds to wait for policy processing to finish. The default is 600 seconds. The value "0" means not to wait. The value "-1" means to wait indefinitely.
`/Logoff`	Causes a logoff after the Group Policy settings are refreshed. This is required for those Group Policy client side extensions that do not process policy during a background refresh cycle but do process policy when a user logs on. Examples include user-targeted Software Installation and Folder Redirection. This option has no effect if there are no extensions called that require a logoff.

(continues)

TABLE 9.1 *Continued*

Value	Description
/Boot	Causes the computer to restart after the Group Policy settings are refreshed. This is required for those Group Policy client-side extensions that do not process policy during a background refresh cycle but do process policy when the computer starts. Examples include computer targeted Software Installation. This option has no effect if no extensions are called that require the computer to restart.
/Sync	Causes the next foreground policy to be done synchronously. Foreground policy applications occur when the computer starts and when the user logs on. You can specify this for the user, computer, or both by using the /Target parameter. The /Force and /Wait parameters are ignored.

We use the gpupdate command in the upcoming exercises to force the immediate application of Group Policy.

> **NOTE**
>
> **Local Only** Gpupdate can only be used to refresh policy on a local machine.

Implementing Local Group Policy Objects

There are two types of GPOs, Local and Domain. Local GPOs are applied to the computer first. However, as we said earlier, the last GPO applied always wins. The exception is if the settings that you configured on the local GPO are not present in any of the other GPOs applied, the local GPO settings are left in place.

Local GPOs are typically used on standalone machines such as those in workgroups. Local computer policies are stored in the %SystemRoot%\System32\GroupPolicy directory because they apply only to the computer on which they're stored and they need not be replicated. Local policies are also more limited in scope and ability compared to domain GPOs.

The Group Policy Object Editor snap-in is used to work with local GPOs. You have the option of adding the snap-in to an existing console or creating a new one. To create a new Group Policy Object Editor console, follow the procedure in Step by Step 9.1.

> **NOTE**
>
> **Local Policy** Perform the following exercises on your member server.

STEP BY STEP

9.1 Creating a Group Policy Object Editor MMC

1. Click Start, Run, and then type in MMC. Click OK.

2. Click Console; then from the pop-up menu, select Add/Remove Snap-In. Click Add.

3. The Add Standalone Snap-In window appears. Scroll down and select the Group Policy Object Editor snap-in, and then click Add.

4. This starts the Group Policy Wizard, as shown in Figure 9.3. Accept the default for Local Computer, and then click the Finish button.

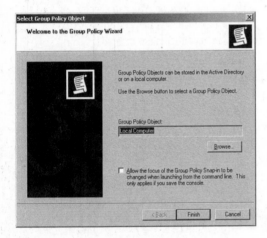

FIGURE 9.3 Select the Local Computer option.

5. If this is the only snap-in that you will be adding, click Close.

6. Click OK to finish.

7. From the Console window select Console, and then click Save As. The Save As window appears.

8. Type in **Group Policy Object Editor** for the filename, and then click Save.

> ### NOTE
>
> **Don't Accept the Default!** When you accept the default save location for an MMC, it gets saved in your user profile. To add it to the Administrative Tools folder for all users, back up a couple of levels and save it to the All Users profile.

Now that we have a console to use to work with the Local Group policies, let's implement and test one. In Windows Server 2003, you can't delete the Guest account, but you can rename it. Let's rename the Guest account to something that can't be guessed by a hacker.

To rename the Guest account using a Local Policy, follow the procedure in Step by Step 9.2.

STEP BY STEP

9.2 Creating a Local Policy

1. Select Start, All Programs, Administrative Tools, Group Policy Object Editor.

2. From the Group Policy Object Editor console, click Computer Configuration, Windows Settings, Security Settings, Local Policies, Security Options.

3. The Security Options folder opens, and displays the definable security options, as shown in Figure 9.4.

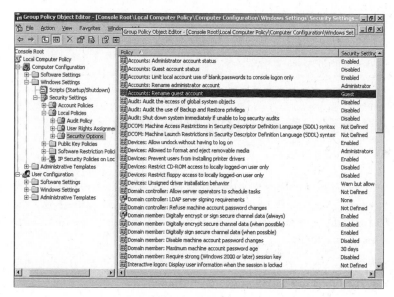

FIGURE 9.4 The Group Policy Object Editor MMC, showing the available security options.

4. Double-click the Rename Guest Account entry. The Properties dialog box appears.

5. Type in an appropriate name for the Guest account, and then click OK.

6. Close the Group Policy Object Editor MMC.

7. Select Start, All Programs, Administrative Tools, Computer Management.

8. In the Computer Management console, click System Tools, Local Users and Groups, Users.

9. The renamed account will be displayed in the right pane, as shown in Figure 9.5.

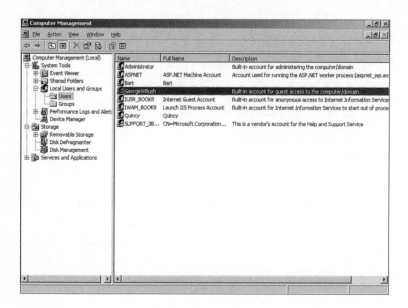

FIGURE 9.5 Using Local Policy to rename the Guest account.

Implementing Group Policy Objects in a Domain

Although being able to configure a single machine via Group Policy is helpful, the real power comes when you're able to create a single GPO and apply the settings in it to hundreds or even thousands of machines! Just imagine the savings in time and expense because you don't have to have a human touch all those machines.

However, with all this power comes great responsibility. For example, although it would be nice to be able to give every user and computer in your organization the same settings, that's really not practical for most environments. In most situations, different users have different needs—and different skill levels. Although a locked-down limited-use desktop might be fine for the mail room, that's probably not going to work for the folks in the software development lab.

When you first set up an Active Directory domain, two default GPOs are created: one that is linked to the domain itself, and therefore affects all users and computers within the domain; and one that is linked to the Domain Controllers OU, which affects all domain controllers within a domain.

Let's expand on Step by Step 9.2 and rename the Guest account, this time at the domain level.

> **NOTE**
>
> **Group Policy** Perform the following exercise using both your domain controller and your member server or workstation.

To rename the Guest account using a GPO, follow the procedure in Step by Step 9.3.

STEP BY STEP

9.3 Creating a GPO

1. On your domain controller, select Start, All Programs, Administrative Tools, Active Directory Users and Computers.

2. In the left pane, right-click the domain name and select Properties from the pop-up menu. This opens the domain Properties dialog box, as shown in Figure 9.6.

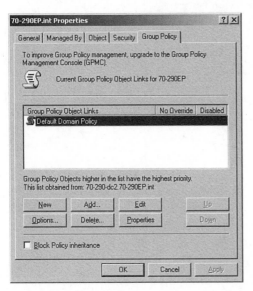

FIGURE 9.6 The Group Policy tab, showing the available options.

3. Click the New button; this adds an entry to the dialog box. Name it Rename Guest Account.

4. Highlight the new entry and click the Edit button. This opens the Group Policy Object Editor with our GPO as the focus.

5. From the Group Policy Object Editor console, click Computer Configuration, Windows Settings, Security Settings, Local Policies, Security Options.

6. The Security Options folder opens, displaying the definable security options.

7. Double-click the Rename Guest Account entry. The Properties dialog box appears.

8. Select the Define this policy setting check box, and then type in an appropriate name for the Guest account, different from the one you selected for the Local Policy exercise, and click OK.

9. Close the Group Policy Object Editor MMC.

10. Close the domain properties dialog box.

11. Go to your member server or workstation, open a command window, and enter the following command: GPUpdate.

12. Close the command window.

13. Select Start, All Programs, Administrative Tools, Computer Management.

14. In the Computer Management console, click System Tools, Local Users and Groups, Users.

15. The renamed account will be displayed in the right pane, as shown in Figure 9.7.

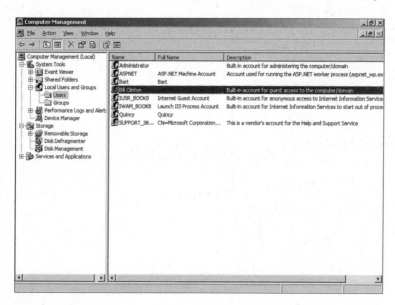

FIGURE 9.7   Using a GPO to rename the Guest account for the domain.

This exercise demonstrated several things about GPOs. The first is that the procedure to create a domain GPO is similar to that of a Local Policy. However, as you may have noticed, the domain GPOs have a lot more settings available. The other point is that the Local Policy was overwritten by the domain GPO. In addition, because we added the new GPO at the domain level, every machine in the domain, and any machines that are added in the future, will have the Guest account renamed.

Managing Policy Objects

Now that we have an idea of what policy is and what it can do for you, let's take a look at how to implement it in your network. Fortunately, Microsoft has supplied a multitude of management features for GPOs, such as inheritance, filtering, and blocking, which we cover in the next sections.

Linking GPOs

When we created the GPO in Step by Step 9.3, we actually performed two operations. We created the GPO and we linked it to the domain. As we saw earlier, all GPOs are stored in Active Directory in a central location. By keeping all the GPOs in a single location, they are easier to manage. When we want to apply a GPO to a domain site or OU, we link it to that object.

By default, only members of the Enterprise or Domain Admins groups can link GPOs to a domain or OU, and only Enterprise Admins can link GPOs to sites. Members of the Group Policy Creator Owners group can create GPOs; however, they cannot link them to an object.

> **NOTE**
>
> **Disabling a Link**   If a GPO no longer should be applied to an object, but is still being used for other objects, you can unlink it.

If you already have a GPO in place that you want to use for an additional OU, you can link it to that OU. In Step by Step 9.4, we will link our Rename Guest Account GPO to the Kansas City OU we created in a previous exercise.

STEP BY STEP

9.4 Linking an existing GPO

1. On your domain controller, select Start, All Programs, Administrative Tools, Active Directory Users and Computers.

2. In the left pane, right-click the Kansas City OU and select Properties from the pop-up menu. This opens the Kansas City Properties dialog box.

3. Click the Add button. This opens the Add a Group Policy Object Link dialog box, as shown in Figure 9.8. From the drop-down box, select the location to look in for the GPO.

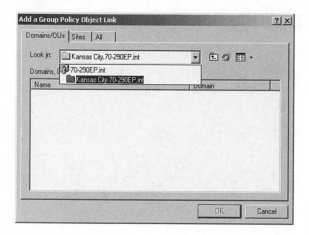

FIGURE 9.8   Select a container to look in for the GPO.

4. Select the domain; the Rename Guest Account GPO should be listed. Highlight the GPO entry and click the OK button. This returns you to the Kansas City Properties dialog box, with the selected GPO displayed.

5. Click OK to save.

NOTE

Containers?   If you look closely in the left pane of the Active Directory Users and Computers MMC, you will notice that all the folder icons are not the same. Some icons are plain—these are containers. The other icons have an open folder label on them—these are OUs. Most of the containers are automatically created by the operating system, and some of them, such as the Users or Computers containers, cannot be linked to GPOs.

Linking GPOs is handy for a variety of reasons. For example, suppose that you have a test OU where you keep your test servers. Part of your testing is to create suitable GPOs to manage these servers. When testing is complete, you can move the servers to your production OU. Instead of manually copying the settings from your test GPOs, you can link them to the production GPO.

Default Group Policy Objects

Windows Server 2003 comes with two default GPOs:

▶ *Default Domain Policy*—This policy is linked to the domain and controls the default Account Policies for things such as Password Policy and Account Lockout.

▶ *Domain Controllers Policy*—This policy is linked to the Domain Controllers OU and contains settings strictly for the domain controllers.

It's best to not edit the default GPOs. Any changes should be implemented in new GPOs.

Group Policy Inheritance

Group Policy in Windows 2003 works according to the hierarchy of site → domain → OU, or *SDOU* for short. As we mentioned earlier, the effects of Group Policy as it is applied are cumulative. As more policies are applied, their settings are merged, with the last setting winning.

What this means is that if you apply a GPO for a site, it will apply to everything in that site. If you apply a GPO to a domain, both the site and the domain GPOs will be applied. This continues down the hierarchy of OUs. For example, take a look at the OU structure in Figure 9.9 that we created in Chapter 2.

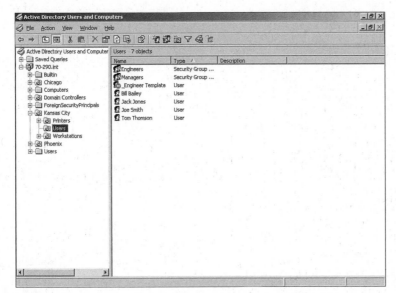

FIGURE 9.9 The OU hierarchy.

When we get to the bottom of our hierarchy, at the Users OU, we could potentially have applied at least four GPOs—one each at the site, domain, Kansas City OU, and the Users OU levels.

NOTE

Active Directory Sites   Sites are handled a little differently from other objects in AD, because they are a physical object and can contain resources from several domains. When an OU is linked to a site, the properties of the OU affect all resources in the site, regardless of their domain membership.

This process is called Inheritance. The Active Directory objects lower in the hierarchy inherit the settings from those higher in the hierarchy.

In addition to inheritance, an Active Directory container can have multiple GPOs linked to it. In addition to the SDOU order, the GPOs linked to the container can be assigned in order. This is configured from the Properties dialog box on the Group Policy tab of the OU, as shown in Figure 9.10.

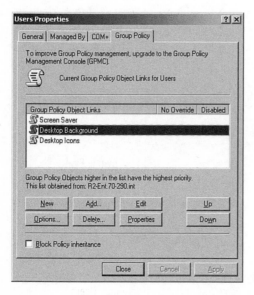

FIGURE 9.10   Setting GPO priority.

As you can see in the figure, changing the priority of the GPOs is a simple as clicking a button.

Blocking Group Policy Inheritance

Although inheritance might sound like a good thing in theory, in practice it can get quite messy. For example, what if you want the users in the Users OU to have different settings from those at the domain level? Or what if you as the system administrator have delegated the management of the Kansas City OU to a junior administrator in that location, and she insists on changing the corporate settings?

In these situations, you have the option of modifying the standard inheritance rules for specific GPOs. The first option is to Block Policy Inheritance. This option is set on a per-container basis and will block the inheritance of *all* policies. It's strictly an all-or-nothing solution.

In Step by Step 9.2 and 9.3, we implemented both a Local and a Group Policy to rename the Guest account. As we left things in Step by Step 9.3, there is a GPO at the domain level that is Renaming the Guest account. In Step by Step 9.5, we will put our member server or workstation in the workstations OU and block inheritance, so that the GPO is not in effect.

STEP BY STEP

9.5 Blocking Group Policy Inheritance

1. On your domain controller, select Start, All Programs, Administrative Tools, Active Directory Users and Computers.

2. Locate the computer account for your test member server or workstation. Move the computer account into the Kansas City\Workstations OU.

3. Right-click the Workstations OU and select Properties from the pop-up menu.

4. Select the Group Policy tab. Select the Block Policy Inheritance check box, as shown in Figure 9.11. Click OK to save.

5. Go to your member server or workstation, open a command window, and enter the following command: *gpupdate*.

6. Close the command window.

7. Select Start, All Programs, Administrative Tools, Computer Management.

8. In the Computer Management console, click System Tools, Local Users and Groups, Users.

9. The account name will be displayed in the right pane. It should not have been set to the name you specified in the blocked GPO.

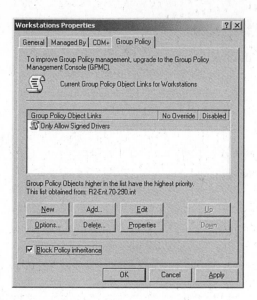

FIGURE 9.11 Enable Block Policy Inheritance.

The Block Policy Inheritance option is useful for situations where the objects in a container require unique settings, and you want to ensure that those settings are not in conflict with inherited settings. In addition, this option can be used when a local administrator is responsible for managing an OU, and she prefers to control her own Group Policy configurations.

However, even when Block Policy Inheritance is turned on, it cannot block the inheritance of a GPO that has the No Override option turned on. We'll look at enforcing Group Policy in the next section.

Challenge

You are the lead system administrator for your company. Upper management has decided that the Phoenix office is going to be allowed to manage its own desktops. However, certain settings in the Default Domain Policy must remain in place. You currently have a single GPO linked to the Phoenix OU named Desktop Settings.

How can you implement this management directive using the least amount of effort?

Try to complete this exercise on your own, listing your conclusions on a sheet of paper. After you have completed the exercise, compare your results to those given here.

1. On your domain controller, select Start, All Programs, Administrative Tools, Active Directory Users and Computers.

(continues)

(continued)

2. In the left pane, right-click the Phoenix OU, and select Properties from the pop-up menu. This opens the Phoenix Proprieties dialog box.

3. Select the Group Policy tab. Highlight the Desktop Settings entry, and then click the Delete button.

4. This opens the Delete dialog box. Select the option to Remove the link from the list, and then click OK.

5. On the Properties dialog box, click OK to save.

In this situation, we couldn't block the inheritance to the OU because we need to retain the Default Domain Policy settings. Also, deleting the Desktop Settings GPO wouldn't be a good idea, because it might be linked to other GPOs. Just deleting the link removes it from the Phoenix OU without affecting anything else.

Enforcing Group Policy

The second way to control Group Policy Inheritance is to select the No Override option. This option is used to prevent a child container from blocking the application of a GPO that is inherited from the parent. Unlike the all or nothing of the Block Policy Inheritance option, the No Override option is set on a per-GPO basis.

> **NOTE**
>
> **Enforced**   The No Override option is renamed to Enforced after the Group Policy Management Console (GPMC) is installed.

The No Override option allows the administrator to enforce specific settings, possibly companywide configuration settings that should take precedence over anything else. A GPO that has the No Override option turned on will take precedence over the settings in the child container, even though traditionally the child settings would take precedence.

On GPOs with the No Override setting enabled, the Block Inheritance setting is ignored.

In Step by Step 9.6, we continue our scenario using the Rename Guest Account GPO. This time we set the No Override option to force the setting in the Kansas City\Workstations OU.

STEP BY STEP

9.6 Enforcing Group Policy inheritance

1. On your domain controller, select Start, All Programs, Administrative Tools, Active Directory Users and Computers.

2. In the left pane, right-click the Kansas City OU and select Properties from the pop-up menu. This opens the Kansas City Properties dialog box.

3. Select the Group Policy tab. Highlight the desired GPO, then click the Options button. This opens the Rename Guest Account Options dialog box, as shown in Figure 9.12.

FIGURE 9.12   Enable the No Override option.

4. Select the No Override check box. Click OK to save.

5. Click Apply to close the Kansas City Properties dialog box.

6. Go to your member server or workstation, open a command window, and enter the following command: **gpupdate**.

7. Close the command window.

8. Select Start, All Programs, Administrative Tools, Computer Management.

9. In the Computer Management console, click System Tools, Local Users and Groups, Users.

10. The account name will be displayed in the right pane. It now should be set to the name configured in the blocked GPO.

Group Policy Management Console

The Group Policy Management Console (GPMC) is a free add-on from Microsoft that can be downloaded from the website at http://www.microsoft.com/downloads/details.aspx? FamilyId=0A6D4C24-8CBD-4B35-9272-DD3CBFC81887&displaylang=en. The GPMC allows you to manage your GPOs via a GUI interface in a more intuitive manner with more functionality than the tools we have been using so far in this chapter.

The GPMC can be installed on either Windows Server 2003 or Windows XP SP1 and can be used to manage GPOs in either a Windows 2000 or a Windows Server 2003 domain. After the GPMC is installed, the Group Policy tab that we've been using in the Active Directory Users and Computers MMC is replaced with a message and a button that opens the GPMC, as shown in Figure 9.13.

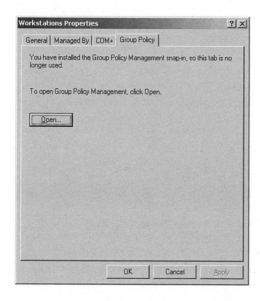

FIGURE 9.13   Click to open the GPMC.

After the GPMC is installed, it can be opened directly by selecting the Group Policy Management icon in the Administrative Tools folder.

EXAM ALERT

To Study or Not to Study?   As this book was going to press, Windows Server 2003 SP2 is being released, and the GPMC was not included in it. It is still just an add-on downloadable from the web. However, it has been added to the exam. We will cover both methods of working with GPOs in this book.

As you can see in Figure 9.14, the GPMC allows you not only to see all of the OUs and GPOs in your domain, but it displays every domain in the forest. If you have the proper permissions, you can copy, back up, restore, import, and link GPOs between and across domains. Another point of interest is the display of the Group Policy Objects container. The GPO container holds all the GPOs in the domain. If you look at the icons for the other GPOs shown in the console, you will notice that they are linked to the other containers. Previously, we knew that the GPO container existed, but it was just a logical entity. We couldn't see it—now we can.

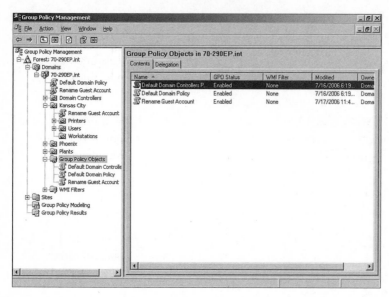

FIGURE 9.14 The GPMC, showing the forest view.

In effect, all the logical things we discussed about Group Policy are now visible.

To find out more about the Group Policy Management Console, consult the online help for the GPMC, and read the GPMC white papers available at http://www.microsoft.com/windowsserver2003/gpmc/default.mspx.

Group Policy Filtering

In Windows Server 2003, the default is for all objects in the container to be affected by all GPOs that are applied to that container. However, there will be situations where you will want some GPOs to apply only to certain users, computers, or groups. This process is called Group Policy Filtering.

Group Policy Filtering works by applying permissions on the GPO so that it can be used only by certain users, computers, or groups. For a Group Policy to be applied to an object, that object must have at least Read permissions for the GPO. The default permissions for a GPO are the following:

▶ *Authenticated Users*—Read, Apply Group Policy

▶ *Domain Admins, Enterprise Admins, SYSTEM*—Read, Write, Create All Child Objects, Delete All Child Objects

▶ *Creator Owner*—Special Permissions

As you can see, because the Authenticated Users group has Read and Apply permissions on all GPOs, they apply by default to everything on the network. There are two ways to filter GPOs:

▶ *Explicitly Deny*—In this method, a new security group is created and assigned the Deny Apply Group Policy permission. Objects that should not be affected by this GPO are added to the group.

▶ *Remove Authenticated Users*—In this method, the Authenticated Users group is removed from the DACL for the GPO. A new security group is created and given Read and Apply Group Policy permissions to the GPO. The desired objects are added to this group.

Either method works the same in practice; it's strictly a matter of preference.

In Step by Step 9.7, we will use the Group Policy Management Console to use the Explicitly Deny method to keep the Rename Guest Account GPO from being applied to our member server or workstation.

STEP BY STEP

9.7 Filtering Group Policy

1. On your domain controller, select Start, All Programs, Administrative Tools, Active Directory Users and Computers.

2. Create a domain local security group and name it Deny Rename.

3. Add the computer account of your workstation or member server to this security group.

4. Select Start, All Programs, Administrative Tools, Group Policy Management.

5. In the left pane, expand the domain, and then expand the Group Policy Objects container. Select the Rename Guest Account GPO.

6. In the right pane, select the Scope tab. Click the Add button in the Security Filtering area, as shown in Figure 9.15. From the Select User, Computer, or Group dialog box, enter the Deny Rename group. Click OK to save.

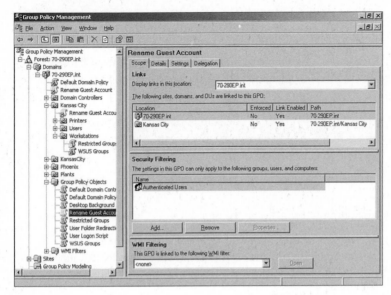

FIGURE 9.15 By default, the settings in the GPO apply to all Authenticated users.

7. In the right pane, select the Delegation tab.

8. Highlight the entry for the Deny Rename group and select the Advanced button. This opens the Rename Guest Account Security settings dialog box shown in Figure 9.16.

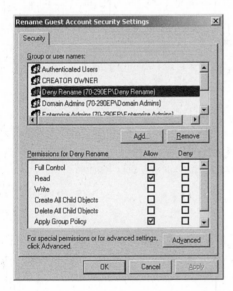

FIGURE 9.16 Set the security on the Deny Rename group to deny Full Control.

9. Highlight the entry for the Deny Rename group and select Deny Full Control.

10. Click OK to save, and then click Yes in the Security Warning prompt.

11. Go to your member server or workstation, open a command window, and enter the following command: **gpupdate**.

12. Close the command window.

13. Select Start, All Programs, Administrative Tools, Computer Management.

14. In the Computer Management console, click System Tools, Local Users and Groups, Users.

15. The account name will be displayed in the right pane. It should not be set to the name configured in the GPO.

Chapter Summary

In this chapter, we looked at implementing Group Policy. With the release of Windows Server 2003, Microsoft has greatly expanded the functionality and scope of Group Policy and has added new tools to implement these additional functions.

Make sure that you have a thorough understanding of the basics of Group policy implementation that were demonstrated in this chapter, as you delve deeper into Group Policy in the next chapter.

Key Terms

▶ Group Policy

▶ Group Policy Object

▶ Group Policy Management Console (GPMC)

▶ Group Policy Inheritance

▶ SDOU

▶ Group Policy Filtering

Apply Your Knowledge

Exercises

9.1 Filtering Group Policy

In this exercise, you will create a GPO and then filter it to apply only to the Managers Group. This exercise uses the Group Policy Management Console.

Estimated Time: 20 minutes

1. From the Start menu, click Start, Control Panel, Administrative Tools, Group Policy Management.

2. In the left pane, expand the domain, and then expand the Kansas City\Users container. Right-click the Users OU and select Create and Link a GPO Here.

3. When prompted, name the GPO Desktop Background.

4. In the GPO container, right-click the new GPO and select Edit from the pop-up menu.

5. This opens the Group Policy Object Editor. Select User configuration, Administrative Templates, Desktop, Active Desktop. In the right pane, double-click the Active Desktop Wallpaper entry.

6. This opens the Active Desktop Wallpaper Properties dialog box. Select the Enable button, and then enter `c:\windows\greenstone.bmp` in the Wallpaper Name field. Click OK to save.

7. In the right pane, double-click the Enable Active Desktop entry.

8. This opens the Active Desktop Properties dialog box. Select the Enable button, and then click OK to save.

9. Close the Group Policy Object Editor.

10. Back in the GPMC, with the Desktop Background GPO selected, click the Delegation tab.

11. Highlight the Authenticated Users entry and click the Remove button.

12. Click the Add button, add the Managers group, and give them Read permissions.

13. On your test server or workstation, log on using any user account.

14. Open a command window and run the gpupdate command. Close the command window.

15. Log off the test machine.

16. Log on the test machine using an account that is a member of the Managers group. You should see the Greenstone desktop background.

17. Log off the test machine.

18. Log on the test machine using an account that is not a member of the Managers group. You should see the default desktop background.

Exam Questions

1. You are the network administrator for FlyByNight Airlines. The network consists of a single Active Directory domain. The functional level of the domain is Windows 2000 native. All network servers run Windows Server 2003, and all client computers run Windows XP Professional.

   Some of your users are complaining that because you implemented a set of new group policies, it's taking noticeably longer for them to log on to their computers. You check your GPOs and notice that the affected users are having 10 GPOs applied—5 with users settings and 5 with computer settings. What can you do to speed up their logon times?

   ○ **A.** Change the order of the GPOs.

   ○ **B.** Raise the functional level of the domain to Windows Server 2003.

   ○ **C.** Disable the Computer section in the GPOs with User settings.

   ○ **D.** Disable the User section in the GPOs with Computer settings.

2. You are the network administrator for FlyByNight Airlines. The network consists of a single Active Directory domain. The functional level of the domain is Windows 2000 native. All network servers run Windows Server 2003, and all client computers run Windows XP Professional.

   You assign one of your junior administrators to create a GPO that changes the desktop on all the PCs in the Maintenance OU. He will need to link it to that GPO when it's completed.

   Which of the following default groups must he be assigned to?

   ○ **A.** Domain Admins

   ○ **B.** GPO Admins

   ○ **C.** Group Policy Creator Owners

   ○ **D.** Maintenance Admins

3. You are the network administrator for FlyByNight Airlines. The network consists of a single Active Directory domain. The functional level of the domain is Windows 2000 native. All network servers run Windows Server 2003, and all client computers run Windows XP Professional.

   You assign one of your junior administrators to create a GPO that changes the desktop on all the PCs in the Kansas City Site. He will need to link it to that GPO when it's completed.

   Which of the following default groups must he be assigned to?

   ○ **A.** Domain Admins

   ○ **B.** GPO Admins

   ○ **C.** Group Policy Creator Owners

   ○ **D.** Enterprise Admins

4. You are the network administrator for CheapRides.com. The network consists of a single Active Directory domain, with a mixture of Windows XP Professional and Windows NT clients.

   The general manager calls and says that he wants all users to have a standard desktop background with the company logo.

   What would you do to accomplish this task?

   ○ **A.** Edit the Default Domain GPO to load the standard desktop background on all computers.

   ○ **B.** Create a new GPO and call it Desktop Background. Edit this GPO to load the standard desktop background on all computers. Link the GPO to the domain container.

   ○ **C.** Create a new GPO and call it Desktop Background. Edit this GPO to load the standard desktop background on all computers.

   ○ **D.** None of the above are correct.

5. You are the network administrator for CheapRides.com. The network consists of a single Active Directory domain. All network servers run Windows Server 2003, and all client computers run Windows XP Professional.

The general manager of the Kansas City location wants his users to have their own custom desktop settings. There is already a Corporate GPO in place with the corporate settings. The Kansas City users and computers are located in a separate OU named Kansas City.

Which two actions should you perform? (Each correct answer presents part of the solution. Choose two.)

- ○ **A.** Create a Kansas City GPO and add the requested settings to it. Link it to the Kansas City OU.

- ○ **B.** Create a Kansas City GPO and add the requested settings to it. Link it to the domain.

- ○ **C.** Configure the properties of the Kansas City OU to block inheritance.

- ○ **D.** Configure the properties of the Corporate GPO to block inheritance.

- ○ **E.** Configure the properties of the domain to block inheritance.

Answers to Exam Questions

1. **D.** Because the computer section of the GPO is applied at machine startup, and the user section is applied at user logon, the best solution is to disable the user section in the GPOs that contain only computer settings. This would keep the system from trying to process them, and cut down on the logon overhead. Changing the order of the GPOs wouldn't help because everything still needs to be processed. The functional level of the domain is not the cause of the problem. See "Group Policy Overview."

2. **A.** By default, only members of the Enterprise or Domain Admins groups can link GPOs to a domain or OU, and only Enterprise Admins can link GPOs to sites. Members of the Group Policy Creator Owners group can create GPOs; however, they cannot link them to an object. The other groups are not default groups. See "Linking GPOs."

3. **D.** By default, only members of the Enterprise or Domain Admins groups can link GPOs to a domain or OU, and only Enterprise Admins can link GPOs to sites. Members of the Group Policy Creator Owners group can create GPOs; however, they cannot link them to an object. The other group is not a default group. "See Linking GPOs."

4. **D.** Group Policy is not supported on pre-Windows 2000 clients, so the task cannot be accomplished with the listed options. See "Group Policy Overview."

5. **A and C.** To accomplish this task, you will need to configure a new GPO, link it to the Kansas City OU, *and* block GPO inheritance on the properties page of the OU. See "Blocking Group Policy Inheritance."

Suggested Readings and Resources

1. *Group Policy Management Console Step-by-Step Guide.* Microsoft Corporation. http://www.microsoft.com/technet/prodtechnol/windowsserver2003/technologies/directory/activedirectory/stepbystep/gpmcinad.mspx.

2. *Group Policy Operations Guide.* Microsoft Corporation. http://technet2.microsoft.com/WindowsServer/en/Library/ed6131df-efca-4337-9594-583e19ca3b761033.mspx?mfr=true.

3. *Group Policy Resource Center.* http://www.gpanswers.com/.

4. Morimoto, Rand, et. al. *Microsoft Windows Server 2003 Unleashed R2 Edition.* Sams Publishing, 2006. ISBN 0672328984.

5. *Windows Server 2003 Deployment Guide.* http://technet2.microsoft.com/WindowsServer/en/Library/c283b699-6124-4c3a-87ef-865443d7ea4b1033.mspx?mfr=true Microsoft Corporation.

6. *Windows Server 2003 Resource Kit.* Microsoft Press, 2005. ISBN 0735614717.

CHAPTER TEN

Managing the User Environment by Using Group Policy

Objectives

This chapter covers information that you will most likely see on the test—and on the job. However, it doesn't cover any specific objectives on the Microsoft Managing and Maintaining a Microsoft Windows Server 2003 Environment exam.

Outline

Study Strategies

▶ In studying this section, be sure to practice all the activities described. Become very familiar with the Group Policy Management Console, how it is installed, and its capabilities and limitations.

▶ To perform the exercises in this chapter, you should have the domain controller that you built in previous chapters and at least one other machine, either a workstation or a server.

▶ The exercises in this chapter continue the use of the users and the Organizational Unit (OU) structure that we first created in Chapter 2, "Managing User and Computer Accounts." If you do not already have them in place, review the exercises in that chapter and re-create them.

▶ Some of the exercises in this chapter have been written to reflect the use of the Group Policy Management Console. Most of them can still be performed from the Group Policy tab of the OU or domain object in the Active Directory Users and Computers Microsoft Management Console (MMC).

▶ Although it would seem that because Microsoft didn't devote any bullet points for Group Policy on the Skills Measured by Exam 70-290 listing on its website, it might not be covered on the exam. This is far from the case. Historically, Group Policy has been featured on the 70-290 exams, and it is an essential part of your duties as a system administrator.

Introduction

The major mission of Group Policy is to manage the user and network environment. This includes the look and feel of the users' desktop, and controlling what they can and can't do when they are logged on to the network. In essence, Group Policy allows you, the system administrator, to ensure that users have what they need to perform their jobs, but not allow them to corrupt their or other users' environments.

In this chapter, we're going to continue our coverage of Group Policy. We will look at more of the things that you can do with Group Policy, and we will also look at the tools needed to manage Group Policy Objects (GPOs).

Assigning Scripts with Group Policy

Scripts, in one form or another, have existed for years on just about all computer platforms from mainframes down to the PC. There has always been a common need to automatically configure a user session without user or administrator intervention.

Group Policy can be used to assign scripts to run when the user logs on or off or when the computer is started or shut down. Script settings are provided in both the User and the Computer sections of the GPO.

Benefits of GPO Scripts

A script can allow you either to standardize the setup of various users or computers or to supply a custom setup for certain users. It just depends on which script is assigned. Typically, a script will be written in whatever command language is available on the platform.

Using Group Policy scripts allows the system administrator to centralize control over the application and data locations that aren't already defined by Folder Redirection. By defining drive mappings via a script instead of letting the user attempt to do it, the administrator is assured that all users will be working with an identical configuration. Because Group Policy scripts can be applied to a large number of users, the administrator can easily make changes to the configuration by just changing a script instead of having to visit each individual desktop.

Scripts can also be used for various system maintenance activities. The administrator can add routines to delete the files in temporary directories, run disk utilities in the background, and various other activities.

Group Policy scripts can be assigned to a user, a computer, a group of users, or all the users in an Organization Unit (OU), site, or domain. There can be different scripts for different departments or locations. If you are using some of the more featured batch languages for your scripts, you can have the script perform a different set of tasks, depending on what group or OU the user or computer may be assigned to.

How Group Policy Scripts Work

In Windows Server 2003, Group Policy scripts are stored in the Group Policy template stored with the GPO. This way, the script is automatically replicated among all the domain controllers. This is a big improvement from the previous versions of Windows NT, where the system administrator placed the scripts in the logon share and then had to manually configure the replication pattern for the network. This method was error prone, and the replication mechanism was infamous for replication failures, without presenting any errors.

After the script is stored in the GPO, the system administrator assigns the script to one or more users or computers. This can be accomplished by applying the script via a Group Policy. When the user logs on to the domain or the computer is started, the script will run and perform whatever tasks the system administrator has coded in it.

> **NOTE**
>
> **Logon Scripts**   Although assigning a logon script to a user profile is still supported in Windows Server 2003, it can be quite tedious to assign scripts to a large number of users. In addition, it can be a nightmare to manage if the logon script names change frequently. The best solution is to assign logon scripts via Group Policy. This allows all changes to be performed in one place, and when assigning scripts using a Group Policy, you have the option of also assigning a logoff script. Unfortunately, Group Policies can be used only with Windows 2000 or later clients.

In Step by Step 10.1 we're going to create a new GPO and use it to assign a logon script to an OU that we created in the exercises in Chapter 2.

To perform this exercise, you will need to do the following:

- ▶ Create a share on your server and name it **Payroll**. Accept the default permissions.

- ▶ Create a logon script and name it **logon.bat**. The contents of the script will be **net use P: ***yourservername***\Payroll**.

STEP BY STEP

10.1 Assigning a logon script using Group Policy

1. Open the Group Policy Management Console. Right-click the Kansas City\Users OU and select Create and Link a GPO Here from the pop-up menu, as shown in Figure 10.1.

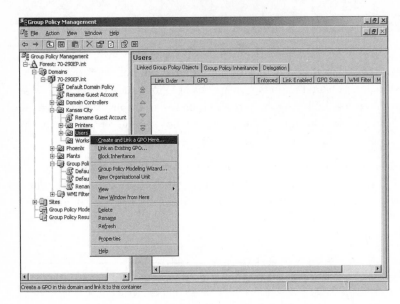

FIGURE 10.1 The GPMC allows you to configure most GPO settings. Select the option to Create and Link a GPO.

2. When the New GPO prompt appears, enter the name **User Logon Script**, and click OK.

3. The new GPO will appear in the Group Policy Objects container, as a linked object under the OU folder, as shown in Figure 10.2.

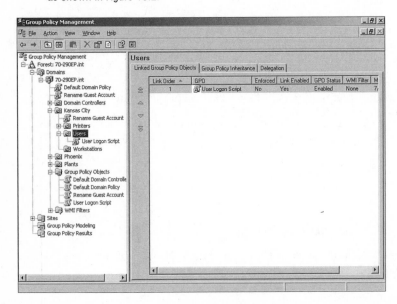

FIGURE 10.2 Right-click the GPO to edit.

4. Right-click the new GPO and select Edit from the pop-up menu. The Group Policy Editor MMC appears.

5. Click the User Configuration icon, and then click the Windows settings folder.

6. Click the Scripts (Logon/Logoff) icon.

7. In the right pane of the console window, double click the Logon icon.

8. The Logon Properties window opens, as shown in Figure 10.3.

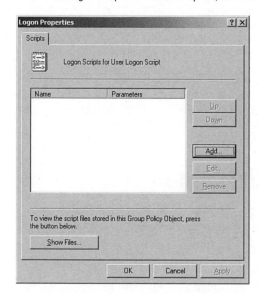

FIGURE 10.3 The Logon Properties dialog box. This is where you add files to the GPT.

9. Click the Show Files button. This opens the GPT folder. Drag and drop the `logon.bat` file to this folder; then close it and return to the Logon Properties dialog box.

10. On Logon Properties, click Add; the Add a Script window appears, as shown in Figure 10.4.

FIGURE 10.4 The Add a Script dialog box. You can enter the script here and any required command-line parameters.

11. In the Add a Script window, you can either type in the name of the logon script, or you can click Browse to locate it. Type in **logon.bat**. Click OK.

12. Click OK again to close the Properties window.

13. On your test server or workstation, log on using one of the user accounts in the Kansas City\Users OU.

14. Open a command window and run the `gpupdate` command. Close the command window.

15. Verify that the Payroll folder was successfully mapped to drive P.

Startup and Shutdown scripts are assigned to a computer, in contrast to the logon and logoff scripts, which are assigned to users. The startup and shutdown scripts are useful for making customizations to the computer that are not user specific.

A good example of where a Group Policy Shutdown script would be useful is on a mail or a database server where background services must be stopped before the system can shut down.

The procedure to assign Group Policy Startup and Shutdown scripts is similar to the steps covered in the Step by Step. They are assigned via the Group Policy console, under the Computer Configuration section.

Configuring Folder Redirection

Another feature in Group Policy in Windows Server 2003 is Folder Redirection. Folder Redirection allows the administrator to redirect the folders that are part of the user profile to a file share, typically on a server. When this user data is stored on a server, the user can access it from any workstation to which the user logs on.

In addition, Folder Redirection makes it easier for the system administrator to secure and back up the user data. This is because the data is stored on a server that the administrator has full control of, which allows the system administrator to monitor the security of the files, monitor the content, and set quotas and file screens as appropriate.

The following folders can be redirected via Group Policy:

▶ *My Documents*—This folder normally holds the user files. By redirecting it to a server, it can be easily backed up, and it should be more secure.

▶ *Application Data*—Redirecting this folder allows the users' application configuration to be available to them if they move to another computer.

▶ *Desktop*— Redirecting this folder allows the users' desktop with all the file folders and shortcuts on it to be available to them if they move to another computer.

▶ *Start Menu*—Redirecting this folder allows users to have a common Start menu and subfolders available to them if they move to another computer.

These folders are automatically created by Windows Server 2003 and are part of the user profile associated with each user account.

There are two types of folder redirection:

> ▶ *Basic*—Basic Folder Redirection offers two options: redirecting all users to a common folder or redirecting all users to a common root and creating a private folder for each user under the root. The second option is recommended for a folder such as My Documents, which might contain sensitive data.

> ▶ *Advanced*—The Advanced Folder Redirection has the same options as basic; however, users can be assigned different paths depending on group membership. This is handy when you're setting up a common GPO where different departments or locations would have their file shares on different servers.

In Step by Step 10.2, we're going to create a new GPO, and use it to assign a Folder Redirection GPO to the Users OU that we created in a previous exercise.

To perform this exercise, you will need to create a share on your server and name it Users. Configure the permissions on the share Authenticated Users—Full Control.

STEP BY STEP

10.2 Configuring folder redirection using group policy

1. Open the Group Policy Management Console. Right-click the Kansas City\Users OU and select Create and Link a GPO Here from the pop-up menu.

2. When the New GPO prompt appears, enter the name **User Folder Redirection**, and click OK.

3. The new GPO will appear in the Group Policy Objects container and as a linked object under the OU folder.

4. Right-click the new GPO and select Edit from the pop-up menu. The Group Policy Editor MMC appears.

5. Click the User Configuration icon, and then click the Windows settings folder.

6. Click the Folder Redirection icon.

7. In the right pane of the console window, right-click the My Documents icon and select Properties from the pop-up menu.

8. The My Documents Properties window opens.

9. In the My Document Properties dialog box, select Basic from the drop-down menu. This enables the other fields, as shown in Figure 10.5. Leave the default for the Target Folder location, and enter the path to the Users share on your server, as shown.

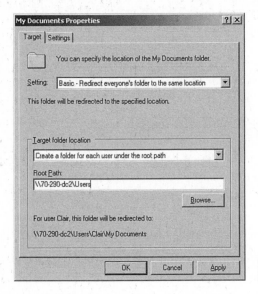

FIGURE 10.5 The My Documents Properties dialog box. Specify where you want the folder redirected to.

10. Click the Settings tab. This tab (see Figure 10.6) displays several additional features. For now, accept the defaults. Click OK to save. Close the Group Policy Object Editor.

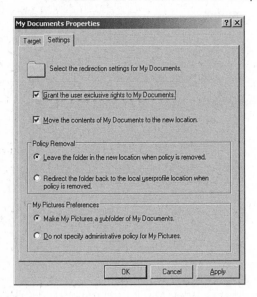

FIGURE 10.6 The My Document Properties dialog box. You can allow the server to move the existing contents of My Documents to the server, among other options.

11. On your test server or workstation, log on using one of the user accounts in the Kansas City\Users OU.

12. Open the My Documents folder, create a text file, and name it **Test-FR.txt**.

13. Open a command window and run the gpupdate command. Close the command window.

14. Reboot the test machine.

15. Log on to the test machine.

16. Right-click the My Documents icon, and select Properties from the pop-up menu. The target folder location should point to the server, as shown in Figure 10.7. The test file should have been moved to the server.

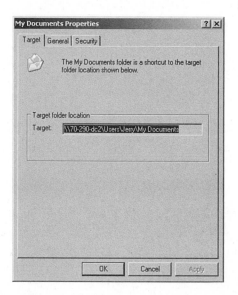

FIGURE 10.7 The My Document Properties dialog box. Note that the target folder path now points to the server.

NOTE

Initial Folder Security For best results, let the operating system create the user folders and the initial security settings for Folder Redirection.

After Folder Redirection is enabled, end users typically will not notice that their data is no longer on their local hard drive.

NOTE

Windows XP Because of the fast user logon feature in Windows XP, you might have to log on two or three times before the folder redirection policy is applied.

Restricting Group Membership

A new Group Policy feature introduced in Windows Server 2003 is Restricted Groups. The Restricted Groups feature allows an administrator to control the membership of the local groups on workstations and member servers. Domain Controllers are not included because they don't have local groups.

The administrator is able to control the membership in the group by specifying the members of the group in the GPO. Any additional members that may have been added to the group are removed during the Group Policy refresh. The administrator is also able to specify what groups the restricted group is a member of.

There are two ways to apply a Restricted Groups Policy:

▶ Via a Security Template. Security Template are discussed in Chapter 16, "Implementing Administrative Templates and Audit Policy."

▶ Via a GPO.

In Step by Step 10.3, we're going to create a new GPO and use it to assign a Restricted Groups GPO to the Workstations OU that contains our test server.

To perform this exercise, you will need to create a share on your server and name it Users. Configure the permissions on the share Authenticated Users—Full Control.

STEP BY STEP

10.3 Configuring a Restricted Groups GPO

1. Open the Group Policy Management Console. Right-click the Kansas City\Workstations OU and select Create and Link a GPO Here from the pop-up menu.

2. When the New GPO prompt appears, enter the name `Restricted Groups`, and click OK.

3. The new GPO will appear in the Group Policy Objects container, and as a linked object under the OU folder.

4. Right-click the new GPO and select Edit from the pop-up menu. The Group Policy Editor MMC appears.

5. Click the Computer Configuration icon; then click the Windows settings folder.

6. Right-click the Restricted Groups icon and select Add Group.

7. In the Add Group dialog box, enter `Administrators`, and then click OK.

8. The Administrators Properties window opens, as shown in Figure 10.8. Click the Add button, and add a user to the group. Click OK to save.

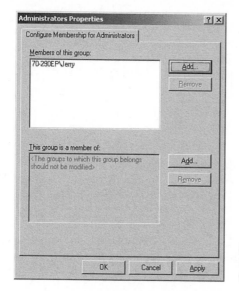

FIGURE 10.8 The Administrators Properties dialog box. Add members to the group, or make the group a member of other groups.

9. On your test server or workstation, log on using the administrator account.

10. Open the Computer Management MMC, and select Local Users and Groups. Open the Groups folder, and then double-click the Administrators entry. The Administrator should be the only account listed. Close the Properties window.

11. Open a command window and run the `gpupdate` command. Close the command window.

12. Double-click the Administrators entry. The account you just added to the GPO should be listed.

By limiting membership to important local groups on your server, such as the Administrators and Power Users groups, you can reduce your security exposure by making sure that unauthorized users accounts aren't present in these groups, either accidentally or intentionally.

Determining Applied GPOs

Group Policy was a wonderful addition when it was first included in Windows 2000. With the new functionality added in Windows Server 2003, it's even better. However, now that we've come to rely on Group Policy to assist us in managing our networks, it has become essential that we keep it configured properly.

Fortunately, Microsoft has provided several tools to assist in managing Group Policy. In the following sections, we'll take a brief look at a few of them.

NOTE

Know It All As we mentioned in Chapter 9, "Implementing Group Policy," as of SP2, Microsoft still was not including the Group Policy Management Console with Windows Server 2003. It is available only as a download from the website. However, this tool makes managing Group Policy a lot easier, and you should expect to see it on the exam.

GPResult

GPResult is a command-line tool that was originally part of the Windows 2000 Server Resource kit, but is now included with the operating system in Windows XP and Windows Server 2003. GPResult allows you to display the Group Policy settings and the Resultant (RSoP) for a computer or user.

Group policy can be applied to a user or computer at the site, domain, or OU, and multiple GPOs can be applied at each level. Because of these different overlapping levels of policies, it's helpful, if not essential, to have a tool that can tell you what the final outcome—the RSoP—really is.

This Resultant Set of Policy information is *extremely* important when you're trying to figure out why a Group Policy setting doesn't seem to be applied, or when it is being applied when it shouldn't be!

Table 10.1 shows the available command-line options for the tool.

TABLE 10.1 Command-Line Options for `gpresult`

Parameter	Description
`/s Computer`	The name or IP address of a remote computer. The default is the local computer.
`/u Domain\User`	Runs the command in the context of the user that is specified by Domain\User. The default is the current user.
`/p Password`	Specifies the password of the user account that is specified in the /u parameter.
`/user TargetUserName`	Specifies the username of the user whose RSoP data is to be displayed.
`/scope {user | computer}`	Displays either user or computer results. If you omit the /scope parameter, both user and computer settings are displayed.
`/v`	Displays verbose policy information.
`/z`	Specifies that the output display all available information about Group Policy. This parameter produces a lot of information and redirects output to a text file when you use it.
`/?`	Displays help.

As you can see from the command options, gpresult can be run either locally or remotely. It can also be limited to either Computer or User settings.

One item that might not be apparent is that you must enter the computer name where the user has logged on, even in those cases where you don't want to see the computer settings. You also will not be able to get any data for a user who has never logged on. This is because most user policies cannot be applied until the user logs on at least once.

In Step by Step 10.4, we're going to use the gpresult tool to see the effects of the multiple GPOs that we assigned to the users in the Kansas City\Users OU.

STEP BY STEP

10.4 Using gpresult to determine RSoP

1. Log on to your test server as Administrator.

2. Open a command window.

3. Enter the following command: **gpresult /user *username* /scope user /v**. (For *username*, enter the name of the user account that you have been using for the previous exercises).

4. The output of the command will appear in the command window, as shown in Figure 10.9.

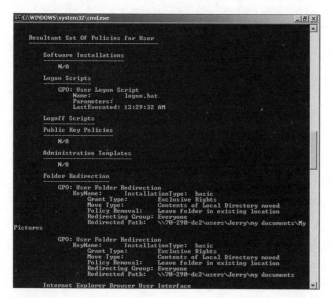

FIGURE 10.9   Part of the output using the /v option for the gpresult command.

As you can see, the `gpresult` command supplies a lot of data not only about the GPOs, but also about the user. Run the command again with a variety of command-line options using both the /v for verbose output and the /Z for full output. You might want to pipe the output to a text file for easier reading.

NOTE

Domain Type   You'll notice that the gpresult tool will display the domain type as Windows 2000. It looks like Microsoft hasn't updated the tool to recognize Windows Server 2003 domains yet.

Group Policy Results

Now that we've had a chance to review the data from the gpresult tool, let's take a look at a similar report using the Group Policy Management Console.

The Group Policy Results function of the GPMC presents much of the same data as the gpresult tool, but it produces it using a GUI wizard that prompts you for the desired parameters so that you don't need to memorize any obscure command-line options. In addition, it also produces a nice multicolored report suitable for printing that can be exported in HTML or XML, so that it can be displayed on a web page or added to a report for your management.

The limitation of the Group Policy Reports function is that it can report only on Windows XP or Windows Server 2003 machines. Windows 2000 servers or workstations are not supported.

In Step by Step 10.5, we're going to use the Group Policy Results Function of the GPMC to see the effects of the multiple GPOs that we assigned to the users in the Kansas City\Users OU. Use the same user and computer names that you used in Step by Step 10.4 so that you can compare results.

STEP BY STEP

10.5 Using the Group Policy Results Function of the GPMC to determine RSoP

1. Open the Group Policy Management Console. Right-click the Group Policy Results node and select Group Policy Results Wizard from the pop-up menu.

2. This starts the Group Policy Results Wizard. Click Next to continue.

3. The Computer Selection dialog box appears, as shown in Figure 10.10. Select the Another Computer option button, and enter the name of the computer. Also select the Do Not Display Policy Settings for the Selected Computer check box. Click Next to continue.

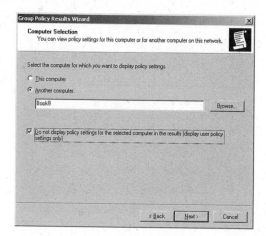

FIGURE 10.10 You must enter the computer name where the user has logged on, even though you don't want to see the computer settings.

4. The User Selection dialog box appears, as shown in Figure 10.11. Select the desired user, and then click the Next button.

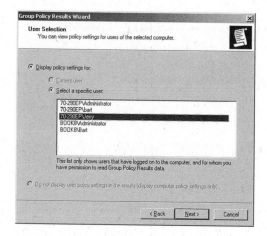

FIGURE 10.11 Select the desired user. Notice that only the users who have previously logged on to the computer are displayed.

5. On the Summary of Selections screen, review your choices. If you need to make any changes, click the Back button; otherwise, click Next.

6. When the Completing the Group Policy Wizard screen appears, click Finish.

7. The report will appear in the right pane of the console window. Click the Settings tab to see the settings that were applied to the user account.

8. The Group Policy Results are displayed (see Figure 10.12).

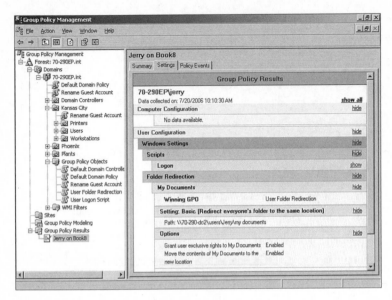

FIGURE 10.12 The settings applied to the user account. Compare these with the results from the gpresult tool.

The three tabs of the query results are as follows:

▶ *Summary*—This page lists the GPOs, the security group membership, and any WMI filters.

▶ *Settings*—This is a complete list of the policy settings applied to the user or computer.

▶ *Events*—This lists all the policy-related events found in the event viewer on the targeted machine.

After the report has been run, it can be saved to a file for future reference.

Group Policy Reporting

As you've probably noticed from working with GPOs, it's hard to tell at a glance what all the settings are. It can be quite tedious to open up the Group Policy Object Editor and expand every folder in every branch of every node in the GPO so that you can see what is enabled and what is not.

Fortunately, Microsoft has supplied a Group Policy Reporting function in the Group Policy Management Console. This function allows you to display all the settings for a GPO in an HTML window, and like the Results report, you can save it to a file for future use.

In Step by Step 10.6, we're going to use the Group Policy Reporting of the GPMC to examine the settings of one of the GPOs that we assigned to the users in the Kansas City\Users OU.

STEP BY STEP

10.6 Using The Group Policy Reporting function of the GPMC

1. Open the Group Policy Management Console. Expand the Kansas City OU, and select the Users OU underneath it.

2. Click the GPO link for the User Folder Redirection GPO. When prompted whether you are using a link, click Yes.

3. The User Folder Redirection configuration is displayed in the right pane of the GPMC. Select the Settings tab.

4. As shown in Figure 10.13, all the configuration settings for the GPO are displayed.

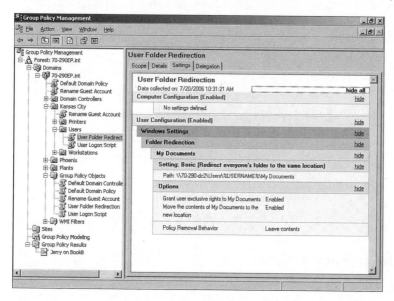

FIGURE 10.13 The Group Policy Management Console, displaying the settings for a GPO.

The four tabs displayed for each GPO contain the following:

▶ *Scope*—This page lists the OUs that the GPO is linked to, Security Filtering, and any WMI filters.

▶ *Settings*—This is a complete list of the policy settings contained in the GPO.

▶ *Delegation*—This tab shows the permissions that users and groups have for the GPO.

▶ *Details*—This lists all the system statistics for the GPO, such as the owner, when it was created and modified, the GUID, and the version number. This tab also allows you to disable the entire GPO or just the User or the Computer section.

After the report has been run, it can be saved to a file for future reference.

Challenge

You are the network administrator for your company. The network consists of a single Active Directory domain. All network servers run Windows Server 2003, and all client computers run Windows XP Professional.

As typical with most administrators, you're overworked. A new application has been released that has to be installed on 50 workstations before the end of the week. You don't have the time, so you recruit a couple of temp employees to do it for you. The new application requires the installer to have local administrator rights on the workstation, but you don't want temporary employees to have domain administrator rights. How do you handle this?

Try to complete this exercise on your own, listing your conclusions on a sheet of paper. After you have completed the exercise, compare your results to those given here.

1. Create a global group and name it **Temporary Admins**. Add the user accounts of the temporary employees to this group

2. Open the Group Policy Management Console. Right-click the OU that the PCs are located in and select Create and Link a GPO Here from the pop-up menu.

3. When the New GPO prompt appears, enter the name **Restricted Groups**, and click OK.

4. The new GPO will appear in the Group Policy Objects container and as a linked object under the OU folder.

5. Right-click the new GPO and select Edit from the pop-up menu. The Group Policy Editor MMC appears.

6. Click the Computer Configuration icon, and then click the Windows settings folder.

7. Right-click the Restricted Groups icon and select Add Group.

8. In the Add Group dialog, enter Administrators, and then click the OK button.

9. The Administrators Properties window opens (just like the one we showed earlier in Figure 10.8). Click the Add button, and add the Temporary Admins global group to the group. Click OK to save.

(continues)

(continued)

Giving temporary employees domain administrator rights is generally not a good idea. By assigning them to the local administrators group, they will have the ability to install software on all machines affected by the GPO. In addition, if they should add any other users to the local administrators group, either purposely or accidentally, those user accounts will be removed at the next Group Policy refresh cycle.

Chapter Summary

Group Policy is used in Active Directory environments to centrally manage the users and computers in the enterprise. Policies can be set for an entire organization at the site or domain level, or things can be decentralized by setting policies for each department at the OU level.

Group Policy can be used to make sure that users have the necessary environment, with the tools needed to perform their jobs. Additionally, you can lower the total cost of ownership by controlling the user and computer environments, thereby reducing the level of technical support and user productivity lost because of user error.

Key Terms

▶ Folder Redirection

▶ gpresult

▶ Restricted Groups

Apply Your Knowledge

Exercises

10.1 Using the gpresult tool

You just configured and applied a new GPO for your member servers. You need to make sure that it has been applied properly and is not in conflict with other GPOs. Because you haven't installed the Group Policy Management Console yet, you need to do it with command-line tools.

Estimated Time: 10 minutes

1. Log on to one of your member servers as Administrator.

2. Open a command window.

3. Enter the following command: **gpupdate /Force**. This command will force a refresh of all GPOs to make sure that all the applicable GPOs are loaded.

4. Enter the following command: **gpresult /scope computer /v**.

5. The output of the command will appear in the command window.

Exam Questions

1. You are the network administrator for FlyByNight Airlines. The network consists of a single Active Directory domain. The functional level of the domain is Windows 2000 native. All network servers run Windows Server 2003, and all client computers run Windows XP Professional.

   You have just finished adding 20 new users, assigned them to a new OU, and assigned a couple of GPOs with several user-related configuration settings to that OU. You want to make sure that the GPOs are being applied correctly and that there are no conflicts. What should you do?

   ○ **A.** Run the `gpresults` command-line tool with the `/user` parameter.

   ○ **B.** Run the Group Policy Results Wizard in the Group Policy Management Console.

   ○ **C.** Run the `gpupdate` command-line tool.

   ○ **D.** None of the above.

2. You are the network administrator for FlyByNight Airlines. The network consists of a single Active Directory domain. The functional level of the domain is Windows 2000 native. All network servers run Windows Server 2003, and all client computers run Windows 2000 Professional.

   A week ago, you added 20 new users, assigned them to a new OU, and assigned a couple of GPOs with several user-related configuration settings to that OU. You stop by the department and notice that the settings have not taken effect. What should you do to troubleshoot the problem?

   ○ **A.** Run the `gpresults` command-line tool with the `/user` parameter.

   ○ **B.** Run the Group Policy Results Wizard in the Group Policy Management Console.

   ○ **C.** Run the `gpupdate` command-line tool.

   ○ **D.** None of the above.

3. You are the network administrator for your company. The network consists of a single Active Directory domain. All network servers run Windows Server 2003, and all client computers run Windows XP Professional.

   You have decided to implement Folder Redirection for your users' My Document folders. You configure the GPO and link it to your test OU. However, when you log on to your Windows XP Professional test machine, you see that the My Documents folder is still pointing to your local hard drive. What should you do to correct the problem?

   ○ **A.** Log off, then log back on again.

   ○ **B.** Run the OUupdate command-line tool.

   ○ **C.** Move the settings to the Default Domain policy.

   ○ **D.** Manually change the settings for My Documents.

4. You are the network administrator for your company. The network consists of a single Active Directory domain. All network servers run Windows Server 2003, and all client computers run Windows XP Professional.

A user has called and requested to have a software application installed on her PC. You're too busy to do it yourself, so you add the user's account to the local Power Users group on her machine so that she will have the necessary permissions to install the software.

The next morning when she tries to install the software, she gets an error message indicating that she doesn't have the appropriate permissions. When you check her PC, you see that she is no longer a member of the Power Users group. What is the cause of this problem?

- ○ **A.** She is not a member of the Local Administrators group.
- ○ **B.** You have Enforced Groups enabled.
- ○ **C.** She is not a member of the Software Installers group.
- ○ **D.** You have Restricted Groups enabled.

Answers to Exam Questions

1. **D.** You will not be able to get any data for a user who has never logged on. This is because most user policies cannot be applied until the user logs on at least once. In this case, neither the gpresult tool nor the Group Policy Results Wizard would have any user data. The gpupdate tool is used only for refreshing Group Policy. See "GPResult."

2. **A.** The only solution is to run the gpresult command-line tool. The Group Policy Results Wizard in the Group Policy Management console doesn't support Windows 2000 clients. The gpupdate tool is used only for refreshing Group Policy. See "Group Policy Results."

3. **A.** Because of the fast user logon feature in Windows XP, you might have to logon 2 or 3 times before the Folder Redirection policy is applied. Moving the settings to the Default Domain policy is not necessary, and typically not a good idea, as is changing the settings manually. The OUupdate tool doesn't exist. See "Configuring Folder Redirection."

4. **D.** The Restricted Groups feature allows an administrator to control the membership of the local groups on workstations and member servers. The administrator is able to control the membership in the group by specifying the members of the group in the GPO. Any additional members that may have been added to the group are removed during the Group Policy refresh. Because the PC sat overnight, it's likely that the Group Policy was refreshed, thereby removing her user account from the Power Users group. See "Restricting Group Membership."

Suggested Readings and Resources

1. Group Policy Management Console Step-by-Step Guide. Microsoft Corporation. http://www.microsoft.com/technet/prodtechnol/windowsserver2003/technologies/ directory/activedirectory/stepbystep/gpmcinad.mspx.

2. Group Policy Resource Center. http://www.gpanswers.com/.

3. How to Use the Group Policy Results (gpresult.exe) Command Line Tool. Microsoft Corporation. http://www.microsoft.com/windowsxp/using/setup/expert/gpresults.mspx.

4. Morimoto, Rand, Noel, Michael, Lewis, Alex. *Microsoft Windows Server 2003 Unleashed R2 Edition*. Sams Publishing, 2006. ISBN 0672328984.

5. Performing Resultant Set of Policy Queries with the GPRESULT Tool. WindowsNetworking.com. http://www.windowsnetworking.com/articles_tutorials/ Resultant-Set-Policy-Queries-GPRESULT.html.

6. Windows Server 2003 Deployment Guide. Microsoft Corporation. http://technet2.microsoft.com/WindowsServer/en/Library/c283b699-6124-4c3a-87ef-865443d7ea4b1033.mspx?mfr=true.

7. *Windows Server 2003 Resource Kit*. Microsoft Press, 2005. ISBN 0735614717.

CHAPTER ELEVEN

Managing and Maintaining Terminal Services

Objectives

This chapter covers the following Microsoft-specified objectives for the "Managing and Maintaining Access to Resources" section of the Managing and Maintaining a Microsoft Windows Server 2003 Environment exam:

Troubleshoot Terminal Services.

▸ **Diagnose and resolve issues related to Terminal Services security.**

▸ **Diagnose and resolve issues related to client access to Terminal Services.**

▸ The purpose of this objective is to teach you how to work with the Windows Server 2003 version of Terminal Services. This includes both Application Server and Remote Desktop for Administration modes.

Outline

Study Strategies

▶ This chapter covers the management and configuration of Terminal Services. In addition to knowing how to properly configure Terminal Services to access your server, you need to be able to diagnose and resolve problems in your environment that are specific to Terminal Services.

▶ It is important that you set up a test Terminal Services server and work through all the exercises at least once. Pay particular attention to permissions, especially those needed to log on to a Terminal Services server, and be sure you have a good understanding of the Session Directory feature. Session Directory is new in Windows Server 2003, so expect to be tested heavily on it.

Introduction

As some old timers in the computer field have said, Terminal Services is a throwback feature. In the beginning days of computing, users had a green-screen dumb terminal sitting on their desk, which was used to connect to a mainframe somewhere down the hall or across the country. All the processing was done in that far away place, and all the users saw was the simple user interface presented to them.

Well, times have changed, and here we are going back to the future. Users are now sitting in front of a pretty multicolored screen, with the actual processing done either down the hall or somewhere across the country. Although having a PC on everyone's desk isn't totally a bad idea, it costs time and money to support each individual PC. By moving all processing back to the server room, most companies are able to cut down on desktop visits and maintenance because all application installation, configuration, and patching are performed in a central location.

In this chapter we will look at the advantages and disadvantages of Terminal Services, along with guidance on how to configure and maintain it.

Using Windows Server 2003 Terminal Services

Windows Server 2003 Terminal Services is designed to provide a multiuser environment, which makes it possible for several users to connect to a server and run applications concurrently.

Terminal Services consists of three major components:

- *Multiuser server core*—This is a modified version of the Windows Server 2003 kernel that allows the operating system to support multiple concurrent users and share resources.

- *Client software*—The Remote Desktop Connection (RDC) client software provides the user interface. It can be installed on a PC, a Windows terminal, or a handheld device. It provides the look and feel of the standard Windows interface.

- *Remote Desktop Protocol (RDP)*—This is the protocol that provides communication between the server and the client software. It runs only on TCP/IP.

Windows Terminal Services is designed to distribute the Windows 32-bit desktop to clients that are usually not able to run it. Although for the client it appears that the application is running locally, all processing actually occurs on the server. The only processing that occurs at the client involves displaying the user interface and accepting input from the keyboard and mouse.

Although the application is run on the server, the information needed to control the user interface, such as keystrokes and mouse clicks, is sent over the connection to the client. The data rate of the connection is very small, generally less than 16KB. This makes Terminal Services well suited for low-bandwidth connections, such as low-speed dial-up lines.

The RDP clients supplied with Windows Server 2003 Terminal Services can be used on most Windows PCs and Windows terminals. A 32-bit client is used with Windows 9x, NT, 2000, and XP.

NOTE

Additional Clients   Clients for the Macintosh and a Terminal Services (not RDC) client for the Pocket PC are not included on the Windows Server 2003 CD-ROM, but they are available for download from the Microsoft website at http://www.microsoft.com/downloads.

Linux

An open-source RDP client, called Rdesktop, is available for the Linux platform. It is available from www.rdesktop.org.

The RDC client provides the standard Win32 desktop to users. It is a Windows-based application and runs only on Windows platforms. However, it is a very small application (generally less than 2MB in size) and can run on machines with very limited processor and memory resources.

This client provides the following features:

- ▶ *Roaming disconnect support*—This allows a user to disconnect her session and then reconnect to the server—either from the same PC or terminal or from any other PC or terminal—and her session resumes just where she left it, without any data loss.

- ▶ *Multiple login support*—This allows a user to be connected to multiple sessions simultaneously.

- ▶ *Local resources are available*—The RDC 5.1 client allows you to connect to most of the resources attached to the local PC that is running the RDC client. This includes drives, smart cards, printers, and the Clipboard. For instance, files can be opened, saved, and printed to the user's local PC, regardless of whether the application is running locally or remotely.

▶ *Automatic session reconnection*—If a user is disconnected from the server because of a local problem, such as a communications line failure, the RDC client automatically attempts to reconnect to the user's session on the Terminal Services server.

Terminal Services Advantages and Disadvantages

Terminal Services offers many advantages. Here are a few of them:

▶ *Windows Terminal Services runs Windows applications*—Most Windows applications run on Terminal Services without any modifications.

▶ *The client is very small*—This allows the client to run on low-powered terminals or PCs.

▶ *The client can be used with older technology*—This allows older machines, which would normally be sent to the scrap heap, to be used as clients.

▶ *The responsibility for processing is put in the server room*—Everything to do with the support of the server and applications is directly controlled by the system administrator in the server room. Users have fewer opportunities to "help" the administrator. This results in fewer problems. In addition, because just about everything is controlled from a centralized location, expensive, time-consuming visits to the desktop are rare.

Terminal Services also has a couple of disadvantages, as follows:

▶ *Hardware*—Terminal Services requires much more hardware than the typical file and print server needs. You can use lower-end systems for the client, but you have to spend more money on the server.

▶ *Security*—You must be aware of the security weaknesses introduced with Terminal Services. For example, Terminal Services users are, in effect, given the equivalent of Log On Locally access to your server, so you need to be especially vigilant in limiting access to sensitive files and folders. In addition, because of this level of access, you should never install Terminal Services in Application Server mode on a domain controller.

Environments for Which Terminal Services Is Recommended

Terminal Services is recommended for use in a variety of environments. The following are some examples:

▶ *Harsh environments*—Terminal Services is very good for harsh environments, such as manufacturing facilities. This allows you to utilize a low-cost Windows terminal that has no moving parts and would normally be susceptible to damage or contamination.

▶ *Remote access*—Because of the low-bandwidth requirements, remote Terminal Services users usually see the same relative performance as if they were running applications locally. In addition, the remote user doesn't have to have frequent software and hardware updates, because all updates are performed on the server by the administrator(s).

▶ *Public access terminals*—A Windows terminal used as a kiosk is very secure because Terminal Services allows administrators to lock down applications and system access.

▶ *Customer service*—Users running a single or a few task-based applications are ideal candidates for Terminal Services because they can be supplied with a low-cost Windows terminal for far less money than a PC, which would likely be overkill for their needs.

▶ *Wireless applications*—Because of the low-bandwidth requirements, Terminal Services is especially good for providing server applications to wireless users, especially users of handheld devices.

Terminal Services Is Not Recommended For...

Here are some applications for which the use of Windows Terminal Services is not recommended:

▶ *Applications requiring heavy calculations*—Typical examples are Computer Aided Drafting (CAD) applications.

▶ *Applications that identify users or sessions by IP address or machine name*—Examples include some terminal-emulator applications.

▶ *Applications with memory leaks or that perform constant keyboard polling*—These problems are common with older DOS applications.

▶ *Applications using animation*—Passing screen updates for large, detailed bitmaps uses a lot of bandwidth and takes time for the user to see the painted bitmap.

▶ *Publishing and drawing programs*—Although the Terminal Services clients supported in Windows Server 2003 can support more than 256 colors, the excess color depth requires more processing and network bandwidth. In addition, all graphics screen updates have to be passed over the connection, which can get pretty slow.

Working with Terminal Services

Terminal Services is available in two modes: Remote Desktop for Administration (formerly called Remote Administration mode) and Application Server mode. Application Server mode configures Windows Server 2003 to operate similar to the previous version of Windows NT Terminal Server 5.0. Remote Desktop for Administration mode is used to provide remote server management. Unlike in Windows 2000, where the Remote Administration mode was an option, the Remote Desktop for Administration mode is automatically installed in Windows Server 2003. However, incoming connections are disabled by default.

Using Terminal Services in Remote Desktop for Administration Mode

The Terminal Services (TS) Remote Administration mode was first available in Windows 2000. The previous version of Windows NT 5.0 Terminal Server did not have this feature. With Windows Server 2003 Terminal Services in Remote Desktop for Administration mode, you are allowed two concurrent sessions, plus a console session to the Windows server. These sessions can be used to remotely access any programs or data on the server.

Using the Terminal Services client is just like working on the server console. The Remote Desktop for Administration mode allows you to have two concurrent TS sessions without any additional Client Access Licenses required. The beauty of the Remote Desktop for Administration mode is that it allows you to manage your server from just about anywhere and from just about any computer. Because the TS client is supported on a variety of Windows platforms, including Windows CE and Pocket PC 2002 and later, you can load the client on any Windows box that you have available and manage your server. Imagine managing your server from your Pocket PC!

In addition, because the RDC connection between the server and the client requires a minimum of bandwidth, you are not limited to a high-speed LAN connection. The Terminal Services client can access the servers via a dial-up connection, the Internet, or even a wireless connection. Again, think about managing your servers from your Pocket PC while sitting on a warm, sandy beach.

NOTE

Switching Between Terminal Services Modes   Although it is possible to switch from one mode to another, it is necessary to reinstall all applications.

In addition to the two virtual sessions, a new feature in Windows Server 2003 provides the capability to connect to the real console of the server. In the past, a lot of tools and applications could not be run remotely, because they were written to interact directly with "session 0," or the physical server console. Also, most system messages are routed to the console automatically, so if you were trying to manage the server remotely and a pop-up error message was sent, you wouldn't be able to see it.

Working with Terminal Services in Remote Desktop for Administration mode is covered at length in the "Managing Servers Remotely" section of Chapter 5, "Administering Windows Server 2003."

Terminal Services in Application Server Mode

The purpose of Application Server mode in Windows Server 2003 Terminal Services is to enable applications to be shared and managed from a central location. The Terminal Services Application Server mode changes the characteristics of the server. Normally, a server is tuned to give best performance to the background processes that are running. This enables server-type applications, such as databases and mail servers, to perform better. However, when Windows is configured for Terminal Services Application Server mode, the server is tuned to give the best performance to the foreground processes. This is similar to the way a workstation operating system is tuned, because those are the types of tasks the operating system is now handling. With Terminal Services, each user is assigned an individual session of 2GB of virtual memory on the server. Performance depends on the capacity of the server, how many users are logged on, and what applications are running.

The Application Server mode of Terminal Services allows the system administrator to load common applications that can be shared by multiple users. The users can be granted the ability to connect to a specific application or a complete desktop environment.

This can greatly decrease the support costs associated with an organization because there are fewer visits to the end user. There is no need for upgrade visits, and there are fewer visits for application issues because everything is located and controlled centrally.

Unlike Remote Desktop for Administration mode, in which there are only two concurrent connections plus the console allowed, Application Server mode allows you to have an unlimited number of concurrent connections, subject to server capacity and licensing. The number of users supported varies widely, depending on the type of applications in use and the hardware configuration of the server. Typically, on the same hardware, you can support far more users running terminal emulator–type applications than users who are using CAD applications.

To install Terminal Services in Application Server mode, follow the procedure outlined in Step by Step 11.1.

STEP BY STEP

11.1 Installing Terminal Services in Application Server Mode

1. Click Start, All Programs, Control Panel, Add or Remove Programs.

2. Click the Add/Remove Windows Components button in the left pane of the Add or Remove Programs dialog box.

3. The Windows Components Wizard appears. Select the Terminal Server check box.

4. If Internet Explorer Enhanced Security Configuration is enabled (it is enabled by default), you will receive the Configuration Warning prompt. After you read and understand this warning, click the Yes button to continue.

5. This returns you to the Windows Components Wizard. Click the Next button to continue.

6. The Terminal Server Setup warning appears, as shown in Figure 11.1. Read and understand the warnings before clicking the Next button to continue.

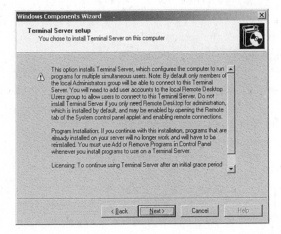

FIGURE 11.1 The Terminal Server Setup warning prompt alerts you to the requirements of a Terminal Server.

7. The Terminal Server Setup screen appears. This screen allows you to select the Full Security mode, which is new to Windows Server 2003, or the Relaxed Security mode, which is roughly equivalent to the security on a Windows 2000 Terminal Services server. Click the desired option button, and then click the Next button to continue.

8. The Terminal Server License dialog box appears, as shown in Figure 11.2. You are prompted as to what license server to use. For now, select the option to specify a license server within 120 days. Click the Next button.

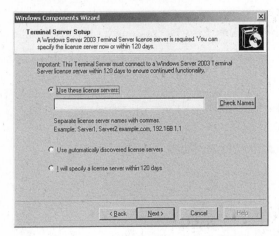

FIGURE 11.2 The Terminal Server Setup licensing prompt asks you what license server to use.

9. Next, you are prompted as to whether to use per-device or per-user licensing. Select Per User, and then click Next.

10. When the Completing the Windows Components Wizard screen appears, click the Finish button. You will be prompted to reboot the server.

Terminal Services Licensing

Application Server mode requires that each remote connection have a Windows Server 2003 Terminal Services user or device Client Access License (TS CAL). These licenses are separate from the normal Windows Client Access Licenses (CALs) and must be installed and managed using a Terminal Services licensing server. Terminal Services Licensing Server is an option that is installed from the Add/Remove Programs applet in the Control Panel.

Windows Server 2003 offers two types of Terminal Services licensing servers:

▶ *Enterprise license server*—An enterprise license server should be used when you have Windows Server 2003 Terminal Services servers located in several domains. This is the default.

▶ *Domain license server*—A domain license server is used if you want to segregate licensing by domain, or if you're supporting a Windows NT 4.0 domain or a workgroup.

To install a Terminal Services licensing server, follow the procedure outlined in Step by Step 11.2.

STEP BY STEP

11.2 Installing a Terminal Services licensing server

1. Click Start, All Programs, Control Panel, Add or Remove Programs.

2. Click the Add/Remove Windows Components button in the left pane of the Add or Remove Programs dialog box.

3. The Windows Components Wizard appears. Select the Terminal Server Licensing check box.

4. The Terminal Server Licensing Setup screen appears (see Figure 11.3). This screen allows you to choose the type of licensing server to install and the location of the license database. Make a selection and then click the Next button to continue.

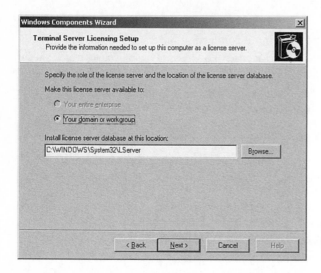

FIGURE 11.3 Choose the type of licensing server to install on the Terminal Server Licensing Setup screen.

5. When the Completing the Windows Component Wizard screen appears, click the Finish button.

NOTE

TS CALS New with Windows Server 2003 are the concepts of a user Client Access License and a device Client Access License. Separating licensing in this way allows organizations additional license options. For example, if a Terminal Services user connects via multiple devices, such as a PC and a handheld device, the organization would need to purchase a user license instead of a device license. The standard TS CAL is valid only for connections to Windows 2000 Terminal Services servers.

Unlike the Windows 2000 license server, which had to be installed on a domain controller in an Active Directory environment, the Windows Server 2003 Terminal Services license server can be installed on any domain controller, member server, or standalone server. This license server can support an unlimited number of Terminal Services servers, and it can issue Terminal Services 2000 Internet Connector licenses, TS 2003 user CALs, TS 2003 device CALs, and temporary TS CALs. The Internet Connector CALs are for non-employees who connect to your Windows 2000 Terminal Services servers over the Internet. A temporary TS CAL is issued when there are no TS user or device CALs available on the license server. A temporary TS CAL allows the client to connect to the Terminal Services server for 120 days. A Terminal Services server can initially operate for up to 120 days without being serviced by a TS licensing server. However, after this grace period expires, the server no longer accepts any TS connections until it is associated with a valid licensing server.

The new licensing setup is only for Windows Server 2003 Terminal Services. As you can see, it is somewhat different from Microsoft's previous Terminal Services licensing methods. Fortunately, Microsoft has provided a whitepaper that gives an overview of the new licensing rules and processes. It can be obtained from the Microsoft Web site at http://www.microsoft.com/windowsserver2003/techinfo/overview/termservlic.mspx.

> **NOTE**
>
> **TS External Connector**   Another new licensing feature is the Windows Server 2003 Terminal Server External Connector license. This is a license that is purchased to allow an unlimited number of external users access to your Terminal Services server. This replaces the Internet Connector license that was available for Windows 2000 Terminal Services.

Installing Applications

For each user to have his own application configurations, Terminal Services monitors the changes that the application makes to the Registry as the program is being installed, and it watches for changes to the `%windir%` folder. Once captured, these changes are copied to a home folder that Terminal Services maintains for each user. When the user logs on to Terminal Services, these Registry settings are transferred to the user-specific Registry keys.

To install applications on a Terminal Services server, you must be in Install mode. This can be accomplished by installing programs via the Add/Remove Programs applet in the Control Panel or via the `Change User` command.

The `Change User /install` command places Terminal Services in Install mode, so that all user-specific mapping is turned off, and the system can monitor the installation process. After the application is installed, use the `Change User /execute` command to restore user-specific mapping. This also moves any newly installed user-specific files to the user's home folder.

To install an application on a Terminal Services server in Application Server mode, follow the procedure outlined in Step by Step 11.3.

STEP BY STEP

11.3 Installing an application on a Terminal Services server

1. Click Start, All Programs, Control Panel, Add or Remove Programs.

2. Click the Add New Programs button in the left pane of the Add or Remove Programs dialog box.

3. Click the CD or Floppy button.

4. When prompted, insert the CD-ROM or floppy disk and click the Next button to continue.

5. If the application isn't found automatically, you can click the Browse button on the Run Installation Program screen to search for it. Click the Next button when you're finished.

6. As the installation starts, the screen shown in Figure 11.4 appears. Do not click the Next button until the application's installation procedure has been completed.

FIGURE 11.4 The After Installation Program screen. Click the Next button after the installation is complete.

7. When the Finish Admin Install screen appears, click the Finish button.

Although not all applications install or run properly in a multiuser environment, some manufacturers are supplying Terminal Services configuration files so that their applications install properly. An example is Microsoft, which has supplied a transform file with Office 2000 so that it can be properly installed on Terminal Services. This file is named TERMSRVR.MST and is available in the Office 2000 Resource Kit.

> **NOTE**
>
> **Terminal Services–Aware Applications**   Current applications may be Terminal Services aware. For example, Office XP or 2003 no longer needs either compatibility scripts or transform files to be installed in Windows Server 2003 Terminal Services.

Microsoft has also supplied several application-compatibility scripts for several common applications that are run after application installation to change their installed configuration to allow them to operate properly in a multiuser environment. These scripts are located in the %systemroot%\Application Compatibility Scripts\Install folder. These scripts are typically run after the initial installation of the application and are used to move user-specific files and configuration information to the user's home folder. These scripts can be run at every logon by adding a reference to them in USRLOGON.CMD, which is run whenever a user logs on to Terminal Services, or via an individual user's Terminal Services logon script. A close examination of these scripts can give you ideas on how to create compatibility scripts for your own applications.

> **NOTE**
>
> **Application Installation in Remote Desktop for Administration Mode**   There are no special steps necessary to install applications in Windows Server 2003 TS Remote Desktop for Administration mode.

Managing User Sessions in Terminal Services

Terminal Services comes with a variety of administrative tools. The Terminal Services Manager is the tool that is used to monitor and manage the Remote Desktop sessions. From this tool, the system administrator has the ability to perform the following tasks on a user session:

- Remote control the user session.

- Observe and terminate user processes.

- Reset the session.

- Disconnect the session.

- Connect to the user session.

- Send messages to the user.

As shown in Figure 11.5, when a user connects to a Remote Desktop session, this connection is displayed in the Terminal Services Manager MMC. This view shows the status for all the connections, including the following:

- *User*—The user ID of the user who started the session.

- *Session*—The type of session. This will be either RDP-TCP# or Console. Note that the special listener port is designated as just RDP-TCP.

- *State*—The current state of the connection. This will be Active, Disconnected, or, in the case of the listener session, Listening.

- *Type*—This is the type of connection. It will be either Console or the client version.

- *Client Name*—This is the name of the client machine on which the connection software is running.

- *Idle Time*—This is the time since there was any activity on the connection.

- *Logon Time*—This is the time and date of the initial connection.

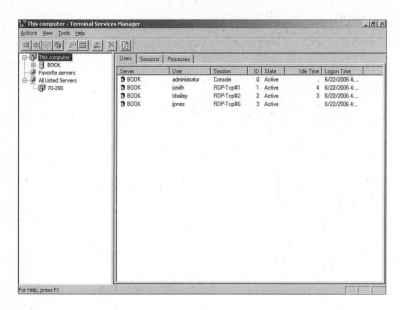

FIGURE 11.5 The Terminal Service Manager MMC, showing the connected sessions.

To manage a user session, right-click the connection from the Sessions tab and select an option from the pop-up menu, as shown in Figure 11.6. Descriptions of the various options are listed in the following sections.

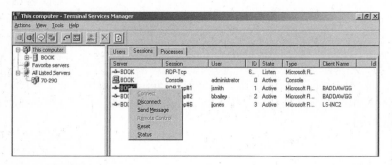

FIGURE 11.6 The Terminal Service Manager MMC, showing the session-management options.

NOTE

Terminal Services Manager Restrictions   The Remote Control and Connect to Session features of the Terminal Services Manager tool are available only when the tool is run in a Terminal Services session. These features are not available when the Terminal Services Manager is run from the server console.

Disconnecting and Reconnecting a Session

To disconnect a session, click Disconnect on the Action menu. Disconnecting a session closes the connection between the server and client; however, the user is not logged off and all running programs remain. If the user logs on to the server again, the disconnected session is reconnected to the client. A disconnected session shows Disc in the State field.

To connect to the disconnected session, click the session in Terminal Services Manager and select Connect from the Action menu. The current session is disconnected, and the selected session is connected to your terminal.

Your session must be capable of supporting the video resolution used by the disconnected session. If the session does not support the required video resolution, the operation fails.

Sending Messages

You can send a message to users informing them of problems or asking them to log off the server. To send a message, right-click an active session and then select Send Message from the Action menu. If you select multiple users, the message is sent to each user.

Remote Controlling a User's Session

You can monitor the actions of users by remote controlling their sessions. The remote-controlled session is displayed in the controller's session, and it can be controlled by the mouse and keyboard of the remote control terminal. By default, the user being controlled is asked to allow or deny session remote control. Keyboards, mice, and notification options can be controlled from the Active Directory Users and Computers MMC.

To remote control a session, right-click the session from the Sessions tab and then select Remote Control from the Action menu.

The remote control session must be capable of supporting the video resolution used by the shadowed session. If the remote control session does not support the required video resolution, the operation fails.

Resetting a Session or Connection

You can reset a session in case of an error. Resetting the session terminates all processes running on that session. To reset a user session, right-click the user from the Users tab of the Terminal Services Manager MMC and then select Reset from the Action menu. If you select multiple users, each user session is reset.

Resetting a session may cause applications to close without saving data. If you reset the special RDP-TCP Listener session, all sessions for that server are reset.

Logging Users off the Server

You can forcefully end a user's session by right-clicking the user from within the Users tab and then selecting Logoff from the Action menu. If you select multiple users, each user is logged off.

> **CAUTION**
>
> **Data Loss!** Logging off or resetting a user's session without giving her a chance to close her applications can result in data loss.

Terminating Processes

To end a user or system process, right-click the process from the Process tab and then select Terminate from the Action menu. If you select multiple processes, each process is terminated.

> **CAUTION**
>
> **Termination Instability!** Terminating a user process can result in the loss of data and can also cause the server to become unstable.

Using the Remote Desktop Connection Client

The Remote Desktop Connection client is installed by default on Windows Server 2003. You can open an RDC session by clicking Start, All Programs, Accessories, Communications, Remote Desktop Connection.

This opens the RDC client, as shown in Figure 11.7. In the Computer field, you can type either the IP address or the name of the remote computer to which you want to connect. If you have previously connected to this computer, you can click the drop-down list, and you will see a list of the computers to which you have made connections.

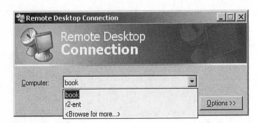

FIGURE 11.7   You can select a previous RDC connection via the drop-down list in the Remote Desktop Connection dialog box.

If you do not see the name or IP address listed, and you cannot remember it, you can click <Browse for more...>, and all the Terminal Services servers you are able to connect to will be listed.

NOTE

Remote Desktop for Administration Mode Doesn't Advertise   By default, only Windows Server 2003 computers running Terminal Services in Application Server mode advertise their presence to the browse list. To enable a Windows Server 2003 server running in Remote Desktop for Administration mode to advertise itself as a Terminal Services server in the browse list, change the value of the `HKEY_LOCAL_MACHINE\` `System\CurrentControlSet\Control\Terminal Server\TSADVERTISE` key from 0 to 1.

After selecting a connection, click Connect and you will see the logon prompt for the remote server. Enter the proper credentials, and you will log on to a desktop from the remote server (see Figure 11.8).

Figure 11.8   After you successfully connect remotely, you will see a Remote Desktop window.

From this window, you can run the programs on the remote server, just as if you were sitting in front of the server console. If you would prefer to see the remote desktop in full-screen mode, click the Maximize button in the upper-right corner of the window. When running RDC in full-screen mode, it is hard to tell that this is a virtual session.

When it's time to end your session, you have two choices: You can either log off or disconnect the session. You log off the session by clicking Start, Shutdown, and then Logoff from the Security dialog box. To disconnect the session, select Disconnect from the Security dialog box or click the Close button in the upper-right corner of the window. If you log off a session, any programs running are automatically shut down for you, just as if you were using your own computer. However, if you disconnect a session, any programs that are running remain running. The next time you log in to the server, the session will be just as you left it.

> **NOTE**
>
> **Terminal Services Etiquette** The default configuration of a Terminal Services server is to maintain disconnected sessions indefinitely. However, even when a session is disconnected, it still uses resources on the server. Unless you have a good reason for leaving a session running, such as running a batch job or a long-running database function, it is usually best to log off when you are finished. Logging off allows the server to release the session, and the resources associated with keeping it active will be available for other processes.

Using the Remote Desktop Client

In the previous section, we logged on to a Remote Desktop session using the default settings. However, the RDC client has many configuration options available that allow you to configure it for the optimum performance in many different situations.

To access these settings, open the RDC client and click the Options button. The settings on the General tab allow you to preconfigure the server, username, password, and domain to connect to.

The RDC client also allows you to export your client configuration settings to a file that can be used on other machines. Just click Save As under Connection Settings.

The display settings are available from the Display tab (see Figure 11.9). The screen display can be configured in the following resolutions:

- ▶ 640×480
- ▶ 800×600
- ▶ 1024×768
- ▶ 1152×864
- ▶ 1280×1024
- ▶ 1600×1200

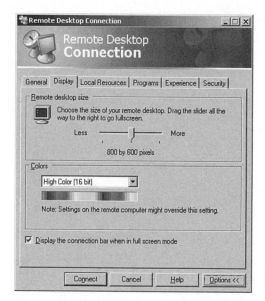

FIGURE 11.9 You configure display settings for Remote Desktop Connection via the Display tab.

You can also set the color resolution, up to a maximum of True Color (24 Bit); however, the higher the resolution, the more data that has to go over the link between the client and the remote server. You will probably want to keep this as low as possible over low-speed links. It's important to remember that the settings on the Terminal Services server always override the RDC client settings.

There is also an option to display the connection bar when you are in full-screen mode. The icons on the connection bar allow you to quickly minimize or maximize your session. The connection bar appears when you move your mouse to the top of the screen. To always display the connection bar at the top of the screen, click the push pin. The connection bar was shown earlier in Figure 11.8.

NOTE

Display Characteristics The maximum values that you can configure the display resolution to will be equal to the settings on your client computer. For example, if the client is configured for 800×600 with 256 colors, you won't be able to configure the RDC session to 1024×768 with 16-bit resolution. The client has to have a desktop resolution either equal to or higher than the RDC session.

The Local Resources tab, shown in Figure 11.10, allows you to configure the interface characteristics of the session, such as sound, keyboard, and device mapping. The Remote Computer Sound option allows you to hear the sounds generated by the remote server session through your local computer. Although this is useful for applications that use sounds as prompts, it's not a good idea to play MP3s over a low-speed connection because sound uses a significant amount of bandwidth. For slow connections, it's recommended that you set this to Do Not Play.

FIGURE 11.10 You can configure interface characteristics for the Remote Desktop connection via the Local Resources tab.

The Local Devices option allows you to specify which of the devices attached to your local computer will be available in your RDC session. This allows you to access your local drives, printers, the Clipboard, or any devices attached to your serial port.

For example, you can cut and paste data from the RDC session to the local computer, and vice versa. You can also copy files from the local drives to the drives of the Windows Server 2003 Terminal Services server, if you have the proper NTFS permissions.

The Keyboard option allows you to specify how the standard Windows key combinations are handled while you are in a remote session. For example, if you are running a remote session and you select the Alt+Tab key combination, the local computer will respond to the keystrokes. You can choose to have the Windows keys assigned to one of the following:

▶ The local computer

▶ The remote computer

▶ The remote computer, only when the session is in full-screen mode

The Programs tab allows you to specify the name and location of a program to run when you connect to the remote session. You will have access only to the program and will not get the Windows desktop. When you close the application, your session will be automatically logged off.

The Experience tab, shown in Figure 11.11, allows you to tailor the performance of your RDC session to the speed of your connection. For example, on a slow dial-up connection, you should turn off all the options except for Bitmap Caching. The Bitmap Caching feature improves performance by using your local disk to cache frequently used bitmaps to reduce the RDP traffic. The visual features listed here greatly affect the amount of data that has to be carried over the link between the server and the client.

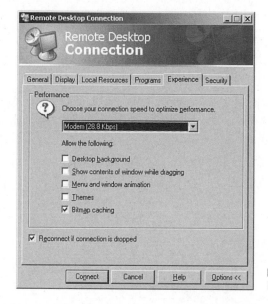

FIGURE 11.11 You can configure additional options for Remote Desktop Connection via the Experience tab.

You will notice as you select the different connection speeds, different options are selected. These are Microsoft's recommendations for each link speed. You can create your own configuration by selecting Custom. Unless you are connecting locally via a LAN, it's usually best to turn off all the options except for Bitmap Caching.

Configuring Terminal Services Connections

Although the default Terminal Services configuration settings are fine for the average installation, the Terminal Services Configuration MMC allows you to fine tune Terminal Services to provide the best combination of performance and features for your installation. The Terminal Services Connection MMC is used to configure the Remote Desktop Protocol–Transmission

Control Protocol (RDP-TCP) used to communicate between the Windows Server 2003 server and the RDC client.

The RDP-TCP connection can be configured by right-clicking the connection entry in the Terminal Services Connection MMC and selecting Properties from the pop-up menu.

From the General tab, shown in Figure 11.12, you can add a comment to describe the connection, configure the encryption level of the connection, or select whether to use Windows authentication. The settings for encryption are as follows:

▶ *Low*—This setting encrypts the data traveling over the connection using 56-bit encryption. However, only the data sent from the client to the server is encrypted; data sent from the server to the client is not. This option is useful because it encrypts the user password as it is sent from the client to the server.

▶ *Client Compatible*—This option automatically encrypts all data sent between the client and the server at the maximum key strength supported by the client. This option is useful in an environment where different types of clients are supported.

▶ *High*—This option encrypts all data using 128-bit encryption. This option can be used in an environment that supports only the RDC client; all other connections will be refused.

▶ *FIPS Compliant*—This option encrypts all data using the Federal Information Processing Standard (FIPS) encryption algorithms.

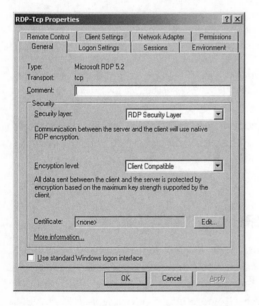

FIGURE 11.12 The RDP-TCP Properties dialog box, showing the options on the General tab.

> **NOTE**
>
> **Per User Settings**   The settings described in this section apply to all users. The settings for an individual user can be configured via the Terminal Services tab of the user object in the Active Directory Users and Computers MMC.

The Use Standard Windows Authentication option needs to be selected only in those cases where a third-party authentication mechanism has been installed and you want to use the Windows Standard Authentication method for RDP connections.

From the Logon Settings tab, you can select to have all users automatically log on to the Terminal Services server by using a common username and password that you enter here. In addition, you can select to prompt them for a password when using this common account by selecting the Always Prompt for Password option. The default is for the user to provide logon credentials.

From the Sessions tab, shown in Figure 11.13, you can select the default session timeout and reconnection settings. These settings are used to determine what action, if any, to take for sessions that have been connected longer than a specified time or have been disconnected. The options are as follows:

▶ *End a Disconnected Session*—This option determines what to do with a disconnected session. A session can become disconnected by a user or because of a communication failure between the server and the RDC client. Even though a session is in the disconnected state, any applications that were running will continue to run. However, these applications will continue to use resources on the server. This option can be used to automatically terminate sessions that remain in a disconnected state for a configured period of time. After the disconnected session is terminated, any resources it was using will be available for other sessions. However, this option can cause the loss of user data if any user files are open when the session is terminated.

▶ *Active Session Limit*—This setting allows you to configure the maximum time that a session can be active before it is either terminated or disconnected, depending on the setting of the When Session Limit Is Reached or Connection Is Broken option.

▶ *Idle Session Limit*—This setting allows you to configure the maximum time a session can be idle before it is either terminated or disconnected, depending on the setting of the When Session Limit Is Reached or Connection Is Broken option.

▶ *When Session Limit Is Reached or Connection Is Broken*—This option allows you to configure the action to take when a session is disconnected or when a session limit is reached. In the case of the session limit being reached, the session is either disconnected or terminated, depending on this setting. When this option is selected, a disconnected session will automatically be terminated.

▶ *Allow Reconnection*—This option is used only with the Citrix-ICA connection. The default for the RDP-TCP connection in Windows Server 2003 is to allow reconnection from any client when a session is in the disconnected state.

The Sessions tab allows you to override any configuration settings that were made in the user profile, RDC, or Terminal Services client using the options on the tabs of the RDP-TCP Properties dialog box.

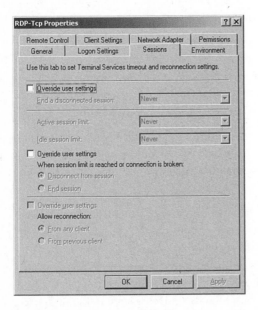

FIGURE 11.13 You can override user settings via the RDP-TCP Properties dialog box's Sessions tab.

The Remote Control tab allows you to configure the Remote Control feature of Windows Server 2003 Terminal Services. The available options are as follows:

▶ *Use Remote Control with Default User Settings*—This is the default option, and it uses the configuration from the user account to determine whether Remote Control is allowed and how it is configured.

▶ *Do Not Allow Remote Control*—This option turns off Remote Control for all sessions.

▶ *Use Remote Control with the Following Settings*—This option turns on Remote Control and is used to select whether the user will be prompted when the administrator attempts to control a remote session, and what level of control the administrator will have.

The Client Settings tab, shown in Figure 11.14, allows you to configure the client experience features of Windows Server 2003 Terminal Services.

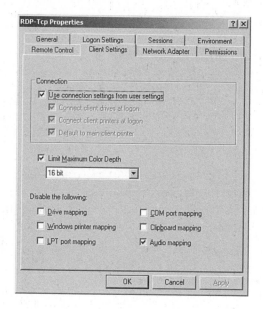

FIGURE 11.14 Client Settings allows you to map local resources to your session.

The Connection area allows you either to use the connection settings chosen on the Local Resources tab of the RDC client (the default) or to configure the settings individually. These options control whether the various devices configured on the computer that the RDC client is installed on will be available in the RDC session.

The options in the Disable the Following area allow you to enable/disable various actions, such as printing from the RDC session to the printers attached to the client computer on which you are running the RDC client. As shown in Figure 11.15, when drive mapping is enabled, the drives on the local client are available within an RDC session, listed under the Other section.

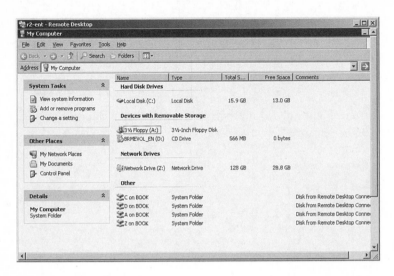

FIGURE 11.15 My Computer, showing the mapped client devices listed under Other.

The Network Adapter tab allows you to limit the number of concurrent RDC client connections by network adapter.

The Permissions tab allows you to configure which users or groups are allowed to connect to Windows Server 2003 Terminal Services and what permissions they will have. The recommended method of allowing users to connect to Windows Server 2003 Terminal Services is to add their user accounts to the Remote Desktop Users group. This group has already been granted the necessary permissions, including the Allow Logon Through Terminal Services, which is necessary to connect via a Terminal Services or RDC client.

> **EXAM ALERT**
>
> **Remote Desktop Users Group**   Do not confuse the Log on Locally right with the rights granted by adding a user to the Remote Desktop Users group. The Log on Locally right allows users to log on to the server at the console, thereby allowing them direct access to the server. Adding a user to the Remote Desktop Users group allows a user to log on to the server over the network using the Terminal Services interface. The amount of access that members of the Remote Desktop users group have to the server can be strictly controlled by the administrator. Knowing the differences between these two functions is important in the field and for the exam.

In addition to the settings available from the property pages of the RDP-TCP connection are the configuration options listed under the Server Settings folder.

These settings are as follows:

▶ *Delete Temporary Folders on Exit*—This option deletes all temporary folders created by RDC sessions as they are exited. This option is turned on by default.

▶ *Use Temporary Folders Per Session*—This option allows you to create a temporary folder for each session. This option is turned on by default.

▶ *Licensing*—This option allows you to select either per-device or per-user licensing. This option is set to Per Device by default. On a Terminal Services server in Remote Administration for Desktops mode, this attribute is displayed as Remote Desktop and is not configurable.

▶ *Active Desktop*—This option is used to enable/disable the Active Desktop in RDC sessions. It is disabled by default. This option should not be enabled because the additional overhead required to support Active Desktop in RDC sessions impacts performance.

▶ *Permission Compatibility*—This option is set to Full Security by default. Full Security is equivalent to the default security settings present on Windows Server 2003. Because most folders and the Registry are locked down, a lot of older applications cannot be installed or run in this configuration. The other option provided is Relaxed Security, which is equivalent to running on a Windows 2000 Terminal Server. For the best security, set this option to Full Security and use only Windows Server 2003–compatible applications.

▶ *Restrict Each User to One Session*—This option keeps users from connecting to multiple sessions via multiple RDC clients. This option is enabled by default.

Challenge

You are the administrator of a network that includes a Windows Server 2003 server configured for Terminal Services Application Server mode. The programming staff has just finished loading a new application on the Terminal Services server. However, the staff needs your assistance. It seems that this new application requires the users to respond to audio signals that are output through their PC speakers. Unfortunately, although the program is running fine on client workstations, the staff has never tested it on a Terminal Services server before and doesn't know the proper way to configure sound.

What is the best way to solve this issue in Windows Server 2003 Terminal Services? On your own, try to develop a solution that would involve the least amount of configuration changes.

If you would like to see a possible solution, follow these steps:

1. On the Windows Server 2003 Terminal Services server, click Start, All Programs, Administrative Tools, Terminal Services Configuration.

(continues)

(continued)

2. In the right pane of the Terminal Services Configuration MMC, double-click the Connections folder.

3. Right-click the RDP-TCP connection and then select Properties from the pop-up menu.

4. Click the Client Settings tab of the RDP-TCP Properties dialog box.

5. On the Client Settings tab, deselect the Audio Mapping check box under Disable the Following in the lower-right section of the dialog box.

6. Click the OK button to Save. Close the MMC.

7. On the client computer, start the RDC client.

8. From the RDC client prompt, click the Options button.

9. From the Options dialog box, click the Local Resources tab.

10. Change the Remote Computer Sound drop-down list to Bring to This Computer.

11. Click Connect.

Audio mapping is turned off by default in Windows Server 2003 Terminal Services, so you have to enable it on the server and on the client. In addition, there must be a sound card with the proper drivers loaded on both the server and the client. Typically, sound is not used in Terminal Services sessions because it can demand a lot of bandwidth over the RDP connection.

Managing Windows Server 2003 Terminal Services via Group Policy

Although Windows Server 2003 Terminal Services can be managed using the Terminal Services Connection MMC, if you have multiple Terminal Services servers, this can become a nightmare. Fortunately, Microsoft has included some additions to Group Policy in Windows Server 2003 to support Terminal Services configuration. These policies can be found under the Computer Configuration section of Group Policy, as shown in Figure 11.16.

The options available include not only the options from the Terminal Services Manager and the Terminal Services Connection MMC, but also various user interface options applicable in the Terminal Services environment. This simplifies Terminal Services configuration by putting the majority of configuration options in a centralized location.

You should create an Organizational Unit (OU) to hold all your Windows Server 2003 Terminal Services servers, and then configure the Computer Configuration settings in the Group Policy object, instead of configuring each individual server. Group Policies override the settings configured with the Terminal Services Configuration tool.

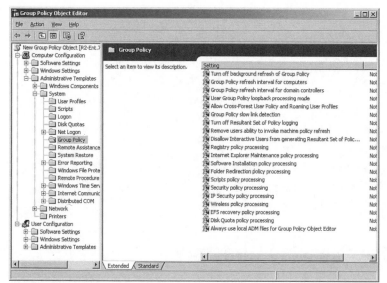

FIGURE 11.16 You can configure settings for multiple Terminal Services servers via the Group Policy MMC's Terminal Services folder.

NOTE

Only for Windows Server 2003 Group Policy can be used to manage only Windows Server 2003 Terminal Services servers. Windows 2000 and Windows NT Terminal Services are not supported.

Challenge

You are the administrator of a network that includes a Windows Server 2003 server configured for Terminal Services Application Server mode. The server is configured properly and should have enough capacity for the projected number of users. However, lately you have noticed that performance seems to decrease toward the end of the day. After some checking around, you discover that some of the users are disconnecting their sessions instead of properly logging off. Therefore, their disconnected sessions use up valuable system resources.

What is the best way to solve this issue in Windows Server 2003 Terminal Services? On your own, try to develop a solution that would involve the least amount of configuration changes.

If you would like to see a possible solution, follow these steps:

1. Click Start, All Programs, Administrative Tools, Terminal Services Configuration.

2. In the right pane of the Terminal Services Configuration MMC, double-click the Connections folder.

3. Right-click the RDP-TCP connection and then select Properties from the pop-up menu.

(continues)

(continued)

4. Click the Sessions tab of the RDP-TCP Properties dialog box.

5. On the Sessions tab, click the Override User Settings check box in the upper-left section of the dialog box.

6. From the End a Disconnection Session drop-down list, select the length of time you want Terminal Services to wait before terminating a disconnected session.

7. Click the OK button to Save. Close the MMC.

Because there is only one Windows Server 2003 Terminal Services server, it's just as easy to set the disconnection settings in the Terminal Services Configuration MMC as it would be to accomplish the same thing via Group Policy.

Terminal Services Session Directory

Even though you can support quite a few user sessions per processor using Windows Server 2003 Terminal Services, there will always be certain applications that are CPU hogs or that need to be available to a large number of users. You can set up multiple Windows Server 2003 Terminal Services machines and assign groups of users to each one, but this doesn't provide any redundancy. In addition, what if one server has 200 users and is starting to slow down under the load, while another server is loafing along with only 10?

You can use a process called *load balancing* to spread the application load across two or more servers. This prevents one server from becoming overloaded while another is loafing. This also provides redundancy for your applications because the failure of a single server does not prevent your users from completing their work.

Windows Server 2003 Network Load Balancing is a feature included in all the Microsoft Windows Server 2003 operating systems. The Network Load Balancing (NLB) feature is used to enhance the scalability and availability of mission-critical, TCP/IP-based services such as web, Terminal Services, virtual private networking, and streaming media servers. NLB requires no additional hardware or software components.

NLB works by distributing IP traffic across multiple Windows Server 2003 servers. Load balancing works on the principle that if a server is busy or unavailable, a client connection is routed to the next available server. Unlike clustering, load balancing does not require that you have identical servers. It also does not require any special disk units or other hardware, so it is an economical configuration. However, you are required to install identical applications in exactly the same manner on each server that is to be balanced.

To the client, it looks like a single server is handling requests because the client sees a single virtual IP address and hostname. NLB is also capable of detecting host server failures and automatically redistributing traffic to the surviving servers. NLB can support up to 32 servers in a balanced configuration.

When you set up an NLB configuration, you can either allow the load to be equally distributed among the servers or specify the load percentages for individual servers. By specifying individual load percentages, you can use dissimilar servers in your balanced configuration. Incoming client requests are distributed among the servers according to this configuration.

All the servers in the balanced configuration exchange heartbeat messages, so they know when a server enters or leaves the configuration. When a server is added or leaves the configuration by either configuration change or failure, the other servers automatically adjust and redistribute the workload. In the current version of Windows Server 2003 Network Load Balancing, the load balance is a static percentage and does not change in response to the actual load of the server, as determined by CPU or memory usage.

Most server failures are detected within 5 seconds, and the recovery and redistribution of the workload are accomplished within 10 seconds. However, the RDC client loses its connection and must reconnect. As long as IP affinity, which automatically redirects a client session to the last server it was connected to, is turned on in NLB, this isn't a problem. Because NLB uses the IP address of the client when routing, it can reconnect to a disconnected session. However, in those situations where the user has moved to another computer or received a different IP address via DHCP, the user receives a new session chosen at random from the group of servers.

To solve this dilemma, Microsoft has included the Terminal Services Session Directory Service as a new feature in the Windows Server 2003 Enterprise and Datacenter editions. The Session Directory Service creates a database on a server that contains a record of the current sessions being hosted by a load-balanced cluster of Windows Server 2003 Terminal Services servers. The session directory database indexes the sessions using the username instead of the IP address. This allows disconnected sessions to be reconnected by using the username to look up the location of a disconnected session when the user is trying to log on to the Terminal Services server again. After it is determined which server is hosting the session that the user was disconnected from, his logon is routed to that server.

The Session Directory (SD) doesn't have to be on a server that has Terminal Services installed. In large Windows Server 2003 Terminal Services installations, it's recommended that SD be hosted on a separate high-availability server.

The Session Directory Service is not enabled by default. To enable it, use the procedure outlined in Step by Step 11.4.

STEP BY STEP

11.4 Enabling the Session Directory Service

1. Click Start, All Programs, Administrative Tools, Services.

2. Right-click the Terminal Services Session Directory entry in the right pane and select Properties from the pop-up menu.

3. Click the Start button. As shown in Figure 11.17, select Automatic from the Startup Type drop-down list.

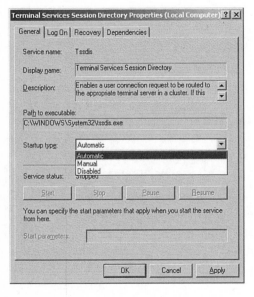

FIGURE 11.17 You enable the Session Directory Service via the Terminal Services Session Directory dialog box.

4. Click OK to save.

After the Session Directory Service is started, you will have to add the Windows Server 2003 Terminal Services servers that you want to use with the service to an OU. After the servers are added to this OU, you will need to use Group Policy to enable SD for the Terminal Services servers in this OU.

To enable SD for a group of servers, use the procedure outlined in Step by Step 11.5.

STEP BY STEP

11.5 Enabling the Session Directory for a group of servers

1. Click Start, All Programs, Administrative Tools, Active Directory Users and Computers.

2. In the right pane, right-click the OU that contains the Windows Server 2003 Terminal Services servers that you want to be controlled by the Session Directory Service. Then select Properties from the pop-up menu.

3. From the Properties dialog box, select the Group Policy tab. Click the Add button to add a new policy.

4. From the Group Policy MMC, shown in Figure 11.18, navigate to the Administrative Templates, Windows Components, Terminal Services, Session Directory folder.

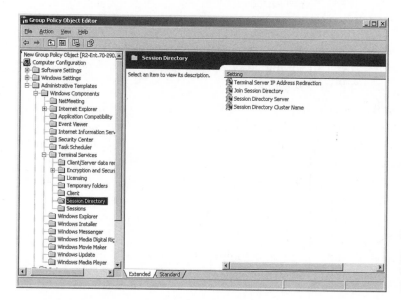

FIGURE 11.18 The Group Policy MMC, showing the options available for the Terminal Services Session Directory.

5. Double-click the Join Session Directory entry, and then select the Enabled option from the Properties dialog box. Click OK.

6. Double-click the Session Directory Server entry and then type in the name of the SD server in the Properties dialog box. Click OK.

7. Double-click the Session Directory Cluster Name entry and then type in a name for the SD cluster in the Properties dialog box. Click OK.

8. Close the Group Policy MMC.

Although it is a best practice to use Group Policy to manage your Terminal Services Session Directory, you can add the servers that are running Terminal Services that you want included in the farm to the Session Directory Computers local group on the server that is designated as the SD server.

Troubleshooting Terminal Services

Objective:
Troubleshoot Terminal Services

▶ Diagnose and resolve issues related to Terminal Services security.

▶ Diagnose and resolve issues related to client access to Terminal Services.

Windows Terminal Services is dependent on the common services on the network, such as TCP/IP and domain services. If you are having problems with Terminal Services, make sure no other functions on the network are failing.

A common problem with Terminal Services involves connecting to the server with the older RDP 5.0 client instead of the RDC 5.0 client, which is included with Windows 2000, or the RDC 5.1 client, which is included with Windows XP and Windows Server 2003. The clients look and function in a similar manner; however, the advanced functionality that is enabled in RDC 5.1, such as improved encryption, audio support, and keyboard mapping, are not available with the older RDP clients.

The multiple-monitor support in Windows XP/2003 can cause problems when you're connecting to one of these machines. If the application that you want to work with was last displayed or is currently displayed on the secondary monitor, you will not be able to see it.

To move the application to your RDC session, use the procedure outlined in Step by Step 11.6.

STEP BY STEP

11.6 Moving an application to your RDC session

1. Select the application's icon on the taskbar.

2. Hold down the Alt key and press the spacebar to open the Window menu. (You won't be able to see it.)

3. Press the M key (Move) and use the arrow keys to move the application window into your RDC session, as shown in Figure 11.19.

4. After the application window is within your session window, press the Enter key to lock it down.

FIGURE 11.19 Moving a window back onto the viewable desktop.

When trying to diagnose a possible Terminal Services problem, sometimes you need to know what mode the server is in. To determine which mode a Terminal Services server is using, follow the procedure outlined in Step by Step 11.7.

STEP BY STEP

11.7 Determining the Terminal Services mode

1. Select Start, All Programs, and then click Administrative Tools.

2. Select Terminal Services Configuration.

3. Select Server Settings.

4. Locate the Licensing entry in the right pane. The mode is listed in the Attribute column, as shown in Figure 11.20.

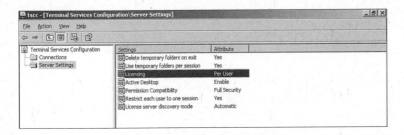

FIGURE 11.20 Identifying the Terminal Services mode.

There are many applications, including some from Microsoft, that you cannot install on the Terminal Services computer from a Remote Desktop session. You have to install these programs from the server console connection. This includes SQL, most of the service packs for Windows, and other Microsoft applications.

Challenge

You are putting together a business plan for a startup company. Your goal is to run a small application service provider (ASP) that caters to several local small businesses that can't afford to have their own server farm and IT staff. You plan for all your clients to access your server farm over the Internet, either through a VPN or via one of the web servers.

You are, in effect, running the business for a number of small companies. It is essential that you provide these companies with reliable access to their data as well as ensure that their data is not accessible by other companies, both those sharing your resources and those external to your network.

Try to complete this exercise on your own, listing your conclusions on a sheet of paper. After you have completed the exercise, compare your results to those given here.

1. You should set up a cluster of load-balanced Windows Server 2003 Terminal Services servers, with identical applications installed on each server. These load-balanced Terminal Services servers should have the Session Directory Service enabled so that a disconnected user (common over Internet connections) will be automatically routed back to her existing session.

2. To ensure that users from one company cannot access the data of another, you should set up different user groups for each company. Each company should be configured with its own file shares and folders. Each company's file shares should grant Deny Read permission to the groups from the other companies.

Chapter Summary

This chapter covered the capability for supporting the Windows Server 2003 desktop on devices that would not normally be able to run Windows Server 2003 applications. To summarize, this chapter contained the following main points:

- *Using Terminal Services*—This includes installing, configuring, and maintaining the two Windows Server 2003 Terminal Services modes.

- *Troubleshooting Terminal Services*—This includes diagnosing and resolving problems specific to the Terminal Services environment.

Key Terms

- Remote Desktop Protocol
- Remote Desktop for Administration mode
- Application Server mode
- Session Directory
- Remote Control

Apply Your Knowledge

Exercises

11.1 Installing Terminal Services in Application Server Mode

In this exercise, you will install Terminal Services in Application Server mode and install a sample application.

Estimated Time: 40 minutes

1. Click Start, All Programs, Control Panel, Add or Remove Programs.

2. Click the Add/Remove Windows Components button in the left pane of the Add or Remove Programs dialog box.

3. The Windows Components Wizard appears. Select the Terminal Server check box.

4. If Internet Explorer Enhanced Security Configuration is enabled (it is enabled by default), you will receive the Configuration Warning prompt. After you read and understand this warning, click the Yes button to continue.

5. This returns you to the Windows Components Wizard. Click the Next button to continue.

6. The Terminal Server Setup warning appears. Read and understand the warning, and then click the Next button to continue.

7. The Terminal Server Setup screen appears. This screen allows you to select Full Security mode, which is new to Windows Server 2003, or Relaxed Security mode, which is roughly equivalent to the security on a Windows 2000 Terminal Services server. Click the desired option button and then click the Next button to continue.

8. When the Completing the Windows Component Wizard screen appears, click the Finish button. You will be prompted to reboot the server.

9. After the server has rebooted, log on as a member of the Administrators group.

10. Click Start, All Programs, Control Panel, Add or Remove Programs.

11. Click the Add New Programs button in the left pane of the Add or Remove Programs dialog box.

12. Click the CD or Floppy button.

13. When prompted, insert the CD-ROM or floppy disk, and click the Next button to continue.

14. If the application isn't automatically found, click the Browse button and search for it. Click the Next button when you're finished.

15. As the installation starts, a screen appears. Do not click the Next button until the application's installation procedure has been completed.

16. When the Finish Admin Install screen appears, click the Finish button.

11.2 Securing a local folder

Because all users accessing a Windows Server 2003 Terminal Services in Application Server mode server are granted the Log On Locally right, you will need to use local security to prevent them from accessing certain folders. In this exercise, you will secure a local folder so that only selected users can access its contents.

Estimated Time: 40 minutes

1. Verify that the volume the desired folder is on is an NTFS volume. If it is not, use the CONVERT command to change it to NTFS.

2. Open either My Computer or Windows Explorer. Navigate to the folder on which you want to configure security.

3. Right-click the object and select Properties from the pop-up menu. Click the Security tab on the resulting dialog box.

4. From the Security tab, click the Add button.

5. The Select Users or Groups dialog box appears. This dialog box allows you to select either a local or domain user or group to assign permissions to. Enter the user or group and then click OK.

6. This returns you to the Folder Properties dialog box. Note that, by default, the user or group just added has been granted Read and Execute, List Folder Contents, and Read permissions for the folder.

7. In the Permissions section of the Folder Properties dialog box, select the desired permissions and then click the OK button to save.

11.3 Configuring the disconnect timeout via Group Policy

In this exercise, you will use Group Policy to set the Windows Server 2003 Terminal Services client disconnect timeout.

Estimated Time: 20 minutes

1. Click Start, All Programs, Administrative Tools, Active Directory Users and Computers.

2. In the right pane, right-click the OU that contains the Windows Server 2003 Terminal Servers that you want to be controlled by the Session Directory Service. Then select Properties from the pop-up menu.

3. From the Properties dialog box, select the Group Policy tab. Click the Add button to add a new policy.

4. From the Group Policy MMC, navigate to the Administrative Templates, Windows Components, Terminal Services, Sessions folder.

5. Double-click the item Set Time Limit for Disconnected Sessions in the right pane of the MMC.

6. From the Properties dialog box, select the Enabled option button and then select a time from the End a Disconnected Session drop-down list.

7. Click OK to save. Close the MMC.

Exam Questions

1. Mary is the network administrator for a loan company. As part of her duties, she built a new Windows Server 2003 server and configured Terminal Services in Application Server mode. Users report that when they try to connect to the Terminal Services server, they receive the following error message: The local policy of this system does not allow you to log on interactively. When Mary attempts to log on to the Terminal Services server from a user's computer, she is able to log on successfully. How can Mary enable the users to log on to the Terminal Services server?

   ○ **A.** Grant the users the right to log on locally.

   ○ **B.** Add the users to the TSUsers group.

   ○ **C.** Grant the users the right to log on over the network.

   ○ **D.** Add the users to the Remote Desktop Users group.

2. You are the administrator of a small network. You have configured a Windows Server 2003 server to run Terminal Services in Application Server mode. What is the maximum number of users that can be supported?

   ○ **A.** The same amount as the number of Terminal Server licenses that were purchased

   ○ **B.** Two, plus one for the console

   ○ **C.** About 100 on Windows Server 2003 Standard Edition and 200 on Windows Server 2003 Enterprise Edition

   ○ **D.** As many as the performance of the server will support

3. You are the administrator of a small network. You have configured a Windows Server 2003 server to run Terminal Services in Application Server mode. What is the proper way to install applications?

   ○ **A.** Open Windows Explorer, navigate to the folder where the installation files are stored, and then double-click the MSI file.

   ○ **B.** Open Add/Remove Programs, navigate to the folder where the installation files are stored, and then double-click the MSI file.

   ○ **C.** Open a command prompt and navigate to the folder where the installation files are stored. Enter the command install. Run the MSI file from the command line.

   ○ **D.** Open Windows Explorer and navigate to the folder where the installation files are stored. Open a command prompt, enter the command change mode /install. Then double-click the MSI file in Windows Explorer.

4. You are the administrator of a small network. You have configured a Windows Server 2003 server to run Terminal Services in Remote Desktop for Administration mode. What is the proper way to install applications?

○ **A.** Open Windows Explorer, navigate to the folder where the installation files are stored, and then double-click the MSI file.

○ **B.** Open Add/Remove Programs, navigate to the folder where the installation files are stored, and then double-click the MSI file.

○ **C.** Install the applications just like on any other server.

○ **D.** Open Windows Explorer and navigate to the folder where the installation files are stored. Open a command prompt, enter the command `change user /install`. Then double-click the MSI file in Windows Explorer.

5. You have just finished building a new Windows Server 2003 server. Your plan is to manage it remotely using Terminal Services Remote Desktop for Administration mode, just like you've been doing with your Windows 2000 servers. However, when you open the RDC client and try to browse to the new server, you don't see it in the list. What is the most likely cause of the problem?

○ **A.** A bad network interface card.

○ **B.** The personal firewall is blocking the ports for the browse list.

○ **C.** Remote Desktop for Administration mode has not been enabled.

○ **D.** Windows Server 2003 in Terminal Services Remote Desktop for Administration mode doesn't advertise to the browse list.

6. You are the network administrator for FlyByNight Airlines. The network consists of a single Active Directory domain. All network servers run Windows Server 2003 Standard Edition. A Terminal Services farm is installed on your network. FBM1, the first server in the farm, acts as the session directory server. All terminal servers are operating at maximum capacity.

An increasing number of users report slow response times when they use these servers. You need to improve the performance of the terminal server farm. You plan to use a server named FBM4, which has hardware identical to that of the other terminal servers in the farm. First, you add FBM4 to the Session Directory Computers OU. What should you do next?

○ **A.** Add FBM4 to the Session Directory Computers local group on FBM1.

○ **B.** Add FBM4 to the Session Directory Computers global group on FBM1.

○ **C.** On FBM4, install the Session Directory service.

○ **D.** On FBM4, create a new session directory server.

7. You are the network administrator for FlyByNight Airlines. The network consists of a single Active Directory domain. All network servers run Windows Server 2003 Standard Edition. A Terminal Services farm consisting of 10 servers is installed on your network. All Terminal Services servers are located in an OU named FBN-TS.

   An increasing number of users report slow response times when they use these servers. You notice that there are at least 100 disconnected Terminal Services sessions. You want all your Terminal Services servers to end disconnected sessions after 15 minutes of inactivity. You want to achieve this using the minimal amount of administrative effort. What should you do?

   ○ **A.** Log on the console of each terminal server. In the RDP-TCP connection properties, set the End a Disconnected Session option to 15 minutes.

   ○ **B.** Edit the GPO to set the time limit for disconnected sessions to 15 minutes.

   ○ **C.** On each Terminal Server, run the `tsdiscon` command to disconnect all 100 users.

   ○ **D.** In Active Directory Users and Computers, set the End a Disconnected Session option for all domain user accounts to 15 minutes.

8. You are the administrator of a small network. You have configured two Windows Server 2003 servers to run Terminal Services in Application Server mode. You add a domain group named Mechanics to the Remote Desktop Users group on both terminal servers.

   One week later, you discover that files on both servers were deleted by a user named Mitch, who is a member of the Mechanics group. You need to prevent Mitch from connecting to any of the terminal servers. What should you do?

   ○ **A.** On both terminal servers, modify the RDP-TCP connection permissions to assign the Deny—Users Access and the Deny—Guest Access permissions to the Mechanics group.

   ○ **B.** On both terminal servers, modify the RDP-TCP connection permissions to assign the Deny—Users Access permissions to the Mechanics group.

   ○ **C.** In the properties of Mitch's user account, disable the Allow Logon to a Terminal Server option.

   ○ **D.** Remove Mitch's user account from the Mechanics group.

9. You are the network administrator for FlyByNight Airlines. The network consists of a single Active Directory domain running in Windows 2003 interim level. Network servers are a mixture of Windows Server 2003 and Windows NT 4.0. A Terminal Services farm is installed on your network. The TS farm is used to host secure documents. All users in the domain have access to the Terminal Servers by membership in the TS-Secure global group.

Your company is hiring 20 summer interns. You need to make sure that the interns can't access the TS farm. What should you do?

○ **A.** Modify the Default Domain Group Policy object (GPO). Configure a computer-level policy to prevent the temporary employees from connecting to the terminal servers.

○ **B.** Modify the Default Domain Group Policy object (GPO). Enable the user-level Terminal Server setting Sets Rules for Remote Control of Terminal Services user sessions.

○ **C.** On the Terminal Services Profile tab of the user properties for each account, disable the option to log on to terminal servers.

○ **D.** In the security policy for domain controllers, disable the computer-level Terminal Server setting Allow Users to Connect Remotely Using the Terminal Server.

○ **E.** None of the above.

Answers to Exam Questions

1. **D.** Although granting the users the right to log on locally will work, this can get unwieldy if there are a large number of users. The proper way is to add the users that need to log on to the Terminal Services server to the Remote Desktop Users group. See the "Configuring Terminal Services Connections" section for more information.

2. **A.** The number of concurrent Terminal Services connections on all versions of Windows Server 2003 is limited to the number of licenses that are installed. However, performance will suffer as the hardware capacity is reached. See the "Terminal Services in Application Server Mode" section for more information.

3. **B.** Applications can be installed on a Windows Server 2003 server running in Terminal Services Application Server mode in two ways: from Add/Remove Programs and, after setting the server in Install mode, by entering the command change user /install. See the "Installing Applications" section for more information.

4. **C.** Applications can be installed on a Windows Server 2003 server running in Terminal Services Remote Desktop for Administration mode just like they would on any other server. This is because it is not a multiuser environment. See the "Installing Applications" section for more information.

5. **D.** Unlike in Windows 2000 Server, Windows Server 2003 Terminal Services servers in Remote Desktop for Administration mode will not be advertised, so they can't be browsed using the RDC client. You will need to enter either the IP address or the server name. See the "Using the Remote Desktop Connection Client" section for more information.

6. **A.** When a new server is added to a Terminal Services Farm, it must either be added to an OU, if you are managing the farm via Group Policy, or to the Session Directory Computers local group on the server hosting the Session Directory role. Although the service is installed by default on all Windows Server 2003 servers, it should be enabled only on a single server per farm. See the "Terminal Services Session Directory" section for more information.

7. **B.** Although it is possible to log on to each server and configure the settings manually, it's more efficient to manage settings that will affect all the Terminal Servers via Group Policy. Running the tsdisconn command would drop all current disconnected sessions, but would not prevent more from occurring. Reconfiguring the user accounts would apply only to existing users, not new ones. See the "Managing Windows Server 2003 Terminal Services via Group Policy" section for more information.

8. **C.** Although removing Mitch from the Mechanics group will work, we don't know what other permissions we would be affecting by doing so. The best way to accomplish our task is to disable TS logons in Mitch's user account. This setting overrides any other permissions to the Terminal Services servers he has been granted. The other solutions would block everyone from logging on to terminal services. See the "Configuring Terminal Services Connections" section for more information

9. **E.** None of the above. Because the domain is running in the Windows 2003 Interim level, and the TS users are assigned via a global group, it's clear that for any new users to be added to that group, they will have to be assigned manually because at that level, you can't add a group to a global group. Disabling logons via the user account would work, but it's not necessary. See "Configuring Terminal Services Connections" and "The Four Domain Functional Levels" in Chapter 3.

Suggested Readings and Resources

1. Anderson, Christa. *Windows Terminal Services*. Sybex, 2002. ISBN 0782128955.

2. Boswell, William. *Inside Windows Server 2003*. New Riders, 2003. ISBN 0735711585.

3. Madden, Brian. *Terminal Services for Windows Server 2003*. Brianmadden.Com Publishing Group, 2004. ISBN 0971151040.

4. Matthews, Marty. *Windows Server 2003: A Beginners Guide*. McGraw-Hill, 2003. ISBN 0072193093.

5. Microsoft Session Directory Whitepaper: http://www.microsoft.com/ windowsserver2003/docs/SessionDirectory.doc.

6. Microsoft Terminal Services Overview Whitepaper: http://www.microsoft.com/ windowsserver2003/docs/TerminalServerOverview.doc.

7. Microsoft Windows 2003 File Server Best Practices: http://www.microsoft.com/ technet/treeview/default.asp?url=/technet/prodtechnol/windowsserver2003/proddocs/ entserver/file_srv_bestpractice.asp?frame=true.

8. Minasi, Mark, et al. *Mark Minasi's Windows XP and Server 2003 Resource Kit*. Sybex, 2003. ISBN 0782140807.

9. Minasi, Mark, et al. *Mastering Windows Server 2003 Server*. Sybex, 2003. ISBN 0782141307.

10. Shapiro, Jeffrey, et al. *Windows Server 2003 Bible*. John Wiley & Sons, 2003. ISBN 0764549375.

11. Tritsch, Bernard. *Microsoft Windows Server 2003 Terminal Services*. Microsoft Press, 2003. ISBN 0735619042.

12

Managing Server Storage Devices

Objectives

This chapter covers the following Microsoft-specified objectives for the "Managing and Maintaining Physical and Logical Devices" section of the Managing and Maintaining a Microsoft Windows Server 2003 Environment exam:

Manage basic disks and dynamic disks

▶ When working in a Windows Server 2003 environment, you need to have a thorough understanding of the different types of disks available. In addition, it is important to understand how they are used and how to manage them.

Optimize server disk performance

▶ **Implement a RAID solution**

▶ **Defragment volumes and partitions**

▶ The purpose of this objective is to teach you how to create, manage, and troubleshoot problems with the various RAID solutions available in Windows Server 2003. In addition, you should be familiar with maintaining volumes and partitions using the Disk Defragmenter utility.

Outline

Study Strategies

▶ The sections in this chapter outline features that are basic to using and managing Windows Server 2003. The proper use of and recovery from problems with storage have always been major points on Microsoft exams. Expect the Windows Server 2003 exams to continue that tradition. Make sure you have a complete understanding of the capabilities of basic and dynamic disks, especially as to how they are similar and how they are different.

▶ Most of the disk-related questions on the test will probably concern the use of dynamic disks. Although basic disks can be used in Windows Server 2003, the advanced storage functionality is supported only on dynamic disks. Make sure you understand the various capabilities of dynamic disks, how they are configured, and how to recover from failures. However, there are still applications where dynamic disks are not recommended. Know what they are and why. Expect to see questions about this topic on the exam.

▶ This chapter contains a lot of hands-on exercises. Make sure that you work through most, if not all, of them to become familiar with the Disk Management MMC, and working with both dynamic and basic disks. A server or virtual software with multiple drives is highly recommended.

Introduction

One of the primary roles of Windows Server 2003 is that of a data repository, or file server. Many administrative tasks are involved in creating, configuring, and managing a file server. This can range from deciding what types of volumes or partitions to use to recovering from a physical disk failure. This chapter covers the tasks required to maintain data on Windows Server 2003. This type of information is crucial for a job as a system administrator, and it is also very important for the exam.

Managing Basic Disks and Dynamic Disks

Objective:

Manage basic disks and dynamic disks

Windows Server 2003 supports two types of physical disk configurations: *basic* and *dynamic*. A single physical disk must be one type or the other; however, you can intermingle the physical disk types in a multiple disk server.

Introduction to Basic Disks

When a new disk is installed in Windows Server 2003, it is installed as a basic disk. The basic disk type has been used in all versions of Microsoft Windows dating back to 1.0, OS/2, and in MS-DOS. This configuration allows a basic disk created in Windows Server 2003 to be recognized by these earlier operating systems.

A basic disk splits a physical disk into units called *partitions*. Partitions allow you to subdivide your physical disk into separate units of storage. There are two types of partitions: *primary* and *extended*.

A primary partition can be used to store a boot record so that you can boot your server from that partition. A hard disk can be configured with one to four primary partitions. You can use these partitions to boot multiple operating systems, or to just contain data. Although multiple primary partitions can contain boot records, only one primary partition can be marked *active*. When a primary partition is marked as active, the system BIOS looks for the boot files needed to start the system in that partition.

The other type of partition is the *extended partition*, which allows you to create a theoretically unlimited number of logical drives inside that partition. Using older operating systems limits the number of drive letters that are available; however, in the later versions of Windows NT/2000/2003/XP, these logical drives can be mounted without a drive letter. The downside is that logical drives created inside an extended partition are not bootable.

You can have up to four primary partitions, or three primary partitions and an extended parti-tion, on a single physical hard disk. The basic disk was the only type supported in versions of Windows prior to Windows 2000.

> **NOTE**
>
> **Watch the Terminology**   Beginning with Windows XP, Microsoft has started to refer to primary partitions and the logical drives that are contained in extended partitions as *basic volumes*. Do not confuse this with *simple volumes*, which are discussed later in the chapter. In addition, remember that a basic disk is a phys-ical entity and that a basic volume is a logical one.

> **EXAM ALERT**
>
> **Know Your Partitions**   Be familiar with the two types of partitions, logical drives, and which drives are bootable.

Before a physical hard disk can be used with an operating system, it must be *initialized*. The initialization process is used to write the master boot record (MBR) to the first sector of the hard drive. The MBR contains a small amount of startup code and a partition table that lists the configuration of the partitions. The hard drive can be initialized during a clean installation of Windows 2003 or by using the command-line utility FDISK.

When a Windows Server 2003 server is started, its basic input/output system (BIOS) reads the MBR on the physical hard drive that is used to start the server. The MBR contains a pointer to the location of the active partition on the hard drive and the code needed to begin the startup process. The active partition is also referred to as the *system partition*. On an Intel-based system, the system partition contains the BOOT.INI, NTDETECT.COM, and NTLDR files. These files tell the server how to start the operating system.

> **NOTE**
>
> **NTBOOTDD.SYS**   Another file that might be included is NTBOOTDD.SYS. This file is needed only if you are using a SCSI controller that has its BIOS disabled.

The BOOT.INI file, shown in Figure 12.1, contains the physical path to the location of the folder that contains the operating system files. The BOOT.INI file can contain paths to multi-ple operating systems. At boot, you are presented with a menu that allows you to choose which operating system to start. In the example shown, there is an additional option to boot to the Recovery Console.

```
boot.ini - Notepad
File  Edit  Format  View  Help
[boot loader]
timeout=30
default=multi(0)disk(0)rdisk(0)partition(1)\WINDOWS
[operating systems]
multi(0)disk(0)rdisk(0)partition(1)\WINDOWS="Windows Server 2003, Standard" /noexecute=optout /fa:
C:\CMDCONS\BOOTSECT.DAT="Microsoft Windows Recovery Console" /cmdcons
```

FIGURE 12.1 A typical BOOT.INI file, showing the location of the system partition.

> **NOTE**
>
> **More on the Recovery Console**   The Recovery Console is covered in Chapter 17, "Managing and Implementing Disaster Recovery."

The partition that contains the operating system files is referred to as the *boot partition*. Of course, you don't have to have separate boot and system partitions. You can use a single partition to contain both the boot and the operating system files; for example, the common configuration for most servers is for both partitions to be located on the C: drive.

> **EXAM ALERT**
>
> There might be scenarios on the exam where you must understand the logical relationship between boot partitions and system partitions.

Although the system partition must be located on a physical partition, the boot partition can be contained on a logical drive in the extended partition. It is important to remember that although physical and extended partitions are physical entities, active, system, and boot partitions are logical entities.

Using the DISKPART Utility

A new feature in Windows Server 2003 is the capability to extend partitions on basic disks. This allows you to extend either primary or logical partitions into unallocated, adjacent, contiguous space. In Windows 2000, only dynamic volumes could be extended.

Extending partitions on a basic disk is performed using the DISKPART utility. DISKPART is a command-line utility that can be used to perform a variety of disk-management tasks. Because it is a command-line utility, it can be included in scripts or run from a remote session.

Although you use the Disk Management snap-in to perform the majority of disk-related tasks, DISKPART can perform more operations than the Disk Management snap-in. For example, extending a basic volume can be performed only through the DISKPART utility.

However, whereas the Disk Management snap-in prevents you from performing operations that might result in data loss, DISKPART has no safeguards and allows you to perform just about any operation on your disk with little or no warning. Here is a partial list of the operations that can be performed using the DISKPART utility:

- ▶ Set a partition to active.

- ▶ Add, create, and delete disks, partitions, and volumes, both basic and fault tolerant.

- ▶ Add or break mirrored volumes (RAID-1).

- ▶ Repair mirrored sets (RAID-1) or fault-tolerant volumes (RAID-5).

- ▶ Import foreign disks.

- ▶ List the size, configuration, and status of the physical and logical disks in the server.

In Windows Server 2003, a basic volume can be extended into the next contiguous, unallocated space on that disk. The limitations are that you cannot extend the system or boot partitions you used to start the current session, and the partition must be formatted with NTFS.

> **NOTE**
>
> **Required Permissions** To perform disk-management tasks on a Windows Server 2003 server, you must be a member of either the Administrators or Server Operators local group on the server. Alternatively, if the server is a member of a domain, you should be a member of the Domain Admins group.

To extend a basic volume on a basic disk using the DISKPART utility, follow Step by Step 12.1.

STEP BY STEP

12.1 Using DISKPART to extend a basic volume

1. From the Start menu, select Run. From the command line, enter DISKPART and press the Enter key.

2. A command window opens with DISKPART in command mode. You need to select the disk and partition on which you want to perform operations. You can accomplish this by entering the list disk command to obtain a list of physical disks in your server, as shown in Figure 12.2. Note that an asterisk appears next to the disk, if any, that has the current focus.

FIGURE 12.2 Output from the DISKPART utility, showing the results of the list disk command.

3. After you determine the number of the disk you want to perform the operation on, you can set the focus to that disk by entering select disk x, where x is the number of the disk.

4. After you have set the focus to the desired disk, you can list the partitions or volumes on the disk by entering the list partition or the list volume command, as shown in Figure 12.3.

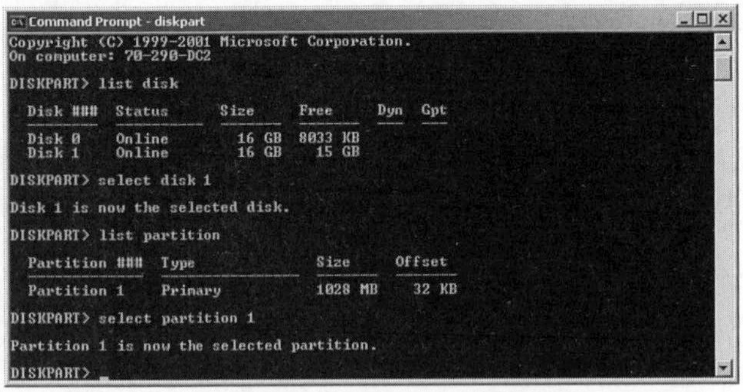

FIGURE 12.3 Output from the DISKPART utility, showing the results of the list partition command.

5. After you determine the number of the partition or volume you want to perform the operation on, set the focus to it by entering either select partition x or select volume x, as appropriate, where x is the number of the partition or volume.

6. After the desired disk and partition/volume are selected, use the `extend` command to extend the selected partition into the contiguous unallocated space. At the command prompt, enter `extend size=x`, where *x* is the amount in megabytes (MB) that you want to extend the partition or volume, as shown in Figure 12.4. If no size is specified, all the contiguous allocated space is added to the existing partition or volume.

7. You can verify the results by entering the `list partition` or `list volume` command and then checking the new size.

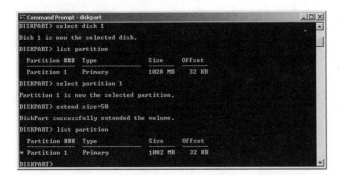

FIGURE 12.4 Output from the `DISKPART` utility, showing the results of the `extend` command. The asterisk is displayed next to the partition or volume that has the focus.

NOTE

Use the Proper Identification On basic disks, you can specify the volume or partition by using the number, drive letter, or mount point. On dynamic disks, you can use only the volume number.

EXAM ALERT

Know the Uses for DISKPART Be familiar with the things that `DISKPART` can do that can't be accomplished via the Disk Management MMC.

Introduction to Dynamic Disks

Dynamic disks were first introduced in Windows 2000 and are the preferred disk type for Windows Server 2003. Unlike a basic disk, a dynamic disk is divided into *volumes* instead of partitions. Although a clean installation of Windows Server 2003 creates a basic disk by default, any additional disks can be added as basic or dynamic disks. In addition, after the initial installation, the basic disk can be converted to a dynamic disk.

Unlike basic disks, which use the original MS-DOS–style master boot record (MBR) partition tables to store primary and logical disk-partitioning information, dynamic disks use a private RAID-5 set of the disk to maintain a *Logical Disk Manager (LDM)* database. The LDM contains volume types, offsets, memberships, and drive letters of each volume on that physical disk. The information in the LDM database is also replicated to all the other dynamic disks so that each dynamic disk knows the configuration of every other dynamic disk. The disks that share the same configuration information are known as a *Disk Group*.

The Disk Group feature makes dynamic disks more reliable and recoverable than basic disks. This extra reliability and recoverability means that a disk move or failure does not cause the disk configuration to be lost. The LDM database is stored in a 1MB reserved area at the end of every dynamic disk.

In addition, configuration changes can be made to dynamic disks without rebooting the server. Dynamic volumes can be created, deleted, and expanded, all without a reboot.

The following are the five types of volumes available using dynamic storage disks:

▶ *Simple volumes*—Simple volumes are similar to a partition on a basic disk.

▶ *Spanned volumes*—Spanned volumes can take various amounts of disk space, from 2 to 32 physical disks, and use that space to create a single large volume. Spanned volumes provide no fault tolerance. In fact, they can be more prone to failure than other types of volume because if any disk fails, the entire set is lost. The advantage of spanned volumes is that you can quickly add more storage space.

▶ *Striped volumes*—Striped volumes can be created from 2 to 32 physical disks. Striped volumes write data to these disks in 64KB sequential stripes. The first stripe is written to the first disk, the second stripe is written to the second disk, and so forth. Striped volumes, also known as *RAID-0*, provide no fault tolerance. The advantage provided by striped volumes lies in the overall disk I/O performance increase of the computer because the total disk I/O is split among all the disks in the volume.

▶ *Mirrored volumes*—Mirrored volumes, also known as *RAID-1* volumes, provide fault-tolerant data storage using two physical disks. Data is written simultaneously to each physical disk so that they contain identical information. If one of the drives in a mirrored volume fails, the system continues to run using the other volume. The total volume capacity will be equal to that provided by one of the physical disks.

▶ *RAID-5 volumes*—RAID-5 volumes are similar to striped volumes in that they use multiple disks—in this case, from 3 to 32 physical disks of the same size. The total volume capacity is equal to that provided by the number of physical disks minus one. Data is written sequentially across each physical disk and contains both data and parity information. For example, if you create a volume using four 1GB disks, your usable storage would be 3GB, because 1GB is devoted to storing the parity information. The parity information from the set is used to rebuild the set should one disk fail, thus providing fault tolerance. RAID-5 volumes in Windows Server 2003 cannot sustain the loss of more than one disk in the set while still providing fault tolerance.

After Windows Server 2003 is installed, you can convert a basic disk to a dynamic disk using the Disk Management snap-in or the DISKPART command-line utility. Using the Disk Management utility to convert disks is covered later in this chapter.

Limitations of Dynamic Disks

After reading about the wonderful features of dynamic disks, you're probably thinking that you should always use dynamic disks instead of basic disks. However, dynamic disks have some limitations, and there are situations in which they can't be used at all. Here are some of the limitations of dynamic disks:

- ▶ You cannot use dynamic disks if you want to dual boot a computer with an older operating system such as Windows 9x or Windows NT 4.0. Unfortunately, these older operating systems cannot access a dynamic disk, either as a boot device or for file storage. Only Windows 2000, 2003, and XP machines recognize dynamic disks. However, a dynamic disk can be accessed over the network by older operating systems.

- ▶ You can't set up multiple boot partitions on a dynamic disk.

- ▶ If you convert a basic disk that was configured to multiboot two or more operating systems to a dynamic disk, that disk is no longer bootable from any of the operating systems on it.

- ▶ Dynamic disks are not supported in laptops or removable disks, such as Zip disks or disks connected via a Universal Serial Bus (USB) or FireWire (IEEE 1394) interface. In addition, dynamic disks are not supported on disks used in shared Cluster Array configurations.

- ▶ Windows Server 2003 cannot be installed on a dynamic volume that was created from unallocated space on a dynamic disk.

- ▶ You can install Windows Server 2003 only on a basic disk, or on a dynamic volume that was converted from a basic boot volume/partition.

- ▶ After a basic disk is converted to a dynamic disk, it can't be converted back to a basic disk. The only way to revert to a basic disk is to back up the data, reinitialize the disk, repartition it, and restore the data.

- ▶ When installing Windows Server 2003 on a dynamic disk, you can't change the volume or partition sizes during the setup procedure.

> **EXAM ALERT**
>
> **Accessing Disks Over the Network**   When accessing a disk over the network, the client PC doesn't know or care whether it's accessing a basic or dynamic disk, using FAT or NTFS. This could easily be part of an exam question.

Most of the dynamic disk limitations in the Windows 2000/2003/XP family are due to the requirement of these operating systems that the boot partition have an entry in the partition table. After a basic disk is converted to a dynamic disk, you cannot change the partition table to mark a volume as an active volume.

> **NOTE**
>
> **Legacy Volumes**   In Windows NT 4.0, basic disks could be created in the following configurations:
>
> ▶ Spanned volume sets
> ▶ Mirrored volumes (RAID-1)
> ▶ Striped volumes (RAID-0)
> ▶ Striped volumes with parity (RAID-5)
>
> Windows Server 2003 does not support the creation or use of any of these configurations on a basic disk. If any of these volumes are present in a server that is upgraded to Windows Server 2003 or are added after Windows 2003 is installed, they will no longer be accessible. These volumes must be mounted in either Windows NT 4.0 or Windows 2000 Server to recover the data. For more information, see the Microsoft Knowledge Base Article Q328520, "Disk Management Displays Previous FTDisk Volumes As 'Unknown' with No Drive Letter."

Using the Disk Management Console to Manage Disks

Regardless of what type of disk you are using in Windows Server 2003, the majority of management tasks are performed using the Disk Management snap-in. The Disk Management snap-in is an extremely useful GUI tool for performing the required management tasks on your computer's hard drives and volumes. Disk Management can be accessed in several ways, the easiest of which is via the Computer Management console, as outlined in Step by Step 12.2.

STEP BY STEP

12.2 Starting the Disk Management snap-in

1. From the Start menu, select All Programs, Administrative Tools, Computer Management.

2. In the left pane of the Computer Management MMC, left-click the Storage entry and then select the Disk Management entry. This starts the Disk Management snap-in, as shown in Figure 12.5.

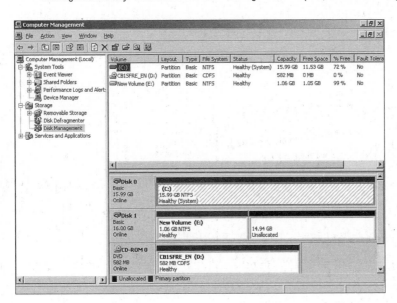

FIGURE 12.5 The Disk Management snap-in, shown here as part of the Computer Management MMC.

3. By default, Disk Management opens with the volume list displayed in the top-right pane and the graphical view displayed in the bottom-right pane. To change the view, for example, to display the disk list in the bottom-right pane, from the menu bar, select View, Bottom, Disk List (see Figure 12.6).

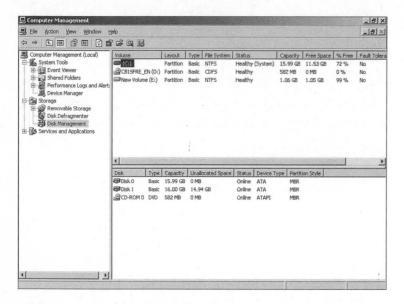

FIGURE 12.6 The Disk Management snap-in, showing the disk list in the bottom-right pane. The disk list displays the physical characteristics of the disks.

The Disk Management utility provides the following information:

▶ The type of disk, such as basic or dynamic

▶ The health status of each disk

▶ The partitions and/or volumes installed

▶ The health status of each partition or volume

▶ The file systems in use, such as FAT32 and NTFS

▶ The total size and free space for each disk, partition, or volume

Monitoring and Configuring Disks and Volumes

The bulk of your hard disk- and volume-management tasks are performed with the Disk Management utility. It can be used to perform the following tasks:

▶ Determine disk and volume information, such as size, file system, and other pertinent information.

▶ Determine disk health status.

▶ Convert basic storage to dynamic storage.

▶ Create new partitions and volumes.

▶ Format partitions and volumes.

▶ Delete partitions and volumes.

▶ Extend the size of dynamic volumes.

▶ Assign and change drive letters or paths to hard drives and removable storage drives.

▶ Add new physical disks.

Although you most commonly access the Disk Management utility from the Computer Management console, you can access Disk Management in any one of the following three ways, depending on your preferences:

▶ On the command line, enter **+**.

▶ On the command line, enter **MMC**. In the empty console, add the Disk Management snap-in. This can be useful for creating powerful, customized MMC consoles for a variety of management tasks.

▶ From within the Computer Management console, click Disk Management.

Viewing Disk Properties

You can quickly determine the properties of each physical disk in your computer by right-clicking the disk in question (see Figure 12.7) in the bottom area of the Disk Management window and selecting Properties from the shortcut menu.

As shown in Figure 12.7, the Disk Device Properties dialog box shows you the following information about your disks:

▶ The disk number, such as 0 or 1

▶ The type of disk (either basic or dynamic)

▶ The status and health of the disk

▶ The total capacity of the disk

▶ The unallocated space remaining on the disk

▶ The device type (either IDE or SCSI)

▶ The vendor of the hard disk, such as Maxtor or Fujitsu

▶ The adapter channel, such as primary IDE or secondary IDE

▶ The volumes or partitions that are located on the physical disk, such as C and D

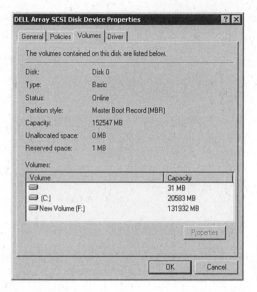

FIGURE 12.7 The Disk Device Properties dialog box, showing the Volumes tab. Most of the physical data about the disk configuration can be obtained here.

Viewing Volume Health Status

The health status of each volume is provided in the volume properties pane under the volume size in Disk Management (refer back to Figure 12.5). The following are some of the more common items displayed in this area:

▶ *Online*—The disk is operating normally with no known problems.

▶ *Healthy*—The volume is operating normally.

▶ *Healthy (At Risk)*—The volume is operating but is experiencing I/O errors.

▶ *Online (Errors)*—Used only for dynamic disks, this status indicates that I/O errors have been detected.

▶ *Offline or Missing*—Used only for dynamic disks, this status indicates that the disk is not accessible.

▶ *Failed Redundancy*—One of the fault-tolerant volumes has failed.

▶ *Foreign*—Used only for dynamic disks, this status indicates that a dynamic disk was removed from a Windows 2000/2003/XP computer and placed into this Windows 2003 computer, but has not yet been imported.

▶ *Unreadable*—The disk is not accessible.

▶ *Unrecognized*—The disk is not recognized (for example, a disk that was used in a Linux or a Unix system).

▶ *No Media*—Used only for removable-media drives such as CD-ROM and Zip drives. The status changes to Online when readable media is inserted into the drive.

Correcting problems with drives is discussed further in the "Recovering from Disk Failures" section, later in this chapter.

Viewing and Configuring Volume Properties

To gather information about a specific volume, right-click the desired volume in the lower pane of the Disk Management window and select Properties from the shortcut menu. As shown in Figure 12.8, the volume's Properties dialog box shows you the following information about your volumes (from the General tab):

▶ The volume label

▶ The type of volume—Either local disk (basic storage) or simple, spanned, or striped (dynamic storage)

▶ The file system in use (either as FAT32 or NTFS)

▶ The amount of space in use on the volume

▶ The amount of free space on the volume

▶ The total capacity of the volume

▶ Whether the volume has been configured for volume-level NTFS file and folder compression

▶ Whether the volume has been configured for indexing by the Indexing Service

If you click the Disk Cleanup button, the Disk Cleanup utility starts, which is discussed later in this chapter. From the Hardware tab (see Figure 12.9) of the volume's Properties dialog box, you can quickly get a summary of all installed storage devices in your computer. To open a troubleshooting wizard for a particular device, select it and click the Troubleshoot button. To view a device's properties, select the device and click the Properties button. The device's Properties dialog box opens. Device properties are discussed in Chapter 15, "Managing and Troubleshooting Hardware Devices."

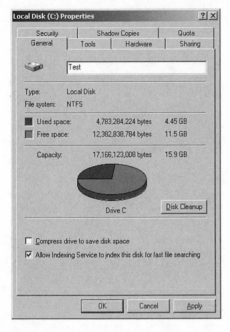

FIGURE 12.8 The General tab of Disk Properties displays the logical configuration of the individual volume.

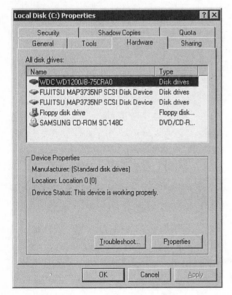

FIGURE 12.9 The Hardware tab of Disk Properties displays information about all the physical drives in the server.

The Sharing tab of the volume's Properties dialog box allows you to configure sharing of a volume for use by network clients across the network. Working with shared folders was discussed in Chapter 4, "Managing and Maintaining Access to Resources." The Security tab allows you to configure the NTFS permissions for the root of the volume; NTFS permissions are also discussed in Chapter 4.

The Quota tab allows you to configure and enforce disk usage quotas for your users. Working with disk quotas is discussed in the "Managing Disk Quotas" section of Chapter 13.

The last tab in the volume's Properties dialog box is the Web Sharing tab. If you have IIS installed on your computer, you will see this tab. The Web Sharing tab allows you to enable the volume or folder you selected as a virtual folder that can be accessed from a website hosted on your server.

Managing Disks on a Remote Computer

Because Disk Management is an MMC snap-in to the Computer Management MMC, it inherits the capabilities of all the Computer Management MMC's snap-ins to manage remote computers. This allows you to perform disk-management operations on any remote Windows 2000/2003/XP computer to which you have the required administrative authority.

To perform disk-management tasks on a remote computer, you must be a member of either the Administrators or Server Operators local group on the remote computer. If the remote computer is a member of a domain, you should be a member of the Domain Admins group.

If the user has the proper permissions, any computer in the Windows 2000/2003/XP family can manage other family members. For example, a Windows 2000 Professional computer can be used to manage a Windows Server 2003 computer or a Windows XP Professional computer. Only the features that are supported on the remote computer are available in the MMC. For example, if you are using a Windows Server 2003 computer to manage a Windows XP Professional computer, the selection for RAID-5 will not be available because it is not supported on the remote computer, which in this case is Windows XP Professional.

Adding a New Disk

When you add a new disk to a Windows Server 2003 server, it must be initialized and a disk signature and MBR written to it before it can be used. When you open the Disk Management snap-in for the first time after the new disk has been installed, the Initialize and Convert Disk Wizard displays a list of any new disks detected by the operating system, and it prompts you as to whether you want to install the new disk as a basic disk or as a dynamic disk.

Step by Step 12.3 walks you through adding a new disk to your server using the Initialize and Convert Disk Wizard.

STEP BY STEP

12.3 Adding a new disk

1. From the Start menu, select All Programs, Administrative Tools, Computer Management.

2. In the left pane of the Computer Management MMC, left-click the Storage entry and then select the Disk Management entry. This starts the Disk Management snap-in, which starts the Initialize and Convert Disk Wizard.

3. Click Next to continue. The next screen displays a list of disks that require initialization before they can be used. Select the desired disks and then click Next to continue.

4. The next screen allows you to select which of the new disks, if any, you want to convert to dynamic disks. If you don't make a selection here, the new disks are configured as basic disks. Click Next to continue.

5. On the next screen, confirm that the selected settings are correct. If you need to make any changes, click the Back button. If everything is correct, click Finish.

> **NOTE**
>
> **A Rescan Might Be Necessary**   If for some reason the Initialize and Convert Disk Wizard doesn't start automatically, the server might not have recognized the presence of the new disk. This sometimes happens with hot-plug disks. You can force the server to recognize the new disk by starting the Disk Management snap-in and then selecting Action, Rescan Disks from the system menu.

Working with Basic Disks

Unless you convert it after the initial installation of Windows Server 2003, the physical disk that the operating system is installed on will be configured as a basic disk with a single partition. If you choose to leave this disk configured as a basic disk, you need to understand how to work with basic disks. This section discusses how to perform the following tasks:

- Create primary partitions on a basic disk.
- Create extended partitions on a basic disk.
- Create logical drives in an extended partition on a basic disk.
- Delete partitions on a basic disk.
- Format a partition.
- Change the drive letter of a partition.
- Set a partition to active.

Creating a Primary Partition on a Basic Disk

As discussed earlier in this chapter, when Windows Server 2003 is initially installed on a new machine, it is installed on a basic disk in a primary partition. Usually, after the initial installation of the operating system, unallocated free space is still available on the disk. This space can be used to create additional drives.

On a basic disk, you can have either four primary partitions or three primary partitions and an extended partition. Step by Step 12.4 walks you through creating a primary partition on a basic disk.

STEP BY STEP

12.4 Creating a primary partition

1. From the Start menu, select All Programs, Administrative Tools, Computer Management.

2. In the left pane of the Computer Management MMC, left-click the Storage entry and then select the Disk Management entry. This starts the Disk Management snap-in.

3. In the lower-right pane of the Computer Management MMC, right-click the unallocated space on the drive that you want to add a primary partition to (see Figure 12.10).

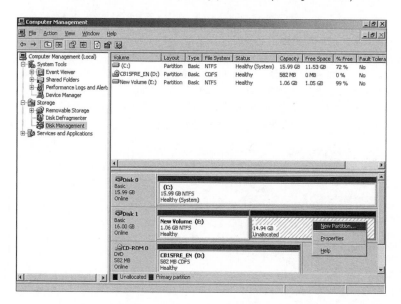

FIGURE 12.10 The Disk Manager snap-in, showing how to start the New Partition Wizard.

4. From the pop-up menu, select New Partition. This starts the New Partition Wizard. Click Next to continue.

5. The next screen (shown in Figure 12.11) prompts you to select the type of partition to create. Select the Primary Partition option button and then click Next to continue.

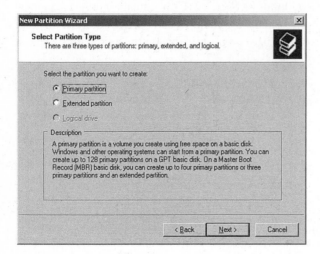

FIGURE 12.11   The New Partition Wizard, showing how to select the partition type. Notice that the logical drive selection is available only when an extended partition is selected.

6. The next screen prompts you to select the size of the new partition. The size can be anything from 8MB up to the size of the available free space. Enter the desired size and then click Next to continue.

7. The next screen allows you to select the drive letter or NTFS folder to assign the new partition to. You also have the option to not assign it, opting instead to come back and do it later. Most of the time you will assign a drive letter. Click Next to continue.

8. The Format Partition screen of the New Partition Wizard allows you to specify whether you want to format the partition and what file system and cluster size to use. There is also a selection to configure the new partition for file and folder compression. Normally, most partitions in Windows Server 2003 are formatted as NTFS with the default cluster size and no compression, as shown in Figure 12.12. The different file system formats are covered later in this chapter. Click Next to continue.

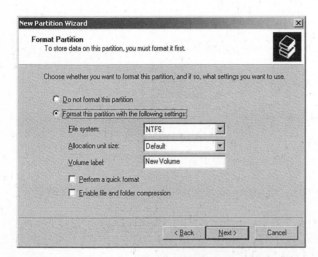

FIGURE 12.12   The Format Partition screen allows you to select from NTFS, FAT, and FAT32 formats.

9. Look over the settings on the Completing the New Partition Wizard screen. Confirm that the selected settings are correct. If you need to make any changes, click the Back button. If everything is correct, click Finish.

Creating an Extended Partition on a Basic Disk

If you need to create more than four partitions on a basic disk, you must create an extended partition so that you can create logical drives inside it. Step by Step 12.5 walks you through creating an extended partition on a basic disk.

STEP BY STEP

12.5 Creating an extended partition

1. From the Start menu, select All Programs, Administrative Tools, Computer Management.

2. Left-click the Storage entry and then select the Disk Management entry. This starts the Disk Management snap-in.

3. In the lower-right pane of the Computer Management MMC, right-click the unallocated space on the drive to which you want to add an extended partition.

4. From the pop-up menu, select New Partition. This starts the New Partition Wizard. Click Next to continue.

5. The next screen prompts you to select the type of partition to create. Select the Extended Partition option button and then click Next to continue.

6. The next screen prompts you to select the size of the new extended partition. The size can be anything from 8MB up to the size of the available free space. Typically, the extended partition is the last partition created on the disk, so you will accept the default, which is the maximum. Click Next to continue.

7. Look over the settings on the Completing the New Partition Wizard screen. Confirm that the selected settings are correct. If you need to make any changes, click the Back button. If everything is correct, click Finish.

Creating a Logical Drive on a Basic Disk

By itself, an extended partition isn't worth much. However, within an extended partition, you can create a theoretically unlimited number of logical drives.

Step by Step 12.6 outlines how to create a logical drive.

STEP BY STEP

12.6 Creating a logical drive

1. From the Disk Management snap-in, right-click the extended partition entry on the drive to which you want to add a logical drive partition.

2. From the pop-up menu, select New Logical Drive. This starts the New Partition Wizard. Click Next to continue.

3. The next screen prompts you to select the type of partition to create. Notice that the Logical Drive selection is available only when an extended partition is selected. Select the Logical Drive option button and then click Next to continue.

4. The next screen prompts you to select the size of the new partition. The size can be anything from 8MB up to the size of the available free space. Enter the desired size and then click Next to continue.

5. The next screen allows you to select the drive letter or NTFS folder to assign the new partition to. You also have the option to not assign it, opting instead to come back and do it later. Most of the time you will assign a drive letter. Click Next to continue.

6. The Format Partition screen of the New Partition Wizard allows you to specify whether you want to format the partition and what file system and cluster size to use. There is also a selection to configure the new partition for file and folder compression. Normally, most partitions in Windows Server 2003 are formatted as NTFS with the default cluster size and no compression. The different file system formats are covered later in this chapter. Click Next to continue.

7. Look over the settings on the Completing the New Partition Wizard screen. Confirm that the selected settings are correct. If you need to make any changes, click the Back button. If everything is correct, click Finish.

Deleting a Partition

Deleting a partition or logical drive is far easier than creating one. However, it is important to remember that when a partition or logical drive is deleted, the data that was on that drive or partition is gone. It cannot be recovered by any utility that is included with Windows Server 2003. Before deleting a partition or logical drive, always make sure you have a current backup!

> **NOTE**
>
> **Delete In the Proper Order**   You cannot delete an extended partition until all the logical drives inside it have been deleted.

Step by Step 12.7 show you how to delete a partition or logical drive.

STEP BY STEP

12.7 Deleting a partition or logical drive

1. From the Disk Management snap-in, right-click the partition or logical drive that you want to delete and select Delete Partition or Delete Logical Drive from the shortcut menu.

2. Acknowledge the warning dialog box notifying you that all data will be lost by clicking Yes.

Windows Server 2003 is self-preserving in that it does not allow you to delete the system or boot partitions from within the Disk Management GUI.

File Systems and Formatting a Partition

Before you can store data on a drive, it has to be formatted with a file system. Two main file systems are recognized by Windows Server 2003: File Allocation Table (FAT16 and FAT32) and the NT File System (NTFS). Although other file systems are in use in Windows Server 2003, such as the Universal Disk Format (UDF) and the CD-ROM File System (CDFS), they are read-only file systems and do not truly support detailed access controls. For this reason, this section—and the Microsoft exam—focuses on the capabilities and features of the FAT and NT file systems.

The File Allocation Table (FAT) File System

The FAT file system is recognized by Windows Server 2003 to provide legacy support for earlier Windows operating systems. Because FAT was originally designed to support disks that were much smaller than the devices in use today, it is not very efficient at handling large disks or files. Windows Server 2003 is able to read partitions formatted in two versions of FAT—the

16-bit version (FAT16) supported by early versions of MS-DOS and the 32-bit version (FAT32) first introduced with Windows 95 OEM Service Release 2 (OSR2). The first version of the FAT file system, FAT12, used in the earliest versions of MS-DOS, is not supported in Windows Server 2003.

Because FAT predates Windows NT and Windows 2000/2003/XP, it does not include support for extensive security or enhanced partition features such as compression. From a practical perspective, the biggest difference between FAT16 and FAT32 is the maximum supported partition size. This is achieved by doubling the size of the File Allocation Table from 16 bits to 32 bits. For FAT16 partitions, the maximum size is 4GB, even though most operating systems limit FAT16 to 2GB partitions. In theory, FAT32 partitions support a maximum size of 2,047GB. However, there is a 32GB limitation on creating FAT32 partitions in Windows 2003.

The NT File System (NTFS)

Introduced with the first versions of Windows NT, the NT File System (NTFS) is designed to provide a high-performance, secure file system for Windows NT Servers. Windows Server 2003 includes the same version of NTFS included with Windows 2000.

Here are some of the benefits of NTFS over FAT:

▶ *Recoverability*—To ensure data is consistently written to the volume, NTFS uses transaction logging and advanced recovery techniques. In the event of a failure, NTFS uses checkpoint and data-logging information to automatically maintain the consistency of the data on the volume.

▶ *Compression*—NTFS supports selective file, folder, and volume compression, which is not available on FAT volumes.

▶ *Encrypting File System (EFS)*—EFS is similar to NTFS compression in that it allows the user to selectively encrypt files and folders as desired. After a file is encrypted, all file operations continue transparently for the user who performed the encryption. However, unauthorized users cannot access the files. EFS is covered in detail in Chapter 13, "Managing Data Storage."

▶ *Disk quotas*—NTFS volumes include the use of disk quotas to limit the amount of drive space a user can consume.

▶ *Mounted drives*—NTFS allows you to attach volumes or partitions to a folder on an existing drive. This allows you to increase the size of the existing drive, and it doesn't use any additional drive letters.

▶ *Permissions*—NTFS allows you to assign security at the file level.

The selectivity of the NTFS compression settings allows administrators the ability to pick and choose whether specific file system objects are compressed. Although data compression reduces the drive space required on the volume, it puts a greater burden on the system's resources. A small amount of processing overhead is involved in compressing and uncompressing files during system operation. Providing the option to selectively compress entire volumes, folders, or individual files ensures that the drive space is used as efficiently as possible, while still maintaining timely file services.

In an effort to provide the fastest file services available, NTFS uses smaller clusters and has been designed to require fewer disk reads to find a file on the volume. NTFS also supports significantly larger volumes than FAT—up to 16TB (terabytes) on a single volume.

Perhaps more importantly, individual files, folders, and volumes can be secured at the user and group level. This is significantly more secure than FAT, which is limited to three very basic permission settings (and then only when the volume is accessed via shared folders): Read, Change, and Full Control. Securing folders and, when possible, files is discussed in greater detail in Chapter 4.

Because NTFS offers such improvements over FAT, Microsoft (and just about anyone else you talk to) recommends that all Windows Server 2003 volumes be formatted with NTFS. However, there are some situations where this is not possible. For example, most multiple-boot configurations require a FAT file system on the boot partition. If you need to maintain a FAT volume on the server, it is important that you understand the security implications of the configuration.

> **EXAM ALERT**
>
> **Mutually Exclusive**   Remember that EFS and compression are mutually exclusive. Both EFS and compression are covered in Chapter 13.

Formatting the Partition or Logical Drive

After you decide which file system to use, you have to format your drives. During the initial installation of Windows Server 2003, the installation procedure formatted the installation drive for you. In addition, when manually creating a partition or logical drive, the wizard prompts you for the file type and then formats the drive for you.

If you need to manually format a partition or logical drive, follow the procedure provided in Step by Step 12.8.

STEP BY STEP

12.8 Formatting a partition or logical drive

1. From the Disk Management snap-in, right-click the partition or logical drive that you want to format. Then select Format from the shortcut menu.

2. From the Format dialog box, as shown in Figure 12.13, enter the volume name, the file system desired, and the allocation unit size. You can adjust the cluster size to tune performance for a specific disk size. However, NTFS compression is not supported for cluster sizes larger than 4,096 bytes. It's usually best to accept the default cluster size unless you have a specific reason not to. You can also select to perform a Quick Format, which removes the files but does not scan for bad sectors. This option should be used only on a disk that has been previously formatted and has no bad sectors. There is also an option to enable file and folder compression on the drive. This causes every file and folder either copied or created on this drive to be compressed. Select the desired options and then click OK to continue.

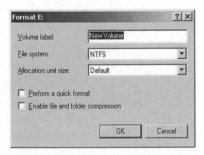

FIGURE 12.13 Drive formatting options.

3. Acknowledge the warning dialog box notifying you that all data will be lost by clicking Yes.

Remember, Windows Server 2003 is self-preserving in that it does not allow you to format the system or boot partitions from within the Disk Management GUI.

Changing the Drive Letter of a Partition

In Windows Server 2003, only the system and boot partitions are required to maintain specific drive letters. Any other drives can be assigned the letters C–Z. Drive letters A and B are reserved for floppy drives; however, you can assign B to a network drive if you want. The only caveat is that if you have installed a program on a drive or if a program is looking for its data in a specific location, you might not be able to access it after you change the drive letter. This happens because many programs store their location in the Registry. When you change a drive letter, the program entries in the Registry aren't updated with the changes.

If you want to rearrange drive letters, it should be done immediately after the initial installation of Windows Server 2003 and before you install any programs.

Use the procedure outlined in Step by Step 12.9 to change drive letter assignments.

STEP BY STEP

12.9 Changing a drive letter

1. From the Disk Management snap-in, right-click the drive that you want to reconfigure and select Change Drive Letter and Paths from the shortcut menu.

2. From the Change Drive Letter and Paths For dialog box, click the Change button.

3. From the Change Drive Letter or Path dialog box, click the drop-down list and choose a new drive letter. Click OK to continue.

4. When the warning prompt appears, click Yes to confirm the change.

Using Mounted Drives

A feature of NTFS is the capability of mounting a partition or volume as a folder on an existing drive. This is especially useful on data drives. For example, suppose that your user data drive is rapidly running out of free space. You could always go out and buy a larger drive and then move all the files over to the new drive. However, by using a mounted drive, you can mount the new drive as a folder on the existing drive, thereby adding additional space to the existing drive. This saves you from having to move the user files. The end users won't see any difference because they still access everything via the same drive letter or share. Additionally, you can create a volume from free space on an existing drive and then mount that volume as a folder.

> **NOTE**
>
> **Mount Points**   In some of the Windows Server 2003 documentation, you might see Mounted Drives referred to as Mount Points. This was the terminology used in previous versions of Windows. Same technology, just a different name.

An additional advantage of mounted drives is that they don't use a drive letter. As we mentioned earlier, there are only 24 letters available. You also are not limited to mounting other NTFS volumes. Other file systems can be mounted, such as a CD or DVD, or a FAT volume.

You can mount multiple drives to a volume and move them to different folders, if needed. For example, when a mounted volume is moved, deleted, or dismounted, the files and folders on the volume are not deleted. This allows you to move the drive to a different folder or to another computer.

Use the procedure outlined in Step by Step 12.10 to create a mounted drive.

STEP BY STEP

12.10 Mounting a drive

1. From the Disk Management snap-in, right-click the drive that you want to mount and select Change Drive Letter and Paths from the shortcut menu.

2. From the Change Drive Letter and Paths For dialog box, select the Mount in the following empty NTFS folder option button.

3. Either type in the folder that you want to mount the drive to or click the Browse button to locate it.

4. Click OK when finished.

EXAM ALERT

Mounted Drives   A mounted drive can only be mounted to an empty folder. You will need to know this for the exam.

Marking a Partition As Active

When an Intel-based computer starts, it looks for the active partition to start the system. This can be either a primary partition on a basic disk or a simple volume on a dynamic disk. However, the simple volume must have previously been created and marked as the active partition before the disk was converted from basic to dynamic. Although the active partition can be changed on a basic disk, it cannot be changed on a dynamic disk. Follow the procedure outlined in Step by Step 12.11 to mark a primary partition as Active.

STEP BY STEP

12.11 Marking a primary partition as Active

1. From the Disk Management snap-in, right-click the partition that you want to mark as Active.

2. Select Mark Partition as Active from the shortcut menu.

3. When the warning prompt appears, click Yes to confirm the change. The results are shown in Figure 12.14.

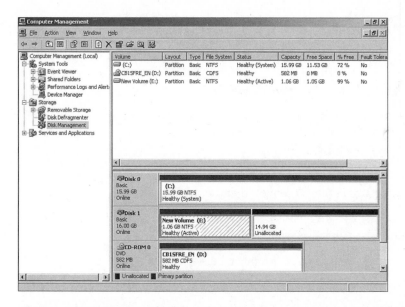

FIGURE 12.14 Disk Management snap-in, showing the results of marking disk 1, partition 1 as Active.

Working with Dynamic Disks

Although the initial installation of Windows Server 2003 configures a new hard disk as a basic disk, you are not required to leave it that way. Unless you have to maintain a dual-boot configuration and have older operating systems accessing partitions on that disk, you can convert the disk to a dynamic disk and take advantage of the extended capabilities available.

As discussed earlier, dynamic disks offer more features and flexibility than basic disks. For example, fault-tolerant disk configurations are supported only on dynamic disks.

In this section you will learn how to perform the following tasks:

- ▶ Convert a basic disk to a dynamic disk.
- ▶ Create simple volumes on a dynamic disk.
- ▶ Extend a dynamic volume.
- ▶ Create a spanned volume.
- ▶ Create a mirrored volume.
- ▶ Create a striped volume.
- ▶ Create a RAID-5 (stripe with parity) volume.

Converting a Basic Disk to a Dynamic Disk

Should you want to take advantage of the capabilities offered by dynamic disks in Windows Server 2003, you must convert your basic disk to a dynamic disk. The conversion is performed on an entire physical disk, not just one particular partition.

Basic disks can be converted to dynamic disks at any time without data loss, provided that you meet all the following requirements. However, you cannot revert a dynamic disk back to a basic disk without complete data loss on the disk.

In addition to the limitations discussed earlier in the chapter, make sure your disks meet the following conditions before attempting to convert them to dynamic disks:

▶ A master boot record (MBR) disk must have at least 1MB of free space available at the end of the disk for the dynamic disk database to be created.

▶ Dynamic storage cannot be used on removable media such as Zip disks.

▶ Hard drives on portable computers cannot be converted to dynamic storage.

▶ The sector size on the hard disk must be no larger than 512 bytes for the conversion to take place. Use the following command on an NTFS volume, where *x :* is the volume in question, to determine the sector size:

```
fsutilfsinfo ntfsinfo x:
```

> **CAUTION**
>
> **Multiboot Limitations**   Dynamic disks can be utilized only by one operating system. If you plan on multi-booting your computer with operating systems other than Windows 2000 or Windows 2003, do not convert your basic disks to dynamic disks.

Step by Step 12.12 guides you through the process to convert a basic disk to a dynamic disk.

STEP BY STEP

12.12 Upgrading a basic disk to a dynamic disk

1. From the Disk Management snap-in, right-click the disk indicator that you want to convert on the left side of the bottom-right pane and select Convert to Dynamic Disk from the shortcut menu.

2. When the Convert to Dynamic Disk dialog box appears, verify that the disk you want to convert is selected and then click OK.

3. The Disks to Convert dialog box lists the volumes on the disks you have selected. Click Convert to continue.

4. The Disk Management dialog box appears, warning you that you will not be able to start other operating systems from this disk. Click Yes to continue.

5. A warning prompt appears, notifying you that any file systems existing on the disk will be dismounted as part of the convert process. Click Yes to proceed—this is your last chance to abort the process.

6. Click Yes to confirm the change. If you are converting the disk that contains the boot or system partition or a volume that is currently in use, you may be required to reboot. After the conversion is completed, the disk will be relabeled as Dynamic, and the partitions are labeled as Simple Volumes, as shown in Figure 12.15.

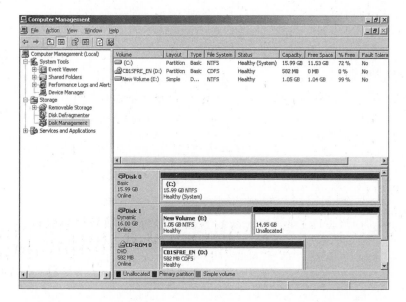

FIGURE 12.15   After the conversion is completed, the disk status bar changes color, and the disk is labeled as Dynamic with Simple Volumes.

CAUTION

Do Not Convert to Dynamic If You May Need to Boot an Older Operating System   Because dynamic disks are unique to the Windows 2000/2003/XP family, they will not be readable or bootable from other operating systems.

Creating Simple Volumes on a Dynamic Disk

Should you happen to have any unallocated (free) space on one of your disks, you can create a new volume in that space. Creating a new dynamic volume follows the same basic process as does creating new basic disk partitions, with the exception that you can choose from one of the available volume types as previously mentioned in the "Introduction to Dynamic Disks" section. You are also given the opportunity to select the total size of the volume to be created in the case of a spanned volume. To create a new partition out of free space on a dynamic disk, refer to Step by Step 12.13.

STEP BY STEP

12.13 Creating a simple volume

1. From the Start menu, select All Programs, Administrative Tools, Computer Management.

2. In the left pane of the Computer Management MMC, left-click the Storage entry and then select the Disk Management entry. This starts the Disk Management snap-in.

3. In the lower-right pane of the Computer Management MMC, right-click the unallocated space on the drive that you want to add a simple volume to.

4. From the pop-up menu, select New Volume. This starts the New Volume Wizard. Click Next to continue.

5. The next screen prompts you to select the type of volume to create. Select the Simple Volume option button and then click Next to continue. It is important to note that in a server with a single dynamic disk, Simple Volume is the only selection available. All the other choices require the presence of two or more dynamic disks.

6. On the Select Disks screen, the disk is preselected for you because there is only one dynamic disk available. You have the option of selecting the size of the volume up to the maximum available. Click Next to continue.

7. The next screen allows you to select the drive letter or NTFS folder to assign the new partition to. You also have the option to not assign it, opting instead to come back and do it later. Most of the time you will assign a drive letter. Click Next to continue.

8. The Format Volume screen allows you to specify whether you want to format the volume and what cluster size to use. There is also a selection to configure the new volume for file and folder compression. Dynamic volumes in Windows Server 2003 can be formatted only as NTFS. Click Next to continue.

9. Look over the settings on the Completing the New Volume Wizard screen. Confirm that the selected settings are correct. If you need to make any changes, click the Back button. If everything is correct, click Finish.

NOTE

FAT Is Dead   Although you can format a dynamic disk as FAT using the command-line format utility or via My Computer, there is no valid reason to do so. Typically, the only reason to format a drive as FAT would be to allow access to older operating systems. However, down-level operating systems cannot recognize a dynamic volume, regardless of the file format.

Challenge

You are the administrator of a network for a manufacturing company that has multiple Windows Server 2003 servers used for applications and file and print services. The Research and Development department has installed a new application on one of its servers. Unlike most intelligently designed applications, this one is hard-coded to save all its files in a folder on the boot volume.

Although there is currently sufficient free space on the boot volume on this server, this application, along with other applications that might be added in the future, could easily shrink the current amount of free space.

You will need to find a way to provide more free space for this application so that other applications can be installed on the boot volume in the future.

What is the best way to solve this issue in Windows 2003? On your own, try to develop a solution that would involve the least amount of downtime and expense.

If you would like to see a possible solution, follow the procedure outlined here.

This is a fairly easy solution. You can use one of the niftiest (but generally underutilized) features of NTFS—mounted drives. Mounted drives allow you to mount a volume to a folder on an existing volume, thereby adding additional space to that volume. Here are the steps to follow:

1. Shut down your server and install an additional hard drive.

2. Restart the server. From the Start menu, select All Programs, Administrative Tools, Computer Management.

3. Click the Storage entry and then select the Disk Management entry. This starts the Disk Management snap-in.

4. In the lower-right pane of the Computer Management MMC, right-click the unallocated space on the drive to which you want to add a simple volume.

5. From the pop-up menu, select New Volume. This starts the New Volume Wizard. Click Next to continue.

6. The next screen prompts you to select the type of volume to create. Select the Simple Volume option button and then click Next to continue.

(continues)

(continued)

7. On the Select Disks screen, you have the option of selecting the size of the volume, up to the maximum available. Select the desired size and then click Next to continue.

8. The next screen allows you to select the drive letter or NTFS folder to assign the new partition to. Select the desired folder and then click Next to continue.

9. The Format Volume screen allows you to specify whether you want to format the volume and what cluster size to use. There is also a selection to configure the new volume for file and folder compression. Accept the defaults and then click Next to continue.

10. Look over the settings on the Completing the New Volume Wizard screen. Confirm that the selected settings are correct. If you need to make any changes, click the Back button. If everything is correct, click Finish.

The nice thing about the Windows Server 2003 implementation of mounted drives is that it allows you to add additional space to an existing volume, instead of the usual process of replacing the volume and having to back up and restore your files.

Extending Dynamic Volume Size

One of the advantages of dynamic volumes is that they can be extended after their creation to add more space. The dynamic volume can be extended using free space on the same or other disks. This can be accomplished without a reboot.

However, here are some restrictions as to which dynamic disks cannot be extended:

▶ The volume either must not be formatted or must be formatted as NTFS.

▶ The volume must not be a system or boot volume.

▶ Dynamic volumes that were converted from basic volumes on Windows 2000 cannot be extended.

▶ RAID-1 (mirrored) or RAID-5 volumes cannot be extended.

▶ A volume that is extended onto another disk becomes a spanned volume.

Following are the types of dynamic disks that can be extended:

▶ Simple and spanned volumes

▶ Dynamic volumes that were converted from basic volumes on Windows Server 2003 or Windows XP Professional

The procedure for extending a dynamic volume is covered in Step by Step 12.14.

STEP BY STEP

12.14 Extending a dynamic volume

1. Open the Disk Management snap-in.

2. In the lower-right pane of the Disk Management snap-in, right-click the drive that you want to extend.

3. From the pop-up menu, select Extend Volume. This starts the Extend Volume Wizard. Click Next to continue.

4. On the Select Disks screen, shown in Figure 12.16, the disk that contains the partition you are extending is preselected for you. The free space on that disk is displayed. You have the option of adding space on the volume, up to the maximum available, and/or selecting space from another disk. Click Next to continue.

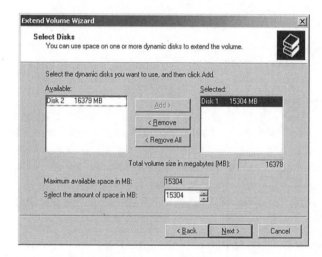

FIGURE 12.16 The partition size can be extended up to the maximum amount of the free space available on several disks.

5. Look over the settings on the Completing the Extend Volume Wizard screen. Confirm that the selected settings are correct. If you need to make any changes, click the Back button. If everything is correct, click Finish. If you look at the Disk Management snap-in, as shown in Figure 12.17, you will notice that whereas a single volume is displayed in the Volume view in the top-right pane, the graphical view in the bottom-right pane shows the actual configuration—two physical drives assigned the same logical drive letter.

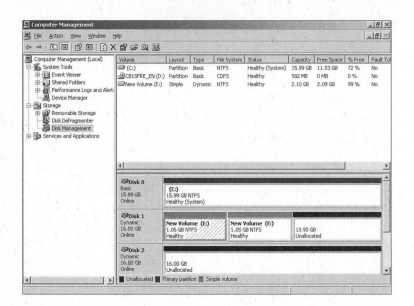

FIGURE 12.17 The graphical view shows the physical volume configuration.

Creating a Spanned Volume

Dynamic disks allow you to create spanned volumes. A spanned volume can contain up to 32 pieces of free space of various sizes from multiple physical hard disks. This allows you to create a volume that is larger than your physical disks. In addition you can create a logical drive of a useful size from smaller pieces that would be useless by themselves. Consolidating the available free space in this manner allows you to have a bigger disk represented by a single drive letter.

Unfortunately, a spanned volume is not fault tolerant. If anything, it becomes more susceptible to failure with every additional piece that is added. This is because if you lose a single hard disk or section, the entire volume is lost.

A spanned volume can be created by extending a volume across multiple disks, similar to the procedure covered in the previous section, or it can be created from scratch. Step by Step 12.15 shows how to create a new spanned volume.

STEP BY STEP

12.15 Creating a spanned volume

1. Open the Disk Management snap-in.

2. In the lower-right pane of the Disk Management snap-in, right-click the first section of unallocated free space that you want to use to create the volume.

3. From the pop-up menu, select New Volume. This starts the New Volume Wizard. Click Next to continue.

4. The next screen, as shown in Figure 12.18, prompts you to select the type of volume to create. Select the Spanned Volume option button and then click Next to continue. It is important to note that in a server with a single dynamic disk, the Simple Volume entry would have been the only selection available. All the other choices require the presence of two or more dynamic disks.

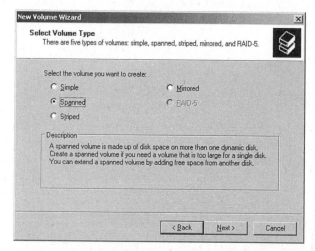

FIGURE 12.18 The New Volume Wizard, showing the types of volumes that you can configure. Note that this server obviously has multiple dynamic disks.

5. On the Select Disks screen, the disk you clicked is preselected for you, with all the available free space entered for you. You can highlight additional drives and click the Add button to add space from them. You have the option of selecting as much free space as you like from each disk, up to the maximum available. Make your selections and then click Next to continue.

6. The next screen allows you to select the drive letter or NTFS folder to assign the new partition to. You also have the option to not assign it, opting instead to come back and do it later. Click Next to continue.

7. The Format Volume screen allows you to specify whether or not you want to format the volume and what cluster size to use. There is also a selection to configure the new volume for file and folder compression. Dynamic volumes in Windows Server 2003 can only be formatted as NTFS. Click Next to continue.

8. Look over the settings on the Completing the New Volume Wizard screen. Confirm that the selected settings are correct. If you need to make any changes, click the Back button. If everything is correct, click Finish.

Implementing RAID Solutions

Objective:

Optimize server disk performance

▶ Implement a RAID solution

As we mentioned earlier in the chapter, there are advantages to using the various RAID solutions, from fault tolerance to increased performance, depending on which version of RAID you're implementing. In this section, we will create the various RAID sets supported in Windows Server 2003.

Creating a Striped Volume

In theory, striped volumes are similar to spanned volumes—they both combine space from multiple physical disks to form a larger logical drive. Striped volumes also have the same Achilles heel—if you lose one physical disk, the entire logical volume is lost.

> **EXAM ALERT**
>
> **Drawbacks of Striped Volumes**   Remember that striped volumes don't provide any fault tolerance. If you lose a single drive, you lose the entire volume. Also, striped volumes cannot contain the system/boot partition.

However, there are additional benefits to striped volumes other than the capability to create a large logical disk. Windows Server 2003 writes the data alternately across the drives using a set block size (RAID-0), hence the term *striping*. This results in the best write performance of any of the volume configurations available in Windows Server 2003, as well as read performance equal to the RAID-5 configuration. Striped volumes require at least two physical disks, with the disks preferably being of the same size, manufacturer, and model. You can add up to 32 dynamic disks to the volume. Striped disks cannot be extended or mirrored.

A striped volume can be created using the procedure outlined in Step by Step 12.16.

STEP BY STEP

12.16 Creating a striped volume

1. Open the Disk Management snap-in.

2. In the lower-right pane of the Disk Management snap-in, right-click the first section of unallocated free space that you want to use to create the volume.

3. From the pop-up menu, select New Volume. This starts the New Volume Wizard. Click Next to continue.

4. The next screen prompts you to select the type of volume to create. Select the Striped option button and then click Next to continue.

5. On the Select Disks screen shown in Figure 12.19, the disk you clicked is preselected for you, with all the available free space entered for you. You can highlight additional drives and click the Add button to add space from them. You have the option of selecting as much free space as you like from each disk, up to the smallest amount of free space available on any of the disks. For example, if you have two disks, and one has 900MB of free space and the other has 800MB of free space, the maximum amount of space you can use on each disk is 800MB. The volume sizes have to be identical on each disk. Make your selections and then click Next to continue.

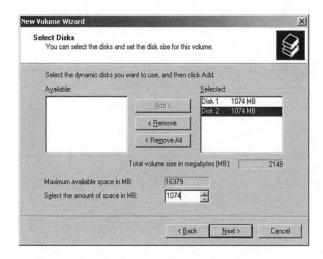

FIGURE 12.19 The size of the striped volume can be configured to be up to the maximum amount of the free space available on the smallest disk.

6. The next screen allows you to select the drive letter or NTFS folder to assign the new partition to. You also have the option to not assign it, opting instead to come back and do it later. Most of the time you will assign a drive letter. Click Next to continue.

7. The Format Volume screen allows you to specify whether you want to format the volume and what cluster size to use. There is also a selection to configure the new volume for file and folder compression. If you're using the stripe set for performance purposes, don't use compression. Dynamic volumes in Windows Server 2003 can be formatted only as NTFS. Click Next to continue.

8. Look over the settings on the Completing the New Volume Wizard screen. Confirm that the selected settings are correct. If you need to make any changes, click the Back button. If everything is correct, click Finish.

EXAM ALERT

Know the Characteristics of Striped Volumes   Remember that striped volumes require at least two disks and can contain up to 32 disks. Also remember that a striped volume is configured with equal space from each disk, even if some of the disks are larger than the others.

Creating a Mirrored Volume

A mirrored volume, also known as *RAID-1*, is one of the two fault-tolerant disk configurations available in Windows Server 2003. A mirrored volume consists of two separate physical disks that are written to simultaneously. If one of the disks fails, the system keeps running using the other disk.

It is best to use two identical disks for the mirror. For additional fault tolerance and better performance, you can install the two disks on separate disk controllers. This practice is known as *duplexing*. This configuration removes the disk controller as a potential single point of failure.

NOTE

Dynamic Volume Mirroring   It might be helpful to point out that Windows Server 2003 uses dynamic *volume* mirroring. This means that you are mirroring a volume, and not necessarily the physical disk, unless of course you configure the volume to be equal to the size of the physical disk. This allows you to have other volumes on the mirrored disk, if you desire. However, the other volumes will not be fault tolerant.

Mirrored volumes can be used as system or boot partitions. However, they cannot be extended. Refer to the previous sections in this chapter to see the restrictions that apply to having system and boot partitions on dynamic volumes.

EXAM ALERT

Usable Capacity It is important to remember that when you're using mirrored drives, a loss of 50% of the capacity of the mirrored drives occurs because of the redundancy. For example, if you mirror two 9GB drives (18GB total capacity), only 9GB will be available because you are, in effect, making two complete copies of your data.

A mirrored volume can be created using the procedure outlined in Step by Step 12.17.

STEP BY STEP

12.17 Creating a mirrored volume from free space

1. Open the Disk Management snap-in.

2. In the lower-right pane of the Disk Management snap-in, right-click the first section of unallocated free space that you want to use to create the mirror.

3. From the pop-up menu, select New Volume. This starts the New Volume Wizard. Click Next to continue.

4. The next screen prompts you to select the type of volume to create. Select the Mirrored option button and then click Next to continue.

5. On the Select Disks screen, the disk you clicked is preselected for you, with all the available free space entered for you. Highlight an additional drive and click the Add button to add it to the mirrored set. You have the option of selecting as much free space as you like from each disk, up to the smallest amount of free space available on any of the disks. For example if you have two disks, and one has 900MB of free space and the other has 800MB of free space, the maximum space you can use on each disk is 800MB. The volume sizes have to be identical on each disk. Make your selections and then click Next to continue.

6. The next screen allows you to select the drive letter or NTFS folder to assign the new partition to. You also have the option to not assign it, opting instead to come back and do it later. Click Next to continue.

7. The Format Volume screen allows you to specify whether you want to format the volume and what cluster size to use. There is also a selection to configure the new volume for file and folder compression. Dynamic volumes in Windows Server 2003 can be formatted only as NTFS. Click Next to continue.

8. Look over the settings on the Completing the New Volume Wizard screen. Confirm that the selected settings are correct. If you need to make any changes, click the Back button. If everything is correct, click Finish.

In addition to creating a mirrored volume from scratch, a mirrored volume can be created by mirroring an existing volume. This is how you mirror your system and boot partitions.

A mirrored volume can be created from a simple volume using the procedure outlined in Step by Step 12.18.

STEP BY STEP

12.18 Creating a mirrored volume from a simple volume

1. Open the Disk Management snap-in.

2. In the lower-right pane of the Disk Management snap-in, right-click the simple volume that you want to mirror.

3. From the pop-up menu, select Add Mirror.

4. The next screen prompts you to select the location of the drive to add to the mirror. Select a disk to add to the mirror and then click the Add Mirror button.

5. On the Disk Management screen shown in Figure 12.20, the disk you added to the mirrored set has been assigned the same drive letter as the simple volume and is synchronized with it.

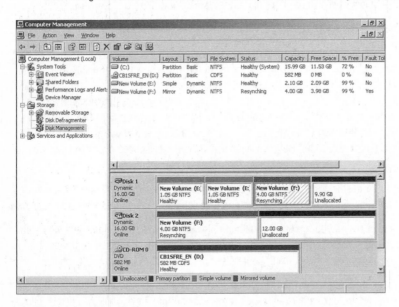

FIGURE 12.20   After you select the Add Mirror button, the new volume will be synchronized with the existing volume.

Creating a RAID-5 (Stripe with Parity) Volume

The RAID-5 volume, also known as *striping with parity*, is the second type of fault-tolerant disk configuration available in Windows Server 2003. A RAID-5 volume consists of 3 to 32 separate physical disks that are written to sequentially in fixed blocks, or *striped*. Along with the data, parity information is also written across the disks. If one of the disks fails, the system keeps running using the other disks because it can re-create the missing data using the parity information.

RAID-5 volumes have read performance equivalent to that of RAID-0, or *striped volumes*. However, because of having to generate the parity information, write performance is impacted. RAID-5 volumes cannot be extended or mirrored. In addition, they cannot contain the system or the boot volumes.

> **EXAM ALERT**
>
> **Usable Capacity**   Similar to mirrored drives, when you're using RAID-5 volumes, a loss of one drive occurs because of the parity overhead. For example, if you configure five 9GB drives (45GB total capacity), only 36GB will be available because, in effect, you are dedicating one drive to containing parity information.

A RAID-5 volume can be created using the procedure outlined in Step by Step 12.19.

STEP BY STEP

12.19 Creating a RAID-5 volume

1. Open the Disk Management snap-in.

2. In the lower-right pane of the Disk Management snap-in, right-click the first section of unallocated free space that you want to use to create the volume.

3. From the pop-up menu, select New Volume. This starts the New Volume Wizard. Click Next to continue.

4. The next screen prompts you to select the type of volume to create. Select the RAID-5 option button and then click Next to continue.

5. On the Select Disks screen, the disk you clicked is preselected for you, with all the available free space entered for you. Highlight the additional drives and click the Add button to add them to the volume. You have the option of selecting as much free space from each disk as you like, up to the smallest amount of free space available on any of the disks. For example, if you have three disks, and two have 900MB of free space and the other has 800MB of free space, the maximum space you can use on each disk is 800MB. The volume sizes have to be identical on each disk. Make your selections and then click Next to continue.

6. The next screen allows you to select the drive letter or NTFS folder to assign the new partition to. You also have the option to not assign it, opting instead to come back and do it later. Click Next to continue.

7. The Format Volume screen allows you to specify whether you want to format the volume and what cluster size to use. There is also a selection to configure the new volume for file and folder compression. Dynamic volumes in Windows Server 2003 can be formatted only as NTFS. Click Next to continue.

8. Look over the settings on the Completing the New Volume Wizard screen. Confirm that the selected settings are correct. If you need to make any changes, click the Back button. If everything is correct, click Finish.

Recovering from Disk Failures

Unfortunately, hard disks can and do fail. This alone is a very solid reason for ensuring that you have a well thought out and practiced disaster-recovery plan in place (see Chapter 17 for more information on using the Windows Backup utility). If your data was on a basic storage disk or a simple, spanned, or striped dynamic volume, you have no choice but to replace the disk and restore the data from the last backup. If you experience failure of a disk in a mirrored volume or a RAID-5 array, fault tolerance is in place and you can recover your data.

Recovering a Failed Mirrored Drive

If one of the drives in a mirrored set happens to fail, you will be provided with a graphical indication in Disk Management. Fortunately, because mirrored volumes are fault tolerant, your server continues to operate normally, albeit with slower read performance. You can schedule your repairs at a convenient time.

The process to repair the mirror depends on whether the disk that failed was part of a mirrored set that contained the system or boot partition.

NOTE

Simulating an Error   The error condition in this Step by Step can be simulated by unplugging one of your physical drives if you're using dedicated hardware. If you're using a virtual product such as VMWare or Virtual PC, you can delete or disable one of your virtual drives.

If the failed disk did not contain the system or boot partition (only data), you can restore the mirror by following the procedure outlined in Step by Step 12.20.

STEP BY STEP

12.20 Repairing a mirrored volume

1. Open the Disk Management snap-in. You should have an error indication similar to that shown in Figure 12.21. The failed disk usually shows a status of Missing, and the volume set shows a status of Failed Redundancy.

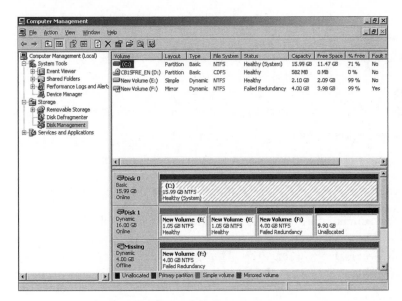

FIGURE 12.21 The Disk Manager snap-in indicates a problem with the mirrored set and flags the failed device.

2. In the lower-right pane of the Disk Management snap-in, right-click the failed mirrored volume and select Remove Mirror from the shortcut menu.

3. In the Remove Mirror dialog box, shown in Figure 12.22, select the disk that is to be removed and click Remove Mirror.

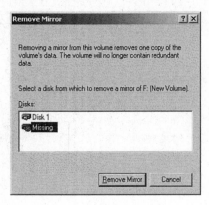

FIGURE 12.22   After you highlight the failed drive and select the Remove Mirror button, the volume will be removed from the mirrored set.

4.   Confirm that you want to remove the mirror by clicking OK when prompted with a dialog box.

5.   Power down the computer, replace the hard disk, and restart the computer.

6.   Create a new mirrored volume using the previous mirrored disk and the replacement disk. Refer to the procedure for creating a mirror earlier in this chapter.

If the mirrored volume that contains the boot or system partition fails and it's the primary drive that has failed, you most likely will not be able to boot your server. This is because the BOOT.INI file is still configured to look for that drive. This will not affect the operation of your server because the server is able to access the files it needs to continue running from the other half of the mirror.

However, unless you have hot-swap drives and can replace the failed disk without shutting down the server, eventually you will need to power down, replace the failed disk, and then restart the server. The easiest way to reboot and repair the server is to create a Windows Server 2003 boot floppy that contains the system files and a copy of the BOOT.INI file that points to the secondary disk in the mirrored set.

Technically speaking, the floppy you are creating is not really a boot floppy because it doesn't contain the operating system. Earlier in the chapter we discussed the Windows Server 2003 boot process. When the server is started, it looks for the files in the Windows Server 2003 system partition. We will re-create the system partition on a floppy disk and edit the BOOT.INI file to point to the operating system files that are on the surviving secondary mirrored volume.

If the failed disk contained the system or boot partition, you can restore the mirror by following the procedure outlined in Step by Step 12.21.

STEP BY STEP

12.21 Repairing a mirrored boot/system volume

1. Open the Disk Management snap-in. You should have an obvious error indication. The failed volume usually shows a status of Missing.

2. Determine which mirrored disk failed. If the secondary disk failed (the disk that contains the mirrored data), you can replace it as outlined previously. If the primary disk failed (the disk that contains the original data), you must proceed with these steps.

3. If you have another Windows Server 2003 computer available (it must have a similar disk configuration) or if your server is still up and running, format a 3 1/2 inch floppy disk. (This disk must be formatted in Windows Server 2003 so that it has the correct MBR.) Copy the NTLDR, NTDETECT.COM, and BOOT.INI files to the floppy disk. You will need to edit the BOOT.INI file as shown in step 6 to reflect the location of your secondary drive.

4. If you do not have another Windows Server 2003 computer available or if your server is down, copy the NTDETECT.COM file from the I386 folder on a Windows Server 2003 Setup CD-ROM to a blank, formatted 3-1/2 floppy. You also need to expand the NTLDR file from this same location by entering the following command from the command line:

   ```
   expand Ntldr._ Ntldr
   ```

5. If your server uses SCSI drives that have the BIOS disabled (not common), you must include the driver ntbootdd.sys on your boot floppy. If used, this file is specific to your SCSI controller and will be present on your server.

6. Finally, create a BOOT.INI file that points to the secondary drive in your broken mirror. (For more help on working with ARC paths, see http://support.microsoft.com/default.aspx?scid=kb;en-us;Q102873.) Following is an example:

   ```
   boot loader]
   timeout=30
   default=multi(0)disk(0)rdisk(0)
   ➥partition(1)\WINNT
   [operating systems]
   multi(0)disk(0)rdisk(0)partition(1)\
   ➥WINNT="Microsoft Windows Server 2003"
   ➥/fastdetect
   ```

7. Power down the computer, replace the hard disk, and restart the computer.

8. Use your boot disk to start your Windows Server 2003 computer.

9. Remove and re-create the mirror as discussed in the previous procedure.

Prebuild the Recovery Floppy

When you initially configure your boot/system drives in a mirrored configuration, that's when you should build your recovery boot floppy. You should configure the boot floppy and then use it for a few test boots to make sure you have the paths configured correctly in the BOOT.INI file. Then make two or more copies of it and put them away in a safe place.

When the server has crashed and the phones are ringing off the hook is not the proper time to learn how to build and test a recovery floppy.

Recovering a Failed RAID-5 Drive

Recovering from a disk failure in a RAID-5 array is a fairly simple process thanks to the fault tolerance provided by the array. Remember that RAID-5 arrays can provide fault tolerance for only one failed disk, so be sure to replace the failed disk as soon as possible. While the disk is failed and not replaced, you can still use the RAID-5 array; however, I/O performance will be severely degraded because the missing data must be re-created from the parity information. Again, you should replace a failed disk in a RAID-5 array as soon as you can by performing the procedure outlined in Step by Step 12.22.

STEP BY STEP

12.22 Repairing a RAID-5 volume

1. Open the Disk Management snap-in. The failed volume usually shows a status of Failed Redundancy.

2. Power down the server, if necessary. Replace the failed disk. Restart the server, if necessary. If the disk is hot swappable, rescan the disks.

3. In the lower-right pane of the Disk Management snap-in, right-click one of the volumes in the failed RAID-5 set (it will be marked as Failed Redundancy) and select Reactivate Volume from the shortcut menu.

4. When the confirmation prompt appears, click Yes to confirm that you want to reactivate the failed volume.

5. When prompted, select the new disk you installed and click OK to begin the rebuilding process.

Importing Foreign Disks

Dynamic disks can be moved from any Windows 2000 computer or later to Windows Server 2003. When a dynamic disk is moved from one computer to another, it is marked as a Foreign Disk. This is because it's not a member of the disk group on the receiving computer. Before the disk can be used, it must join the disk group on the new computer by *importing* it. After the disk is imported, you can access any volumes that are on it.

Importing a foreign disk can be accomplished by using the diskpart utility or via the Disk Manager MMC. When moving a single disk, or the entire disk group to another computer, the process is fairly straightforward. Just right-click the entry for the foreign disk in the Disk Manager MMC and click Import.

NOTE

Rescan Disks It is imperative that you rescan disks after you move hard disks between computers. When Disk Management rescans disk properties, it scans all attached disks for changes to the disk configuration. It also updates information about removable media, CD-ROM drives, basic volumes, file systems, and drive letters. Without a rescan, your new disks probably won't be recognized.

However, the situation becomes more complicated when fault tolerant or nonredundant volumes that span multiple disks are moved. For example, if you move one volume of a mirror, and then move the other volume at a later date, they will both appear to be in synch, but in reality they could possibly have different contents.

A second example is if you move one of the volumes of a RAID-0 array. This volume will appear as disabled, even after you attempt to import it. It can be brought back online after you move the remaining volumes over, or you can just delete it and reuse it.

Optimizing Server Disk Performance

Objective:

Optimize server disk performance

▶ Defragment volumes and partitions

Windows Server 2003 comes with three fairly robust, built-in tools that you can use to perform basic troubleshooting, cleanup, and repair operations:

▶ *Disk Cleanup*—This utility removes temporary files and other "deadwood" that may be on your computer's disks.

▶ *Check Disk*—This utility checks the file and folder structure of your hard disk. You can also have Check Disk check the physical structure of your hard disk. Check Disk can perform repairs as required.

▶ *Disk Defragmenter*—This utility defragments your hard disks by moving all pieces of each file into a continuous section on the hard disk.

We examine each of these tools in the following subsections.

Using the Disk Cleanup Utility

The Disk Cleanup utility can remove temporary files, installation logs, Recycle Bin items, and other deadwood that accumulates on your volumes over time. You can start the Disk Cleanup utility in three ways, depending on your needs:

▶ On the General tab of the volume's Properties dialog box, click the Disk Cleanup.

▶ From the Start menu, click All Programs, Accessories, System Tools, Disk Cleanup.

▶ On the command line, enter `cleanmgr /d X`, where *X* represents the volume to be cleaned. The /d switch is mandatory and specifies the volume to be cleaned.

Step by Step 12.23 details how to run the Disk Cleanup utility.

STEP BY STEP

12.23 Running Disk Cleanup

1. Open either My Computer or Windows Explorer. Right-click the drive that you want to run Disk Cleanup on and select Properties.

2. From the Properties page, select the General tab and click the Disk Cleanup button.

3. From the Disk Cleanup dialog box, select the files to delete or compress and then click OK.

4. When the Disk Cleanup finishes, click OK.

By selecting the More Options tab in the Disk Cleanup dialog box, you are presented with other options to create free space on your drive, such as removing Windows components or other programs that you don't use. The Disk Cleanup utility can be configured for scheduled cleaning by using the Scheduled Tasks Wizard located in the Control Panel.

Using the Check Disk Utility

The Check Disk utility can be used to check the file and folder structure of your hard disks as well as to check the physical structure of your hard disks. Check Disk can also be configured to automatically correct any errors located. Check Disk can be launched by using one of the following methods:

▶ As a GUI utility, Check Disk can be launched from the Tools tab of the volume's Properties dialog box.

▶ As a command-line utility, Check Disk can be launched by entering **chkdsk** on the command line.

Step by Step 12.24 details how to run the GUI version of the Check Disk utility.

STEP BY STEP

12.24 Running Check Disk from the GUI

1. Open either My Computer or Windows Explorer. Right-click the drive that you want to run Check Disk on and select Properties.

2. From the Properties page, select the Tools tab and click the Check Now button.

3. From the Check Disk New Volume dialog box, shown in Figure 12.23, select the desired checking options and then click Start.

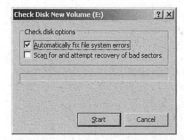

FIGURE 12.23 Select the disk tests to run.

4. When the Check Disk utility finishes, click OK.

The GUI version of Check Disk can fix most minor problems. However, there are times when you need to have more options available for checking your disks. The command-line Check Disk utility, CHKDSK.EXE, offers more flexibility.

The chkdsk command has the following syntax:

```
chkdsk [volume[[path]filename]]] [/F] [/V] [/R]
  [/X] [/I] [/C] [/L[:size]]
```

Table 12.1 presents the options for use with the chkdsk command.

TABLE 12.1   The Options for the chkdsk Command

Switch	Description
volume	Specifies the drive letter, mounted drive, or volume letter.
filename	Specifies the files to check for fragmentation (FAT only).
/F	Specifies that errors are to be fixed if found on the disk.
/V	Specifies that clean-up messages are to be displayed.
/R	Specifies that bad sectors are to be recovered. Requires the /F switch.
/L:[size]	Specifies the log size to be created.
/X	Specifies that the selected volume is to be dismounted if required. Requires the /F switch.
/I	Specifies that less vigorous checking of index entries is to be performed.
/C	Specifies that checking of cycles within the folder structure is to be skipped.

Using the Disk Defragmenter Utility

It was once thought that NTFS could not become fragmented. However, it was soon discovered that NTFS becomes fragmented the same as FAT and FAT32 do. Starting with Windows 2000, Microsoft includes a "light" version of Executive Software's Diskeeper, relabeled as the Disk Defragmenter utility, that is used for performing disk defragmentation.

The purpose of a defragmentation tool is to analyze a volume or partition and determine whether each file occupies a contiguous space. During the normal operation of a server, files are written, deleted, and rewritten. If a file needs to be added to, it must be given space wherever free space is available, and the free space might not necessarily be located next to the space that the file currently occupies. As a file is rewritten over and over, parts of it may be scattered all over the volume. This can slow down the access time for the file because it has to be read from various locations. In addition, new files and programs may be installed in pieces because there is no contiguous free space left on the drive large enough to store the new program. Over time, this slows the I/O performance of the volume.

After the defragmentation program has analyzed the volume, it can then consolidate the files and folders by moving the data around until the each of the files and folders are located in contiguous space on the volume. In addition, the defragmentation program consolidates the free space at the end of the volume so that new programs and files can be installed in contiguous space. The defragmentation utility included with Windows Server 2003, Disk Defragmenter, can defrag both NTFS and FAT volumes and partitions.

> **NOTE**
>
> **Free Space Limitations**   The GUI version of the Disk Defragmenter in Windows Server 2003 will not defragment a disk that has less than 15% free space.

You can access the Disk Defragmenter utility by following any one of these five methods:

▶ On the Tools tab of the volume's Properties dialog box, click the Defragment Now button.

▶ From the Start menu, click All Programs, Accessories, System Tools, Disk Defragmenter.

▶ From within the Computer Management console, click Disk Defragmenter, as shown in Figure 12.24.

▶ On the command line or from the Run dialog box, enter `dfrg.msc`.

▶ On the command line or from the Run dialog box, enter `MMC`. In the empty console, add the Disk Defragmenter snap-in. This can be useful for creating powerful, customized MMC consoles for a variety of management tasks.

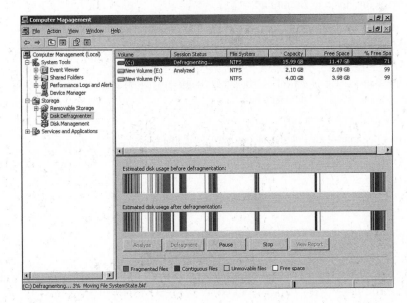

FIGURE 12.24   Disk Defragmenter in the Computer Management console.

No matter which way you start Disk Defragmenter, your options are the same. To analyze a volume, click the Analyze button. You can defragment a volume, with or without first analyzing it, by clicking the Defragment button. The View Report button shows the analysis report again. You can pause or stop a running defragmentation.

The Disk Defragmenter utility can be configured for scheduled cleaning by using the Scheduled Tasks Wizard located in the Control Panel.

TIP

Check out the full version of Diskeeper at www.executivesoftware.com/diskeeper/diskeeper.asp.

In addition to the GUI defragmentation utility, there is also a command-line utility. The command-line version of Disk Defragmenter can be used in scripts, and it also has an option to force a defragmentation to take place when there is less than 15% free space on the volume or partition.

When started from the command line, the `defrag.exe` command has the following syntax:

```
defrag [volume[[path]filename]]] [/A] [/V] [/F]
```

Table 12.2 presents the options for use with the `defrag` command.

TABLE 12.2   The Options for the `defrag` Command

Switch	Description
`volume`	Specifies the drive letter, mounted drive, or volume letter.
`filename`	Specifies the files to check for fragmentation (FAT only).
`/A`	Performs an analysis of the volume, displays a summary report, and indicates whether a defragmentation is required.
`/V`	Verbose. Displays a full analysis report.
`/F`	Forces a defragmentation of the volume, even if the free space is less than 15%.

Chapter Summary

This chapter covered a lot of ground, including the following:

▶ *Working with partitions and volumes*—This includes knowing the types of partitions available on a basic disk (primary, extended, and logical) and the types of volumes available on a dynamic disk (simple, spanned, mirrored, striped, and striped with parity). Know when and how to use them.

▶ *Implementing a RAID solution*—This includes knowing how to configure, troubleshoot, and repair the various RAID configurations available in Windows Server 2003.

▶ *Optimizing server disk performance*—This includes knowing which of the partitions/ volumes provide the best performance and how to configure and maintain them.

▶ *Defragmenting volumes and partitions*—This is part of maintaining and optimizing server disk performance.

Key Terms

▶ Boot disk

▶ Boot partition

▶ System partition

▶ Basic disk

▶ Dynamic disk

▶ Mirror volume

▶ RAID-0

▶ RAID-1

▶ RAID-5

▶ `BOOT.INI`

▶ Extended partition

▶ Spanned volume

▶ Fault tolerant

▶ Defragmentation

▶ NTFS

▶ FAT32

▶ Striped volume

Apply Your Knowledge

Exercises

12.1 Creating and testing a boot disk

This exercise demonstrates how to create a boot disk. This boot disk can be used to start the server when your system files are corrupted or when you need to boot to recover a failed mirrored set. This exercise requires a blank floppy disk.

Estimated Time: 20 minutes.

1. Format the floppy disk, either from the command line or from Windows Explorer or My Computer.

2. Using either Windows Explorer or My Computer, confirm that your view settings allow you to see hidden and system files.

3. From the system partition, copy `BOOT.INI`, `NTDETECT.COM`, `NTLDR`, and `NTBOOTDD.SYS` (if present) to your floppy disk. Remove the floppy disk.

4. Delete `NTDETECT.COM` on the system partition.

5. Reboot your server. The reboot should fail.

6. Insert your floppy disk and reboot the server. The reboot should be successful. Copy `NTDETECT.COM` from the floppy to your system partition.

12.2 Repairing a mirrored volume

This exercise demonstrates how to repair a mirrored volume. This exercise assumes that you are repairing the mirrored volume in a server that uses hot-plug drives. For a procedure for use in a server that does not have hot-plug drives, see Step by Step 12.20, "Repairing a Mirrored Volume."

Estimated Time: 30 minutes.

1. Create a mirrored volume using the steps outlined earlier in this chapter.

2. Remove one of the drives in the mirror volume. This will simulate a failure.

3. Open the Disk Management snap-in and check the status of the mirrored volume. It should show a status of Failed Redundancy.

4. In the Disk Management snap-in, right-click the mirrored volume and select Remove Mirror.

5. When the Remove Mirror dialog box appears, select the disk that you removed and click Remove Mirror. Select Yes to confirm.

6. Replace the drive that you removed earlier. In the Disk Management snap-in, select Re-Scan Disks.

7. Right-click the remaining disk from the mirror and select Add Mirror. When the Add Mirror dialog box appears, select the disk that you just added. Click Add Mirror.

12.3 Defragmenting a volume

This exercise demonstrates how to defragment a volume. This exercise is nondestructive, so it can be used on any volume.

Estimated Time: 20 minutes.

1. Using either Windows Explorer or My Computer, display the root of the volume that you want to defragment.

2. Right-click the volume and select Properties.

3. On the Tools tab of the volume's Properties dialog box, click the Defragment Now button.

4. When the Disk Defragmenter screen is displayed, select Analyze.

5. When you are presented with the dialog box asking whether you want to view the report or close, click the Defragment button.

6. After the defragmentation process completes, you can view the report.

Exam Questions

1. Davin has decided to configure a RAID-5 array on one of his servers to use for file storage. He has five 50GB SCSI hard disks available. What is the total amount of disk space that will be available after he finishes his configuration?

   ○ **A.** 250GB

   ○ **B.** 250MB

   ○ **C.** 200GB

   ○ **D.** 225GB

   ○ **E.** 245GB

2. John has been assigned to build five Windows Server 2003 servers. His boss has specified that the system volume has to be fault tolerant. What type of volume can he configure in Windows Server 2003 to attain fault tolerance of the system volume?

   ○ **A.** Simple volume

   ○ **B.** Spanned volume

   ○ **C.** Mirrored volume (RAID-1)

   ○ **D.** Striped volume (RAID-0)

   ○ **E.** Striped volume with parity (RAID-5)

3. Shelly is the junior system administrator for Travel Inc. She has been assigned to compress the files and folders that contain the travel arrangements for Company B for the last quarter. She opens Windows Explorer and navigates to the necessary folders and selects the properties for the folders, but does not see the option to enable compression. What could be the possible cause of this?

○ **A.** Shelly is not a member of the Disk Administrators group.

○ **B.** The folders are encrypted using EFS.

○ **C.** Shelly is accessing a RAID-5 volume.

○ **D.** The volume is formatted using FAT32.

4. Joe wants to add fault tolerance to the storage disks on his Windows Server 2003 servers. His budget is tight this fiscal year, so he has to be able to balance fault tolerance with available storage capacity. Which of the following disk configurations will give Joe the best combination of fault tolerance and storage capacity?

○ **A.** Striped volume

○ **B.** Spanned volume

○ **C.** Mirrored volume

○ **D.** Striped with parity (RAID-5) volume

5. Jeff needs to add more space to his boot/system partition. The partition resides on a basic volume formatted with NTFS. What are Jeff's options to expand the partition?

○ **A.** Open the Disk Management snap-in and select Extend Partition.

○ **B.** Use the command-line utility `DISKPART.EXE` and use the commands to extend the partition.

○ **C.** Convert the partition to a dynamic volume and then open the Disk Management snap-in and select Extend Volume.

○ **D.** The partition cannot be expanded.

6. Joe needs to build a Windows Server 2003 server to host a mission-critical SQL database. What type of disk configuration should he use for the boot/system partition?

○ **A.** Striped volume

○ **B.** Spanned volume

○ **C.** Mirrored volume (RAID-1)

○ **D.** Striped with parity (RAID-5) volume

7. Joe needs to build a Windows Server 2003 server to host a mission-critical SQL database. He has already decided on the optimum configuration for his boot/system partition. However, he still needs to make a decision on the optimum configuration for the disks used to store his database. His database will be mostly read with batch updates after business hours. What type of disk configuration should he use for the database?

○ **A.** Striped volume

○ **B.** Spanned volume

○ **C.** Mirrored volume (RAID-1)

○ **D.** Striped with parity (RAID-5) volume.

8. Loren is responsible for monitoring an organization that has more than 2,000 Windows Server 2003 servers. While making his daily check of the servers, he discovers that one of them has suffered the failure of a mirrored volume. Because the server supports hot-plug drives, what are the first steps that he should perform to accomplish the repair after breaking the mirror?

○ **A.** Replace the drive, open the Disk Management snap-in, and select Re-Scan drives.

○ **B.** Power down the server, replace the drive, and then power up the server.

○ **C.** Replace the drive and open the Add/Remove Hardware Wizard.

○ **D.** Replace the drive, open the Disk Management snap-in, and create a new mirrored volume.

9. You are the network administrator for Skelly Inc. All network servers run Windows Server 2003. A server named FileSrv1 contains a simple volume that stores mission-critical data files. FileSrv1 experiences hardware failure and stops functioning. Replacement parts will be available within 72 hours. A second file server named FileSrv2 is available. However, FileSrv2 has insufficient disk space to hold the data on FileSrv1. You need to provide immediate access to the data on FileSrv1. First, you install the disks from FileSrv1 on FileSrv2 and restart FileSrv2. However, the disks do not appear in Disk Management.

Which action or actions should you perform? (Choose all that apply.)

○ **A.** Install the disks from FileSrv1 on FileSrv2. In Disk Management, initialize the disks.

○ **B.** Install the disks from FileSrv1 on FileSrv2. In Disk Management, rescan the disks.

○ **C.** In Disk Management, select each disk from FileSrv1. Then select the option to import foreign disks.

○ **D.** In Disk Management, select each disk from FileSrv1. Then select the option to repair the volume.

○ **E.** On FileSrv2, run the mountvol /p command from a command prompt.

○ **F.** On FileSrv2, convert the dynamic disks to basic disks.

10. You are the network administrator for Skelly Inc. All network servers run Windows Server 2003. A server named FileSrv1 contains a RAID-5 volume that stores mission-critical data files. Routine Monitoring reveals that one of the volumes in your RAID-5 array has failed. During your maintenance window, you shut down the server and replace the failed volume. After you restart the server, you need to ensure that another disk failure doesn't cause the users to lose access to their data. What should you do?

○ **A.** Initialize the new disk. Select the failed RAID-5 set, and then select the Repair Volume option.

○ **B.** Import the foreign disk. Select the failed RAID-5 set, and then select the Repair Volume option.

○ **C.** Select the failed RAID-5 set, and then select the Reactive Volume option.

○ **D.** Import the foreign disk. Select the failed RAID-5 set, and then select the Reactive Disk option.

Answers to Exam Questions

1. **C.** 200GB is the correct answer. A RAID-5 array will always use the equivalent space of one of the disks in the array for parity information. See "Implementing RAID Solutions."

2. **C.** The only type of volume that supports fault tolerance that can contain a system volume is a mirrored volume (RAID-1). See "Implementing RAID Solutions."

3. **D.** Compression is supported only on NTFS volumes. Although EFS and compression are mutually exclusive, the compression option will still be displayed. See "The NT File System (NTFS)."

4. **D.** The striped with parity volume will give Joe the best combination of fault tolerance and storage capacity. Of the choices available, only RAID-1 (mirrored volume) and RAID-5 offer fault tolerance. Whereas RAID-1 results in a 50% cost in disk space, RAID-5 exacts less overhead. For example, in a configuration of four drives of 10GB each, RAID-5 will require 10GB for parity, or 25%. See "Implementing RAID Solutions."

5. **C.** The Disk Management snap-in cannot be used to extend a partition on a basic disk. Although DISKPART.EXE can be used to expand a partition on a basic disk, it cannot extend the partition from which the system was booted. A basic partition must be converted to a dynamic volume before it can be extended. The Disk Management snap-in can be used to extend a volume on a dynamic disk, even the one that the system was booted from. See "Introduction to Basic Disks."

6. **C.** Of the choices available, only RAID-1 and RAID-5 offer fault tolerance. However, only the RAID-1 configuration can be used for boot partitions. See "Implementing RAID Solutions."

7. **D.** Of the choices available, only RAID-1 and RAID-5 offer fault tolerance. Of these two configurations, RAID-5 offers the best read performance because the data is striped across multiple volumes, thereby increasing read efficiency. However, because RAID-5 has to write parity information with the data, write performance is not optimal. Fortunately, updates to the database will be performed during off hours, so that should not be a problem. See "Implementing RAID Solutions."

8. **A.** The proper way to start the procedure on a server that uses hot-plug drives is to replace the drive and then perform a rescan in the Disk Management snap-in. This will start the Disk Initialization Wizard. Answer B would work in some circumstances. However, if the primary drive of a mirrored volume that is being used for the boot/system partition fails, you will not be able to restart your server without a fault-tolerant boot floppy. See "Recovering a Failed Mirrored Drive."

9. **B and C.** Without a rescan, your new disks probably won't be recognized. When you move a dynamic disk from one computer to another, Windows Server 2003 considers the disk as a foreign disk by default. When Disk Manager indicates the status of a new disk as foreign, you have to import the disk before you can access volumes on the disk. Either initializing or converting the disks will erase all your data. Repairing the disk isn't necessary, and the Mountvol command is a way to link volumes without requiring a drive letter, which wouldn't do you any good because the volume hasn't been scanned and imported yet. See "Importing Foreign Disks."

10. **C.** Because this is a new volume and not a foreign disk, it will not have to be imported. Because we are adding it to an array, the Reactivate Volume option will initialize the volume automatically. Remember that RAID-5 arrays can provide fault tolerance for only one failed disk, so be sure to replace the failed disk as soon as possible. See "Recovering a Failed RAID-5 Drive."

Suggested Readings and Resources

1. Boswell, William. *Inside Windows Server 2003*. Addison-Wesley, 2003. ISBN: 0735711585.

2. Matthews, Marty. *Windows Server 2003: A Beginners Guide*. McGraw-Hill, 2003. ISBN: 0072193093.

3. Microsoft Knowledgebase article: Best Practices for Using Dynamic Disks on Windows Server 2003-based Computers. http://support.microsoft.com/default.aspx?scid=kb;en-us;816307.

4. Microsoft Knowledgebase article: Description of Disk Groups in Windows Disk Management. http://support.microsoft.com/default.aspx?scid=kb;en-us;222189.

5. Morimoto, Rand, et. al. Creating a Fault-Tolerant Environment in Windows Server 2003. http://www.informit.com/articles/article.asp?p=174367&rl=1.

6. Minasi, Mark, et al. *Mark Minasi's Windows XP and Server 2003 Resource Kit.* Sybex, 2003. ISBN: 0782140807.

7. Minasi, Mark, et al. *Mastering Windows Server 2003 Server.* Sybex, 2003. ISBN: 0782141307.

8. Shapiro, Jeffrey, et al. *Windows Server 2003 Bible R2 Edition.* John Wiley and Sons, 2006. ISBN: 0764549375.

13

Managing Data Storage

Objectives

This chapter covers the following Microsoft-specified objectives for the "Monitor File and Print Servers" section of the Managing and Maintaining a Microsoft Windows Server 2003 Environment exam:

Monitor file and print servers. Tools might include Task Manager, Event Viewer, and System Monitor.

▶ **Monitor disk quotas.**

▶ The purpose of this objective is to teach you how to implement and monitor disk quotas, using the various tools available in Windows Server 2003, with an emphasis on the new tools available in the R2 release.

Outline

Study Strategies

▶ Although there currently are not any listings on the exam guidelines that mention file compression or file encryption, they will make an appearance on the exam nonetheless. You will need to know how to implement file and folder compression, what the advantages and limitations are, and when it cannot be used. Make sure that you set up and configure the compression scenarios in this chapter and observe the operation closely.

▶ With the current emphasis on security, it is essential to become familiar with the Windows Server 2003 version of file and folder encryption, especially the features added with the R2 release.

▶ One of the centerpieces in the R2 release of Windows Server 2003 is the File Server Resource Manager. Make sure you are familiar with its operation, what differences it provides in quotas versus using straight New Technology File System (NTFS) quotas, and how to run the reports. In addition, get some hands-on experience setting up templates and using file screening.

▶ The disk quota questions will probably be related to how quotas are applied to users and what happens when a file is moved or copied. Make sure you understand the limitations of the Microsoft version of disk quotas and how to monitor and configure them.

▶ Test your encryption skills using the provided exercises, make sure that you are comfortable with creating keys, recovering keys, and know what happens when an encrypted file is moved to another volume, or the owner's user account is deleted.

▶ To get the full benefit of the exercises in this chapter, create folders on your test servers, add files to them, and assign the files to different owners. This will allow you to experience the compression, file quotas, encryption, and reports sections in a more realistic manner.

File Compression in Windows Server 2003

Windows Server 2003 includes two types of file and folder compression: NTFS-based file system compression and the compressed folders feature, which is equivalent to the various Zip file utilities that have been available from sources other than Microsoft.

Compression allows you to store more files on a volume because a compressed file takes up less space. Typically, files such as text files, documents, spreadsheets, and bitmaps will gain the most benefit from compression, because they generally contain a lot of blank space and redundant data. Other files such as compressed graphics files (JPEG, PNG), video files, or Zip files provide the least benefit because they already use their own form of compression.

Using either method to compress files and folders gives you the same result: decreasing the amount of space that a file, folder, or program uses on your hard drive or removable media.

Configuring NTFS File and Folder Compression

NTFS compression allows you to compress a single file or even the entire volume. Because compression is built in to the file system, working with compressed files and folders is invisible to the end user. When you open a file, Windows Server 2003 automatically decompresses the file, and when you close the file, it is recompressed.

Because NTFS compression is a property of a file, folder, or volume, you can have uncompressed files on a compressed volume or a compressed file in an uncompressed folder.

Native file and folder compression is one of the many benefits of using NTFS; native compression is not available on the File Allocation Table (FAT) file system. Unfortunately, this capability comes at a price—NTFS compression and Encrypted File System (EFS) encryption are mutually exclusive. That is, you cannot both compress and encrypt a file or folder at the same time.

You can manage compression from the command line by running the compact command or from the Windows GUI in the applicable folder or file Properties dialog box. Step by Step 13.1 outlines how to enable NTFS compression on a folder.

STEP BY STEP

13.1 Compressing a folder on an NTFS volume

1. Open either My Computer or Windows Explorer. Right-click the folder that you want to compress and select Properties from the pop-up menu.

2. From the folder's Properties page, click the Advanced button, as shown in Figure 13.1.

FIGURE 13.1   Compression is an attribute of a folder.

3. In the Advanced Attributes dialog box, shown in Figure 13.2, select the Compress Contents to Save Disk Space check box. Click OK to save.

FIGURE 13.2   To compress a folder, select the Compress Contents to Save Disk Space check box. Notice that you can check either Compress Contents or Encrypt Contents, but not both.

4. Click OK on the folder's Properties page.

5. If the Confirm Attribute Changes dialog box appears, as shown in Figure 13.3, choose whether you want to apply the changes to only the selected folder or to the folder and all its subfolders and files. Click OK.

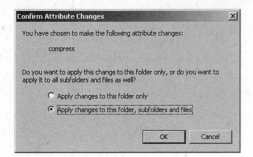

FIGURE 13.3   Select what you want compressed.

As mentioned earlier, you can choose to compress a single file, or a group of files, without compressing the folder or the volume that the file resides in. To compress a single file or group of files, consult Step by Step 13.2.

STEP BY STEP

13.2 Compressing a file on an NTFS volume

1. Open either My Computer or Windows Explorer. Right-click the file that you want to compress and select Properties from the pop-up menu.

2. From the file's Properties page, click the Advanced button.

3. In the Advanced Attributes dialog box, select the Compress Contents to Save Disk Space check box. Click OK to save.

4. Click OK on the file's Properties page.

If you need to conserve a lot of space, you can choose to compress an entire NTFS volume. However, remember that it takes a certain amount of system overhead to work with compressed files, so you probably won't want to compress a volume that contains files that are frequently accessed, such as your boot drive. Also, there will always be certain files in use that cannot be compressed, such as ntoskrnl and pagefile.sys.

To compress an NTFS volume, follow the procedure outlined in Step by Step 13.3.

STEP BY STEP

13.3 Compressing an NTFS volume

1. Open either My Computer or Windows Explorer. Right-click the drive that you want to compress and select Properties from the pop-up menu.

2. From the local disk's Properties page shown in Figure 13.4, click the Compress Drive to Save Disk Space check box.

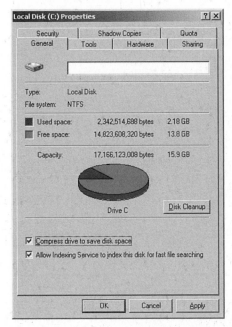

Local Disk (C:) Properties	? X

Security	Shadow Copies	Quota
General	Tools	Hardware	Sharing

Type: Local Disk
File system: NTFS

| Used space: | 2,342,514,688 bytes | 2.18 GB |
| Free space: | 14,823,608,320 bytes | 13.8 GB |

Capacity: 17,166,123,008 bytes   15.9 GB

Drive C   Disk Cleanup

☑ Compress drive to save disk space
☑ Allow Indexing Service to index this disk for fast file searching

OK   Cancel   Apply

FIGURE 13.4   Compressing a volume.

3. From the Confirm Attribute Changes dialog box, choose whether you want to turn compression on for the volume or compress all its subfolders and files. Click OK.

4. Click OK on the local disk's Properties page.

By looking at the Properties page for the file or folder, you can determine how much physical space was saved by comparing the entries for Size and Size on Disk, as shown in Figure 13.5.

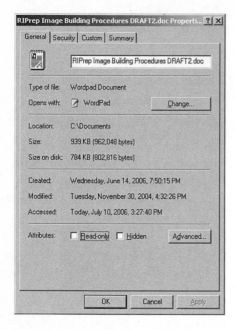

FIGURE 13.5 Comparing compressed and uncompressed sizes.

It's important to note that if you compress a volume or folder, you can choose to not compress the files and subfolders. However, any new files or folders created on a compressed volume or in a compressed folder will be compressed. New objects automatically inherit the compression attribute of the container in which they are created.

Challenge

You are the administrator of a network for a manufacturing company that includes multiple Windows Server 2003 servers used for file and print services. Your company is currently having financial problems, so the hardware budget for this fiscal year is limited.

The legal department is required to have all its documents available for at least 10 years because of a pending wrongful-death lawsuit. Unfortunately, you are running out of drive space and the voluminous amount of data consumed by these documents isn't going away anytime soon.

You must find a way to provide more free space for your users while keeping the documents for the legal department readily available—all without funding for new hardware!

What is the best way to solve this issue in Windows Server 2003? On your own, try to develop a solution that would involve the least amount of downtime and expense.

If you would like to see a possible solution, follow the procedure outlined here.

This is a fairly straightforward decision, mainly because without a budget, you can't use features such as remote storage and offline backups, which require additional hardware. Your only option is to compress

(continues)

(continued)

the old documents using the file and folder compression feature in Windows Server 2003. Fortunately, document files usually have a high compression ratio, so you should be able to gain a large amount of free space.

Here are the steps to follow:

1. Using either Windows Explorer or My Computer, navigate to the folder on the volume you want to compress.

2. Right-click the folder and select Properties. From the Properties dialog box, write down the Size and the Size on Disk entries.

3. Click the Advanced box. From the Advanced Attributes dialog box, select Compress Contents to Save Space, and then click OK.

4. Click OK again to close the dialog box.

5. When you are presented with the dialog box asking whether you want to apply the changes to the selected folder or to the folder, subfolder, and all files, select the check box to apply the changes to the folder, subfolder, and all files. Click OK to save.

6. After the compression completes, right-click the folder, select Properties, and compare the Size on Disk entry with the numbers you recorded earlier.

The nice thing about the Windows Server 2003 implementation of compression is that it allows you to apply compression at the volume, folder, or file level. This allows you to selectively compress older files that are not frequently used, yet you do not disrupt the files that are always in use.

Copying or Moving Compressed Files or Folders

Several rules apply when you move or copy compressed files and folders. The possible outcomes of moving or copying NTFS compressed files or folders are as follows:

▶ Moving an uncompressed file or folder to another folder on the same NTFS volume results in the file or folder remaining uncompressed, regardless of the compression state of the target folder.

▶ Moving an uncompressed file or folder to another folder on a different NTFS volume results in the file or folder inheriting the compression state of the target folder.

▶ Moving a compressed file or folder to another folder on the same NTFS volume results in the file or folder remaining compressed after the move, regardless of the compression state of the target folder.

▶ Moving a compressed file or folder to another folder on a different NTFS volume results in the file or folder inheriting the compression state of the target folder.

▶ Copying a file to a folder causes the file to take on the compression state of the target folder, whether on the same or a different volume.

▶ Overwriting a file of the same name causes the copied file to take on the compression state of the target file, regardless of the compression state of the target folder.

▶ Copying a file from a FAT folder to an NTFS folder results in the file taking on the compression state of the target folder.

▶ Copying a file from an NTFS folder to a FAT folder results in all NTFS permissions being lost.

Identifying Compressed Objects

So that you can easily identify files and folders that have been compressed, you can turn on a view property in Windows Explorer or My Computer. When this property is turned on, files and folders that are compressed are displayed in blue text. To enable this option, use the instructions in Step by Step 13.4.

STEP BY STEP

13.4 Changing the view property to identify compressed objects

1. Open either My Computer or Windows Explorer. From the system menu, click Tools, Folder Options.

2. In the Folder Options dialog box, click the View tab.

3. In the Advanced Settings window of the Folder Options dialog box, shown in Figure 13.6, select the Show Encrypted or Compressed NTFS Files in Color check box. Click OK to save.

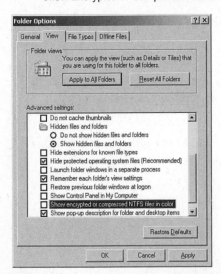

FIGURE 13.6 Turn on the view property for compressed objects.

Managing Compression from the Command Line

In addition to the GUI method of compressing files, Windows Server 2003 also has a command-line utility, `COMPACT.EXE`. The command-line utility is handy for use with scripting, or it can be used in those situations where you want to compress only certain types of files. For example, if you wanted to compress only the document files on your volume, you could use wildcards to specify that only those types of files should be compressed.

The `compact` command has the following syntax:

```
compact [{/c|/u}] [/s[:dir]] [/a] [/i] [/f]
 [/q] [FileName[...]]
```

Table 13.1 presents the available options for use with the `compact` command.

TABLE 13.1 The Options for the `compact` Command

Switch	Description
/c	Specifies that the directory or file is to be compressed.
/u	Specifies that the directory or file is to be decompressed.
/s	Specifies that the compression action is to be performed on all subdirectories of the specified directory.
/a	Specifies the display of hidden or system files.
/I	Specifies that errors are to be ignored during the compression process.
/f	Specifies that the compression operation is to be forced on the specified directory or file. This is useful in cases in which a directory is only partly compressed.
/q	Specifies that only the most essential information is to be reported.
FileName	Specifies the file or directory. You can use multiple filenames and wildcard characters (* and ?).

EXAM ALERT

Expect a compact Question   Expect at least one exam question that deals with compressing files and folders from the command line.

Compressed (Zipped) Folders

The second form of compression available in Windows Server 2003 is compressed folders. As stated earlier, the compressed folders feature uses the industry-standard Zip format to compress files into a folder. Unlike NTFS compression, compressed folders can be copied or moved to other computers, and they retain their compressed format.

Compressed folders can be created in My Computer or Windows Explorer using the procedure outlined in Step by Step 13.5.

STEP BY STEP

13.5 Creating a compressed folder

1. Open either My Computer or Windows Explorer. Highlight the drive or folder that you want to create the compressed folder in. Then, from the system menu, select File, New, Compressed (Zipped) Folder, as shown in Figure 13.7.

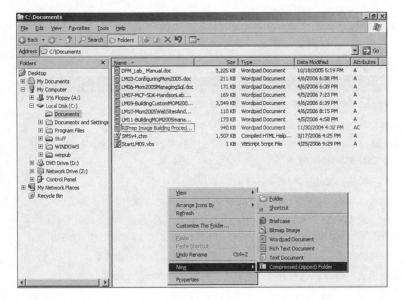

FIGURE 13.7 Creating a compressed folder.

2. Key in a name for the new folder, and then press Enter to save.

After you have created the compressed folder, shown in Figure 13.8, you can add and remove files and folders to and from it by dragging and dropping, just like any other folder in Windows Server 2003. In addition, you can run most programs and open and edit files in the compressed folder. For extra security, you can password protect the compressed folders.

Because compressed folders are essentially just common Zip files, they can also be manipulated by most third-party Zip utilities.

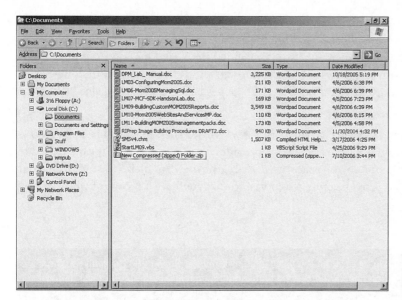

FIGURE 13.8 Compressed folders are identified by the zipper icon.

Best Practices for Compressed Files and Folders

File compression isn't a panacea for file storage problems—it's just another tool that should be used in association with the other tools in this chapter. However, used properly, it can help you to manage your storage efficiently.

There are certain points to remember:

▶ *Compress only file types that will benefit from compression*—This includes text files, documents, spreadsheets, and bitmaps.

▶ *Don't use compression for compressed files*—This includes files such as compressed graphics files (JPEG, PNG), video files, or other files that already use some form of compression.

▶ *Don't compress live data*—This includes databases that host a lot of write activity and other files that are constantly changing.

File Server Resource Manager

No matter how much storage you have on your file servers, users always manage to fill it up. Even if you restrict Internet access so that they can't download their favorite games and pictures, they still pack your servers with various documents and other assorted business-related and "other" files that they just can't live without. Is it really necessary to retain WordPerfect 5.0–formatted documents from 1993?

In most environments, the administrator must have a mechanism to monitor and control the amount of space that users are allocated. Although there have always been third-party utilities available to control disk usage, Microsoft finally included the Disk Quota feature in its operating systems starting with Windows 2000. Previous to the R2 release of Windows Server 2003, the Disk Quota feature in Windows Server 2003 was largely unchanged since the initial version.

The File Server Resource Manager (FSRM) is a new MMC snap-in available in Windows Server 2003, starting with the R2 release. FSRM provides a variety of tools that can be used to monitor and control the amount of space used and control what files are stored on your servers. In addition, it also provides storage reports, so that you have a record of who's storing what and where.

> **EXAM ALERT**
>
> **R2 Only**   Although the domain can still be Windows 2000 or Windows Server 2003 without R2, the server the FSRM is installed on and all the servers that will be managed via the FSRM must be at R2 or later.

To install the File Server Resource Manager on a Windows Server 2003 R2 server, follow the procedure in Step by Step 13.6.

STEP BY STEP

13.6 Installing the File Server Resource Manager

1. From the Start menu, click Start, Control Panel, Add or Remove Programs.

2. In the Add or Remove Programs window, as shown in Figure 13.9, click Add/Remove windows.

3. This starts the Windows Components Wizard. From the Windows Components dialog box, select the check box for Management and Monitoring tools, and then click the Details button.

4. In the Management and Monitoring Tools dialog box, select the File Server Resource Manager subcomponent, as shown in Figure 13.10. Click OK to return to the wizard.

FIGURE 13.9 Installing Windows components.

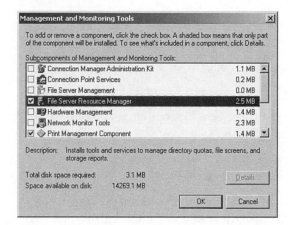

FIGURE 13.10 Select the File Server Resource Manager subcomponent.

5. On the Windows Components dialog box, click the Next button to continue.

6. When prompted, insert the requested Windows Server 2003 R2 CDs. (You might need both CD1 and CD2.)

7. The necessary files are loaded. When completed, click the Finish button.

8. When prompted, restart the server.

After the FSRM is installed, it can be opened by selecting the File Server Resource Manager icon in the Administrative Tools folder.

The FSRM MMC, as shown in Figure 13.11, takes advantage of the new functionality in MMC version 3.0 by displaying the additional Actions pane on the far right.

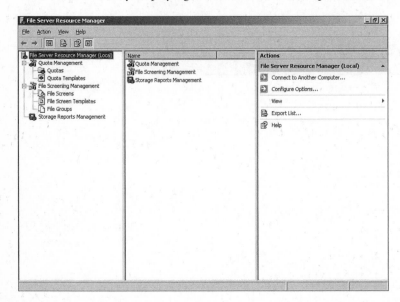

FIGURE 13.11   The File Server Resource Manager MMC.

As you can see in Figure 13.11, there are three major nodes in the FSRM MMC:

▶ *Quota Management*—Used to create and manage quotas on volumes and folders.

▶ *File Screening Management*—Used to create file screens that prevent users from saving blocked file types in managed volumes and folders.

▶ *Storage Reports Management*—Used to create and schedule storage reports.

Before we can use the FSRM MMC, we need to set up a few configuration options. To access the configuration, right-click the File Resource Manager entry in the left pane, and select Configure Options from the pop-up menu. This opens up the options dialog box, shown in Figure 13.12.

On the Email Notifications tab, enter the SMTP server, the email address of the administrators that you want notifications sent to, and the From e-mail address. Click the Test E-mail button to test your configuration.

On the File Screen Audit tab, shown in Figure 13.13, you have the option to record all file screening activity in an auditing database. This database is used to create the File Screen Audit Report.

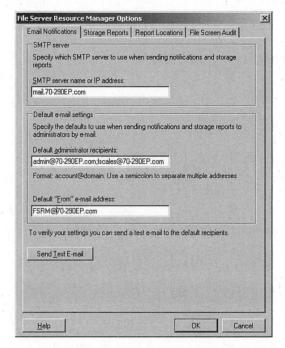

FIGURE 13.12 You can set the FSRM notification configuration from the Email Notifications tab.

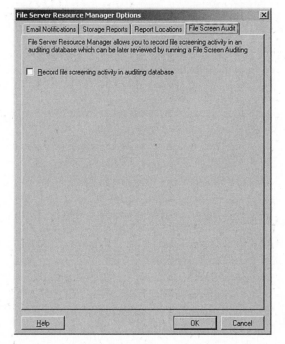

FIGURE 13.13 File Screen auditing is enabled by selecting the check box.

> **NOTE**
>
> **Performance Hit**   Enabling file screen auditing adds a certain amount of overhead to the file screening process. Make sure that you actually need this functionality before turning it on.

Now that we have the initial configuration of the File Server Resource Manager completed, let's take an in-depth look at what we can accomplish with it.

Implementing and Monitoring Disk Quotas

Objective:

Monitor file and print servers. Tools might include Task Manager, Event Viewer, and System Monitor.

▶ Monitor disk quotas.

Disk quotas are a method of controlling the amount of space a user has access to on a file server. You can also use the Disk Quota feature to monitor the space in use by your users. As we mentioned earlier, both the Windows 2000 and Windows Server 2003 operating systems support disk quotas, which are used to track and control disk usage per user on NTFS volumes.

Quotas can be configured in one of two ways: as a monitoring tool so that the administrator can track disk usage by user or as a tool to prevent the user from saving files to the disk when a specified limit is reached.

There are two types of disk quotas in Windows Server 2003 starting with the release of version R2:

▶ *NTFS Quotas*—These are the old-style quotas that have been used since Windows 2000.

▶ *FSRM Quotas*—These are the new-style quotas that were introduced in R2.

NTFS Quotas

NTFS quotas are set on a per-volume basis and are assigned to each user, but unfortunately they cannot be assigned by folder or by group. Similar to encryption and compression, quotas can be used only on NTFS-formatted partitions and volumes. When you enable disk quotas for a volume, volume usage is automatically tracked for all users from that point on.

NTFS quotas have the following features and limitations:

▶ Disk quotas do not apply to members of the local Administrators account.

▶ The files contained on a volume converted from FAT to NTFS do not count against user quotas, because they are initially owned by the local administrator. Files created or moved to the volume after the conversion has been completed are owned by the user.

▶ Disk quotas cannot be applied on a per-folder basis. They can only be applied per volume.

▶ If a physical disk has multiple volumes, a quota can be applied separately to each volume.

▶ Even if a volume consists of multiple physical disks, the quota for the volume applies to the entire volume.

▶ Disk usage is based on all files that the user creates, copies, or takes ownership of.

▶ File compression cannot be used to prevent users from exceeding their quota. Disk quotas are based on the actual file size, not the compressed file size.

▶ Disk quotas affect the free size that an installed application sees during the installation process.

▶ Disk quotas can be enabled on local or network volumes and removable drives formatted with NTFS.

▶ Disk quotas are not available on any volume or partition formatted using a version of Windows prior to Windows 2000. Disk quotas are available only on NTFS volumes or partitions formatted by Windows 2000 or later.

▶ When quotas are exceeded, notification is via an entry in the event logs.

Implementing NTFS Disk Quotas

EXAM ALERT

Which Disk Quotas? We are presenting material on the older NTFS Quotas because questions pertaining to them might appear on the exam, and your environment might include pre-R2 versions of Windows Server 2003. However, if you are using a Windows Server 2003 R2 server, you should use the new style quotas implemented via the FSRM.

NTFS Quotas are applied at the volume level from the Volume Properties dialog box of the NTFS volume. In addition to turning quotas on or off, the following options are available on the Quota Properties tab:

▶ *Deny Disk Space to Users Exceeding Quota Limit*—This option causes users who have exceeded their limit to receive an "insufficient disk space" message when they try to save a file. They will be unable to add any more data to the volume until they free up space by moving or deleting some existing files.

▶ *Limit Disk Space To*—This setting is used to configure the amount of space to which new users are limited.

▶ *Log Event When a User Exceeds Their Quota Limit*—When a user exceeds his or her quota, an event is written to the System log. These events are queued and written hourly.

▶ *Log Event When a User Exceeds Their Warning Level*—When a user exceeds his or her warning level, an event is written to the System log. These events are queued and written hourly.

The default in Windows Server 2003 is for quotas to be turned off. To set NTFS quota limits on a volume, perform the procedure outlined in Step by Step 13.7.

STEP BY STEP

13.7 Setting NTFS Quota Limits on a volume

1. From My Computer or Windows Explorer, right-click the volume you want to enable quotas on and select Properties from the pop-up menu.

2. On the Disk Properties dialog box, select the Quota tab.

3. On the Quota tab, select the Enable Quota Management check box, as shown in Figure 13.14.

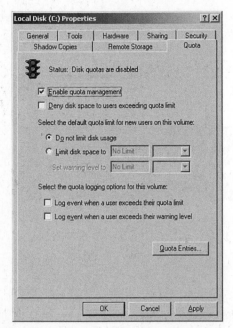

FIGURE 13.14 You can configure quotas from the Quota tab.

4. In the Disk Properties dialog box shown in Figure 13.14, select the Limit Disk Space To option button and add limit and warning levels.

5. Click OK.

6. When you receive the warning dialog box shown in Figure 13.15, read it, and then click OK.

FIGURE 13.15   This warning dialog box tells you that the drive will be scanned so that the file ownership can be inventoried and the disk usage can be credited to each user.

After you turn on disk quotas, the volume is scanned and the file space is calculated, depending on the Creator Owner of each file. Although all users are assigned, by default, the quota limit you just configured (see Figure 13.16), you can change the quota configuration of an existing user.

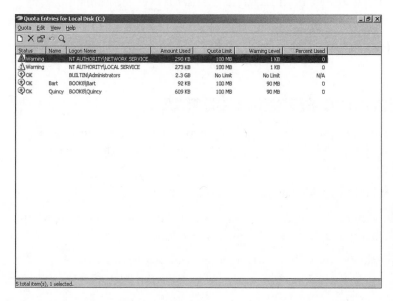

FIGURE 13.16   The Quota Entries window from a drive that just had quotas enabled. Note that there is no limit on the administrators account.

Managing NTFS Disk Quotas

After disk quotas have been implemented on your server, most of the work required in managing them involves monitoring the disk space that the users have allocated and making adjustments when a user has a good reason to receive more disk space.

A lot of this monitoring can be performed from Event Viewer if you selected the option to write an entry in the event logs when a user crosses the warning threshold or exceeds the hard limit. The applicable entries in the event logs can be found by performing a search or filtering for the event IDs 36 (for warning threshold) and 37 (for over the limit), with a source entry of NTFS.

Quotas can be configured so that when users reach a preset warning level, an event is recorded in the event log. The users can continue to save files to the volume until they reach their quota limit. At that time, they will be unable to save any more files to the volume, and they will receive an "insufficient disk space" message. This will also record an event in the event log.

The second major task associated with disk quotas involves monitoring the space each user has available. This can be accomplished by opening the Quota Entries window and sorting the space entries to find out which users have exceeded their limits and which users are near their limits, as shown previously in Figure 13.16.

This is made easier by referring to the icons to the left of the entries. The following icons are used so that you can see the status at a glance:

▶ *Green*—This means the user is below the warning threshold.

▶ *Yellow triangle with exclamation point*—This means the user is over the warning threshold but under the limit.

▶ *Red circle with exclamation point*—The user has exceeded the limit.

File Server Resource Manager Quotas

Although NTFS Quotas are still available in Windows Server 2003 R2, it's much better to implement your quotas using the File Server Resource Manager (FSRM). The differences are as follows:

▶ Quotas can be set at both the folder and volume level.

▶ Quotas are calculated using the actual disk space used, so compressed files are now calculated using the actual size on disk, not the uncompressed size.

▶ Quotas can be implemented on multiple servers by copying a template between servers.

▶ Quotas can be automatically created for subfolders as they are added.

▶ Notifications have been enhanced to include not only Event Logging, but also the capability to send an email, run a file or script, or generate a storage report.

To implement a quota using the File Server Resource Manager, follow the procedure in Step by Step 13.8.

STEP BY STEP

13.8 Implementing a quota using the File Server Resource Manager

1. From the Start menu, click Start, Control Panel, Administrative Tools, File Server Resource Manager.

2. In the File Server Resource Manager MMC, right-click Create Quota in the Actions pane.

3. This opens the Create Quota dialog box, as shown in Figure 13.17. Either enter the desired path in the Quota Path field, or click the Browse button to locate it.

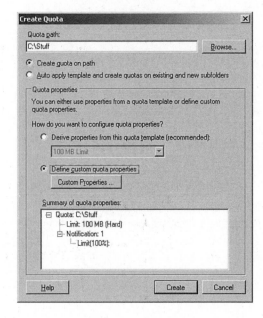

FIGURE 13.17 You can either accept the defaults or create custom properties.

4. Click the Custom Properties button.

5. This opens the Quota Properties dialog box, as shown in Figure 13.18. Enter the desired Space Limits, and then click the OK button.

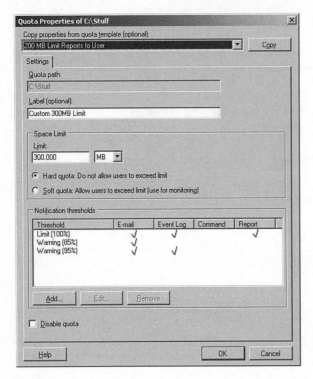

FIGURE 13.18 The properties dialog box allows you to configure space limits and notifications.

6. On the Create Quota dialog box, click the Create button to save your quota.

7. When the Save Custom Properties as a Template dialog box appears, as shown in Figure 13.19, select the Save the Custom Quota Without Creating a Template option button, and then click the OK button.

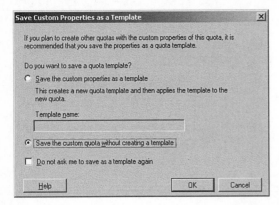

FIGURE 13.19 You have the option of saving your settings as a template that can be reused and copied to other servers.

8. The quota is displayed in the FSRM MMC, as shown in Figure 13.20.

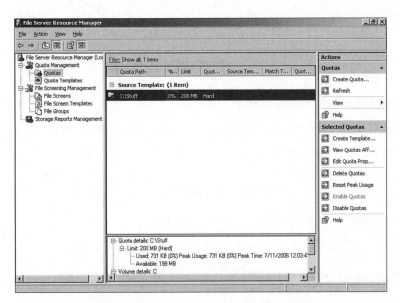

FIGURE 13.20 The completed quota will apply to all users who save files in the folder.

That was a quick example of how to set up a simple quota. However, if you have an environment with tens, hundreds, or even thousands of volumes and folders to set quotas on, that process would become tedious very quickly.

Fortunately, Microsoft has included the Quota Templates feature with the FSRM. A quota template can contain the following information:

▶ *Space*—The allowed disk space can be defined in any increment from kilobytes to terabytes. Quotas can be applied to either new or existing volumes or folders.

▶ *Limits*—Quotas can be set to either Hard or Soft. A hard quota will prevent the user from saving any more files. Unlike some third-party software, there is no grace period; when the limit is reached, the user is effectively blocked from using any more space. A soft quota will warn users, but will let them continue to save files. The soft quotas are typically used for space monitoring purposes.

▶ *Notifications*—You can configure notifications to let the user and/or administrator know when the users' space nears or reaches their quota limit. These notifications can be saved to the event log, emailed, or can cause a program or script to be run.

You can either use the quota templates as is, or you can use them as a basis for your own custom template. In Step by Step 13.9, we will copy an existing template and configure it for our needs.

STEP BY STEP

13.9 Implementing a quota using a quota template

1. From the Start menu, click Start, Control Panel, Administrative Tools, File Server Resource Manager.

2. In the File Server Resource Manager MMC, click the Quota Templates entry in the left pane.

3. This displays a list of the predefined Quota templates, as shown in Figure 13.21. Right-click the 200 MB Limit Reports to User template and select Create Quota from Template from the pop-up menu.

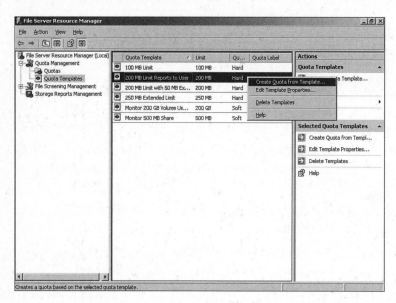

FIGURE 13.21 The FSRM comes supplied with a selection of predefined templates that you can use as the basis for your own custom templates.

4. This opens the Create Quota dialog box. Enter the desired path into the Quota Path field or click the Browse button to locate it. Notice in the bottom part of the dialog box that the predefined quota properties are shown (see Figure 13.22).

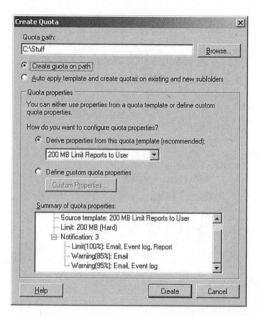

FIGURE 13.22 The predefined properties are listed for the selected quota template.

5. Select the Define Custom Quota Properties option button, and then click the Custom Properties button. This opens the Quota Properties dialog box, as shown in Figure 13.23. In the Copy Properties field, select the 200MB Limit template from the drop-down list, and then click the Copy button. This copies the settings from the existing template. Enter a label as shown.

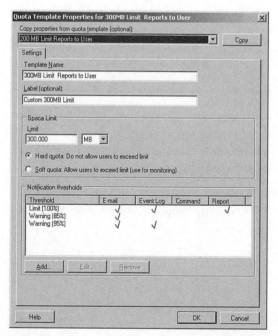

FIGURE 13.23 You can copy the existing settings to your custom template.

6. Change the Space Limit to 300MB, and then click the Add button to add another warning email notification at 90%.

7. Click the OK button. When you return to the Create Quota dialog box, notice that the quota properties reflect your changes.

8. Click the Create button to save your quota.

9. When the Save Custom Properties as a Template dialog box appears, enter a suitable name, and then click the OK button.

10. The quota is displayed in the FSRM MMC, as shown in Figure 13.24.

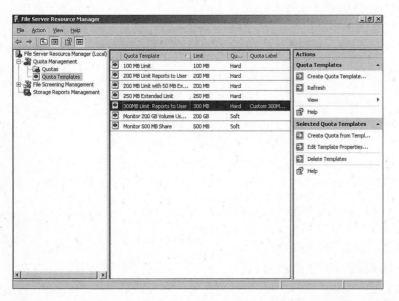

FIGURE 13.24   The completed quota will apply to all users who save files in the folder.

Templates are handy for a couple of reasons. First, you can reuse them for other volumes or folders, without having to go to the trouble of defining a new configuration. Second, if you have a change that needs to be made to all templates, you can specify to automatically make the change to all templates that were derived from the original templates.

For example, suppose we want to add an email notification at 65% to the users that we just assigned the previous template to. Follow the procedure in Step by Step 13.10 to update all the quotas derived from the original 200MB limit quota.

STEP BY STEP

13.10 Updating a quota derived from a quota template

1. From the Start menu, click Start, Control Panel, Administrative Tools, File Server Resource Manager.

2. In the File Server Resource Manager MMC, click the Quota Templates entry in the left pane.

3. This displays a list of the predefined quota templates. Double-click the 200 MB Limit Reports to User template.

4. This opens the Quota Template Properties dialog box. Click the Add button and add the 65% Threshold. Click OK to save.

5. The Update Quotas Derived from Template dialog box opens, as shown in Figure 13.25. Select the Apply Template to All Derived Quotas option, and then click the OK button.

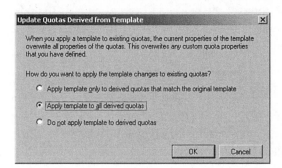

FIGURE 13.25 You can apply your changes to all the templates derived from this one.

6. Double-click the template that we created in the previous Step by Step and observe that the new notification has been added.

Referring to Figure 13.25, the three settings are

▶ *Apply Template Only to Derived Quotas That Match the Original Template*—This option will push your changes to any derived quotas, but only if you haven't manually customized them since they were derived.

▶ *Apply Template to All Derived Quotas*—This option pushes your changes to your derived templates, whether or not they have been manually edited since they were derived.

▶ *Do Not Apply Template to Derived Quotas*—This option does exactly what it says. It saves the changes you made to the template, and then exits.

File Screening with the FSRM

The second major feature that the File Server Resource Manager brings to the table is file screening. As we discussed earlier, file screening allows you to prevent users from saving blocked file types to your servers.

Just like with quotas, file screens can be built from scratch, or you can use and modify the supplied templates. You have the ability to apply file screens to a volume or folder while configuring exceptions so that certain users can save some of the blocked file types. Similar to quotas, you can configure file screening to block users from saving certain types of files, let them save them and notify you that they were saved, or both.

File Groups

File screens are configured through the use of File Groups. A File Group defines the files that should or should not be blocked. In addition, a File Group can be configured for specific exceptions that will override the blocking rule. Windows Server 2003 includes the following prebuilt file groups:

▶ Audio and Video Files

▶ Backup Files

▶ Compressed Files

▶ E-Mail Files

▶ Executable Files

▶ Image Files

▶ Office Files

▶ System Files

▶ Temporary Files

▶ Text Files

▶ Web Page Files

Let's create a File Group specifically for those nonbusiness files that users like to store on servers, such as .mpg, .wma, and .mp3. Follow the procedure in Step by Step 13.11 to accomplish this.

STEP BY STEP

13.11 Creating a File Group

1. From the Start menu, click Start, Control Panel, Administrative Tools, File Server Resource Manager.

2. In the File Server Resource Manager MMC, click to expand File Screening Management, and then click the File Groups entry.

3. Click Create File Groups in the Actions pane as shown in Figure 13.26.

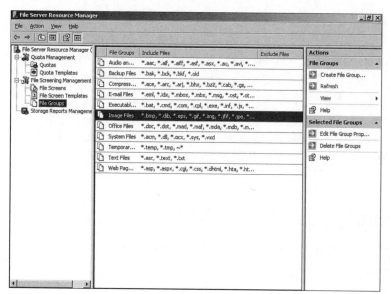

FIGURE 13.26 The FSRM showing the preconfigured file groups and the included file extensions.

4. This displays the Create File Group Properties dialog box shown in Figure 13.27.

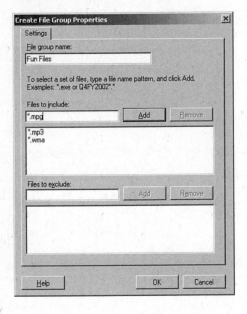

FIGURE 13.27 Enter the extensions of the files to block.

5. Enter a name for the File group, and then enter the extensions of the files to block, using the format `*.mp3`. Click the Add button to add the file to the list.

6. When you're finished, click OK to save. The new file group will be displayed in the FSRM MMC with the preconfigured file groups.

File Screen Templates

The File Groups are used as the basis for the following default file screen templates that are included with Windows Server 2003 R2:

▶ Block Audio and Video Files

▶ Block E-Mail Files

▶ Block Executable Files

▶ Block Image Files

▶ Monitor Executable and System Files

You probably noticed that all the templates were titled "Block," except for the last one. Similar to the functionality of quotas, we have the ability to just monitor file save activity and notify the administrator when a specified file type is saved to the volume or folder.

Although we have the ability to create a simple file screen to apply to a single folder or volume, the best method is either to use one of the supplied templates, or use these templates as the basis for a custom template. Follow the procedure in Step by Step 13.12 to create a custom file screen template.

STEP BY STEP

13.12 Creating a file screen template

1. From the Start menu, click Start, Control Panel, Administrative Tools, File Server Resource Manager.

2. In the File Server Resource Manager MMC, click to expand File Screening Management, and then click the File Screen Template entry.

3. Click the Create File Screen Template entry in the Actions pane. This displays the Create File Screen Template dialog box shown in Figure 13.28.

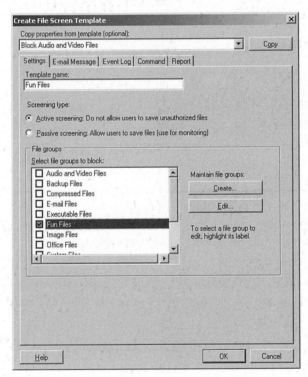

FIGURE 13.28 Select the file group to use, or click the Create button to make a new one.

4. Enter the name of the template, and then select the file group we created in Step by Step 13.11. Make sure that the Active Screening option button is selected.

5. Click the E-Mail Message tab. Select the options to send an email to both the administrators and the user, as shown in Figure 13.29.

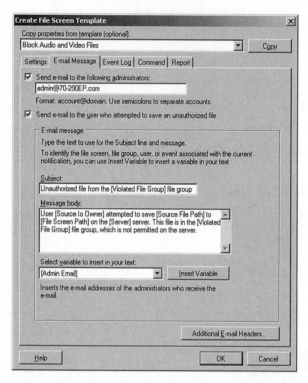

FIGURE 13.29 Select the options to send a notification message.

6. When you're finished, click the OK button to save the template.

The template we just created will block the saving of the files that we specified in the file group and will send the user and the administrator an e-mail when the user attempts to save one of the file types.

Now that we have created a template, we need to apply it to a volume or folder. In Step by Step 13.13, we will set up a file screen on the root of the user's home folders to block the saving of any unauthorized files in their home folders.

STEP BY STEP

13.13 Applying a file screen

1. From the Start menu, click Start, Control Panel, Administrative Tools, File Server Resource Manager.

2. In the File Server Resource Manager MMC, click to expand File Screening Management, and then click the File Screen entry.

3. Click the Create File Screen entry in the Actions pane; this displays the Create File Screen template dialog box shown in Figure 13.30.

Figure 13.30 Select the file screen path, and then select the template to use.

4. Enter the file path, and then select the file screen template we created in the previous step by step. Click OK to save.

5. When you're finished, click the Create button to save.

File Screen Exceptions

Like everything else, the one-size-fits-all analogy doesn't always work for file screening. For example, what if the marketing department has a specific need to store video files, possibly outtakes for a commercial they are producing? Because you've already blocked *.mpg files, how are they going to be able to store their files on the servers?

When there is a need to allow files that other file screens are blocking, you need to create a file screen exception. A *file screen exception* is a file screen that is used to override the screening for a folder and its subfolders. This is done by attaching a file group to the screen, just as we have done with regular file screens.

> **NOTE**
>
> **No Exceptions** You cannot apply a file screen exception on a folder that you have already applied a file screen to. The exception must either be assigned to a subfolder or the original file screen must be changed.

In Step by Step 13.14, we will set up a file screen exception on the root of the user's home folders to allow the saving of *.mpg files in the Marketing folder.

STEP BY STEP

13.14 Creating a file screen exception

1. From the Start menu, click Start, Control Panel, Administrative Tools, File Server Resource Manager.

2. In the File Server Resource Manager MMC, click to expand File Screening Management. Then, right-click the File Screen entry and select Create File Screen Exception from the pop-up menu.

3. This displays the Create File Screen Exception dialog box shown in Figure 13.31. Enter the exception path as shown.

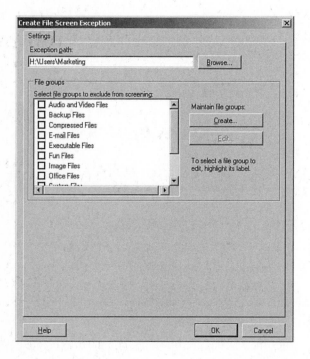

FIGURE 13.31 Enter the exception path, and then click the Create button.

4. Because there is not a predefined file group that contains only the *.mpg file type, click the Create button to open the Create File Group Properties dialog box, as shown in Figure 13.32.

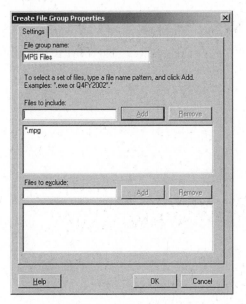

FIGURE 13.32 Enter the desired extension.

5. Click OK to save. This returns you to the Create File Screen Exception dialog box. Select the check box for the File Group that you just created, and then click OK to save. The File Screen and its associated exception is shown in Figure 13.33.

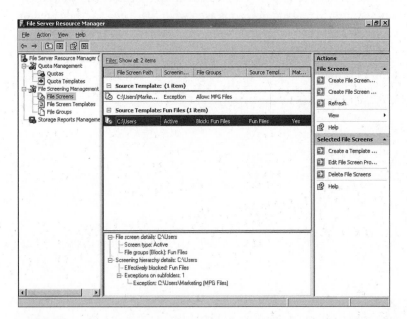

FIGURE 13.33 FSRM MMC showing a File Screen and its associated File Screen Exception.

Generating Storage Reports with FSRM

To monitor the success—or failure—of quotas and file screen activity, the FSRM is able to generate a series of reports. The available reports are the following:

- ▶ Duplicate files
- ▶ File screening audit
- ▶ Files by file group
- ▶ Files by owner
- ▶ Large files
- ▶ Least recently accessed files
- ▶ Most recently accessed files
- ▶ Quota usage

These reports can either be generated on a scheduled basis or on demand. They can be quite helpful because they are not only designed to give the system administrator a view of how the quotas and file screening are performing, but they point out other file server management issues, such as identifying large files, duplicate files, or files that aren't currently being used. This assists the system administrator in making decisions as to what files need to be deleted or moved to offline storage.

Report tasks are used to schedule reports that are generated on a regular schedule. A report task consists of the following information:

- ▶ What reports are to be generated
- ▶ The report parameters
- ▶ The volumes and folders to report on
- ▶ The schedule to generate the reports
- ▶ The output format of the reports

In Step by Step 13.15, we will create a report task that will run a couple of reports at 11:25 every evening.

STEP BY STEP

13.15 Creating a report task

1. From the Start menu, click Start, Control Panel, Administrative Tools, File Server Resource Manager.

2. In the File Server Resource Manager MMC, right-click the Storage Reports Management entry and select Schedule a New Report Task from the pop-up menu.

3. This displays the Storage Reports Task Properties dialog box shown in Figure 13.34.

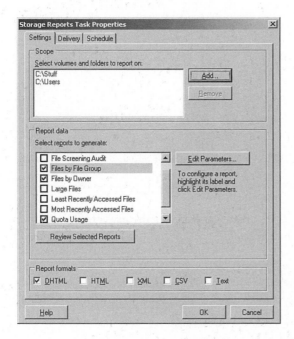

FIGURE 13.34 The Storage Report Tasks Properties dialog box allows you to specify the desired reports and the volumes and folders to report on.

4. Enter the volumes and folders that you want to report on. Next, select the reports that you want to see. You can review the report parameters by highlighting a report and selecting the Review Selected Reports button. Also, select the desired report format.

5. Click the Delivery tab. If desired, enter an email address that you want the reports to be mailed to. The default is to save them in the %systemdrive%\StorageReports\Scheduled folder.

6. Click the Schedule tab. Click the Create Schedule button.

7. This opens the Schedule dialog box shown in Figure 13.35. Click the New button and fill out the desired start time for the reports you selected. Note that you can select multiple schedules for the reports. Click OK when finished.

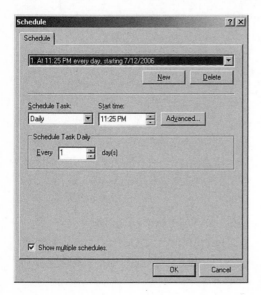

FIGURE 13.35   Enter the desired schedule.

8. This returns you to the Schedule tab. Verify that the correct schedule is displayed, and then click the OK button to save your schedule.

As you can see in Figure 13.36, the scheduled report task is listed by the name of the reports, what is to be reported on, and the report schedule.

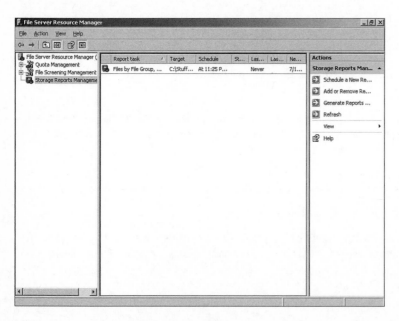

FIGURE 13.36   The FSRM listing the Report Task.

There will be times when you want a snapshot of what is happening with your disk storage. The FSRM allows you to generate an on-demand report that gathers current data to display.

In Step by Step 13.16, we will create an on-demand report and view it in a browser.

STEP BY STEP

13.16 Creating an on-demand report

1. From the Start menu, click Start, Control Panel, Administrative Tools, File Server Resource Manager.

2. In the File Server Resource Manager MMC, right-click the Storage Reports Management entry and select Generate a New Report Now from the pop-up menu.

3. This displays the Storage Reports Task Properties dialog box.

4. Enter the volumes and folders that you want to report on. Next, select the reports that you want to see. You can review the report parameters by highlighting a report and selecting the Review Selected Reports button. Also, select the DHTML report format.

5. Click the OK button. You will be prompted as to whether you want the reports to be generated immediately or to be run as a background process. Select the option to run them immediately.

6. The report output will be displayed in a browser window, as shown in Figure 13.37.

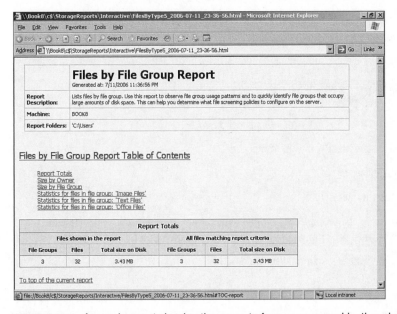

FIGURE 13.37 A sample report showing the amount of space consumed by the selected file groups.

As you have seen in the preceding sections, the File Server Resource Manager can be extremely helpful in managing your file servers. In summary, FSRM provides the following benefits:

▶ *Quotas*—FSRM allows the system administrator to limit the space used by volume or folder and can notify the user when the limits are approached or exceeded. Quotas can be applied to either new or existing volumes or folders.

▶ *File Screening*—File screens can be created to prevent users from saving unapproved file types, and notifications can be sent when users attempt to save blocked files.

▶ *Templates*—Quota and file-screening templates can be created to apply to new volumes or folders added to the organization.

▶ *Reporting*—Reports of storage usage can either be generated on a scheduled basis or on demand.

Challenge

You are a lead system administrator who is responsible for monitoring the storage space on all the file servers in your enterprise. You've given one of your junior administrators the task of reducing the storage space used by at least 15%. Because he is fairly new to storage administration, you suggest that he run a report to identify the files that each user owns. How would he accomplish this?

Try to complete this exercise on your own, listing your conclusions on a sheet of paper. After you have completed the exercise, compare your results to those given here.

1. From the Start menu, click Start, Control Panel, Administrative Tools, File Server Resource Manager.

2. In the File Server Resource Manager MMC, right-click the Storage Reports Management entry, and then select Generate a New Report Now from the pop-up menu.

3. This displays the Storage Reports Task Properties dialog box.

4. Enter the volumes and folders that you want to report on.

5. Next select the files by owner report.

6. Select the DHTML report format.

7. Click the OK button. You will be prompted as to whether you want the reports to be generated immediately or to be run as a background process. Select the option to run them immediately.

8. The report output will be displayed in a browser window.

Encrypting File System (EFS)

One of the hot items in the news lately has been data theft. There have been far too many cases of thieves either accessing sensitive data over the Internet or stealing laptop computers that contain thousands of names, Social Security numbers, bank account numbers, and the like. Too many people assume that as long as an asset is password protected that their data is safe. This is far from the case.

Any amateur with a password-cracking program can gain access to a computer, and accessing data from a stolen computer is as simple as installing a new operating system on the hard drive, or just adding the hard drive to another computer. After files are accessed, they can be read or copied.

The Encrypting File System (EFS), first introduced in Windows 2000, has been updated for Windows Server 2003. EFS is an extension to NTFS and provides file-level encryption. EFS uses public/private key technology, which makes it difficult, but not necessarily impossible, to crack. As is typical with this key technology, the public key is used to encrypt the data, and a private key is used for decryption.

The public key is just that—public. It can be passed around and is used to encrypt a file or an email message. Public keys are good for information exchange, such as secure mail. A user can publish her public key, and people can use this key to encrypt any mail they are sending to her. They can be assured that no one else can read the message, because it can be decrypted and read only by using the private key, which is kept secure by the receiver.

> **EXAM ALERT**
>
> **Public/Private Key Technology**   This technology is covered at length on the 70-298 Designing Security for a Microsoft Windows Server 2003 Network exam. More information about this technology can be found at http://windowssdk.msdn.microsoft.com/en-us/library/ms732314.aspx.

Encryption in EFS works by using a public/private key pair with a per file encryption key. When a user encrypts a file, EFS generates a file encryption key (FEK) and uses the public key to encrypt it. When the user wants to read or decrypt the file, the FEK is decrypted using the private key. The FEF is used to decrypt the file.

> **NOTE**
>
> The file encryption and compression attributes are mutually exclusive. You can apply one or the other to a file, but not both.

Although you can mark a folder as encrypted, the folder itself is not actually encrypted. EFS provides only file-level encryption. By marking a folder as encrypted, any files that are created or moved into the folder are automatically encrypted. Any existing files in the folder at the time that you set the encryption attribute are not automatically encrypted unless you select the option to apply changes to the folder, subfolder, and files on the Confirm Attribute Changes dialog.

The first time a user selects the encryption attribute from the properties dialog box of a file or folder, EFS will automatically generate a public key pair; then the private key is certified by a Certificate Authority (CA). If a CA is not available, the public key is self signed. All this is transparent to the user.

In Step by Step 13.17, we will use EFS to encrypt a folder, create a file in that folder, and then copy a file to that folder to see the effects of the encryption process.

STEP BY STEP

13.17 Encrypting a file or folder

1. In Windows Explorer, create a folder and name it **Secure**. Create a file in this folder and name it **Test1.txt**.

2. In Windows Explorer, right-click the folder you just created and select Properties from the pop-up menu.

3. This displays the Advanced Attributes dialog box shown in Figure 13.38.

FIGURE 13.38 The Advanced Attributes dialog box allows you to turn on either compression or encryption.

4. Click the OK button twice to save the changes and close the Properties dialog box.

5. Create a text file in the root directory and name it **Secure1.txt**. Move the file to the Secure folder.

6. Create a text file in the Secure folder and name it **Secure2.txt**.

7. Observe in Windows Explorer that both new files in the Secure folder (`Secure*.txt`) are displayed in green and that the original file is unchanged, as shown in Figure 13.39. This indicates that they are encrypted.

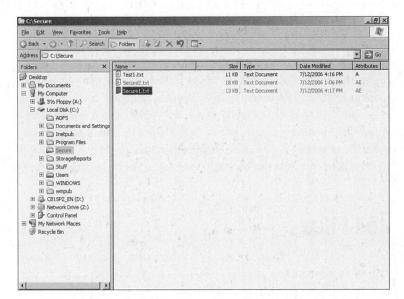

FIGURE 13.39 Encrypted files and folders will be displayed in green.

8. Log off the server, and then log back on again using a domain user (not administrator account). Try to open the secure files in the secure folder. You should receive the message `Access is denied`.

As you saw in the exercise, turning on encryption for a file or folder is pretty simple. In addition, after encryption is turned on for a folder, every file that is created or moved into that folder is automatically encrypted, without any user intervention. Any existing files are not affected.

The following conditions apply when moving or copying encrypted files:

▶ When a folder is encrypted, all files and subfolders added to that folder are automatically encrypted.

▶ If an encrypted file or folder is moved or copied to another folder on an NTFS formatted volume, it remains encrypted.

▶ If an encrypted file or folder is moved or copied to a FAT or FAT32 formatted volume, it is decrypted.

▶ If an encrypted file or folder is moved or copied to a floppy, it is decrypted.

▶ If a user other than the one who encrypted the file or folder attempts to copy it, he will receive the message `Access is denied`.

- ▶ If a user other than the one who encrypted the file attempts to move it to a folder that was encrypted by the original user, she will be successful.

- ▶ If a user other than the one who encrypted the file or folder attempts to move or copy it to another volume (NTFS, FAT, or FAT32), he will receive the message `Access is denied`.

After encryption is configured, the encrypt/decrypt process is transparent to the user and to applications. When a user opens a file, it is automatically decrypted and will be reencrypted when the user saves it. Because encryption is a file-level process, the application is unaware that it is working with an encrypted file. However, you must be careful to set the encryption attribute on for the folder that the file is stored in, because some applications, such as Microsoft Word, will create temporary files, and they will not be encrypted unless they are in an encrypted folder.

Sharing Encrypted Files

In some situations, the data in a file will need to be shared with other users, or possibly a group of users. However, it will still be important to keep the contents secure. In this situation, you can specifically share the encrypted file with other users. However, keep the following points in mind:

- ▶ After the user is given permission to the file, he or she can also grant others permission to use the file.

- ▶ Encrypted files can be shared, but not encrypted folders. Note that this refers only to EFS sharing, and an encrypted folder can always be an NTFS file share.

- ▶ Any user who is being granted access must have an EFS certificate. This certificate can reside in Active Directory, in the user's roaming profile, or in the user's profile on the server where the shared file is located.

> **NOTE**
>
> **Certificate Required**   As we mentioned earlier, all users that are being granted access must have a certificate. The easiest way to get a certificate is to encrypt a file or folder, which will automatically generate an EFS certificate for that user.

To share an encrypted file, follow the procedure in Step by Step 13.18.

STEP BY STEP

13.18 Sharing an encrypted file

1. Open Windows Explorer and navigate to the Secure folder.

2. In Windows Explorer, right-click the `Secure2.txt` file and select Properties from the pop-up menu.

3. This displays the Advanced Attributes dialog box.

4. Click the Details button; this opens the Encryption Details dialog box, as shown in Figure 13.40.

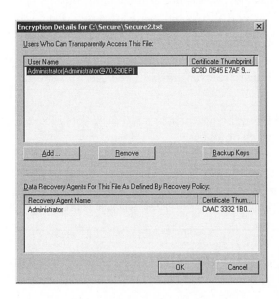

FIGURE 13.40   The Encryption Details dialog box allows you to authorize users and recovery agents for an encrypted file.

5. Click the Add button and use the Select User dialog box (see Figure 13.41) to add a user to the encrypted file. Click OK three times to return to Windows Explorer.

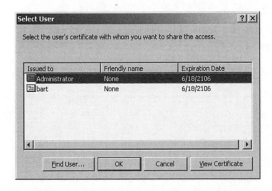

FIGURE 13.41   The Select User dialog box lists the users who have certificates installed on the local machine.

6. Log off the server, and then log back on again using the user that you shared the file with. Try to open the files in the secure folder. The file should open without any problems.

EFS Recovery Agents

So how can encrypted data be recovered if users lose their private key or leave the company? On standalone Windows servers and workstations (not members of a domain), the Data Recovery Agent (DRA) role must be manually assigned—it is not created automatically. In a domain, the domain administrator's account will automatically be granted this role.

Because this account is designated as the DRA, a recovery key is generated and saved in the local administrators' certificate store that can be used by the local administrator to recover the encrypted data. This recovery key can be used only to recover the data. The user's private key is never revealed.

If the DRA role is removed by a configuration error, the system assumes that no data recovery policy is in place and will refuse to encrypt any files or folders.

> **NOTE**
>
> The user account with recovery agent rights will be able to copy the file to his/her computer to perform recovery operations.

Any user can be a recovery agent; no other rights are required.

Creating a Domain DRA

After a user has encrypted a file, an EFS certificate is automatically created for them. This certificate is needed before the user can be designated as a recovery agent.

In the following Step by Step, we will perform the two steps needed to create a DRA: First, publish the certificate to the user account, and then add the user account as an EFS Recovery Agent.

STEP BY STEP

13.19 Adding an EFS Recovery Agent

1. Open the Active Directory Users and Computers MMC. From the View menu, select Advanced Features.

2. Locate the user you want to add, right-click the entry, and select Properties.

3. On the User Properties dialog box, select the Published Certificates tab.

4. Click the Add from Store button; this displays the Select Certificate dialog box shown in Figure 13.42.

FIGURE 13.42 Select the entry for the desired user that lists the EFS certificate.

5. Select the entry for the user that lists the EFS certificate, and then click the OK button.

6. This returns you to the User Properties dialog box. The certificated should be shown under the list of certificates published for the account, as shown in Figure 13.43. Click OK to close.

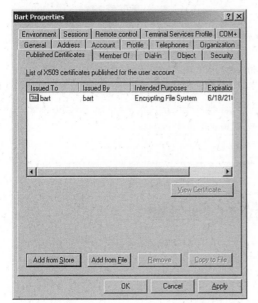

FIGURE 13.43 The certificate is published to the user account.

7. In Active Directory Users and Computers, right-click the domain entry and select Properties from the pop-up menu. On the Properties dialog box, click the Group Policy tab.

8. On the Group Policy tab, highlight the Default Domain Policy entry, and then click the Edit button. This opens the Group Policy Editor.

9. In the Group Policy Editor, expand Computer Configuration, Windows Settings, Security Settings, Public Key Policies, and then highlight the entry for Encrypting File System (see Figure 13.44).

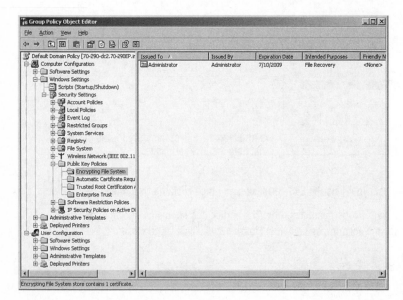

FIGURE 13.44 The administrator's certificate is published by default.

10. Right-click the Encrypting File system entry, and then select Add Recovery Agent from the pop-up menu. This starts the Add Recovery Agent Wizard. Click Next to continue.

11. On the Select Recovery Agents dialog box, click the Browse Directory button. From the Select Users dialog box, enter the name of the user account you want to add, and then click OK.

12. Click Next, and then click Finish.

Recovering an Encrypted File or Folder

To recover an encrypted file or folder, the recovery agent must copy the file to his computer, if in a domain, or log on to the computer with the local administrator account on a standalone computer.

To recover a file or folder, follow these steps:

1. Log on to the test server as a local administrator.

2. Right-click the file or folder and select Properties.

3. Click the Advanced button.

4. From the Advanced Attributes dialog box, deselect the Encrypt Contests to Secure Data check box.

5. Click OK twice to save.

If the computer is a member of a domain, move the file back to the user's computer.

Encryption Using the Cipher Command

The cipher command-line utility is supplied so that you can work with encrypted files and folders from the command line. This is handy when you are encrypting or decrypting a large number of files or folders, because you can use wildcards or run the utility from a script.

The cipher command options are listed in Table 13.2.

TABLE 13.2   Cipher Command-Line Options

Option	Meaning
No parameters	Displays the encryption state of the files in the current folder
/e	Encrypts the specified folder(s)
/d	Decrypts the specified folder(s)
/s:dir	Performs the operation on the current folder and all subfolders
/a	Encrypts/decrypts the files in all the folders that were specified
/i	Continues when an error occurs
/f	Forces all specified files to be encrypted
/q	Nonverbose reporting
/h	Displays hidden or system files
/k	Creates a new key; all other options are ignored

EXAM ALERT

You might encounter EFS questions on the exam. You should know how to encrypt and decrypt files and folders using both the GUI and the cipher utility. In addition, you should be familiar with the key recovery process.

Chapter Summary

As a systems administrator, one of your main tasks is to manage the data on your storage devices. Compressing files, folders, and programs decreases their size and reduces the amount of space they use on your storage devices.

Of course, one of the best ways to manage your storage is to not store unnecessary files on your servers in the first place. The file screening features introduced in Windows Server 2003 R2 help you prevent users from storing unauthorized file types that have no business use, and that take up large amounts of your precious (and expensive!) storage space.

In concert with file screening are disk quotas. Quotas are use to prevent users from storing more than a specified amount of data, which ensures that the users—not the system administrator—are responsible for determining what files are important to the individual user.

Last, but certainly not least, is File Encryption. With the emphasis put on security in the network environment these days, having a built-in method of encrypting and securing important files and folders is essential.

Key Terms

- Disk quota
- Hard Limit
- Soft Limit
- Quota Template
- File Screen Exception
- Report Tasks
- Quota Limit
- Recovery Key
- Encrypting File System

Apply Your Knowledge

Exercises

13.1 Configuring user disk quotas

A common problem when managing file servers is running out of free space. Users typically have to be reminded that the amount of space available is not infinite. As a system administrator, it is your job to allocate disk space to users and make sure they don't use more space than they should.

To simplify this task, as the administrator, you should put some of the onus of managing disk space constraints back on the users. After all, they know more about which files need to be deleted than you do.

What is the best way to accomplish this in Windows Server 2003? On your own, try to develop a solution that involves limited ongoing management by the system administrator.

If you would like to see a possible solution, follow these steps:

Estimated Time: 20 minutes

1. From My Computer or Windows Explorer, right-click the volume you want to enable quotas on and select Properties from the pop-up menu.

2. On the Properties dialog box, select the Quota tab.

3. On the Quota tab, select the Enable Quota Management check box.

4. In the Quota Properties dialog box, select the Limit Disk Space To option button and add limit and warning levels. Click OK.

5. A warning dialog box appears. It tells you that the drive will be scanned so that the file ownership will be inventoried and the disk usage can be credited to each user. Click OK.

6. In the Quota Entries window, from the system menu, select Quota, and then click New Quota Entry from the drop-down menu.

7. The Select Users dialog box appears. From here you can select one or more users from the local or domain database. Add a user and then click OK.

8. The Add New Quota Entry dialog box appears. Set the desired limits and then click OK.

9. The new users are added with the configured settings.

13.2 Configuring compression on a volume

This exercise demonstrates how to configure NTFS compression for an entire volume. This exercise requires an empty NTFS volume.

Estimated Time: 20 minutes.

1. Using either Windows Explorer or My Computer, create a folder on the volume that you want to compress.

2. Copy the contents of the Windows folder to this folder. Include all files and subfolders.

3. Using either Windows Explorer or My Computer, display the root of the volume that you want to compress.

4. Right-click the volume and select Properties. From the Properties dialog box, write down the Size and the Size on Disk entries.

5. Click the Advanced box. From the Advanced Attributes dialog box, select Compress Contents to Save Space and then click OK.

6. Click OK again to close the dialog box.

7. When you are presented with the dialog box asking you whether you want to apply the changes to the selected folder or to the folder, subfolder, and all files, select the check box to apply the changes to the folder, subfolder, and all files. Click OK to save.

8. After the compression completes, right-click the root of the volume, select Properties, and compare the Size on Disk entry with the numbers you recorded earlier.

13.3 Configuring a File Group

After blocking all the popular formats of music and video files, the MALM (Make Administrators' Life Miserable) foundation has come out with a new format for music files with a different file extension. You will need to add this new extension to the existing Audio and Video File Group so that it will be distributed with your existing File Screen templates.

Estimated Time: 10 minutes.

1. From the Start menu, click Start, Control Panel, Administrative Tools, File Server Resource Manager.

2. In the File Server Resource Manager MMC, click to expand File Screening Management, and then click the File Groups entry.

3. Double-click the Audio and Video File Group entry.

4. This displays the File Group Properties dialog box.

5. Enter the extension of the files to block, using the format *.xxx. Click the Add button to add the extension to the list.

6. When you're finished, click OK to save. The file group will be displayed in the FSRM MMC with the new extension added to the list of files to block.

Exam Questions

1. Jill, a junior system administrator, decided to move some old files to a new server that was purchased to hold old files. After carefully calculating the space that was needed, she created a volume to hold the old files. After moving the files, she noticed that the disk still had plenty of free space. What did Jill do wrong?

    ○ **A.** She didn't calculate the needed space properly.

    ○ **B.** She moved the wrong files.

    ○ **C.** Compression was enabled on the new volume.

    ○ **D.** The new server is more efficient than the old server.

2. Kevin, another junior system administrator, decided to move some old compressed files to a new server that was purchased to hold old files. After carefully calculating the space that was needed, he created a volume to hold the old files. Halfway through moving the files, he received the message that the disk had run out of free space. What was Kevin's problem?

    ○ **A.** He didn't calculate the needed space properly.

    ○ **B.** He moved the wrong files.

    ○ **C.** He didn't enable compression on the new volume.

    ○ **D.** The new server compressed files using a different method than the old server.

3. What user account has the default recovery agent role on a standalone server?

    ○ **A.** Power Users Group

    ○ **B.** DRA User

    ○ **C.** Domain Administrator account

    ○ **D.** Local Administrator

    ○ **E.** None of the above.

4. Which users can read an encrypted file?

   ○ **A.** User with DRA rights

   ○ **B.** DRA Users

   ○ **C.** User who encrypted the file

   ○ **D.** Domain Admins

5. The Human Resources manager was recently terminated. Because of the sensitive nature of her files, they were all encrypted. What utility can you use to decrypt her files?

   ○ **A.** Cipher

   ○ **B.** Decrypt

   ○ **C.** Unencrypt

   ○ **D.** RecoverPass

6. John is trying to take some work home with him. Unfortunately, when he tries to copy a 1MB text file from the Windows Server 2003 R2 file server to a freshly formatted floppy disk, he keeps getting an insufficient space error. What could be his problem?

   ○ **A.** The floppy disk is bad.

   ○ **B.** He needs to delete some of the files on the floppy to gain more space.

   ○ **C.** The file is compressed.

   ○ **D.** He's not authorized to copy the file.

7. Sally works in the production department for BigDawg Inc. She's working late one night and is trying to save a video file to her home folder, but she keeps getting an access denied message. What's the most likely cause of her problem?

   ○ **A.** Her file has a virus.

   ○ **B.** She doesn't have permissions on the folder.

   ○ **C.** She has only read permissions on the folder.

   ○ **D.** File screening is enabled.

8. John, a junior system administrator, decided to move some old Zip files to a new server that was purchased to hold old files. The new server is running Windows Server 2003, and NTFS compression is enabled on the storage volumes.

   After carefully calculating how much less space was needed, he created a volume to hold the old files. While moving the files, he ran out of free space. What did John do wrong?

   ❍ **A.** He's not authorized to copy the files.

   ❍ **B.** He doesn't have permissions on the volume.

   ❍ **C.** Zip files can't be compressed.

   ❍ **D.** The Zip files were encrypted.

9. Frank is the system administrator for the State of Kansas. His file servers are running out of space. He needs to free up at least 10% of his volumes for a new application. What technology can he use to get things back into shape?

   ❍ **A.** FAT Quotas

   ❍ **B.** NTFS Screening

   ❍ **C.** File Screening

   ❍ **D.** NTFS Compression

   ❍ **E.** None of the above

Answers to Exam Questions

1. **C.** When a file is moved from an uncompressed volume to a compressed volume, it will be compressed. A file that is moved or copied to another volume will always receive the attributes of the container that it is moved or copied into. See "Copying or Moving Compressed Files or Folders."

2. **C.** When a file is moved from a compressed volume to an uncompressed volume, it will be uncompressed. A file that is moved or copied to another volume will always receive the attributes of the container that it is moved or copied into. See "Copying or Moving Compressed Files or Folders."

3. **E.** By default, no accounts are granted the recovery agent role on standalone workstations and servers. See "EFS Recovery Agents."

4. **A and C.** Only the user who owns the encrypted file and the user account with recovery agent rights are able to read an encrypted file. See "EFS Recovery Agents."

5. **A.** Cipher is the command-line utility that can be used to decrypt files and folders. The other utilities do not exist. See "Encryption Using the Cipher Command."

6. **C.** When a file is moved from a compressed volume to an uncompressed volume, it will be uncompressed. When using the Windows Server 2003 R2 version of compression, the size on disk is listed, not the uncompressed size of the file. Because text files can be compressed up to 75%, it's likely that the 1MB file is actually a lot larger than his 1.44MB floppy disk. See "File Compression in Windows Server 2003."

7. **D.** The most likely cause is that file screening is enabled. Because she's trying to save to her home folder, it's likely that she would have full permissions. See "File Screening with the FSRM."

8. **C.** Zip files are already compressed, so they can't be compressed again. Not having the proper permissions or trying to move an encrypted file would not result in an out-of-space error. See "Configuring NTFS File and Folder Compression."

9. **D.** Because Frank already has a space problem, he needs to use NTFS compression to gain a little breathing room. Although File Screening will provide him some benefits in the future, it won't help him reduce space now if the files are already present on his servers. There is no such thing as FAT Quotas or NTFS screening. See "Configuring NTFS File and Folder Compression," and "File Screening with the FSRM."

Suggested Readings and Resources

1. Boswell, William. *Inside Windows Server 2003*. New Riders, 2003. ISBN 0735711585.

2. File server management dos and don'ts. Techtarget.com. http://searchwinit.techtarget.com/originalContent/0,289142,sid1_gci786333,00.html.

3. File Server Resource Feature Overview. Microsoft Corporation. http://technet2.microsoft.com/WindowsServer/en/Library/3cb63d86-964f-45e8-a76f-1bf72676b0751033.mspx?mfr=true.

4. File Server Resource Manager Step-by-Step Guide. Microsoft Corporation. http://technet2.microsoft.com/WindowsServer/en/Library/b158948f-d5ee-4275-9616-1d38a27013ef1033.mspx?mfr=true.

5. Public/Private Key Pairs Microsoft Corporation. http://windowssdk.msdn.microsoft.com/en-us/library/ms732314.aspx.

6. Windows Server 2003 Deployment Guide. Microsoft Corporation. http://technet2.microsoft.com/ WindowsServer/en/Library/c283b699-6124-4c3a-87ef-865443d7ea 4b1033.mspx?mfr=true.

7. *Windows Server 2003 Resource Kit*. Microsoft Press, 2005. ISBN 0735614717.

CHAPTER FOURTEEN

Monitoring and Optimizing Server Performance

Objectives

This chapter covers the following Microsoft-specified objectives for the "Monitoring and Optimizing Server Performance" section of the Managing and Maintaining a Microsoft Windows Server 2003 Environment exam:

Monitor and analyze events. Tools might include Event Viewer and System Monitor.

▶ The purpose of this objective is to teach you how to use the System Monitor to track the performance of your Windows Server 2003 computer.

Monitor file and print servers. Tools might include Task Manager, Event Viewer, and System Monitor.

▶ **Monitor server hardware for bottlenecks.**

▶ The purpose of this objective is to teach you how to use the various tools available in Windows Server 2003 to assist in identifying performance bottlenecks.

Monitor system performance.

▶ When working in a Windows Server 2003 environment, it is important that you have a thorough understanding of the performance characteristics of your servers. This makes it easier to identify potential problems before they cause outages.

Monitor and optimize a server environment for application performance.

▶ **Monitor memory performance objects.**

▶ **Monitor network performance objects.**

▶ **Monitor process performance objects.**

▶ **Monitor disk performance objects.**

▶ The purpose of this objective is to teach you how to monitor and optimize your Windows 2003 server by monitoring the four basic performance objects.

Outline

Study Strategies

▶ The proper use of the performance-monitoring tools to identify problems with and to optimize server subsystems has always been a major point on Microsoft exams. Expect the Windows Server 2003 exams to continue that tradition. Make sure that you have a complete understanding of the capabilities of both the System Monitor and the Performance Logs and Alerts tool. In addition, you should be very familiar with Task Manager, especially how it is similar to System Monitor and how it is different.

▶ To get real-world experience in your lab environment, get a copy of leakyapp.exe and cpustres.exe. These two applications will simulate memory and CPU loads so that you can get more in-depth experience monitoring the performance counters. Both applications are available in either the Windows 2000 or Windows XP Resource kits.

Introduction

No matter what role your Windows Server 2003 server has in your network, if it does not perform well, you're not doing your job as a system administrator. A good system administrator can use the monitoring and troubleshooting tools included in the operating system to identify and diagnose problems.

This chapter covers the tools, tasks, and procedures required to monitor, collect, and review operational and performance data on a Windows Server 2003 server. This type of information is not only crucial for a job as a system administrator, it is also important for the exam.

Monitoring Performance

Objective:

Monitor system performance.

Monitoring the performance of your Windows Server 2003 servers is an essential task that is often overlooked until something goes wrong. Fortunately Windows Server 2003 comes with a variety of tools that can be used to track the performance of your server and assist in quickly diagnosing any performance-related problems.

Using Task Manager

The Task Manager utility is included in Windows Server 2003 to give administrators a way to monitor and manage the state of currently running applications and processes. Almost a mini performance utility, this tool provides a quick glance into a system's health. In addition, Task Manager provides the administrator with a summarized view of the basic system resources in use.

The Task Manager can be used to monitor the state of active applications, including a real-time view of the system resources assigned to each application. Task Manager also allows you to observe applications that have stopped responding and to terminate them.

Task Manager can be started several ways:

- ▶ Right-click the taskbar and click Task Manager on the pop-up menu.
- ▶ Press Ctrl+Shift+Esc.
- ▶ Press Ctrl+Alt+Del to open the Windows Security dialog box and then click the Task Manager button.

The Task Manager window has five tabs: Applications, Processes, Performance, Networking, and Users. Each tab is discussed in the sections that follow.

Applications Tab

The Applications tab, shown in Figure 14.1, displays a list of the currently active applications, along with their status—either Running or Not Responding. The default status for a program is Running; however, there are times when a program temporarily displays a status of Not Responding. This usually occurs when another program or programs have a higher priority and receive the bulk of the system resources, or if a program is performing a computationally heavy task and is too busy to acknowledge any requests.

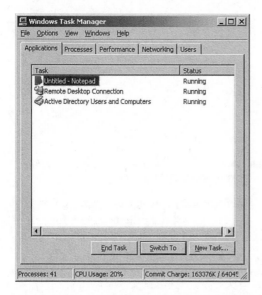

FIGURE 14.1 The Task Manager's Applications tab, showing running applications.

If the application not responding is not automatically restored to Running status after the other applications have completed, you probably need to terminate it manually. This can be accomplished by right-clicking the application and selecting End Task from the pop-up menu or by clicking the End Task button at the bottom of the Task Manager window. Unfortunately, if the application has any files open, your data will not be saved. Task Manager also allows you to terminate running applications.

There are also three methods to start applications using Task Manager:

▶ From the Task Manager window menu bar, select File, New Task (Run).

▶ Select Start, Run, and then type **taskmgr**.

▶ From the Task Manager's Applications tab, click the New Task button in the lower-right corner of the window.

Processes Tab

The Processes tab, shown in Figure 14.2, displays a list of the currently active processes, along with the resources they are using. Even on a system that displays few applications running, there will always be multiple processes running in the background.

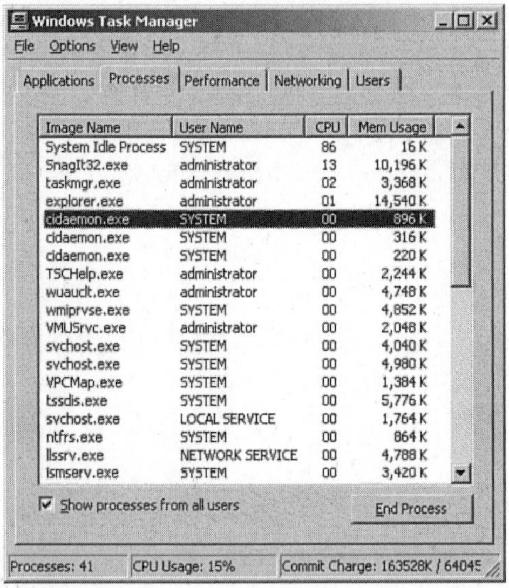

FIGURE 14.2 The Task Manager's Processes tab, showing processes sorted by CPU time.

There are two reasons for this. First, operating system processes won't be displayed on the Applications tab. The second reason is that if you start an application called go.exe, for example, odds are the application will start multiple background processes. This is where the Processes tab can be pretty handy because the main application might not be using a lot of resources, but one of the background processes could be maxing out the CPU!

The default view shows the processes running for the currently logged-on user, but the processes for all users can be shown by selecting the Show Processes from All Users check box in the lower-left corner of the dialog box. The default resources displayed are CPU % (abbreviated as CPU) and Memory Usage. However, additional items, such as Page Faults, I/O Writes, and Peak Memory Usage, can be added by selecting View, Set Columns from the Task Manager menu bar.

Using the Processes tab, you can immediately see which processes are using the majority of the system resources. In the default view, you can sort the processes by name (Image Name), username, CPU percentage used (CPU), or memory used (Mem Usage).

For example, to sort the processes by the amount of CPU percentage used, click the CPU heading twice. This allows you to identify a process that is hogging the resources and starving the other processes. This can indicate a process that is having a problem and needs to either be terminated or set to a lower priority. Under normal conditions, the System Idle Process should have the highest percentage in the CPU column.

Understanding Priority

Windows Server 2003 provides a fast, reliable, multitasking environment that supports preemptive multitasking and the execution of applications in separate address spaces. In preemptive multitasking, the operating system controls which application has access to the CPU and for how long. The operating system is free to switch resources at any time to an application with a higher priority. This also allows the operating system to revoke resources from a defective or a poorly designed program that tries to dominate resources.

Windows Server 2003 supports multiple units of execution for a single process, using a process called *multithreading*. In a multithreaded environment, a process can be broken up into subtasks, called *threads*, which can execute independently of the main process. This allows a program to perform multiple tasks simultaneously instead of sequentially. For example, when you are using Microsoft Outlook, you can read messages or create a new message while downloading or sending messages. Multithreading means one process does not have to wait for another to finish.

In a preemptive multitasking system, individual tasks cannot dictate how long they use the system resources. This means that some type of priority system is necessary to ensure that critical tasks get a larger share of the processor's time. The priority system is part of the operating system, but the individual tasks can tell the OS what priority they need. This works well in theory, but there are always situations in which a system might get loaded with high-priority tasks that keep the low-priority tasks from getting any system resources at all.

Windows Server 2003 uses a dynamic priority system that allows it to adjust the priority of tasks to reflect constantly changing system conditions. For example, if a low-priority task is passed over in favor of a high-priority task, Windows Server 2003 increases the priority of the low-priority task until it gets some system resources. After a high-priority task runs for a while, Windows Server 2003 lowers that task's priority. The dynamic priority system ensures that some tasks get more system resources than others and that every task gets at least some system resources.

A *foreground application* is one that is made active by selecting it on the Windows Server 2003 desktop, thus bringing it to the foreground. All other applications running are then termed *background applications*, with respect to the foreground application. By default, Windows Server 2003 assigns more resources and a higher priority to a background application than to foreground applications in the same priority class. This is, of course, because Windows Server 2003 is a server operating system, and servers typically host background operations such as file sharing and print services.

Windows Server 2003 uses priority to allocate processor time in small chunks to applications. This is called *time slicing*. Windows Server 2003 allocates multiple, short, variable-length time slices to foreground applications, while allocating longer, fixed-length, but less-frequent time slices to background applications or services.

To change the default behavior, open the System applet in the Control Panel (see Figure 14.3). From the Advanced tab, click the Settings button in the Performance area. From the Performance Options dialog box, you can select the Advanced tab to optimize the responsiveness of your system. Two choices are available: Programs and Background Services. The default is Background Services, in which the server assigns more resources to applications running in background sessions, such as mail or database servers. This results in a more responsive system, and it's recommended for servers that are not running foreground applications.

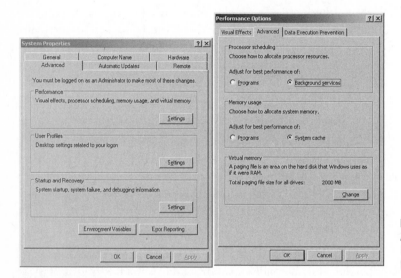

FIGURE 14.3 The Advanced tab of System Properties, showing performance options.

NOTE

Processor Scheduling   On a server, there is rarely a good reason to change the configuration to adjust performance for programs, except on Terminal Servers running in Application mode.

Windows Server 2003 further subdivides processing time to applications using different classes of priority levels. Priority levels are assigned numbers from 0 to 31. Applications and noncritical operating system functions are assigned levels of 0 to 15, whereas real-time functions, such as the operating system kernel, are assigned levels of 16 to 31. The normal base priority is 8.

By default, priority levels are not displayed in the Task Manager window. To configure Task Manager to display the priority level of running applications, perform the procedure outlined in Step by Step 14.1.

STEP BY STEP

14.1 Configuring Task Manager to display priority levels

1. Right-click the taskbar and then click Task Manager in the pop-up menu.

2. From the Task Manager window, select the Processes tab.

3. On the Task Manager system menu, select View, Select Columns. This opens the Select Columns dialog box shown in Figure 14.4.

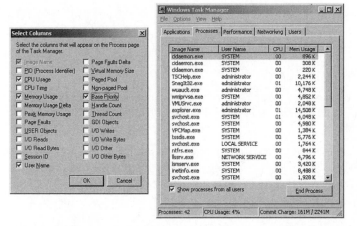

FIGURE 14.4 The Select Columns dialog box allows you to select the information you want displayed on the Processes tab of Task Manager.

4. Click the Base Priority check box shown in Figure 14.4. Click OK to save. The result is shown in Figure 14.5.

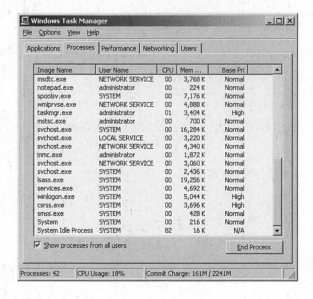

Image Name	User Name	CPU	Mem ...	Base Pri
msdtc.exe	NETWORK SERVICE	00	3,768 K	Normal
notepad.exe	administrator	00	224 K	Normal
spoolsv.exe	SYSTEM	00	7,176 K	Normal
wmiprvse.exe	NETWORK SERVICE	00	4,888 K	Normal
taskmgr.exe	administrator	01	3,404 K	High
mstsc.exe	administrator	00	700 K	Normal
svchost.exe	SYSTEM	00	16,284 K	Normal
svchost.exe	LOCAL SERVICE	00	3,220 K	Normal
svchost.exe	NETWORK SERVICE	00	4,340 K	Normal
mmc.exe	administrator	00	1,872 K	Normal
svchost.exe	NETWORK SERVICE	00	3,060 K	Normal
svchost.exe	SYSTEM	00	2,436 K	Normal
lsass.exe	SYSTEM	00	19,256 K	Normal
services.exe	SYSTEM	00	4,692 K	Normal
winlogon.exe	SYSTEM	00	5,044 K	High
csrss.exe	SYSTEM	00	3,696 K	High
smss.exe	SYSTEM	00	428 K	Normal
System	SYSTEM	00	216 K	Normal
System Idle Process	SYSTEM	82	16 K	N/A

☑ Show processes from all users   End Process

Processes: 42   CPU Usage: 18%   Commit Charge: 161M / 2241M

FIGURE 14.5 Task Manager reconfigured to display the priority of all processes.

If a process is running at a low priority, and a real-time process is started, the real-time process receives more system resources than the process running at low priority. This can sometimes cause the application that the lower-priority process is controlled by to show a status of Not Responding on the Task Manager's Applications tab.

To keep a real-time process from starving a lower-priority process, you can manually set the priority of the lower-priority process to a higher value.

To set a process to a higher priority, perform the procedure outlined in Step by Step 14.2.

STEP BY STEP

14.2 Setting a process to a higher priority

1. Right-click the taskbar and then click Task Manager in the pop-up menu.

2. From the Task Manager window, select the Processes tab.

3. On the Task Manager system menu, right-click the process that you want to change the priority of (in this case, notepad.exe) and select Set Priority from the pop-up menu, as shown in Figure 14.6.

4. After selecting a priority, you receive the warning message shown in Figure 14.7. Click Yes if you're sure that this is what you want to do.

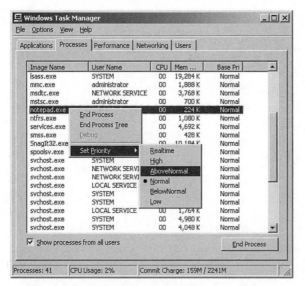

FIGURE 14.6   Select the desired priority from the pop-up menu. Only administrators can set a process to Realtime.

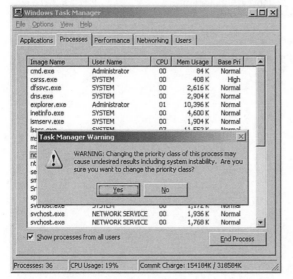

FIGURE 14.7   Be sure you understand the implications of changing priorities of running processes before you select Yes.

5. As shown in Figure 14.8, the priority of the process has been successfully changed.

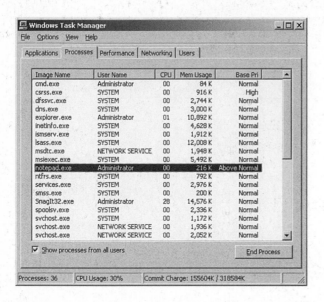

FIGURE 14.8 The selected process now is running at Above Normal priority.

As you might have noticed in the previous exercise, Task Manager does not allow you to set a process to a specific number: It allows you to set only priority classes. The priority classes are as follows:

▶ *Realtime*—Priority 24

▶ *High*—Priority 13

▶ *AboveNormal*—Priority 9

▶ *Normal*—Priority 8

▶ *BelowNormal*—Priority 7

▶ *Low*—Priority 4

Using Task Manager to tune an application in this manner is a temporary fix because after you reboot your system or stop and start the application, you lose the priority properties.

EXAM ALERT

Real-Time Rights   To use the Realtime option, you must be logged on as a user with Administrator rights. It is important to know this for the exam.

Normally, there should be no need to change the priority of processes. However, suppose you have a database query process that cannot complete because the process is not getting enough CPU time. In this case, you can temporarily change the priority of the process to High to enable the task to complete successfully. Be warned that if you run applications at High priority, this can slow overall performance because other applications get less I/O time.

> **CAUTION**
>
> **Be Careful with Realtime** Changing the base priority of an application to Realtime makes the priority of the application higher than the process that monitors and responds to keyboard input. If the process you set to Realtime completes successfully, fine. However, if it requires any input for processing or recovery, your only option is to reboot the system.

In some situations, a process must be terminated. You can either terminate a specific process or terminate the process and all other processes linked to it. This is accomplished by right-clicking the process entry in the Processes tab of the Task Manager and selecting End Process to terminate a specific process or by selecting End Process Tree to terminate that process and any other processes it has started. For example, if you terminate the process for a word processing program, you can select End Process Tree to additionally terminate the spell checker and grammar processes started by the word processor process.

> **EXAM ALERT**
>
> **Expect Process-Related Questions** Not all processes can be terminated using Task Manager. The Kill utility, included in the Windows Server 2003 Resource Kit, terminates most processes, including services or system processes. Use it very carefully because terminating system processes can make your server unstable.

On a multiprocessor server, an additional menu item called Set Affinity appears on the pop-up menu on the Processes tab. The Set Affinity command allows you to limit a process to a specific CPU.

To set a process to use a specific CPU, perform the procedure outlined in Step by Step 14.3.

STEP BY STEP

14.3 Setting processor affinity

1. Right-click the taskbar and then click Task Manager in the pop-up menu.

2. From the Task Manager window, select the Processes tab.

3. On the Task Manager system menu, right-click the process that you want to assign to a specific processor and select Set Affinity from the pop-up menu.

4. From the Processor Affinity dialog box shown in Figure 14.9, select the processor you want to run the process on. Click OK to save.

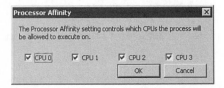

FIGURE 14.9 Make sure you understand the implications of setting processor affinity before you select OK.

> **CAUTION**
>
> **Processor Affinity** The processor affinity option should be used with care because it could potentially decrease the performance of the process. This can occur in a situation where the processor that you have selected starts to get overloaded. Unlike other processes that can use time slices from any processor, your process is locked on to the overloaded processor.

Performance Tab

The Performance tab, shown in Figure 14.10, displays the CPU and memory usage for your server. The display includes graphs of the current usage, plus additional histograms showing recent usage. Below the graphs are numerical statistics for the CPU and memory usage.

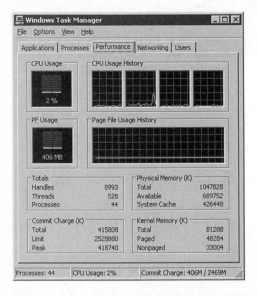

FIGURE 14.10 The Task Manager's Performance tab, showing server-usage statistics on a multi-processor system.

The information shown here can give you a quick overview of the performance characteristics of your server. Any abnormalities displayed here indicate that you should investigate further using some of the other Windows Server 2003 utilities.

Networking Tab

The Networking tab is displayed if you have a NIC installed. The default view displays the state, link speed, and network utilization of each NIC, as shown in Figure 14.11.

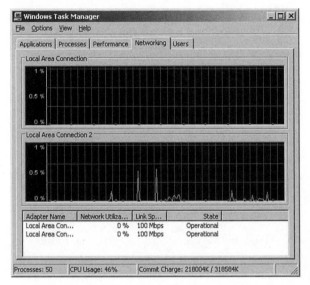

FIGURE 14.11 The Task Manager's Networking tab, showing network-utilization statistics.

The information available on the Networking tab gives you an overview of the performance of your network connections. At a glance, you can see what connections are active, how much bandwidth is being consumed, and which connection is seeing the most traffic. This information can be helpful in your initial problem determination because you can immediately see how your network connections are performing.

As with the other tabs in Task Manager, a multitude of additional items can be displayed. For a complete listing, from the System menu click View, Select Columns.

Users Tab

The Users tab displays the users currently logged on to your server. This includes users logged on to the console, users connected via the Remote Desktop Protocol (RDP) client in Remote Administration mode, and Terminal Services users connected in Application mode. Each session is assigned a session ID, with session 0 always representing the console session. In addition to the username session ID and session type, the status of the session and the name of the client computer are displayed, as shown in Figure 14.12.

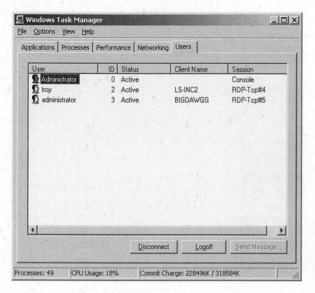

FIGURE 14.12 The Task Manager's Users tab, showing the users who are logged on to the server. You have the option to log off, disconnect, or send messages to the user sessions.

It is important to remember that if your Windows Server 2003 server is not running in Terminal Services Application mode, only three connections are allowed into your server. Two of these are remote administrative sessions, and the third is the console session, which can be either local or connected via RDP. If an administrator logs on to one of the sessions, and then goes off to lunch (or otherwise keeps the session active), other administrators are prevented from connecting to that server. From this interface, you have the option to send the administrator a message asking him to log off. Alternatively, if he is away from his workstation, you can either log him off or disconnect his session.

Monitoring and Optimizing a Server Environment for Application Performance

Objective:

Monitor file and print servers. Tools might include Task Manager, Event Viewer, and System Monitor.

▶ Monitor server hardware for bottlenecks.

In Windows Server 2003, Microsoft has included the Configure Your Server Wizard, which tunes your server for specific roles on your network. Even though Microsoft has done a fairly good job with defining the server roles and configuring the performance options for each role, you can always do better. In this section, we examine the tools and utilities you can use to optimize your server's performance.

EXAM ALERT

Configure Your Server Wizard The Configure Your Server Wizard is not included in the Windows Server 2003 Web Edition operating system, which is logical because that version is intended to be used only for web servers, and it comes optimized for that role out of the box. As an administrator, you should be familiar with the capabilities of all versions of Windows Server 2003 for the exam.

Monitoring System Resources

Although Task Manager can give you a quick overview of system performance, there are situations in which a more thorough investigation is needed. This is where the Performance tool comes in handy. The Performance tool is actually made up of two separate Microsoft Management Console (MMC) snap-ins: System Monitor and Performance Logs and Alerts.

The Performance tool is started by following the procedure outlined in Step by Step 14.4.

STEP BY STEP

14.4 Starting the Performance Tool in System Monitor view

1. From the Start menu, click Start, All Programs, Administrative Tools, Performance.

2. As shown in Figure 14.13, the Performance tool opens with the System Monitor view displayed.

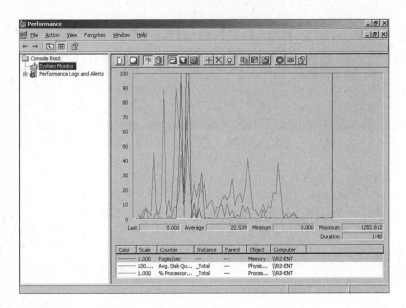

FIGURE 14.13 The Windows Server 2003 Performance tool showing the System Monitor view.

System Monitor

The System Monitor snap-in allows you to view real-time performance data contained in the counters from your domain controllers, member servers, or workstations on your network. In addition, System Monitor allows you to review performance data that is stored in a log file created with the Performance Logs and Alerts snap-in.

Windows Server 2003 is a modular, object-oriented operating system. Each subsystem within Windows Server 2003 is an object. For example, the CPU is an object, the memory is an object, the storage subsystem is an object, and so on. As your computer performs various tasks, each of these objects generates performance data.

Each object has several monitoring functions called *counters*. Each counter offers insight into a different aspect or function of the object. For example, the memory object has counters that measure % Committed Bytes in Use, Available Bytes, Page Faults/sec, and more. System Monitor takes the readings from these counters and presents the information to you in a human-readable format (numbers or graphs). Each counter is displayed as a colored line. Multiple counters from the same system or from remote systems can be viewed simultaneously.

In addition, objects can be separated by instance. *Instance* is the terminology used to refer to multiple occurrences of the same type of object, such as in a multiprocessor server. A separate instance exists for each processor.

By default, System Monitor is started with the following counters displayed:

▶ Memory: Pages per Second

▶ Physical Disk: Average Disk Queue Length

▶ Processor: % Processor Time

Numerous other counters can be added to give you a more thorough view of your server's performance. To add additional counters to be monitored, perform the procedure outlined in Step by Step 14.5.

STEP BY STEP

14.5 Adding additional performance counters

1. From the Start menu, click Start, All Programs, Administrative Tools, Performance.

2. The Performance tool opens with the System Monitor view displayed. As shown in Figure 14.14, right-click anywhere on the graph in the System Monitor view. Select Add Counters from the pop-up menu.

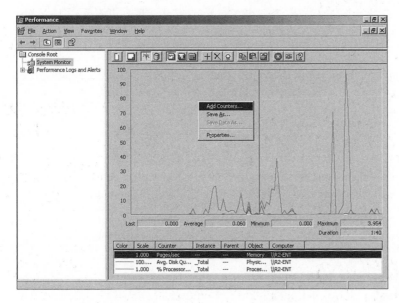

FIGURE 14.14 Select Add Counters from the pop-up menu or click the + icon in the toolbar.

3. From the Add Counters dialog box shown in Figure 14.15, select Memory from the Performance Object drop-down list and then select Pages/sec from the Select Counters from List area.

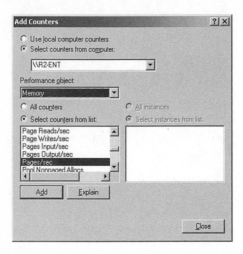

FIGURE 14.15 Select the desired Performance object and then select the counters and instance to monitor. Clicking the Explain button provides an explanation of what each counter records.

4. Click the Add button to add the object and counter to the view. Repeat for any additional counters as desired. Then click the Close button to save.

As you saw in this Step by Step procedure, the Add Counters dialog box allows you to make choices from several areas to customize your monitoring needs. The choices found on this dialog box are as follows:

▶ *Computer*—This option allows you to select whether to add counters from the local computer or any remote computer on your network. You add remote computers using their Universal Naming Convention (UNC) computer name.

▶ *Performance Object*—This is a drop-down list that displays all the objects available for monitoring.

▶ *Counters*—This option allows you to select either all counters or individual counters from a list. Hold down the Shift or Ctrl key and click to select multiple items.

▶ *Instance*—If an object has multiple instances (for example, your server might have multiple network cards), you can select each individual instance or all instances.

After selecting each counter, click the Add button to add the counter to the System Monitor display. For a description of each counter, highlight the counter and click the Explain button. When you're finished, click the Close button.

The number of objects available for monitoring varies by system. Most server services and applications, such as DNS, DHCP, and mail servers, install their own counters that can be used to monitor the performance of those functions.

Each counter can be displayed as a colored line in one of the graph views. Multiple counters from the same system or from remote systems can be viewed simultaneously. Figure 14.16 shows you an example of what one of the graph views, of which there are several, may look like on your system.

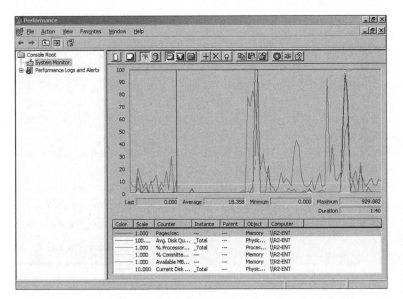

FIGURE 14.16 The Windows Server 2003 System Monitor showing several additional server-usage counters.

Of all the items you can monitor on a typical server, here are the objects you need to monitor closely for performance issues:

- ▶ Memory
- ▶ Processor
- ▶ Physical disk
- ▶ Network

These counters provide instant insight into the overall performance on a system. When these counters get too high, it's a good indication that you need to upgrade the system or segment the network.

The Performance Logs and Alerts Snap-In

Although System Monitor provides far more system-monitoring information than Task Manager, it still provides only a snapshot view of system performance. To perform a more thorough evaluation of system performance, you need to view the system statistics over a period of time. You can find these statistics in the Performance Logs and Alerts tool, located under System Monitor in the Performance tool MMC. The following two subsections detail the logging and alert features you can use to capture performance data over an extended time period.

Performance Logs

The Performance Logs and Alerts MMC snap-in allows you to log performance data over a period of time and save it to a log file for later viewing. Two logging options are available: Counter Logs and Trace Logs. Counter logs allow you to record data about hardware usage and the activity of system services from local or remote computers. You can configure logging to occur manually or automatically based on a defined schedule. Trace logs record data as certain activity, such as disk I/O or a page fault, occurs. When the event occurs, the provider sends the data to the log service.

EXAM ALERT

Trace Logs   Trace logs are commonly used for developers to trace an application's interaction with the operating system. It will probably not be covered on the exam.

The snap-in allows you to save log data in the following file formats:

- *Text file (CSV)*—Comma-delimited format, for import into spreadsheet or database programs.

- *Text file (TSV)*—Tab-delimited format, for import into spreadsheet or database programs.

- *Binary file*—This is the default for use with the System Monitor snap-in. Data is logged into this file until it reaches the maximum limit. The default maximum file size is 1MB, but this can be changed when you configure settings for the file from the Log Files tab of the Log Properties dialog box by clicking the Configure button.

- *Binary circular file*—Data is logged into this file until it reaches the maximum limit. Then the file is overwritten, starting at the beginning of the file. The default maximum file size is 1MB, but this can be changed when you configure settings for the file from the Log Files tab of the Log Properties dialog box by clicking the Configure button.

- *SQL*—Data is logged directly into an existing SQL database.

Because the data is available in so many common formats, you have the option of analyzing the data using the default Microsoft tools or importing it into the tool of your choice.

> **NOTE**
>
> **Establishing a Baseline**   You should take a measurement of your system during its normal operation to establish a baseline. This baseline provides something to compare counters to when the system experiences problems. A baseline comparison provides a quick way to pinpoint problem areas.

The Performance utility allows you to log on an object basis and on a counter basis. This means you can configure a log to record all the data for an object instead of using individual counters. Therefore, after a log file is recorded, you can select any counter from an object to examine. After you determine what to record, you need to determine two time-related issues: the measurement interval and the length of time to record the log file. These issues are detailed as follows:

- ▶ The measurement interval determines how often a performance reading is taken. Too short an interval can produce spurious results and can cause an additional workload on your system. Too long an interval might hide performance changes. Although most readings are insignificant, frequent readings can cause significant performance degradations.

- ▶ The length of time over which a log file is recorded should be long enough to capture all the normal operational activities. This typically means recording a log file for at least a week. A shorter time period might not offer you a complete picture of your system's normal weekly performance.

The sample log is defined with the following basic counters:

- ▶ Memory: Pages per Second
- ▶ Physical Disk: Average Disk Queue Length
- ▶ Processor: % Processor Time

Note that these are the same counters that appear in the initial System Monitor view. You can create your own logs with the counters you specify.

To create a new counter log, perform the procedure outlined in Step by Step 14.6.

STEP BY STEP

14.6 Creating a new counter log

1. From the Start menu, click Start, All Programs, Administrative Tools, Performance.

2. The Performance tool opens with the System Monitor view displayed. Right-click Counter Logs under Performance Logs and Alerts in the left pane and then select New Log Settings from the pop-up menu (see Figure 14.17).

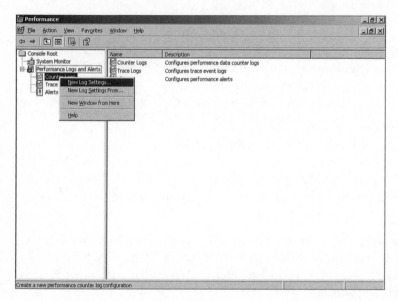

FIGURE 14.17 Right-click Counter Logs and then select New Log Settings from the pop-up menu.

3. In the New Log Settings dialog box, enter the name for the new log and then click OK.

4. In the Log Properties dialog box, shown in Figure 14.18, click the Add Objects button or the Add Counters button to add the desired objects and counters to the log. Repeat this step for any additional counters desired. Notice that an option is available that allows you to run the logs using a different user ID and password.

5. Click the Log Files tab.

6. On the Log Files tab, enter the desired log file name, type, and location, if the defaults are not what you want. Change the maximum log file size if desired (see Figure 14.19).

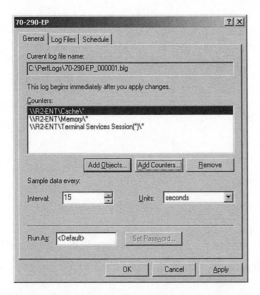

FIGURE 14.18 Adding counters and objects to the new log. The procedure is similar to adding counters in System Monitor.

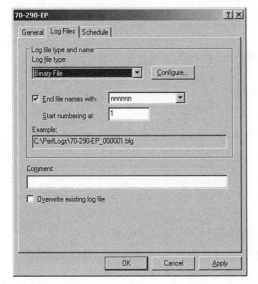

FIGURE 14.19 The Log Files tab showing counter log file configuration.

7. Click the Schedule tab. On the Schedule tab, you can select the start and stop times for logging or select to manually start and stop the log (see Figure 14.20).

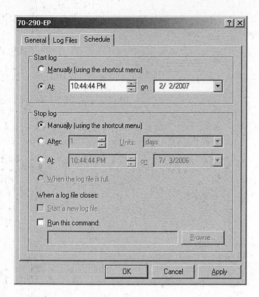

FIGURE 14.20   The Schedule tab showing the counter log schedule.

8. Click OK to save the log.

If you selected to manually start the counter log, you can start it by right-clicking the log entry in the right pane of the Performance Logs and Alerts snap-in and selecting Start. The icon for the log is *green* when running and *red* when stopped.

After you have recorded data in your log file, you can view it within System Monitor. To open your log file, use the procedure outlined in Step by Step 14.7.

STEP BY STEP

14.7 Viewing counter logs

1. From the Start menu, click Start, All Programs, Administrative Tools, Performance.

2. The Performance tool opens with the System Monitor view displayed. Right-click anywhere in the right pane and select Properties from the pop-up menu.

3. In the System Monitor Properties dialog box, select the Source tab. On the Source tab, shown in Figure 14.21, select the Log Files option button and then click the Add button to browse for the log file. After locating the file, click the Open button.

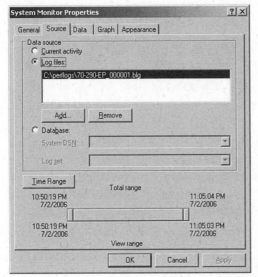

FIGURE 14.21 The System Monitor Properties dialog box showing the Source tab.

4. In the System Monitor Properties dialog box, click the Time Range button to adjust the time window that you want to view within the log file. Click OK when finished.

A *time window* is a selected block of time from a log file. When a log file is used as the source of data, the System Monitor utility automatically sets every data point within the log file as active—that is, it views the data from the start to the end of the log file. Through the use of a time window, you can shorten or otherwise alter the data in use. The Source tab from the Log Properties dialog box reveals the Time Range settings. From this dialog box, you can slide the start and end points manually to select your start or stop points. Only the data in the selected time frame (between the start and stop points and shaded gray) is used by the System Monitor utility.

While a log is being recorded, don't try to view the log file from the same instance of the Performance utility that is performing the logging. If you need to view the contents of the open log file, use another instance of the Performance utility. You can view all data points up to the point when you opened the log file, and new data continues to be recorded into the file by the first instance of the Performance utility.

After a log file is recorded, you can append and resample the file to combine multiple files or to remove spurious readings. To record new data into an existing log file, just specify the path to the existing file in the Log Options dialog box.

The only limitation to log file recording is the free disk space on the destination drive; if your hard disk is full, the log file cannot record unless it is emptied or deleted.

Naming Log Files

You should always name your log files with as much description as possible within the 255-character file-name limitation. Try to include the name of the system, the start and end date/time, and the object names recorded. A properly labeled log file is easy to use and locate.

Trace Logs

The second type of logs is trace logs. Trace logs are used to track lower level events supplied by data providers that are part of the .NET Framework. Trace logs are set up exactly like counter logs, except they will have the extension `.etl`. A major difference between trace and counter logs is that while counter logs take samples, trace logs track events continuously. Trace logs are used by developers and require special software tools to read them. You can find out more about trace logs at http://msdn.microsoft.com.

Performance Alerts

The Alerts container is used to define threshold alerts. These can be used with real-time measurements or with historical log files. An alert is issued when a specific counter crosses a defined threshold value. When this occurs, a trigger event is initiated.

Creating an alert is similar to configuring a counter log. To create an alert, perform the procedure outlined in Step by Step 14.8.

STEP BY STEP

14.8 Creating an alert

1. From the Start menu, click Start, All Programs, Administrative Tools, Performance.

2. The Performance tool opens with the System Monitor view displayed. Right-click the Alerts entry under Performance Logs and Alerts in the left pane of the snap-in and select New Alert Settings from the pop-up menu.

3. In the New Alert Settings dialog box, enter the name for the new alert.

4. In the Alert Properties dialog box, shown in Figure 14.22, click the Add button to add additional objects and counters or click the Remove button if the wrong counters have been selected.

5. After you have selected the desired counters to monitor, set the alert condition using the Alert Value drop-down field. Notice that an option is available that allows you to monitor the alerts using a different user ID and password.

6. If you click the Action tab, shown in Figure 14.23, you can select the action to take when the threshold is reached.

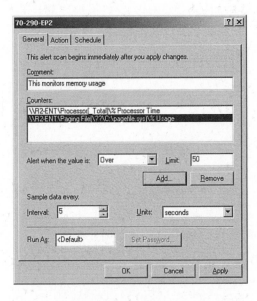

FIGURE 14.22 Add or remove counters.

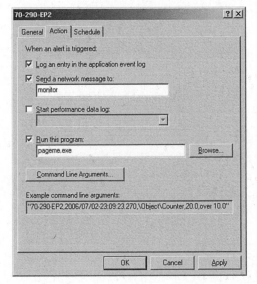

FIGURE 14.23 Alert properties showing the Action tab.

7. Click the Schedule tab. On the Schedule tab, you can select the start and stop times for monitoring or select to manually start and stop the log, as shown in Figure 14.24.

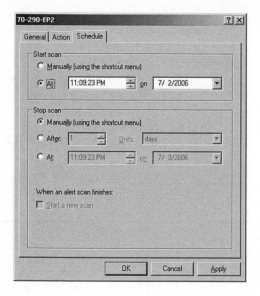

FIGURE 14.24 Showing the alerts log schedule.

8. Click OK to save the log.

You can select several actions to be performed when an alert threshold is reached, as follows:

▶ *Log an Entry in the Application Event Log*—If a threshold is reached, Windows Server 2003 creates an entry in this log, and you can view it in the application event log found in the Event Viewer.

▶ *Send a Network Message To*—This allows you to send a message to a user via the Messenger service.

▶ *Start Performance Data Log*—This starts logging to a predefined counter log. This is useful if you are trying to see what happens to system performance when a specific event occurs.

▶ *Run This Program*—This can be any program that can be run from a command line. For example, it might be a program that performs some type of system maintenance, such as compressing files.

Alerts are most often used to monitor systems in real time. You can set an alert to notify you when a specific event occurs. Some of the conditions that you might want to configure an alert for are low disk space, swap file usage, and task queues for network cards and CPUs. Any of these items can point to a current or potential system problem.

Optimizing System Resources

Objective:
Monitor and optimize a server environment for application performance.

- ▶ Monitor memory performance objects.

- ▶ Monitor network performance objects.

- ▶ Monitor process performance objects.

- ▶ Monitor disk performance objects.

Before you can optimize a server, you must understand its characteristics, including how it operates under a normal load and what areas are stressed when the load increases. This has a lot to do with the application type and load of the server. For example, a web server reacts differently to a load condition than a server that is hosting Terminal Services.

The first step in optimization should be to establish a *baseline*. To establish a baseline for a server, you should log performance data for the server when it is under a normal load for an established period of time. You typically want to log at least a day, and sometimes even a week or more. This allows you to observe the various components of your server under normal load and stress circumstances. You should have a large enough sample so that you can observe all the highs and lows and determine what figures are averages for your server.

After you establish this baseline, the next step is to observe your server under load and to identify any components that are limiting the overall performance of your server. The main four components that cause the majority of the bottlenecks in a server are the memory, disk, processor, and network interface. The following four subsections discuss optimizing resources associated with these vital server objects.

Monitoring Memory Performance Objects

The Windows Server 2003 memory system uses a combination of physical memory and a swap file stored on the hard disk to provide space for the applications to run. Data in memory is written to the swap file through a process called *paging*. Paging is used to increase the amount of memory available to applications. Windows Server 2003 performs paging to make it seem to applications that the computer has more physical memory than is installed. The amount of virtual memory available on a computer is equal to its physical memory plus whatever hard disk space is configured for use as paging files.

Because accessing data from a hard disk is many times slower than accessing it from memory, you want to minimize the frequency with which the server has to swap data to the hard drive. This can usually be accomplished simply by adding more physical memory.

Here are some counters to watch to monitor memory performance:

▶ *Memory: Pages Input/sec*—When this counter remains at a low value (2 or less), it indicates that all operations are occurring within physical RAM. This means that paging is not occurring and therefore is not the cause of the performance degradation.

▶ *Memory: Cache Faults/sec*—Indicates how frequently the system is unable to locate data in the cache and must search for it on disk. If this number grows steadily over time, your system is headed into constant thrashing. This means every bit of information required by the system must be retrieved directly from the disk. This condition usually indicates an insufficient amount of RAM on your system. However, it can also be caused by running a combination of applications, such as a read-intensive application (typically a database that is performing a large number of queries) at the same time as an application that is using an excessive amount of memory. In this case, you can either schedule the applications to not run at the same time or move one of them to another system.

▶ *Memory: Page Faults/sec*—Similar to Cache Faults/sec, except that it also measures faults when a requested memory page is in use by another application. If this counter averages above 200 for low-end systems or above 600 for high-end systems, excess paging is occurring.

▶ *Memory: Available Bytes*—Indicates the amount of free memory available for use. If this number is less than 4MB, you do not have sufficient RAM on your system, so the system performs excessive paging.

▶ *Paging File: % Usage Peak*—Indicates the level of paging file usage. If this number nears 100% during normal operations, the maximum size of your paging file is too small, and you probably need more RAM. If you have multiple drives with multiple paging files, be sure to view the Total instance of this counter.

Monitoring Disk Performance Objects

The disk subsystem can be a bottleneck, either directly or indirectly. If the access speed of the disk is slow, it negatively affects the load time of applications and the read and write time of application data. In addition, because Windows Server 2003 relies on virtual memory, a slow disk subsystem indirectly affects memory performance.

> **NOTE**
>
> **No More DISKPERF**   In previous versions of Windows, you were required to use the DISKPERF utility to enable the disk counters. Windows Server 2003 enables the counters by default.

Here are some key performance counters for the disk subsystem:

- *PhysicalDisk: Avg. Disk Queue Length*—Tracks the number of system requests waiting for disk access. The number of queued requests should not exceed the number of spindles in use plus 2. Most drives have only a single spindle, but RAID arrays have more (and Performance Monitor views RAID arrays as a single logical drive). A large number of waiting items indicates that a drive or an array is not operating fast enough to support the system's demands for input and output. When this occurs, you need a faster drive system.

- *PhysicalDisk: % Disk Time*—Represents the percentage of time that the disk is actively handling read and write requests. It is not uncommon for this counter to regularly hit 100% on active servers. Sustained percentages of 90% or better, however, might indicate that a storage device is too slow. This usually is true when its Avg. Disk Queue Length counter is constantly above 2.

- *PhysicalDisk: Avg. Disk sec/Transfer*—Indicates the average time in seconds of a disk transfer.

> **NOTE**
>
> **Keep Your Data Accurate**   When you're recording a log file for the Disk objects, be sure not to record the file to the same drive being measured. You are not recording accurate values if you do, because the act of reading the object and writing to the drive adds a significant amount of workload.

Monitoring Process Performance Objects

The processor is the heart of your server. Most operations in the server are controlled either directly or indirectly by the processor. Most processor bottlenecks are caused by multiple processes running at the same time, requiring more cycles than the processor can deliver efficiently. This can be alleviated by replacing the processor with a faster model or by adding an additional processor in a multiprocessor-capable server.

To identify problems with the processor, monitor the following counters:

▶ *Processor: % Processor Time*—Indicates the amount of time the CPU spends on non-idle work. It's common for this counter to reach 100% during application launches or kernel-intensive operations (such as SAM synchronization). If this counter remains above 80% for an extended period, you should suspect a CPU bottleneck. (There will be an instance of this counter for each processor in a multiprocessor system.)

▶ *Processor: % Total Processor Time*—Applies only to multiprocessor systems. This counter should be used the same way as the single CPU counter. If any value remains consistently higher than 80%, at least one of your CPUs is a bottleneck.

▶ *System: Processor Queue Length*—Indicates the number of threads waiting for processor time. A sustained value of 2 or higher for this counter indicates processor congestion. This counter is a snapshot of the time of measurement, not an average value over time.

Monitoring Network Performance Objects

Although not as common as processor, disk, or memory bottlenecks, thanks to the preponderance of high-performance 100MB and even 1,000MB NICs, there are occasions when the network card is a bottleneck. This is most likely to occur on web servers or terminal servers.

To identify performance problems with the network interface, monitor the following counters:

▶ *Network Interface: Bytes Total/sec*—Indicates the rate at which data is sent to and received by a NIC (including framing characters). Compare this value with the expected capacity of the device. If the highest observed average is less than 75% of the expected value, communication errors or slowdowns might be occurring that limit the NIC's rated speed.

▶ *Network Interface: Current Bandwidth*—Estimates a NIC's current bandwidth, measured in bits per second (bps). This counter is useful only for NICs with variable bandwidth.

▶ *Network Interface: Output Queue Length*—Indicates the number of packets waiting to be transmitted by a NIC. If this averages above 2, you are experiencing delays.

▶ *Network Interface: Packets/sec*—Indicates the number of packets handled by a NIC. Watch this counter over a long interval of constant or normal activity. Sharp declines that occur while the queue length remains nonzero can indicate protocol-related or NIC-related problems.

Other network-related counters that may be worth monitoring include protocol-specific objects, such as ICMP, IP, TCP, and UDP.

Make sure you understand the common performance counters and their meanings. In addition, know what ranges are normal and what values indicate that a specific hardware component needs to be upgraded.

Monitoring Server Hardware for Bottlenecks

Objective:

Monitor file and print servers. Tools might include Task Manager, Event Viewer, and System Monitor.

▶ Monitor server hardware for bottlenecks.

As you know, a *bottleneck* is a component in a computer system that is preventing some other part of the system from operating at its optimum performance level. However, a bottleneck does not necessarily refer to components operating at 100% of their capability. It is possible for components operating at only 60% to slow down other components. Bottlenecks can never be fully eliminated; there *always* is a slowest or limiting component. The goal of removing bottlenecks is to attempt to make the user the most significant bottleneck rather than having a computer component as the bottleneck. This way, the system is faster than its user.

Bottleneck discovery and elimination is not an exact science. In fact, it's not even an automated process. Through a comparison of a baseline and current or recorded activity, you need to decipher the clues that might indicate a bottleneck. The objects and counters discussed in the previous sections of this chapter are a good start to monitor for conditions that can indicate a bottleneck.

Every system is different. You need to use the methods discussed in this chapter and learn to apply them to your own unique situation. A measurement value that indicates a bottleneck on one system might not be a bottleneck on another. Typically, you want to look for areas of your computer that are operating outside of your normal baseline measurements or that are affecting other components adversely. After you identify a trouble spot, you need to take action through software configuration or hardware replacement to improve the performance of the suspect area. Don't just look for low-throughput measurements. Table 14.1 shows some common counters and the settings that indicate there might be a potential problem.

TABLE 14.1   Common Performance Indicators

Component	Counter	Measurement
Memory	Pages Input/sec	A measure of 2 or more indicates that paging is occurring.
Memory	Available Bytes	Less than 4MB indicates that you need to increase RAM.
Paging File	% Usage Peak	A measure of 80% or more indicates that you need to increase the size of the paging file.
PhysicalDisk	Avg. Disk Queue Length	The number of queued requests should not exceed the number of spindles in use plus 2.
PhysicalDisk	% Disk Time	Sustained percentages of 90% or better might indicate that the disk is too slow.
Processor	% Processor Time	If this counter remains above 80% for an extended period, you should suspect a CPU bottleneck.
System	Processor Queue Length	A sustained value of 2 or higher indicates processor congestion.
Network Interface	Bytes Total/sec	If the highest observed average is less than 75% of the expected value, communication errors or slowdowns might be occurring that limit the NIC's rated speed.
Network Interface	Output Queue Length	If this averages above 2, you are experiencing delays.

Other common telltale signs of bottlenecks include long task queues, resource request patterns, task frequency, task duration, task failures, retransmissions or re-requests, and system interrupts. With a little practice and by using some of our suggestions, you are sure to get a feel for bottleneck discovery.

> **EXAM ALERT**
>
> **Know the Common Performance Counters**   A common scenario question on the exam tests your knowledge of determining bottlenecks. A typical question will present you with a specific set of counters, and you will need to determine the problem area.

Windows Management Instrumentation

All the performance counters can also be accessed via the Windows Management Instrumentation (WMI) interface using any of the scripting languages supported in Windows Server 2003. This allows you to create your own custom monitoring applications.

Challenge

As a system administrator, you must monitor and manage various servers and workstations. Most of your job consists of fielding questions and requests, as well as troubleshooting common problems and complaints, such as not being able to print, resetting passwords, and so on.

However, the really challenging part of your job occurs when fielding ambiguous complaints, such as the server seems slow or the database takes forever to update.

How would you address this type of concern? What types of tools are included in Windows Server 2003 that can assist you? On your own, try to develop a strategy to address this type of issue.

After you have completed the exercise, compare your results to those given here.

1. From the Start menu, click Start, All Programs, Administrative Tools, Performance.

2. The Performance tool opens with the System Monitor view displayed. By default, the following counters are displayed:

   ▶ Memory: Pages per Second

   ▶ Physical Disk: Average Disk Queue Length

   ▶ Processor: % Processor Time

3. The default counters can help you to quickly determine if one or more of the monitored areas are a bottleneck. For more in-depth study, you can add more counters.

4. Right-click anywhere on the graph in the System Monitor view. From the pop-up menu, select Add Counters.

5. From the Add Counters dialog box, select additional counters from the Performance Object dropdown list, using the guidelines in the chapter. At the very least, add one of the suggested network objects because the default counters do not include a network object.

6. Click the Add button to add the object and counter to the view. Repeat this step for any additional counters desired. Finally, click the Close button to save.

Remote Monitoring

The process of monitoring a server adds a certain amount of overhead. This additional over-head can cause the data collected to be somewhat inaccurate. This problem can be solved by monitoring your servers remotely.

The Performance console can be run from a Windows XP workstation or another Windows Server 2003 server. However, if you're tracking the performance of certain applications that supply their own counters, such as Microsoft Exchange or SQL Server, you will need to load the Administrative Tools for those products on the monitoring computer so that the appro-priate counters are loaded.

The process to monitor a server remotely is not much different from local monitoring. The remote monitoring procedure is demonstrated in Step by Step 14.9.

STEP BY STEP

14.9 Monitoring a remote server

1. On the monitoring workstation, click Start, All Programs, Administrative Tools, Performance.

2. The Performance tool opens with the System Monitor view displayed. Right-click anywhere on the graph in the System Monitor view. Select Add Counters from the pop-up menu.

3. From the Add Counters dialog box, enter the remote server name in the field, as shown in Figure 14.25. Next, select the desired counter.

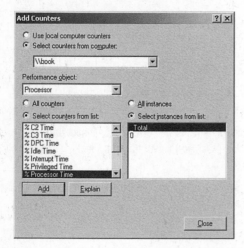

FIGURE 14.25 Select the remote server and then select the counters and instance to monitor. Clicking the Explain button provides an explanation of what each counter records.

4. Click the Add button to add the object and counter to the view. Repeat for any additional counters and remote servers as desired. Then click the Close button to save.

Chapter Summary

When working in a Windows Server 2003 environment, it is important that you have a thorough understanding of the performance characteristics of your servers.

Windows Server 2003 provides two tools that provide real-time views of server performance: Task Manager and System Monitor. Whereas Task Manager is useful for a quick and dirty look at system performance for instant troubleshooting, System Monitor provides access to far more counters to provide a more through view of system performance.

System Monitor is part of the Performance console. The other monitoring tool in the Performance console is Performance Logs and Alerts. The Performance Logs and Alerts tool allows you to monitor performance over a period of time and save the results to log files that can be read by System Monitor or other third-party tools.

The Performance Logs and Alerts tool also allows you to send an alert when a preset performance-related trigger is reached.

Key Terms

▶ Counters

▶ Instance

▶ Event ID

▶ Bottleneck

▶ Trigger

▶ System Monitor

Apply Your Knowledge

Exercises

14.1 Setting Performance Alerts

One of the most common monitoring scenarios is tracking down a reported "slow" network. Typically, users will call the help desk and complain that the access to a file or application server seems slow. You suspect that the network adapter is being overwhelmed with traffic. You will need to positively identify this issue and preferably take an in-depth look at the server when it occurs.

What is the best way to accomplish this in Windows Server 2003? On your own, try to develop a solution that involves limited ongoing management by the system administrator.

If you would like to see a possible solution, follow these steps:

Estimated Time: 20 minutes

1. From the Start menu, click Start, All Programs, Administrative Tools, Performance.

2. The Performance tool opens with the System Monitor view displayed. Right-click the Alerts entry under Performance Logs and Alerts in the left pane of the snap-in and select New Alert Settings from the pop-up menu.

3. In the New Alert Settings dialog box, enter the name for the new alert.

4. In the Alert Properties dialog box, click the Add button to add the performance object Network Interface. Select the desired instance, and then click the Close button.

5. After you have selected the counters to monitor, set the alert condition using the Alert Value drop-down field. For this exercise, set the value to 80%.

6. Click the Action tab and select the option to send a network message to your workstation.

7. Click the Schedule tab. On the Schedule tab, you can select the start and stop times for monitoring or select to manually start and stop the log.

8. Click OK to save the log.

Exam Questions

1. Mary is a developer for a small software firm. She is testing a new server-based product that updates a SQL database and then prompts the administrator for information that it then sends to an email server. Because Mary is running Windows Server 2003 on a desktop computer, the performance is not very good. She wants to increase the performance of the application to an acceptable level. Which should Mary do?

   ○ **A.** Use Task Manager to increase the priority of the database application to AboveNormal.

   ○ **B.** Use Task Manager to increase the priority of the test application to Normal.

   ○ **C.** Use Task Manager to increase the priority of the database application to Realtime

   ○ **D.** Use Task Manager to increase the priority of the test application to Realtime.

2. Davin is a new system administrator for an engineering firm. The engineering firm recently fired its previous system administrator because the performance of the firm's file server was always poor. The server is configured with a hardware RAID-5 array with three disks. The disk cabinet has space available for three more disks. Davin decides that he is going to retain his job, so he fires up System Monitor and observes the performance of his file server.

The first thing that he notices is that the PhysicalDisk: %Disk Time and the Paging File: %Usage Peak counters are both pegged at 100%.

What can he do to improve the performance of the file server?

    ◯ **A.** Add more free space to the file server.

    ◯ **B.** Add two more drives to the drive array.

    ◯ **C.** Convert the drive array to RAID-1 for better performance.

    ◯ **D.** Add more RAM to the file server.

3. John is having what he thinks are disk performance problems on his new Windows Server 2003 server. He decides to use System Monitor to look at the disk counters to see how everything is performing. What must he do to enable the counters for the logical disks?

    ◯ **A.** At the command line, type **DISKPERF -y**, and then restart the server.

    ◯ **B.** At the command line, type **DISKPERF -yd**, and then restart the server.

    ◯ **C.** At the command line, type **DISKPERF -y**.

    ◯ **D.** Nothing, the counters are already enabled.

4. James is having performance problems on one of his database servers. He ran System Monitor for a couple of days and came up with the following average values:

    ▶ Processor: %Processor Time: 80%

    ▶ System Processor Queue Length: 5

    ▶ PhysicalDisk: Avg. Disk Queue Length: 2

    ▶ Memory: Pages Input/sec: 2

What should James do?

    ◯ **A.** Add more RAM.

    ◯ **B.** Add a faster disk.

    ◯ **C.** Add an additional processor.

    ◯ **D.** Get a better NIC.

5. Stuart is running a database application that runs in the background but requires a lot of processor time. He is running this application on a server with several other applications, but they are neither critical nor time sensitive. What can Stuart do to improve the performance of his database application?

   ○ **A.** Install more memory in his server.

   ○ **B.** Install a faster disk subsystem in his server.

   ○ **C.** Install a faster NIC in his server.

   ○ **D.** Use Task Manager to set his application to a higher priority.

6. You are the administrator for a small sporting goods company. The Human Resources manager of your company loads an application on a Windows Server 2003 Terminal Server which is located in an OU named Terminal Servers. The users of the terminal server report unacceptable response times. To investigate, you log on to the server and start up Task Manager, and you see that the average CPU usage is more than 80%. However, when you look at the Processes tab, none of the processes shown are showing any measurable activity.

   What should you do to make the offending process visible?

   ○ **A.** In Task Manager, select the Show Processes from All Users option.

   ○ **B.** From a command prompt, run the query process command.

   ○ **C.** Open the Terminal Services Manager. Select the server from the list of servers, and then select the Processes tab.

   ○ **D.** Edit the Group Policy object (GPO) for the Terminal Servers OU and add your user account to the "Profile a single process" policy. Then use Task Manager to reexamine the server.

7. You are the network administrator for your company. You have a file server that is heavily used. Users are complaining about excessive slowdowns, usually during the evening. You have examined the processor, memory and disk performance, but everything seems to be within normal limits. What should you do?

   ○ **A.** Use Task Manager to review network utilization.

   ○ **B.** Use Task Manager to record network utilization for later review.

   ○ **C.** Use System Monitor to record network utilization for later review.

   ○ **D.** Use Performance Logs and Alerts to record network utilization for later review.

8. As part of a server consolidation, you are moving a group of shared folders to a new Windows Server 2003 server. Unfortunately, this new server has significantly less space than the server it replaced. You will need to store older files offline when the free space falls below a specific amount. What is the most efficient way to track free space?

○ **A.** Start System Monitor. Configure it to monitor PhysicalDisk:%Free Space. Set it to send a message when the Free Space falls below a specified percentage.

○ **B.** Start System Monitor. Configure it to monitor LogicalDisk:%Free Space. Set it to send a message when the Free Space falls below a specified percentage.

○ **C.** Start Performance Logs and Alerts. Configure it to monitor LogicalDisk:%Free Space. Set it to send a message when the Free Space falls below a specified percentage.

○ **D.** Start Performance Logs and Alerts. Configure it to monitor PhysicalDisk:%Free Space. Set it to send a message when the Free Space falls below a specified percentage.

9. Frank is the system administrator for Fudge Inc. His users have been complaining about the response time on one of his Windows Server 2003 file and print servers. He ran Performance Logs and Alerts for a couple of days and came up with the following average values:

  ▶ Processor: %Processor Time: 80%

  ▶ System Processor Queue Length: 2

  ▶ PhysicalDisk: Avg. Disk Queue Length: 6

  ▶ Memory: Pages Input/sec: 5

What should Frank do?

○ **A.** Add more RAM.

○ **B.** Add a faster disk.

○ **C.** Add an additional processor.

○ **D.** Get a better NIC.

10. You are the network administrator for FlyByNight Airlines. The network consists of a single Active Directory domain. All network servers run Windows Server 2003 Standard Edition.

Your company has just bought a smaller airline, and you need to make sure that the employees from the new airline can access the HR application with decent performance. The HR application typically produces a high volume of disk activity. What counter should you monitor?

○ **A.** The % Disk Time counter for the PhysicalDisk performance object

○ **B.** The Average Disk Queue Length counter for the PhysicalDisk performance object

○ **C.** The Free Gbytes counter for the LogicalDisk performance object

○ **D.** The File Transfers/sec counter for the LogicalDisk performance object

Answers to Exam Questions

1. **C.** When a process is set to Realtime, it is unable to respond to external input. Changing the base priority of an application to Realtime makes the priority of an application higher than the process that monitors and responds to keyboard input. The second step in Mary's application test requires keyboard input. The application, therefore, would hang, and Mary would be required to reboot. However, the database application doesn't need keyboard input, so setting it to Realtime wouldn't be a problem. See the "Understanding Priority" section for more information.

2. **D.** Although the Disk Time counter is excessively high, so is the Paging File usage. When the paging file usage is extremely high, that means that the server is constantly swapping to disk, which is a pretty good indication that the server is running out of physical memory. See the "Monitoring Memory Performance Objects" section for more information.

3. **D.** Nothing, all disk counters are enabled by default in Windows Server 2003. See the "Monitoring Disk Performance Objects" section for more information.

4. **C.** Both the processor time and the processor queue length are suspect. An average processor time of 80% by itself would be a problem, but the processor queue length should never get above 2 for an extended period of time. See the "Monitoring Process Performance Objects" section for more information.

5. **D.** Because you weren't given any performance measurements in this question, you have no way of knowing whether any of the components mentioned are being stressed. However, because the database application is a background process and is running with other applications, setting Stuart's database application to a higher priority should give it a little more processing time. See the "Understanding Priority" section for more information.

6. **A.** The default view shows the processes running for the currently logged-on user, but the processes for all users can be shown by selecting the Show Processes from All Users check box in the lower-left corner of the dialog box. See the "Processes Tab" section for more information.

7. **D.** The only workable answer is D. Performance Logs and Alerts can be set to automatically record performance data for later review, which is good because the problem occurs in the evening when you probably won't be working. System Monitor and Task Manager are mostly used for looking at real-time events. See the "Performance Logs" section for more information.

8. **C.** The Alerts function of Performance Logs and Alerts is used to define threshold alerts. These can be used with real-time measurements or with historical log files. An alert is issued when a specific counter crosses a defined threshold value. When this occurs, a trigger event is initiated. Free Space is tracked by LogicalDisk, not PhysicalDisk. See the "Performance Alerts" section for more information.

9. **A.** Although the processor utilization is high, the Memory :Pages Input/sec and Physical Disk: Avg. Disk Queue Length results indicate that most processes are being swapped out to disk. This indicates that the server doesn't have enough RAM. See the "Monitoring Memory Performance Objects" section for more information.

10. **A.** The Disk Time counter tracks the percentage of time that the drive is servicing R/W requests. A high number indicates that the disk is extremely busy. The other counters listed do not exist. See the "Monitoring Disk Performance Objects" section for more information.

Suggested Readings and Resources

1. Morimoto, Rand; Noel, Michael; Lewis, Alex. *Microsoft Windows Server 2003 Unleashed (R2 Edition)*. Sams Publishing, 2006. ISBN 0672328984.

2. *Performance Monitoring Best Practices*. http://technet2.microsoft.com/WindowsServer/ en/Library/204bb1a3-713b-4ba3-9a9b-98ca46a3076b1033.mspx?mfr=true.

3. Stanek, William. *Microsoft Windows Server 2003 Administrator's Pocket Consultant*. Microsoft Press, 2003. ISBN 0735613540.

4. Windows Server 2003 Deployment Guide. Microsoft Corporation. http://www.microsoft.com/windowsserver2003/techinfo/reskit/deploykit.mspx.

5. Windows Server 2003 Performance Tuning. http://www.windowsnetworking.com/ articles_tutorials/Windows-Server-2003-Performance-Tuning.html.

6. Windows Server 2003 Resource Kit. Microsoft Corporation. Look for a link to it on the Technical Resources for Windows Server 2003 page. http://www.microsoft.com/windowsserver2003/techinfo/default.mspx.

15

Managing and Troubleshooting Hardware Devices

Objectives

This chapter covers the following Microsoft-specified objectives for the "Managing and Maintaining Physical and Logical Devices" section of the Managing and Maintaining a Microsoft Windows Server 2003 Environment exam:

Install and configure server hardware devices

▶ **Configure driver-signing options.**

▶ **Configure resource settings for a device.**

▶ **Configure device properties and settings.**

▶ Windows Server 2003 operates much as Windows Server 2000 and Windows XP do in working with hardware devices. We explain how you control the way the system deals with unsigned device drivers and how to configure driver settings for hardware devices.

Monitor server hardware

▶ In managing your server, you will need to monitor its hardware. We explain how to monitor your system using the Device Manager, Hardware Troubleshooting Wizard, and Control Panel items, including the Add Hardware, Mouse, and Printers and Faxes applets.

Troubleshoot server hardware devices

▶ **Diagnose and resolve issues related to hardware settings.**

▶ **Diagnose and resolve issues related to server hardware and hardware driver upgrades.**

▶ If there's one thing sure in computing, it's that there will be problems with the computer hardware. We provide some methods for determining what devices are at fault and describe how to resolve issues that occur because of hardware settings and hardware device drivers.

Outline

Study Strategies

▶ To understand hardware devices so that you can manage and troubleshoot them, you need to understand what properties and settings can be managed, as well as when manual configuration is necessary. You should have access to a Windows Server 2003 computer, but you won't be missing much if you investigate on a Windows XP computer instead.

▶ Make sure you are familiar with Plug and Play and how it ties in with the Advanced Configuration and Power Interface (ACPI) standard.

▶ Run File Signature Verification and work with the Control Panel applets to become familiar with their settings.

Introduction

The devices (or components) that make up a computer must communicate effectively, without interference. Having two or more devices trying to use the same communication channel causes errors or even system crashes, so it's critical that the devices are configured correctly.

In the early days of network administration, it was common for configuration errors to occur because these settings were performed manually, and the work was error prone. The development of the Plug and Play specification and the Advanced Configuration and Power Interface (ACPI) standard for system boards made the whole process automatic. It is very worthwhile for an administrator to insist that only devices that conform to these standards be used.

This chapter discusses installing and configuring hardware devices, ensuring that the drivers loaded to operate the devices are uncorrupted and come from reputable sources, and troubleshooting hardware issues.

Installing and Configuring Hardware Devices

Objective:
Install and configure server hardware devices

In an ideal world, if you wanted to install a new device in your server, you would simply power down the server, insert the new device, make sure it has power and signal cable attachments, and then power up the server. The new device would be ready immediately.

That is the goal of the people who design hardware architecture, and, actually, with modern hardware and modern operating systems, we're almost there. With a motherboard that meets the ACPI standard, Windows Server 2003 recognizes and configures all hardware that is built to the Plug and Play specification.

However, this is not an ideal world. If you have older devices, particularly devices that were built to the Industry Standard Architecture (ISA) specifications, Plug and Play won't be able to help you. (Some Plug and Play drivers were written for later ISA devices, but they don't always work effectively.) Sometimes the device is not recognized, or the device driver is corrupted or not available. That's where the skills covered in this section will come in handy.

ISA Free

A lot of workstations and almost all servers shipping these days are designed without ISA slots. This makes working with hardware much easier because you only have to deal with the different flavors of Peripheral Component Interconnect (PCI).

What's the ACPI Standard?

ACPI is the current standard for communication with a motherboard's basic input/output system (BIOS). The BIOS is the mechanism that allows an operating system to communicate with the devices on the computer. In older standards, Plug and Play negotiation and configuration was handled in hardware, but in an ACPI system, the configuration is handled by the operating system.

With ACPI, all devices that have power-management capabilities (such as sleep mode or hibernation) can be controlled by the operating system. This allows the operating system to selectively shut down devices not currently in use, which gives maximum battery life to portable computing devices. ACPI is also needed for the OnNow Device Power Management initiative, which allows a computer to be started by simply touching any key on the computer's keyboard. ACPI is installed only if all components detected during setup support power management. This is because older components that do not support ACPI typically exhibit erratic behavior and can potentially cause system crashes.

How Does the Operating System Manage a Device?

A server contains many hardware devices: disk drives, network cards, display adapters, and any of a large number of peripherals. For them to be usable by the system, each must be identified by the operating system, and the appropriate device driver must be loaded.

A *device driver* is a program that passes requests between the operating system and the device. For example, the user presses the A key on the keyboard, and the keyboard device driver notifies the operating system that A has been pressed on that device. Or, the program or operating system sends data to a disk drive: The device driver receives the data from the operating system and transfers it to the disk drive.

Where Do Device Drivers Come From?

Device drivers are critical to the proper operation of hardware devices, so it's important that you understand where they come from. If the device is listed on the Hardware Compatibility List (HCL) for an operating system, the device driver may have been written by the device manufacturer, shipped to Microsoft, and supplied on the distribution CD-ROM for the operating system. Alternatively, for common devices, Microsoft may provide a generic driver, and manufacturers write additions to control specific features of their devices.

If you can't find a driver for a particular device on the Windows Server 2003 distribution CD-ROM, the device may have been produced after the Windows Server 2003 CD-ROM was made. In that case, the driver may be available on the Microsoft website or on the manufacturer's website.

Quick Fix

If a device is not acting properly, a possible solution is to download the latest driver from the manufacturer's website. This may fix the problem right away, and even if it doesn't, you can be sure the first thing the manufacturer's technical support staff will ask you is the version of the driver. However, before installing any new drivers, be sure to examine the supporting documentation for known issues.

What Drivers Are Running on My Computer?

If you want to find out what drivers are currently running on your system, the command-line utility driverquery.exe nicely lists the running drivers for you. At a command prompt, enter **driverquery >c:\driverquery.txt** to put the output into the c:\driveryquery.txt file. Then you can read it with Notepad. This utility is available only in Windows XP and Windows Server 2003.

If you use the /fo csv switch, the output from driverquery.exe will be created in comma-separated variable (CSV) format, making it suitable for loading into a database or a spreadsheet for analysis. Using the /s switch allows you to specify a remote system, and the /si switch provides information about signed drivers (see the next section). The following command provides a listing in CSV format (fo csv) of the drivers running on the remote system MERCURY (/s mercury), including information about signed drivers (/si):

```
driverquery /fo csv /s mercury /si
```

The first few lines of the output are as follows:

```
"DeviceName","InfName","IsSigned","Manufacturer"
"Advanced Configuration and Power Interface (ACPI) PC",
➡"hal.inf","TRUE","(Standard computers)"
"Microsoft ACPI-Compliant System","acpi.inf","TRUE","Microsoft"
"Processor","cpu.inf","TRUE","(Standard processor types)"
```

Updating Device Drivers

From time to time, hardware manufacturers will release new versions of their device drivers, usually to fix bugs, but sometimes to add functionality or increase the performance of the hardware device.

When new drivers are released, your job as a system administrator is to download them from the web, and then install them on your server.

Follow the procedure in Step by Step 15.1 to see how to update a device driver.

STEP BY STEP

15.1 Updating a device driver

1. Click Start, right-click my Computer, and select Properties.

2. On the Properties window, select the Hardware tab.

3. Click the Device Manager button. This opens the Device Manager MMC, as shown in Figure 15.1.

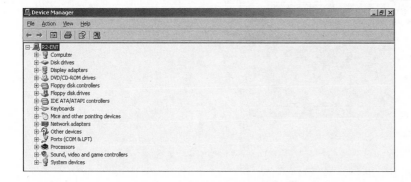

FIGURE 15.1 The Device Manager MMC, listing all installed devices.

4. Expand the entry of the device that you want to select.

5. Right-click the device and select Upgrade Driver from the pop-up menu.

6. This starts the Hardware Update Wizard. When prompted as to whether to connect to Windows Update, select No. Click Next.

7. When prompted whether to install the software automatically or from a specific location, select specific location.

8. When prompted for location, select Don't Search. I Will Choose the Driver to Install, as shown in Figure 15.2. Click Next.

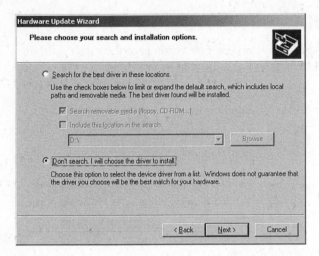

FIGURE 15.2   Select the location where the new driver is located.

9. On the next screen, highlight the device in the dialog box, then click the Have Disk button, as shown in Figure 15.3.

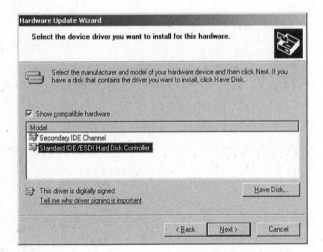

FIGURE 15.3   Select the device, and then click the Have Disk button.

10. Navigate to the location of the new driver files, then Click OK to load them.

11. Click Next, and then click Finish when prompted.

What Is Driver Signing and Why Should I Care?

Device drivers are heavily used and very close to the kernel of the operating system. As a result, it is important that the device drivers in use are supplied by reputable sources. (Imagine the chaos caused by the installation of a bad driver for a backup tape drive. A seemingly perfect backup might turn out to be totally unusable!)

Microsoft requests that manufacturers submit their drivers to be tested by the Windows Hardware Quality Labs (WHQL). Drivers submitted to WHQL that pass the certification tests for Windows Server 2003 are given a Microsoft digital signature. When the driver finishes the testing phase and is approved, a catalog (`*.cat`) is created. The CAT file is a hash of the driver binary file and other relevant information. This CAT file is then digitally signed with the Microsoft private key.

When Windows Server 2003 inspects the driver, it examines the catalog file that is included. If the signature is authenticated, this is a guarantee that the driver was created by the owner of the catalog file and that the driver has not been tampered with since it was created. Signed driver files are distributed through the following methods, as well as on the Windows Server 2003 CD-ROM:

▶ Windows service packs

▶ Hotfix distributions

▶ Operating system upgrades

▶ Windows Update

For the greatest device driver security, many administrators want to ensure that only signed device drivers are loaded. To achieve this situation, Windows Server 2003 can be configured to refuse to load unsigned drivers.

Configuring Driver-Signing Options for a Single Computer

Objective:
Configure driver-signing options

Normally, you would want to have only signed device drivers on your system. That is definitely the most secure way of operating. But what if you want to use a device driver that for some reason has not been signed? It might be a hot-off-the-press driver from the manufacturer's technical support staff, for example, that you need to try. Or it might be the only driver available for a particular device that you must use. In that case, you can change the default behavior of Windows Server 2003 to allow unsigned drivers to be loaded. Step by Step 15.2 walks you through this process.

STEP BY STEP

15.2 Configuring Windows Server 2003 to allow loading of unsigned drivers

1. Click Start, Control Panel, System, and then click the Hardware tab.

2. Click Driver Signing.

3. In the Driver Signing Options dialog box, in the What Action Do You Want Windows to Take? section, click Ignore—Install the Software Anyway and Don't Ask for My Approval, as shown in Figure 15.4.

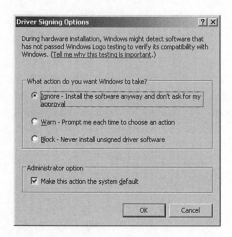

FIGURE 15.4 To instruct Windows Server 2003 to allow loading of unsigned drivers, click Ignore—Install the Software Anyway and Don't Ask for My Approval.

EXAM ALERT

Only for Administrators Only administrators can reduce the security level or turn off driver signing.

Of course, it's not recommended that you leave your server configured this way. This is because with this type of configuration, the operating system would allow any unsigned driver to be installed. You should check back with your hardware vendor frequently to get a signed version of the driver as soon as possible, and you should reconfigure the driver-signing options when the signed driver is installed. Alternatively, to sidestep the problem completely, consider removing the problem device from the computer and substituting a device for which signed drivers are available.

As soon as you have installed the unsigned driver, you should return to the Driver Signing Options dialog box and choose Block—Never Install Unsigned Driver Software.

Configuring Driver-Signing Options for Several Computers at Once

What if you want to ensure that there will be no unsigned drivers at all in your network? As you have seen, it's not difficult to change the driver-signing options on a few servers by following the steps just given on each one. But if you have hundreds or thousands of Windows 2000 or later workstations and/or Windows 2000 or later servers on your network, and you want to protect all of them from unsigned drivers, that would be a huge task. If you're like most administrators, you would prefer to manage all these computers at once, instead of configuring each one individually. Not only is this faster, it's also easier than keeping track of which computers have been configured.

This is a job for Group Policy! You can create a Group Policy Object (GPO) and apply it to computers in a given part of the Active Directory tree. We can create a Group Policy Object to ensure that no unsigned drivers can be loaded. Step by Step 15.3 shows how to do this, starting with creating the necessary OU structure. Note that you must be a domain administrator, or have limited administrator rights delegated to you, to be able to create and manage GPOs.

STEP BY STEP

15.3 Creating a Group Policy Object to prohibit the loading of unsigned drivers

1. Click Start, Administrative Tools, Active Directory Users and Computers.

2. In the left pane, click the domain object

3. Select the Kansas City OU, choose Action, New, Organizational Unit, and type **Workstations**.

4. Click Start, Administrative Tools, Group Policy Management. In the left pane, expand the domain, and then expand the Kansas City\Workstations container. Right-click the Workstations OU and select Create and Link a GPO Here from the popup menu.

5. When prompted, name the new Group Policy Object **Only allow signed drivers**.

6. Click Edit and navigate to Computer Configuration, Windows Settings, Security Settings, Local Policies, Security Options.

7. In the right pane, select Devices: Unsigned Driver Installation Behavior, as shown in Figure 15.5.

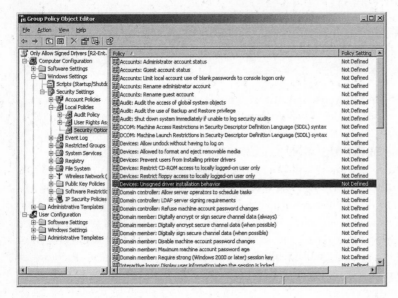

FIGURE 15.5 To control the operation of Windows Server 2003 when asked to load an unsigned driver, choose the policy Devices: Unsigned Driver Installation Behavior and get its properties.

8. Select Actions, Properties and then select Define This Policy Setting. Ensure that Do Not Allow Installation is showing in the drop-down box and then click OK. You'll see that the Policy Setting column now shows Do Not Allow Installation for this policy.

9. Close the Group Policy dialog boxes until you are back to the main Group Policy Management window.

10. Open a command prompt, type **GPUDATE** /**force**, and press Enter to apply the new policy immediately.

Because this policy is linked to the Workstations OU, it will be applied to each of the computers whose accounts are located in that OU or in any OUs subordinate to the Workstations OU. Also, now that the policy has been created, it can be linked to any other OU in the Active Directory, such as to the Phoenix Workstations OU when it is created.

EXAM ALERT

Group Policy Microsoft highly recommends using Group Policy to configure common settings such as driver signing. For the exam, be sure you know how to create a GPO and what settings to configure for driver signing.

Determining Whether a Computer Has Unsigned Drivers

Imagine you've just been made administrator of a network, and you want to know if there are any unsigned drivers on the computers you're responsible for. Microsoft has provided a tool with Windows 2003, Windows 2000, and Windows XP to check for exactly this situation. That tool is File Signature Verification, and you access it by using Start, Run, `sigverif.exe`.

As you can see from the Advanced dialog box, shown in Figure 15.6, you can have File Signature Verification check only system files or check the file types you specify in a folder you browse to.

FIGURE 15.6 Normally you would want to check the files in the Windows folder and its subdirectories, but you can choose to verify specific file types and folders.

As you can see in Figure 15.6, the Advanced settings allow you to narrow your search to specific file types and locations.

When you click OK in the File Signature Verification dialog box, there will be a delay of a minute or more while every system file is checked for a signature. As you can see from Figure 15.7, several unsigned files exist on the sample Windows Server 2003 computer. These are Windows 2000 unsigned drivers for the HP OfficeJet printer.

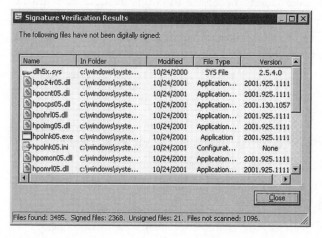

FIGURE 15.7 The sample Windows Server 2003 computer has 21 unsigned files.

Other Methods for Protecting Device Drivers

Device drivers and other system files are automatically protected against improper replacement by the Windows File Protection facility. This facility runs in the background (invisible to the user and the administrator) and is alerted whenever a file in a protected folder is changed. It determines whether the new version of the file is signed, and if not, Windows File Protection automatically rolls back the file to the version kept in the %systemroot%\ system32\dllcache folder. If the desired version of the file is not in the dllcache folder, Windows File Protection asks for the Windows Server 2003 CD-ROM to be mounted, and it copies the file from there.

Windows File Protection

For some reason, when Windows File Protection asks for the Windows Server 2003 CD, it really wants that CD! Just having a handy copy of the i386 directory on a file share doesn't seem to work.

An administrator can run the System File Checker (sfc.exe) to explicitly schedule a scan of the system files immediately, at the next reboot, or at every reboot. Also, if the dllcache folder is corrupted or needs to be repopulated for some other reason, the administrator can run the System File Checker (SFC) with the /purgecache switch to cause the folder to be emptied and reloaded.

Configuring Resource Settings for a Device

Objective:

Configure resource settings for a device.

On a Windows Server 2003 machine, it is rarely necessary to configure devices manually, because most hardware sold since 1995 complies with the Plug and Play specification. The operating system identifies any conflicts and configures the devices to avoid them. However, you should know how to configure settings, in case you need to resolve a conflict on non-Plug and Play devices.

What Are Resource Settings?

Resource settings are mechanisms by which the device can communicate with other hardware or the operating system. The following list describes some resources in greater detail:

▶ Direct memory access (DMA) allows a device to read from the computer's memory, or write to it, without using the computer's processor (CPU). Each device using DMA must have a DMA channel dedicated for its use.

▶ An interrupt request (IRQ) line is a hardware channel line over which a device can interrupt the CPU for service. Some devices can share an IRQ line; others must have a dedicated IRQ.

▶ An input/output (I/O) port is another channel through which data is transferred between a device and the CPU. It acts like an area of memory that can be read from and written to by the device and the CPU. I/O ports cannot be shared.

▶ A memory address is an area of memory allocated to the device driver, for communication between the device and the operating system.

If two devices attempt to use the same resources, and the particular resource is not sharable, one or both of the devices may be unusable.

Configuring Device Properties and Settings

Objective:
Configure device properties and settings.

In general, there is no need to change the configured settings of a device. What might require you to do so is a situation in which one or more of the communications channels used by a device is already in use by another device. This is known as a *conflict*.

To configure a device's properties and settings, the tool to use is Device Manager. Device Manager is available as a snap-in to a Microsoft Management Console (MMC), as a subentry under Computer Management, and from the Hardware tab of System Properties. If you need another way to get to Device Manager, you can create a desktop shortcut, giving `devmgmt.msc` as the location of the item.

It's a good idea to start Device Manager occasionally, to check that all devices are working properly. Figure 15.8 shows Device Manager with one device in an error state. (Devices that are not working properly are shown with a yellow question mark icon. Devices that are disabled have a red X over the icon.)

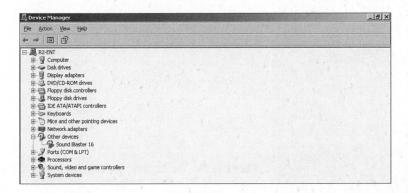

FIGURE 15.8 From within Device Manager, double-click a device's icon to see its properties.

To see the properties of a device, double-click its icon in the Device Manager listing. Figure 15.9 shows the General tab of the PS/2 Compatible Mouse Properties dialog box.

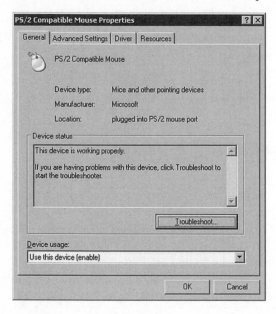

FIGURE 15.9 The General tab shows basic information about the device, has a Troubleshoot button in case there are problems, and allows you to enable or disable the device in the current configuration.

Click the Advanced Settings tab, if there is one, to see special settings for this type of device. See Figure 15.10 for the advanced settings for the PS/2 mouse.

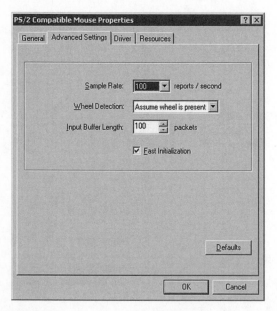

FIGURE 15.10 The Advanced Settings tab allows you to make changes to the special settings for a device.

Select the Resources tab to see what system resources are reserved for the device. Figure 15.11 shows this tab.

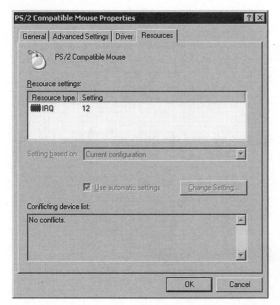

FIGURE 15.11 The Resources tab for the PS/2 mouse is very simple. Only one resource, the IRQ level, is used, and it cannot be changed.

A more complex set of resources is allocated to the display driver. In Figure 15.12, you'll see that IRQ, I/O port, and memory resources are allocated.

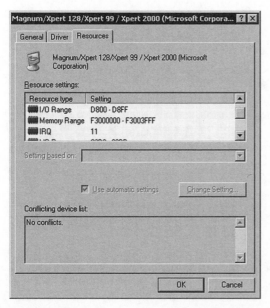

FIGURE 15.12 A display driver is substantially more complex than a mouse. It uses several channels to communicate with the CPU.

Note the check box Use Automatic Settings, which is set by default. If this check box is enabled, it can be cleared, and then you can manually select the settings you want to use.

NOTE

Automatic Settings   For most devices, you will find that the Use Automatic Settings check box is checked, meaning that automatic settings will be used, and dimmed, meaning that you cannot access the check box. This happens when there are no alternative settings for that resource on the device or the device's resources are controlled by Plug and Play.

If all combinations of settings result in conflicts, you may find that it is impossible to use that combination of devices, and one of them will have to be removed or disabled.

To see the resources assigned on your computer, open Device Manager; on the View menu, choose Resources by Type. Then click the plus sign beside each resource type. Figure 15.13 shows the IRQ assignments on the sample server.

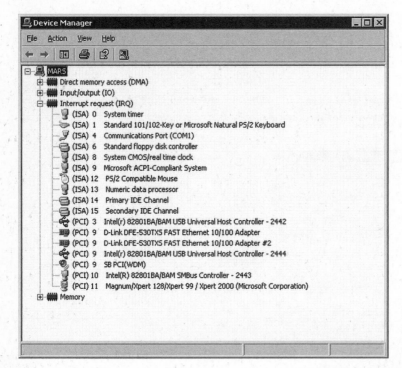

FIGURE 15.13   The assigned IRQ resources are visible by choosing View, Resources by Type.

NOTE

Managing Drivers for Printers and Faxes   Device Manager does not manage device drivers for printers and fax devices. They are managed through the Printers and Faxes applet in Control Panel. This procedure was covered back in Chapter 6, "Implementing Printing."

Challenge

You are a system administrator who is responsible for managing all the servers in your office. You have heard that the drivers for the new SCSI cards you installed last week have been updated with a later version, but since you just installed them last week, you are somewhat doubtful. How can you make sure that your SCSI cards are using the latest drivers?

Try to complete this exercise on your own, listing your conclusions on a sheet of paper. After you have completed the exercise, compare your results to those given here.

To work with a device's properties and settings, the tool to use is Device Manager. Device Manager is available as a snap-in to a Microsoft Management Console (MMC), as a subentry under Computer Management, and from the Hardware tab of System Properties.

To check the version of the driver installed for your SCSI cards, double-click its icon in the Device Manager listing. Next select the Driver tab, and then select the Driver Details button. This will open the Properties window, which will list the following:

▶ Driver File Name(s) and location

▶ Driver Provider

▶ Driver Date

▶ Driver Version

▶ Driver Signer

This information can be used to compare the version of the installed driver with those listed on the SCSI card manufacturer's website.

Monitoring Server Hardware

Objective:

Monitor server hardware

The administrators of a well-run computing organization perform regularly scheduled tasks to ensure that the computing infrastructure is operating properly. One of these tasks is to check that all devices on each of the servers in the organization are functional. Device Manager is the tool to use for checking the functionality of the devices on a server.

Using Device Manager

To start Device Manager, right-click My Computer, choose Manage, and in the left pane, under System Tools, select Device Manager. If any devices are not working properly, they will be identified with a yellow question mark icon, as shown in Figure 15.14.

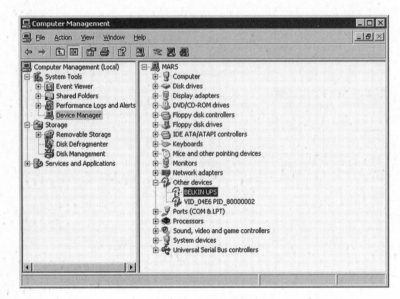

FIGURE 15.14 Under Other Devices, you will see that the Belkin UPS has a question mark beside it. To see the reason for the question mark, double-click the device.

As you can see from Figure 15.15, the drivers have not been installed for the Belkin UPS. When you click Reinstall Driver, you'll be able to browse to the CD-ROM where the drivers are located.

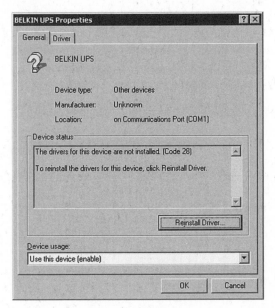

FIGURE 15.15   The reason for the error condition is that the drivers have not been loaded.

The driver supplied is not signed, and from its name it appears that it was written for Windows 2000, not Windows Server 2003. See the warning in Figure 15.16.

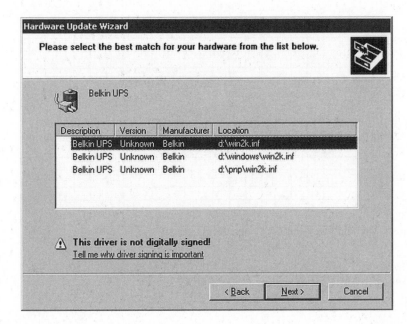

FIGURE 15.16   The three drivers listed are all unsigned.

Now we have a dilemma. Do we install an old driver that may not work well (or may even cause system instability), or do we work without the capability to control the UPS? Because we think control of the UPS is very important and we know the change we have just made (in case there is a problem and we need to back out the change), we decide to proceed. After a minute the driver is installed, and the yellow question mark has disappeared from Device Manager

We should remember to go to the Belkin website periodically to search for a signed driver written for Windows Server 2003.

NOTE

Nonpresent Devices   An interesting problem that occurs occasionally concerns IP address conflict messages when a new network interface card (NIC) is installed on a computer and is assigned the static address of a removed NIC. In that case, the old NIC's settings are still stored in the Registry, and you can assign a different address to the new NIC. You will want to remove the old NIC, but because it is absent, the device does not show up in the list of devices, even after you choose View, Show Hidden Devices.

The solution? Choose Start, Run and in the Open box type `Devmgmt.msc set DEVMGR_SHOW_NONPRESENT_DEVICES=1`. The absent NICs will be visible under Network Adapters, and you will be able to delete them.

Troubleshoot Server Hardware Devices

Objectives:

▶ Diagnose and resolve issues related to hardware settings

▶ Diagnose and resolve issues related to server hardware and hardware driver upgrades

When a device is causing problems, it is often helpful to use the Hardware Troubleshooter, which is available from within Device Manager. As you can see in Figure 15.17, the Hardware Troubleshooter offers to help you with problems with the following issues:

▶ Storage devices (disk drives, CD-ROMs, DVD-ROMs)

▶ Network adapters

▶ Input devices (mouse, keyboard, camera, scanner, infrared)

▶ Game controllers

▶ Universal Serial Bus (USB) devices

▶ Display adapters

▶ Modems

▶ Sound cards

The Hardware Troubleshooter also can help you resolve a hardware conflict on your computer. This is useful when two devices use the same resource (DMA channel, IRQ line, memory range, or input/output port). The wizard walks you through a series of questions aimed at determining what is wrong with the device

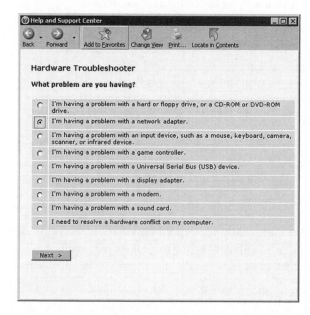

FIGURE 15.17 Choose the type of device you want to troubleshoot.

The Hardware Troubleshooter can help you solve problems that might have cost you hours of troubleshooting time, and it can help you save the money you might have spent on technical support calls.

Using Control Panel Applets

The Control Panel provides several applets (small, single-purpose applications) that can help you manage hardware; they are as follows:

▶ *Add Hardware*—This starts the Add Hardware Wizard, which can both help you install new hardware and help you troubleshoot existing hardware.

▶ *Display*—This applet allows you to control the way your display operates.

▶ *Game Controllers*—This applet allows you to install and configure game controller hardware.

▶ *Mouse*—This applet manages mouse settings.

▶ *Phone and Modem Options*—This applet allows you to configure phone and modem settings.

▶ *Printers and Faxes*—This applet is used to configure printer and fax settings.

▶ *Sounds and Audio Devices*—This applet enables you to configure speakers and recording devices.

NOTE

Get Some Hands-On Experience   The Windows Server 2003 Control Panel applets are very close in function to the Windows XP applets, so if you're concerned that you might interfere with the operation of your Windows Server 2003 computer, you can experiment with the applets on your Windows XP system instead and get essentially the same experience.

The following sections describe how to use the Control Panel applets.

Using the Add Hardware Wizard

Initially, the Add Hardware Wizard searches for recently added hardware that has not yet been installed. If it finds no new hardware, it asks you whether the device is installed, and if it is, it shows you a list of the installed devices so that you can select the one that is having problems.

If Windows Server 2003 can recognize the problem, it will suggest remedies for it, such as reinstalling the driver, changing settings, or disabling or removing the device. If Windows Server 2003 cannot identify a problem with the device, it will offer to start the appropriate troubleshooter.

Using the Display Applet

If there are problems with the display, go directly to the Settings tab. (All the other tabs control how the display looks to the users.) You can access advanced settings from the Advanced button, or you can load the troubleshooter by selecting the Troubleshoot button.

Using the Game Controllers Applet

Although it's extremely unlikely that you will be running games on a server, there may be management devices that use the game controller interfaces. To manage them, use the Game Controllers applet.

Using the Keyboard Applet

The Keyboard applet allows you to specify how the keyboard operates. You can determine how long you must hold down a key before it starts to repeat (the repeat delay), and how quickly it repeats (the repeat rate). There's a handy test area that allows you to test your settings. You can also change the rate at which the cursor blinks.

Using the Mouse Applet

The Mouse applet lets you choose whether the left or right mouse button is the primary button. It allows you to set the double-click speed—dragging the slider to the left allows two slower clicks to be counted as a double-click. And it allows you to turn on ClickLock, which lets you highlight items, or drag selected items, without holding down the mouse button (see Figure 15.18).

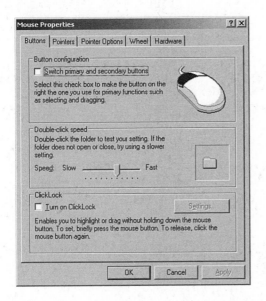

FIGURE 15.18 Use the Buttons tab of the Mouse applet to control button allocation, double-click speed, and ClickLock.

The Pointer Options tab of the Mouse applet allows you to control the speed on movement of the pointer, automatically move the pointer to a dialog box's default command button, display pointer trials (particularly useful on LCD screens), hide the pointer when you are typing into a window, and (if the pointer is hidden) show where it is when you press Ctrl.

Using the Sounds and Audio Devices Applet

On the Hardware tab of the Sounds and Audio Devices Control Panel applet, you will see a listing for any sound, video, or game controllers. This is a central management point for all such devices. If you are having problems with any of the listed devices, you can select the device and choose Troubleshoot to start the Troubleshooting Wizard for that device. Figure 15.19 shows the contents of the Hardware tab.

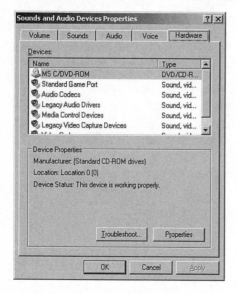

FIGURE 15.19 Select a device in the Devices window and then click Troubleshoot or Properties.

For example, suppose you are having trouble with the sound card on your computer. Choosing the SB PCI card and selecting Properties brings up the Properties dialog box for the sound card. From there, you may choose Troubleshoot to start the Troubleshooting Wizard, or you may choose the Properties, Settings, or Driver tab to enable or disable capabilities of the device, to configure settings, or to update its driver.

Troubleshooting Server Hardware

A hardware device might stop working because of a mechanical or electronic failure, such as a disk head crash or a surge in the power. Any hardware component, especially ones with moving parts such as disk drives, will fail eventually. But it's much more common that a device will become unusable because of incorrect device settings or because of wrong or corrupted device drivers.

In this section, we talk about issues caused by hardware settings and about issues caused by upgrades to hardware and to hardware drivers.

Smooth Power Saves Lives!

Hardware lives, that is! When you realize the very high speeds and fine tolerances that are used in modern computer hardware components, it's easy to see that smooth power is a must for system reliability. A small disturbance at the wrong moment in the power supplied to a disk drive can cause data corruption. And a spike in the voltage across any electronic device can damage or destroy the device.

That's why it's essential that any production computing environment be carefully protected against power fluctuations (under-voltage, over-voltage, spikes, or drops) that can damage components. An uninterruptible power supply (UPS) is your first line of defense. A UPS will provide smooth power isolated from the fluctuations that exist in any power utility's service. Some production environments have power supplied from two different grids and have their own onsite emergency generators. These two steps ensure that power is available. Then they feed that power into large banks of batteries and run the data center equipment from the batteries. The result: smooth, reliable power, and hardware with a long and happy life.

Diagnosing and Resolving Issues Related to Hardware Settings

Objective:

Diagnose and resolve issues related to hardware settings

As discussed earlier, hardware devices make use of system resources to communicate with other components and with the operating system. These resources—direct memory access (DMA), interrupt request (IRQ), input/output (I/O) port, and memory address—can be shared by newer Plug and Play–compatible devices, and the devices can receive configuration settings from the operating system.

Each device responds to a query from the operating system with a list of settings it can use for each of the resources and whether the resources can be shared. The operating system then mediates between competing devices and sends configuration settings to each of them so that there is no conflict.

Some older devices, such as most Industry Standard Architecture (ISA) bus expansion cards, cannot share resources, however. And many of them, even with a Plug and Play driver, cannot have their resource settings configured by the operating system.

What happens if a computer starts up and finds two non-Plug and Play devices that both want to use IRQ 5? Although the computer might not start at all, it's more likely that one or both of the devices will not work. To resolve this situation, we would go to our friend the Device Manager and look for yellow question mark "problem" icons.

When you find a device with a problem icon and double-click it, you will see a statement that the device is not working due to a conflict. The Resources tab shows which resource is in conflict and usually will indicate which other device it is conflicting with. Then it's up to you to find settings for the two devices that don't result in a conflict.

> **NOTE**
>
> **Using Manual Settings** If the check box Use Automatic Settings has been cleared, you have told Windows (or somebody else has) not to try to configure the devices. Your first action in this case should be to select that check box and see if the problem goes away. If it does, you can pat yourself on the back. If it doesn't, you will either have to find nonconflicting settings or remove one of the conflicting devices.

Diagnosing and Resolving Server Hardware Issues

In general, if hardware issues are not caused by incorrect settings, they are caused by unsupported hardware or inappropriate device drivers.

Unsupported Hardware

As mentioned earlier, the HCL should be the first source you consult when you are looking for a new component for your production Windows Server 2003 computer. It's possible that devices not on the HCL will work without a problem on your computer, but why take the chance? You're risking the reliability of your organization's computing system, and your own reputation. Just say "no" to unsupported hardware.

An efficient way to test the hardware on a computer for its suitability for use with Windows Server 2003 is to run the compatibility checker program. You can run the compatibility checker on the computer on which you intend to install Windows Server 2003 by inserting the Windows Server 2003 CD-ROM and choosing Check System Compatibility, or by executing this command from the I386 folder:

```
winnt32 /checkupgradeonly
```

The resulting report will identify devices and applications that are not compatible with Windows Server 2003. With this information, you can decide whether to remove or replace the incompatible devices. Do not overlook this situation: You will cause yourself problems (system instability or device failures) if you do.

You can also search the online version of the HCL, which is always up-to-date at http://www.microsoft.com/whdc/hcl/search.mspx.

Managing Hardware Device Driver Upgrades

Suppose you have bought a new tape drive (having checked that it is listed on the HCL) and installed it on your computer, but the computer didn't recognize the tape drive when it rebooted. Chances are good that the driver installed by the operating system is not up-to-date. Device Manager should show a yellow question mark icon, and selecting Reinstall Driver from the General tab of the Device Properties dialog box, or Update Driver from the Drivers tab, will allow you to specify an updated driver.

Where do you find these updated drivers? One popular source is Windows Update, the Microsoft site from which security patches, new features, and driver updates can be manually or automatically downloaded (http://windowsupdate.microsoft.com/). These drivers will be digitally signed, so they will be protected by Windows File Protection. They may come from a website maintained by the device manufacturer, whose drivers may or may not be signed. And they might come from a third-party website, which makes drivers from many manufacturers available to its visitors.

By preference, you should always take the signed drivers from the Windows Update site before unsigned manufacturers' drivers, and both of these before drivers from a third-party website.

Dealing with a Device Driver Upgrade Problem

Occasionally, while performing maintenance on your computer, you may install a driver that causes problems. The following sections will outline a few methods to deal with this issue.

Device Driver Roll Back

In earlier versions of the operating system, if you decided to back out a driver upgrade, you might have difficulty finding the previous version: "Where did I put that CD-ROM?"

A very useful enhancement in Windows Server 2003 is the Device Driver Roll Back facility. When you select the Driver tab on the Properties dialog box for a device in Device Manager, one of the available buttons is Roll Back Driver. Its caption describes its purpose well: "If the device fails after updating the driver, roll back to the previously installed driver." Information about the previous driver is stored by Windows Server 2003, and when Device Driver Roll Back is invoked, the current driver is uninstalled and the previous driver is reinstalled. Follow the procedure in Step by Step 15.4 to see how to roll back a device driver.

STEP BY STEP

15.4 Rolling back a device driver

1. Click Start, Administrative Tools, Computer Management.

2. In the left pane, click the Device Manager entry.

3. In the right pane, expand the entry of the device that you want to select.

4. Right-click the device, and then select Properties from the pop-up menu.

5. Click the Drivers tab, and then click the Roll Back Driver button, as shown in Figure 15.20.

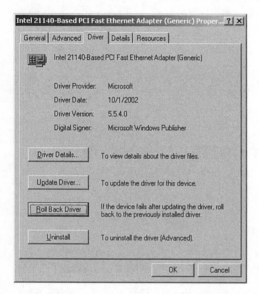

FIGURE 15.20 Select Roll Back Driver to go to the previous driver for this device.

6. When prompted, select Yes to confirm that you want to roll back to the previous driver.

Sometimes a driver upgrade will make the computer unable to boot up. In this case, use the F8 key during system startup and choose the option to start the system in Safe Mode. When the computer is running in Safe Mode, run Device Manager to find the problem device and on the Driver tab of the Properties dialog box, select Roll Back Driver.

Disabling or Uninstalling a Device Driver

Because servers are usually important in most companies, and downtime should be kept to a minimum, what happens if your server has a nonessential hardware device that is impacting your server's performance? For example, suppose that you have a fax board in your file and print server that gets used only occasionally. If the fax board is not going to be used for a month or so, but its driver is taking up a large amount of memory, what can you do?

In this situation, you have two choices:

▶ *Disable the device*—If you disable the device, the device is still physically connected, but the entries in the system Registry that tell Windows to load the driver are disabled. The drivers are still physically on the server, but won't be reloaded, even on reboot of the server.

▶ *Uninstall the driver*— The drivers are still physically on the server and will be reloaded on the next reboot of the server, unless you remove the device from the server.

In this situation, you can disable the device using the Device Manager MMC and reenable it when needed. The drivers will not be reloaded, even when the server is rebooted.

When you have no more use for the fax board, you can uninstall the device driver, then shut down the server, and physically remove it from the server.

To disable or uninstall a device driver, follow the procedure in Step by Step 15.5.

STEP BY STEP

15.5 Disabling or uninstalling a device driver

1. Click Start, Administrative Tools, Computer Management.

2. In the left pane, click the Device Manager entry.

3. In the right pane, expand the entry of the device that you want to select.

4. Right-click the device, and select the desired option from the pop-up menu (see Figure 15.21).

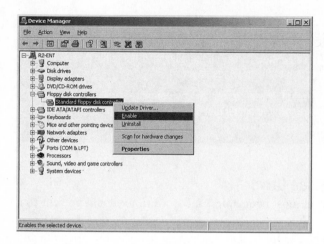

FIGURE 15.21 The device pop-up menu allows you to select driver options such as Update, Disable, or Uninstall.

5. When prompted, select Yes to confirm that you want to perform the requested action.

Trying to Use a Non-HCL Device

When our server was first installed, there were two problem devices. The first one, the Belkin UPS, was taken care of by installing a Windows 2000 driver. That approach often works because Windows 2000 and Windows Server 2003 are similar operating systems, but you shouldn't depend on such solutions. It's much better to use only devices on the Windows Server 2003 HCL and find a Windows Server 2003 driver for the device.

Still, sometimes we have no choice and must try to use the out-of-date or unsupported hardware, as the following example illustrates. Figure 15.22 shows the Device Manager display with one problem device.

Let's take a look at the cryptically identified VID_04E6 PID_80000002. A little research with a search engine establishes that this is an external HP Colorado 5GB tape drive. It's a few years old, and it's not found on the Windows Server 2003 HCL. With that knowledge, another search discovers Windows 2000 drivers for this device on a third-party website, which we downloaded into `C:\System manage-ment\Drivers\Colorado 5GB`.

Again we are considering whether to use a Windows 2000 driver in a Windows Server 2003 system. Again we decide that it's better to have something than nothing, so we install the driver, accepting warnings that the driver is unsigned, so Windows can't ensure that it isn't replaced improperly. In Figure 15.23 you see the dialog box in which we give the path where the drivers were downloaded.

(continues)

(continued)

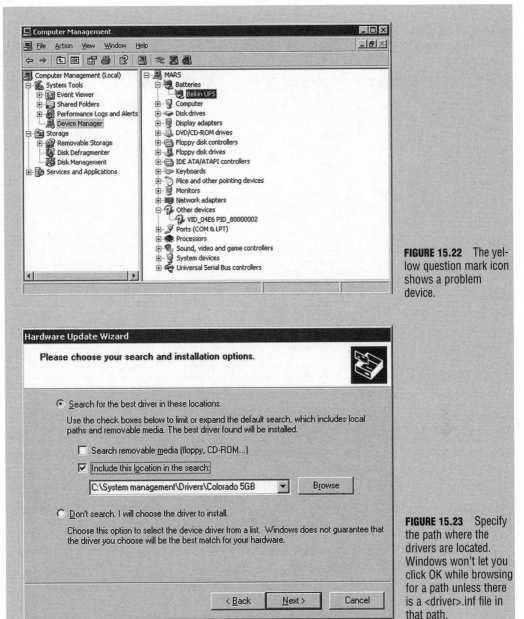

FIGURE 15.22 The yellow question mark icon shows a problem device.

FIGURE 15.23 Specify the path where the drivers are located. Windows won't let you click OK while browsing for a path unless there is a <driver>.inf file in that path.

(continues)

(continued)

Finally, the driver for the tape drive is installed, and Device Manager has given us a clean bill of health (see Figure 15.24).

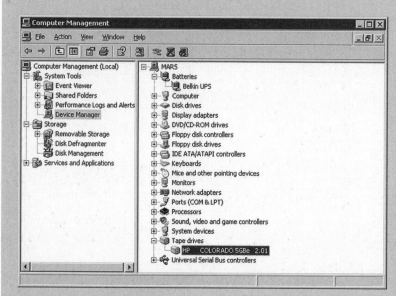

FIGURE 15.24 When there are no red or yellow icons in the Device Manager display, Windows Server 2003 is satisfied that all the devices are working fine.

However, don't think your troubles are over just because Device Manager has no complaints. Just after this screenshot was taken, the computer was rebooted, and it would not complete the bootup. When the external tape drive was removed, bootup proceeded normally. Even Device Manager can be fooled!

The lesson to be learned from this exercise is that the decision to try to proceed with unsupported hardware was unwise. Remember that your first priority as a system administrator is to ensure that the computers you maintain are always online and always functioning properly. Do not compromise this priority by deciding (or agreeing, even under pressure) to use unsupported hardware.

Challenge

You are the administrator of a network that includes multiple Windows Server 2003 servers that are used for remote access and telephony services. The Customer Service department is a very heavy user of both inbound and outbound faxes, the capability of which is controlled by an older server with a set of proprietary ISA fax cards. This old server has been having hardware-related problems, and it's not cost effective for it to be repaired. Therefore, you order a new server—luckily, one of the few available that still has a few ISA slots.

However, now it's up to you to make these old fax cards work with Windows Server 2003.

What is the best way to solve this issue in Windows Server 2003? On your own, try to develop a solution that would involve the least amount of downtime.

If you would like to see a possible solution, follow the procedure outlined here.

Unfortunately, you're going to have to work around two separate issues: older unsigned drivers and non–Plug and Play devices. First you're going to have to install the fax cards in your server and make sure they're not trying to use resources allocated to other devices. Then you're going to have to load an unsigned driver. Here are the steps to follow:

1. Consult the documentation that came with the fax boards to determine the resource configuration.

2. Click Start, Control Panel, System, and then click the Hardware tab.

3. Click the Device Manager button.

4. In Device Manager, check to make sure the required resources are available. You can accomplish this by selecting the Resources by Connection entry in the View menu. If the necessary resources are not available, try to reconfigure the fax cards for some that are.

5. Power down the server.

6. Install the fax cards in the new server.

7. Boot the server.

8. Click Start, Control Panel, System, and then click the Hardware tab.

9. Click the Device Manager button.

10. In Device Manager, expand the entry for the fax device.

11. Right-click the fax device and select Properties from the pop-up menu.

12. Click the Resources tab.

13. Select the resource setting you want to modify.

14. Clear the Use Automatic Settings check box if it is selected.

15. Click the Change Setting button.

(continues)

(continued)

16. Configure the resource settings to the settings that the fax card is configured for.

17. Click OK to save. Repeat this process for the other fax cards.

18. Close Device Manager.

19. This returns you to the Hardware tab of the System Properties dialog box. Click Driver Signing.

20. In the Driver Signing Options dialog box, in the What Action Do You Want Windows to Take? section, click Ignore—Install the Software Anyway and Don't Ask for My Approval.

21. Click OK and then click OK again on the System Properties dialog box to save.

22. Install the driver for the fax cards according to the manufacturer's instructions.

As soon as you have installed the unsigned driver, you should return to the Driver Signing Options dialog box and choose Block—Never Install Unsigned Driver Software.

Chapter Summary

One of the most important parts of the system administrator's job is to understand the relationship between the operating system and the various system devices. The majority of installation configuring and troubleshooting tasks are performed using the Device Manager snap-in. It will be important to know Device Manager thoroughly.

In addition, pay attention to the following tips:

▶ To ensure the stability of your servers and to have all your devices operate properly, it is critical that the devices be compatible with Windows Server 2003 and that you use only signed drivers from reputable sources.

▶ Modern system boards (motherboards) meet the Advanced Configuration and Power Interface (ACPI) standard, which means the operating system running in that system will be able to recognize and configure all installed hardware that is built to the Plug and Play specifications.

▶ A device with an ACPI-compliant motherboard can have its devices selectively powered down or put into sleep mode. This allows battery-powered computers to have maximum battery life.

▶ Older hardware, particularly devices that were built to the Industry Standard Architecture (ISA) specifications, cannot be managed by Windows Server 2003, so manual configuration is necessary to make sure the resource usage by these devices does not conflict with other devices on the computer.

▶ Device drivers are software components that allow communication between the operating system and devices. They run very close to the kernel of the operating system, so it is crucial that they be trustworthy. Driver signing assures the administrator that the drivers running on a computer are legitimate. Running unsigned drivers compromises the stability of your computer.

▶ You can ensure that no unsigned drivers can be installed on your computer by configuring the driver-signing options on the computer. For large numbers of computers, it's recommended that you create a Group Policy Object to automate this configuration.

▶ To check whether there any unsigned drivers on your computer, run File Signature Verification, which you access by using Start, Run, `sigverif.exe`.

▶ Windows Server 2003 includes an important service, Windows File Protection, that automatically removes any unsigned system files and replaces them with signed files.

▶ For any hardware device, as many as four different resources can be defined: direct memory access (DMA), interrupt request (IRQ), input/output (I/O) port, and memory address. It is important to avoid conflicts between devices attempting to use the same settings for a given device. If the devices are Plug and Play compatible, these conflicts will not arise. If they are not, you may have to perform some manual configuration.

▶ To determine the settings for a device, or to configure devices manually, you use the Device Manager tool. When you start Device Manager, devices that are not working properly are shown with a yellow question mark icon. Devices that are disabled have a red X over the icon. Device Manager does not manage device drivers for printers and fax devices.

▶ Occasionally you will find that an error message is displayed when you attempt to assign the same IP address to a new network card, if you did not uninstall the old card before you removed it from the computer. You must start Device Manager with a special parameter to make the absent network card visible and capable of being deleted.

▶ There are methods by which you can override the warnings that Device Manager presents if you try to install old or unsigned drivers. We don't recommend you do this, however, if you want to maintain the reliability of your computer.

▶ Use the Add Hardware Wizard to install devices that are not automatically recognized and installed by the operating system.

▶ You will be unable to deselect Use Automatic Settings on the Resources tab for a device's properties if the device is Plug and Play compatible and being managed by the operating system.

▶ Use the Hardware Compatibility List (HCL) or the compatibility checker program to determine whether any devices in a computer are incompatible with Windows Server 2003.

▶ Remember to "Just Say No" if you are tempted (or asked) to use unsupported devices or unsigned drivers on your computer.

Key Terms

▶ Advanced Configuration and Power Interface (ACPI)

▶ Plug and Play

▶ Basic input/output system (BIOS)

▶ OnNow Device Power Management

▶ Device driver

▶ Hardware Compatibility List (HCL)

▶ Driver signing

- ▶ Group Policies

- ▶ File Signature Verification

- ▶ Windows File Protection

- ▶ System File Checker

- ▶ Resource settings

- ▶ Device Manager

- ▶ Hardware Troubleshooter

- ▶ Uninterruptible power supply (UPS)

- ▶ Direct memory access (DMA)

- ▶ Interrupt request (IRQ)

- ▶ Input/output (I/O) port

- ▶ Memory address

- ▶ Compatibility checker

- ▶ Windows Update

- ▶ Device Driver Roll Back

Apply Your Knowledge

Exercises

15.1 Checking for unsigned drivers

This exercise demonstrates how to determine whether there are any unsigned drivers on your computer. We accomplish this in two ways: by using File Signature Verification and by using `driverquery.exe`.

Estimated Time: 10 minutes

1. Select the Start menu, click Run, and in the Open dialog box type **sigverif**.

2. You want to perform the default verification, so click Start to begin the file checking. Wait while the verification program runs.

3. Review the listing of unsigned drivers. Determine the source of the drivers.

4. (Optional) Browse the website of the manufacturer of the device for which the unsigned drivers were loaded. See if any signed drivers exist for the devices in question.

5. Open a command prompt.

6. Enter **driverquery /?** and review the help information.

7. Enter **driverquery /fo table /s *<computername>* /si** to show a list of loaded drivers on the computer.

8. Enter **driverquery /fo csv /s *<computername>* /si >c:\dr.csv** to write a comma-separated values table of loaded drivers on the computer to the file `c:\dr.csv`.

9. (Optional) Run a spreadsheet program or a database program and load the output from step 8. Consider how a database of driver information for each of the servers in your network might be useful.

15.2 Determining the DMA channels in use

This exercise demonstrates how to determine what DMA channels are in use on your computer. We'll use Device Manager.

Estimated Time: 5 minutes

1. To start Device Manager, right-click My Computer and choose Manage.

2. In the Explorer pane, click Device Manager.

3. In the View menu, choose Resources by Type.

4. Click the plus sign beside Direct Memory Access (DMA).

5. Review the channels in use on your computer.

Exam Questions

1. You have been asked whether an older computer will operate properly with Windows Server 2003. What feature of the computer must be present for device resource settings to be assigned automatically by Windows Server 2003?

   ○ **A.** APM

   ○ **B.** SFC

   ○ **C.** ACPI

   ○ **D.** PnP

2. After installing a new driver for a printer, you find that it is not functioning properly, and you decide to return to the previous driver. What procedure(s) will give you the desired results?

- ○ **A.** Uninstall the printer and then start again with the most recent functioning driver you can find.

- ○ **B.** Use Device Manager to invoke Driver Roll Back.

- ○ **C.** Run Driver Roll Back from Administrative Tools.

- ○ **D.** On the Advanced tab of the printer's Properties dialog box, choose New Driver and use Have Disk to select the source of the previous driver.

3. A colleague has sent you a new driver for your server's RAID controller, which he says makes the drives it controls run more efficiently. You want to ensure that the driver is from a reputable source. How do you do that?

- ○ **A.** Look for the driver on the manufacturer's website.

- ○ **B.** Run Windows File Protection to determine the creator of the driver.

- ○ **C.** Run `sigverif.exe`, and on the Advanced tab, choose to search on `*.sys` files in the folder where you saved the driver.

- ○ **D.** Run `driverquery` with the `/fo csv` switch against the folder where you saved the file.

4. You are the administrator of a small network. You use Group Policy to limit what the users can do on their workstations. What action should you take to warn users about unsigned drivers, but not block the installation?

- ○ **A.** Put the warning in the company policy manual and distribute it via email.

- ○ **B.** Configure the driver signing policy for Notify When Installing Unsigned Drivers.

- ○ **C.** Configure the driver signing policy for Warn When Installing Unsigned Drivers.

- ○ **D.** Configure the driver signing policy for Alert When Installing Unsigned Drivers.

5. You are the administrator of a small network. One of your junior administrators calls and says she is having a problem with one of the modems in the remote access servers. You go look at the server and open Device Manager. You notice that the entry for the modem has a question mark with a red X. What action should you take to correct this problem?

- ○ **A.** Use Device Manager to enable the device.

- ○ **B.** Reinstall the drivers for the device.

- ○ **C.** Reassign the resources for the device.

- ○ **D.** Nothing. The device is not compatible with Windows Server 2003.

6. You are having problems getting some of the specialized hardware devices in a new server to work properly with Windows Server 2003, after installing the hardware and downloading the drivers from the Internet. You call Microsoft support, and the first thing that they ask you is whether you are using any unsigned drivers. What is the easiest way to find this out?

   ○ **A.** Run `sigverif.exe` with the default options.

   ○ **B.** Run `sigverif.exe` with the advanced options.

   ○ **C.** Run `driverquery` with the `/fo csv` switch.

   ○ **D.** Run `driverquery` with the `/fo cvs` switch.

7. One of your junior administrators inadvertently installed an older application on one of your Windows Server 2003 servers that overwrote some of the system DLLs. Fortunately, Windows Server 2003 comes with the Windows File Protection feature so that the system files are automatically replaced with the correct ones. Unfortunately, WFP can't seem to find the necessary files in the `%systemroot%\system32\dllcache` folder. Where can you obtain the proper files?

   ○ **A.** Windows Update

   ○ **B.** Windows service packs

   ○ **C.** Windows Server 2003 CD-ROM

   ○ **D.** Hotfix distributions

8. You are building a new print server using Windows Server 2003. All the printer drivers have loaded successfully except for an older Windows NT driver that may or may not be supported on Windows Server 2003. What utility should you use to troubleshoot this driver problem?

   ○ **A.** Device Manager

   ○ **B.** Computer Management

   ○ **C.** Printers applet

   ○ **D.** Printers and Faxes applet

9. You are the network administrator for Skelly Inc. All network servers run Windows Server 2003, and all client computers run Windows XP Professional.

   Several users report that they cannot access a server named FileSrv1. First, you verify that the network adapter on FileSrv1 has the correct driver installed. Then, you open Device Manager on FileSrv1. You see a red X by the network adapter entry.

   Now you need to use Device Manager to restore network connectivity on FileSrv1. What should you do?

   ○ **A.** You must enable the network adapter.

   ○ **B.** You need to change the network adapter IRQ setting.

   ○ **C.** You have to change the network adapter's IP address.

   ○ **D.** Adjust the link speed of the network adapter to match the link speed of the network.

   ○ **E.** Resolve all possible hardware conflicts between the network adapter and the unknown device.

10. You are the administrator of a Windows Server 2003 computer named FilePrt1. There is a driver conflict on FilePrt1. You suspect that an unsigned driver has been installed for one of the hardware devices. You need to locate any unsigned drives. What should you do?

    ○ **A.** Use the advanced options of the File Signature Verification tool to scan the contents of the Systemroot\System32 folder and all subfolders.

    ○ **B.** Run the `drivequery / si` command, and examine the output.

    ○ **C.** Use the advanced options of the File Signature Verification tool to scan the contents of the Systemroot\System folder and all subfolders.

    ○ **D.** Run the `ver` command.

Answers to Exam Questions

1. **C.** ACPI must be present on the computer for Windows Server 2003 to be able to take over the configuration of devices. APM (Advanced Power Management) is a predecessor to ACPI that does not perform automatic configuration as completely as ACPI. SFC (System File Checker) is a tool for scheduling a run of the system files to identify any that are unsigned. PnP (Plug and Play) is a specification that states how devices should identify themselves and respond to configuration commands. See the "Installing and Configuring Hardware Devices" section for more information.

2. **A, D.** You must remove the existing driver and install one that you know works. You can do this explicitly, by deleting the printer and reinstalling it, or with the help of the Add Printer Driver Wizard. Device Manager does not function with printer drivers, and Driver Roll Back is not available for printer drivers. See the "Managing Drivers for Printers and Faxes" section for more information.

3. **C.** File Signature Verification will inspect the files in the location you specify, and it will tell you if they are unsigned. Looking for the driver on the manufacturer's website is probably safer than using the one your colleague supplied, but a driver you find there may yet be unsigned. Windows File Protection replaces unsigned drivers with signed ones from the dllcache. Running `driverquery.exe` with the `/fo csv` switch shows the running drivers—it does not inspect drivers that are not running. See the "What Drivers Are Running on My Computer?" section for more information.

4. **C.** Although distributing the policy via email seems like a good idea, you will need something more reliable. By selecting the Warn option, the user will be instructed that he or she is installing an unsigned driver and will be informed of the potential consequences; however, the user will still be able to install it. The Notify and Alert options do not exist. See the "What Is Driver Signing and Why Should I Care?" section for more information.

5. **B.** The icon displayed usually indicates that the drivers are either missing or corrupt. Reinstalling the drivers should correct the problem. See the "Diagnosing and Resolving Issues Related to Hardware Settings" section for more information.

6. **A.** Running `sigverif.exe` with the default options generates a list of all unsigned system files and drivers on the server. Getting similar information from `driverquery.exe` requires the `/si` switch. See the "Determining Whether a Computer Has Unsigned Drivers" section for more information.

7. **C.** If the desired version of the file is not in the dllcache folder, Windows File Protection asks for the Windows Server 2003 CD-ROM to be mounted, and it copies the files from there. Obtaining the files from Windows Update, a service pack, or a hotfix would be an option only if the required files have been updated, and you have no guarantee that you're installing the proper version. See the "Other Methods for Protecting Device Drivers" section for more information.

8. **D.** Neither Device Manager nor any other components of the Computer Management MMC manage device drivers for printers and fax devices. They are managed through the Printers and Faxes applet in Control Panel. The Printers applet does not exist in Windows Server 2003. See the "Managing Drivers for Printers and Faxes" section for more information.

Apply Your Knowledge

9. **A.** The red X indicates that the network card is disabled. The question also mentions that the correct driver is installed. Therefore, enabling the network adapter will render it operational. If the IRQ was wrong, the network adapter would have an exclamation mark in a yellow circle over it. If the IP address was wrong or the link speed was set incorrectly, there would be no indication in Device Manager. If there was a hardware conflict, the network adapter status would be marked with an exclamation mark with a yellow circle over it. See the "Configuring Device Properties and Settings" section for more information.

10. **A.** The File Signature Verification tool generates the report of unsigned drivers with the least administrative effort. Using the `driverquery` command with the `si` parameter will display the properties of signed drivers, but not the location of unsigned drivers. In Windows Server 2003, Systemroot\System folder is not a protected folder and will not indicate whether the driver is signed. The `Ver` command is useless unless you specify what you want to verify. See the "Determining Whether a Computer Has Unsigned Drivers" section for more information.

Suggested Readings and Resources

1. OnNow Device Power Management. Microsoft Corporation whitepaper. http://www.microsoft.com/whdc/hwdev/tech/onnow/devicepm.mspx.

2. Windows Server 2003 Deployment Guide. Microsoft Corporation. http://www.microsoft.com/windowsserver2003/techinfo/reskit/deploykit.mspx.

3. Windows Server 2003 Resource Kit. Microsoft Corporation. Look for a link to it on the Technical Resources for Windows Server 2003 page: http://www.microsoft.com/windowsserver2003/techinfo/default.mspx.

16

Implementing Administrative Templates and Audit Policy

Objectives

This chapter covers the following Microsoft-specified objectives for the "Monitor File and Print Servers" section of the Managing and Maintaining a Microsoft Windows Server 2003 Environment exam:

Monitor and analyze events. Tools might include Event Viewer and System Monitor.

▶ The purpose of this objective is to teach you how to use the system tools to locate and identify errors and security events using the Event Viewer logs. In addition, you will need to be able to manage the security logs for the purpose of auditing system events.

Outline

Study Strategies

▶ The sections in this chapter outline how to monitor and enforce security in both a stand-alone and a domain environment. Make sure that you have a complete understanding of how to work with the Event Logs, and especially the Security and Analysis tool. Perform the supplied exercises, and look at the supplemental reading to get more of an understanding of its capabilities.

▶ Most of the Event Viewer questions will probably be related to the use of the Security log and auditing. Although auditing is turned on by default in Windows Server 2003, you still have to configure auditing on the individual objects. Make sure you understand the various auditing capabilities, how to enable auditing for an object, and how to configure and archive the event logs.

▶ In addition to the capabilities we discussed in previous chapters, Group Policy can also be used to implement security. You should perform the exercises that make security changes, and observe both how they are applied and their effects on standalone servers and member servers.

Introduction

We start this chapter by looking at how to configure and apply security using the Active Directory security model. We then look at the tools that can be used to monitor and audit security events and analyze whether the steps taken will be sufficient to protect the enterprise.

Security in Windows Server 2003

Similar to the security model in previous versions of Windows dating back to Windows NT, the domain remains the security boundary in a Windows Server 2003 network. Any security configurations that are made apply only to the domain that they were configured in; they do not automatically cross from one domain to another. Each domain will have its own security policies.

In Windows Server 2003, the foundation of the Active Directory security model is the association of an Access Control List (ACL) with each object, attribute, and container to control access to these items by users and groups. In Chapter 4, "Managing and Maintaining Access to Resources," we briefly examined how the network administrator is able to assign individual users and groups varying levels of permissions for objects and their attributes, and even hide those attributes from certain groups of users. This type of security provides the network administrator with a high degree of control over individual objects and their attributes.

As networks get larger and grow in scope, having this type of granular security control is more important. In addition, in the larger organization it is essential to be able to have this type of control to be able to implement a comprehensive organizational security plan. Because of the different needs of each department or location, there might need to be a distinct security plan for each separate entity. For example, the security needs for the accounting department will usually be far greater and more complex than those needed in the mailroom.

As the complexity of the organizational security plan grows, there is a need to simplify the implementation of security as much as possible to ensure that the proper policies are implemented in the proper areas, and for the proper users. Fortunately, Active Directory comes with several tools that can be used to simplify the configuration and management of network security. We examine some of these tools and show you how to implement them in the Active Directory environment.

Applying Security Policies

In Chapter 9, "Implementing Group Policy," we covered the use of Group Policies in a Windows Server 2003 network. In addition to creating Group policies that control users and computers, we can create Security policies that control the security configuration of Active Directory and its objects. The settings contained in these security policies are used to define the security behavior of the network.

Windows Server 2003 uses the Group Policy Object to apply security permissions. Security configurations are created within the Group policy object to control various security areas of Windows Server 2003 clients. By default, Group Policies are applied when the computer starts up, and they are periodically refreshed to pick up any changes that are made to the policies.

Configuring Security Policies

Security policies can be found in two places in the Group Policy snap-in of the Active Directory Users and Computers console. The computer configuration policies are contained in the Computer Configuration container. These policies are used to control the security configuration of computers on the network. These policies will be applied to the computer as its operating system is initialized.

The other security policy is used to enforce lockdown policies on users on the network. These policies are contained in the User Configuration container. These policies will be applied whenever a user logs on to the network.

The Group Policy snap-in allows you to define security policies with the Security Settings extension. The Security Settings extension allows you to define the security configuration for local computers, the domain, and the site within a Group Policy Object. Using a group policy simplifies security administration by allowing the administrator to specify the security settings once, and then apply these settings to all the objects in a container as part of the Group Policy enforcement.

Nine security areas can be configured. These settings are located in the Security Settings node of a Group Policy object, as shown in Figure 16.1. They are

- ▶ Account Policies
- ▶ File System
- ▶ Local Policies
- ▶ Event Log
- ▶ IP Security Policies
- ▶ Public Key Policies
- ▶ Registry
- ▶ Restricted Groups
- ▶ Software Restriction Policies
- ▶ Wireless Network
- ▶ System Services

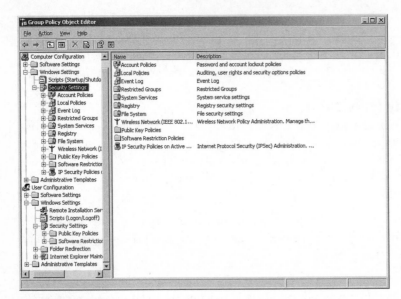

FIGURE 16.1 Group Policy console showing Security Policy areas.

Although most of the policy areas can be applied at the site, domain, or organizational unit (OU) level, there are some policy areas that apply only at the domain. For example, you cannot define different account or public key policies for different OUs in the same domain. All other policy areas can be specified at the level of the site or the OU. Unlike domain controllers, which receive their policies directly from Active Directory, workstations and member servers are allowed to define their own local policies.

Account Policies

Account policies are used to configure the security attributes for the user accounts in the domain. This policy will be the default policy for any machines that are members of the domain. However, you can set an account policy at the OU level, but these settings will apply only to the *local* user accounts of the nondomain controller computers contained in that Organizational Unit (OU).

These attributes are the following:

▶ *Account Lockout Policy*—This policy disables a user account after a specified number of failed logon attempts. There are three settings that can be configured:

▶ *Lockout Count*—This is the number of failed logon attempts permitted before the account is disabled.

▶ *Lockout Reset Time*—This is the time interval between attempts before the lockout count is returned to zero.

▶ *Lockout Duration*—This is the time interval after the account is locked out that the account will remain disabled.

▶ *Password Policy*—Several options are available for password policy. For example, both the minimum password length and maximum password age can be specified. In addition, Windows Server 2003 allows you to require the use of Complex Passwords. Complex Passwords have to be at least six characters long and must contain a mix of different characters. A complex password cannot contain any part of the username or the user's full name. You can also prevent users from reusing passwords or simple variations of previous passwords.

▶ *Kerberos Authentication Policy*—You can modify the default Kerberos settings at the domain level. This can include the ticket lifetime and enforcement of user logons.

NOTE

Account Policies It is not necessary to apply an account policy to organization units that don't contain computers. The account policies that apply to the users in the organizational unit can only be applied as a domain policy.

To modify the Account Policies, follow the procedure in Step by Step 16.1.

STEP BY STEP

16.1 Modifying Account Policies

1. Click Start, All Programs, Administrative Tools, Domain Security Policy.

2. From the Domain Security Policy snap-in, click Security settings, and then click Account Policies.

3. Click Password Policies, and then in the right pane of the console, right click Minimum Password Length (see Figure 16.2).

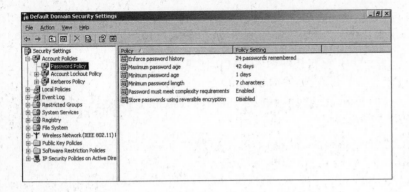

FIGURE 16.2 Default Domain Security Settings MMC, showing Windows Server 2003 default Password Policy.

4. From the pop-up menu, click Security.

5. The Security Policy Setting window appears. Select the Define This Policy Setting check box.

6. Set the password length in the Characters box to 7.

7. Click OK to save.

When configuring the account policies, it is best to balance the level of security desired with the overhead created by having security policies that are too restrictive. Although no one wants to have a network that is vulnerable to security breaches, having an overly restrictive lockout policy can create an excessive workload for the user help desk personnel. In addition, if the password format and length is too difficult to remember, most users will write down their passwords, potentially leaving them where an unauthorized user could find them. Usually, a password length of seven characters is optimum both for security exposure and user convenience.

Remember that password, lockout, and Kerberos policies are applied at the domain level only. A Windows Server 2003 domain controller will ignore any policies defined at the OU or site level.

Event Log Policies

The Event Log policies are used to configure the application, system, and security event logs on Windows Server 2003 computers. For example, you can specify the following:

▶ Access rights for each type of log

▶ Maximum log size

▶ Length of retention

▶ Log retention methods

The settings for the event logs can be controlled at the site, domain, or OU level. Generally, domain controllers should be configured with larger logs, and they should be retained longer than the logs on workstations. In addition, you might want to configure the access rights of the event logs on domain controllers so that they can be viewed only by administrators. Event and security logs will be covered at length later in the chapter.

File System Policies

File system policies can be used to configure security for files and folders. For example, to ensure that only administrators can modify system files and folders on all the computers in the domain, you can configure a policy that will grant full control over system files and folders to administrators while giving users read permission only. In addition, file system policies can also be used to prevent users from being able to see certain files and folders.

This type of security configuration can be specified once in the file system policy and then applied to all the computers in the domain. This can save the network administrator a lot of time and effort when locking down the file system on a large number of computers.

File System policies can also be used to control the security auditing of user access to certain files and folders when auditing is enabled. You can specify which users and which user events are logged for both failed and successful events. We will look at this at greater length in the section on Audit Policy.

Local Computer Policies

Local computer policies are used to control the security of the local computer. The policies that will affect the local computer and its users are stored in the *\%systemroot%\system32\GroupPolicy folder*. Local computer policies allow the administrator to control and audit a variety of events and tasks. These events and tasks can be broken down into three areas:

- ▶ Audit Policy
- ▶ User Rights Assignment
- ▶ Security Options

Local Computer Policies allow the network administrator to control the security of the individual computers from a central location. By applying this policy to a domain, site, or organizational unit it saves the administrator time and effort since there is no need to visit individual computers. By separating different types of computers such as domain controllers, member servers, and user workstations into different organizational units, the administrator can tailor the policies for each type of machine. In addition, by assigning different user rights to different user groups, this also allows the administrator to grant more extensive rights that might be needed in the Developers group while limiting the rights of users in the Warehouse group.

Audit Policy

The Audit policy is used to specify which security events will be logged in the Security log on the local computer. This can include events such as logons and user access of specified files and folders. You can audit successful attempts, unsuccessful attempts, or both. Auditing and audit policies will be covered at length later in this chapter.

Using the Event Logs

Objective:

Monitor and analyze events. Tools might include Event Viewer and System Monitor.

The Event Viewer in Windows Server 2003, shown in Figure 16.3, is available in the Computer Management MMC or as a standalone MMC snap-in. This Windows Server 2003 utility records information about various system occurrences. The Event Viewer is not only the first place you should look when you're having problems, but you must also review it regularly to monitor regular server operations and events.

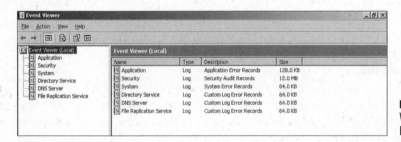

FIGURE 16.3 The Windows Server 2003 Event Viewer.

The Event Viewer is used to view event log files that are updated by the operating system and various services and applications running on your server. Typically, events are written to the logs for any significant occurrence that a user or administrator should be aware of. Reading the contents of these log files can assist you in determining the status of your server and as a first step in diagnosing problems.

As in previous versions of Windows, all servers have the following three log files: System, Security, and Application. Although these three logs have been carried over from previous versions of Windows, the Event Viewer has been expanded to allow other components or third-party applications to use it as the global location for log files. The logs that appear in your installation of Windows Server 2003 vary depending on the components installed. For example, the Domain Name Service maintains its own log in the Event Viewer. All Windows Server 2003 systems have at the very least the following three logs:

▶ *System log*—This file records events related to system operation, most often associated with device drivers and services such as DHCP and WINS. Most of the information here relates to the stopping and starting of services or the failure of a system component.

▶ *Application log*—This file records events related to applications, programs, and utilities, usually not native Windows Server 2003 components. Examples are database programs, email servers, and print messages. The information that is recorded here is determined by the application developer, and it usually consists of informational messages, errors, or warnings. This log is also used to store the alerts generated by the Performance Logs and Alerts tool.

▶ *Security log*—This file records events related to security and auditing. Typical events include valid or invalid logon attempts and the accessing of resources such as the opening, reading, or deleting of a file or folder. The types of events recorded in this log can be configured via the audit policy. In previous versions of Windows, the security log would not record any information until an audit policy was enabled. In Windows 2003, security logging is enabled by default.

If the DNS service is installed on your server, the DNS log is also available. It records events related to the operation of the DNS service. If you're having name-resolution problems on your network, this is the first place to look.

In addition, Active Directory domain controllers have the following logs:

▶ *Directory Service log*—This file records events related to the operation of the Active Directory service. Typical events in this log are related to communication between domain controllers and Global Catalog servers.

▶ *File Replication Service log*—This file records events related to replication of the SYSVOL and the DFS tree, as well as other applications that use FRS, such as DFS.

Understanding the Event Logs

As mentioned earlier, event logs can be very useful, not only for monitoring server operations but also as a first step in diagnosing a problem. It is helpful to become familiar with the normal events that occur on a daily basis because some errors normally reoccur and are not an indication of a problem.

The event logs contain five main types of events that range from informational messages that do not require any action to serious events, such as hardware or service failures, that require your immediate attention. As shown in Figure 16.4, each type of event is visually cued by an icon. This allows you to quickly recognize events that require your attention.

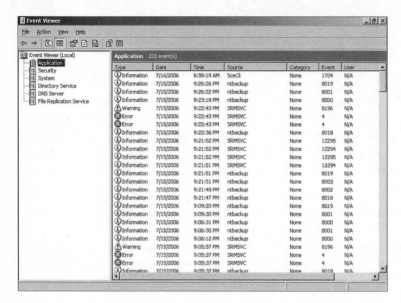

FIGURE 16.4 The Windows Server 2003 Event Viewer, showing the icons for various types of events.

The five types of events and their related icons are as follows:

▶ *Error events*—These are displayed as an X in a red circle. An error event is usually serious and can lead to data loss or a loss of functionality. Typical examples of error events are services that have stopped or failed to load on system startup and disk read or write failures.

▶ *Warning events*—These are displayed as an exclamation point on a yellow triangle. A warning event is usually not critical but indicates that you might have to take action in the future. Typical examples of warning events are low disk space conditions or failures in synchronization of the time service.

▶ *Information events*—These are displayed as a lowercase i on a bubble. Most information events are just to let you know that a task has been completed successfully. For example, when a service is started, it might write an information event to the log. Although the majority of informational events are benign, if you have Alert Logging turned on, that service writes an information message to the log when an alert has been triggered, which is a condition that requires follow-up.

▶ *Success audits*—These are displayed as a key icon. Successfully logging on to the server or accessing an audited resource are examples of things that would generate a success audit event.

▶ *Failure audits*—These are displayed as a padlock icon. If a user tries and fails to log on to a server or access an audited resource that he or she has not been granted access to, a failure audit event is generated.

Each entry in the event log, regardless of type, contains the following information:

- ▶ A description of the event (usually, but not always)

- ▶ The date and time that the event was logged

- ▶ The type of event (one of the five types we discussed earlier)

- ▶ The source of the event—usually the service, component, or application that posted the event to the log

- ▶ The username—either the user ID of the logged-on user for a security event or the process name for system events

- ▶ The name of the server where the event occurred

- ▶ The category of the event, which is typically used only in the Security log for events such as logon/logoff, object access, and policy changes

- ▶ The event ID, which is used to identify the event type, which is a number that can be used to aid in the troubleshooting of server problems

As shown in Figure 16.5, some events provide a URL that you can click. This URL links you to the Microsoft website. If there is more information available for your event, it is displayed. If you don't understand an error message and there is no URL, write down the event ID. The event ID can be used to perform a search using the Microsoft Knowledge Base at http://support.microsoft.com. The articles in the Knowledge Base can sometimes be useful in figuring out a problem, or they can at least give you more information to work with.

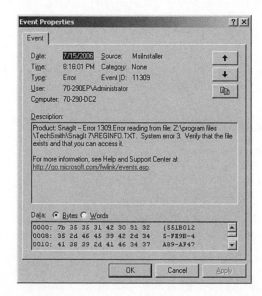

FIGURE 16.5 Log entries aren't always as clear as this one, so you will sometimes be able to click a URL for more information.

EventID.net

EventID.net is a third-party website that collects definitions for most of the common events. Basic searches and information are free. This site also provides troubleshooting information and extra documentation for subscribers. This is a good reference if you can't locate any useful information on an event in the Microsoft Knowledge Base. The site is accessible at www.eventid.net.

Working with the Event Logs

Although the System and Application logs can be viewed by anyone, the Security log is restricted to administrators. To open and view an event log, perform the procedure outlined in Step by Step 16.2.

STEP BY STEP

16.2 Opening the Event Viewer and viewing the System log

1. Click Start, All Programs, Administrative Tools, Event Viewer.

2. In the left pane of the Event Viewer MMC, click the entry for the System log.

3. Find an event with a source of EventLog and an Event ID of 6005. Double-click the entry to open it.

As you can see in Figure 16.6, an event is written to the System log when the event log service is started. The event log service is started every time the server is started, so that gives you a good starting point when you want to look for errors that have occurred since the last system restart.

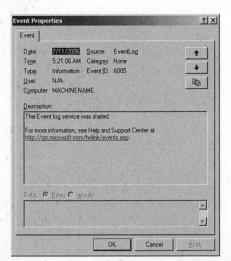

FIGURE 16.6 A System log event is recorded every time the server is started.

Viewing Logs on Another Computer

You can view the log files from a remote system on your network using the Connect to Another Computer command from the Event Viewer menu. This feature simplifies administrative tasks by allowing you to diagnose a system remotely via Event Viewer rather than requiring you to sit at that computer's keyboard. You must be a member of the Administrators group on the remote computer to view its event logs.

To open and view an event log on a remote computer, perform the procedure outlined in Step by Step 16.3.

STEP BY STEP

16.3 Opening the Event Viewer on a remote computer

1. From the Start menu, click Start, All Programs, Administrative Tools, Event Viewer.

2. In the left pane of the Event Viewer MMC, right-click the Event Viewer (Local) entry. Select Connect to Another Computer from the pop-up menu.

3. From the Select Computer dialog box shown in Figure 16.7, you can either enter the name of the remote computer (without the leading \\) or click the Browse button to locate it on your network if you're not sure of the computer name. Click the Browse button to continue.

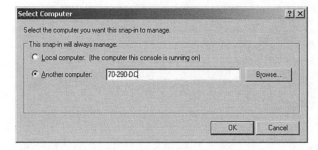

FIGURE 16.7 Remember to enter the computer name without the leading backslashes.

4. From the next Select Computer dialog box, click the Advanced button.

5. From the Select Computer dialog box, click the Locations button to select the domain to browse. Then click the Find Now button to search for computers.

6. Select a computer and then click OK twice to connect.

Configuring Log Properties

When you open a log in the Event Viewer, a snapshot of the log is displayed. Any new information that is written to the log as you are viewing it is not displayed until you click the Refresh icon on the toolbar. When you switch between logs, the view is refreshed automatically.

Several configuration settings determine how much information can be stored in the event logs and how long the information is retained before it is overwritten. You can change the event log retention options through the Event Log Properties dialog box, shown in Figure 16.8, accessed from the Log menu. Each log file has its own size and day limit settings.

In addition to the setting for log size, three additional settings determine the retention properties of the logs:

▶ *Overwrite Events As Needed*—When the log is full, new events overwrite the oldest events.

▶ *Overwrite Events Older Than X Days*—This prevents the information in the logs from being overwritten until the specified time has elapsed. If the log becomes full, no events are recorded until there are events older than the specified period.

▶ *Do Not Overwrite Events*—This option prevents the logs from ever being overwritten, even if they become full. It should be used only if you clear or archive the logs on a regular basis. This option is typically used for the Security logs on highly secure networks, where access records must be maintained indefinitely. Increasing the maximum size of the log file is a good idea to ensure the server does not stop functioning in the event that the log reaches its maximum size and is set to avoid overwriting older events.

CAUTION

Be Careful When Setting Retention Time   If you are not careful when configuring your event log retention settings, you could configure your logs so that important events are missed. For example, if you set the overwrite period too short, or turn on Overwrite Events as Needed with too small of a log size, as the log fills up, events will be overwritten. In addition, if you set the log size too small and then turn on Do Not Overwrite Events, after the log fills up, no events will be logged.

The default settings for the logs restrict each log file to a maximum of 16,384KB. When the fixed file size is reached, the oldest events are overwritten by new events, as needed. If you need to retain events for longer time periods, you should increase the file size and the retention time.

To configure the retention settings for an event log, perform the procedure outlined in Step by Step 16.4.

STEP BY STEP

16.4 Configuring the event log retention settings

1. From the Start menu, click Start, All Programs, Administrative Tools, Event Viewer.

2. In the left pane of the Event Viewer MMC, right-click the desired event log. From the pop-up menu, select Properties.

3. From the Application Log Properties dialog box shown in Figure 16.8, you can adjust the log size, set the retention time, or clear the log manually. After making the desired changes, click the OK button to save.

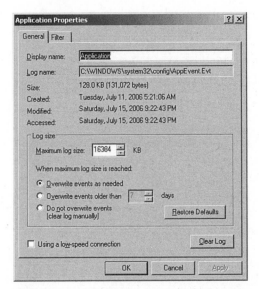

FIGURE 16.8   Changing the event log retention settings.

EXAM ALERT

Event Log Defaults   The event logs in Windows 2000 defaulted to 512KB and would overwrite events older than 7 days. The Windows Server 2003 defaults, however, are a much more practical 16,384KB and overwrite events only as needed. The change in size is a significant difference, and it's something you might see on the exam.

Clearing and Saving Logs

In addition to the retention settings, the Event Log Properties dialog box has an option to clear the log files. This option allows you to clear all entries from the selected log file. The option is also available from the pop-up menu when you right-click a log file in the Event Viewer MMC.

To clear a log file from the Event Viewer MMC, perform the steps outlined in Step by Step 16.5.

STEP BY STEP

16.5 Clearing an event log

1. From the Start menu, click Start, All Programs, Administrative Tools, Event Viewer.

2. In the left pane of the Event Viewer MMC, right-click the desired event log. From the pop-up menu, select Clear All Events.

3. After you elect to clear events, the confirmation dialog box appears.

4. From the Save Log As dialog box, specify a name and location for the saved log, and then click the Save button.

As part of your regular maintenance, even if you have the logs set to overwrite as needed, you can manually archive them without clearing them. You can save the logs by right-clicking a log file entry in Event Viewer and selecting Save Log File As. You can save logs to an event file (.evt) or in a format that can be used with other applications (.txt). You can load the EVT file type into another Event Viewer. The log's TXT file can be saved in either standard mono-space-columned or comma-delimited format. These formats can be used in common word processing or spreadsheet programs.

Log Viewing Options

The default view of the Event Viewer is to display the newest entry at the top. A handy feature of the Windows Server 2003 Event Viewer is its capability to sort the logs based on the columns displayed in the utility. For example, to sort the logs based on event ID, click the Event column heading, and the information is sorted in either ascending or descending order, depending on whether you click the column heading once or twice (see Figure 16.9).

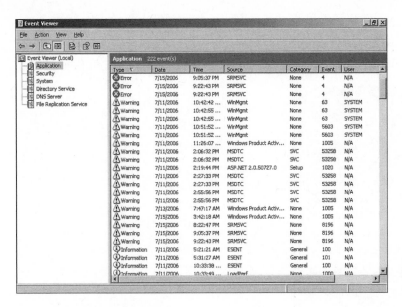

FIGURE 16.9 Click one of the column headings to sort the event files.

Filtering Events

By default, the Event Viewer shows the entire contents of the log file. This can be quite overwhelming, especially on a busy server, because a lot of informational messages are usually irrelevant when you are searching for the cause of a problem.

In these situations, you can use the Filter command from the View menu to quickly locate events of a certain type or pertaining to a particular source, category, user, computer, event ID, or date range. For example, you might want to see how many warnings have been recorded.

To filter a log file from the Event Viewer MMC, perform the steps outlined in Step by Step 16.6.

STEP BY STEP

16.6 Filtering an event log

1. From the Start menu, click Start, All Programs, Administrative Tools, Event Viewer.

2. In the left pane of the Event Viewer MMC, right-click the desired event log. From the system menu, select View, Filter.

3. After you select Filter, the Properties dialog box shown in Figure 16.10 appears.

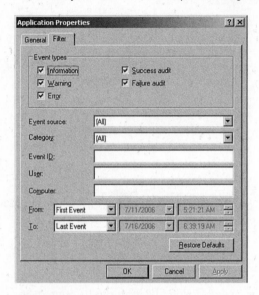

FIGURE 16.10 Select the desired filtering options, and then click OK.

4. From the Event Log Properties dialog box shown in Figure 16.10, deselect all the event types, except for Warning, and then click OK. The results after filtering are shown in Figure 16.11.

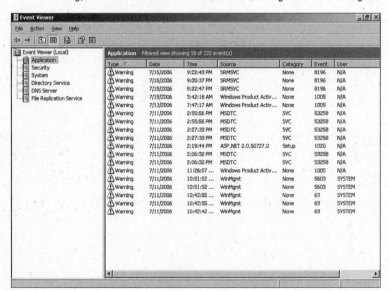

FIGURE 16.11 The log file after filtering.

5. To return to the default view that shows all events, from the system menu select View, All Records.

The filtering options are very flexible; you can select either one or multiple filters to display only those entries that apply to the area you are working on.

The available filters are as follows:

▶ *Event Types*—This allows you to filter based on the type of events. For example, you might want to just see events that relate to a problem, such as warnings or errors. If you're working with Security logs, you would be more interested in success or failure audits, such as multiple failed logons, which might indicate an intrusion attempt.

▶ *Event Source*—This option allows you to filter events from a specific source, such as a driver, system component, or service.

▶ *Category*—This option allows you to filter events from a specific category. This filter is mostly useful with the Security log because it uses the category field more than the other logs do. This allows you to quickly filter the user logon type events from resource access and system events. Typical categories for the Security log are Account Logon, Logon/Logoff, System Event, and Policy Change.

▶ *Event ID*—Filters the log to display only a single event ID.

▶ *User*—Filters the log to show events that are associated with a particular user. Not all events have a user entry.

▶ *Computer*—Filters the log to show events that are associated with a particular computer. Because the initial release of Windows Server 2003 lets you display the log from only one computer at a time, this option is not commonly used.

▶ *From and To*—Filters the log to show only events that are included in the specified time/date range.

New Log View

As discussed in the previous section, sometimes a specific view of the logs makes it easier for you to do your job. Microsoft has supplied an option for the Event Viewer named New Log View. Using this option, you can customize a view of any of the logs, including filtering, size, and so on. You can then save this view under another name. This allows you to customize your view of the event logs without affecting the default views or the logs themselves.

A new view can be added for any log by highlighting the log and then right-clicking it. From the pop-up menu, select New Log View. The new log entry will appear in Event Viewer and can be renamed and configured like any other log.

Finding Specific Events

There might be times when you must find a specific event, or series of events, that can't be easily grouped using filtering. For example, if you want to see how many and what types of disk errors have been occurring on your server, filtering might not find all the events you are searching for because of the specific nature of filters. In cases like these, it is useful to search the logs using the options available for filtering with the added ability to search using keywords.

To search through the contents of the selected log for an event by keywords, use the Find command from the View menu. As you can see in the Find dialog box shown in Figure 16.12, you have similar options to those you used for filtering, in addition to the option to search for specific keywords in the Description field. Because the Find command does not allow you to search using a specific date range, it allows you to search backward and forward in a log. It displays a single entry at a time; use the Find Next button to move to the next entry.

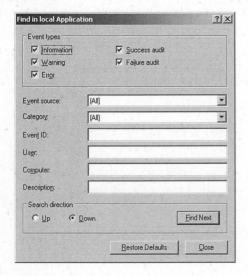

FIGURE 16.12 Select the desired Find options, and then click Find Next.

To find a specific log entry, perform the procedure outlined in Step by Step 16.7.

STEP BY STEP

16.7 Finding an event

1. From the Start menu, click Start, All Programs, Administrative Tools, Event Viewer.

2. In the left pane of the Event Viewer MMC, right-click the desired event log. From the system menu, select View, Find.

3. After you select Find, the Find dialog box shown back in Figure 16.12 appears.

4. From the Find dialog box shown in Figure 16.12, deselect all the event types except for Failure Audit, and then click OK.

5. The first log entry that matches the Find criteria is highlighted. You can double-click the entry to display it, or you can click Find Next to move to the next matching entry.

Loading a Saved Event Log

In most high-security environments, archiving the Security log is required. This is so that a record is maintained of previous security and auditing events. In addition, there might be situations where you will archive other logs for error-tracking purposes. After a log is archived, it can be imported into the Event Viewer on any Windows 2000/2003/XP computer.

To load a saved log file, perform the procedure outlined in Step by Step 16.8.

STEP BY STEP

16.8 Loading a saved event log

1. From the Start menu, click Start, All Programs, Administrative Tools, Event Viewer.

2. In the left pane of the Event Viewer MMC, right-click Event Viewer (Local). From the pop-up menu, select Open Log File.

3. In the Open dialog box shown in Figure 16.13, select the file to open. Saved event logs have an *.evt filename.

FIGURE 16.13 Select the saved event log that you want to view. Make sure that you specify the log type.

4. Click Open to load the saved log file. As you can see in Figure 16.14, the saved file is added as an additional entry in the Event Viewer.

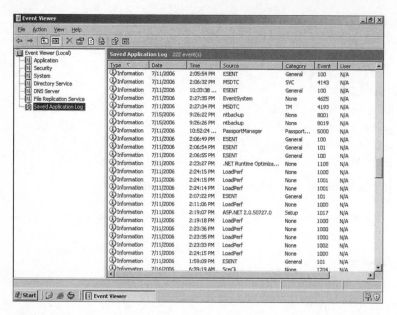

FIGURE 16.14 The log file is displayed as an additional entry. It does not replace the existing logs.

Third-Party Solutions

Event Viewer can record a significant amount of useful, if not vital, information, but extracting or even locating the data within the log files can be a daunting task. You may want to invest in an event-consolidation and event-reporting utility that can automatically and semi-intelligently scan Event Viewer. These tools look for patterns of failure, intrusion, or degradation of the system and then report the findings to you in a concise format.

Microsoft included a useful tool in the Windows 2000 Resource Kit, called `dumpel.exe`, which filters the event logs for specific events using a variety of search criteria. For some reason, it was left out of the Windows 2003 Resource Kit. However, it can still be downloaded from http://www.microsoft.com/downloads/details.aspx?FamilyID=c9c31b3d-c3a9-4a73-86a3-630a3c475c1a&DisplayLang=en.

Managing Security Logs

Earlier in the chapter, we examined how to use the Event Viewer to work with various log files. Most of the other log files, such as the Application and System log files, can be viewed by all users. However, the Security log can be viewed only by administrators.

You can make various configuration changes to the Security log, the most important of which is to increase the size of the log. The default size is 16,384KB, which is sufficient for light logging in small- to medium-sized organizations but becomes quickly filled in larger organizations that perform a lot of auditing.

Although we covered how to manually increase the size of the event logs earlier in the chapter, it would be time consuming to make this change on every server in your enterprise. To make the configuration of the event logs consistent on the computers in your organization, you can create an Event Log Settings policy. This policy can be created via the Group Policy snap-in. After the policy is configured, it can be applied to the desired computers just like any other policy.

To configure the Security log size for all computers in the domain, perform the procedure outlined in Step by Step 16.9.

STEP BY STEP

16.9 Creating a Security log policy

1. From the Start menu, click Start, All Programs, Administrative Tools, Domain Security Policy.

2. From the Default Domain Security Settings MMC, shown in Figure 16.15, click Security Settings, Event Log.

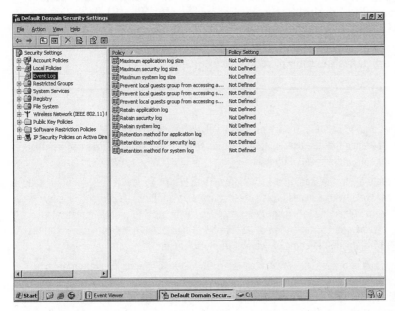

FIGURE 16.15 The Default Domain Security Settings MMC, showing the available settings for the event logs.

3. The policies available for the object are displayed. Double-click the Maximum Security Log Size policy. This opens the Properties dialog box shown in Figure 16.16.

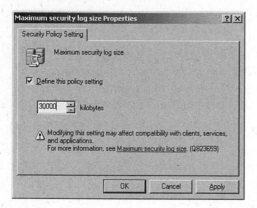

FIGURE 16.16 Select Define This Policy Setting, and then increase the default value to 30,000.

4. Set the log size to 30,000. Note that the settings are in kilobytes. Click OK to save.

5. Close the Default Domain Security Settings MMC.

Recording security events is used as a form of intrusion detection. When security auditing and the Security logs are configured properly, it is possible to detect some types of network break-ins before they succeed. An example of this is a password attack, which in a network with a good password policy can take some time to perform successfully. The Security log is also invaluable after a break-in has occurred, so you can track the movements and actions of the intruder and how he was able to enter your system. Above all, security logging is effective only if the network administrator takes the time to review it frequently.

Best Practices

It is important to realize that a good security implementation involves the coordination of many network functions. Above all, it is imperative that the user is able to log on to the network and locate and use the appropriate resources without an undue level of difficulty.

Critical network servers should always be kept in a secure area. The odds of a system break-in are greatly increased if a skilled intruder has physical access to a server console. In addition, having critical servers in an open area can make them vulnerable to a disgruntled employee with nothing more sophisticated than a baseball bat or a bucket of water. Attacks do not have to be sophisticated to be damaging, and historically most losses occur from inside the company versus from the outside.

One of the best security policies is proper user education. Users should be aware of how important it is to protect company resources and the implications of what could happen if critical information falls into the wrong hands. Users should be educated about how to keep their passwords confidential and secure. A good idea is to publish a clearly worded security policy and require everyone, including network administrators, to review it periodically.

Configuring Auditing

Now that we've covered the basics of using the Event Viewer and managing Security Logs, we are going to put this knowledge to use. One of the primary uses of the event logs, specifically the Security log, is to monitor the access of server resources by users and processes. In the current climate of security breaches and what seems like weekly security exploits, it's very important to know who is using your servers and for what purposes.

Auditing is the process of recording user and system activities on the network. These events are recorded in the Windows Server 2003 Security Log, which is one of the logs contained in the event log we examined earlier in this chapter.

Just about any activity involving a Windows Server 2003 object can be recorded in the Security log. When you configure auditing, you decide what activities, called *events*, you want to track and against what object. Typical activities that can be tracked are valid or invalid logon attempts, creating or opening files, and changes in user rights. After the audited events are recorded in the Security log, you can use the Event Viewer utility to view and analyze them.

In Windows Server 2003, the *security descriptor* is used to control access to objects. In addition to storing permissions information, a security descriptor also contains auditing information. The portion of the security descriptor that contains this auditing information is known as a *System Access Control List (SACL)*. The SACL is used to specify what attributes of the object are audited and what events associated with the attributes are audited.

It is just as important to audit user account-management tasks as it is to audit the accesses of important network resources. The entries saved to the Security log provide the network administrator with a summary of network operations, showing what tasks were attempted and by whom. Not only does this help to detect intrusions by malicious invaders, but the logs can also show more mundane problems, such as careless users who inadvertently delete important files.

As shown in Figure 16.17, a typical entry in the Security log shows the following:

- ▶ The time and date the event occurred
- ▶ The event performed
- ▶ The user account that performed the event
- ▶ The success or failure of the event

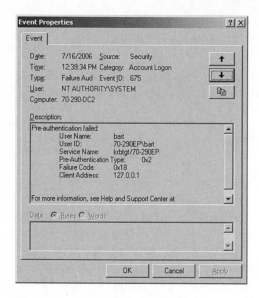

FIGURE 16.17 A typical Security log entry showing a failed logon.

Using Audit Policies

To simplify the configuration of auditing, Windows Server 2003 allows you to create an *audit policy*, which is used to define the events that are recorded in the Windows Server 2003 Security logs. Audit policies are created and applied similar to the other types of policies using the Group Policy snap-ins. Unlike previous versions of Windows, when Windows Server 2003 is first installed, auditing is turned on. By turning on various auditing event categories, you can implement an auditing policy that suits the security needs of your organization.

> **NOTE**
>
> **Check for Inheritance** Auditing policies are subject to policy inheritance, so the policies that you set on your local computer could be overshadowed by policies set for the domain as a whole.

The first step in creating an audit policy is deciding which events and users should be audited and on which computers. Generally, the audit policies are different depending on the role, or type of computer, that is being audited. For example, the audit policy would most likely be more extensive for a domain controller than for a workstation. In addition, audit policies can be applied at different levels, so you need to decide whether to apply them at the site, the organizational unit, or the domain level.

The next step is to decide what attributes of the events you are auditing that you want to track. For example, if you are tracking logon attempts, you must decide if you want to record successful logons, failed logons, or both. As part of this step, you must consider that the more events that are audited, the larger the Security logs become. Although you can configure the Security logs to be larger, this makes it more difficult to find specific events.

After you have decided what events to audit, and how you want them audited, you must specify your choices using the Audit Policy container in the Group Policy snap-in. After you have made your choices, you can use the Group Policy snap-in to apply the audit policy to the desired objects.

The type of events that can be audited by Windows Server 2003 are separated into the following event categories:

▶ *Account Logon Events*—This event is recorded when a domain controller receives a request to validate a user account. This provides the network administrator with a record of user accounts that have logged on to the network, when they logged on, and what privileges they were given.

▶ *Account Management*—This event monitors the actions of the network administrator. It records any changes that the administrator makes to the attributes of a user, a group, or a computer account. It also records an event when the administrator creates or deletes an account. This option is of the most use in networks with multiple administrators, especially when you have inexperienced administrators that need to be monitored closely.

▶ *Directory Service Access*—This event monitors user access to the Directory Service objects. Auditing has to be turned on for the specific object for this activity to be logged.

▶ *Logon Events*—This event monitors logons and logoffs at the local console as well as network connections to the computer.

▶ *Object Access*—This event monitors user access to objects on the network, such as files, folders, or printers. Auditing has to be turned on for the specific object for this activity to be logged.

▶ *Policy Change*—This event monitors changes in any of the policies that have been applied in the domain. This includes changes to user security options, user rights, and audit policies. This option can be very handy when certain permissions-related operations stop working. You can search back through the log to see if any policies have been changed inadvertently.

▶ *Privilege Use*—This event monitors the use of user rights. Typical examples are the administrator viewing or working with the Security log, or a user changing the system time. The entry in the log shows the account name, the time, and exactly which right was used.

▶ *Process Tracking*—This event is used to monitor executable files, such as EXE, DLL, and OCX files, and is generally used by programmers who want to track program execution. It can also be used for virus detection. In most cases, better tools are available for doing both tasks.

NOTE

Auditing Is Object Specific   The types of events that can be audited for an object are determined by the type of object to be audited. For example, the auditing features for files and directories require the use of an NTFS file system.

▶ *System Events*—This is a catchall event monitor. It is used to track events such as users restarting or shutting down computers, services starting and stopping, and any events that affect overall Windows Server 2003 security. An example of this is if the audit log fills up.

Creating an Audit Policy

Audit policies are created using the Group Policy snap-in or from the Active Directory Users and Computers snap-in, if your server is a member of a domain.

To create an audit policy, perform the procedure outlined in Step by Step 16.10.

STEP BY STEP

16.10 Creating an audit policy for logon failure events

1. From the Start menu, click Start, All Programs, Administrative Tools, Domain Controller Security Policy.

2. Click Local Policies, Audit Policy. The Audit Policy settings are displayed in the right pane, as you can see in Figure 16.18.

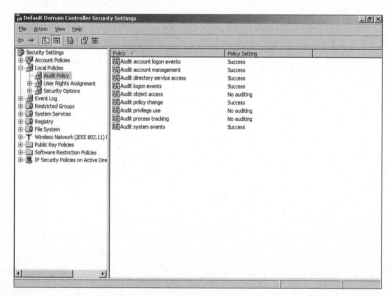

FIGURE 16.18   The default audit policies available for the domain controller. Note that several are turned on by default.

3. Right-click the Audit Account Logon Events audit policy.

4. The Audit Policy Properties dialog box appears, as shown in Figure 16.19. Select the Define These Policy Settings check box and then select both the Success and the Failure check boxes. This turns on auditing for any logon event.

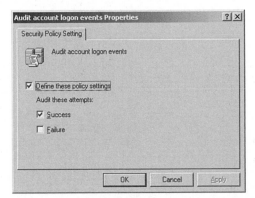

FIGURE 16.19 Auditing successful logons is turned on by default. Turn on failure auditing for this exercise.

5. Click OK to save.

It is important to remember that for objects, auditing is a two-step process. First, you have to enable the specific auditing category that includes the object you want to audit. Second, you have to enable auditing of specific events on this object from the properties page of the object itself.

For example, if you want to audit the access of the Payroll folder on one of your file servers, you must turn on auditing for object access, either at the site, domain, OU, or local level. Next, select the properties page of the folder and enable auditing for that folder.

In Step by Step 16.11, we first turn on auditing for object access at the domain level using the Domain Security Policy MMC; then we enable auditing on the Payroll folder.

STEP BY STEP

16.11 Creating an audit policy for object access

1. From the Start menu, click Start, All Programs, Administrative Tools, Domain Security Policy.

2. From the Default Domain Security Policy MMC, shown in Figure 16.20, click Local Properties, Audit Policy.

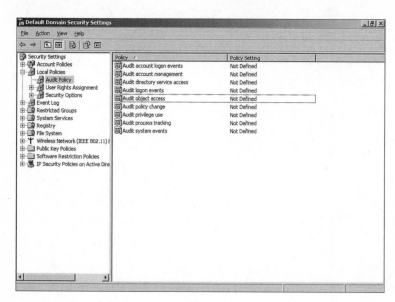

FIGURE 16.20 Double-click the desired audit policy to configure it. Note that by default, nothing is enabled at the domain level.

3. The policies in effect for the object are displayed. Double-click the Audit Object Access policy. This opens the Properties dialog box.

4. Under Audit These Attempts, select Define These Policy Settings to enable the policy, and then select the Failure check box. Enabling this will record an entry in the Security log anytime an unauthorized attempt to access an object is made. Click OK to save.

5. Close the Default Domain Security Policy MMC.

6. Open a command window and enter the GPUpdate command. Close the command window.

7. Open either Windows Explorer or My Computer and navigate to the Payroll folder. Right-click the Payroll folder and select Properties.

8. From the resulting Properties dialog box, select the Security tab. From the Security tab, click the Advanced button.

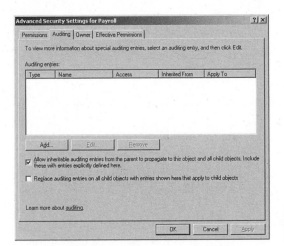

FIGURE 16.21 The Auditing tab displays the type of auditing enabled, who it applies to, whether it was inherited, and from where.

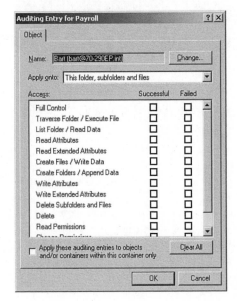

FIGURE 16.22 The Auditing Entry dialog box allows you to select both the events and the objects on which to enable auditing.

9. This opens the Advanced Security Settings dialog box. Select the Auditing tab, shown in Figure 16.21.

10. On the Auditing tab, click the Add button. From the Select User or Group dialog box that appears, enter the user or group for which you would like to track access to the resource. If you don't know the exact name, you can click the Advanced button to browse for a user or group name. Click OK when you're finished.

11. The Auditing Entry dialog box appears, as shown in Figure 16.22. Notice that you can select from a variety of events for success, failure, or both. In addition, you have the option to apply the auditing settings to the folder only, the folder and its files, and a variety of other options. This turns on auditing for any logon event.

12. Click OK three times to save.

When you're defining your audit policy, it is important to know what you plan to do with all the data that is collected. If you are using the audit policy for resource planning, you might want to increase the log size so that you can store data for a longer length of time, or you can archive logs from time to time so that you can keep an ongoing record of system and resource usage.

Always audit the files and folders that contain sensitive data, while ignoring common files that most users access regularly. Quantity of data does not always equal quality of data. In addition, auditing does create overhead, both in processing time and disk space.

The Everyone group should be used to audit resource access instead of using the Users group. Remember that *most* user accounts are added to the Everyone group by default. However in Windows Server 2003, the Everyone group no longer includes anonymous users.

Don't forget to audit all administrative tasks performed by the administrative groups. This allows you to spot problems created by inexperienced administrators. In addition, the Administrator account is a favorite target for intruders. By monitoring the administrative accounts, you should be able to spot the erratic activity that is common to an improperly trained or unauthorized user.

Challenge

In the world we live in today, security has become a major concern. A good system administrator must not only be wary of threats from the outside, but must also guard against inside threats. Recent statistics have shown that a server is more likely to be attacked from inside the firewall than from the outside.

Some parts of your network need to be more secure than others. For example, anything that has to do with trade secrets, proprietary company information, or employee data should have the strongest security applied.

(continues)

(continued)

But how do you know whether your security measures are effective? Are you suffering from a false sense of security? (No pun intended!) What types of tools are included in Windows Server 2003 that can reassure you? On your own, try to develop a strategy to address this type of issue.

If you would like to see a possible solution, follow the next steps.

Estimated Time: 20 minutes

One way to attack this problem is to turn on auditing for specific files and folders. A good practice is to always audit the files and folders that contain sensitive data, while ignoring common files that most users access regularly.

On the server that contains the objects you want to audit, follow these steps:

1. From the Start menu, click Start, All Programs, Administrative Tools, Local Security Policy.

2. From the Local Security Policy MMC, click Local Properties, Audit Policy.

3. The policies in effect for the object are displayed. Double-click the Audit Object Access policy; this opens a Properties dialog box.

4. Under Audit These Attempts, select the Failure check box. Click OK to save.

5. Close the Local Security Policy MMC.

6. Open either Windows Explorer or My Computer and navigate to the folder that you want to audit. Right-click the folder and select Properties.

7. From the resulting Properties dialog box, select the Security tab. From the Security tab, click the Advanced button.

8. This opens the Advanced Security Settings dialog box. Select the Auditing tab.

9. The Auditing tab displays the type of auditing enabled, who it applies to, whether it was inherited, and from where. On the Auditing tab, click the Add button.

10. From the Select User or Group dialog box that appears, enter the user or group for which you want to track access to the resource. For security auditing, select the Everyone group. Click OK when you're finished.

11. The Auditing Entry dialog box appears. Notice that you can select from a variety of events for success, failure, or both. In addition, you have the option to apply the auditing settings to the folder only, to the folder and its files, and a variety of other options.

12. Click OK three times to save.

EXAM ALERT

Logon Auditing   When a user logs on to a domain where auditing is enabled, the authenticating domain controller will log an event in its security log. It is likely that multiple domain controllers have authenticated the user at different times—therefore, you must examine the security log on each domain controller. In Event Viewer, you can set various filters to simplify the search for information.

User Rights Assignment

We have looked at how to control access to objects such as files, folders, and printers in Windows Server 2003 through the use of permissions. The network administrator can also control the tasks that users can perform by assigning user rights. Although permissions are used to control objects, user rights control users and groups.

User rights give or deny users or groups the ability to perform specific tasks on local computers that may have an effect on security. These rights cover everything from the ability to perform system backups to who is able to shut down the system. When the network administrator is setting up security policies for a network, this is where the most time will be spent.

Generally, most rights will be preassigned to either the Administrators or the Power Users local groups. However, there will be occasions when the network administrator will need to reassign rights for better security or just to allow the user to perform certain tasks.

Although you can assign these rights to an individual user account, to simplify manageability and accountability it is best to assign them at the group level.

There are a large number of rights available. Some of the commonly used ones are

- ▶ *Access This Computer from the Network*—By default this right is granted to most local groups, including the Everyone group. This right gives users the ability to access shared resources such as folders, printers, and web services from the network. For greater control, remove this right from the Everyone user group, create a new group, and add this right to it. You can then specifically add the users that you want to access the computer.

- ▶ *Act as Part of the Operating System*—This is not a right that will normally be given to a user. The common use for it is to grant it to the user ID that is assigned to control a service. This is typically used with server-based programs such as mail or database servers. Most installation programs will configure this right for you; however, during disaster recovery, it will sometimes be necessary to assign it manually.

- ▶ *Add Workstations to the Domain*—As covered in Chapter 2, "Managing User and Computer Accounts," Windows NT and Windows 2000 computers must have accounts in the domain. This account can be created during the installation of the computer or manually at any other time. Without this account being present, the computer cannot join the domain. This right is valid only on domain controllers, and by default, only the Domain Admins group will have it. If a group that doesn't have administrator rights is in charge of installing computers on the network, you can either add the computer accounts before they install the computers, or you can assign them to an Install Users group and grant that group this right.

> **NOTE**
>
> **Backup Rights**   You can either add the users responsible for backups to the Backup Operators group or create a new group and assign this right to it. This right will also be granted to the service account for your backup program.

▶ *Backup/Restore Files and Directories*—This right is by default assigned to only the Administrators and the Backup Operators groups. Improper granting of this right can create a security exposure by allowing unauthorized users the access to copy confidential files from your computers. Although a user may not have been explicitly granted access to confidential files and folders, the right to perform a backup takes precedence.

▶ *Bypass Traverse Checking*—This is by default granted to the Everyone group. This allows users to get to a folder that is part of a tree that is restricted. An example is if the root folder is restricted, and users need to get to folders under it. This option should always be left on. This option is present only for POSIX compatibility.

▶ *Change System Time*—The default is for only Administrators to have this right. In previous versions of Windows NT, users were generally granted this right so that the time could be synchronized via login script using the NET TIME command. In Windows 2000, the time of Windows 2000 Server and Professional clients is automatically synchronized.

▶ *Create a Pagefile*—By default, this right is assigned only to the Administrators group. Normally, this will not need to be changed unless you configure the security option to automatically delete the paging file at logoff time.

▶ *Force Shutdown from a Remote System*—The default is for this right to be granted to only Administrators and Backup Operators. This right allows utilities such as Shutdown.exe to be used to reboot computers remotely.

▶ *Increase Scheduling Priority*—This is normally granted to Administrators only. This right allows the user to change the scheduling priority of individual processes using the Task Manager utility.

▶ *Load and Unload Device Drivers*—By default, this right is granted only to the Administrators group. This will have to be available if your users need to load printer drivers.

▶ *Log On as a Batch Job*—This allows a .bat or .cmd file to access the system in the background.

▶ *Log On as a Service*—This right is typically granted to the service accounts for server applications that run background threads, such as mail and database servers. (See the bullet item "Act as Part of the Operating System.")

▶ *Log on Locally*—This right is normally assigned to every default group except for Users and Power Users. The main use for it is to keep unauthorized users from logging on to the server console. The exception to this will be on a server that is running Terminal Services. Because Terminal Services users will be, logically speaking, logging on to a virtual server console, any Terminal Services users will need to be granted this right.

▶ *Manage Auditing and Security Log*—This right grants the permission to manage and configure the Security log. The default is for only Administrators to have this right.

▶ *Profile System Performance*—This right is necessary to allow users to monitor system performance using tools such as Performance Monitor.

▶ *Shut Down the System*—For servers, only Administrators and Backup Operators will have this right. If the server is running Terminal Services in Application Mode, Power Users will have it, too.

▶ *Take Ownership of Files and Other Objects*—This right grants the permission to take the ownership of objects away from an owner. By default, only Administrators are granted this right.

As we mentioned previously, just a few of the user rights can be configured. For a complete listing, consult the online help in Windows Server 2003.

To assign user rights via a Local Security policy, follow the procedure in Step by Step 16.12.

STEP BY STEP

16.12 Assigning user rights via the Local Security Policy

1. Select Start, All Programs, Administrative Tools, Local Security Policy.

2. From the Local Security Policy snap-in, shown in Figure 16.23, click User Rights Assignment. In the right pane, all the available User Rights are displayed.

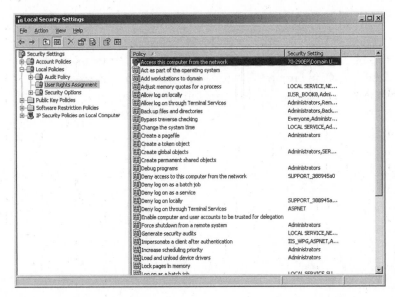

FIGURE 16.23 The Local Security Settings MMC, showing the default settings for a member server.

3. To change a User Right, right-click the listing, and then select Security from the pop-up menu.

4. The Local Security Policy Setting window appears. This window shows a more detailed view of the users and groups that have been assigned this User Right. From this window, you can deselect those users that you no longer want to have this right. This will affect only the local policy. If there is a domain policy, the domain policy will always override the local policy. Click the Add button.

5. The Select Users or Groups window appears. From this window, you can add additional users to be granted this right. They can be added from the local accounts database or from the Active Directory database.

6. Click OK twice when finished.

In Figure 16.23, look at the top entry in the right pane. Notice that it has a domain icon. This tells you that the setting for this entry was set at the domain level, and because of the SDOU rule, it overrides any setting at the local level.

Using Security Templates

Security Templates are preconfigured files that store typical security configurations for workstations and servers. Windows Server 2003 is shipped with a selection of templates that are stored in the `%systemroot%\security\templates` directory. The supplied templates cover a wide selection of security scenarios, from a typical low security domain client to a high security domain controller. The attributes of the templates can be copied, pasted, imported, or exported into other templates. This allows the templates to be used as is, or they can be used as the basis for a custom security scheme.

A security template can be imported into a local or a nonlocal Group Policy Object, so that any computer or user accounts that the Group Policy Object controls will receive the security settings. If security settings have already been configured in the Group Policy Object, they can be exported to create a new security template that can be applied to other objects.

The predefined security templates that are supplied with Windows Server 2003 are designed to provide an appropriate level of security on a Windows Server 2003 domain controller, server, or client computer. However, you must be aware that the default clean-install permissions given to user groups in Windows Server 2003 provide a significant increase in security over previous versions of Windows NT. The local Power Users group in Windows Server 2003 will have security settings roughly equivalent to those granted to the Local Users group in Windows 4.0. The security settings for the Administrators group has not changed.

This can create a problem if your network is running applications that are not fully Windows Server 2003 compatible. Part of the specification for applications designed for Windows Server 2003 is that the applications are required to be designed to operate in a more secure environment, by users with fewer security rights. If all your applications are Windows Server 2003 compatible, the security rights that are granted to members of the Users group should be sufficient. If you are still running noncompliant applications on your network, it is possible that your users will have to be members of the Power Users group in order to have the rights necessary to run these applications.

> **NOTE**
>
> **Default Security Settings** The default security settings are not automatically applied to Windows Server 2003 systems that have been upgraded from Windows NT 4.0 or earlier. On these systems, whatever security was already in place still applies. The default security settings are applied only when Windows Server 2003 is clean-installed onto an NTFS partition. If Windows Server 2003 is installed onto a FAT file system, the security templates cannot be applied.

The security templates are supplied for several security levels:

▶ *Default*—The Default security templates (`Setup Security.inf`) are configured with the default security settings for Windows Server 2003 computers. These templates are created during the installation process and will differ depending on whether the install was a clean install or an upgrade. Although this template can be used as a basis for other servers and workstations, it cannot be applied to domain controllers. This template is very large, so it should not be applied via Group Policy.

▶ *Domain Controller Default Security*—This template (`DC Security.inf`) is created when a member server is promoted to a domain controller.

▶ *Compatible*—To provide backward compatibility, the default in Windows Server 2003 is for users to be members of the Power Users group. This allows the users to have access to most legacy applications. Most network administrators are not going to allow this because the Power Users group has far more rights than are necessary to run legacy applications. By using the Compatible template (`Compatws.inf`), the Users group is granted sufficient rights to run most legacy applications. In addition, the security levels are lowered on the files, folders, and Registry keys that are commonly used by legacy applications. In addition, all members of the Power Users group will be removed.

▶ *Secure*—The Secure template (`Securedc.inf` or `Securews.inf`) modifies security settings for areas of the operating system that are not covered by permissions. This includes tighter settings for password policy, auditing, and any security-related Registry keys. Access Control Lists are not modified, because the secure configurations assume that the default Windows Server 2003 security settings are in place. However, it does remove all members from the Power Users group.

▶ *Highly Secure*—The priority of the Highly Secure template (`Hisecdc.inf` or `Hisecws.inf`) is to lock down the security of the network without regard for performance, operational ease of use, or connectivity. This template can be used only in a native Windows Server 2003 environment because no pre-Windows 2000 clients or servers are supported. All network communications are digitally signed and encrypted.

▶ *System Root Security*—This template (`Rootsec.inf`) is used to reapply the Windows Server 2003 default system root permissions to a system drive.

Creating Security Templates

The Security Templates snap-in is used to work with security templates. You have the option of adding the snap-in to an existing console or creating a new one. To create a new Security Templates console, follow the procedure in Step by Step 16.13.

STEP BY STEP

16.13 Creating a Security Templates MMC

1. Click Start, Run, and then type in MMC. Click OK.

2. Click Console; then from the pop-up menu, select Add/Remove Snap-In. Click Add.

3. The Add Standalone Snap-In window appears. Scroll down and select the Security Templates snap-in, and then click Add.

4. If this is the only snap-in that you will be adding, click Close.

5. Click OK to finish.

6. From the Console window select Console, and then click Save As. The Save As window appears.

7. Type in **Security Templates** for the filename, and then click Save.

Now that you have a console to use to work with the security templates, you have the following options:

▶ Create a new security template

▶ Import a security template into a Group Policy Object

▶ Export Security settings to a security template

▶ Customize one of the supplied security templates

Customizing Security Templates

One of the quickest ways to apply security is to use one of the templates that Microsoft supplies as a foundation for your own security policy. Then you can just make the necessary configuration changes to fit the needs of your organization.

To customize a supplied or existing security template, follow the procedure in Step by Step 16.14.

STEP BY STEP

16.14 Customizing a security template

1. Select Start, All Programs, Administrative Tools, Security Templates.

2. From the Security Templates console, click Security Templates, and then click the %windir%\Security\Templates folder (see Figure 16.24).

3. The Templates folder opens and displays the predefined security templates.

4. Right-click the desired template. Then select Save As from the pop-up menu.

5. Type in an appropriate name for the new template, and then click Save.

6. In the right pane of the Security Templates console, right-click the template that you just saved. When the pop-up menu appears, select Set Description.

7. The Security Template Description window appears. Type in a description for the template, and then click OK.

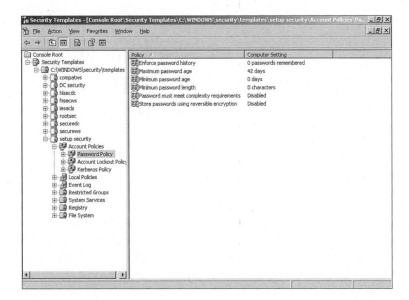

FIGURE 16.24 The Security Templates MMC, showing the default templates for a domain controller.

8. In the Security Templates console, double-click the template that you created, and then select the Event Log node.

9. We want to change an entry for the Application Log size, so we double-click the Application Log entry in the right pane.

10. The Maximum Application Log Size window appears. Select the define this policy check box, and then enter 40000, as shown in Figure 16.25. Click OK to save.

11. If this is the first setting that relates to this particular category, you might get an additional prompt to adjust the values of related settings. If so, accept the required adjustments (you can always change them later), and then click OK to continue.

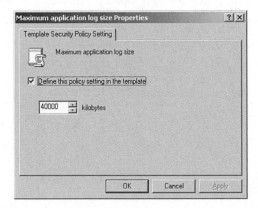

FIGURE 16.25 Using the Security Templates MMC to change the default value for the Application log.

12. Right-click the name of the template and select Save from the pop-up menu.

Now that we have a custom security template, we need to apply it to a workstation or member server to test it. This is where the Security Configuration and Analysis Tool comes in.

Using the Security Configuration and Analysis Tool

Managing the security of a network is an ongoing task. There will always be those occasions where, for the sake of expediency a security setting might have been changed to allow a user temporary access or to allow a process to run. These temporary changes often are forgotten and not restored to their proper state. There will also be users or junior network administrators that will make unauthorized changes that are detrimental to network security. These types of incidents can cause a security exposure that could prove costly to your network.

The Security Configuration and Analysis tool will compare the security settings of a computer to those of a template, view the results, and resolve any discrepancies that were revealed by the analysis. The tool allows you to perform comparisons with either the standard templates or custom templates that you have created. The tool can also be used to import or configure security settings and apply them to the Group Policy Object for a computer or multiple computers.

The Security Configuration and Analysis tool is a standard MMC snap-in that uses a database of security configuration settings to perform its analysis and configuration functions. The database allows templates to be imported or exported, multiple templates to be combined into a common template, and new templates to be created.

After the templates are stored in the database, they can be used as the basis for a security analysis. When performing an analysis, the administrator is presented with the current system settings, and the areas where the current settings do not match the template are flagged. While performing the analysis, any discrepancies can be corrected.

The Security Configuration and Analysis snap-in is used to work with security templates. You have the option of adding the snap-in to an existing console, or creating a new one.

To create a new Security Configuration and Analysis console, follow Step by Step 16.15.

STEP BY STEP

16.15 Creating a Security and Configuration Analysis MMC

1. Click Start, Run, and then type in MMC. Click OK.

2. Click Console, and then from the pop-up menu, select Add/Remove Snap-In. Click Add.

3. The Add Standalone Snap-In window appears. Scroll down and select the Security Configuration and Analysis snap-in, and then click Add.

4. If this is the only snap-in that you will be adding, click Close.

5. Click OK to finish.

6. From the Console window select Console, and then click Save As. The Save As window appears.

7. Type in Security Configuration and Analysis for the filename, and then click Save.

Now that we have a console to use to work with the Security Configuration and Analysis tool, we have the following options:

▶ Create a new security database

▶ Import a security template into the security database

▶ Export security database settings to a security template

▶ Configure system security

▶ Perform a system security analysis

▶ Work with the results of the Security Analysis

Before the Security Configuration and Analysis console can be used, you will have to create a database to store the security configuration settings.

To create a new Security Configuration and Analysis console, follow Step by Step 16.16.

STEP BY STEP

16.16 Creating a Security and Configuration Analysis database

1. Select Start, All Programs, Administrative Tools, Security Configuration and Analysis.

2. From the Security Configuration and Analysis console, right-click Security Configuration and Analysis. From the pop-up menu, select Open Database.

3. The Open Database dialog box appears. Type in the desired name and directory, and then click open.

4. Because we are creating a new database, the Import Template dialog box appears. This will allow us to import a security template to use as a basis for our analysis. Select `test.inf` (the template we created in the previous exercise), and then click Open.

> **NOTE**
>
> **Clear This Database**   There is a check box on the Import Template dialog box labeled Clear This Database Before Importing. This is selected if you want to delete the previous templates that were being used for analysis and start fresh. This does not delete the template files from the disk; it removes them only from the database.

After the template is imported into the database, you can change the configuration, import attributes from other templates, or merge it with other templates. The steps needed to configure the settings of the template are similar to those performed when using the other policy tools.

Now that we have added the template to the database, we are ready to use it as a basis for the analysis of a computer. The Security Configuration and Analysis tool will compare the settings in the database with those on the chosen system and flag the differences. Then you can use the tool to make configuration changes to the machine, if desired.

To analyze system security using the Security Configuration and Analysis tool, follow the procedure in Step by Step 16.17.

STEP BY STEP

16.17 Analyzing system security

1. Select Start, All Programs, Administrative Tools, Security Configuration and Analysis.

2. From the Security Configuration and Analysis console, right-click Security Configuration and Analysis. From the pop-up menu, select Open Database.

3. The Open Database dialog box appears. Type in the desired name and directory, and then click open.

4. Right-click Security Configuration and Analysis, and then from the pop-up menu, select Analyze Computer Now.

5. The Perform Analysis dialog box appears. This prompts you for the path and name for the log file. The default path is fine. Click OK to continue.

6. The status window appears, and indicates the progress of the various processes. When the process is complete, you will be returned to the main console window.

7. In the left pane, click the Event Log node.

8. The detail pane of the console displays the analyzed policies along with the results of the comparisons. As you can see in Figure 16.26, one column shows the settings from the database and another column shows the actual settings on the machine. In addition, to the left of the policy name is an icon representing the status of the analysis. The following describes what the icons indicate:

   ▶ A green check mark indicates that the settings were the same.

   ▶ A red X means there was a difference.

   ▶ No icon means that the policy was not included in the template and no analysis was performed.

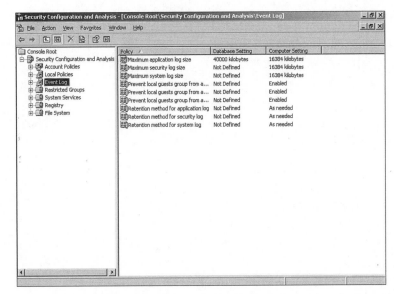

FIGURE 16.26 The results of the comparison.

9. If you want the settings on the computer to be configured to match the template in the database, right-click Security Configuration and Analysis; then from the pop-up menu, select Configure Computer Now.

10. The Configure System dialog box appears. This prompts you for the path and name for the `error.log` file. The default path is fine. Click OK to continue.

11. To verify that the security settings were applied correctly, repeat the analysis steps.

To provide a properly secured network, it is important to perform a regular security analysis of each computer. By using the Security Configuration and Analysis tool and database to keep a record of what the proper settings are, this allows the administrator to quickly detect any security exposures and easily correct them.

The proper use of security templates requires the network administrator to not only analyze the needs of the users, but also the needs of the installed base of applications. Certain templates are dependent on the presence of only Windows Server 2003 applications and could conceivably prevent legacy applications from running, or they could prevent the users from having access to them. Because the security templates can also modify operating system settings, it is essential that they be thoroughly tested on a test network before they are applied in a production network.

Chapter Summary

This chapter has covered a lot of ground; here are the main points:

In this chapter, you learned what Security Policies are available in Windows Server 2003 and how to configure them. This includes how to apply them, when to apply them, and their effects in both standalone and domain environments.

Next, you had an in-depth look at managing and configuring event logs, including knowing the types of event logs available on both a domain controller and a member server. You also learned how to configure, search, filter, delete, and archive the data contained in the event logs.

You learned how to use auditing to monitor security-related events, and you worked with security templates that can be used to not only set the baseline security settings for an organization, but to determine what settings have been changed.

Key Terms

- ▶ Audit policy
- ▶ Security log
- ▶ Event ID
- ▶ Account Policies
- ▶ Local Policies
- ▶ Event Log
- ▶ Security Configuration and Analysis

Apply Your Knowledge

Exercises

16.1 Creating a new log view

It can be helpful to have a custom view of the event logs so that you can easily find specific events. For example, to quickly find quota events, you can filter the event logs. By saving a custom view of the logs, you can easily identify these events without having to reconfigure the filter on the logs every time you want to monitor quotas.

What is the best way to accomplish this in Windows Server 2003? On your own, try to develop a solution that involves limited ongoing management by the system administrator.

If you would like to see a possible solution, follow these steps:

Estimated Time: 20 minutes

1. From the Start menu, click Start, All Programs, Administrative Tools, Event Viewer.

2. In the left pane of the Event Viewer MMC, right-click the System log. From the pop-up menu, select New Log View.

3. A new log entry appears in the left pane of the Event Viewer MMC. Right-click the entry and select Rename from the pop-up menu. Change the name to **Quota**.

4. Right-click the Quota log. From the system menu, select View, Filter.

5. After you select Filter, the Properties dialog box appears. From the Log Properties dialog box, select the event ID 36 and a source of NTFS and then click OK.

This gives you a custom log that can be used to track Quota events.

Exam Questions

1. Jason is the system administrator for a small bank. The bank requires that he maintain a log of all logon events in the domain and retain it for a period of no less than 7 years. What must Jason do to obtain and archive this data?

   ○ **A.** Auditing is automatically turned on in Windows Server 2003. He must clear and archive the Security logs weekly.

   ○ **B.** In the domain GPO, he must turn on the option Audit Account Logon Events for both success and failure. He must also clear and archive the Security logs weekly.

   ○ **C.** In the domain GPO, he must turn on the option Audit Logon Events for both success and failure. He must also clear and archive the Security logs weekly.

   ○ **D.** In the domain GPO, he must turn on the option Audit Account Logon Events and the option Audit Logon Events for both success and failure. He must also clear and archive the security logs weekly.

2. You are the network administrator for FlyByNight Airlines. The network consists of a single Active Directory domain. All network servers run Windows Server 2003, and all client computers run Windows 2000 Professional. One of the members of the network security department calls and says that he can't access the security event logs on your file and print server FandP. All members of the network security department are members of the ITSecurity global group. You need to grant the ITSecurity global group the minimum rights necessary to view the security event log on FandP. What should you do?

- ○ **A.** Assign the Generate Security Audits user right to the ITSecurity global group.

- ○ **B.** Assign the Manage Auditing and Security Logs user right to the ITSecurity global group.

- ○ **C.** Assign the Allow Logon through Terminal Services user right to the ITSecurity global group.

- ○ **D.** Assign the Act as Part of the Operating System user right to the ITSecurity global group.

3. You are the network administrator for FlyByNight Airlines. The network consists of a single Active Directory domain with 20 sites. All network servers run Windows Server 2003, and all client computers run Windows XP Professional. One of the users in another office has been complaining that when she comes in every Monday morning, her user account is locked out. You suspect that someone is trying to break into your network using her user account. Where should you search for information?

- ○ **A.** Only in the Security Event log of a domain controller in your site.

- ○ **B.** Only in the Security Event logs of the domain controllers in the user's site.

- ○ **C.** In the Security Event logs of all domain controllers in all sites.

- ○ **D.** Only in the Security Event log of the user's computer.

4. You are the network administrator for Cheap Stuff Inc. The network consists of a single Active Directory domain with 20 sites. All network servers run Windows Server 2003, and all client computers run Windows XP Professional. You have three departments, and each department has its resources located in a separate OU. The manager of the Marketing department is complaining that his user's accounts are being locked out after three unsuccessful logon attempts. He wants the setting changed to five attempts. The other two department managers don't want their settings to be changed. What must you do?

- ○ **A.** Change the Account Lockout Threshold for the domain to five unsuccessful attempts.

- ○ **B.** Change the Account Lockout Threshold for the Marketing OU to five unsuccessful attempts.

- ○ **C.** Change the Account Lockout Threshold for the Marketing users group to five unsuccessful attempts.

- ○ **D.** None of the above.

5. You are the network administrator for the Kansas City office of Cheap Stuff Inc. The network consists of a single Active Directory domain with 20 sites. All network servers run Windows Server 2003, and all client computers run Windows XP Professional. Each site has its own OU. Cheap Stuff's network security department has implemented a new policy that requires a specific configuration for the size and retention settings for the Security event log of all file servers. The rule also specified that local administrators on servers cannot override the changes you make to the settings for the Security event log.

   You need to define a method to modify the Security event log settings on each file server in the Kansas City office to meet the security department's requirements. What should you do?

   ○ **A.** Modify the local security policy on each file server to define the size and retention settings for the Security event log.

   ○ **B.** Create a security template on one of the file servers by using the Security Configuration and Analysis tool. Define the size and retention settings for the Security event log in the template. Import the security template into the local security policy of all your file servers.

   ○ **C.** Use Event Viewer to modify the event log properties on each file server. Define the size and retention settings for the Security event log.

   ○ **D.** Create a new Group Policy object (GPO) and link it to the Kansas City OU. In the GPO, define the size and retention settings for the Security event log.

6. You are the network administrator for FlyByNight Airlines. The network consists of a single Active Directory domain. All network servers run Windows Server 2003, and all client computers run Windows 2000 Professional. One of the junior administrators is attempting to diagnose a problem on one of your servers. However, when he tries to open the Security event log, he receives an Access Denied error.

   Which of the following should you do to enable him to complete his tasks?

   ○ **A.** Add the junior administrator's user account to the Server Operators domain group.

   ○ **B.** Add the junior administrator's user account to the local Administrators group on the file server.

   ○ **C.** Add the junior administrator's user account to the Power Users local group.

   ○ **D.** Assign the junior administrators user account the Allow Logon through Terminal Services user right for the file server.

7. You are the network administrator for FlyByNight Airlines. The network consists of a single Active Directory domain with four domain controllers. All network servers run Windows Server 2003, and all client computers run Windows XP Professional. The domain's audit policy ensures that all account logon events are audited. A temporary employee uses a client computer named FBN0431. When the temporary user's assignment concludes, his employment is terminated.

Now you need to learn the times and dates when the temporary employee logged on to the domain. You need to accomplish this goal by reviewing the minimum amount of information. What should you do?

- ○ **A.** Log on to FBN0431 as a local Administrator, and use the Event Viewer to view the local security log. Use the Find option to list only the events for the employee's user account.

- ○ **B.** Log on to FBN0431 as a local Administrator, and use the Event Viewer to view the local security log. Use the Find option to list only the events for the FBN0431 computer account.

- ○ **C.** Use the Event Viewer to view the security log on each domain controller. Use the Find option to list only the events for King's user account.

- ○ **D.** Use the Event Viewer to view the security log on each domain controller. Set a filter to list only the events for King's user account.

- ○ **E.** Use Event Viewer to view the security log on each domain controller. Set a filter to list only the events for the FBN0431 computer account.

8. You are the network administrator for Cheap Stuff Inc. The network consists of a single Active Directory domain with 20 sites. All network servers run Windows Server 2003, and all client computers run Windows XP Professional. You install an application on one of your servers. The application fails to start because the default NTFS permissions on your server are too restrictive. You use a security template from the manufacturer of the application to modify the NTFS permissions on your server to allow the application to work.

A new update to the application is released. The application no longer requires the modified NTFS permissions. You need to restore the default permissions to restore the original level of system security.

Which security template should you import into the local security policy of your server?

- ○ **A.** The `Syssetup.inf` template.

- ○ **B.** The `Setup Security.inf` template.

- ○ **C.** The `Defltsv.inf` template.

- ○ **D.** The `Netserv.inf` template.

9. You are the network administrator for Cheap Stuff Inc. The network consists of a single Active Directory domain. All network servers run Windows Server 2003. Confidential files are stored on a member server named CSI5. The computer object for CSI5 resides in an OU named Confidential. A Group Policy object named GPO1 is linked to the Confidential OU.

To audit access to the confidential files, you enable auditing on all private folders on CSI5. Several days later, you review the audit logs. You discover that auditing is not successful. You need to ensure that auditing occurs successfully. What should you do?

○ **A.** Start the System Event Notification Service (SENS) on CSI5.

○ **B.** Start the Error Reporting service on CSI5.

○ **C.** Modify the Default Domain Controllers GPO by selecting Success and Failure as the Audit Object Access setting.

○ **D.** Modify GPO1 by selecting Success and Failure as the Audit Object Access setting.

10. You are the network administrator for the Kansas City office of Cheap Stuff Inc. The network consists of a single Active Directory domain with 20 sites. All network servers run Windows Server 2003, and all client computers run Windows XP Professional. Each site has its own OU. Cheap Stuff's network security department has implemented a new policy that requires that all new servers be configured with specified predefined security settings when the servers join the domain. These settings differ slightly for the various company offices.

You plan to install Windows Server 2003 on 10 new computers, which all function as file servers. You need to ensure that the security configuration of the new file servers meets the new company standards. The network security department has implemented these settings on a test server in the Kansas City office.

You export a copy of this server's local security policy settings to a template file. You need to configure the security settings of the new servers, and you want to use the minimum amount of administrative effort. What should you do?

○ **A.** Use the Security Configuration and Analysis tool on one of the new servers to import the template file.

○ **B.** Use the default Domain Security Policy console on one of the new servers to import the template file.

○ **C.** Use the Group Policy Editor console to open the Kansas City OU and import the template file.

○ **D.** Use the default Local Security Policy console on one of the new servers to import the template file.

Answers to Exam Questions

1. **D.** For all logon events on all workstations to be collected in the Security logs on the domain controllers, both Audit Account Logon and Audit Logon Events must be turned on. Although auditing is turned on by default in Windows Server 2003, Audit Account Logon and Audit Logon Events are turned on only for success events, not failure events. See "Configuring Auditing."

2. **B.** By default, the ability to view the Security event log is restricted to administrators. The Manage the Security Event log user right is a powerful user privilege that should be closely guarded. Users with this right can clear the security log, possibly erasing important evidence of unauthorized activity. Neither the ability to generate audits or act as part of the operating system would enable the security group to access the security logs, as would logging on via Terminal Services. See "Working with the Event Logs."

3. **C.** When a user logs on to a domain where auditing is enabled, the authenticating domain controller will log an event in its security log. You will need to check the Security Event logs of all the domain controllers in all the sites, because it could be that the attack is being launched from outside of the office where the user is located. Checking just the user's computer or a limited number of domain controllers wouldn't give you a complete picture. See "Managing Security Logs."

4. **D.** The Account Lockout Threshold setting can be applied only at the domain level, so any changes there would affect the other departments, which was not allowed. See "Account Policies."

5. **D.** Any of the listed methods would work to set the configuration of the Security Event logs. But D is the only method that can't be overridden by the local administrators. See "User Rights Assignment" in this chapter.

6. **B.** By default, the ability to view the Security event log is restricted to administrators. The Manage the Security Event log user right is a powerful user privilege that should be closely guarded. Users with this right can clear the security log, possibly erasing important evidence of unauthorized activity. The ability to log on via Terminal Services wouldn't add any additional access rights. See "Working with the Event Logs."

7. **D.** When a user logs on to a domain where auditing is enabled, the authenticating domain controller will log an event in its security log. It is likely that multiple domain controllers have authenticated the user at different times; therefore, we must examine the security log on each domain controller. In Event Viewer, you can set various filters to simplify the search for information. In this case, we can filter the logs to show events for only the user's account. See "Creating an Audit Policy."

8. **B.** The default security template (*Setup Security.inf*) is configured with the default security settings for Windows Server 2003 computers. This template is created during the installation process. See "Using Security Templates."

9. **D.** For objects such as folders, auditing is a two-step process. First, you have to enable the specific auditing category that includes the object you want to audit. Second, you have to enable auditing of specific events on this object from the properties page of the object itself. Because we want to audit only this server, we would enable it at the OU level. See "Using Audit Policies."

10. **C.** Importing the template into a GPO linked to the Kansas City OU is the best solution. Because we need to apply the settings to all the servers in Kansas City and not to the other servers in the domain, using the Security and Configuration and Analysis tool wouldn't be sufficient, because it does only one server at a time. Also, importing the template into the Default Domain policy would affect all the servers in the domain. See "Using Security Templates."

Suggested Readings and Resources

1. *Security Policy Settings*. Microsoft Corporation.
   http://technet2.microsoft.com/WindowsServer/en/Library/bcd7ea4c-f989-4cee-969a-920f62f555111033.mspx?mfr=true.

2. Shinder, Deb. *Understanding the Roles of Server 2003 Security Policies*.
   http://www.windowsecurity.com/articles/Understanding-Roles-Server-2003-Security-Policies.html.

3. *Windows Server 2003 Deployment Guide*. Microsoft Corporation.
   http://technet2.microsoft.com/WindowsServer/en/Library/c283b699-6124-4c3a-87ef-865443d7ea4b1033.mspx?mfr=true.

4. *Windows Server 2003 Resource Kit*. Microsoft Press, 2005. ISBN 0735614717.

5. *Windows Server 2003 Security Policy*. Microsoft Corporation.
   http://technet2.microsoft.com/windowsserver/en/technologies/secpol.mspx.

17

Managing and Implementing Disaster Recovery

Objectives

This chapter covers the following Microsoft-specified objectives for the "Managing and Implementing Disaster Recovery" section of the Managing and Maintaining a Microsoft Windows Server 2003 Environment exam:

Manage backup procedures

▶ **Verify the successful completion of backup jobs.**

▶ **Manage backup storage media.**

▶ The purpose of this objective is to teach you how to use the various tools available in Windows Server 2003 to back up your server. In addition, you should be familiar with the various strategies for dealing with backup media rotations.

Restore backup data

▶ When working in a Windows Server 2003 environment, it is important that you not only have a thorough understanding of backup procedures but also of restoring the data on a server.

Schedule backup jobs

▶ When working in a Windows Server 2003 environment, it is important that you have a thorough understanding of the performance characteristics of your servers. This way, it is easier to identify potential problems before they cause outages.

Perform system recovery for a server

▶ **Implement Automated System Recovery (ASR).**

▶ **Restore data from shadow copy volumes.**

▶ **Back up files and system state data to media.**

▶ **Configure security for backup operations.**

▶ The purpose of this objective is to teach you how to recover both system and user data on your Windows Server 2003 server. You must be able to use the built-in tools to ensure that your data is available at all times.

Recover from server hardware failure

▶ Although not as common as it once was, because of the improvements in server hardware reliability over the years, server hardware failure is an event that you must still be prepared to handle. Hardware failures can range from a simple disk failure to the destruction of a server because of a catastrophe.

Outline

Study Strategies

▶ The sections in this chapter outline features that are essential to using and managing a Windows Server 2003 environment. The backup and restoration of data are common tasks that you can expect to be heavily emphasized on the test.

▶ Expect to see a number of questions on two new features introduced in Windows Server 2003: Automated System Recovery (ASR) and the Volume Shadow Copy Service (VSS). Know how both features work, under what circumstances they should be used, and how to implement them.

▶ Understand the different types of system recovery available and under what circumstances each one should be used. Know the differences between Safe Mode, the Recovery Console, and Last Known Good Configuration, as well as when each should be used.

▶ Know how to use the Windows Server 2003 Backup utility, including how to back up and restore both user data and the system state information. Know what data is saved as system state data on domain controllers and member servers. In addition, know how to schedule the backup to run unattended.

Introduction

Managing and maintaining the performance of a Windows Server 2003 environment is only part of the typical duties a system administrator will perform. No matter how well maintained the environment remains, the system administrator must eventually deal with the inevitability of a situation that causes data loss.

The system administrator needs to know how to handle these situations by preparing for them in advance and knowing what steps to perform when the inevitable occurs.

This chapter covers the tools, tasks, and procedures required to back up, restore, and recover both system and user data on Windows Server 2003. This type of information is not only crucial for a job as a system administrator, but it also is very important for the exam.

Using Windows Backup

Backing up data is the simple process of copying the files and folders located on a server to another location. This provides a safety blanket of sorts in the event of a drive or server failure, power outage, virus infection, or user error. With a proper backup, you can rest assured that important files are still available in the event something catastrophic happens.

Windows Server 2003 provides a more advanced backup program than what was included with Windows NT. Starting with Windows 2000, Microsoft opted to license backup software from Veritas Software (formerly Seagate Software). Compared to the Windows NT backup utility, this tool is a big step forward.

Windows Server 2003 Backup allows you to create backup jobs that you can run manually or schedule to run unattended. Unlike the Windows NT 4.0 Server backup, which could back up only to tape, you can now back up to disk, Zip drives, CD-R/RW, or any other media available via the Windows Server 2003 file system.

Windows Backup also allows you to back up files from other computers. However, it cannot back up the Registry or system state data from other computers. The Backup utility allows you to back up a single file, a folder, a drive, or multiple drives. Also, all the backup and restore functions can be performed manually or via wizards.

More About Windows Backup

Although using the Windows Backup utility to back up the Registry and system state data on remote computers is not supported, there is an unofficial workaround. Just use the Windows Backup program on the remote computer to back up the Registry and system state data to disk. Then the backup file can be backed up remotely.

Windows Backup allows you to back up files and folders on FAT16, FAT32, or NTFS volumes. However, if you have backed-up data on an NTFS volume restoring to either type of FAT volume, this results in loss of configured file and folder permissions, in addition to the loss of encrypted files and compression attributes.

To perform a backup or restore on a Windows Server 2003 server, you must be a member of the local Administrators or Backup Operators group. If you are a member of the local Administrators or Backup Operators group on a domain controller, you can back up and restore files on any computer that is a member of the domain or that has a two-way trust relationship with the domain. If you are not a member of either of these groups, you can back up only the files you are the owner of or that you have at least Read permissions for. To restore a file or folder, you must have Write permission. In addition, administrators and backup operators can back up and restore encrypted files and folders. The files and folders will not be decrypted during the backup and restore process.

NOTE

User Rights You can grant other users and/or groups the ability to back up and restore files using user rights. Assigning user rights is covered later in the chapter in the section "Configuring Security for Backup Operations."

Volume Shadow Copy

Using Volume Shadow Copy, you are now able to back up most open files. In previous versions of Windows, including Windows 2000, open-file backup was available only using third-party utilities. For example, most database programs (such as Microsoft SQL Server and Microsoft Access), user files (such as Word documents and Excel spreadsheets), and even common files (such as the WINS and DHCP databases) would not be backed up by the Windows Backup utility. This is because most programs lock access to files that they are updating to prevent data corruption. Therefore, when the backup program attempted to open these files, its request was rejected. Most of the time, the Backup utility would keep trying to open the file until it either received access to the file or the retry timeout period expired. This would slow down the backup procedure, or in the case of some unattended backup procedures, the backup process would terminate without completing a full backup.

When Volume Shadow Copy is used during a backup and an open file is encountered, a snapshot is taken of the file. This is an exact copy of the file that is saved to another area on the disk. This copy is then saved via the Backup utility.

Volume Shadow Copy has the following advantages:

▶ Users cannot be locked out by the backup program.

▶ Open files are not skipped.

▶ The backup completes faster.

▶ Applications can write data to a file during a backup.

▶ The need for additional third-party software in most cases is eliminated.

▶ Backups can be performed during business hours.

Volume Shadow Copy is enabled by default in the Windows Backup program and is part of the Volume Shadow Copy Service feature covered in depth later in this chapter.

Types of Backups

Windows Server 2003 has five backup options: Normal, Copy, Daily, Differential, and Incremental. Each type varies as to what is backed up and whether the archive bit is set. The *archive bit* is a file attribute that is turned on when a file is created or modified, and it can be cleared, depending on the type of backup, whenever a file is successfully backed up. It is used to let the backup software know what files need to be backed up based on whether the file has just been created or whether modifications to a previously backed-up file have happened since the last backup.

Normal

A *normal* (sometimes referred to as a *full backup*) *backup* is used to back up all the files and folders that you select, regardless of the setting of the archive bit. It then clears the archive bit of the files to show that they were backed up. The disadvantage of a normal backup is that it takes longer than some of the other backup types because it backs up all the files and folders. However, it does have the advantage of requiring only a single media (or set of media) for a full restore. To minimize backup time, the normal backup is typically used in a rotation with incremental or differential backups.

Copy

A *copy backup* is typically used to make an archival copy of data and does not interrupt your current backup set. It does not read or change the archive bit.

Daily

A *daily backup* is used to back up only the files and folders that have been created or modified on that day. It does not read or change the archive bit. A daily backup is typically used to make a quick snapshot of the daily activity. This is useful when you need to perform a task on the server and want to have a current backup available.

Differential

A *differential backup* is used to back up only the files and folders that have been created or modified since the last normal or incremental backup. It does not change the archive bit. However, it reads the archive bit to determine which files need to be backed up. A differential backup is typically used between instances of a normal backup. For example, if you perform a normal backup on Monday, you can perform differential backups the rest of the week. The differential backup takes longer and longer each day because it backs up all the files and folders that have been created and modified since the last normal backup. A differential backup has the advantage that it takes less time than a normal backup, but more than an incremental backup. When you perform a full restore, it requires the media for both the last normal backup and the last differential backup.

Incremental

An *incremental backup* is used to back up only the files and folders that have been created or modified since the last normal or incremental backup. It reads the archive bit to determine which files have been changed and need to be backed up. It then changes the archive bit of the files that were backed up so that the next time the backup program is run, these files will not be backed up again unless they were changed. An incremental backup is typically used between instances of a normal backup. Unlike the differential backup, the backup times typically do not get longer each day, because the incremental backup only backs up the files and folders that were modified since the last incremental backup. An incremental backup has the advantage of taking less time than a normal backup, but when you perform a full restore, it requires the media for the normal backup and all the incremental backups performed since the normal backup (which can be time consuming, depending on how many incremental backups you must restore).

Although in some situations you might perform a normal backup daily, this is not common except for the smallest of organizations. Typically, most organizations perform a normal backup once a week and then an incremental or differential backup on the other days.

EXAM ALERT

Know Your Backups!   You should be familiar with the various types of backups, when each one should be used, and what data is restored during a recovery procedure.

To back up data files using the Backup or Restore Wizard, perform the procedure outlined in Step by Step 17.1.

STEP BY STEP

17.1 Backing up data using the Backup or Restore Wizard

1. From the Start menu, click Start, All Programs, Accessories, System Tools, Backup.

2. The Backup or Restore Wizard appears, as shown in Figure 17.1.

FIGURE 17.1 The Backup or Restore Wizard's opening screen. You can switch to Advanced mode and deselect the option to start in Wizard mode from this screen.

3. From the Backup or Restore screen, you can select to either back up or restore files and settings. Select Backup Files and Settings and then click the Next button to continue.

4. From the What to Back Up screen, shown in Figure 17.2, you can select to back up all the information on the computer, or you can choose what to back up. Select the option to choose what to back up, and then click the Next button to continue.

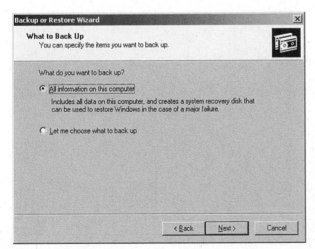

FIGURE 17.2 The What to Back Up screen allows you to select the option to back up all information on the computer, which includes a system recovery disk, or you can choose what to back up.

5. From the Items to Back Up screen, shown in Figure 17.3, you can select the files and folders to back up. Select the desired files and folders and then click the Next button to continue.

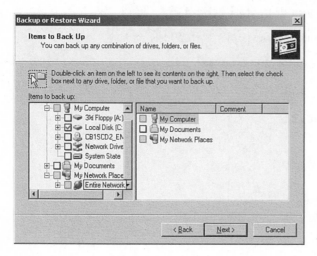

FIGURE 17.3 You can select files and folders on remote computers if you have a connection to them.

6. From the Backup Type, Destination, and Name screen, you can select to back up to a tape or file, specify where to save the backup, and provide a name for the backup. Select the desired options and then click the Next button to continue.

7. From the Completing the Backup or Restore Wizard screen, examine the selected backup settings. If any settings are not correct, click the Back button to reconfigure them. If everything is correct, click the Finish button.

8. If you clicked the Advanced button, you will see the Type of Backup screen, shown in Figure 17.4. This screen allows you to select from the following types of backups: Normal, Copy, Incremental, Differential, and Daily. Select the desired type of backup and then click the Next button to continue.

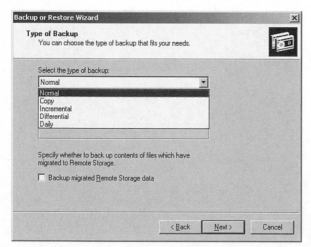

FIGURE 17.4 The Type of Backup screen. The default is a normal backup.

9. From the How to Back Up screen, shown in Figure 17.5, you can select verification, hardware compression, and Volume Shadow Copy options. Select the desired options and then click the Next button to continue.

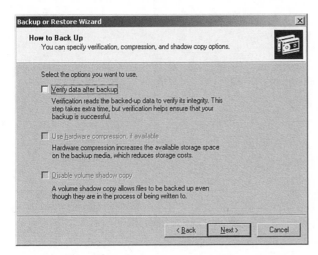

FIGURE 17.5   The How to Back Up screen. This screen allows you to select whether to use Volume Shadow Copy and hardware compression and whether to verify the data after the backup.

10. From the Backup Options screen, you can select to overwrite or append to an existing backup. From this screen, you have the additional option of setting more security for the backup by selecting the check box to restrict access to the backup set to the administrator and the owner. Select the desired options and then click the Next button to continue.

11. From the When to Back Up screen, you can select to run the backup job immediately or schedule it to run later. Select the desired option and then click the Next button to continue.

12. From the Completing the Backup or Restore Wizard screen, examine the selected backup settings. If any settings are not correct, click the Back button to reconfigure them. If everything is correct, click the Finish button.

13. The backup starts and the Backup Progress window appears. When the backup completes, the Report button will appear.

14. Click the Report button to open the backup report, shown in Figure 17.6, which displays the status of the backup.

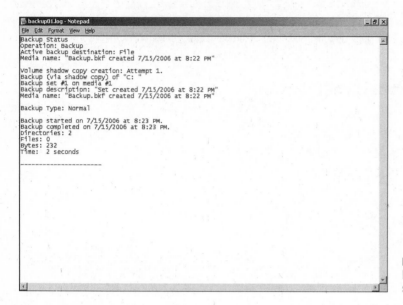

FIGURE 17.6 The backup log, showing the backup status.

15. Close all windows when finished.

To shorten the steps required for backups in the future, you can preconfigure most of the settings configured after selecting the Advanced button. These settings are located on the Options tab in the Backup program.

To configure the default options for a backup, perform the procedure outlined in Step by Step 17.2.

STEP BY STEP

17.2 Configuring the default options for the backup program

1. From the Start menu, click Start, All Programs, Accessories, System Tools, Backup.

2. The Backup or Restore Wizard appears. Click the Advanced Mode hyperlink.

3. From the Backup Utility Advanced Mode screen, shown in Figure 17.7, select Tools, Options.

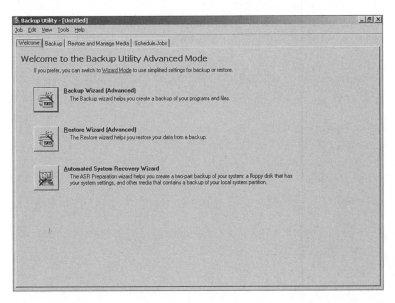

FIGURE 17.7 The Backup
Utility Advanced Mode
screen.

4. The Options dialog box appears. From here, you can set the defaults for your backups and restores (see
Figure 17.8).

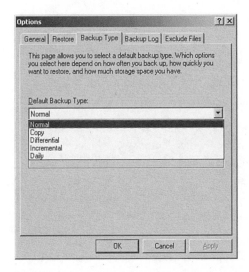

FIGURE 17.8 The Options dialog box's Backup Type tab.

The five tabs on the Options dialog box allow you to set the defaults for your backup and
restore jobs. This way, you can use the wizard to quickly set up a backup or restore job with
the preconfigured settings.

The Backup Type tab shown in Figure 17.8 allows you to select the default type of backup to perform. The selections are the standard five types of backups: Normal, Copy, Differential, Incremental, and Daily.

The General tab, shown in Figure 17.9, allows you to set the default actions for the backup procedure and the alerts presented for various conditions.

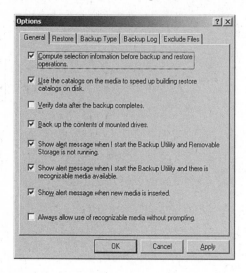

Figure 17.9   The Options dialog box's General tab.

Here's a list of the options and their explanations:

▶ *Compute Selection Information Before Backup and Restore Operations*—This option displays the number of files and the total size of the files and folders selected.

▶ *Use the Catalogs on the Media to Speed Up Building Restore Catalogs on Disk*—This option forces the restore to use the catalog saved with the media. A *catalog* is an inventory of the files and folders that were backed up, along with their locations. This file is normally saved on the last volume of the backup media. This option should be deselected only if the catalog is damaged or missing, because rebuilding the catalog can take a long time for a large backup.

▶ *Verify Data After the Backup Completes*—This option is not selected by default. If it is selected, after the completion of the backup, Windows Backup compares the information on the backup media to the files on the hard drive to verify that they were backed up properly. This step can double the length of the backup procedure, but it is good insurance for important files.

▶ *Back Up the Contents of Mounted Drives*—This option tells Windows Backup to back up the contents of drives that are mounted as folders on an NTFS volume.

▶ *Show Alert Message When I Start the Backup Utility and Removable Storage Is Not Running*—This option should be checked only if you are using a tape drive for backup. The Removable Storage service manages the tape drives for you. If it is not running, the backup will fail.

▶ *Show Alert Message When I Start the Backup Utility and There Is Recognizable Media Available*—This option should be checked only if you are using a tape drive for backup. This message option generates an alert if a compatible tape is mounted when you start the backup utility.

▶ *Show Alert Message When New Media Is Inserted*—This option should be checked only if you are using a tape drive for backup that is managed by Removable Storage. This message option generates an alert if a compatible tape is mounted when you start the backup utility.

▶ *Always Allow Use of Recognizable Media Without Prompting*—Does just what it states. If the proper media is in place, the backup starts automatically.

The Restore tab allows you to set the default actions for the restore procedure to take when restoring a file that is already present. Here are the available options:

▶ Do Not Replace the File on My Computer.

▶ Replace the File on Disk Only if the File on Disk Is Older.

▶ Always Replace the File on My Computer.

The Backup Log tab, shown in Figure 17.10, allows you to set the amount of information that is to be recorded in the backup log. The default is to create a summary log that only records the actions taken. The other options available are to keep a detailed log that includes the names of all files and folders that were backed up, and to not create a backup log at all.

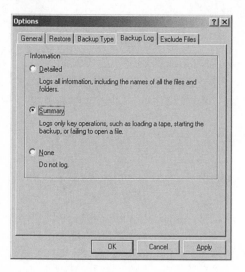

FIGURE 17.10 The Options dialog box's Backup Log tab.

The Exclude Files tab, shown in Figure 17.11, allows you to define the files that should not be backed up, both for all users (top window) and the current user (bottom window). By default, files such as the page and hibernate files are excluded.

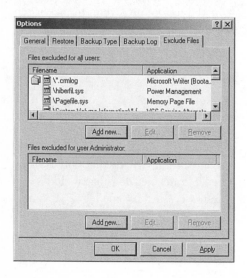

FIGURE 17.11 The Options dialog box's Exclude Files tab.

System State Backups

Objective:

Back up files and system state data to media

All backups of a Windows Server 2003 server should include the *system state data*. System state data is a collection of data that contains the operating system configuration of the server. For all Windows Server 2003 operating systems, the system state data includes the following:

▶ Registry

▶ COM+ class registration database

▶ System boot files

▶ The system files included in the Windows File Protection area

For Windows Server 2003, the system state data also includes the Certificate Services database

(if the server is operating as a certificate server). If the server is a domain controller, the system state data also includes the Active Directory services database and the SYSVOL directory. In addition, the system state data includes the IIS Metabase or the Cluster Service configuration if these features are installed on the server.

The system state backup procedure automatically backs up all the system state data relevant to your server configuration. Because of their interdependencies, these components cannot be backed up or restored separately.

It's important to back up the system state data for each server and domain controller. The system state backup from one server or domain controller cannot be restored to a different server or domain controller.

There are two types of system state backup/restore procedures: local and remote. A *local* backup/restore is used when the backup media is hosted on the server being restored. A *remote* restore is performed when the backup media is located on another machine. The Windows Server 2003 Backup program is capable of backing up and restoring the system state data only on the local server.

To back up system state data on a Windows Server 2003 server, perform the procedure outlined in Step by Step 17.3.

STEP BY STEP

17.3 Backing up system state data

1. From the Start menu, click Start, All Programs, Accessories, System Tools, Backup.

2. The Backup or Restore Wizard appears.

3. From the Backup or Restore screen, you can select to either back up or restore files and settings. Select Backup Files and Settings and then click the Next button to continue.

4. From the What to Back Up screen, you can select to back up all the information on the computer, or you can choose what to back up. Select the option to choose what to back up and then click the Next button to continue.

5. From the Items to Back Up screen, shown in Figure 17.12, click the My Computer entry to expand the tree. Select the System State entry and then click the Next button to continue.

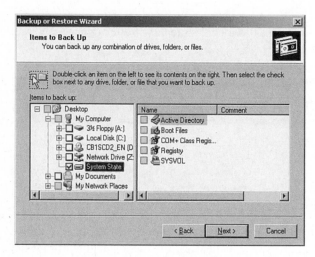

FIGURE 17.12 The Backup or Restore Wizard showing the System State check box selected. Note that on the right, the items present indicate that this is a domain controller.

6. From the Backup Type, Destination, and Name screen, you can select to back up to a tape or file, specify where to save the backup, and provide a name for the backup. Select the desired options and then click the Next button to continue.

7. From the Completing the Backup or Restore Wizard dialog box, examine the selected backup settings. If any settings are not correct, click the Back button to reconfigure them. If everything is correct, click the Finish button.

The system state data can be backed up separately or as part of a complete server backup.

Scheduling Backup Jobs

Objective:

Schedule backup jobs

A backup job runs faster and more efficiently when fewer users are on the server. In addition, even with the Volume Shadow Copy service, it's better to back up a closed file rather than an open one. This ensures that the most current version of the file is backed up. Unfortunately, in most environments the period of least usage is either in the middle of the night or on weekends. Most system administrators would prefer to work more conventional hours.

Fortunately, Windows Backup includes a built-in scheduling service. This feature allows the administrator to schedule backups to run unattended anytime in the future. Jobs can be scheduled to run once, or they can be repeated using the following options:

- ▶ Daily
- ▶ Weekly
- ▶ Monthly
- ▶ At System Startup
- ▶ At Logon
- ▶ When Idle

Scheduling backups with the native Backup utility no longer requires the use of the Task Scheduler service. You no longer need to use the AT.EXE utility to schedule the backup (although you still can if you really want to). Instead, you click the Set Schedule button when creating a backup job using the advanced backup options of the Backup or Restore Wizard (see Figure 17.13), or you use the Schedule Jobs tab of the Backup utility (shown later in Figure 17.14).

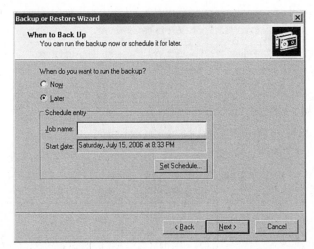

FIGURE 17.13 The When to Back Up screen. This screen is part of the advanced tasks of the Backup or Restore Wizard. From this screen you can set a backup schedule by clicking the Set Schedule button.

To configure an unattended backup, perform the procedure outlined in Step by Step 17.4.

STEP BY STEP

17.4 Scheduling an unattended backup job

1. From the Start menu, click Start, All Programs, Accessories, System Tools, Backup.

2. The Backup or Restore Wizard appears. Click the Advanced Mode hyperlink to open the Backup utility.

3. From the Backup utility's Advanced Mode screen, select the Schedule Jobs tab, shown in Figure 17.14.

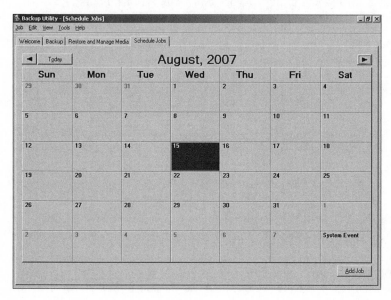

FIGURE 17.14 The Backup utility's Advanced Mode screen displaying the Schedule Jobs tab.

4. From the Schedule Jobs tab, double-click the date on which you want to run a backup job. This starts the Backup Wizard. On the Backup Wizard's opening screen, click Next to continue.

5. The What to Back Up screen appears, as shown in Figure 17.15. Select one of the options and then click Next to continue.

6. The Items to Back Up screen appears. Select the files and folders to be backed up and then click Next to continue.

7. The Backup Type, Destination, and Name screen appears. Select the backup type and where to save it and then give it a job name. Click Next to continue.

8. The Type of Backup screen appears. This screen allows you to select from the following types of back-ups: Normal, Copy, Differential, Incremental, and Daily. Select the desired type of backup and then click the Next button to continue.

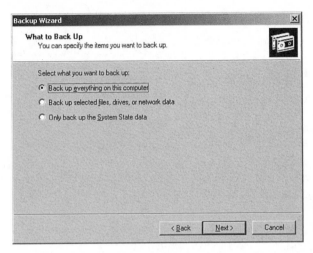

FIGURE 17.15 Select what you want to back up. You can choose to back up everything, selected files and folders, or system state data.

9. The How to Back Up screen appears. You can select verification, hardware compression, and Volume Shadow Copy options. Select the desired options and then click the Next button to continue.

10. From the Backup Options screen, you can select to overwrite or append to an existing backup. From this screen, you have the additional option of setting more security for the backup. Select the desired options and then click the Next button to continue.

11. From the When to Back Up screen, you can select to run the backup job immediately or schedule it to run later. Click the Set Schedule button.

12. The When to Back Up dialog box appears with the date that you selected from the calendar, as shown in Figure 17.16. Enter an appropriate name for the job. To change the time, click the Set Schedule button.

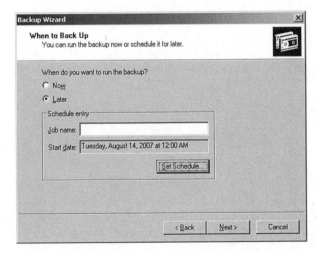

FIGURE 17.16 Select when you want the backup to run. Notice that the date you clicked on the calendar is filled in for you.

13. The Schedule Job dialog box appears, as shown in Figure 17.17. Select the desired options and then click the Settings button.

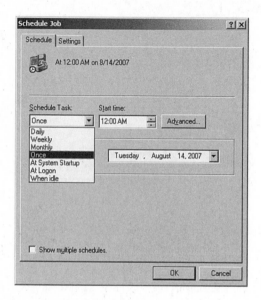

FIGURE 17.17 The Schedule Job dialog box presents you with more granular scheduling parameters.

14. On the Settings tab, as shown in Figure 17.18, you can specify additional options, such as what to do if the task runs longer than a certain time, and start the task only if the computer is idle. Select the desired options and then click the OK button.

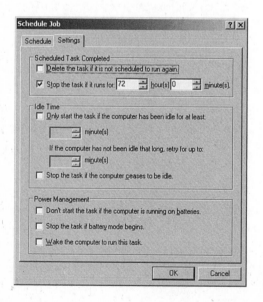

FIGURE 17.18 Select additional parameters for your scheduled task.

15. Back on the When to Back Up dialog box, click Next. The Set Account Information dialog box appears. Enter the user account and password that you want the backup job to run as. Then click the OK button.

16. Back at the When to Back Up screen, click Next to continue.

17. From the Completing the Wizard screen, examine the selected backup settings. If any settings are not correct, click the Back button to reconfigure them. If everything is correct, click the Finish button.

Back Up from the Command Line

In addition to the GUI we have been working with, Windows Server 2003 has a command-line version of the Backup program called `ntbackup.exe`. The command-line version allows you to schedule a backup either from the command line or in a batch file or script. Prior to Windows 2000, this method was very popular because at that time Windows Backup did not have the built-in scheduler service it has now.

There will always be a use for command-line utilities. For example, if you need to run a backup as part of another process, and this process requires automation, it is simple to include the command-line Backup utility in a batch file or script.

Here is the syntax for the `ntbackup` command:

```
ntbackup backup [systemstate] "@FileName.bks" /J {"JobName"}
➥[/P {"PoolName"}] [/G {"GUIDName"}] [/T { "TapeName"}]
➥ [/N {"MediaName"}] [/F {"FileName"}] [/D {"SetDescription"}]
 [/DS {"ServerName"}]  [/IS {"ServerName"}] [/A] [/V:{yes | no}]
➥ [/R:{yes | no}] [/L:{f | s | n}] [/M {BackupType}]
➥[/RS:{yes | no}] [/HC:{on | off}][/SNAP:{on | off}]
```

Table 17.1 defines the command-line parameters available for a command-line backup.

TABLE 17.1 Command-Line Parameters for `ntbackup.exe`

Parameter	Description
`systemstate`	Backs up the system state data. This option forces the backup to be either a normal or a copy type.
`@FileName.bks`	Specifies the name of the backup selection file. The selection file contains the names of the files and folders you want to be backed up. The selection file must be created using the GUI version of Windows Backup.
`/J {"JobName"}`	The name of the job to be recorded in the log file.
`/P {"PoolName"}`	The media pool from which to use media.
`/G {"GUIDName"}`	The tape, referred to by its Globally Unique Identifier (GUID). Do not use this switch with `/P`.

(continues)

TABLE 17.1 *Continued*

Parameter	Description
/T {"*TapeName*"}	The tape, referred to by its name. Do not use this switch with /P.
/N {"*MediaName*"}	Specifies a new name for the tape. Do not use with /A.
/F {"*FileName*"}	The logical path and filename. Do not use with /P, /G, or /T.
/D {"*SetDescription*"}	Specifies a label for each backup set.
/DS {"*ServerName*"}	Backs up the Directory Service database for the specified Exchange Server.
/IS {"*ServerName*"}	Backs up the Information Service database for the specified Exchange Server.
/A	Appends to an existing backup. Must be used with either /G or /T. Cannot be used with /P.
/V:{yes|no}	Verifies the backup.
/R:{yes|no}	Restricts access to the tape to members of the Administrators group or the owner.
/L:{f | s | n}	Specifies the type of log file, either f (full), s (summary), or n (none).
/M {*BackupType*}	Specifies the type of backup: Normal, Copy, Differential, Incremental, or Daily.
/RS:{yes | no}	Backs up the Remote Storage database.
/HC:{on | off}	Turns on/off hardware compression, if supported.
/SNAP:{on | off}	Enables or disables Volume Shadow Copy.
/?	Displays help.

The command-line options automatically default to whatever is configured via the GUI version of Backup. Any options specified override the GUI settings for that instance only.

The following is a sample ntbackup command with the parameters explained:

```
Ntbackup backup "@c:\full.bks" /J "Full Backup" /t "Week1Full"
➥ /V:yes /L:f /HC:on
```

This command line specifies that ntbackup will back up the file and folders specified in the backup selection file c:\full.bks. The job name will be Full Backup, and the tape used is Week1Full. The data will be verified after the backup is complete, the log type is full, and hardware compression is turned on for the tape drive.

To create a backup selection file to be used with the command-line version of Backup, perform the procedure outlined in Step by Step 17.5.

STEP BY STEP

17.5 Creating a backup selection file

1. From the Start menu, click Start, All Programs, Accessories, System Tools, Backup.

2. The Backup or Restore Wizard appears. Click the highlighted Advanced Mode link to open the Backup utility.

3. From the Backup utility's Advanced Mode window, shown in Figure 17.19, select the Backup tab.

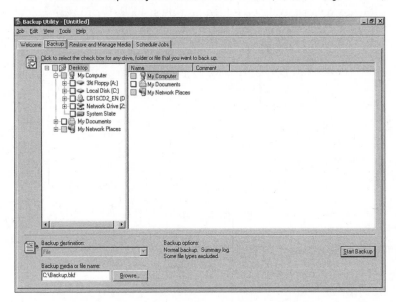

FIGURE 17.19 The Backup utility's Advanced Mode window, displaying the Backup tab. From here, select the files and folders you want to back up.

4. From the Backup tab, select the files and folders you want to include in the backup job. This starts the Backup Wizard. On the Backup Wizard's opening screen, click Next to continue.

5. From the system menu, select Job, Save Selections. From the Save As dialog box, enter a file and path for the selection file. It must have an extension of *.bks.

6. Click Save.

EXAM ALERT

Know the Capabilities   You probably do not need to memorize the various command-line parameters for the test. However, you should have a general idea of the capabilities of ntbackup from the command line and how to create the backup selection file.

Configuring Security for Backup Operations

Objective:
Configure security for backup operations

Earlier in this chapter, we discussed that to back up and restore a Windows Server 2003 server, you must be a member of the Administrators or the Backup Operators group. If you are not a member of one of these groups, you can back up only the files that you own or that you have at least Read permissions for. To restore a file or folder, you must have Write permission. These permissions are assigned via the Backup Files and Directories and the Restore Files and Directories user rights. These rights can be assigned via Group Policy.

To assign other users the Backup Files and Directories right, follow the procedure outlined in Step by Step 17.6.

STEP BY STEP

17.6 Assigning other users the Backup right

1. From the Start menu, click Start, All Programs, Administrative Tools, Domain Security Policy.

2. From the Default Domain Security Settings MMC, shown in Figure 17.20, click Local Policies and then User Rights Assignment.

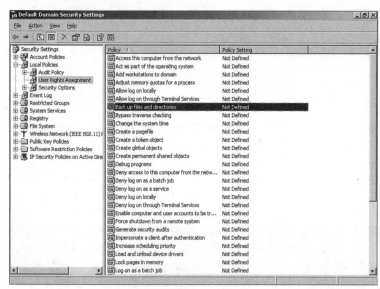

FIGURE 17.20 Double-click the desired user right to configure it.

3. The users and groups that possess Backup rights, if any, are displayed in Figure 17.21. If not already selected, click the Define These Policy Settings check box. Note that the groups that have these rights by default will not be displayed.

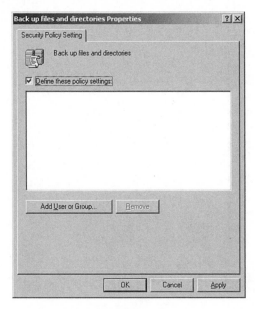

FIGURE 17.21 The users and groups with Backup rights are displayed.

4. Click the Add User or Group button. This opens the Select Users or Groups dialog box. Add users or groups from the local or domain accounts database. Click OK to save.

5. Click OK to save.

6. Close the Default Domain Security Settings MMC.

NOTE

Local Policy In the preceding Step by Step, we demonstrated changing Group Policy for the domain. If you want to grant these rights only on a single server, you can change the same settings via the Local Security Policy MMC on that server.

The Restore Files and Directories right can be configured using the same procedure. In addition to restricting backup and restore access to files and folders via Group Policy, you can also control who has the ability to restore backed-up files during the backup process. This is accomplished by selecting the Allow Only the Owner and the Administrator Access to the Backup Data option from the Backup Options dialog box, shown in Figure 17.22, during the backup configuration. This option prevents anyone other than an administrator or the person performing the backup from restoring the information that is being backed up.

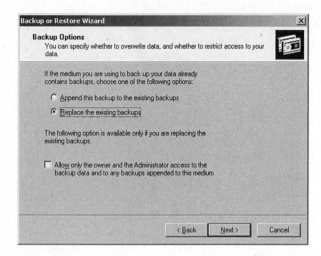

FIGURE 17.22 The option to restrict restore rights is displayed.

Verifying the Successful Completion of Backup Jobs

Objective:

Verify the successful completion of backup jobs

After a backup or restore job completes, you can verify its completion by clicking the Report button that appears on the Backup Progress dialog box at the completion of a backup or restore.

Clicking the Report button opens the backup log, as shown in Figure 17.23. This is a sample log from the backup of system state data. Full logging was turned on so that all the files and folders that were backed up are listed, along with their paths and attributes.

```
backup02.log - Notepad                                              _ 8 x
File  Edit  Format  View  Help
Backup Status
Operation: Backup
Active backup destination: File
Media name: "Backup5.bkf created 7/15/2006 at 9:05 PM"

Volume shadow copy creation: Attempt 1.
Backup (via shadow copy) of "C: "
Backup set #1 on media #1
Backup description: "Set created 7/15/2006 at 9:05 PM"
Media name: "Backup5.bkf created 7/15/2006 at 9:05 PM"

Backup Type: Normal

Backup started on 7/15/2006 at 9:06 PM.
Backup completed on 7/15/2006 at 9:06 PM.
Directories: 227
Files: 339
Bytes: 13,503,021
Time:  18 seconds
Backup (via shadow copy) of "System state"
Backup set #2 on media #1
Backup description: "set created 7/15/2006 at 9:05 PM"
Media name: "Backup5.bkf created 7/15/2006 at 9:05 PM"

Backup Type: Copy

Backup started on 7/15/2006 at 9:06 PM.
Backup completed on 7/15/2006 at 9:09 PM.
Directories: 224
Files: 2496
Bytes: 527,301,673
Time:  2 minutes and  59 seconds

-----------------------
```

FIGURE 17.23 The backup log showing full reporting.

Notice that the summary at the bottom of the file lists the number of files and directories that were backed up, along with the total bytes and total elapsed time. If there had been any errors, they would be listed here.

If you want to see the results of a backup job after it has completed and you forgot to click the Reports button or you ran an unattended job from the command line, you can access the report from the Backup utility. Click Tools, Reports from the system menu. This opens the Backup Reports dialog box, shown in Figure 17.24. From this dialog box you can view or print any of the saved reports for previously run backup jobs.

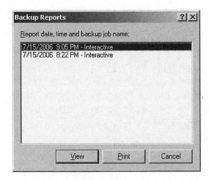

FIGURE 17.24 The Backup Reports dialog box allows you to select from previously saved backup logs.

Restoring Backup Data

Objective:

Restore backup data

It doesn't do you any good to back up all this data if it can't be restored. Fortunately, the Windows Server 2003 Backup program is also capable of restoring the data that you backed up. The restore procedures work similar to the backup procedures—as a matter of fact, most use the same wizards, and it's just a matter of selecting different options. The two major differences are that there is no command-line equivalent to the GUI version of the program, and a restore can't be scheduled to run unattended.

To restore data files using the Restore Wizard, perform the procedure outlined in Step by Step 17.7.

STEP BY STEP

17.7 Restoring data using the Restore Wizard

1. From the Start menu, click Start, All Programs, Accessories, System Tools, Backup.

2. The Backup or Restore Wizard appears. From the Backup or Restore screen, you can select to either back up or restore files and settings. Select Restore Files and Settings and then click the Next button to continue.

3. From the What to Restore screen, shown in Figure 17.25, select the files and backup set to restore and then click the Next button to continue.

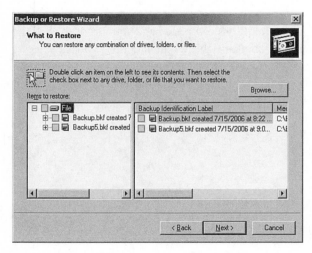

FIGURE 17.25 The What to Restore screen allows you to select the files, folders, and backup set to use to restore your data. You can click the Browse button to catalog the backup media.

4. From the Completing the Backup or Restore Wizard screen, examine the selected restore settings. If any settings are not correct, click the Back button to reconfigure them. If everything is correct, click the Finish button.

5. If you click the Advanced button, the Where to Restore screen, shown in Figure 17.26, opens. This screen allows you to select from the following options: Original Location, Alternate Location, and Single Folder. Select the location for the restore and then click the Next button to continue.

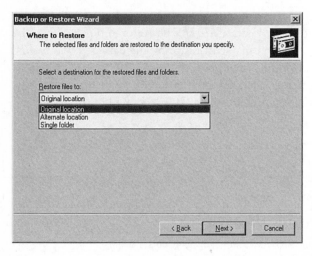

FIGURE 17.26 The Where to Restore screen. These options allow you to restore the files to an alternate location so that the original files will not be overwritten. You can also select to restore all selected files to a single folder.

6. From the How to Restore screen, shown in Figure 17.27, you can select how the restore process handles existing files. The default is not to overwrite them. Select the desired option and then click the Next button to continue.

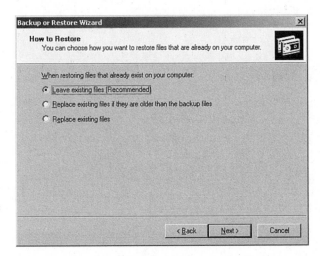

FIGURE 17.27 The How to Restore screen. The options here allow you to leave the existing files, replace them, or replace them only if they are older than the files on the backup media.

7. From the Advanced Restore Options screen, shown in Figure 17.28, you can select other restore options. You can restore the files using the security settings they were saved with (this is only for NTFS volumes). You can also select to restore junction points, which are logical pointers to files and folders on other drives, or you can select whether to preserve the volume mount points. Select the desired options and then click the Next button to continue.

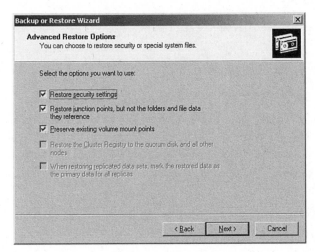

FIGURE 17.28 The Advanced Restore Options screen. These are the miscellaneous options that don't fit anywhere else.

8. From the Completing the Backup or Restore Wizard screen, examine the selected restore settings. If any settings are not correct, click the Back button to reconfigure them. If everything is correct, click the Finish button.

9. The Restore Progress dialog box appears, displaying the progress of the restore.

Restoring System State Data

As discussed earlier, the Backup program in Windows Server 2003 allows you to restore the system state data only on a local computer. You are not allowed to back up and restore the system state on a remote computer. Although you can't selectively back up components of the system state, you can restore the following system state components to an alternate location:

▶ Registry

▶ SYSVOL folder

▶ System boot files

▶ Cluster configuration (if installed)

The Active Directory, IIS Metabase, COM+ Class Registration, Certificate services databases, and the Windows File Protection folder cannot be restored to an alternate location.

To restore the system state data on a Windows Server 2003 server (not a domain controller), perform the procedure outlined in Step by Step 17.8.

STEP BY STEP

17.8 Restoring system state data using the Restore Wizard

1. From the Start menu, click Start, All Programs, Accessories, System Tools, Backup.

2. The Backup or Restore Wizard appears. From the Backup or Restore screen, you can select to either back up or restore files and settings. Select Restore Files and Settings and then click the Next button to continue.

3. From the What to Restore screen, select System State from the backup set to restore. Then click the Next button to continue.

4. From the Completing the Backup or Restore Wizard screen, examine the selected restore settings. If any settings are not correct, click the Back button to reconfigure them. If everything is correct, click the Finish button.

5. If you click the Advanced button, the Where to Restore screen opens. This screen allows you to select from the following options: Original Location, Alternate Location, and Single Folder. Select the location for the restore and then click the Next button to continue.

6. If you've selected to restore to the original location, you receive a warning that system state data will be overwritten. Click OK to acknowledge the warning.

7. From the How to Restore screen, you can select how the restore process handles existing files. The default is not to overwrite them. Note that these options do not apply to the system state restore; they are shown by default. Click the Next button to continue.

8. From the Advanced Restore Options screen, you can select other restore options. You can restore the files using the security settings they were saved with (this is only for NTFS volumes). You can also select to restore junction points, which are logical pointers to files and folders on other drives, or you can select whether to preserve the volume mount points. Note that these options apply only if you are restoring other files with your system state data. Ignore them. Then click the Next button to continue.

9. From the Completing the Backup or Restore Wizard screen, examine the selected restore settings. If any settings are not correct, click the Back button to reconfigure them. If everything is correct, click the Finish button.

10. The Restore Progress dialog box appears, displaying the progress of the restore.

11. After the restore completes, restart the server.

NOTE

For More Information   For information on how to restore system state data on a domain controller, see the section titled "Using Directory Services Restore Mode to Recover System State Data," later in this chapter.

Challenge

It is very important to always have a current backup of system state data, especially for domain controllers. The Windows Server 2003 Backup utility includes a built-in scheduler that allows you to schedule the backup to occur on a recurring basis.

For this exercise, your job is to automate the backup of system state data on your server. The data should be backed up every weekday evening at 11:00 p.m.

What is the best way to accomplish this in Windows Server 2003? On your own, try to develop a solution that involves the least amount of downtime.

If you would like to see a possible solution, follow these steps:

1. From the Start menu, click Start, All Programs, Accessories, System Tools, Backup.

2. The Backup or Restore Wizard appears.

3. From the Backup or Restore screen, select Backup Files and Settings and then click the Next button to continue.

(continues)

(continued)

4. From the What to Back Up screen, select the option to choose what to back up. Then click the Next button to continue.

5. From the Items to Back Up screen, click the My Computer entry to expand the tree. Select the System State entry and then click the Next button to continue.

6. From the Backup Type, Destination, and Name screen, you can select to back up to a tape or file, specify where to save the backup, and provide a name for the backup. Select the desired options and then click the Next button to continue.

7. From the Completing the Backup or Restore Wizard screen, examine the selected backup settings. If any settings are not correct, click the Back button to reconfigure them. If everything is correct, click the Advanced button.

8. From the Type of Backup screen, click the Next button to continue.

9. From the How to Back Up screen, click the Next button to continue.

10. From the Backup Options screen, click the Next button to continue.

11. From the When to Back Up screen, click the Set Schedule button.

12. The Schedule Job dialog box appears. Select the option to run the task daily at 11:00 p.m. Select the desired days to run the backup. When you're finished, click OK to save.

13. Back on the Schedule Job dialog box, click the OK button.

14. The Set Account Information dialog box appears. Enter the user account and password that you want the backup job to run as. Then click the OK button.

15. Back at the When to Back Up screen, click Next to continue.

16. From the Completing the Backup or Restore Wizard screen, examine the selected backup settings. If any settings are not correct, click the Back button to reconfigure them. If everything is correct, click the Finish button.

Using Other Recovery Tools

Although a good backup can allow the system administrator to recover from a variety of problems, a full server restore can be time consuming. Sometimes a server might have a problem that can be repaired by changing its configuration or replacing a small number of files. Windows Server 2003 includes a number of utilities that allow the system administrator (and even a user, in the case of Volume Shadow Copy) to recover from various problems. In this section, we examine these utilities and show how and when they are used.

Restoring Data from Shadow Copy Volumes

Although hardware errors can sometimes result in data loss, industry studies have shown that at least one third of all data loss is caused by human error, usually accidental file deletion or modification. Although these types of errors can be rectified by restoring the affected file or folder from a current backup, this requires the intervention of a system administrator or other overworked IT professional.

The other problem with restoring from a backup is that backups are usually performed outside of normal business hours, usually at night. If, at 4:00 p.m., a user accidentally overwrites a file that he has been working on all day, the version on the backup tape does not reflect any changes made that day, so all the changes will be lost.

This situation can be averted using the Volume Shadow Copy service in Windows Server 2003. The Volume Shadow Copy service allows users to view the contents of shared folders as they existed at specific points in time and to restore a previous copy of a file. This reduces the calls to administrators to restore accidentally deleted or overwritten files.

The Volume Shadow Copy feature in Windows Server 2003 works by setting aside a configurable amount of space, either on the same or a different volume. This space is used to save any changes to the files accessed via a share on the volume that Volume Shadow Copy is enabled on. These changes are added by making a block-level copy of any changes that have occurred to files since the last shadow copy. Only the changes are copied, not the entire file. As new shadow copies are added, the oldest one is purged either when you run out of allocated space or when the number of shadow copies reaches 64.

Shadow copies are turned on for an entire volume, not just for specific files and folders. When the Volume Shadow Copy service runs, it takes a snapshot of the files and folders on the volume. When a file is changed and saved to a shared folder, Volume Shadow Copy writes the previous version of the file to the allocated space. If the file is saved again before Volume Shadow Copy has run again, a second copy is not saved to the Shadow Copy storage area. A second copy cannot be saved to the storage area until the service has run again. The Volume Shadow Copy service can be configured to run at any time; the default schedule is for it to run weekdays at 7:00 a.m. and 12:00 p.m.

Shadow copies are configured on a Windows Server 2003 server. Before they are configured, you should plan how they should be configured. The following guidelines apply:

▶ Volume Shadow Copy is enabled for all shared folders on a volume; you can't just select a few.

▶ The minimum storage space you can allocate for shadow copies is 100MB.

▶ The storage space can be allocated on the same or on another volume.

▶ The default storage size allocated is 10% of the volume; however, you can increase the size at any time.

▶ When estimating the size to allocate, you must consider both the number and size of the files in the shared folders as well as how often they will be updated.

▶ Remember that when the storage limit is reached, the oldest shadow copies will be deleted.

▶ If you decide to store your shadow copies on another volume, the existing shadow copies will be deleted.

▶ The default configuration values for shadow copies are 100MB of space, with a scheduled update at 7:00 a.m. and 12:00 p.m. on weekdays.

▶ Using a separate volume to store shadow copies is highly recommended for heavily used file servers.

▶ Performing a shadow copy more than once an hour is not recommended.

▶ Shadow copies do not work properly on dual-boot systems.

To configure Volume Shadow Copy on a volume, perform the procedure outlined in Step by Step 17.9.

STEP BY STEP

17.9 Turning on Shadow Copy

1. From Windows Explorer or My Computer, right-click the root of the volume on which you want to enable Volume Shadow Copy.

2. The New Volume Properties dialog box appears. From this Properties dialog box, click the Shadow Copies tab. This displays the view shown in Figure 17.29.

3. From the Shadow Copies tab, highlight the volume on which you want to enable shadow copies and then click the Enable button. The Enable Shadow Copies confirmation box shown in Figure 17.30 is displayed. Read the text, and then click the Yes button to continue.

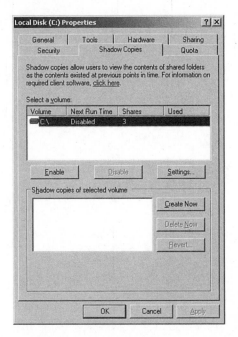

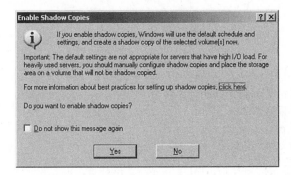

FIGURE 17.30 The shadow copies confirmation
box. Make sure you understand the conditions
and then click Yes.

4. After the volume is processed, the information on the Shadow Copies tab is updated, as shown in
Figure 17.31. From this tab you can force an update of the shadow copies by clicking the Create Now
button.

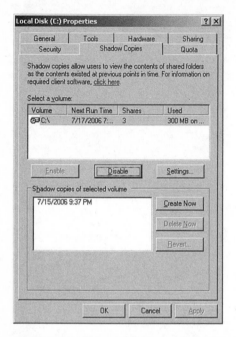

FIGURE 17.31   The updated Shadow Copies tab. As you can see, the default space and schedule items were configured.

After Volume Shadow Copy is enabled on the server, a client must be installed on the workstation so that the previous versions of the files are visible. Microsoft supplies a Shadow Copy client for Windows XP, Windows 2000 Professional, and Windows 98 users. The client is located in the `%systemroot%\system32\clients\twclient` folder on Windows Server 2003. The client software is referred to as Previous Versions. Windows Server 2003 and later operating systems have the Previous Versions client built in. The installation file, `twcli32.msi`, is a Microsoft installer file; you can copy it to a share that is accessible by your users.

To view files using the Previous Versions client, perform the procedure outlined in Step by Step 17.10.

STEP BY STEP

17.10 Restoring previous versions

1. Map to a share on the volume for which you enabled Volume Shared Copies. Right-click the share and select Properties.

2. The Folder Properties dialog box appears. From this Properties dialog box, click the Previous Versions tab, as shown in Figure 17.32.

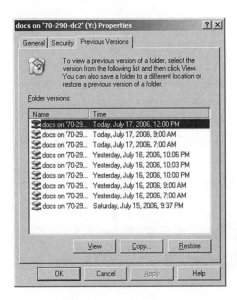

FIGURE 17.32 The Previous Versions tab, showing the versions available. You can view or copy the various versions of files in the shared folder to another location, or you can restore them to the shared folder.

3. From the Folder Properties dialog box, select the version to restore and then click the Restore button to continue.

4. The Previous Versions confirmation prompt appears. Remember that restoring a folder overwrites every file in that folder. Click Yes to continue.

The following buttons are available from the Previous Versions tab:

▶ *View*—This button allows you to view the contents of the selected version of the shared folder. You can only view the files; you cannot edit them.

▶ *Copy*—This button allows you to copy some or all of the files to a different location.

▶ *Restore*—This button restores the files in the shared folder to their state at the time the selected version was made. This overwrites all the existing files in the shared folder with the previous versions. Use this option with care.

Shadow copies are good for the following scenarios:

▶ *Recovering files that were accidentally deleted*—If someone accidentally deletes a file, he or she can recover a previous version using the Previous Versions client.

▶ *Recovering files that were overwritten*—If someone normally creates new files using the Save As method, sometimes he or she might click Save instead and overwrite the original file. The user can recover a previous version of the file using the Previous Versions client.

▶ *Checking the changes made between file versions*—The user can look at the previous versions of the file to see what changes have been made.

Shadow copies work with compressed or encrypted files and retain whatever permissions were set on these files when the shadow copies were taken.

NOTE

Keep Your Backup Plan　Using shadow copies is *not* a valid replacement for a well-planned backup procedure.

EXAM ALERT

Volume Shadow Copy Clients　Volume Shadow Copy clients are not available for Windows 95, Me, or any version of NT.

Advanced Options Menu

The Advanced Options menu allows you to select from a variety of options that can be used to troubleshoot and repair server startup and driver problems. The following options are available on the Windows Server 2003 Advanced Options menu, as shown in Figure 17.33:

▶ *Safe Mode*—This option starts Windows Server 2003 with the basic drivers for the mouse, video, monitor, mass storage, and keyboard. This option is recommended when you suspect that a recently installed application is causing problems. You can boot into this mode and uninstall the application.

▶ *Safe Mode with Networking*—This option starts Windows Server 2003 with the basic drivers, plus the network drivers. This option is handy for testing basic network connectivity.

▶ *Safe Mode with Command Prompt*—This option starts Windows Server 2003 with the basic drivers and opens a command prompt window instead of the desktop. This option is useful when the first two Safe Mode options are unable to start the server.

▶ *Enable Boot Logging*—This option starts Windows Server 2003 normally, but logs a list of all device drivers, services, and their status that the system attempts to load to %systemroot%\ntblog.txt. This is a good option to select to diagnose system startup problems.

▶ *Enable VGA Mode*—This option starts Windows Server 2003 normally but forces it to load the basic VGA driver. This option is useful for recovering from the installation of a bad video driver.

▶ *Last Known Good Configuration*—This option starts Windows Server 2003 with the contents of the Registry from the last time the user logged on to the system. This is helpful when recovering from a configuration error. For example, if you install a new driver and then the system crashes or fails to start, you can remove these changes by selecting Last Known Good Configuration when rebooting. When this option is selected, any configuration changes made after the last logon are lost. It is important to note that as soon as you log on to the server, the current drivers and Registry information become the last known good configuration. Therefore, if you suspect a driver problem, don't reboot and log on because you cannot roll back the changes using this option.

▶ *Directory Services Restore Mode*—This option is used to restore the Active Directory database and SYSVOL on a domain controller. It is listed only on a domain controller.

▶ *Debugging Mode*—This option starts Windows Server 2003 normally but sends debugging information over a serial cable to another computer. This option is for software developers.

▶ *Disable Automatic Restart on System Failure*—The default in Windows Server 2003 is to reboot on failure. If there is a stop message, it might not be displayed long enough to read it. This option will stop the system if there is an error, so that you can read any error messages.

▶ *Start Windows Normally*—This option bypasses the menu options and starts Windows Server 2003 without any modifications.

▶ *Reboot*—This option reboots the computer.

▶ *Return to OS Choices Menu*—If multiple operating systems are installed, selecting this option returns you to the boot menu.

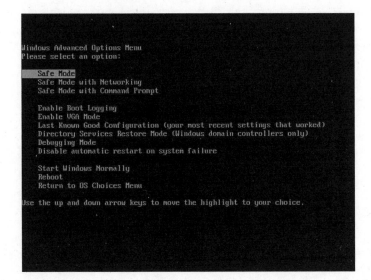

FIGURE 17.33 The Windows Server 2003 Advanced Options Menu screen showing the Safe Mode option selected.

Although Microsoft recommends using Last Known Good Configuration as the first step in diagnosing a problem, you can also start and log on to the server using one of the Safe Mode options. Unlike a normal logon, the Safe Mode options do not update the Last Known Good Configuration information, so it's still an option if you try Safe Mode first.

If your startup problem does not appear when you start the system in Safe Mode, you can eliminate the default settings and minimum device drivers as problems. Using Safe Mode, you can diagnose the problem and remove the faulty driver, or you can restore the proper configuration.

NOTE

Other Recovery Options   If your server does not start properly using Safe Mode or Last Known Good Configuration, you might have to boot to the Recovery Console or restore your system files using the Automated System Recovery (ASR) feature.

Last Known Good Configuration

The Last Known Good Configuration option allows you to restore the system to the state it was in at the time of the last logon. Whenever a user logs on to the console of a server, the hardware configuration and settings are stored in the Registry key `HKLM\System\CurrentControlSet`. This configuration is then backed up to another key, usually `ControlSet001`. If you install a driver or make a configuration change after you log on, this new information is saved to the `CurrentControlSet` key. If your changes result in a blue screen or other problems, you can restart your server and then go into the Advanced Options Menu and select Last Known Good Configuration. This allows you to select and boot with the configuration information backed up from the `CurrentControlSet` key at the last logon. This should allow you to boot properly, although the new drivers will no longer be present.

You must remember that the previous configuration information is overwritten with the current configuration every time you complete a logon to a server. Therefore, if you reboot and log on to the server, the good configuration entry will have been overwritten by the bad configuration entry. Make sure you understand the sequence of system events so that you don't lose this recovery option.

To reboot a server using the Last Known Good Configuration option, perform the procedure outlined in Step by Step 17.11.

STEP BY STEP

17.11 Using the Last Known Good Configuration

1. Restart the server. If Windows Server 2003 is the only operating system installed, you have to press F8 early in the boot process, just after the POST screen disappears. Otherwise, when you see the prompt Please Select the Operating System to Start, press the F8 key at the first OS screen.

2. The Advanced Options Menu screen appears, as shown previously in Figure 17.33. On the Advanced Options Menu screen, use the arrow keys to select the Last Known Good Configuration option.

3. You're now back at the operating system screen, as shown in Figure 17.34. Select the operating system you want to start and then press the Enter key.

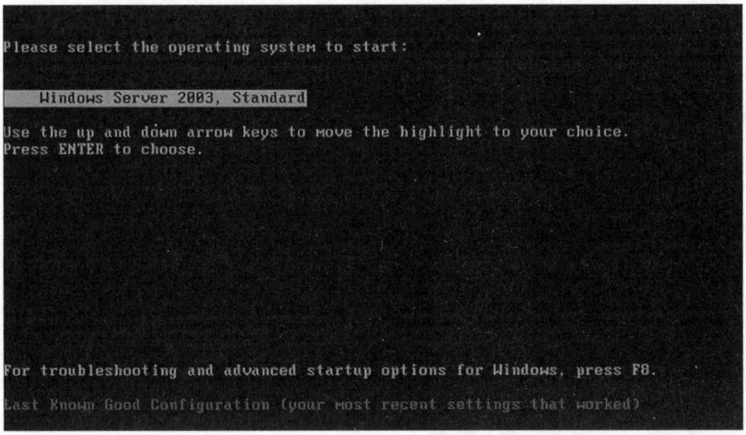

FIGURE 17.34 The boot menu screen again. Note that it informs you that you're in Last Known Good Configuration mode.

After the server boots, it should run normally. However, any configuration or driver changes made since the last logon are gone.

Safe Mode

The Windows Server 2003 Safe Mode option is a recovery tool carried over from the Windows 9x product line. This tool allows you to start your system with a minimal set of device drivers and services loaded.

Safe Mode is useful for those situations in which you load a new driver or software program or make a configuration change that results in an inability to start your system. You can use Safe Mode to start your system and remove the driver or software that is causing the problem.

To get into Safe Mode, perform the procedure outlined in Step by Step 17.12.

STEP BY STEP

17.12 Starting in Safe Mode

1. Restart the server. If Windows Server 2003 is the only operating system installed, you have to press F8 early in the boot process, just after the POST screen disappears. Otherwise, when you see the prompt Please Select the Operating System to Start, press the F8 key at the first OS screen.

2. The Advanced Options Menu screen appears. On the Advanced Options Menu screen, use the arrow keys to select one of the Safe Mode startup options, and then press Enter.

3. You're now back at the operating system screen. Select the operating system you want to start and then press the Enter key. The server boots.

4. When you come to the logon screen shown in Figure 17.35, log on to the server.

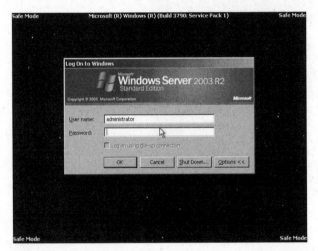

FIGURE 17.35   The Windows Server 2003 logon screen in Safe Mode. Notice that you're in VGA mode.

Remember that the capabilities vary depending on which Safe Mode option you select. For instance, the Safe Mode with Command Prompt option presents you with a command prompt window, and the Windows GUI will not be started, as shown in Figure 17.36.

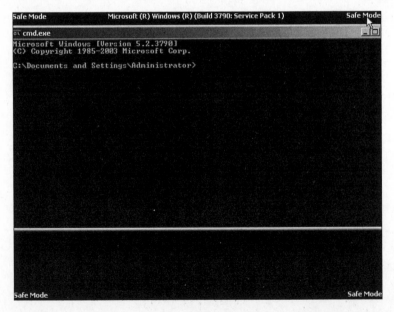

FIGURE 17.36   Windows Server 2003 server in Safe Mode with Command Prompt mode. Notice that you're in VGA mode and are limited to a command prompt window.

Recovery Console

For those situations in which the tools and methods available via Safe Mode are not enough to recover from a server failure, or if Safe Mode will not boot the server, Microsoft has provided an additional tool called the *Recovery Console*. The Recovery Console is a DOS-like command-line interface in which you can perform a limited set of commands and disable system services. Unlike booting from a DOS disk, the Recovery Console allows you limited access to files on an NTFS-formatted volume.

The Recovery Console is not installed by default; you must install it manually after you have installed Windows Server 2003 or run it from the product CD. To install the Recovery Console, perform the procedure outlined in Step by Step 17.13.

STEP BY STEP

17.13 Installing the Windows Server 2003 Recovery Console

1. Load the Windows Server 2003 CD-ROM.

2. Open a command prompt, access the Windows Server 2003 CD-ROM, and enter the `\i386\winnt32 /cmdcons` command.

3. Click the Yes button when the Windows Setup window, shown in Figure 17.37, appears.

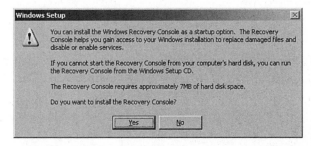

FIGURE 17.37 The Recovery Console confirmation prompt. Click Yes to install.

4. When the setup procedure completes, restart the server.

The Recovery Console option is added to the Windows Server 2003 boot menu, as shown in Figure 17.38.

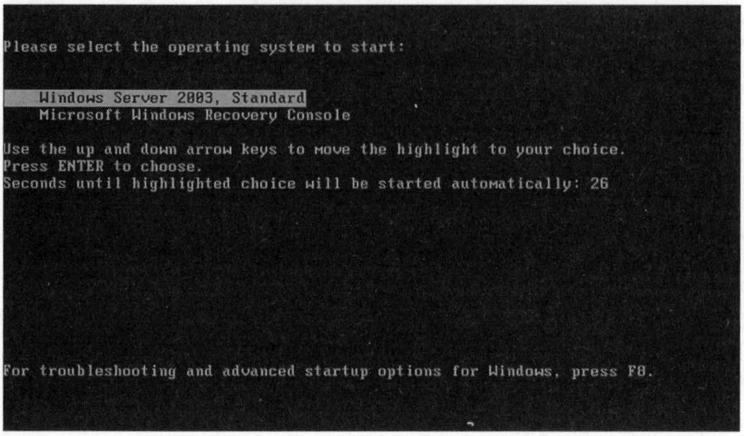

```
Please select the operating system to start:

   Windows Server 2003, Standard
   Microsoft Windows Recovery Console

Use the up and down arrow keys to move the highlight to your choice.
Press ENTER to choose.
Seconds until highlighted choice will be started automatically: 26




For troubleshooting and advanced startup options for Windows, press F8.
```

FIGURE 17.38 The Windows Server 2003 boot menu showing the addition of the Recovery Console.

If your system fails and you don't have the Recovery Console installed, or if you are having startup problems, you can run Recovery Console from the Windows Server 2003 CD-ROM.

NOTE

No More Boot Floppies Windows Server 2003 does not come with startup floppies, or with any method of creating them.

To run the Recovery Console from a CD-ROM perform the procedure outlined in Step by Step 17.14.

STEP BY STEP

17.14 Running the Recovery Console from a CD-ROM

1. Insert the desired media type and start the server.

2. In the Windows Server 2003 Setup procedure, select the option to repair the operating system.

3. Select Recovery Console as your repair method.

4. The system boots to the Recovery Console screen shown in Figure 17.39.

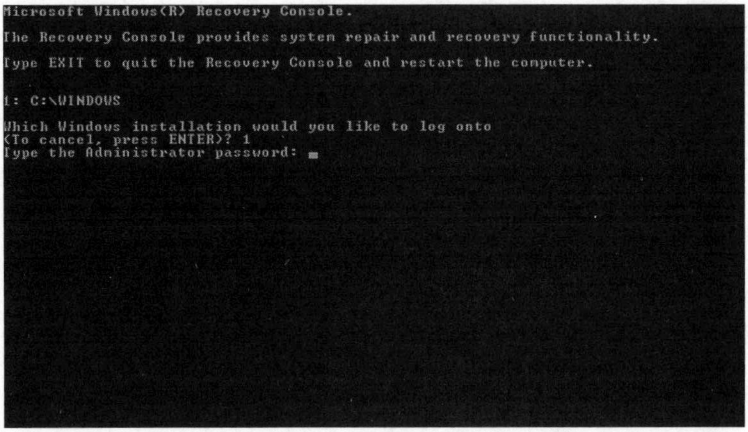

FIGURE 17.39   The Windows Server 2003 Recovery Console showing the logon screen.

After you start the Recovery Console, either from a CD or from the hard disk, you will be prompted for the operating system number to log on to and the Administrator password, as shown in Figure 17.39. On a member server, this is the local Administrator password. However, on a domain controller this is not the domain or local Administrator password; instead, it's the Directory Services Restore Mode password that you were prompted to create during the dcpromo procedure you used to install Active Directory.

After you log on, the commands listed in Table 17.2 are available.

TABLE 17.2   Recovery Console Commands

Command	Description
Attrib	Changes the attributes of files and folders.
Batch	Used to execute commands from a text file.
Bootcfg	Used to query, configure, or change the boot.ini file.
CD	Used to change the directory.
Chdir	Used to change the directory.
Chkdsk	Repairs disk errors.
Cls	Clears the screen.
Copy	Copies a file.
Del	Deletes files.
Delete	Deletes files.
Dir	Used to display a list of files and directories.
Disable	Used to disable a service or driver.
Diskpart	Used to manage partitions and volumes.

(continues)

TABLE 17.2 *Continued*

Command	Description
Enable	Used to enable a service or driver.
Exit	Closes the console and reboots the server.
Expand	Extracts a file from the Windows CAB files.
Fixboot	Writes a new boot sector.
Fixmbr	Used to repair the master boot record.
Format	Used to format a drive.
Help	Lists the available commands.
Listsvc	Lists the installed services and drivers.
Logon	Used to log on to another Windows installation.
Map	Displays a list of mapped drives.
MD	Used to create a directory.
Mkdir	Used to create a directory.
More	Used to display a text file. Same as Type.
RD	Used to delete a directory.
Ren	Used to rename a file.
Rename	Used to rename a file.
Rmdir	Used to delete a directory.
Set	Used to display and set environment variables.
Systemroot	Sets the current directory to the systemroot.
Type	Used to display a text file. Same as More.

As you can see, the Recovery Console allows you to perform a variety of tasks, such as formatting a drive, copying, deleting, or renaming files, and starting and stopping services. However, there are some limitations:

▶ You have access only to %systemroot% and its subfolders, the root partitions of %systemdrive%, any other partitions, floppy drives, and CD-ROMs.

▶ You cannot copy a file from the hard disk to a floppy, but you can copy a file from a floppy, a CD-ROM, or another hard disk to your hard disk.

Using Directory Services Restore Mode to Recover System State Data

On a domain controller, the Active Directory files are restored as part of the system state. The system state on a domain controller consists of the following items:

▶ Active Directory (NTDS)

▶ The boot files

▶ The COM+ Class Registration database

▶ The Registry

▶ The system volume (SYSVOL)

▶ Files in the Windows File Protection folder

The individual components cannot be backed up or restored separately; they can be handled only as a unit, as we discussed previously in the section "System State Backups."

When a single domain controller fails, and the other domain controllers are still operational, it can be repaired and the data restored using a current backup tape. After Active Directory is restored, the domain controller coordinates with the other domain controllers to synchronize any changes that were made to the Active Directory on the other domain controllers since the backup tape was created. This process is called a *nonauthoritative restore* and is the type of system state restore we performed earlier in this chapter.

Windows Server 2003 assigns an Update Sequence Number (USN) to each object created in Active Directory. This allows Active Directory to track updates and prevents it from replicating objects that have not changed. When you perform a normal file restore of the Active Directory, all the data that is restored is considered old data and will not be replicated to the other domain controllers. This data is considered to be nonauthoritative (old and out-of-date) because the objects have lower USNs. All the objects contained in the other copies of Active Directory on the other domain controllers that have higher USNs than the objects in the restored data will be replicated to the restored domain controller so that all copies of Active Directory are consistent. A nonauthoritative restore is the default restore mode for Active Directory and is used most often.

However, in specific circumstances, such as the accidental deletion of a group or an Organizational Unit (OU), it may be necessary to perform an authoritative restore. When you perform an authoritative restore, the USNs on the objects in the copy of the Active Directory database that is restored to the domain controller are reset to a number higher than the current USNs so that all the data that is restored is no longer considered old data. This allows the objects in the restore job to overwrite newer objects on the other domain controllers.

> **NOTE**
>
> **Authoritative Restore**   An authoritative restore cannot be performed while a domain controller is online—the domain controller must be restarted into Directory Services Restore Mode, which is an option available from the Advanced Options Menu.

To restore an object, you must know its common name (CN), the Organization Unit (OU), and the domain (DC) in which the object was located. For example, to restore the ABC St. Louis User OU in the abc.com domain during an Authoritative Restore, you would enter the following command:

```
Restore Subtree "OU=ABC St. Louis User,DC=abc,DC=com"
```

This command restores all the objects that have been deleted in the ABC St. Louis User OU since the backup tape was created.

To restore a user, you would use the following command:

```
Restore Subtree "CN=JDoe,OU=ABC St. Louis User,DC=ABC,DC=com"
```

To restore a printer, you would use this command:

```
Restore Subtree "CN=DeskJet 3rdfloor,OU=ABC St. Louis User,DC=abc,DC=com"
```

After the command has completed, enter **quit** twice and reboot the domain controller. The domain controller now replicates the restored Active Directory object to the other domain controllers.

To perform an authoritative restore of a deleted OU, perform the procedure outlined in Step by Step 17.15.

To set up this exercise, open the Active Directory Users and Computers MMC, create an OU, and name it Test.

STEP BY STEP

17.15 Performing an authoritative restore

1. Restart the server. If Windows Server 2003 is the only operating system installed, you have to press F8 early in the boot process, just after the POST screen disappears. Otherwise, when you see the prompt Please Select the Operating System to Start, press the F8 key at the first OS screen.

2. The Advanced Options Menu screen appears, as shown in Figure 17.40. On the Advanced Options screen, use the arrow keys to select Directory Services Restore Mode.

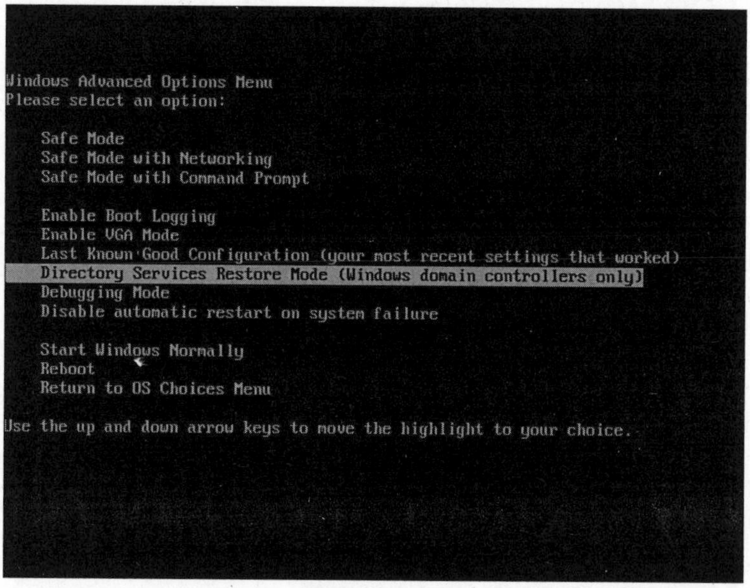

```
Windows Advanced Options Menu
Please select an option:

    Safe Mode
    Safe Mode with Networking
    Safe Mode with Command Prompt

    Enable Boot Logging
    Enable VGA Mode
    Last Known Good Configuration (your most recent settings that worked)
    Directory Services Restore Mode (Windows domain controllers only)
    Debugging Mode
    Disable automatic restart on system failure

    Start Windows Normally
    Reboot
    Return to OS Choices Menu

Use the up and down arrow keys to move the highlight to your choice.
```

FIGURE 17.40 The Advanced Options Menu screen showing the selection of Directory Services Restore Mode.

3. You're now back at the operating system screen. Select the operating system you want to start and then press the Enter key. The server boots.

4. The server boots into Directory Services Restore Mode. From the Windows Server 2003 logon screen, log on using the Directory Services Restore Mode password. This is not the normal Administrator password. This is the password that was entered during the dcpromo procedure.

5. Start the Windows Server 2003 Backup program by selecting Start, All Programs, Accessories, System Tools, Backup.

6. The Backup or Restore Wizard appears. Click the highlighted Advanced Mode link to open the Backup utility.

7. From the Backup utility's Advanced Mode window, select the Restore and Manage Media tab.

8. From the Restore and Manage Media tab, double-click the backup set that contains the backup of the system state data that you want to restore.

9. In the right pane of the Restore and Manage Media tab, shown in Figure 17.41, select System State and then click the Start Restore button to continue.

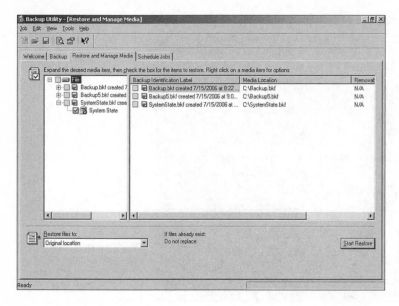

FIGURE 17.41 The Restore and Manage Media tab. Select the desired backup set and then select System State.

10. A confirmation prompt warns you that your current system state data will be overwritten. Click OK to continue.

11. When the Confirm Restore dialog box appears, click the Advanced button.

12. From the Advanced Restore Options dialog box, shown in Figure 17.42, select the When Restoring Replicated Data Sets, Mark the Restored Data as the Primary Data for All Replicas check box, and then click the OK button.

FIGURE 17.42 The Advanced Restore Options dialog box showing the authoritative restore selection.

13. Click the OK button in the Confirm Restore dialog box.

14. When the restore is complete, click Close.

15. When prompted to reboot, select No.

16. Open a command prompt window and type **ntdsutil**. Then press Enter.

17. At the command prompt, type **Authoritative Restore** and then press Enter.

18. Type **Restore Subtree "OU=Test,DC=70-290,DC=local"** and then press Enter. When prompted, click OK and then click Yes.

19. After the command has completed, the ntdsutil utility will display the number of objects restored and whether the restored objects have backlinks that need to be restored. If there are backlinks that need to be restored, make a note of the location of the `.txt` and `.ldf` files.

20. Because our OU was empty, there were no backlinks to be restored. On the command line, enter **quit** twice and reboot the domain controller. The domain controller now replicates the restored Active Directory object to the other domain controllers.

An authoritative restore is used most often in situations where an Active Directory object such as a user, group, or OU has been accidentally deleted and needs to be restored. If only a single Active Directory object is accidentally deleted, it is possible to restore only that object from a backup tape by performing a *partial* authoritative restore. This is accomplished by restoring from the last backup before the object was deleted. The procedure to perform this type of restore is very similar to the full Active Directory authoritative restore shown in the previous section.

CAUTION

Partial Authoritative Restores   When you're performing a partial authoritative restore, it is very important that you restore only the specific item that needs to be restored. If the entire Active Directory is restored, you could inadvertently write over newer objects. For example, the naming context of Active Directory contains the passwords for all the computer accounts and trust relationships. These passwords are automatically changed approximately every 30 days. If the existing values are overwritten by the restore, and the passwords have been renegotiated since that backup was created, the computer accounts will be locked out of the domain and the trust relationships will be dropped. For more information, see Microsoft Knowledge Base Article Q216243, "Impact of Authoritative Restore on Trusts and Computer Accounts."

More About Authoritative Restores and Backlinks

In some situations, restoring user and/or group objects will not restore the corresponding group backlinks. For more information on how to work around this issue, see Microsoft Knowledge Base Article Q280079, "Authoritative Restore of Groups Can Result in Inconsistent Membership Information Across Domain Controllers."

NOTE

Containers, Not OUs   The default Active Directory folders shown in the root of the Active Directory Users and Computers MMC are actually containers and not Organizational Units:

▶ Users

▶ Builtin

▶ Computers

When referencing these containers, you have to use the CN= attribute and *not* the OU= attribute.

Challenge

You are the administrator of a network that includes multiple Windows Server 2003 servers used for file and print services for a small chemical company. You have a small but well-trained staff of senior administrators, with a couple junior administrators you are training.

One of the junior administrators is processing a request from Human Resources to delete the user account of an employee who has left the company. This user was named John Betty, and he worked in Executive Services. Unfortunately, there is a lady named Betty John who also works in Executive Services, and the junior administrator accidentally deleted her user account instead of John Betty's. What's even worse, Betty John is one of the senior vice presidents.

What is the best way to restore the deleted user account in Windows Server 2003? On your own, try to develop a solution that would involve the least amount of downtime.

If you would like to see a possible solution, follow these steps:

Estimated Time: 40 minutes

1. Restart one of the domain controllers. If Windows Server 2003 is the only operating system installed, you have to press F8 early in the boot process, just after the POST screen disappears. Otherwise, when you see the prompt Please Select the Operating System to Start, press the F8 key at the first OS screen.

2. The Advanced Options Menu screen appears. On the Advanced Options screen, use the arrow keys to select Directory Services Restore Mode.

3. You're now back at the operating system screen. Select the operating system you want to start and then press the Enter key. The server boots.

4. The server boots into Directory Services Restore Mode. From the Windows Server 2003 logon screen, log on using the Directory Services Restore Mode password. This is not the normal Administrator password. This is the password that was entered during the dcpromo procedure.

5. Start the Windows Server 2003 Backup program by selecting Start, All Programs, Accessories, System Tools, Backup.

6. The Backup or Restore Wizard appears. Click the highlighted Advanced Mode link to open the Backup utility.

7. From the Backup utility's Advanced Mode window, select the Restore and Manage Media tab.

8. From the Restore and Manage Media tab, double-click the backup set that contains the backup of the system state data that you want to restore.

(continues)

(continued)

9. In the right pane of the Restore and Manage Media tab, select System State and then click the Start Restore button to continue.

10. A confirmation prompt warns you that your current system state data will be overwritten. Click OK to continue.

11. When the Confirm Restore dialog box appears, click the Advanced button.

12. From the Advanced Restore Options dialog box, select the When Restoring Replicated Data Sets, Mark the Restored Data as the Primary Data for All Replicas check box, and then click the OK button.

13. Click the OK button in the Confirm Restore dialog box.

14. On the Windows Server 2003 boot menu, select the operating system to start and press Enter.

15. The server boots into Directory Services Restore Mode. From the Windows Server 2003 logon screen, log on using the Directory Services Restore Mode password. This is not the normal Administrator password. This is the password that was entered during the `dcpromo` procedure.

16. Open a command prompt window and type **ntdsutil**. Then press Enter.

17. At the command prompt, type **Authoritative Restore** and then press Enter.

18. Type **Restore Subtree "CN=Betty John,OU=Executive Services,DC=yourcompany, DC=com"**, and then press Enter. When prompted, click OK and then click Yes.

19. After the command has completed, enter **quit** twice and reboot the domain controller. The domain controller now replicates the restored Active Directory object to the other domain controllers.

Implementing Automated System Recovery (ASR)

Objective:
Implement Automated System Recovery (ASR)

Most of the recovery procedures we have looked at so far are not much use if more than a handful of the boot partition files are missing or damaged. Although in certain modes you have the ability to copy files from the operating system CD-ROM, this can become a nightmare if your boot partition has sustained major damage.

Previous versions of Windows used the emergency repair disk (ERD) to assist in this type of situation; however, beginning in Windows 2000, it became unwieldy to save enough files to a floppy to restore the Registry and other files necessary to rebuild a boot partition. To rectify this situation, Windows Server 2003 includes a new feature called Automated System Recovery (ASR). ASR works by making a backup of the system and boot partitions (if different) to tape or other media. It then saves the catalog and other operating system information, such as system state, and disk partition information to a floppy disk.

When a problem occurs that cannot be fixed by using any of the other repair and recovery methods, or if you have replaced a failed boot drive, you need to restore the boot partition. Using ASR, this is as simple as booting your server from the Windows Server 2003 CD-ROM, and then inserting the floppy disk and the backup media created by the ASR process. The boot partition is automatically restored for you.

> **NOTE**
>
> **System and Boot Partitions** Remember from Chapter 12, "Managing Server Storage Devices," that the boot partition contains the operating system files, whereas the system partition contains the startup files, such as `Ntldr` and `Ntdetect.com`. In most situations, the system and boot partitions are on the same volume.

ASR installs a generic installation of Windows Server 2003 and then uses this generic installation to mount and restore your boot partition from the backup media created by ASR. This process not only restores the information on your boot drive, it also restores the disk signatures and re-creates the boot partition or volume, if necessary. It does not recover or delete any data volumes.

The advantage of using ASR is that it automates the restoration of your server. For example, in previous versions of Windows NT and Windows 2000, after a disk failure, you would be required to do the following:

1. Repartition and format the new hard drive.

2. Load a generic installation of Windows, including any specialized drivers.

3. Restore the system and boot partitions from a backup tape.

With ASR, after booting from the Windows Server 2003 CD-ROM, you insert the ASR floppy and the backup tape, and all these steps are performed for you.

ASR should be run regularly so that the backup media contains the most current configuration to be used for server recovery. ASR is implemented using the Windows Server 2003 Backup utility's Automated System Recovery Wizard.

The ASR Wizard can be used to create an ASR backup set using the procedure outlined in Step by Step 17.16.

STEP BY STEP

17.16 Creating an ASR backup

1. From the Start menu, click Start, All Programs, Accessories, System Tools, Backup.

2. The Backup or Restore Wizard appears. Click the highlighted Advanced Mode link to open the Backup utility.

3. From the Backup utility's Advanced Mode window, shown in Figure 17.43, select the Automated System Recovery Wizard button.

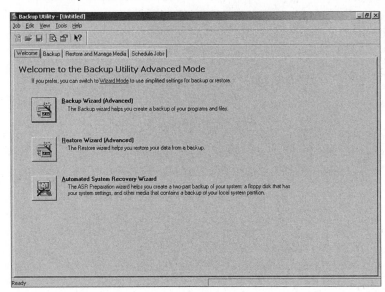

FIGURE 17.43   The Backup utility's Advanced Mode screen, displaying the ASR Wizard button.

4. The ASR Wizard opening screen appears. Click Next to continue.

5. The Backup Destination screen appears. Select the desired options and then click Next to continue.

6. The Completing the Wizard screen appears. Click Finish to continue.

7. The Backup program backs up the boot partition to your selected media. When prompted, insert a blank, formatted floppy disk.

To repair your system using ASR, you must start from the Windows Server 2003 CD. During the setup process, select F2, when prompted, and then insert the floppy disk and the backup media.

When needed, ASR can be used to restore a server using the procedure outlined in Step by Step 17.17.

STEP BY STEP

17.17 Restoring an ASR backup

1. Load the Windows Server 2003 CD-ROM in your CD-ROM drive.

2. Restart the server. When you see the prompt shown in Figure 17.44, press the F2 key.

Windows Setup

Press F2 to run Automated System Recovery (ASR)...

FIGURE 17.44 Press the F2 key to start ASR.

3. When prompted, insert the floppy disk and press the Enter key.

ASR uses the setup configuration files stored on the floppy disk to restore the boot partition to its state at the time the ASR media set was built.

> **EXAM ALERT**
>
> **Know the Recovery Methods** You should be familiar with the various recovery methods for Windows Server 2003, as well as when and how to use each one.

Slipstreaming Operating System CD-ROMs

Several of the procedures in this section refer to using the original installation CD-ROM to copy files from or as part of the recovery procedure. However, after a server has been operational for a while, you have probably installed a service pack or two (or three), and the files on the original CD-ROM no longer match the ones on your server. Because some of the recovery procedures require you to overwrite operating system files on the server with files from the operating system CD-ROM, it's best to use a slipstream CD-ROM that contains a service pack–updated version of the operating system instead of the original CD-ROM. Instructions on how to create a slipstreamed operating system CD-ROM can usually be found in the Readme file included with the service packs.

Planning for Disaster Recovery

Objective:

Managing and implementing disaster recovery

In this chapter we have covered a variety of tools and procedures that can be implemented in Windows Server 2003 to protect your servers and data in case of a disaster. However, disaster planning and recovery involves more than learning a few procedures; it has to be part of an overall strategy. Just firing up Windows Backup and filling up media with data does not make a good disaster-recovery plan. You have to have a plan in place for what to do with your backups when you need them.

A good disaster-recovery plan starts with the basics:

▶ What kind of disasters are you planning for?

▶ What are you going to do when a disaster occurs?

When making your disaster-recovery plan, you should prepare not only for common daily occurrences, such as users or administrators accidentally deleting files, but also more serious problems, such as tornadoes, hurricanes, and extended power outages.

Your disaster-recovery plan should be documented. If the chief technology officer walks into your office and starts asking what-if questions, you should be able to reach into your desk and pull out a binder that contains a detailed layout of what disasters you have planned for, what the contingencies are, who to contact, and where the materials you need (such as spare parts, offsite media, passwords, and so on) are stored and how to obtain them.

Copies of this disaster-recovery "cookbook" should be distributed to the personnel who have a part in recovery. In addition, this cookbook should be updated frequently as new hardware and software are added to your network or as additional personnel are added or removed. This should be a "living" document.

To keep this document effective, you should schedule frequent test runs to verify that the procedures work and that necessary personnel are comfortable with them. Feel free to make liberal use of screenshots in the documentation. Just like the old adage says, "A picture is worth a thousand words," especially when you're in the middle of a disaster and trying to recover.

Implementing and Using Good Backup Procedures

As part of your disaster-recovery plan, you should have solid backup and restore procedures. Here are some of the recommended best practices for backups:

▶ *Test your backups*—This can help to identify not only bad tapes but also bad procedures.

▶ *Train additional personnel*—In the case of a disaster, you might need to replace administrators who are busy elsewhere.

▶ *Preinstall the Recovery Console on all servers*—This allows you to recover quicker because you won't need to hunt down the Windows Server 2003 CD-ROM.

▶ *Back up both the system state and the data together*—This allows you to protect yourself from a hard disk failure and makes it easier for you to locate backup sets because everything should be on a single set.

▶ *Use the Automated System Recovery feature*—This not only protects you from the failure of a boot disk, but because the restore is fully automated, it allows you to work on other things while the process completes.

▶ *Always create and review the backup logs*—This lets you know whether a backup procedure has failed. There is nothing worse than starting the restore on a critical server and finding out that the backup media is blank because the backup failed.

▶ *Don't disable the Volume Shadow Copy backup feature*—The Volume Shadow Copy backup feature allows you to back up open files. If this option is turned off, some files will not be backed up.

▶ *Rotate your backup media*—Rotating backup media helps to insulate you from media failures.

Managing and Rotating Backup Storage Media

Objective:
Manage backup storage media.

After spending a lot of time and effort backing up your servers, it can all be negated by a bad tape or a tape that was overwritten when it shouldn't have been. There are several standard industry practices for managing and rotating backup storage media. For proper disaster-recovery protection, they should be followed.

For example, if you use the same tape or tapes every day, they soon become worn out. There is nothing worse than being in the middle of restoring critical files when you discover that a backup tape cannot be read because of an error. Best practices for working with backup tapes recommend that you cycle tapes so that they are not used too frequently, and that you track their in-service date. You should have a plan in place for the tapes to be replaced either when they are showing errors in the backup log or sometime before their "end of life," as recommended by the manufacturer of the tape.

Let's look at a typical weekly backup schedule and the differences in the media required for a full restore (see Tables 17.3 and 17.4).

TABLE 17.3   Weekly Backup Schedule Using Normal and Incremental Backups

Day	Backup Type	Media Required for Full Restore
Monday	Normal	Monday
Tuesday	Incremental	Monday and Tuesday
Wednesday	Incremental	Monday, Tuesday, and Wednesday
Thursday	Incremental	Monday, Tuesday, Wednesday, and Thursday
Friday	Incremental	Monday, Tuesday, Wednesday, Thursday, and Friday

TABLE 17.4   Weekly Backup Schedule Using Normal and Differential Backups

Day	Backup Type	Media Required for Full Restore
Monday	Normal	Monday
Tuesday	Differential	Monday and Tuesday
Wednesday	Differential	Monday and Wednesday
Thursday	Differential	Monday and Thursday
Friday	Differential	Monday and Friday

In both cases, you should use five media sets (one or more tapes) each week. These tapes should be stored in a fireproof media safe during the week, and the previous week's backup should be stored offsite in a secure, climate-controlled location. A common practice is to have three or four sets of backup media so that there is a longer period before older data is over-written. This protects the system administrator from a user who deletes a file just before he leaves for a two-week vacation and then wants his file back when he returns to work. These backups can be supplemented by a monthly, quarterly, or even yearly normal backup that can be kept for a longer period of time.

Chapter Summary

This chapter covered the main features in Windows Server 2003 used for protecting and restoring server configurations and data in case of disasters of various types. To summarize, this chapter contained the following main points:

▶ *Planning for disaster recovery*—This includes planning for and working with the procedures involved in creating a disaster-recovery plan.

▶ *Using Windows Backup*—This includes saving and recovering both system state data and user data.

▶ *Using recovery tools*—This includes using the disaster-recovery tools built in to Windows Server 2003, such as Automated System Recovery, Last Known Good Configuration, the Recovery Console, and Safe Mode.

Key Terms

▶ Incremental backup

▶ Differential backup

▶ Backup selection file

▶ Recovery Console

▶ Safe Mode

▶ System state

▶ Last Known Good Configuration

▶ Automated System Recovery (ASR)

Apply Your Knowledge

Exercises

17.1 Using Last Known Good Configuration

A very common problem in Windows is the installation and recovery from the effects of bad device drivers. The effects of a faulty device driver can range from poor performance to a blue screen. As a system administrator, you need to be able to recover from this type of incident.

What is the best way to accomplish this in Windows Server 2003? On your own, try to develop a solution that involves the least amount of downtime.

If you would like to see a possible solution, follow these steps:

Estimated Time: 20 minutes

1. Open Regedit. Delete the Registry key `HKLM\SYSTEM\CurrentControlSet\Control\SystemBootDevice`.

2. Restart the server. You should get a blue screen, possibly with the message "Inaccessible Boot Device."

3. Restart the server. If Windows Server 2003 is the only operating system installed, you have to press F8 early in the boot process, just after the POST screen disappears. Otherwise, when you see the prompt Please Select the Operating System to Start, press the F8 key at the first OS screen.

4. The Advanced Options Menu screen appears. On this screen, use the arrow keys to select the Last Known Good Configuration option.

5. You're now back at the operating system screen. Select the operating system you want to start and then press the Enter key. The server boots normally.

17.2 Using the Recovery Console

Another common problem in Windows is the corruption of system files. This prevents a server from booting properly, or it can result in a system stop error. It is important to understand the capabilities and limitations of the tools used to correct these types of situations.

For this exercise, one of the Windows Server 2003 system files is corrupt. The server will no longer boot. Even Safe Mode is not available. Your job is to fix the server while incurring the least amount of downtime.

What is the best way to accomplish this in Windows Server 2003? On your own, try to develop a solution that involves the least amount of downtime.

If you would like to see a possible solution, follow these steps:

Estimated Time: 20 minutes

1. Open either My Computer or Windows Explorer. Select Tools, Folder Options, and then click the View tab. Unhide the hidden files.

2. In the root folder on the boot drive, remove the read-only attribute from the `boot.ini` file.

3. Make a copy of `boot.ini` and name it **boot.sav**.

4. Open `boot.ini` with a text editor and delete all the lines under `[operating systems]`.

5. Save the file.

6. Reboot the server. You should get a boot error, most likely "Cannot find NTLDR."

7. Insert the Windows Server 2003 CD-ROM and start the server.

8. In the Windows Server 2003 Setup procedure, select the option to repair the operating system.

9. Select Recovery Console as your repair method.

10. The system boots to the Recovery Console screen.

11. Select the operating system to load. This will probably be number 1.

12. Enter the Administrator password.

13. From the command prompt, type **del boot.ini**.

14. From the command prompt, type **ren boot.sav boot.ini**.

15. Type **Exit** to restart the server. It should boot normally.

Exam Questions

1. Mary scheduled Windows Backup to run unattended during the night to back up her server. When she came in the next day, she examined the backup logs, and the backup not only took a lot longer to complete than she thought it would, but there were also messages in the log about skipped open files. What is Mary's problem?

   ○ **A.** She left too many files open.

   ○ **B.** She ran the command-line version of Backup instead of the GUI version.

   ○ **C.** Volume Shadow Copy was disabled.

   ○ **D.** She forgot to dump her SQL database before starting the backup.

2. Volume Shadow Copy is enabled on a volume that hosts the user data files. On Friday, a user tries to use the Previous Versions client to access a copy of a file that she has been working on every day that week. However, she has versions only from Wednesday forward. What is the most likely problem?

   ○ **A.** The Volume Shadow Copy Service wasn't enabled until Wednesday.

   ○ **B.** The user doesn't have the proper rights to see all the files.

   ○ **C.** The area designated for Volume Shadow Copy is too small.

   ○ **D.** She hasn't saved a copy of the file since Wednesday.

3. John, a junior system administrator, just loaded new video drivers on a Windows Server 2003 server. After the installation, he rebooted the server and immediately received a blue screen. What's the quickest way for John to recover from this problem?

○ **A.** Rebuild the server using Automated System Recovery (ASR).

○ **B.** Go into Safe Mode, delete the driver, and reboot.

○ **C.** Boot into the Recovery Console, delete the driver, and reboot.

○ **D.** Boot the server and select Last Known Good Configuration.

4. Jane is one of the network administrators for Big Company, Inc. Jane is responsible for managing and maintaining all the database servers in the organization. As part of her duties, Jane maintains current backups of all the servers she is responsible for, along with various boot disks and other items necessary for recovery purposes.

One day, Jane comes to work and one of her servers has blue screened. It seems that one of the junior administrators was upgrading device drivers and, after he rebooted, got a blue screen. Jane proceeds to try Last Known Good Configuration, then Safe Mode, and then the Recovery Console, but those methods don't seem to repair the problem. What is her next step?

○ **A.** Rebuild the server using Automated System Recovery (ASR).

○ **B.** Go into Safe Mode, restore the system state data, and reboot.

○ **C.** Boot into the Recovery Console, restore the system state data, and reboot.

○ **D.** Repair the server using the emergency repair disk (ERD).

5. Fred reboots one of his Windows Server 2003 domain controllers and receives the message that NTOSKRNL.EXE cannot be found. What is the quickest way to repair this problem?

○ **A.** Boot his server from a DOS disk and copy the NTOSKRNL.EXE file from the Windows Server 2003 CD-ROM.

○ **B.** Boot his server from the Recovery Console and copy the NTOSKRNL.EXE file from the Windows Server 2003 CD-ROM.

○ **C.** Boot his server from Safe Mode and copy the NTOSKRNL.EXE file from the Windows Server 2003 CD-ROM.

○ **D.** Boot his server from the Windows Server 2003 CD-ROM and select the Repair option. Then copy the NTOSKRNL.EXE file from the Windows Server 2003 CD-ROM.

6. Your Windows Server 2003 uses a SCSI adapter that is not included on the Hardware Compatibility List (HCL). You install an updated driver for the SCSI adapter. When you start the computer, you receive the following STOP error:

"INACCESSIBLE_BOOT_DEVICE."

Which of the following procedures can you use to resolve the problem?

- ○ **A.** Start the computer in Safe Mode. Reinstall the old driver for the SCSI adapter.

- ○ **B.** Start the computer by using a Windows Server 2003 bootable floppy disk. Reinstall the old driver for the SCSI adapter.

- ○ **C.** Start the computer by using the Windows Server 2003 CD-ROM. Load the Recovery Console and replace the SCSI driver.

- ○ **D.** Recover the system and boot partitions using ASR.

7. You are trying out a TCP/IP Registry hack that you saw in a magazine. After carefully making the change using Regedit, you reboot your server. However, it hangs on the logon screen. What is the best way to correct this problem?

- ○ **A.** Restart the server in Safe Mode. Undo the Registry change.

- ○ **B.** Restart the computer and boot to the Recovery Console. Undo the Registry change.

- ○ **C.** Restart the server and select Last Known Good Configuration from the Advanced Options Menu screen.

- ○ **D.** Restart the server in Safe Mode with Networking. Undo the Registry change.

8. You are the administrator of a Windows Server 2003 Active Directory domain with multiple sites. As part of your job, you perform daily system state backups on your domain controllers. Unfortunately, one of your junior administrators opened a file that contains a virus on one of your domain controllers. This virus seems to have deleted several users and groups in your Active Directory database on one of your domain controllers. What action should you take?

- ○ **A.** Quickly unplug the domain controller from the network, format the hard drive, and recover from backup.

- ○ **B.** On one of the other domain controllers, use Windows Backup to restore the system state data. Run Ntdsutil.

- ○ **C.** On one of the other domain controllers, boot into Directory Service Restore mode. Use Windows Backup to restore the system state data. Run Ntdsutil.

- ○ **D.** On one of the other domain controllers, boot into Safe Mode. Use Windows Backup to restore the system state data. Run Ntdsutil.

9. You are the administrator of a Windows Server 2003 Active Directory domain with multiple sites. As part of your job, you perform daily system state backups on your domain controllers. Unfortunately, one of your junior administrators opened a file that contains a virus on one of your domain controllers. This virus seems to have deleted several users and groups in your Active Directory database on several domain controllers. What action should you take?

    ○ **A.** Unplug the domain controller from the network, format the hard drive, and recover from backup.

    ○ **B.** On one of the other domain controllers, use Windows Backup to restore the system state data. Run Ntdsutil.

    ○ **C.** On one of the other domain controllers, boot into Directory Service Restore mode. Use Windows Backup to restore the system state data. Perform an authoritative restore.

    ○ **D.** On one of the other domain controllers, boot into Safe Mode. Use Windows Backup to restore the system state data. Run Ntdsutil.

10. Bob is the system administrator for Good Times Inc., a manufacturer of various leisure-time accessories. The Good Times network consists of 12 Windows Server 2003 servers, 10 Windows 2000 servers, and 700 Windows XP Professional clients. The Recovery Console is installed on each domain controller.

Every Friday at 11:00 p.m., you run the Automated System Recovery (ASR) Wizard in conjunction with removable storage media. Every night at midnight, you use third-party software to perform full backups of user profiles and user data on removable storage media. One Friday at 8:00 p.m., an administrator reports that the CA database on a domain controller named GT1 is corrupted. You need to restore the database as quickly as possible.

Which two actions should you perform? (Each correct answer presents part of the solution. Choose two.)

    ○ **A.** Restart GT1 by using Directory Services Restore Mode.

    ○ **B.** Restart GT1 by using the installation CD-ROM.

    ○ **C.** Perform a nonauthoritative restoration of Active Directory.

    ○ **D.** Perform an authoritative restoration of Active Directory.

    ○ **E.** Use the ASR disk to restore the contents of the ASR backup file.

Answers to Exam Questions

1. **C.** When Volume Shadow Copy is enabled, and the backup process encounters an open file, a snapshot of the file is copied to another area on disk, and that snapshot copy of the file is backed up. Volume Shadow Copy is enabled by default for backups, but it can be deselected if desired. See "Volume Shadow Copy."

2. **C.** The most likely cause is that the Volume Shadow Copy area is too small. Volume Shadow Copy can store only 64 copies, and it starts deleting the oldest versions when it reaches that number or when it runs out of disk space. See "Volume Shadow Copy."

3. **D.** Although any of the other answers would work, the quickest way to recover from a bad driver installation is to boot the server using Last Known Good Configuration. See "Last Known Good Configuration."

4. **A.** The next recovery step to attempt after Jane has tried Last Known Good Configuration, Safe Mode, and the Recovery Console is Automated System Recovery. ASR deletes and reformats the boot partition and then reloads it from backup. Restoring the system state data usually will fix a driver problem because it restores the Registry, but that had already been tried. The ERD doesn't exist in Windows Server 2003 (it has been replaced by ASR). See "Implementing Automated System Recovery (ASR)."

5. **B.** A DOS disk won't be able to read an NTFS disk, which is what's installed by default on a domain controller. Safe Mode won't be available if the NTOSKRNL.EXE file is corrupted or missing. The Repair option from the install procedure requires the ASR recovery media. Because the Recovery Console uses its own miniversion of Windows Server 2003 to boot the server, it can be used to copy and repair system files. See "Recovery Console."

6. **C, D.** Safe Mode does not work because the boot partition is inaccessible because of the driver problem. There is no boot floppy for Windows Server 2003. The Recovery Console has its own copy of Windows Server 2003 so that you can still boot to it. ASR will also work. See "Recovery Console."

7. **C.** Restarting a server and selecting Last Known Good Configuration is the quickest and easiest way to correct most bad Registry edits. See "Last Known Good Configuration."

8. **A.** Because the virus has affected only a single domain controller, you should take it off the network before it replicates changes to the other domain controllers. Then you should rebuild the domain controller from backup. See "Using Directory Services Restore Mode to Recover System State Data."

9. **C.** Because the problem has started replicating to other domain controllers, your only choice is to perform an authoritative restore, which overwrites the bad copy of the AD database with a good copy from your backups. See "Using Directory Services Restore Mode to Recover System State Data."

10. **A and C.** To restore the CA database, which is backed up as part of the System State data, we must restart the server in Directory Services Restore mode. Because we don't need to overwrite any Active Directory data, we will perform a nonauthoritative restore. ASR is not required because the server is still operational. See "Using Directory Services Restore Mode to Recover System State Data."

Suggested Readings and Resources

1. Disaster Recovery Whitepaper. Microsoft Corporation. http://www.microsoft.com/technet/treeview/default.asp?url=/technet/prodtechnol/windowsserver2003/proddocs/deployguide/sdcbc_sto_gqda.asp.

2. How ASR Works. Microsoft Corporation. http://technet2.microsoft.com/WindowsServer/en/Library/7b4f0436-cc90-4b52-b6ab-064f9db8d2721033.mspx?mfr=true.

3. How to Troubleshoot Startup Problems in Windows Server 2003. Microsoft Corporation. http://support.microsoft.com/kb/325375/.

4. Shadow Copy Whitepaper. Microsoft Corporation. http://www.microsoft.com/windowsserver2003/docs/SCR.doc.

18

Managing and Implementing Windows Server Update Services

Objectives

This chapter covers the following Microsoft-specified objectives for the "Managing and Maintaining a Server Environment" section of the Managing and Maintaining a Microsoft Windows Server 2003 Environment exam:

Manage software update infrastructure

► With new security exploits announced what seems to be weekly and with corresponding patches that need to be applied, it is important that you automate as much of this process as possible. Microsoft has made available the Windows Server Update Services (WSUS) to allow you to control the patches and updates applied to the Windows platform.

Outline

Study Strategies

▶ The sections in this chapter outline features that are essential to managing a Windows Server 2003 environment.

▶ Expect to see several questions on an area that is being heavily emphasized in Windows Server 2003: Windows Server Update Services (WSUS) and the various configurations available. Know how the features of WSUS work, under what circumstances they should be used, and how to implement them.

Introduction

When Windows Server 2003 was originally released, the 70-290 Exam featured questions about the Microsoft' software update and patching service called Software Update Services (SUS). SUS has been replaced with Windows Server Software Update Services (WSUS). Microsoft will no longer support WSUS after December 6, 2006, and WSUS hasn't been available as a download from the Microsoft website since August 2005.

Because SUS 1.0 will no longer synchronize or provide new updates after December 6, 2006, the exam should be updated to reflect questions on WSUS.

Therefore, in this chapter we will look at WSUS, examine how it operates, and how best to implement it on Windows Server 2003.

Managing a Software Update Infrastructure

Objective:

Manage software update infrastructure

No matter how well it seems that software is written, there is always a need for bug fixes and security patches. In addition, there never seems to be an end to the need for updated drivers and minor feature upgrades. Sometimes it seems that the system administrator's job never ends.

Microsoft Update

The later versions of Windows included the Windows Update feature, later updated to Microsoft Update. Microsoft Update is used to keep your Windows system and selected components up-to-date by connecting to the Microsoft Update website over the Internet and automatically downloading and installing security fixes, critical updates, and new drivers. These updates are used to resolve known security and stability issues with the Windows operating system.

Although relying on Microsoft Update is fine if you have only a few computers, in an enterprise environment, it leaves much to be desired. Consider the following:

▶ Most of the updates require the user to have administrative rights on the computer. This is rarely allowed in an enterprise environment.

▶ The updates have not been tested in the user's specific environment. If an update has a conflict with other software on the network, it can bring the company to its knees.

▶ Each computer is responsible for downloading its own updates. This can be bandwidth intensive if you have a large environment.

> **NOTE**
>
> **Windows Update**   Although the Windows Update website still exists, the Microsoft Updates website pro-
> vides the same patches in addition to patches for Microsoft Office and the Microsoft line of server-based
> applications.

Windows Server Update Services

Fortunately, Microsoft has provided the Windows Server Software Update Services (WSUS) to assist the system administrator in managing updates in the small- to medium-sized enterprise environment.

Microsoft WSUS is a service that can be installed on an internal Windows 2000 or Windows Server 2003 server that can download all critical updates as they are posted to Microsoft Update. Administrators can also receive email notification when new critical updates have been posted.

The client computers and servers can be configured through Group Policy or the Registry to contact the internal WSUS server for updates, instead of going out over the Internet to the Microsoft servers. WSUS is basically an internal version of the Microsoft Update service, with the exception that the network administrator has the option to control which updates get downloaded from Microsoft and which ones get installed on the computers in the environment.

WSUS allows administrators to quickly and easily deploy most updates to Windows 2000 or Windows Server 2003 servers as well as desktop computers running Windows 2000 Professional or Windows XP Professional.

You can install multiple WSUS servers in your environment, both for load balancing or for test purposes. For example, you can set up a WSUS server to automatically download all the latest updates from Microsoft. After they have been downloaded, you can distribute the updates to test computers to verify compatibility with the existing software. After the updates have been tested, they can be published to the production environment.

A basic WSUS configuration is shown in Figure 18.1. In this example, the WSUS server in the headquarters is configured to run a scheduled synchronization with the Microsoft Update website. The administrator then publishes the updates to a group of test computers. After testing has been completed, the approved updates on the HQ server are distributed to the other WSUS clients in the enterprise.

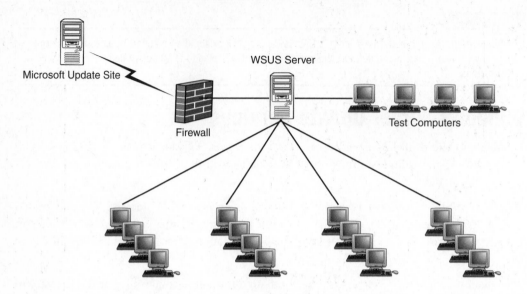

FIGURE 18.1 A basic WSUS configuration, including test computers.

This type of configuration is enabled by utilizing *Computer Groups*. Computer groups allow the administrator to segregate computers in different groups with different deployment rules. In our previous example, the test computers would be in a separate group, and the rest of the computers in the organization would be in a different group.

Another example would be to separate servers from workstations. Although most workstations can be patched just about any evening, servers usually work around the clock, so they would need a scheduled maintenance window.

You can also utilize a downstream WSUS server, as shown in Figure 18.2. In this configuration, the Upstream WSUS server obtains all the updates from the Microsoft website. The downstream servers then receive the approved updates from the upstream website. This configuration is typically used in organizations that have multiple sites connected by a WAN. Because the downstream WSUS servers don't have to access the Internet, and can only download approved updates from the upstream WSUS server, his gives the administrator more control over the patching process, and reduces the required bandwidth. However, the remote administrators will still be allowed to change some configuration settings, including adding additional computer groups.

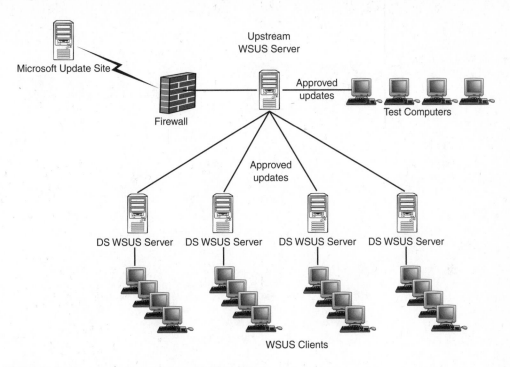

FIGURE 18.2 The upstream server approves all updates.

Another typical configuration is shown in Figure 18.3. In this configuration, traveling laptop users or VPN clients are assigned to a separate computer group on a designated WSUS server. The users assigned to this group will get their approvals from their assigned WSUS server, but they will obtain their updates directly from the Microsoft Update website. This allows the administrator to control which patches are installed on these machines, but doesn't require the administrator to supply the storage space or the bandwidth required to download the patches.

WSUS requires a SQL database to hold its configuration information and a catalog of the updates. A copy of WMSDE for Windows Server 2003 is included with the WSUS installation and should be used for most installations of WSUS. Unlike the previous versions of the Microsoft SQL Desktop Engine (MSDE), WMSDE is not limited to 2GB. Windows 2000 Server installations can either use MSDE for small installations or SQL Server for larger environments.

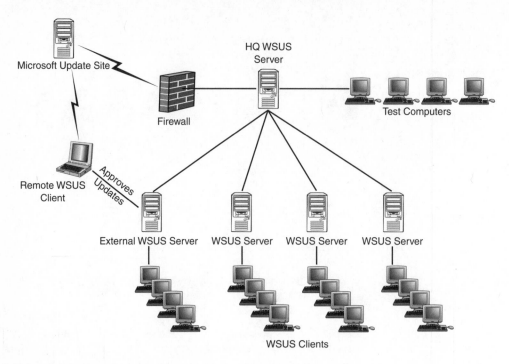

FIGURE 18.3 Remote clients download directly from Microsoft Update.

WSUS allows you two options for storing updates—local or remote storage. In the local storage option, all approved updates are downloaded from Microsoft Updates and stored on your WSUS server. When your clients need an update, they obtain it from the store on the WSUS server. With Remote Storage, no updates are downloaded to your WSUS server. When the clients need an update, they download the approved updates directly from the Microsoft Updates site.

For those remote sites where there isn't an administrator available to manage the WSUS servers, you can install replicas. A WSUS replica server is a mirrored installation of the upstream server. Unlike in the downstream configuration we discussed earlier, you can't add additional Computer Groups to a replica server.

Installing Windows Server Update Services

WSUS is not included with Windows Server 2003; instead, it must be downloaded from the Microsoft website at http://go.microsoft.com/fwlink/?LinkId=47374. The requirements for WSUS for up to 500 clients are as follows:

▶ Windows 2000 Service Pack 2 or later.

▶ IIS 5.0 or later.

▶ Internet Explorer 6.0 or later.

▶ CPU 1GHz or higher.

▶ 1GB RAM.

▶ Both the system partition and the partition on which you install WSUS on must be formatted as NTFS.

▶ 1GB of free space on the System partition formatted as NTFS.

▶ 6GB of hard drive space. 30GB recommended.

▶ Minimum of 2GB of free space on the volume where the Windows SQL Server 2000 Desktop Engine (WMSDE) is installed.

▶ Background Intelligent Service (BITS) 2.0.

▶ Microsoft .NET Framework 1.1 SP1.

▶ Ports 80 and 443 must be open on the firewall between the WSUS server and the Internet.

To install WSUS, use the procedure in Step by Step 18.1.

NOTE

Windows Server 2003 SP1   BITS 2.0 and .NET Framework 1.1 SP1 are included in Windows Server 2003 SP1 and later.

STEP BY STEP

18.1 Installing WSUS

1. Locate the downloaded WSUS installation file and then double-click it to start the installation.

2. From the Setup Wizard screen, click the Next button to continue.

3. Select the I Accept the Terms in the License Agreement option button and click the Next button to continue.

4. On the Select Update Source screen, shown in Figure 18.4, you choose whether to store updates on the WSUS server or have your clients download them from Microsoft Updates. Accept the default, and then click Next.

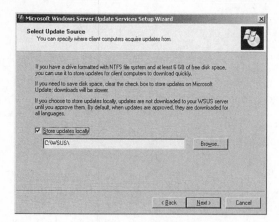

FIGURE 18.4 Choose where to store approved updates.

5. The Database Options screen appears. You have the option of letting WSUS install the WMSDE, or you can point WSUS to an existing SQL server. Accept the default of installing WMSDE by clicking the Next button. This is shown in Figure 18.5.

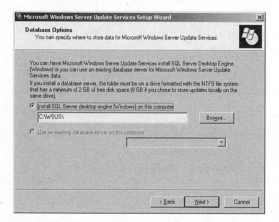

FIGURE 18.5 Choose what database to use.

6. The Web Site Selection screen appears. You can select to use the default website or create your own. Accept the defaults and click the Next button to continue.

7. The Mirror Update Settings screen appears, as shown in Figure 18.6. If you are creating a hierarchy of WSUS servers, you would specify a server to obtain updates from. Because this is the first server in the hierarchy, click the Next button to continue.

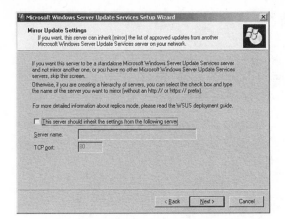

FIGURE 18.6 Enter the original server if creating a WSUS hierarchy.

8. The Ready to Install screen appears. Review the URL and then click the Next button to continue.

9. When the installation completes, click the Finish button to end the procedure.

After the installation procedure has completed, you can connect to the SUS Administration page by entering http://*servername*/WSUSAdmin. From the WSUS Administration page, you can synchronize the server with the Microsoft Update site and configure various options. This initial synchronization is required so that you will be able to view the available updates. By default, the synchronization procedure will display updates for all products in all languages. To save on bandwidth, you can go to the Synchronizations page and select only the products and languages that you want to see.

NOTE

WSUS Administrators The WSUS installation added a new local group, WSUS Administrators. You must be a member of this group or the local Administrators group to configure and manage WSUS.

To synchronize WSUS with the Microsoft Windows Update site, use the procedure in Step by Step 18.2.

STEP BY STEP

18.2 Synchronizing WSUS

1. Enter `http://servername/SUSAdmin` in your web browser. This opens the WSUS Administration web page shown in Figure 18.7.

Chapter 18: Managing and Implementing Windows Server Update Services

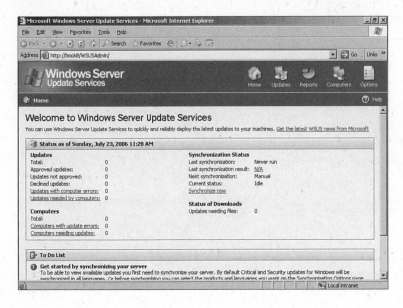

FIGURE 18.7 The WSUS Administration web page.

2. In the upper-right pane of the web page, click the Options icon.

3. The Options page, shown in Figure 18.8, allows you to change the configuration options that you selected during the initial installation of WSUS. In addition, it also provides you with settings to configure the WSUS server to operate behind a proxy server, and assign computer groups. Notice that there is also an option to specify a local WSUS server to synchronize with.

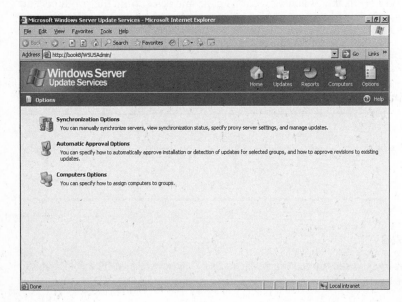

FIGURE 18.8 The Options page allows you to control the configuration of your WSUS server.

4. From the Synchronization Options page, shown in Figure 18.9, you can click the Change buttons under products or Update Classifications to limit the updates that will be downloaded.

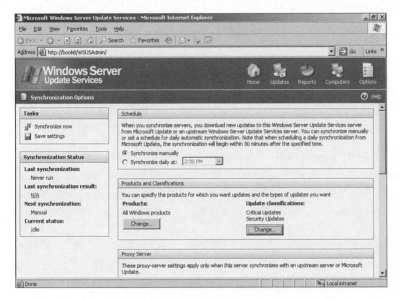

FIGURE 18.9 The Synchronization Options page allows you to filter what updates are downloaded. The default is to download updates for all operating systems in all languages.

5. Scroll down to the bottom of the page and select the Advanced button in the Update Files and Languages area.

6. When prompted, acknowledge the warning message. This opens the Advanced Synchronization Options dialog shown in Figure 18.10. Click OK to save.

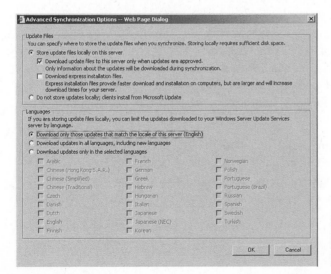

FIGURE 18.10 The Advanced Synchronization Options page. Notice that the default is to download updates only after they have been approved.

7. Select the option to download only those updates that match the locale of this server. Click the OK button to save.

8. This returns you to the Synchronization Options page. You have the option to synchronize immediately or to synchronize on a scheduled basis. Click the Synchronize Now button to continue.

9. The updates are downloaded to your WSUS server. This might take a while depending on the options you've selected and the number of updates currently available. A progress bar is displayed to indicate the progress.

10. When the synchronization with the Microsoft Update site is complete, click the OK button.

There is also an option to specify a local WSUS server to synchronize with. Along with this option is a check box that specifies that only approved items should be synchronized. These options are used in the scenario with multiple WSUS servers that we covered earlier. Using these options allows you to download updates only to a single server. The updates are tested and approved by the HQ WSUS server. By configuring your other WSUS servers to point to this central server and to synchronize only approved updates, you can reduce the traffic on your network.

NOTE

Initial Synch   The initial WSUS synchronization can potentially take a long time, depending on how many products and languages you are supporting. It's best to schedule the first WSUS synchronization for either overnight or over a weekend.

Computer Groups

Earlier in the chapter, we briefly discussed Computer Groups. Computer Groups allow you to target a group of computers with different patches on a different schedule than other groups. This is handy, so that if your development group is in the final stages of readying a release and have "frozen" their test machines, you won't inadvertently install patches that could interfere with their test cycle.

By default, all computers are automatically added to the All Computers Group and the Unassigned Computers group. When a computer is assigned to a specific group, it is automatically removed from the Unassigned Computers group. All computers registered with WSUS will remain in the All Computers group until they are removed from the WSUS environment.

There are two ways to assign a computer to a group in WSUS:

▶ Manually assigning it to a group using the WSUS console

▶ Using Group Policy (or a Registry key) to assign a Computer Group name to the contents of an OU

Unfortunately, you can use one or the other method, but not both. To select the method of assigning computers to groups, use the process in Step by Step 18.3.

STEP BY STEP

18.3 Selecting Group Targeting

1. Enter `http://servername/SUSAdmin` in your web browser. This opens the WSUS Administration web page.

2. In the upper-right pane of the web page, click the Options icon.

3. From the Options page, click the Computers Options icon. This opens the Computers Options page, shown in Figure 18.11.

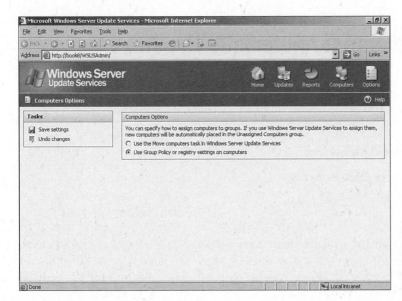

FIGURE 18.11 The Options page allows you to control how you will assign computers to your Computer Groups.

4. Select the Use Group Policy option button, and then click the Save Settings icon.

5. In the upper-right pane of the WSUS console, select the Computers icon. This opens the Computers page, as shown in Figure 18.12.

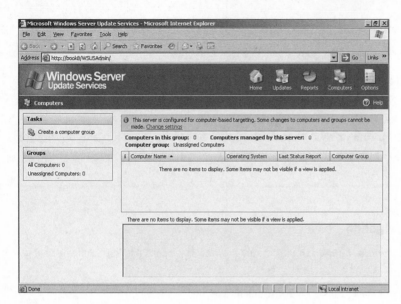

FIGURE 18.12 The Computers page allows you to configure your Computer Groups. Note the warning message.

6. Click the Create a Computer Group icon. Enter a name for your Computer Group, and click OK to save.

Configuring Clients for Automatic Updates

After the updates have been synchronized and approved, and the Computer Groups configured, the updates are ready to be distributed to the clients. To connect to the WSUS server, the client should have the Automatic Update software installed. The correct version is included with the following:

▶ Windows XP Service Pack 1 or later

▶ Windows 2000 Service Pack 3 or later

▶ All versions of Windows Server 2003

These versions of the Automatic Updates client don't support WSUS, but they will automatically self-update to a version that does. Older versions of the Windows Update client do not support WSUS at all. For older operating systems, you will have to download the updated client from the WSUS web page at http://www.microsoft.com/windowsserversystem/updateservices/default.mspx.

By default, the Microsoft Windows client and server operating systems are configured to obtain updates from the Windows Update site; they must be reconfigured to obtain updates from the Microsoft Updates site or a WSUS server.

Although you can manually edit the Registry of Windows servers and clients to use a WSUS server, that process is time consuming and error prone. The most efficient way to make this change is via Group Policy.

We're going to target your test server that's installed in the Workstations OU using the procedure in Step by Step 18.4.

STEP BY STEP

18.4 Configuring a WSUS Groups GPO

1. Open the Group Policy Management Console. Right-click the Kansas City\Workstations OU and select Create and Link a GPO Here from the pop-up menu.

2. When the New GPO prompt appears, enter the name **WSUS Groups**, and click OK.

3. The new GPO will appear in the Group Policy Objects container, and as a linked object under the OU folder.

4. Right-click the new GPO and select Edit from the pop-up menu. The Group Policy Editor MMC appears.

5. Click Computer Configuration, click Administrative Templates, click Windows Components, and then click the Windows Update folder, as shown in Figure 18.13.

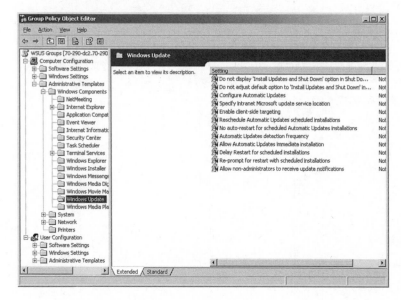

FIGURE 18.13 The Group Policy Object Editor, showing the configurable policy options for Windows Update.

6. Double-click the Enable client-side targeting entry and select Enabled. Enter the name of the computer group you just created, and then click the OK button to save.

7. Double-click the Specify Intranet Microsoft Update Service Location entry and select Enabled. Enter the name of the WSUS computer in the format http://servername in both fields, and then click the OK button to save (see Figure 18.14).

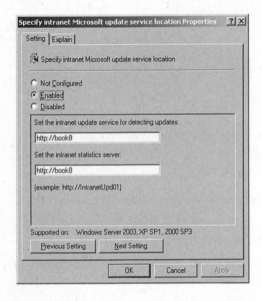

FIGURE 18.14 This policy points your Automatic Update clients to your WSUS server, both for updates and to record statistics.

8. Double-click the Configure Automatic Updates entry, and then select the Enabled option from the Properties dialog box (see Figure 18.15). Configure an appropriate schedule and then click the OK button to save. Close the Group Policy Object Editor.

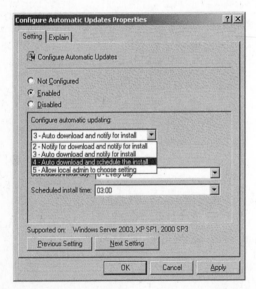

FIGURE 18.15 The Configure Automatic Updates policy, showing the options available for scheduling. The default is every day at 3:00 a.m.

9. On your test server, log on using the administrator account.

10. Open a command window and enter **gpupdate /force**.

11. Wait a minute or so, and then enter **wuauclt /detectnow**. (This command forces the client to contact the WSUS server.)

12. Open the WSUS Administration web page.

13. In the upper-right pane of the web page, click the Computers icon.

14. The computers in the OU that you just applied the GPO to should be displayed.

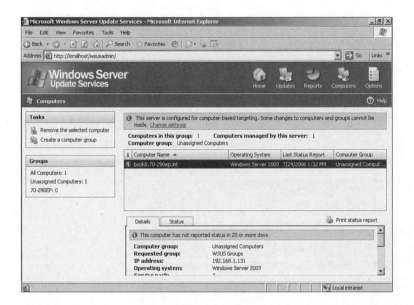

FIGURE 18.16 The Computers page of the WSUS console, showing the assigned computers and their associate groups.

The other Group Policy options shown back in Figure 18.13 are used to control whether the computer performs an autorestart after it installs an update that requires a reboot or waits until a scheduled reboot. The last option controls whether the updates are automatically installed when the computer is first started after it has missed an update window (for example, if the computer was scheduled for an update at 3:00 a.m. but was turned off).

By default, each client computer checks in with the WSUS server at a 22-hour interval with a random offset of 0 to 30 minutes. When the client checks in, it receives any new WSUS configuration settings and saves its individual statistics to the WSUS database. This interval can be changed via Group Policy.

Approving Updates

Not all the updates apply to the computers on your network. Also, there is the possibility that one of the fixes might actually break something in your environment. Fortunately, WSUS can be configured to not make any updates available until after you have approved them. This gives you the opportunity to select which updates you want to distribute and to test them before you release them to your production environment.

To approve WSUS updates so that they can be distributed to your clients, use the procedure in Step by Step 18.5.

STEP BY STEP

18.5 Approving WSUS updates

1. Open the WSUS Administration web page.

2. In the upper-right pane of the web page, click the Updates entry.

3. From the Updates page, shown in Figure 18.17, you can select the updates you want to make available to your clients. After selecting the desired updates, click the Change Approval button.

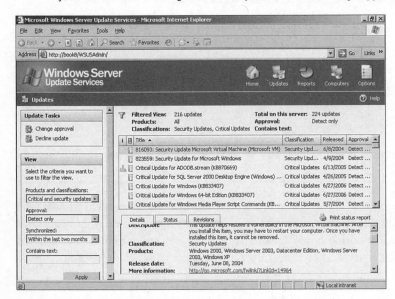

FIGURE 18.17 The Approve Updates page allows you to control which updates are made available to your clients. A brief description of each update is supplied, along with any prerequisites. For more information, you can click the Details hyperlink supplied with each entry.

4. You receive a warning prompt telling you that the selected list will replace all previously approved updates. Click the Yes button to continue.

5. If a license agreement is required for any of the updates, it is displayed. Read the agreement and then click the Yes button. Click the Synchronize Now button to continue.

6. When prompted, click the OK button to save the list.

Managing Updates

Unfortunately, Microsoft doesn't provide much in the way of tools to manage WSUS. WSUS is intended for the small- to medium-sized enterprise. All the configuration options are available from the web console. For larger enterprises, Microsoft recommends that you implement the System Management Server (SMS) product. SMS provides much more powerful update capabilities, including expanded operating system support, hardware and software inventory, and remote control management capabilities.

However, unlike its predecessor, Software Update Services (SUS), WSUS provides four main reports to track the status of updates:

▶ *Status of Updates*—This report lists and provides the status of all approved updates, broken down by computer and computer group.

▶ *Status of Computers*—This report lists the patch status of all computers.

▶ *Synchronization Results*—This report shows the results of the last synchronization, including synchronization errors, new updates available, revised updates, and expired updates.

▶ *Settings Summary*—This report provides a list of the WSUS configuration settings.

To run a Status of Computers report, follow the procedure in Step by Step 18.6.

STEP BY STEP

18.6 Running a WSUS Status of Computers report

1. Open the WSUS Administration web page.

2. In the upper-right pane of the web page, click the Reports entry.

3. From the Reports page, select the Status of Computers icon.

4. As you can see in Figure 18.18, you can select the computer group you want to see, along with other filtering options such as Installed, Needed, and so on. When you've made the appropriate selections, click the Apply button.

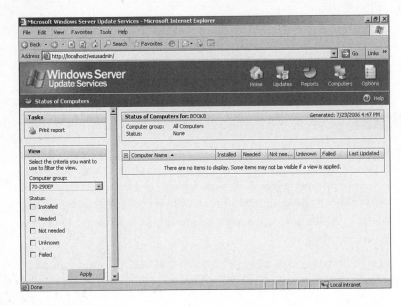

FIGURE 18.18 The Status Of Computers report allows you to control what Computer Group to see and how much information is displayed in the report.

5. If desired, you can select the Print Report icon to obtain a hard copy of the report.

In addition to the previously mentioned reports, WSUS can supply compliance reports to track the compliance status of a computer—whether all the required updates have been installed on that computer, and by Update—whether the update has been installed on all of the computers that require it.

Unlike the other reports that are available from the Reports page, these reports are run by selecting the desired computer on the Computers page and the selected update on the Updates page.

Challenge

You are the administrator of a Windows Server 2003 Active Directory domain with multiple sites. You have installed a WSUS infrastructure with a WSUS server at each site that pulls its patch information from your central WSUS server.

You manager has asked you if the Cincinnati site has installed patch KB32145. He would like to know if all the computers in that site have installed the patch, and if not, how many have not. What do you do?

Try to complete this exercise on your own, listing your conclusions on a sheet of paper. After you have completed the exercise, compare your results to those given here.

1. Open the WSUS Administration web page.

2. In the upper-right pane of the web page, click the Updates entry.

(continues)

(continued)

3. From the Updates page, enter the KB number for the patch in the Contains Text field in the lower-right part of the page, and click the Apply key. The patch entry should appear.

4. Highlight the patch entry, and then click the Print Status Report icon.

WSUS provides on-the-fly status reporting of just about any common metric to allow you to check the patch status of your network. The only caveat is that you should wait at least 22 hours after a patch distribution, so that the clients have a chance to report their statistics. For an individual client, you can expedite the reporting process by entering the **Wuauclt /detectnow** command.

Chapter Summary

It is important to remember that no matter how much work is put into it, no software is perfect. That's where the Windows Server Update Services (WSUS) comes in. WSUS allows the system administrator to set up, control, and monitor an internal version of the Microsoft Windows Update website. This provides the administrator greater control over the patches, security fixes, and other updates that are to be distributed to both servers and client computers.

Key Terms

- ▶ Microsoft Update
- ▶ Windows Update
- ▶ Software Update Service (SUS)
- ▶ Windows Server Update Services (WSUS)

Apply Your Knowledge

Exercises

18.1 Performing an immediate synchronization

The server that runs WSUS is configured to synchronize weekly on Saturday at 12:00 p.m. Because of a virus outbreak, a critical update was released today.

You need to manually update the WSUS server.

Estimated Time: 20 minutes.

1. Enter **http://*servername*/SUSAdmin** in your web browser. This opens the WSUS Administration web page.

2. In the upper-right pane of the web page, click the Options icon.

3. From the Options page, select the Synchronization Options icon.

4. On the Synchronization Options page, click the Synchronize Now icon.

5. The updates are downloaded to your WSUS server. This might take a while depending on the options you've selected and the number of updates currently available. A progress bar is displayed to indicate the progress.

6. When the synchronization with the Microsoft Update site is complete, click the OK button.

18.2 Running a computer status report

One of your remote users reports that she's having trouble connecting to a VPN server. You suspect that her computer didn't receive a recent hotfix.

How can you verify this?

Estimated Time: 20 minutes.

1. Enter `http://servername/SUSAdmin` in your web browser. This opens the WSUS Administration web page.

2. In the upper-right pane of the web page, click the Computers entry.

3. From the Computers page, select the computer that was supposed to receive the hotfix.

4. Click the Print Status Report icon; this will print a report showing every update installed by WSUS on the client computer.

Exam Questions

1. You are the lead administrator for a large manufacturer of farm machinery and related parts based in the upper Midwest. Your company has several small manufacturing plants spread out over a five-state area. Most of the end users are not computer savvy, so the client computers are somewhat locked down. All clients are running Windows XP, and all servers are running Windows Server 2003. The manufacturing plants are connected to headquarters via T1 lines in a hub-and-spoke configuration.

Because of the large number of updates and security fixes that Microsoft is releasing on a regular basis, your staff is becoming overwhelmed with the workload of updating the client computers in the remote locations. You need to identify an automated solution to assist you in keeping your clients up-to-date. What do you do? (Pick two.)

- ○ **A.** Install a Software Update Service (SUS) server in the HQ location. Configure the SUS server at HQ to synchronize with the Microsoft Windows Update website.

- ○ **B.** Install a Software Update Service (WSUS) server in the HQ location. Configure the WSUS server at HQ to synchronize with the Microsoft Update website.

- ○ **C.** Configure the clients to receive and install updates from the SUS server.

- ○ **D.** Configure the clients to receive and install updates from the WSUS server.

- ○ **E.** Configure the clients to receive and install updates from the Microsoft Update website.

2. You are the system administrator for FlyByNight Airlines. Your network consists of a single Active Directory domain, with all servers running Windows Server 2003 and all clients running Windows XP Professional.

   You need to install Windows Server Update Services on a spare server named FlyBy1. FlyBy1 has a minimum amount of free hard drive space available, but you have no other servers, and your clients need to install several critical updates. What should you do?

   ○ **A.** On FlyBy1, make sure that only the locale used is selected.

   ○ **B.** On FlyBy1, select the option to allow updates to be stored on Windows Update.

   ○ **C.** On FlyBy1, select the option to allow updates to be stored on Microsoft Update.

   ○ **D.** Modify the default home page for all clients to http://windowsupdate.microsoft.com.

3. You are the system administrator for FlyByNight Airlines. Your network consists of a single Active Directory domain, with all servers running Windows Server 2003 and all clients running Windows XP Professional.

   You need to implement a solution for managing security updates on client computers. You plan to use a Windows Server 2003 computer to manage security updates. Your solution for managing security updates must meet the following requirements:

   ▶ Security updates must be installed automatically.

   ▶ You must be able to control which updates are available to install.

   ▶ Security updates must synchronize automatically with the latest updates offered by Microsoft.

   You need to implement a solution for managing security updates that meets the requirements. What should you do?

   ○ **A.** Publish the security updates by using a Group Policy object (GPO). Assign the GPO to the client computers that require updates.

   ○ **B.** Install Windows Server Update Services (WSUS). Configure the WSUS software to synchronize daily with Microsoft. Use Group Policy to configure the appropriate Windows Update settings on the client computers.

   ○ **C.** Install Microsoft Internet Security and Acceleration (ISA) Server on a Windows Server 2003 computer.

   ○ **D.** Create a process to run Windows Update on all client computers.

4. You are the lead administrator for a large manufacturer of farm machinery and related parts based in the upper Midwest. Your company has several small manufacturing plants spread out over a five-state area. Most of the end users are not computer savvy, so the client computers are somewhat locked down. All clients are running Windows XP, and all servers are running Windows Server 2003. The manufacturing plants are connected to headquarters via T1 lines in a hub-and-spoke configuration.

You just installed Windows Server Update Services (WSUS) on a server named WSUS1. You enable WSUS1 to obtain and store security patches for distribution on the internal network.

Now you need to ensure that all client computers receive future security patches from WSUS1 only.

You open the Group Policy object (GPO) for the Clients OU. Which setting should you configure?

- ○ **A.** Computer Configuration\Software Settings\Software Installation

- ○ **B.** User Configuration\Software Settings\Software Installation

- ○ **C.** Computer Configuration\Administrative Templates\Windows Components\Windows Installer

- ○ **D.** User Configuration\Administrative Templates\Windows Components\Windows Installer

- ○ **E.** Computer Configuration\Administrative Templates\Windows Components\Windows Update

5. You are the lead administrator for a pet food company based in the Southeast. Most of the end users are not computer savvy, so the client computers are somewhat locked down. All clients are running Windows XP, and all servers are running Windows Server 2003.

You recently installed Windows Server Update Services (WSUS) to manage security updates. The server that runs SUS is configured to synchronize automatically every day at 7:00 a.m. New critical updates were released today at 9:00 a.m. You need to manually update the SUS server. What action should you take?

- ○ **A.** Log on to the WSUS server. Download the new security updates from Microsoft Update.

- ○ **B.** Download the new security updates from Microsoft Update to your local computer. Copy and paste the updates on the WSUS server.

- ○ **C.** On the WSUS home page, synchronize the server.

- ○ **D.** Log on to the WSUS server. Run `Wupdmgr.exe` by using the appropriate command to manually synchronize the server.

- ○ **E.** On the WSUS Synchronization Options page, synchronize the server.

6. You are the administrator of a Windows Server 2003 network that consists of clients ranging from Windows NT 4.0 to Windows XP. You purchase and install a new Windows Server 2003, and install and configure WSUS. Your Windows 2000 SP3 and Windows XP SP2 clients are able to receive patches without any problems. However, it doesn't look like your Windows NT 4.0 SP6 clients are receiving any updates.

   What can you do to receive updates from WSUS for your Windows NT 4.0 clients?

   ○ **A.** Download a new client from the WSUS support page.

   ○ **B.** Reconfigure Group Policy to support the Windows NT 4.0 clients.

   ○ **C.** Manually edit the registry to connect to the WSUS server.

   ○ **D.** Windows NT 4.0 is not supported by WSUS.

7. You are the administrator for a small chemical firm. You currently have 15 Windows 2000 SP2 workstations, 5 Windows XP (no service packs) laptops, and 3 Windows 2003 Servers. You install WSUS on a Windows Server 2003 server named Patch. You must ensure that all client computers receive all Microsoft security patches, critical updates, and service packs. This needs to be accomplished as quickly as possible. What should you do? (Choose three.)

   ○ **A.** Download and install the latest version of the Automatic Updates client on the Windows 2000 workstations.

   ○ **B.** Download and install the latest version of the Automatic Updates client on the Windows XP laptops.

   ○ **C.** Download and install the latest version of the Automatic Updates client on the Windows 2003 servers.

   ○ **D.** Modify the Windows Update settings of the Default Domain Controllers Group Policy object to point the client computers to http://Patches.

   ○ **E.** Modify the Windows Update settings of the Default Domain Policy Group Policy object to point the client computers to http://Patches.

   ○ **F.** Apply service pack 3 to the Windows 2000 SP2 workstations.

8. You are the administrator of a Windows Server 2003 Active Directory domain with multiple sites. You have installed a WSUS infrastructure with a WSUS server at each site that pulls its patch information from your central WSUS server. You check the Microsoft website and see that they have released a critical update. You schedule this update to be applied at 3:00 a.m.

   When you come into the office the next morning, you check the Status of Updates report to see whether the patch application was successful. To your dismay, you see that less than 25% of the computers have the critical patch installed. What should you do to correct this?

   ○ **A.** Schedule WSUS to apply the patch at 3:00 a.m. the next morning.

   ○ **B.** Apply the patch manually.

   ○ **C.** Do nothing, and check the report again tomorrow morning.

   ○ **D.** Call Microsoft Support and open an incident.

Answers to Exam Questions

1. **B and D.** WSUS can provide an automated way to keep your clients updated. SUS is no longer supported by Microsoft. Although you can have each client access the Microsoft Updates website directly, you can't control what patches are installed, or if they get installed. See "Microsoft Update."

2. **C.** Whereas minimizing the amount of locales you download updates for will save a lot of storage space, in a limited storage scenario you want to minimize storage use as much as possible. WSUS supports the use of Remote Storage. This option allows you to approve the updates, and then allow the client computers to download them directly from Microsoft Updates. WSUS does not use Windows Update. See "Microsoft Update."

3. **B.** You can use Windows Server Update Services to download all critical updates to servers and clients as soon as they are posted to the Windows Update website. Although the GPO method would apply updates to the clients, it wouldn't automatically synchronize them with the website. Creating a process for the clients to go to the Windows Update site would bypass the approval process, so it's not a good solution. ISA is a firewall product and would be of no use in this scenario. See "Configuring Clients for Automatic Updates."

4. **E.** Automatic Updates clients can be configured to synchronize from an WSUS server rather than the Windows Update servers by modifying the clients' Registries or, more efficiently, by configuring Windows Update policies in a Group Policy Object (GPO). See "Configuring Clients for Automatic Updates."

5. **E.** To perform an immediate synchronization, select Synchronize Now on the synchronization options page. Downloading the updates manually won't add the required information to the WSUS database. See "Installing Windows Server Update Services."

6. **D.** WSUS doesn't support Windows NT 4.0. See "Configuring Clients for Automatic Updates."

7. **A, B, and E.** Windows 2000 SP2 or earlier clients and Windows XP clients with no service packs are unable to connect to a WSUS server without manually updating the Automatic Updates client to a later version. Windows 2000 SP2 or later, Windows XP SP1 or later, and all versions of Windows Server 2003 clients either have the correct software installed or can connect to the WSUS server and automatically update to a newer version. By adding the WSUS server location to the Default Domain controllers GPO, only domain controllers would receive updates. See "Configuring Clients for Automatic Updates."

8. **C.** WSUS provides on-the-fly status reporting of just about any common metric to allow you to check the patch status of your network. The only caveat is that you should wait at least 22 hours after a patch distribution so that the clients have a chance to report their statistics. For an individual client, you can expedite the reporting process by entering the `Wuauclt /detectnow` command. See "Managing Updates."

Suggested Readings and Resources

1. Deploying Microsoft Windows Server Update Services. Microsoft Corporation. http://technet2.microsoft.com/WindowsServer/en/library/ace052df-74e7-4d6a-b5d4-f7911bb06b401033.mspx?mfr=true.

2. Morimoto, Rand, Noel, Michael, Lewis, Alex. *Microsoft Windows Server 2003 Unleashed R2 Edition*. Sams Publishing, 2006. ISBN 0672328984.

3. Step-by-Step Guide to Getting Started with Microsoft Windows Server Update Services. Microsoft Corporation. http://www.microsoft.com/ downloads/details.aspx?FamilyId=3BA03939-A5A9-407B-A4B0-1290BA5182F8&displaylang=en.

4. Windows Server 2003 Deployment Guide. Microsoft Corporation. http://technet2.microsoft.com/WindowsServer/en/Library/c283b699-6124-4c3a-87ef-865443d7ea4b1033.mspx?mfr=true.

5. *Windows Server 2003 Resource Kit*. Microsoft Press, 2005. ISBN 0735614717.

6. Windows Server Update Services home page. http://www.microsoft.com/windowsserversystem/updateservices/default.mspx.

PART II

Final Review

Fast Facts

Practice Exam

Answers to Practice Exam

Fast Facts

Managing and Maintaining a Microsoft Windows Server 2003 Environment

The facts, methods, and skills that you need to master were covered in the preceding chapters in this book. You should have read the study materials presented in each chapter, worked through the exercises, and practiced using the study suggestions. When you have tackled all this material and have applied your knowledge in a lab or in your workplace, you should be ready to take the exam.

Exam days tend to be stressful, which can be compounded by procrastinating your studies and then cramming all the facts you can into your head at the last minute. Success usually isn't the result of one big action that you perform a single time. Ninety-nine percent of the time, success is the culmination of consistent small actions. When it comes to successfully passing a certification exam, the best approach is to spend a minimum of 15 minutes every day studying. If you study longer, that's great. However, the key is to never skip a day and to study for no less than 15 minutes each day.

After you finish studying Chapters 1 through 18, you should be ready to sign up for the exam. A few days prior and up until the day of the exam, you can brush up on your facts and skills by reading this final chapter.

This book was organized to bracket together the skills that Microsoft Exam 70-290 tests in the same groups Microsoft uses. These Fast Facts highlight the most essential points for you to recognize and process while you are taking the exam. They are by no means a substitute for the rest of this book, but they do provide excellent review material.

Managing and Maintaining Physical and Logical Devices

Windows Server 2003 supports two types of physical disk configurations: basic and dynamic. A single physical disk must be one type or the other; however, you can intermingle the physical disk types in a multiple-disk server.

Basic Disks

When a new disk is installed in Windows Server 2003, it is installed as a basic disk. The basic disk type has been used in all versions of Microsoft Windows since version 1.0, OS/2, and MS-DOS. This allows a basic disk created in Windows Server 2003 to be recognized by these earlier operating systems. A basic disk splits a physical disk into units called *partitions*. Partitions allow you to subdivide your physical disk into separate units of storage. There are two types of partitions: primary and extended. On a single physical hard disk you can have up to four primary partitions, or three primary partitions and an extended partition. The basic disk is the only type supported in versions of Windows prior to Windows 2000.

Dynamic Disks

Dynamic disks were first introduced in Windows 2000 and are the preferred disk type for Windows Server 2003. Unlike a basic disk, a dynamic disk is divided into volumes instead of partitions. Although a clean installation of Windows Server 2003 will create a basic disk by default, any additional disks can be added as basic or dynamic disks. In addition, after the initial installation, the basic disk can be converted to a dynamic disk.

Unlike basic disks, which use the original MS-DOS-style master boot record (MBR) partition tables to store primary and logical disk-partitioning information, dynamic disks use a private region of the disk to maintain a Logical Disk Manager (LDM) database, which contains the volume types, offsets, memberships, and drive letters of the volumes on that physical disk. The important characteristics of dynamic disks are summarized in Table 1.

TABLE 1 Dynamic Volume Types

Volume Type	Number of Disks	Configuration	Fault Tolerance
Boot	N/A	The volume that contains the %Systemroot% files (usually C:\Windows).	N/A
System	N/A	The volume that contains the Ntdetect.com, Ntldr, and Boot.ini files (usually C:\).	N/A

(continues)

TABLE 1 *Continued*

Volume Type	Number of Disks	Configuration	Fault Tolerance
Simple	1	A single region or multiple concatenated regions of free space on a single disk.	None.
Spanned	2 to 32	Two or more regions of free space on 2 to 32 disks linked into a single volume. Can be extended. Cannot be mirrored.	None.
Striped	2 or more	Multiple regions of free space from two or more disks. Data is evenly interleaved across the disks, in stripes. Known as RAID Level 0.	None.
Mirrored	2	Data on one disk is replicated on the second disk. Cannot be extended. Known as RAID Level 1.	Yes, with maximum capacity of the smallest disk.
RAID 5	3 to 32	Data is interleaved equally across all disks, with a parity stripe of data also interleaved across the disks. Known as RAID-5 or striping with parity.	Yes, with maximum capacity of the number of disks minus one. (If you have 5 100GB disks, your volume would be 400GB).

▶ A dynamic disk cannot be read by other operating systems in a dual boot configuration.

▶ Several utilities can help manage the disk partitions:

   ▶ *CHKDSK.EXE*—Command-line utility that verifies and repairs FAT or NTFS formatted volumes.

   ▶ *CLEANMGR.EXE*—a.k.a. Disk Cleanup, a GUI utility that deletes unused files.

   ▶ *DEFRAG.EXE*—a.k.a. Disk Defragmenter, a command-line utility that rearranges files contiguously, recapturing and reorganizing free space in the volume. Optimizes performance.

   ▶ *DFRG.MSC*—a.k.a. Disk Defragmenter, a GUI utility that performs the same actions as DEFRAG.EXE.

   ▶ *DISKPART.EXE*—A command-line utility that can run a script to perform disk-related functions. DISKPART's nearest GUI counterpart is the Disk Management utility.

   ▶ *FSUTIL.EXE*—A command-line utility that displays information about the file system and can perform disk-related functions.

Unlike Windows NT 4.0, Windows Server 2003 does not support the creation or use of any of these configurations on a basic disk. If any of these volumes are present on a basic disk in a server that is upgraded to Windows Server 2003, or if they are added after Windows Server 2003 is installed, they will no longer be accessible.

File Systems

Two main file systems are recognized by Windows Server 2003:

▶ *File Allocation Table (FAT)*—Windows Server 2003 is able to read partitions formatted in two versions of FAT: the 16-bit version (FAT16), supported by early versions of MS-DOS, and the 32-bit version (FAT32), first introduced with Windows 95 OEM Service Release 2 (OSR2). For FAT16 partitions, the maximum size is 4GB. In theory, FAT32 partitions support a maximum size of 2,047GB. However, there is a 32GB limitation on creating FAT32 partitions in Windows Server 2003.

▶ *The NT File System (NTFS)*—NTFS is designed to provide a high-performance, secure file system for Windows Server 2003. It also supports selective file, folder, and volume compression or encryption and auditing. In addition, NTFS supports security assigned at the file, folder, or volume level.

NTFS Compression

Native file and folder compression is one of the many benefits of using NTFS. NTFS compression and EFS encryption are mutually exclusive. That is, you cannot both compress and encrypt a file or folder at the same time. Because NTFS compression is a property of a file, folder, or volume, you can have uncompressed files on a compressed volume or a compressed file in an uncompressed folder.

In addition, several rules apply when you move or copy compressed files and folders. The possible outcomes of moving or copying NTFS-compressed files or folders are as follows:

▶ Moving an uncompressed file or folder to another folder on the same NTFS volume results in the file or folder remaining uncompressed, regardless of the compression state of the target folder.

▶ Moving a compressed file or folder to another folder on the same volume results in the file or folder remaining compressed after the move, regardless of the compression state of the target folder.

▶ Copying a file to a folder causes the file to take on the compression state of the target folder.

- ▶ Overwriting a file of the same name causes the copied file to take on the compression state of the target file, regardless of the compression state of the target folder.

- ▶ Copying a file from a FAT folder to an NTFS folder results in the file taking on the compression state of the target folder.

- ▶ Copying a file from an NTFS folder to a FAT folder results in all NTFS-specific properties being lost.

Troubleshooting Server Hardware Devices

A server contains many hardware devices: disk drives, network cards, display adapters, and any of a large number of peripherals. For them to be usable by the system, each must be identified by the operating system, and the appropriate device driver must be loaded.

A *device driver* is a program that passes requests between the operating system and the device.

Windows File Protection

Device drivers and other system files are automatically protected against improper replacement by the Windows File Protection facility. This facility runs in the background (invisible to the user and the administrator) and is alerted whenever a file in a protected folder is changed. It determines whether the new version of the file is signed. If it isn't, Windows File Protection automatically rolls back the file to the version kept in the `%systemsroot%\system32\dllcache` folder. If the desired version of the file is not in the `dllcache` folder, Windows File Protection asks for the Windows Server 2003 CD-ROM to be mounted and then copies the file from there.

An administrator can run the System File Checker (`SFC.EXE`) to explicitly schedule a scan of the system files either immediately, at the next reboot, or at every reboot. Also, if the `dllcache` folder is corrupted or needs to be repopulated for some other reason, the administrator can run the System File Checker with the `/purgecache` switch to cause the folder to be emptied and reloaded.

Resource Settings

Resource settings are mechanisms by which a device can communicate with other hardware or the operating system. The following list details the four types of resources:

- ▶ *Direct memory access (DMA)*—Allows a device to read from the computer's memory, or to write to it, without using the computer's processor (CPU). Each device using DMA must have a DMA channel dedicated for its use.

▶ *Interrupt request line (IRQ)*—A hardware channel line over which a device can interrupt the CPU for service. Some devices can share an IRQ line; others must have a dedicated IRQ.

▶ *Input/output (I/O) port*—Another channel through which data is transferred between a device and the CPU. It acts like an area of memory that can be read from, and written to, by the device and the CPU. I/O ports cannot be shared.

▶ *Memory address*—An area of memory allocated to the device driver for communication between the device and the operating system.

If two devices attempt to use the same resources, and the particular resource is not sharable, one or both of the devices may be unusable.

Some older devices, such as most Industry Standard Architecture (ISA) bus expansion cards, cannot share resources. And many of them, even with a Plug and Play driver, cannot have their resource settings configured by the operating system. They must be manually configured in the system BIOS.

Driver Signing

Microsoft has provisions in Windows Server 2003 for confirming that device drivers have passed a certain level of testing and that they have not been changed since the testing was accomplished. This is done by including a digital signature in the device driver that combines Microsoft's software-signing certificate and a digest of the code that implements the driver. Signed driver files are distributed through the following methods and can be found on the Windows Server 2003 CD-ROM:

▶ Windows service packs

▶ Hotfix distributions

▶ Operating system upgrades

▶ Windows Update

For the greatest device driver security, many administrators want to ensure that only signed device drivers are loaded. To achieve this, Windows Server 2003 can be configured to refuse to load unsigned drivers.

▶ In Device Manager, you can click the Driver tab to update the driver, roll back the driver to a prior version, remove the driver, and troubleshoot the device.

▶ A jumpy mouse pointer indicates a mouse driver problem or video device driver error.

▶ Configure mouse settings in the Control Panel Mouse applet.

▶ Configure keyboard settings in the Control Panel Keyboards applet.

▶ Scanners and digital cameras use similar processes for transmitting digital media to the computer.

▶ Multilink is a method of aggregating the bandwidth of multiple modem connections using Point-to-Point Protocol (PPP).

▶ Serial Line Internet Protocol (SLIP) is for Unix connections. It does not support the advanced functions or multiple protocols that PPP supports.

▶ Universal serial bus (USB) allows up to five USB hubs to be connected in a chain. If you have too many hubs, you will trigger an error condition.

▶ If you install a device, Windows Server 2003 looks for the driver signature as a part of System File Protection. When it fails to find one, Windows Server 2003 notifies you that the drivers are not signed as part of its default configuration. You can change this behavior to always allow installation or to always block unsigned drivers.

▶ Device Manager does not manage device drivers for printers and fax devices. They are managed through the Printers and Faxes applet in Control Panel.

Managing Users, Computers, and Groups

Here are some points to remember about user accounts:

▶ Every user account is assigned a unique Security Identifier (SID).

▶ SIDs are never reused.

▶ An account can be renamed without losing any of the permissions assigned to it because the SID doesn't change.

▶ User, computer, and group accounts are created and managed using the Active Directory Users and Computers MMC.

▶ Local users and groups are created using the Local Users and Groups snap-in.

▶ csvde and ldifde can be used to import and export users and groups.

Password Complexity

Password complexity is determined by the domain account policies. If enabled, this policy requires that passwords meet the following minimum requirements:

- ▶ They must not contain all or part of the user's account name.

- ▶ They must be at least six characters in length.

- ▶ They must contain characters from three of the following four categories:

    - ▶ English uppercase characters (A through Z)

    - ▶ English lowercase characters (a through z)

    - ▶ Base-10 digits (0 through 9)

    - ▶ Nonalphabetic characters (such as !, $, #, %)

Managing Local, Roaming, and Mandatory User Profiles

The settings for a user's work environment are stored in a file known as the *user profile*. This file is automatically created the first time a user logs on to a computer running any version of Windows, and any changes to the environment (Favorites, Start menu items, icons, colors, My Documents, Local Settings, and so on) are saved when the user logs off. The profile is reloaded when the user logs on again. Table 2 lists the components of a user profile (from Windows Server 2003 Help and Support):

TABLE 2   User Profile Folders and Their Contents

User Profile Folder	Contents
Application Data	Program-specific data (for example, a custom dictionary). Program vendors decide what data to store in this user profile folder.
Cookies	User information and preferences.
Desktop	Desktop items, including files, shortcuts, and folders.
Favorites	Shortcuts to favorite locations on the Internet.
Local Settings	Application data, history, and temporary files. Application data roams with the user by way of roaming user profiles.
My Documents	User documents and subfolders.
My Recent Documents	Shortcuts to the most recently used documents and accessed folders.
NetHood	Shortcuts to My Network Places items.
PrintHood	Shortcuts to printer folder items.

TABLE 2 *Continued*

User Profile Folder	Contents
SendTo	Shortcuts to document-handling utilities.
Start Menu	Shortcuts to program items.
Templates	User template items.

The user profiles facility allows several people to use the same computer running Windows and each to see his or her own desktop. The types of user profiles are shown in Table 3.

TABLE 3   Profile Types

Profile	Created For	How It Works
Roaming profile	Users who log on to different computers on the network	Stored on a server. When a user logs on to a network computer, the profile is copied locally to the computer. When the user logs off the network, any changes to the profile are copied back to the server.
Mandatory profile	Administrative enforcement of settings A user account that is shared by two or more users	Stored on a server. When a user logs on to a network computer, the profile is copied locally to the computer. No changes are ever saved when the user logs off the server. Only the administrator can make changes to the profile.
Local profile	Every user at first logon	When the user logs on to a computer, whether it is connected to the network or not, a local profile is created and saved in the local Documents and Settings folder for that user. All changes are saved when the user logs off.
Temporary profile	Users who were unable to load their profile	When there is an error condition that prevents a user from loading the normal profile, a temporary profile is loaded. When the user logs off, all changes are deleted.
All Users files and folders	All users who log on to the computer	When a user logs on to the computer, the All Users files and folders contents, which include desktop and Start Menu items, are combined with the individual's profile.
Default user profile	Users who log on for the first time	When a user logs on for the first time, the default profile is used as a template to create a new profile for the user.

▶ Each user account has a Profile tab in its Properties sheet where you can specify a network location to use as a roaming profile.

▶ A mandatory profile is a roaming profile that can't be changed by the user. To create a mandatory profile, you create a roaming profile and rename the `Ntuser.dat` file to `Ntuser.man`.

The Four Domain Functionality Levels

The default domain functionality level of a domain installed on a new Windows Server 2003 machine is Windows 2000 mixed (which was called "mixed mode" in Windows 2000). At this level, a domain can contain domain controllers on computers running Windows NT, Windows 2000, or Windows Server 2003.

After you have removed all Windows NT domain controllers from the domain, you can increase the domain functionality level to Windows 2000 native or to Windows Server 2003. At the Windows 2000 native level, you get the improved group capabilities of Active Directory as delivered in Windows 2000, such as the ability to "nest" groups and the availability of groups of Universal scope.

The most advanced level of domain functionality is the Windows Server 2003 level. Only domains where there are no Windows 2000 or Windows NT domain controllers can be raised to this level of domain functionality.

A fourth level of domain functionality is known as *Windows Server 2003 interim*. Both Windows NT and Windows Server 2003 domain controllers can exist in a domain at this level. As with the Windows 2000 mixed level, enhanced group functionality cannot be used!

Group Types

The two types of groups are as follows:

▶ *Distribution*—Used for email distribution lists only. Cannot be used to assign permissions for resource access.

▶ *Security*—Used for the assignment of permissions for resource access and for email distribution.

Group Scope

A way of classifying a group is by defining its *scope*. This means determining what locations the members can come from, and where the resources can be located that the group can be granted access permissions to. In Table 4, the first column lists the scope of the group object (Domain Local, Global, or Universal), the second column lists the object types that can be members of this kind of group, and the third column lists the locations of the resources that a group can be given access to. Note that in several cases, the characteristics of the group object differ depending on the functionality of the domain.

TABLE 4   Group Scopes and Applicable Members and Rights

Scope	Can Include	Can Be Granted Access to Resources In...
Domain Local	Accounts, Global groups, and Universal groups from any domain and Windows 2000 native or in Windows Server 2003 functionality level domains, other Domain Local groups from the same domain as the group object.	The local domain
Global	In domains at the Windows 2000 mixed level or at the Windows Server 2003 interim level, only accounts from the same domain as the group object. In Windows 2000 native or Windows Server 2003 functional level domains, accounts and other global groups from the same domain as the group object.	Any domain in the forest and any domain in any other forest that trusts the local domain
Universal	(Not available in domains at the Windows 2000 mixed level or the Windows Server 2003 interim level.) Accounts, Global groups, and Universal groups from any domain.	Any domain in the forest and any domain in any other forest that trusts the local domain

The following are some important points to remember about groups:

▶ When you grant rights to domain users, the best practice is to use the AGDLP method. This means that you place Accounts in Global groups. Then you place the Global groups into Domain Local groups, to which you grant (or deny) permissions.

▶ When a permission is explicitly denied to a user or group, even if the user is a member of another group where the same permission is explicitly granted, the Deny permission overrides all others and the user will not be allowed access.

▶ Whenever a user requests authorization to use a prohibited object or resource, the user will see an `Access is Denied` message.

Tables 5 and 6 list the default groups included in Windows Server 2003.

TABLE 5   Default Local Groups in Windows Server 2003

Local Group	Default Access	Default Members Locally	Default Domain Members When Joined to a Domain
Administrators	Unrestricted access to the computer	Administrator	Domain Admins Global Group
Backup Operators	Access to run Windows Backup and sufficient access rights that override other rights when performing backup	N/A	N/A
Guests	Limited only to explicitly granted rights and restricted usage of computer	Guest IUSR_machine	Domain Guests Global group
Power Users	Create\modify local user accounts, share resources	N/A	N/A
Users	Limited to use of the computer, personal files and folders, and explicitly granted rights	All newly created users NT Authority\ Authenticated Users special built-in group NT Authority\Interactive special built-in group	Domain Users Global group

TABLE 6   Built-in Special Groups in Windows Server 2003

Built-in Group	Default Access	Default Members Locally	Default Domain Members When Joined to a Domain
Anonymous Logon	Not provided any default access rights.	User accounts that Windows XP cannot authenticate locally	N/A
Authenticated Users	Not given any default access rights.	All users with valid local user accounts on this computer	All Active Directory users in the computer's domain or any trusted domain
Creator Owner	Designated full control over resources created or taken over by a member of the Administrators group.	Administrators group	N/A
Dialup	No specific rights; this group is not shown on systems without configured modems and dial-up connections.	All users who have connected to the computer with a dial-up connection	N/A

(continues)

TABLE 6 *Continued*

Built-in Group	Default Access	Default Members Locally	Default Domain Members When Joined to a Domain
Everyone	Full Control is the default permission granted for all files and folders on NTFS volumes; you must remove this permission to implicitly deny access.	All users who access the computer	N/A
Interactive	No specific rights.	All users who have logged on locally to the computer	N/A
Network	No specific rights.	All users who have established a connection to this computer's shared resource from a remote network computer	N/A

Managing and Maintaining Access to Resources

The process of working with share and NTFS permissions has always been a major focus on Microsoft exams. Make sure you have a complete understanding of how the different permissions are applied when you access a folder over the network versus accessing it from the server console.

Managing File System Permissions

Permissions define the type of access that is granted to a user or group for an object such as a file, folder, or share. Permissions can be assigned to local users or groups, or if the server is a member of a domain, permissions can be assigned to any user or group that is trusted by that domain.

If you are sitting at the server or workstation console, only the NTFS file and folder access permissions apply. However, if you are trying to access the files across the network via a shared folder, both the file and the share permissions apply.

NTFS Permissions

NTFS permissions can be granted to either users or groups. By default, the Administrators group can assign permissions to all files and folders on a server.

The following permissions apply to a file:

- *Read*—This permission allows you to read the contents of a file and its attributes, including file ownership and assigned permissions.

- *Read and Execute*—This permission includes all the Read permissions in addition to the ability to run applications.

- *Write*—This permission includes all the Read permissions in addition to the ability to overwrite the file and change its attributes.

- *Modify*—This permission includes all the Read and Execute and the Write permissions in addition to the ability to modify and delete the file.

- *Full Control*—This permission includes all the Modify permissions in addition to allowing you to take ownership of a file and configure the permissions to it.

The following permissions apply to a folder and to the files and subfolders contained in that folder:

- *Read*—This permission allows you to read the contents of a folder and its attributes, including ownership and assigned permissions.

- *Read and Execute*—This permission includes all the Read permissions in addition to the ability to run applications.

- *Write*—This permission includes all the Read permissions in addition to the ability to create new files and subfolders and change the folder's attributes.

- *Modify*—This permission includes all the Read & Execute and the Write permissions in addition to the ability to modify and delete the folder.

- *Full Control*—This permission includes all the Modify permissions in addition to allowing you to take ownership of a folder and configure the permissions to it.

The creator or owner of a file or folder will automatically have the Full Control permission for that object. In addition to the basic permissions, NTFS also allows you to assign more granular special permissions. Special permissions are generally a subset of the basic NTFS permissions. This allows you to limit access to a file or folder to specific tasks. Special permissions apply to both files and folders. The owner of a file or folder will always have the right to modify permissions.

- Permissions applied to folders are inherited by subfolders unless you select the This Folder Only option when applying the permissions.

- A user's actual permissions are the resulting collective allowed rights that have flowed down from upper-level folders plus explicitly assigned permissions at that level as long as there are no denied rights. Denied rights override allowed rights.

► Conflicting permissions for users who are members of multiple groups are a common problem to encounter on the exam. Not only should you be aware that Deny permissions always override Allowed permissions, but explicit permissions always override inherited permissions.

By default, when you assign file and folder permissions, these permissions are automatically applied to the files and folders underneath them in the hierarchy. This means that any permissions applied at the root of an NTFS drive will flow down to files and folders at the lowest level, unless the inheritance has been removed. In addition, if you create a file or folder in an existing folder, the permissions in effect for that folder will apply to the new objects.

Here are a few key points to remember about inherited permissions:

► Inherited Deny permissions will be overridden by an explicit Allow permission.

► Explicit permissions will always take precedence over inherited permissions.

NTFS file and folder permissions are cumulative. This means that the effective NTFS permissions will be a combination of the permissions granted to the user and those permissions granted to any group the user is a member of. The exception to this is Deny Access, which overrules everything else.

The following are some important points to remember about NTFS file and folder permissions:

► Permissions applied to folders are inherited by subfolders unless you select the This Folder Only option when applying the permissions.

► A user's actual permissions are the resulting collective allowed rights that have flowed down from upper-level folders plus explicitly assigned permissions at that level, as long as there are no denied rights. Denied rights override allowed rights.

► You can display a user's actual rights to use a file by looking at the Effective Permissions tab of the Advanced Security options.

► Conflicting permissions for users who are members of multiple groups are a common problem to encounter on the exam. Not only should you be aware that Deny permissions always override Allowed permissions, but explicit permissions always override inherited permissions.

Table 7 shows the results of copying and moving files and folders on NTFS volumes.

TABLE 7   Moving and Copying Files on NTFS Volumes May Change Permissions

Operation	Resulting Permissions
Move a file or folder to another location on the same NTFS volume.	The file or folder retains its original permissions.
Move a file or folder to a different NTFS volume.	The file or folder inherits new permissions from the new parent folder.
Copy a file or folder to another location on the same NTFS volume.	The file or folder inherits new permissions from the new parent folder.
Copy a file or folder to a different NTFS volume.	The file or folder inherits new permissions from the new parent folder.

Share Permissions

Share permissions apply only when a file or folder is accessed over the network through a shared folder. When a folder is shared, by default the Everyone group is granted Read access. Only members of the Administrators, Server Operators, and Power Users group are permitted to share folders, and only three permissions are allowed for a shared folder:

▶ Read

▶ Change

▶ Full Control

When you're accessing the contents of a shared folder on an NTFS volume, the effective permission for the object is a combination of the share and NTFS permissions applied to the object. The effective permission will always be the most restrictive.

The following are some important items to remember about shares:

▶ Be on the lookout for questions that say that a user can access a file locally, but not across the network. These are indicative of NTFS and Share permission conflicts. In this situation, only NTFS permissions would apply.

▶ You can use the command net share to create or delete a shared folder. To create a new shared folder, type **net share MYSHARE=c:\mydata**.

▶ There are three possible Share permissions to grant or deny: Full Control, Change, and Read.

▶ You can hide shares by adding a $ symbol at the end of the name. All administrative shares are hidden. These are C$, ADMIN$, IPC$, PRINT$, and FAX$.

▶ The Web Distributed Authoring and Versioning (WebDAV) protocol acts as a redirector to enable users to read and save documents via the Hypertext Transfer Protocol (HTTP) when you share Web Folders.

Encrypting File System (EFS)

Encrypting File System (EFS) is similar to NTFS compression in that it allows the user to selectively encrypt files and folders as desired. After a file is encrypted, all file operations continue transparently for the user who performed the encryption. However, unauthorized users cannot access the files. NTFS compression and EFS encryption are mutually exclusive. That is, you cannot both compress and encrypt a file or folder at the same time. Here are some additional points to keep in mind:

▶ Only files and folders on NTFS volumes can be encrypted.

▶ If a folder is encrypted, all files and folders contained in that folder will be automatically encrypted.

▶ Encrypted files will be unencrypted when they are moved or copied to a non-NTFS volume.

▶ Moving or copying encrypted files to an unencrypted folder on an NTFS volume will not decrypt them.

▶ A recovery agent is an authorized individual who is able to decrypt data in the event that the original certificate is unavailable, such as when an employee leaves the company.

▶ A recovery agent can be any user assigned that role.

▶ A Certificate Authority (CA) is required to deploy EFS.

Encrypted files can be shared. However, keep the following points in mind:

▶ After the user is given permission to the file, he or she can also grant others permission to use the file.

▶ Encrypted files can be shared but encrypted folders cannot. Note that this refers only to EFS sharing, and an encrypted folder can always be an NTFS file share.

▶ Any user who is being granted access must have an EFS certificate. This certificate can reside in Active Directory, in the user's roaming profile, or in the user's profile on the server where the shared file is located.

Terminal Services Fundamentals

Windows Terminal Services is designed to distribute the Windows 32-bit desktop to clients that are usually not able to run it. Although at the client it appears that the application is running locally, all processing is actually occurring on the server. The only processing that occurs at the client involves displaying the user interface and accepting input from the keyboard and mouse. Terminal Services consists of three major components:

▶ *Multiuser server core*—This is a modified version of the Windows Server 2003 kernel that allows the operating system to support multiple concurrent users and share resources.

▶ *Client software*—The Remote Desktop Connection (RDC) client software provides the user interface. It can be installed on a PC, Windows terminal, or handheld device. It provides the look and feel of the standard Windows interface.

▶ *Remote Desktop Protocol* (RDP)—This is the protocol that provides communication between the server and the client software. It runs only on TCP/IP.

Terminal Services is available in two modes: Remote Desktop for Administration (formerly called Remote Administration mode) and Application Server mode. Remote Desktop for Administration mode is used to provide remote server management. Unlike in Windows 2000, where the Remote Administration mode was an option, the Remote Desktop for Administration mode is automatically installed in Windows Server 2003. However, incoming connections are disabled by default. With Windows Server 2003 Terminal Services in Remote Desktop for Administration mode, you are allowed two concurrent sessions, plus a console session to the Windows server.

Application Server mode requires each remote connection to have a Windows Server 2003 Terminal Services user or device Client Access License (TS CAL). These licenses are separate from the normal Windows Client Access Licenses (CALs) and must be installed and managed using a Terminal Services licensing server. If a license is not installed within 90 days, the client will no longer be able to access the server.

Two types of Terminal Services licensing servers are built in to Windows Server 2003:

▶ *Enterprise License server*—An Enterprise License server should be used when you have Windows Server 2003 Terminal Services servers located in several domains. This is the default.

▶ *Domain License server*—A Domain License server is used if you want to segregate licensing by domain, or if you're supporting a Windows NT 4.0 domain or a workgroup.

To install applications on a Terminal Services server in Application Server mode, you must be in Install mode. This can be accomplished by installing programs via the Add/Remove

Programs applet in the Control Panel or via the Change User command. When you're connecting via the RDC client, the following resources can be mapped between the server and the client session:

- ▶ Client drives
- ▶ Client printers
- ▶ Clipboard
- ▶ Printers
- ▶ Serial ports
- ▶ Sound

Managing and Maintaining a Server Environment

The purpose of this objective is to teach you how to use the various tools available in Windows Server 2003 to manage your servers.

Remote Assistance

In a Remote Assistance session, you can grant a remote user the ability to observe your desktop as you are working. You can exchange messages via a chat session, or you can talk to each other if you both have the required sound cards and microphones. You can even grant a remote user the ability to take over your desktop to make changes and run programs. After enabling Remote Assistance, you must issue an invitation before anyone can connect to your machine. This invitation can be sent to the other user via one of the following methods:

- ▶ Windows Messenger (the preferred method)
- ▶ Email
- ▶ Disk

If you are accessing a Remote Assistance computer that is behind a firewall, port 3389 must be open.

Internet Information Services (IIS)

IIS is no longer installed as a default component. In addition, even after it is installed, it will present only static pages. If your website requires the use of ASP or other dynamic content, you must manually enable the support for each feature.

During an upgrade from a previous version of Windows, IIS will be installed; however, the service will be disabled, and you must start it manually.

IIS 6.0 allows you to run your web applications in either of two modes:

▶ IIS 5.0 Isolation Mode

▶ Worker Process Isolation Mode

IIS 5.0 Isolation Mode is used to run older IIS 5.0–compatible applications that will not run natively in IIS 6.0. By default, a web server that is upgraded from a previous version of IIS will be enabled in IIS 5.0 Isolation Mode.

In Worker Process Isolation Mode, applications and processes can be separated into *application pools*, which are sets of one or more applications assigned to a set of one or more worker processes. An application pool can contain websites, applications, and virtual directories. Each application pool is isolated from the others. Because of this, a failure or memory leak will affect only the processes running in that application pool and will have no effect on any of the other functions in other application pools.

In Windows Server 2003, you can run either in IIS 5.0 Isolation Mode or Worker Process Isolation Mode, but not both simultaneously on the same server. IIS 6.0 can be managed via the following four methods:

▶ The IIS Manager MMC

▶ Administration scripting

▶ Manually editing the configuration file

▶ The Remote Administration website

IIS Metabase

The IIS Metabase is used to store most configuration information for IIS. The Metabase can be backed up using the IIS Manager MMC. The backup is stored in the `%systemroot%\system32\inetsrv\` folder. By default, IIS will keep the last 10 Metabase backups; these previous backups are stored in the `%systemroot%\system32\inetsrv\history` folder. To restore the IIS Metabase, select Backup, Restore Configuration from the IIS Manager MMC. The backups will be displayed by filename as well as by the date and time they were backed up. The metabase is now an XML file, which makes it easier to edit.

Virtual Servers

When you're hosting multiple websites on a single server, each website must have a unique identity. This is accomplished by using the following identifiers:

▶ *Unique IP address*—Commonly used for websites accessed over the Internet. Required when Secure Sockets Layer (SSL) is being used.

▶ *Host header name*—Commonly used over both the Internet and intranets.

▶ *TCP port number*—Rarely used on production web servers.

When using multiple IP addresses to identify the websites on your server, you can either install multiple network interface cards (NICs), each with a unique IP address, or just assign multiple IP addresses to a single NIC.

Authentication Mechanisms

Authenticated access is used to integrate the web server with Windows security. The user is required to present a user ID and password to access website resources. These user IDs and passwords are stored either as local accounts on the web server or in the Active Directory domain database. When anonymous access is disabled, all users who attempt to access the website will be prompted for a user ID and password. Authentication is also required when the website resources are protected via NTFS permissions.

Four types of authenticated access are available:

▶ *Integrated Windows authentication*—If the web server and the client are members of trusted domains, the browser will pass the user ID and password to the web server automatically and the user will not be prompted for a password. This method does not work through some firewalls but is fine for intranets. The password is transmitted as a hash value.

▶ *Digest authentication*—This method is supported only if the client is using Internet Explorer 5 or later, in an Active Directory domain, and the password must be stored in clear text. However, this method will work through most firewalls. The password is transmitted as an MD5 hash value.

▶ *Basic authentication*—This is the least-secure method because it transmits the password as clear text. However, it is supported by just about any browser available. Basic authentication is usually used in combination with SSL so that the passwords are encrypted.

▶ *.NET Passport authentication*—This is a new feature in Windows Server 2003. This method uses the Passport authentication system that Microsoft is marketing to e-commerce websites. It allows a user to create a single sign-on that is honored across various Passport-enabled sites. Authentication is performed by a central Passport authentication server. When Passport authentication is selected, a default domain must be specified.

Windows Server Update Services (WSUS)

Windows Server Update Services (WSUS) can be installed on an internal Windows 2000 with SP4 or Windows Server 2003 server that can download all critical updates as they are posted to Windows Update. Administrators can also receive email notification when new critical updates have been posted.

The client computers and servers can be configured through Group Policy or the Registry to contact the internal WSUS server for updates, instead of going out over the Internet to the Microsoft servers. The WSUS clients can be configured to point to a specific SUS server. This way, in a WAN environment, they will always receive updates from the server that is closest to them. The client is configured to often check its local WSUS server for updates. Older versions of the Automatic Update client do not support WSUS. The supported versions of the Automatic Update client are included with the following:

▶ Windows XP Service Pack 1 or later

▶ Windows 2000 Service Pack 3 or later

▶ All versions of Windows Server 2003

Monitoring and Optimizing Server Performance

This section summarizes the tools and procedures used to monitor and optimize the performance of a Windows Server 2003 server. Items covered include Event Viewer, Task Manager, Performance Monitor, System Monitor, disc quotas, and print queues.

Event Viewer

The Event Viewer is used to view event log files that are updated by the operating system and various services and applications running on your server. Typically, events will be written to the logs for any significant occurrence that a user or administrator should be aware of. All Windows Server 2003 systems have at the very least these three logs:

▶ *The System log file*—Records events related to system operation, most often associated with device drivers and services such as DHCP or WINS. Most of the information you will find here is related to the stopping and starting of services or the failure of a system component.

▶ *The Application log file*—Records events related to applications, programs, and utilities, usually not native Windows Server 2003 components. Examples are database programs, email servers, and print messages. The information that is recorded here is determined by the application developer, and it will usually consist of informational messages, errors, or warnings. This log is also used to store the alerts that are generated by the Performance Logs and Alerts tool.

▶ *The Security log file*—Records events related to security and auditing. Typical events include valid and invalid logon attempts and the accessing of resources, such as opening, reading, or deleting a file or folder. The types of events recorded in this log can be configured via the audit policy. In previous versions of Windows, the Security log would not record any information until an audit policy was enabled. In Windows Server 2003, security logging is enabled by default.

If the DNS service is installed on your server, the DNS log will be available. The DNS log file records events related to the operation of the DNS service. If you're having name-resolution problems on your network, this is the first place to look.

In addition, Active Directory domain controllers will have the following logs:

▶ *The Directory Service log file*—Records events related to the operation of the Active Directory service. Typical events you will see in this log are related to communication between domain controllers and Global Catalog servers.

▶ *The File Replication Service log file*—Records events related to the replication of the SYSVOL folder.

Auditing

Auditing is the process of recording user and system activities on the network. These events are recorded in the Windows Server 2003 Security log, which is one of the logs contained in the Event log. When you configure auditing, you decide which events you want to track and against what object. Typical activities that can be tracked are valid and invalid logon attempts, creating and opening files, and changes in user rights. A typical entry in the Security log will show the following:

▶ The time and date the event occurred

▶ The event performed

▶ The user account that performed the event

▶ The success or failure of the event

An audit policy is used to define the events that will be recorded in the Windows Server 2003 Security logs. Audit policies are created and applied in ways similar to the other types of policies using the Group Policy snap-in. Auditing is turned on by default in Windows Server 2003.

Task Manager

The Task Manager can be used to monitor and manage the state of active applications, including a real-time view of the system resources assigned to each application. Task Manager also allows you to observe applications that have stopped responding, to increase or decrease their priority, and to terminate them.

Windows Server 2003 subdivides processing time to applications using different classes of priority levels. Priority levels are assigned numbers from 0 to 31. Applications and noncritical operating system functions are assigned levels of 0 to 15, whereas real-time functions such as the operating system kernel are assigned levels of 16 to 31. The normal base priority is 8.

Task Manager does not allow you to set a process to a specific number; it allows you only to set priority classes. The priority classes are as follows:

▶ *Realtime*—Priority 24

▶ *High*—Priority 13

▶ *AboveNormal*—Priority 9

▶ *Normal*—Priority 8

▶ *BelowNormal*—Priority 7

▶ *Low*—Priority 4

Performance Monitor

The Performance Monitor tool is actually made up of two separate Microsoft Management Console (MMC) snap-ins: System Monitor and Performance Logs and Alerts.

System Monitor

Each subsystem within Windows Server 2003 has more than one object that exists in System Monitor. Each object has several monitoring functions called *counters*. Each counter offers insight into a different aspect or function of the object. The System Monitor snap-in allows you to view real-time performance data contained in the counters from your system. In addition, System Monitor allows you to review performance data that is stored in a log file created with the Performance Logs and Alerts snap-in. Here's a list of the objects you need to monitor closely for performance issues:

▶ Memory

▶ Processor

▶ Physical disk

▶ Network

Performance Logs and Alerts

The Performance Logs and Alerts MMC snap-in allows you to log performance data over a period of time and save it to a log file for later viewing. Two logging options are available: Counter Logs and Trace Logs. Counter logs allow you to record data about hardware usage and the activity of system services from local or remote computers. You can configure logging to occur manually or automatically based on a defined schedule. Trace logs record data as a certain activity, such as disk I/O or a page fault, occurs. When the event occurs, the provider sends the data to the log service. The log data can be saved in the following file formats:

▶ *Text file (CSV)*—Comma-delimited format, for import into spreadsheet or database programs.

▶ *Text file (TSV)*—Tab-delimited format, for import into spreadsheet or database programs.

▶ *Binary file*—This is the default for use with the System Monitor snap-in. Data is logged into this file until it reaches the maximum limit. The default maximum file size is 1MB, but this can be changed when you configure settings for the file from the Log Files tab of the Log Properties dialog box by clicking the Configure button.

▶ *Binary circular file*—Data is logged into this file until it reaches the maximum limit. Then the file is overwritten, starting at the beginning of the file. The default maximum file size is 1MB, but this can be changed when you configure settings for the file from the Log Files tab of the Log Properties dialog box by clicking the Configure button.

▶ *SQL*—Data is logged directly into an existing SQL database.

The Alerts container is used to define threshold alerts. These can be used with real-time measurements or with historical log files. An alert is issued when a specific counter crosses a defined threshold value. When this occurs, a trigger event is initiated. You can select several actions to be performed when an alert threshold is reached:

▶ *Log an Entry in the Application Event Log*—If a threshold is reached, Windows Server 2003 will create an entry in this log and you can view it in the Application event log found in the Event Viewer.

▶ *Send a Network Message To*—This allows you to send a message to a user or computer via the Messenger service.

▶ *Start Performance Data Log*—This starts logging to a predefined counter log. This is useful if you are trying to see what happens to system performance when a specific event occurs.

▶ *Run This Program*—This can be any program that can be run from a command line. For example, it might be a program that performs some type of system maintenance, such as compressing files.

Monitoring Memory Performance

Here are some counters to watch to monitor memory performance:

▶ *Memory: Cache Faults/sec*—This condition usually indicates an insufficient amount of RAM on your system. However, it can also be caused by running a combination of apps, such as running a read-intensive application at the same time as an application that is using an excessive amount of memory.

▶ *Memory: Page Faults/sec*—If this counter averages above 200 for low-end systems or above 600 for high-end systems, excess paging is occurring.

▶ *Memory: Available Bytes*—Less than 4MB indicates insufficient RAM on the system, thus causing the system to perform excessive paging.

▶ *Paging File: % Usage Peak*—If this number nears 100% during normal operations, the maximum size of your paging file is too small, and you probably need more RAM.

Monitoring Disk Performance

Unlike in previous versions of Windows, Windows Server 2003 enables the disk counters by default. Here are some key performance counters for the disk subsystem:

▶ *PhysicalDisk: Avg. Disk Queue Length*—The number of queued requests should not exceed the number of spindles in use, plus 2.

▶ *PhysicalDisk: % Disk Time*—It is not uncommon for this counter to regularly hit 100% on active servers. Sustained percentages of 90% or better, however, might indicate that a storage device is too slow. This usually is true when its Avg. Disk Queue Length counter is constantly above 2.

▶ *PhysicalDisk: Avg. Disk sec/Transfer*—Indicates the average time, in seconds, for a disk transfer.

Monitoring Processor Performance

To identify problems with the processor, you should monitor the following counters:

▶ *Processor: % Processor Time*—If this counter remains above 80% for an extended period, you should suspect a CPU bottleneck. (There will be an instance of this counter for each processor in a multiprocessor system.)

▶ *Processor: % Total Processor Time*—If this value remains consistently higher than 80%, at least one of your CPUs is a bottleneck.

▶ *System: Processor Queue Length*—A sustained value of 2 or higher for this counter indicates processor congestion.

Monitoring Network Performance

To identify performance problems with the network interface, you should monitor the following counters:

▶ *Network Interface: Bytes Total/sec*—If the highest observed average is less than 75% of the expected value, communication errors or slowdowns might be occurring that limit the NIC's rated speed.

▶ *Network Interface: Output Queue Length*—If this averages above 2, you are experiencing delays.

▶ *Network Interface: Packets/sec*—Sharp declines that occur while the queue length remains nonzero can indicate protocol-related or NIC-related problems.

File Server Resource Manager

The File Server Resource Manager (FSRM) is a new MMC snap-in available in Windows Server 2003, starting with the R2 release. The FSRM MMC contains the following snap-ins:

▶ *Quota Management*—Used to create and manage quotas on volumes and folders.

▶ *File Screening Management*—Used to create file screens that prevent users from saving blocked file types in managed volumes and folders.

▶ *Storage Reports Management*—Used to create and schedule storage reports.

Although the domain can still be Windows 2000 or Windows Server 2003 without R2, the server on which the FSRM is installed and all the servers that will be managed via the FSRM must be at R2 or later.

Implementing and Monitoring Disk Quotas

Disk quotas provide a method of controlling the amount of space a user has access to on a file server. You can also use the disk quota feature to monitor the space in use by your users. Disk quotas are disabled by default. All events related to disk quotas are sent to the event logs.

There are two types of disk quotas in Windows Server 2003 starting with the release of version R2:

▶ *NTFS Quotas*—These are the old-style quotas that have been used since Windows 2000.

▶ *FSRM Quotas*—These are the new-style quotas that were introduced in R2.

NTFS Disk Quotas

Here are some of the key points to remember about NTFS disk quotas:

▶ Disk quotas do not apply to members of the local Administrators account.

▶ The files contained on a volume converted from FAT to NTFS will not count against user quotas, because they will initially be owned by the local administrator and will count against the administrator's quota. Files created or moved to the volume after the conversion has been completed are owned by the user.

▶ Disk quotas cannot be applied on a per-folder basis. They can only be applied on a per-volume basis.

▶ If a physical disk has multiple volumes, a quota must be applied separately to each volume.

▶ Disk usage is based on all files that the user creates, copies, or takes ownership of.

▶ File compression cannot be used to prevent a user from exceeding his or her quota. Disk quotas are based on the actual file size, not the compressed file size.

▶ Disk quotas affect the free size that an installed application will see during the installation process.

▶ Disk quotas can be enabled on local or network volumes and on removable drives formatted with NTFS.

▶ Disk quotas are not available on any volume or partition formatted using a version of Windows prior to Windows 2000. Disk quotas are available only on NTFS volumes or partitions formatted by Windows 2000 or later.

File Server Resource Manager Quotas

Although NTFS Quotas are still available in Windows Server 2003 R2, it is much better to implement your quotas using the File Server Resource Manager (FSRM). The differences are as follows:

▶ Quotas can be set at both the folder and the volume level.

▶ Quotas are calculated using the actual disk space used, so compressed files are now calculated using the actual size on disk, not the uncompressed size.

▶ Quotas can be implemented on multiple servers by copying a template between servers.

▶ Quotas can be automatically created for subfolders as they are added.

▶ Notifications have been enhanced to include not only Event Logging, but also the capability to send an email, run a file or script, or generate a storage report.

The following are some key points to remember about FSRM Quotas:

▶ *Space*—The allowed disk space can be defined in any increment from kilobytes to terabytes. Quotas can be applied to either new or existing volumes or folders.

▶ *Limits*—Quotas can be set to either Hard or Soft. A hard quota will prevent the user from saving any more files. Unlike some third-party software, there is no grace period; when the limit is reached, the user is effectively blocked from using any more space. A soft quota will warn users but will let them continue to save files. The soft quotas are typically used for space monitoring purposes.

▶ *Notifications*—You can configure notifications to let the user and/or administrator know when the users' space nears or reaches their quota limit. These notifications can be saved to the event log or be emailed, or they can cause a program or script to be run.

File Screening with the FSRM

The second major feature that the File Server Resource Manager brings to the table is file screening. File screening enables you to prevent users from saving blocked file types to your servers.

File screens are configured through the use of File Groups. A File Group defines the files that should or should not be blocked. In addition, a File Group can be configured for specific exceptions that will override the blocking rule. Windows Server 2003 includes the following prebuilt file groups:

▶ Audio and Video Files

▶ Backup Files

▶ Compressed Files

▶ E-Mail Files

▶ Executable Files

▶ Image Files

▶ Office Files

▶ System Files

▶ Temporary Files

▶ Text Files

▶ Web Page Files

When there is a need to allow files that other file screens are blocking, you need to create a file screen exception. A *file screen exception* is a file screen that is used to override the screening for a folder and its subfolders. This is done by attaching a file group to the file screen.

Managing and Monitoring Print Queues

Here are some key terms to remember with regard to print queues:

▶ *Print job*—The sequence of data and print device commands sent to the print device

▶ *Spooler*—The service that manages the documents that are waiting to be printed

▶ *Spool file*—The file that stores the print data while it's waiting to be printed

▶ *Print queue*—The list of print jobs currently in the spooler

▶ *Print server*—A computer, usually a Windows Server 2003 machine, which you install and share the print drivers on

▶ *Printer driver*—The software that enables the operating system to communicate to the printing device

▶ *Print device*—The physical printer

▶ *Local printer*—Any print device that is directly attached to and controlled by the print server

▶ *Network printer*—Any print device that is directly attached to the network

Printer pooling is a form of load balancing in that two or more print devices are represented by a single virtual printer. The users send their print jobs to what looks like a single printer. The print server then queues the print jobs in the order that they were submitted. For printer pooling to work successfully, the following conditions must be met:

▶ *The printers must use the same print driver*—They don't all have to be the same exact model, just as long as they will give the same results using a common printer driver.

▶ *They must all be connected to the same print server*—This is because they have to share the same driver and print queue.

▶ *They should be located in close proximity to each other*—Because the user will have no way of knowing which printer the print job ends up on, it's best to have them all in the same room.

You can set up several logical printers connected to a single physical printer. Each logical printer can have slightly different configurations (but use the same print driver) and can be assigned to different people. For example, different users could be assigned different logical printers with different priorities. The priority sets the default importance of the print jobs in the queue. Priorities can be set from 1 to 99. The job assigned the highest number will be printed first. Table 8 shows the given predefined roles.

TABLE 8   Group-Specific Roles

Group	Print	Manage Documents	Manage Printer
Administrators	X	X	X
Creator Owner		X	
Everyone	X		
Power Users	X	X	X
Print Operators	X	X	X
Server Operators	X	X	X

A printer can be configured with various advanced properties. A summary of these properties is listed in Table 9.

TABLE 9   Configurable Advanced Printer Properties

Setting	Description
Always available and Available from	Enables you to specify the hours of the day when the printer is available. For example, you can configure a printer that accepts large jobs to print only between 6:00 p.m. and 8:00 a.m. so that shorter jobs can be printed rapidly. Jobs submitted outside the available hours are kept in the print queue until the available time.
Priority	Enables you to assign a numerical priority to the printer. This priority ranges from 1 to 99, with higher numbers receiving higher priority. For example, you can assign a printer for managers with a priority of 99 so that their print jobs are completed before those of other employees.
Spool print documents so program finishes printing faster	Enables spooling of print documents. Select from the following: ▶ Start printing after last page is spooled. Prevents documents from printing until completely spooled. Prevents delays when the print device prints pages faster than the rate at which they are provided. ▶ Start printing immediately. The default option, causes documents to be printed as rapidly as possible.
Print directly to the printer	Documents are sent to the print device without being spooled first. Recommended only for unshared printers.
Hold mismatched documents	The spooler holds documents that do not match the available form until this form is loaded. Other documents that match the form can print.
Print spooled documents first	Prints documents in the order that they finish spooling, rather than the order in which they start spooling. Use this option if you have selected the Start printing immediately option.
Keep printed documents	Retains printed jobs in the print spooler. Enables a user to resubmit a document from the print queue rather than from an application.
Enable advanced printing features	Enable additional options such as page order and pages per sheet.
Printing Defaults command button	Selects the default orientation and order of pages being printed. Users can modify this from most applications if desired. Additional print device-specific settings may be present.
Print Processor command button	Specifies the available print processor, which processes a document into the appropriate print job.
Separator Page command button	Enables you to specify a separator page file, which is printed at the start of a print job to identify the print job and the user who submitted it. This is useful for identifying printed output when many users access a single print device.

The print spooler is part of the operating system and runs as the Print Spooler service. The print spooler manages the print queues for all local or network printers that are managed by the server. By default, the spool file is located at `%systemroot%\System32\Spool\Printers`.

Large print jobs can generate a significant impact on the network and print server loads. The print spooler files on a Windows Server 2003 print server can be relocated to a dedicated hard disk if these loads are going to be high.

The Print Management Console is an updated Microsoft Management Console (MMC) snap-in that you can use to view and manage printers and print servers in your organization. You can use Print Management from any computer running Windows Server 2003 R2 or later, and you can manage all network printers on print servers running Windows 2000 Server, Windows Server 2003, or Windows Server 2003 R2.

Print Management Console

The Print Management Console is an updated MMC snap-in, first included in Windows Server 2003 R2, that you can use to view and manage printers and print servers in your organization. You can use Print Management from any computer running Windows Server 2003 R2 or later, and you can manage all network printers on print servers running Windows 2000 Server, Windows Server 2003, or Windows Server 2003 R2.

The Print Management Console is not installed by default. It must be manually installed after your initial installation of Windows Server 2003 R2. In addition, the schema additions for R2 must be installed to support the new Fast Query lookup via LDAP in Active Directory.

The PMC includes the Printer Filters feature. Printer Filters can be used to group your printers according to various criteria, so that they can be found and managed easily There are three preconfigured printer filters:

- ▶ *All Printers*—This list contains all printers in your organization.
- ▶ *Printers Not Ready*—This list shows any printer with a not ready condition because of error, being paused, out of paper, and so on.
- ▶ *Printers with Jobs*—This list shows all printers with print jobs currently in their print queues.

The following are some additional things to remember about printers:

- ▶ When the wrong printer driver is installed, the output is garbled.
- ▶ A print device can be associated with multiple printers to enable custom settings and priorities.
- ▶ A printer pool is a single printer that is associated with multiple print devices in order to simplify the use of identical printers (or similar printers that can use the same print driver) and increase the output performance.

Managing and Implementing Disaster Recovery

This objective covers the tools and procedures necessary to back up and recover your server in the event of a disaster, either large or small.

Windows Backup

Windows Backup allows you to back up files and folders on FAT16, FAT32, and NTFS volumes. However, if you have backed-up data on an NTFS volume, restoring to either type of FAT volume will result in a loss of configured file and folder permissions, in addition to the loss of encryption and compression attributes.

To back up and restore a Windows Server 2003 server, you must be a member of the local Administrators or the Backup Operators group. If you are a member of the local Administrators or the Backup Operators group on a domain controller, you can back up and restore a file on any computer that is a member of the domain or has a two-way trust relationship with the domain. If you are not a member of either of these groups, you will only be able to back up the files you are the owner of or those you have at least Read permissions for.

Windows Server 2003 has five backup options, as detailed in the following list. Each type varies as to what is backed up and whether or not the archive bit is set. The *archive bit* is a file attribute that is turned on when a file is created or modified, and it is cleared whenever a file is successfully backed up. It is used to let the backup software know which files need to be backed up based on whether they have just been created or whether modifications to previously backed-up files have happened since the last backup.

Here's the list of backup options in Windows Server 2003:

▶ *Normal*—A normal backup (sometimes referred to as a *full backup*) is used to back up all the files and folders you select, regardless of the setting of the archive bit. It then changes the archive bit of the files to show that they were backed up.

▶ *Copy*—A copy backup is used to back up the desired files and folders. It does not read or change the archive bit.

▶ *Daily*—A daily backup is used to back up only the files and folders that have been created or modified on that day. It does not read or change the archive bit.

▶ *Differential*—A differential backup is used to back up only the files and folders that have been created or modified since the last normal or incremental backup. It does not change the archive bit. However, it reads the archive bit to determine which files need to be backed up.

▶ *Incremental*—An incremental backup is used to back up only the files and folders that have been created or modified since the last normal or incremental backup. It reads the archive bit to determine which files need to be backed up as well as clears the archive bit of the files that were backed up.

System State Backups

System state data is a collection of data that contains the operating system configuration of the server. For all Windows Server 2003 operating systems, the system state data includes the following:

▶ Registry

▶ COM+ Class Registration database

▶ System boot files

▶ The system files included in the Windows File Protection area

The system state data also includes the Certificate Services database (if the server is operating as a certificate server). If the server is a domain controller, the system state data also includes the Active Directory Services database and the SYSVOL directory. The system state will include the IIS Metabase or the Cluster Service configuration if these features are installed on the server. Due to their interdependencies, these components cannot be backed up or restored separately.

Restoring System State Data

Although you can't selectively back up components of the system state, you can restore the following system state components to an alternate location:

▶ Registry

▶ SYSVOL folder

▶ System boot files

▶ Cluster configuration (if installed)

The Active Directory, IIS Metabase, COM+ Class Registration and Certificate Services databases, and the Windows File Protection folder cannot be restored to an alternate location.

Volume Shadow Copy

By using Volume Shadow Copy with Windows Backup, you can back up most open files. When Volume Shadow Copy is used during a backup and an open file is encountered, a snapshot is taken of the file. This is an exact copy of the file, and it is saved to another area on the disk. This copy is then saved via the Backup utility.

Volume Shadow Copy offers the following advantages:

▶ Users cannot be locked out by the Backup program.

▶ Open files are not skipped.

▶ The backup procedure completes faster.

▶ Applications can write data to a file during a backup.

▶ Volume Shadow Copy eliminates the need for additional third-party software in most cases.

▶ Backups can be performed during business hours.

The Volume Shadow Copy Service (VSS) allows users to view the contents of shared folders, as they existed at specific points in time, and to restore a previous copy of a file. The Volume Shadow Copy feature works by setting aside a configurable amount of space, either on the same or a different volume. This space is used to save any changes to the files on the volume that Volume Shadow Copy is enabled on. These changes are added by making a block-level copy of any changes that have occurred to files since the last shadow copy. Only the changes are copied, not the entire file. As new shadow copies are added, the oldest one will be purged when you either run out of allocated space or the number of shadow copies reaches 64. The following guidelines apply:

▶ Volume Shadow Copy is enabled at the volume level.

▶ The minimum storage space you can allocate for shadow copies is 100MB.

▶ The storage space can be allocated on the same volume that Volume Shadow Copy is enabled on, or on another volume.

▶ The default storage size allocated will be 10% of the volume; however, you can increase the size at any time.

▶ When estimating the size to allocate, you must consider both the number and size of the files on the volume as well as how often they will be updated.

▶ Remember that when the storage limit is reached, the oldest shadow copies will be deleted.

▶ If you decide to store your shadow copies on another volume, the existing shadow copies will be deleted.

- ► The default configuration for shadow copies is for a scheduled update at 7:00 a.m. and 12:00 p.m. on weekdays.

- ► Using a separate volume to store shadow copies is highly recommended for heavily used file servers.

- ► Shadow copies will not work properly on dual-boot systems.

A Volume Shadow Copy client is required for Windows XP, Windows 2000 Professional, and Windows 98 users. The client is located in the `%systemroot%\system32\clients\twclient` folder on Windows Server 2003 systems.

Advanced Options Menu

The Advanced Options menu allows you to select from a variety of options that can be used to troubleshoot and repair server startup and driver problems. The following options are available on the Windows Server 2003 Advanced Options menu:

- ► *Safe Mode*—This option starts Windows Server 2003 with the basic drivers for the mouse, video, monitor, mass storage, and keyboard.

- ► *Safe Mode with Networking*—This option starts Windows Server 2003 with the basic drivers, plus the network drivers.

- ► *Safe Mode with Command Prompt*—This option starts Windows Server 2003 with the basic drivers and opens a command window instead of the desktop.

- ► *Enable Boot Logging*—This option starts Windows Server 2003 normally but logs a list of all the device drivers and services, along with their status, that the system attempts to load. This information is logged to `%systemroot%\ntblog.txt`.

- ► *Enable VGA Mode*—This option starts Windows Server 2003 normally but forces it to load the basic VGA driver.

- ► *Last Known Good Configuration*—This option starts Windows Server 2003 with the contents of the Registry from the last time the user logged on to the system.

- ► *Directory Services Restore Mode*—This option is used to restore the Active Directory database and SYSVOL folder on a domain controller. It will only be listed on a domain controller.

- ► *Debugging Mode*—This option starts Windows Server 2003 normally but sends debugging information over a serial cable to another computer.

- ► *Boot Normally*—This option bypasses the menu options and starts Windows Server 2003 without any modifications.

Unlike a normal logon, the Safe Mode options do not update the Last Known Good Configuration information. Therefore, it will still be an option if you try Safe Mode first.

Recovery Console

The Recovery Console is a DOS-like command-line interface in which you can perform a limited set of commands and start and stop system services. Unlike booting from a DOS disk, the Recovery Console allows you access to files on an NTFS-formatted volume.

The Recovery Console is not installed by default; you must install it manually after you have installed Windows Server 2003. It can also be run from the Windows Server 2003 CD-ROM. After you log on, the commands in Table 10 are available:

TABLE 10 Recovery Console Commands

Command	Description
Attrib	Changes the attributes of files and folders
Batch	Executes commands from a text file
CD	Changes the directory
Chdir	Changes the directory
Chkdsk	Repairs disk errors
Cls	Clears the screen
Copy	Copies files
Del	Deletes files
Delete	Deletes files
Dir	Displays a list of files and directories
Disable	Used to disable a service or driver
Diskpart	Used to manage partitions and volumes
Enable	Used to enable a service or driver
Exit	Closes the console and reboots the server
Expand	Extracts a file from the Windows CAB files or expands compressed files from the Windows Server 2003 CD-ROM
Fixboot	Writes a new boot sector
Fixmbr	Used to repair the master boot record
Format	Used to format a drive
Help	Lists the available commands
Listsvc	Lists the installed services and drivers
Logon	Logs on to the server
Map	Displays a list of local drive partitions and their mappings

(continues)

TABLE 10 *Continued*

Command	Description
MD	Creates a directory
Mkdir	Creates a directory
More	Displays the contents of a text file and pauses when the screen is full
RD	Used to delete a directory
Ren	Used to rename a file
Rename	Used to rename a file
Rmdir	Used to delete a directory
Systemroot	Sets the current directory to the systemroot
Type	Displays the contents of a text file and pauses when the screen is full

There are some limitations, however:

▶ You have access only to %systemroot% and its subfolders, the root partitions of %systemdrive%, any other partitions, floppy drives, and CD-ROMs.

▶ You cannot copy a file from the hard disk to a floppy, but you can copy a file from a floppy, a CD-ROM, or another hard disk to your hard disk.

Recovering System State Data by Using Directory Services Restore Mode

On a domain controller, the Active Directory files are restored as part of the system state. The system state on a domain controller consists of the following:

▶ Active Directory (NTDS)

▶ The boot files

▶ The COM+ Class Registration database

▶ The Registry

▶ The system volume (SYSVOL)

▶ Files in the Windows File Protection folder

The individual components cannot be backed up or restored separately; they can only be handled as a unit.

When Active Directory is in a corrupted state on all the domain controllers, it will be necessary to restore AD from tape and force the replication of the restored data to all the other domain controllers. This type of operation is called an *authoritative restore*. An authoritative restore will cause the data that is restored from tape to overwrite the corrupted data that is stored on all the domain controllers.

If only a single Active Directory object is accidentally deleted, it is possible to restore only that object from a backup tape by performing a partial authoritative restore.

To restore an object, you will need to know its common name (CN), the Organization Unit (OU), and the domain (DC) the object was located in. First, boot into Directory Restore mode and start the NTDSUtil utility. For example, to restore the ABC St. Louis User OU, in the abc.com domain, you would enter the following command:

```
Restore Subtree "OU=ABC St. Louis User,DC=abc,DC=com"
```

Implementing Automated System Recovery (ASR)

Automated System Recovery (ASR) works by making a backup of the boot partition onto tape or other media. It then saves the catalog and other operating system information, such as system state and disk partition information, to a floppy disk.

When a problem occurs that cannot be fixed by using any of the other repair and recovery methods, or if you have replaced a failed boot drive, you will need to boot your server from the Windows Server 2003 CD-ROM and then insert the floppy disk and the backup media that was created by the ASR process.

ASR installs a generic version of Windows Server 2003 that is used to mount and restore your boot partition from the backup media created by ASR. This process not only restores the information on your boot drive, it also restores the disk signatures and re-creates the boot partition or volume, if necessary. It will not recover or delete any data volumes, however.

Group Policy

Group Policy enables you to define a standard collection of settings and apply them to some or all the computers and/or users in your enterprise. Group Policy has the capability to provide centralized control of a variety of components of a Windows network, such as security, application deployment and management, communications, and the overall user experience.

Group Policy is applied by creating an object that contains the settings that control the users' and computers' access to network and machine resources. This Group Policy Object (GPO) is created from templates that are stored on the workstation or server.

These GPOs are linked to a container that holds Active Directory objects such as users, groups, workstations, servers, and printers. The settings in these GPOs will be applied to the objects in the container. The container can be an OU, a domain, or a site. GPOs can also be applied to a single computer through the use of Local Policy. You can apply multiple GPOs to a container—in this case, the settings will be merged. If there is a conflict in the settings between GPOs, the last setting applied wins.

Group Policy works by manipulating Registry and security settings on the workstation or server. Unlike the System Policies used in Windows NT, Group Policy does not permanently (tattoo) change the Registry. After Group Policy is removed, the Registry settings return to their defaults.

Each Group Policy object has two separate sections: User and Computer configuration.

Group Policy for users includes settings for

- ▶ Operating system behavior
- ▶ Desktop settings
- ▶ Security settings
- ▶ Application settings
- ▶ Application installation
- ▶ Folder redirection settings
- ▶ Logon and logoff scripts

User settings are applied at user logon and during the periodic Group Policy refresh cycle. When these settings are applied to a user, they apply to that user at whatever computer the user logs on to.

Group Policy for computers includes settings for

- ▶ Operating system behavior
- ▶ Desktop settings
- ▶ Security settings
- ▶ Application settings
- ▶ Application installation
- ▶ Folder redirection settings
- ▶ Computer startup and shutdown scripts

The following are some important things to remember about Group Policy:

▶ A lot of the same settings are available via both user and computer settings. When the settings between user and computer conflict, user settings generally take precedence.

▶ GPOs are stored in two parts—as part of a Group Policy Template (GPT) and as objects inside a container in Active Directory called a Group Policy Container (GPC).

▶ GPTs contain settings related to software installation policies and deployments, scripts, and security information for each GPO. They are stored in the %SystemRoot%\SYSVOL*domain*\Policies directory on every domain controller. The GPTs usually contain subfolders called Adm, USER, and MACHINE to separate the data to be applied to different portions of the Registry.

▶ The USER portion is applied to keys in HKEY_CURRENT_USER, and the MACHINE portion is applied to keys in HKEY_LOCAL_MACHINE. The Adm portion can contain settings for either branch of the Registry.

▶ GPOs can be used to control only Windows 2000 or later servers and workstations.

Changes made to existing GPOs and new GPOs will be applied during the refresh cycle. The exceptions are the following:

▶ Software installation settings will be updated only at reboot or logon.

▶ Folder redirection settings will be updated only at reboot or logon.

▶ Computer configuration changes will be refreshed every 16 hours whether or not they have been changed.

▶ Domain controllers refresh Group Policy every five minutes, so that critical settings, such as security settings, are not delayed.

Changes can be implemented immediately using the gpupdate tool. Table 11 shows available command-line options for the tool.

TABLE 11 Command-Line Options for Gpupdate

Value	Description
/Target:{Computer	User}	Specifies that only user or only computer policy settings are refreshed. By default, both user and computer policy settings are refreshed.
/Force	Reapplies all policy settings. By default, only policy settings that have changed are reapplied.

(continues)

TABLE 11 *Continued*

Value	Description
/Wait:{*value*}	Sets the number of seconds to wait for policy processing to finish. The default is 600 seconds. The value 0 means not to wait. The value -1 means to wait indefinitely.
/Logoff	Causes a logoff after the Group Policy settings are refreshed. This is required for those Group Policy client-side extensions that do not process policy during a background refresh cycle but do process policy when a user logs on. Examples include user-targeted software installation and folder redirection. This option has no effect if no extensions that require a logoff are called.
/Boot	Causes the computer to restart after the Group Policy settings are refreshed. This is required for those Group Policy client-side extensions that do not process policy during a back ground refresh cycle but do process policy when the computer starts. Examples include computer-targeted software installation. This option has no effect if no extensions that require the computer to restart are called.
/Sync	Causes the next foreground policy to be done synchronously. Foreground policy applications occur when the computer starts and when the user logs on. You can specify this for the user, computer, or both by using the /Target parameter. The /Force and /Wait parameters are ignored.

There are two types of GPOs, Local and Domain. Local GPOs are applied to the computer first. However, as we said earlier, the last GPO applied always wins. The exception is if the settings that you configured on the local GPO are not present in any of the other GPOs applied, the local GPO settings are left in place.

Group Policy in Windows 2003 works according to the hierarchy of site → domain → OU, or *SDOU* for short. The effects of Group Policy as it is applied are cumulative. As more policies are applied, their settings are merged, with the last setting winning.

Windows Server 2003 comes with two default GPOs:

▶ *Default Domain Policy*—This policy is linked to the domain and controls the default account policies for things such as Password Policy and Account Lockout.

▶ *Domain Controllers Policy*—This policy is linked to the Domain Controllers OU and contains settings strictly for the domain controllers.

It's best to not edit the default GPOs. Any changes should be implemented in new GPOs.

The following are some key points to remember about GPOs:

- The Active Directory objects lower in the hierarchy inherit the settings from those higher in the hierarchy.

- The Block Policy Inheritance option is set on a per-container basis and will block the inheritance of *all* policies. It's strictly an all-or-nothing solution.

- The No Override option in Group Policy is used to prevent a child container from blocking the application of a GPO that is inherited from the parent. Unlike the all or nothing of the Block Policy Inheritance option, the No Override option is set on a per-GPO basis.

- Group Policy Filtering is used to restrict the application of a GPO. It works by applying permissions on the GPO so that it can be used only by certain users, computers, or groups. For a Group Policy to be applied to an object, that object must have at least Read permissions for the GPO.

Group Policy Management Console

The Group Policy Management Console (GPMC) is a free add-on from Microsoft that can be downloaded from the Microsoft website. The GPMC can be installed on either Windows Server 2003 or Windows XP SP1 and can be used to manage GPOs in either a Windows 2000 or a Windows Server 2003 domain. After the GPMC is installed, the Group Policy tab that was previously used in the Active Directory Users and Computers MMC to access Group Policy settings is replaced with a message and a button that opens the GPMC MMC.

Practice Exam

Managing and Maintaining a Microsoft Windows Server 2003 Environment

This exam consists of 60 questions that reflect the material covered in the chapters and are representative of the types of questions you should expect to see on the actual exam.

The answers to these questions appear in their own section following the exam. It is strongly suggested that when you take this exam, treat it just as you would an actual exam at the test center. Time yourself, read carefully, and answer all the questions to the best of your ability.

Most of the questions do not simply require you to recall facts, but require deduction on your part to determine the best answer. Most questions require you to identify the best course of action to take in a given situation. Many of the questions are verbose, requiring you to read them carefully and thoroughly before you attempt to answer them. Run through the exam, and for questions you miss, review any material associated with them.

Exam Questions

1. You are building a Windows Server 2003 server that is to be used as a database server for your company. Deciding that hardware RAID is the way to go, you purchase a new controller card that supports RAID-5. After you install the new card and start your server, the controller card does not appear in Device Manager. What do you need to do to get the hardware working correctly?

   ❍ **A.** Shut down the server, reinstall the device, and restart the server.

   ❍ **B.** Use the Add/Remove Programs applet in Control Panel to install the drivers for the controller card.

   ❍ **C.** Use the Add Hardware applet in Control Panel to install the controller card.

   ❍ **D.** Use the Device Manager utility to install the controller card.

2. You are the administrator of a network that has several Windows Server 2003 servers. When starting your mail server, you receive a blue screen. The Recovery Console was not preloaded. How will you boot to it?

   ❍ **A.** By using a PXE-capable NIC.

   ❍ **B.** From the Windows Server 2003 CD-ROM.

   ❍ **C.** From the Windows Server 2003 boot disks.

   ❍ **D.** It's not possible to boot to the Recovery Console if it's not preinstalled.

3. Mary has installed four disks on her Windows Server 2003 server that she wants to configure as a RAID-5 array. However, it doesn't seem to be working. What is the most likely cause of Mary's problem?

   ❍ **A.** The server hard disks are configured as dynamic disks.

   ❍ **B.** The server hard disks are configured as basic disks.

   ❍ **C.** The controller does not support a RAID-5 configuration.

   ❍ **D.** Mary was not made a member of the Enterprise Admins group.

4. You are the network administrator for a small manufacturing firm. Because of a downturn in the economy, you are unable to upgrade your servers, so you must make do with the hardware you currently own. You're running out of disk space on your file server. What steps can you take to keep the file server from becoming full?

   ❍ **A.** Enable disk quotas.

   ❍ **B.** Use the Disk Defragmenter to consolidate free space.

   ❍ **C.** Enable disk quotas and set warning limits.

   ❍ **D.** Enable disk quotas and enable limits.

5. Joe is the network administrator for a mid-sized network that consists of 20 Windows Server 2003 servers and 700 Windows XP workstations. As all good administrators should, he subscribes to several security newsletters. One day he receives a newsletter that tells him that Microsoft has just released an Internet Explorer security patch with a rating of critical. How can Joe get this patch applied to all of his servers and workstations in the least amount of time?

○ **A.** Download the patch from Microsoft and apply it to all his computers.

○ **B.** Use the Windows Update service to apply the patch to his computers.

○ **C.** Use the Windows Server Update Services (WSUS) to apply the patch to all his computers.

○ **D.** Write code to apply the patch via a logon script.

6. You are a user at a small legal firm. While working with a small database, you attempt to save a file and are denied access because you are out of disk space. You check the NTFS disk quotas and see that you have 50MB of free space remaining, but your database file is only 40MB. What is the problem?

○ **A.** You need to reconfigure the NTFS permissions.

○ **B.** You need to reconfigure the disk quotas to give you more space.

○ **C.** The disk is compressed.

○ **D.** You have a virus.

7. You are the administrator of a small network. You have a Windows Server 2003 server that you suspect is going to need a memory upgrade. Which of the following tools allows you to see how much memory is being used by your applications? (Choose all correct answers.)

○ **A.** System Monitor

○ **B.** Performance Logs and Alerts

○ **C.** Task Manager

○ **D.** Performance Monitor

8. You have a Windows Server 2003 server that seems to be sluggish. Which of the following devices should you monitor closely? (Choose all correct answers.)

○ **A.** Memory

○ **B.** Video

○ **C.** Application load time

○ **D.** Processor

○ **E.** Network interface card

9. You are the network administrator for a small advertising firm. Most of the data on your file servers consists of zipped graphics files. You're running out of disk space on your file server. What steps can you take to keep the file server from becoming full?

   ○ **A.** Enable drive compression.

   ○ **B.** Use the Disk Defragmenter to consolidate free space.

   ○ **C.** Enable drive compression and set it to Maximum.

   ○ **D.** Enable disk quotas and enable limits.

10. You are the only system administrator for your company. You have decided to take a long-overdue and well-deserved vacation. Before you go, you want to give one of your users the ability to run backups. To which groups should you add her user account so that she has the proper permissions to perform backups? (Choose all correct answers.)

   ○ **A.** Server Operators

   ○ **B.** Power Users

   ○ **C.** Account Operators

   ○ **D.** Administrators

   ○ **E.** Backup Operators

11. You have just finished building a new Windows Server 2003 server. As part of your build checklist, you need to create an Emergency Repair Disk. Which Windows Server 2003 utility should you use to create an Emergency Repair Disk?

   ○ **A.** Rdisk

   ○ **B.** MakeERD

   ○ **C.** Windows Server 2003 Backup

   ○ **D.** ERDclone

   ○ **E.** None of the above

12. You are the administrator for Widgets, Inc. The Director of Information Security is extremely security conscious. She wants you to install all Microsoft security patches within 48 hours of their release to the Microsoft Update site. On which of the following clients can this be accomplished using WSUS? (Choose all correct answers.)

    ◯ **A.** Windows Server 2003 servers

    ◯ **B.** Computers with Windows XP Service Pack 1

    ◯ **C.** Computers with Windows 2000 Service Pack 1

    ◯ **D.** Computers with Windows NT 4.0 Service Pack 6

13. Your Windows Server 2003 network consists of various client computers, including many Windows 95 and Windows 98 clients. You have a new application that runs only on Windows Server 2003 or Windows XP, to which all your users need access. What can you do to give all your users access to this new application quickly and relatively cheaply?

    ◯ **A.** Upgrade all your client machines to Windows XP and install the new software.

    ◯ **B.** Install a new server with Windows Server 2003 configured in Remote Administration mode, and install the application on the server.

    ◯ **C.** Install a new server with Windows Server 2003 configured in Application mode, and install the application on the server.

    ◯ **D.** None of the above.

14. You are the new junior administrator for a Windows Server 2003 server running IIS 6.0. The CIO is extremely security conscious. She wants you to view the audit logs daily. What utility do you use to view audit information?

    ◯ **A.** Audit Log Viewer

    ◯ **B.** Log Viewer

    ◯ **C.** Event Viewer

    ◯ **D.** Audit Viewer

    ◯ **E.** Event Audit Viewer

15. Mary is the lead administrator for a small manufacturing firm located in the Southeast. A user in one of the branch offices calls Mary and requests her help on a Windows XP problem. Mary attempts to assist the user over the telephone, but the user is having trouble describing what he is seeing on his screen. Which technologies in Windows Server 2003 or Windows XP can Mary use to fix this problem? (Choose all correct answers.)

○ **A.** Remote Desktop for Administration

○ **B.** Terminal Services

○ **C.** Remote Assistance

○ **D.** Remote Administrator

16. You have purchased new hardware and are moving a group of shared folders to a new Windows Server 2003 server. After moving the folders and their contents using Copy, you make the server available again to the users. Soon, your telephone rings with users complaining that they can't see the file shares. What steps must you perform to fix the problem? (Choose all correct answers.)

○ **A.** You need to reconfigure the NTFS permissions.

○ **B.** You need to reconfigure the share permissions.

○ **C.** You need to restart the Server service on the new server.

○ **D.** You need to reshare the shares.

○ **E.** You need to give the shares unique names.

17. You are installing a new network application that requires a configuration script to be run when a user logs on to the network. What is the best way to configure this for a Windows Server 2003–based network?

○ **A.** Configure a startup script on the user's computer.

○ **B.** Add a logon script entry to the user account configuration in Active Directory Users and Groups.

○ **C.** Use Group Policy.

○ **D.** Add a drive mapping to the user profile.

18. You are configuring a Windows NT workstation that you are going to use to manage your Windows Server 2003–based network. Which one of the following tools should you install on your workstation?

○ **A.** The administration tools for Windows Server 2003

○ **B.** The Active Directory Users and Groups MMC

○ **C.** The Terminal Services client

○ **D.** User Manager for Domains

19. Stan is a system administrator who works with a mixture of Windows 2000 and Windows Server 2003 servers. The shipping department has asked him to install a new application that requires a couple different folders that users need Read/Write access to. He installs the application, creates a couple shared folders on a couple different servers, tests the application, and then hands it over to the shipping department. Soon, his phone begins to ring. It seems that users cannot access all the folders. What is the most likely cause of this problem?

   ○ **A.** Stan is using FAT32 volumes.

   ○ **B.** Stan assigned the wrong permissions to the wrong groups.

   ○ **C.** One folder is on Windows 2000; the other is on Windows Server 2003.

   ○ **D.** Stan set quota limits too low.

20. You are the administrator for a utility company. Your company is part of a utility cooperative that shares infrastructure and information to keep costs down. You have published coal and natural gas futures prices on your website. However, because of the sensitive nature of this data, this information must be secure. What steps should you perform to allow other companies access to this data while making it secure from unauthorized users? (Choose all correct answers.)

   ○ **A.** Turn anonymous access off.

   ○ **B.** Configure the website to support Integrated Authentication.

   ○ **C.** Install and configure a certificate and SSL.

   ○ **D.** Configure the website to support Basic Authentication.

   ○ **E.** Encrypt the data in the shared folders.

21. You have attached an external IrDA device on serial port 1 of your Windows Server 2003 server to communicate with a printer. What step should you take to install the device?

   ○ **A.** Install the drivers using Device Manager.

   ○ **B.** Use the Add Hardware Wizard to install the device.

   ○ **C.** Use the Add Printers applet.

   ○ **D.** Restart the server and let Plug and Play detect the device.

22. You are one of the system administrators for a bank with multiple locations. Because of a shortage of employees, your tellers have to rotate between banks, as needed. All banks are connected to the logon and file servers in the headquarters location by 128K lines. The tellers need to always have the same files and desktop available. Which Windows Server 2003 technology should you implement to make this happen?

   ○ **A.** Terminal Services

   ○ **B.** Roaming profiles

   ○ **C.** Mandatory profiles

   ○ **D.** Distributed File System (DFS)

23. You've just installed new SCSI drivers and your server has blue screened. Which Windows Server 2003 server startup option will recover from this problem?

   ○ **A.** Safe Mode

   ○ **B.** Safe Mode with Networking

   ○ **C.** Automated System Recovery

   ○ **D.** Last Known Good Configuration

24. Which of the following methods cannot be used to start the Recovery Console in Windows Server 2003? (Choose all correct answers.)

   ○ **A.** Operating system menu

   ○ **B.** Windows Server 2003 boot disks

   ○ **C.** Windows Server 2003 CD-ROM

   ○ **D.** Network share

25. Mary's boss has been given her the task of saving money. She decides that instead of purchasing new servers, she will set up user quotas and file compression to make the existing servers last longer. Unfortunately, Mary has servers of various vintages. Which operating system cannot use user quotas?

   ○ **A.** Windows NT 4.0

   ○ **B.** Windows Server 2003

   ○ **C.** Windows 2000 Server

   ○ **D.** Windows XP Professional

26. The CIO of your financial services company resigns without warning. Her personal folders contain several files that the Securities and Exchange Commission (SEC) needs access to. The folders have the following permission: CIO: Full Control.

All the user folders, including one for the SEC, are located on a server formatted with NTFS. What's the quickest way to give the SEC access to these files?

- ○ **A.** Reset the password on the CIO's account and then give the SEC the user ID and the new password.
- ○ **B.** Assign ownership of the files to the SEC.
- ○ **C.** Take ownership of the files and give the SEC Full Control permission.
- ○ **D.** Move the files to the SEC's folders.

27. In an effort to conserve space on your file servers, you enable disk quotas on every user volume. However, the user data still seems to be increasing in size. What is the most likely problem?

- ○ **A.** You're using FAT32 volumes.
- ○ **B.** You assigned the quotas to the wrong groups.
- ○ **C.** Quota limits are not enabled by default.
- ○ **D.** The default quota limits are set too high.

28. After scheduling a normal backup to run on Sunday night, you want to back up only the files and folders that have changed the rest of the week. What type of backup should you perform on the other days of the week?

- ○ **A.** Normal
- ○ **B.** Daily
- ○ **C.** Incremental
- ○ **D.** Partial

29. You are working with your Windows Server 2003 server when you receive a blue screen. When you reboot your server you see the following message:

```
Windows cannot access the following registry key:
```

```
HKEY_LOCAL_MACHINE\System
```

What can you do to recover from this error?

- ○ **A.** Rebuild the server using Automated System Recovery (ASR).
- ○ **B.** Go into Safe Mode, delete the SCSI driver, and reboot.
- ○ **C.** Boot into the Recovery Console, delete the video driver, and reboot.
- ○ **D.** Boot the server and select Last Known Good Configuration.

30. You are one of the system administrators for a bank with multiple locations. Because of a shortage of employees, your tellers have to rotate between banks, as needed. The tellers need to always have the same files and desktop available. Which Windows Server 2003 technology should you implement to make this happen?

- ○ **A.** Shared Profiles
- ○ **B.** Roaming profiles
- ○ **C.** Mandatory profiles
- ○ **D.** Distributed File System (DFS)

31. You are the administrator of a Windows Server 2003 network for Widgets, Inc. The Director of Information Services is extremely security conscious. She just read an online article that said that a new virus has been released that takes advantage of a security hole that was fixed by a certain hotfix, but most companies have failed to implement it.

You need to verify that the hotfix is installed on all your servers. What should you do?

- ○ **A.** Open the SUS console, go to the computers page, and run the updates report, specifying the hotfix number.
- ○ **B.** Open the WSUS console, go to the Computers page, and run the updates report, specifying the hotfix number.
- ○ **C.** Open the SUS console, go to the Updates page, and run the updates report, specifying the hotfix number.
- ○ **D.** Open the WSUS console, go to the Updates page, and run the updates report, specifying the hotfix number.

32. You are the proud owner of a Windows Server 2003 server. After you have installed your applications, you have decided to create a baseline of system performance. What is the best tool to use to accomplish this?

- ○ **A.** Performance Monitor
- ○ **B.** Performance Logs and Alerts
- ○ **C.** Task Manager
- ○ **D.** System Monitor

33. Your Windows Server 2003 server seems sluggish. You want to figure out what's wrong, so you run Performance Logs and Alerts and see the following averages:

Processor: % ProcessorTime: 50

System: Processor Queue Length: 1

Memory: Pages/sec: 10

PhysicalDisk: Avg. Disk Queue Length: 4

Paging File: % Usage: 25

What should you do to improve performance?

- ○ **A.** Add memory.
- ○ **B.** Add a faster processor.
- ○ **C.** Add a faster hard disk.
- ○ **D.** Replace the hard disk with a faster one.

34. Your Windows Server 2003 server seems sluggish. You want to figure out what's wrong, so you run Performance Logs and Alerts and see the following averages:

Processor: % ProcessorTime: 95

System: Processor Queue Length: 6

Memory: Pages/sec: 10

PhysicalDisk: Avg. Disk Queue Length: 2

Paging File: %Usage: 25

What should you do to improve performance?

- ○ **A.** Add memory.
- ○ **B.** Add a faster processor.
- ○ **C.** Add a faster hard disk.
- ○ **D.** Replace the hard disk with a faster one.

35. You are the administrator of a Windows Server 2003 Terminal Services load-balanced application farm. You have identical applications installed on all your servers. Everything is running fine, except your database administrators complain that if they start a Terminal Services session where they are doing a database rebuild in the office and then try to reconnect to that session from their home computer, they get a new session. What can you do to fix this issue?

   ○ **A.** Install and configure Session Directory.

   ○ **B.** Increase the disconnect timeout.

   ○ **C.** Increase the idle timeout.

   ○ **D.** Give the database admin administrative rights for the network.

36. After reading about all the new features in Windows Server 2003 Terminal Services, Joe decides to install a new test server to see whether everything he has heard is true. Joe installs and configures the new server, loads a few sample applications, and then requests a few users to try it out. However, it seems that only two people can log on to Terminal Services at a time. What is the most likely cause of this problem?

   ○ **A.** Joe didn't install the Session Directory.

   ○ **B.** Joe didn't install and activate the Terminal Services licensing server.

   ○ **C.** The server is in Remote Desktop for Administration mode.

   ○ **D.** The users are still using the older Terminal Services client.

37. After reading about all the new features in Windows Server 2003 Terminal Services, Joe decides to upgrade all the servers in his Terminal Services farm to Windows Server 2003. After the upgrades are completed, he installs a new application that features audio prompts. When trying to use the application, the end users don't hear anything. What is the most likely cause of this problem?

   ○ **A.** Joe didn't install the Session Directory.

   ○ **B.** Joe didn't enable audio support.

   ○ **C.** Audio support is only available with the Citrix add-on.

   ○ **D.** The users are still using the older Terminal Services client.

38. After Joe gets his Windows Server 2003 Terminal Services servers up and running, he has to work out the licensing issues. If Joe has the following users, what Client Access Licenses (CALs) should he purchase?

▶ 30 computers

▶ 10 handheld devices

▶ 20 users who use both handhelds and computers

○ **A.** 60 Terminal Services CALs

○ **B.** 60 Terminal Services device CALs

○ **C.** 60 Terminal Services user CALs

○ **D.** 20 Terminal Services user CALs and 40 Terminal Services device CALs

39. You are creating a Windows Server 2003 server cluster when you discover that your dynamic disks are not supported. What method can you use to convert your dynamic disks back to basic disks?

○ **A.** You cannot convert a dynamic disk back to a basic disk.

○ **B.** Use Format /basic.

○ **C.** Use Convert /basic.

○ **D.** In the Disk Management snap-in, right-click the disk and select Revert to Basic Disk.

40. You are building a new Windows Server 2003 server to host a SQL database. This server must provide good performance in addition to fault tolerance. How should you configure the disk subsystem?

○ **A.** RAID-5

○ **B.** RAID-0

○ **C.** RAID-1

○ **D.** RAID-3

41. You are trying out the driver-signing feature of Windows Server 2003 in your test lab. You configure Group Policy to block the installation of unsigned drivers by end users. However, when you log in to test the policy, you are able to install an unsigned driver without any problems. What is the most likely cause of this problem?

○ **A.** You logged on as administrator.

○ **B.** You forgot to save the policy.

○ **C.** You forgot to refresh Group Policy after applying the configuration. The changes should take effect after you use the `secedit` command.

○ **D.** You forgot to refresh Group Policy after applying the configuration. The changes should take effect after you use the `gpupdate` command.

42. Your Windows Server 2003 server seems sluggish. You suspect that the disk subsystem is the bottleneck. Using the Performance Logs and Alerts utility, which counters should you be monitoring? (Choose all correct answers.)

○ **A.** % Disk Time

○ **B.** % Disk Queue

○ **C.** Disk Seeks/Sec

○ **D.** Disk Queue Length

43. George is building a new server for a database application. The user of the server wants the server to be fault tolerant, so George decides to use Windows Server 2003's mirroring capabilities to create a mirrored set for the boot/system partition. If George has the following drives available, what will be the effective capacity of his boot/system partition?

▶ Drive 1: 18GB

▶ Drive 2: 9GB

○ **A.** 9GB

○ **B.** 18GB

○ **C.** 27GB

○ **D.** 13.5GB

44. George decides to add a RAID-5 array to the new server he is building for the database application. If George has the following drives available, what will be the effective capacity of his RAID-5 array?

▶ Drive 1: 18GB

▶ Drive 2: 18GB

▶ Drive 3: 36GB

▶ Drive 4: 36GB

○ **A.** 108GB

○ **B.** 72GB

○ **C.** 54GB

○ **D.** 60GB

45. Your Windows Server 2003 server seems sluggish. You suspect that the CPU might be the bottleneck. Using the Performance Logs and Alerts utility, which counters should you be monitoring? (Choose all correct answers.)

○ **A.** % Processor Time

○ **B.** % Processor Page Faults

○ **C.** Processor Interrupts/Sec

○ **D.** Processor Queue Length

46. It's late Friday afternoon and you want to finish a database query so that you can go home. Using Task Manager, what priority can you set the database process to so that it will finish quicker?

○ **A.** Normal

○ **B.** High

○ **C.** AboveNormal

○ **D.** Priority 15

47. You are the administrator for Good Times, Inc. The Director of IT is extremely security conscious. She doesn't want any user being able to use a blank password. Which of the following password policies should you use to accomplish this? (Choose all correct answers.)

○ **A.** Password Length

○ **B.** Passwords Must Meet Complexity Requirements

○ **C.** Minimum Password Length

○ **D.** Require Non-Blank Password

48. In addition to the non-blank passwords requirement, your extremely security-conscious Director of IT wants you to increase the level of audit logging performed for user logons. If there are going to be more items audited, what other step should you take?

- ❍ **A.** Increase the log-retention length.

- ❍ **B.** Increase the size of the Event log.

- ❍ **C.** Increase the size of the Security log.

- ❍ **D.** Increase the size of the Audit log.

49. You're the system administrator for a fairly large corporation. Your corporation has a mix of network clients and platforms. You want to use Windows Server 2003 Terminal Services so that all clients see the same desktop. Which of the following platforms are *not* supported by the Windows Server 2003 version of Terminal Services? (Choose all correct answers.)

- ❍ **A.** Handheld devices (iPAQ, HP, and so on)

- ❍ **B.** Apple Macintosh

- ❍ **C.** Red Hat Linux

- ❍ **D.** Windows for Workgroups

50. You are the lead administrator for a large manufacturer of farm machinery and related parts based in the Upper Midwest. Your company has several small manufacturing plants spread out over a five-state area. Most of the end users are not computer savvy, so the client computers are somewhat locked down. All clients are running Windows XP, and all servers are running Windows Server 2003. The manufacturing plants are connected to headquarters via 128K lines in a hub-and-spoke configuration. A WSUS server is located in each location.

Each WSUS server is configured to synchronize by using the default settings. Because bandwidth at each office is limited, you want to ensure that updates require the minimum amount of time. What should you do? (Choose all correct answers.)

- ❍ **A.** Synchronize the updates with a WSUS server at the central office.

- ❍ **B.** Select only the locales that are needed.

- ❍ **C.** Configure Background Intelligent Transfer Service (BITS) to limit file transfer size to 9 Mb.

- ❍ **D.** Configure Background Intelligent Transfer Service (BITS) to delete incomplete jobs after 20 minutes.

51. You are the network administrator for a small legal firm. Most of the data on your file servers consists of old legal documents. You're running out of disk space on your file server. What steps can you take to keep the file server from becoming full?

    ○ **A.** Enable drive compression.

    ○ **B.** Enable drive compression and set it to maximum.

    ○ **C.** Enable disk quotas.

    ○ **D.** Use the Disk Defragmenter utility to consolidate free space.

52. You are the network administrator for an engineering firm. You are setting up folder permissions for Mary Smith, a new employee.

The Projects folder is configured with the following permissions:

Share Permissions:

Managers: Full Control

Engineering department: Change

Scheduling department: Read

NTFS Permissions

Managers: Full Control

Engineering department: Modify

Scheduling: Read

If Mary is a member of the Engineering department and the Scheduling group, what is her effective permission over the network?

    ○ **A.** Change

    ○ **B.** Modify

    ○ **C.** Read

    ○ **D.** Full Control

53. You are the administrator of a Windows Server 2003 network that consists of clients ranging from Windows NT 4.0 to Windows XP. You purchase and install a new XYZ Color Laser printer and install the Windows 2003 drivers on your print server. Your Windows 2000 and Windows XP clients are able to print without any problems. However, when you try to print from the Windows NT 4.0 clients, you receive a message similar to the following: "The server on which the printer resides does not have a suitable XYZ printer driver installed." What is the best solution?

   ○ **A.** Reinstall the Windows 2003 drivers.

   ○ **B.** Download the Windows NT 4.0 version of the printer drivers from the manufacturers website. Copy them to the \Winnt\System32\printer\sdrivers folder on the Windows 2003 print server.

   ○ **C.** Download the Windows NT 4.0 version of the printer drivers from the manufacturer's website. Change the sharing options on the printer configuration to install additional drivers for Windows NT 4.0.

   ○ **D.** Download the Windows NT 4.0 version of the printer drivers from the manufacturer's website. Install the drivers on each Windows NT 4.0 workstation.

54. Davin is the system administrator for a small accounting firm. He has set up several identical printers in a common area on which users can print their reports. Unfortunately, most users seem to want to use the same printer, so users are constantly standing around waiting for their print jobs to finish.

   What can Davin do to improve the printing process so that users can get their reports faster?

   ○ **A.** Connect the printers to the same print server.

   ○ **B.** Configure two logical printers that are assigned to the same printing device. Assign different priorities and groups to each printer.

   ○ **C.** Configure the printers in a printer pool.

   ○ **D.** Turn on print auditing.

55. Frank is the purchasing officer for the IT department of BigCo, Inc. James, the lead administrator, has requested that Frank purchase four copies of Windows Server 2003 to be used for domain controllers. Which of the following versions of Windows Server 2003 cannot be used for a domain controller?

   ○ **A.** Windows Server 2003, Standard Edition

   ○ **B.** Windows Server 2003, Enterprise Edition

   ○ **C.** Windows Server 2003, Datacenter Edition

   ○ **D.** Windows Server 2003, Web Edition

56. You are the administrator of a Windows 2000 network. You decide to buy a new server and load a copy of Windows Server 2003 SP1 on it. After loading the operating system and logging on for the first time, you inadvertently click the Finish button on the Post Setup Security Updates screen. You still need to install the current updates on the server; how do you return to the Post Setup Security Updates screen?

    ○ **A.** Reboot your server; it will appear when you first log on.

    ○ **B.** Access the Post Setup Security Updates screen from the Manage Your Server utility in the Administrative Tools folder.

    ○ **C.** Access the Post Setup Security Updates utility in the Administrative Tools folder.

    ○ **D.** You cannot; it appears only once.

57. You are the administrator of a Windows 2000 network that consists of clients ranging from Windows NT 4.0 to Windows XP. You purchase and install your first Windows Server 2003 server and join it to your domain. You are able to log on to the server without any problems using your domain account. However, when you try to change the password on the local administrator account to "password," you receive a message similar to the following: "The password does not meet the complexity requirements." This local administrator password works on all your other machines. What is the problem?

    ○ **A.** You mistyped the password.

    ○ **B.** The password doesn't meet the complexity requirements.

    ○ **C.** The server requires a reboot before the password can be changed.

    ○ **D.** Windows Server 2003 servers can't be used in a Windows 2000 domain.

58. You are the system administrator for a small chemical company. One of your department managers just called, and she wants you to give Fred, one of the employee's, read access to an object in Active Directory. What tool should you use to accomplish this?

    ○ **A.** OU Manager

    ○ **B.** Active Directory Object Manager

    ○ **C.** Active Directory Users and Computers

    ○ **D.** Active Directory Object Access

59. You are the administrator of a Windows Server 2003 network that consists of clients ranging from Windows NT 4.0 to Windows XP. You need to delegate management of the users in the Kansas City OU to one of your junior administrators. What is the best way to accomplish this?

   ○ **A.** Assign the junior administrator's user account the necessary special permissions.

   ○ **B.** Assign the junior administrator's user account the necessary permissions using the Delegation of Control Wizard.

   ○ **C.** Add the junior administrator's user account to a group. Assign the group the necessary permissions using the Delegation of Control Wizard.

   ○ **D.** Go to the Security tab of the OU. Assign the junior administrator the necessary permissions.

60. You are the administrator of a Windows Server 2003 network for Widgets, Inc. A Windows Server 2003 computer named FilePrint1 functions as a print server on the network. Several users submit large print jobs to Printer5, which is hosted on FilePrint1. A user reports that the print jobs fails to complete. You examine the print queue on Printer5, and you discover that one of the print jobs is showing an error. You attempt to delete the job, but you are unsuccessful.

   You need to ensure that print jobs submitted to Printer5 complete successfully. What is the first thing you should you do?

   ○ **A.** Configure Printer5 to use a TCP/IP port.

   ○ **B.** Increase the priority of Printer5.

   ○ **C.** Delete all files from the C:\Windows\System32\Spool folder.

   ○ **D.** Restart the spooler service on FilePrint1.

Answers to Practice Exam

1. C	21. B	41. D
2. B	22. A	42. A, D
3. B	23. D	43. A
4. D	24. B, D	44. C
5. C	25. A	45. A, D
6. C	26. B	46. B
7. A, C	27. C	47. B, C
8. A, D, E	28. C	48. C
9. D	29. D	49. C, D
10. D, E	30. B	50. A
11. E	31. D	51. A
12. A, B	32. A	52. A
13. C	33. D	53. C
14. C	34. B	54. C
15. C	35. A	55. D
16. A, B, D	36. C	56. D
17. C	37. D	57. B
18. C	38. D	58. C
19. C	39. A	59. C
20. A, C, D	40. A	60. D

Answers and Explanations

1. **C.** Non–Plug and Play hardware, or hardware that is not automatically recognized, must be added via the Add Hardware applet in the Control Panel. Reinstalling the hardware will not cause it to be recognized; therefore, answer A is incorrect. Installing drivers will not accomplish anything if the hardware is not recognized; therefore, answer B is incorrect. The Device Manager does not assist in installing new hardware directly; therefore, answer D is incorrect. See "Using the Add Hardware Wizard" in Chapter 15, "Managing and Troubleshooting Hardware Devices."

2. **B.** The server can be booted to the Recovery Console using the Windows Server 2003 CD-ROM. Booting from a PXE-capable NIC is used only for the Remote Installation Service (RIS); therefore, answer A is incorrect. Unlike previous versions of Windows, Windows Server 2003 does not come with boot disks; therefore, answer C is incorrect. Answer D is incorrect because you can boot into the Recovery Console using the Windows Server 2003 CD-ROM. See "Recovery Console" in Chapter 17, "Managing and Implementing Disaster Recovery."

3. **B.** The most likely reason for Mary not being able to create a RAID-5 array in this situation is that the disks are basic disks, not dynamic disks. Dynamic disks are required to create RAID-5 arrays; therefore, answer A is incorrect. Because Windows Server 2003 supports software RAID, a hardware RAID controller is not required; therefore, answer C is incorrect. Being a member of the Enterprise Admins group is not a requirement to create a RAID-5 array; therefore, answer D is incorrect. See "Introduction to Dynamic Disks" in Chapter 12, "Managing Server Storage Devices."

4. **D.** To enforce a quota, you must set limits. Just enabling disk quotas tracks usage, but nothing else; therefore, answer A is incorrect. Consolidating free space won't result in any extra space; therefore, answer B is incorrect. Enabling warning limits allows the administrator to see who is running out of configured space; therefore, answer C is incorrect. See "Implementing and Monitoring Disk Quotas" in Chapter 13, "Managing Data Storage."

5. **C.** Although all the listed solutions would work, the quickest and easiest solution is to use the Windows Server Update Services (WSUS) to automatically download the patch from Microsoft and apply it to all the computers; therefore, answers A, B, and D are incorrect. See "Managing Updates" in Chapter 18, "Managing and Implementing Windows Server Update Services."

6. **C.** In addition to disk quotas, a Windows Server 2003 server's NTFS drives support file and folder compression. Disk quotas are based on uncompressed file size; therefore, your database file may take up more than the displayed size-on-disk figure. An NTFS

permissions problem or a virus would not give you an out-of-space message; therefore, answers A and D are incorrect. Users do not have the authority to configure quotas; therefore, answer B is incorrect. See "Implementing and Monitoring Disk Quotas" in Chapter 13.

7. **A, C.** Both System Monitor and Task Manager allow you to see the current performance of your applications. The Performance Logs and Alerts snap-in allows you to log data and create alerts only, and the Performance Monitor utility was used in previous versions of Windows; therefore, answers B and D are incorrect. See "Monitoring Performance" in Chapter 14, "Monitoring and Optimizing Server Performance."

8. **A, D, E.** Although video performance might be important on a workstation, on a server the big four are memory, processor, physical disk, and network; therefore, answer B is incorrect. Answer C is incorrect because application load time is not a device. See "Optimizing System Resources" in Chapter 14.

9. **D.** To enforce a quota, you must set limits. Zip files are already compressed, so disk compression has little, if any, effect; therefore, answers A and C are incorrect. Consolidating free space won't result in any extra space; therefore, answer B is incorrect. See "Implementing and Monitoring Disk Quotas" in Chapter 13.

10. **D, E.** You need to add her user account to the Administrators and Backup Operators groups to provide the proper permissions to perform backups. The Server Operators, Power Users, and Account Operators groups do not have the proper file-level permissions to back up files; therefore, answers A, B, and C are incorrect. See "Default Groups" in Chapter 3, "Managing Groups."

11. **E.** Windows Server 2003 does not use an Emergency Repair Disk; therefore, answers A, B, C, and D are all incorrect. See "Implementing Automated System Recovery (ASR)" in Chapter 17.

12. **A, B.** To support WSUS, client computers must be running the updated Automatic Updates client and Windows 2000 (Service Pack 3), Windows XP, or Window Server 2003; therefore, answers C and D are incorrect. See "Configuring Clients for Automatic Updates" in Chapter 18.

13. **C.** The quickest and probably cheapest way to distribute the application is to set up a Windows Server 2003 server with Terminal Services running in Application Server mode. In Application Server mode, Terminal Services can support multiple concurrent users, whereas Remote Desktop for Administration mode limits you to two concurrent connections. If your desktops are still running Windows 95 and Windows for Workgroups, it's unlikely they could be upgraded to Windows XP quickly or cheaply; therefore, answers A, B, and D are incorrect. See "Using Windows Server 2003 Terminal Services" in Chapter 11, "Managing and Maintaining Terminal Services."

14. **C.** The audit information is recorded in the Security Log under Event Viewer; therefore, answers A, B, D, and E are all incorrect. See "Configuring Auditing" in Chapter 16, "Implementing Administrative Templates and Audit Policy."

15. **C.** Neither Remote Desktop for Administration or Terminal Services allows Mary to work on the Windows XP client because these are Windows Server 2003 specific features. The Remote Assistance feature allows both Mary and the user to see and control the desktop on the client. The Remote Administrator feature does not exist; therefore, answer D is incorrect. See "Remote Assistance" in Chapter 5 "Administering Windows Server 2003."

16. **A, B, D.** When a shared folder is moved, it is no longer shared. When it is moved to a different server, it assumes the NTFS permissions of the target folder, which probably won't be the same as the original folder. Restarting the Server service or giving the shares new names will not cause nonshared folders to appear as shares; therefore, answers C and E are incorrect. See "Copying and Moving Files and Folders" in Chapter 4 "Managing and Maintaining Access to Resources."

17. **C.** Although you can still assign a logon script via the user profile, the recommended method in Windows Server 2003 is to assign logon scripts via Group Policy; therefore, answers A, B, and D are incorrect. See "How Group Policy Scripts Work" in Chapter 10 "Managing the User Environment by Using Group Policy."

18. **C.** You should install the Terminal Services client so that you can access your servers remotely. The Windows Server 2003 administration tools can be installed only on Windows XP and Windows Server 2003 computers; therefore, answer A is incorrect. The Active Directory Users and Groups MMC, whether it is the Windows 2000 or Windows 2003 version, will not run on Windows NT; therefore, answer B is incorrect. Although User Manager for Domains works in a mixed-mode Windows Server 2003 domain, it doesn't provide much functionality; therefore, answer D is incorrect. See "Using Windows Server 2003 Terminal Services" in Chapter 11.

19. **C.** One major difference between Windows 2000 and Windows Server 2003 is the default permissions for file shares. In Windows 2000, the default is Everyone—Full Control. In Windows Server 2003, the default is Everyone—Read. Using Shared folders on a FAT32 volume wouldn't make a difference in access through a share, as long as the permissions were configured correctly. Also, if the permissions were assigned to the wrong groups, that wouldn't explain why the users can access some folders and not others; therefore, answers A and B are incorrect. Quotas were not mentioned; therefore, answer D is incorrect. See "Creating and Managing Shared Folders" in Chapter 4.

20. **A, C, D.** You need to follow these steps to use Secure Sockets Layer (SSL) to require authentication and encrypt all data passing between the user computer and the website; therefore, answers B and E are incorrect.

21. **B.** External devices attached to serial ports must be installed using the Add Hardware Wizard. Only internal devices, or devices attached to certain parallel ports, can be installed using Plug and Play or via Device Manager; therefore, answers A and D are incorrect. The Add Printers applet can be used only to install printers, not communication devices; therefore, answer C is incorrect. See "Using the Add Hardware Wizard" in Chapter 15.

22. **A.** Windows Server 2003 Terminal Services is the only viable option here. It allows the user desktop and files to remain at the headquarters location, and only screen updates and keystrokes are transmitted over the WAN. Although roaming profiles are a nice feature, they tend to get rather large. With such a low-bandwidth link, a typical profile downloading over the WAN would saturate the link; therefore, answer B is incorrect. Although mandatory profiles always present users with the same desktop, their files are not available unless some sort of drive mapping is implemented; therefore, answer C is incorrect. DFS would allow the user files to be stored in multiple locations, but that doesn't affect the desktop, and the file replication between multiple locations could potentially saturate the WAN link; therefore, answer D is incorrect. See "Using Windows Server 2003 Terminal Services" in Chapter 11.

23. **D.** The Last Known Good Configuration option starts the server using the `Hardware` key that was in use the last time the server was successfully booted. It overwrites the new, and potentially bad, SCSI drivers that you just installed. The options in answers A and B will not be effective because they will still be using the defective drivers to boot the server. Automated System Recovery would potentially fix the problem, but only if you had already created a backup set previous to installing the faulty drivers; therefore, answer C is incorrect. See "Last Known Good Configuration" in Chapter 17.

24. **B, D.** The Windows Server 2003 Recovery Console cannot be started from a network share, and Windows Server 2003 no longer includes boot disks. Using the operating system menu and the Windows Server 2003 CD-ROM are both viable options for starting the Recovery Console; therefore, answers A and C are incorrect. See "Recovery Console" in Chapter 17.

25. **A.** Windows NT 4.0 is the only listed operating system that does not support disk quotas. This is because it uses NTFS version 4.0, whereas all the other listed operating systems use NTFS 5.0, which has quota, compression, and encryption support built in; therefore, answers B, C, and D are incorrect. See "Implementing and Monitoring Disk Quotas" in Chapter 13.

26. **B.** Unlike previous versions of Windows, in Windows Server 2003, the administrator can assign the ownership of files and folders. Moving the files would not work because files moved to a different folder on an NTFS partition retain their existing permissions; therefore, answer D is incorrect. The other options would work, but they take more steps; therefore, answers A and C are incorrect. See "Changing Ownership of Files and Folders" in Chapter 4.

27. **C.** When quotas are enabled, they track only the space used by each user. Quota limits are not enabled by default; they must be manually configured. Quotas are not supported on FAT32 volumes; therefore, answer A is incorrect. Quotas cannot be assigned by group, and there are no default quota limits; therefore, answers B and D are incorrect. See "Implementing and Monitoring Disk Quotas" in Chapter 13.

28. **C.** An incremental backup is used to back up only the files and folders that have been created or modified since the last normal or incremental backup. It reads the archive bit to determine which files need to be backed up. It then changes the archive bit of the files that were backed up, so that the next time the backup program is run, the file is not backed up again unless it was changed. A normal backup backs up all the files, whereas a daily backup backs up only the files created or modified that day; therefore, answers A and B are incorrect. A partial backup does not exist; therefore, answer D is incorrect. See "Types of Backups" in Chapter 17.

29. **D.** Restarting a server and selecting Last Known Good Configuration is the quickest and easiest way to correct most problems with the SYSTEM Registry key; therefore, answers A, B, and C are incorrect. See "Last Known Good Configuration" in Chapter 17.

30. **B.** Roaming profiles allow the users' desktop and the contents of their folders, such as My Documents, to follow them from computer to computer. Shared Profiles is not a valid option; therefore, answer A is incorrect. Although mandatory profiles always present users with the same desktop, their files are not available unless some sort of drive mapping is implemented; therefore, answer C is incorrect. DFS would not enable the required functionality; therefore, answer D is incorrect. See "Managing Local, Roaming, and Mandatory User Profiles" in Chapter 2 "Managing User and Computer Accounts."

31. **D.** WSUS can supply compliance reports to track the compliance status of an Update. Unlike the other reports that are available from the reports page, these reports are run by selecting the selected update on the Updates page. SUS doesn't provide a reporting function. See "Managing Updates" in Chapter 18.

32. **B.** The Performance Logs and Alerts tool can be used to capture baseline data that can be viewed in the System Monitor. Performance Monitor was the tool used in Windows NT 4.0; therefore, answer A is incorrect. Task Manager is not suited for baselining; therefore, answer C is incorrect. Although System Monitor is used to display performance data, it can't log it to create a baseline; therefore, answer D is incorrect. See "The Performance Logs and Alerts Snap-In" in Chapter 14.

33. **D.** Typically, a Disk Queue Length of more than 2 is a problem. To fix this, you should replace the disk with a faster one. Although adding a faster disk might help a little, the existing disk will still be a bottleneck; therefore, answer C is incorrect. All the other settings are within an acceptable range; therefore, answers A and B are incorrect. See "Optimizing System Resources" in Chapter 14.

34. **B.** Typically, a Processor Queue Length of more than 2 is a problem, especially if ProcessorTime is more than 80%. All the other settings are within an acceptable range; therefore, answers A, C, and D are incorrect. See "Optimizing System Resources" in Chapter 14.

35. **A.** Because NLB uses the IP address of the client when routing, it can reconnect to a disconnected session. However, in those situations where the user has moved to another computer or received a different IP address via DHCP, the user receives a new session chosen at random from the group of servers. The Session Directory is a database that indexes the sessions using the username instead of the IP address. Session Directory allows disconnected sessions to be reconnected by using the username to look up the location of a disconnected session. Simply prolonging the session by increasing the disconnect and the idle timeout, or granting administrative rights, will have no effect on session routing; therefore, answers B, C and D are incorrect. See "Terminal Services Session Directory" in Chapter 11.

36. **C.** Terminal Services in Remote Desktop for Administration mode supports only two concurrent connections, plus a console session. A new server has a 120-day grace period for client licenses; therefore, answer B is incorrect. Answer A is incorrect because the Session Directory is useful only for session routing among multiple Terminal Services servers. Any Terminal Services client can be used to connect to a Windows Server 2003 Terminal Services server, albeit with less functionality; therefore, answer D is incorrect. See "Using the Remote Desktop Connection Client" in Chapter 11.

37. **D.** A common problem with Terminal Services involves connecting to the server with the older Terminal Services RDP 4.0 client instead of the RDC 5.0 client (included with Windows 2000) or the RDC 5.1 client (included with Windows XP or Windows Server 2003). The clients look and function in a similar manner; however, the advanced functionality that is enabled in RDC 5.0 and 5.1, such as audio support and keyboard mapping, is not available with the older Terminal Services 4.0 RDP clients. Session Directory allows disconnected sessions to be reconnected by using the username to

look up the location of a disconnected session. It has no effect on audio; therefore, answer A is incorrect. Audio support is enabled, by default, and doesn't require the Citrix add-on; therefore, answers B and C are incorrect. See "Using the Remote Desktop Connection Client" in Chapter 11.

38. **D.** New with Windows Server 2003 is the concept of user Client Access Licenses and device Client Access Licenses. These allow organizations additional license options. For example, if a Terminal Services user connects via multiple devices, such as an office PC, a home PC, and a handheld device, he would purchase a user license instead of a device license. PCs or other devices that support multiple users would require a device license; therefore, answers A, B, and C are incorrect. The standard TS CAL is only for Windows 2000 Terminal Services servers. See "Terminal Services Licensing" in Chapter 11.

39. **A.** After a basic disk is converted to a dynamic disk, it can't be converted back to a basic disk. The only way to revert to using a basic disk is to back up the data, reinitialize the disk, repartition it, and restore the data; therefore, answers B, C, and D are incorrect. See "Introduction to Dynamic Disks" in Chapter 12.

40. **A.** RAID-5 provides the best compromise between performance and fault tolerance; therefore, answers B and C are incorrect. RAID-3 is not supported by Windows Server 2003; therefore, answer D is incorrect. See "Introduction to Dynamic Disks" in Chapter 12.

41. **D.** Except for security changes, Group Policies are not immediately applied. Windows Server 2003 uses the `gpupdate` command to apply policies immediately. Administrative privilege is not at issue because you logged in as a regular user to test the policy; therefore, answer A is incorrect. Policies are saved automatically as they are configured; therefore, answer B is incorrect. Previous versions of Windows used the `secedit` command; therefore, answer C is incorrect. See "Gpupdate" in Chapter 9 "Implementing Group Policy."

42. **A, D.** If the Disk Queue Length is above 2, or the % Disk Time is a sustained 80% or better, the disk unit is the most likely bottleneck. Disk Seeks/Sec is not a good indicator of a bottleneck because you would need to correlate the results with the disk access time, and % Disk Queue is not a valid option; therefore, answers B and C are incorrect. See "Optimizing System Resources" in Chapter 14.

43. **A.** The space available is 9GB. When a mirrored set is created, it is sized to be equivalent to the smallest volume; therefore, answers B, C, and D are incorrect. See "Implementing RAID Solutions" in Chapter 12.

44. **C.** The space available is 54GB. When a RAID-5 array is created, it uses no more than the size of the smallest configured area on each volume. In addition, the equivalent of one volume is dedicated to storing parity information; therefore, answers A, B, and D are incorrect. See "Implementing RAID Solutions" in Chapter 12.

45. **A, D.** If the Processor Queue Length is above 2, or the % Processor Time is a sustained 80% or better, the processor is the most likely bottleneck. % Processor Page Faults doesn't exist; therefore, answer B is incorrect. A high value for Processor Interrupts/Sec usually indicates a bad card or system device; therefore, answer C is incorrect. See "Optimizing System Resources" in Chapter 14.

46. **B.** Although setting the process to AboveNormal, which is a priority 9, is better than Normal, which is an 8, the High setting has a priority 13. Therefore, answers A and C are incorrect. Priorities are not assigned via number; therefore, answer D is incorrect. See "Understanding Priority" in Chapter 14.

47. **B, C.** The password complexity rules are rather involved, but require that the minimum length be six characters. Alternatively, you can set the Minimum Password Length policy to 1. This prevents users from attempting to use blank passwords. The options Password Length and Require Non-Blank Password do not exist; therefore, answers A and D are incorrect. See "Account Policies" in Chapter 16.

48. **C.** The Security log is the place where the audit events are stored. Increasing the log-retention time might make things worse if the log is not set to overwrite old data; therefore, answer A is incorrect. There are no logs specifically named Audit or Event; therefore, answers B and D are incorrect. See "Configuring Log Properties" in Chapter 16.

49. **C, D.** Windows for Workgroups and Linux clients are available only from third parties. Pocket PC devices and Apple Macintosh are supported, although you might have to download the client from Microsoft; therefore, answers A and B are incorrect. See "Using the Remote Desktop Client" in Chapter 11.

50. **A, B.** When you install WSUS, by default it downloads multiple languages for the updates, resulting in updates that you probably don't need. In this scenario, we can reduce the bandwidth used by the synchronization by selecting only the required locales. This will avoid downloading and synchronizing multiple copies of the same updates, but in different languages. Because we have a hub and spoke network, configuration synchronizing with the central office server would provide the least amount of traffic over the 128K lines. Also, if you limit the transfer size, or limit the transfer time, you won't receive the larger patches. See "Windows Server Update Services" in Chapter 18.

51. **A.** Enabling drive compression is the best solution. Typically, document files are good candidates for compression, and compressing them should free a large amount of space on the server. There is not a maximum setting for disk compression—it is either enabled or disabled—so B is incorrect. Enabling disk quotas will help you limit the amount of space used by each user, but it will not free any space. Although defragging the files on your disk should improve performance, it will have no effect on the amount of free space available. See "Configuring NTFS File and Folder Compression" in Chapter 13.

52. **A.** Because Mary is accessing the folder through a share, her permissions will be the more restrictive of the combined share and NTFS permissions. Modify is an NTFS permission, not a share permission, so B is incorrect. Answer C is incorrect because the Engineering group has more access than just Read. Answer D is incorrect because Mary is not a member of the Managers group, and their members are the only ones who have full control over the files. See "Combining Share and NTFS Permissions" in Chapter 4.

53. **C.** If you share a printer with users running other versions of Windows (Windows 9x or Windows NT 3.5 and 4.0), you can install additional printer drivers on your computer so those users can connect to your printer without being prompted to install the drivers missing from their systems. Reinstalling the drivers wouldn't help because if the Windows 2000 and Windows XP clients are working, the drivers were installed correctly. Manually copying driver files to the folder will not install the drivers. Although manually installing the drivers on each machine would work, it would be a lot of effort, and not necessary because if you load the drivers on the print server, Windows NT 4.0 and Windows 2000/2003/XP–based clients check the printer driver each time they connect to the printer. If the driver or the current version is not installed, a copy of the driver is downloaded automatically. See "Managing Printer Drivers" in Chapter 6.

54. **C.** Configuring the printer in a printer pool will distribute the print jobs among all the printers in the pool. This should allow print jobs to be completed faster because all printers will be used. Configuring two logical printers with different priorities won't solve the issue because it just results in some print jobs and users having different priorities. Print auditing will not improve the speed of printing reports; it will only tell you who is doing the printing. Connecting the printers to the same print server will not improve the speed of printing reports—and in some cases, it might slow things down. See "Printer Pooling" in Chapter 7.

55. **D.** Windows Server 2003, Web Edition 2003 is tuned for use as a web server. It cannot be used as a domain controller. There are no limitations on roles for the other versions. See "The Windows Server 2003 Family" in Chapter 1.

56. **D**. The main purpose of the Post Setup Security Updates screen is to ensure that all your security patches are up to date before you allow your server to be exposed to your network or the Internet. This screen only appears on the first boot. It will not be available upon another boot or via the Start menu. See "Logging on to Windows Server 2003" in Chapter 1.

57. **B**. By default, a Windows Server 2003 standalone server does not require a user to enter a complex password. However, for domain controllers, and servers and PCs that are members of a network, the password complexity policy is enabled by default.

For a password to meet the complexity requirements, it must adhere to the following format:

▶ It must not contain all or part of the username

▶ It must be at least six characters long

▶ It must contain characters from three of the following four categories:

▶ Lowercase characters (a through z)

▶ Numeric characters (0 through 9)

▶ Nonalphabetic characters (i.e. !,@,#,$,%)

58. **C**. In Windows Server 2003, the permissions for objects and their attributes are configured using the Active Directory Users and Computers snap-in. The other tools listed do not exist. See "Assigning Permissions to Active Directory Objects" in Chapter 8.

59. **C**. Although the network administrator has very granular control over Active Directory objects, trying to keep up with and document the changes to specific attributes of unique objects can easily become a management nightmare. Assigning permissions manually through the Security tab, especially when assigning them to a user account, is not recommended. The proper way to accomplish this task is to assign the permissions to a group using the Delegation of Control Wizard. See "Assigning Permissions to Active Directory Objects" in Chapter 8.

60. **D**. Usually, spooler problems can be corrected by stopping and restarting the Spooler service through the Services applet. If this fails to resolve the problem, check to make sure the spooler's host drive has at least 50MB of free space. If it doesn't, change the spool host drive and reboot the system. In some cases, a simple reboot corrects the spooler problem. In addition, sometimes it's necessary to delete the .SPL files from the spooler and restart; however, that will cause the users to resubmit their print jobs. Configuring the printer to use a TCP/IP port or increasing the priority won't correct the problem. See "Troubleshooting Printing Problems" in Chapter 7.

PART III

Appendixes

APPENDIX A

Accessing Your Free MeasureUp Practice Test— Including Networking Simulations!

This Exam Cram book features exclusive access to MeasureUp's practice questions, including networking simulations! These simulations are yet another excellent study tool to help you assess your readiness for the 70-290 Managing and Maintaining a Microsoft Windows Server 2003 Environment exam. MeasureUp is a Microsoft Certified Practice Test Provider, so these simulations validate your hands-on skills by modeling real-life networking scenarios—requiring you to perform tasks on simulated networking devices. MeasureUp's simulations also assess your ability to troubleshoot and solve realistic networking problems. If you are planning to take the certification exam for 70-290 or 70-291, you should expect to see performance-based simulations on the exam. MeasureUp's Microsoft simulations will ensure that you are prepared.

To access your free practice questions and simulations, follow these steps:

1. Retrieve your unique Registration Key on the inside of the back cover of this book.

2. Go to www.measureup.com.

3. Create a free MeasureUp account or log in to your existing account.

4. On the Learning Locker toolbar, click Register Products.

5. Read and consent to the License Agreement by clicking the check box below the License Agreement.

6. Type your registration key number into the Key box. Do not remove any dashes or substitute any numbers.

7. Click Register.

934

Appendix A: Accessing Your Free MeasureUp Practice Test—Including Networking Simulations!

8. Click the Learning Locker button to display your Personal Test Locker.

9. Click the Practice Test link, and follow the instructions to start your test or the Learning Locker tab to return to your Learning Locker.

For more details about MeasureUp's product features, see Appendix B, "MeasureUp's Product Features."

MeasureUp's Product Features

Since 1997, MeasureUp has helped more than 1 million IT professionals achieve certifications from the industry's leading vendors. Created by content developers certified in their areas and with real-world experience, MeasureUp practice tests feature comprehensive questions (some with performance-based simulations), detailed explanations, and complete score reporting. As a Microsoft Certified Practice Test Provider, MeasureUp's practice tests are the closest you can get to the certification exams!

Multiple Testing Modes

MeasureUp practice tests are available in Study, Certification, Custom, Missed Question, and Non-Duplicate question modes.

Study Mode

Tests administered in Study Mode allow you to request the correct answer(s) and explanation for each question during the test. These tests are not timed. You can modify the testing environment *during* the test by clicking the Options button.

Certification Mode

Tests administered in Certification Mode closely simulate the actual testing environment you will encounter when taking a certification exam. These tests do not allow you to request the answer(s) or explanation for each question until after the exam.

Custom Mode

Custom Mode allows you to specify your preferred testing environment. Use this mode to specify the objectives you want to include in your test, the timer length, and other test properties. You can also modify the testing environment *during* the test by clicking the Options button.

Missed Question Mode

Missed Question Mode allows you to take a test containing only the questions you missed previously.

Non-Duplicate Mode

Non-Duplicate Mode allows you to take a test containing only questions not displayed previously.

Question Types

The practice question types simulate the real exam experience, and include the following:

▶ Create a tree

▶ Select and place

▶ Drop and connect

▶ Build list

▶ Reorder list

▶ Build and reorder list

▶ Single hotspot

▶ Multiple hotspots

▶ Live screen

▶ Command line

▶ Hot area

▶ Fill in the blank

Random Questions and Order of Answers

This feature helps you learn the material without memorizing questions and answers. Each time you take a practice test, the questions and answers appear in a different randomized order.

Detailed Explanations of Correct and Incorrect Answers

You'll receive automatic feedback on all correct and incorrect answers. The detailed answer explanations are a superb learning tool in their own right.

Attention to Exam Objectives

MeasureUp practice tests are designed to appropriately balance the questions over each technical area covered by a specific exam.

Technical Support

If you encounter problems with the MeasureUp test engine on the CD-ROM, you can contact MeasureUp at 678-356-5050 or email support@measureup.com. Technical support hours are from 8 a.m. to 5 p.m. EST Monday through Friday. Additionally, you'll find Frequently Asked Questions (FAQs) at www.measureup.com.

If you'd like to purchase additional MeasureUp products, telephone 678-356-5050 or 800-649-1MUP (1687), or visit www.measureup.com.

Glossary of Technical Terms

In this appendix, we provide definitions for the list of key terms that appeared at the end of each chapter. In addition, we have included some other definitions that might be helpful.

A

Access Control Entry (ACE)   Each entry in an Access Control List is known as an Access Control entry (ACE).

Access Control List (ACL)   An Access Control List is a list of users that can access an object and the specific actions that the user can perform on the object.

account lockout   A security feature that is used to disable an account when certain procedures are violated, such as the number of times a user attempts to log on unsuccessfully.

account policies   Used to configure the security attributes for the user accounts in the domain. This policy will be the default policy for any machines that are members of the domain. However, you can set an account policy at the OU level, but these settings will apply only to the *local* user accounts of the nondomain controller computers contained in that OU.

Active Directory   A centralized resource and security management, administration, and control mechanism in Windows Server 2003 that is used to support and maintain a Windows Server 2003 domain. The Active Directory is hosted by domain controllers.

Active Directory Users and Computers   The MMC used to manage users, groups, computer accounts, and resources, as well as OUs and Group Policies.

Administrative Tools   The included applications that are used to manage the server and network.

Advanced Configuration and Power Interface (ACPI)   ACPI is the current standard for communication with a motherboard's Basic Input/Output System (BIOS). With ACPI, all devices that have power-management capabilities (such as sleep mode or hibernation) can be controlled by the operating system. This allows the operating system to selectively shut down devices not currently in use to give maximum battery life to portable computing devices. ACPI is also needed for the OnNow Device Power Management initiative, which allows a user to start his or her computer by simply touching any key on the computer's keyboard. ACPI is installed only if all components detected during setup support power management.

application pool   A set of one or more applications assigned to a set of one or more IIS worker processes. An application pool can contain websites, applications, and virtual directories. Each application pool is isolated from the others. Because of this, a failure or memory leak will affect only the processes running in that application pool and will have no effect on any of the other functions in other application pools.

Application Server mode   The Application Server mode of Terminal Services allows the system administrator to load common applications that can be shared by multiple users. Although an unlimited number of connections is supported, each connection requires a license, called a *Terminal Server Client Access License (TSCAL)*.

auditing   The recording of the occurrence of a defined event or action.

Audit Policy   A policy used to track access to resources. Typical events include valid or invalid logon attempts and the accessing of resources such as the opening, reading, or deletion of a file or folder.

authentication   The process of being identified by the server and/or network.

Automated System Recovery (ASR)   ASR works by making a backup of the boot partition and System State to tape or other media and then saving the catalog and other operating system information, such as disk partition information, to a floppy disk. When a problem occurs that cannot be fixed by using any of the other repair and recovery methods, or when you have replaced a failed boot drive, you can restore the boot partition by booting your server from the Windows Server 2003 CD and then inserting the diskette and the backup media created by the ASR process.

B

backup selection file This selection file contains the names of the files and folders that you want to be backed up. The selection file must be created using the GUI version of Windows Backup.

basic disk When a new disk is installed in Windows Server 2003, it is installed as a basic disk. The basic disk type has been used in all versions of Microsoft Windows dating back to 1.0, OS/2, and MS-DOS. This allows a basic disk created in Windows Server 2003 to be recognized by these earlier operating systems. A basic disk splits a physical disk into units called *partitions*. Partitions allow you to subdivide your physical disk into separate units of storage.

Basic Input/Output System (BIOS) The interface that allows an operating system to communicate with the hardware devices on the computer.

boot partition The partition that contains the operating system files.

BOOT.INI The BOOT.INI file contains the physical path to the location of the folder that contains the operating system files. The BOOT.INI file can contain paths to multiple operating systems. At boot time, you will be presented with a menu so that you can choose which operating system to start.

bottleneck A component in a computer system that prevents some other part of the system from operating at its optimum performance level.

C

certificate A digital signature issued by a third party (called a *Certificate Authority*, or *CA*) that claims to have verified the identity of a server or an individual.

Check Disk A utility that checks the file and folder structure of your hard disk. You can also have Check Disk check the physical structure of your hard disk. Check Disk can perform repairs as required.

client A computer on a network that requests resources or services from some other computer.

cluster server Clustering is an advanced feature that allows workload to be switched over from one server to another, either manually, or because of a hardware or software failure.

Comma Separated Variable (CSV) A file format that is used by various utilities in Windows Server 2003 for import and export.

compression The process of compacting data to save disk space.

computer account The computer account is a security principal, and it can be authenticated and granted permissions to access resources. A computer account is automatically created for each computer running Windows NT (or later operating systems) when the computer joins the domain.

counters   Each object has several monitoring functions called *counters*. Each counter offers insight into a different aspect or function of the object. For example, the memory object has counters called % Committed Bytes in Use, Available Bytes, Page Faults/sec, and more. System Monitor takes the readings from these counters and presents the information to you in a human-readable format.

D

defragmentation   The process of reorganizing files so that they are stored contiguously on the hard drive.

Delegation of Control Wizard   The Delegation of Control Wizard is used to delegate the control of certain users, groups, and OUs to a user or group.

device driver   A device-specific software component used by an operating system to communicate with a device. The device driver is responsible for passing requests between the operating system and the device.

device driver rollback   The capability to easily restore a device driver to the previous version. This can be accomplished either manually via the Device Manager applet or automatically via Windows File Protection.

Device Manager   A Windows Server 2003 administrative tool used to install, configure, and manage hardware devices.

differential backup   Used to back up only the files and folders that have been created or modified since the last normal or incremental backup. It does not change the archive bit.

digital signature   Used to ensure that the identity of the provider of the signature is who they say they are.

direct memory access (DMA)   DMA allows a device to read or write to the computer's memory without using the computer's processor (CPU). Each device using DMA must have a DMA channel dedicated for its use.

disabled account   An inactive account that cannot be used for accessing resources.

Disk Cleanup   A tool used to regain access to hard drive space through deleting temporary, orphaned, or downloaded files, emptying the Recycle Bin, compressing little-used files, and condensing index catalog files.

Disk Defragmenter   The application built in to Windows Server 2003 for defragmenting hard disks.

Disk Management console   The MMC snap-in that is used to manage the physical and logical disks in a Windows Server 2003 server.

disk quota   Provides a way of controlling or monitoring how much space a user is allowed to use on a volume.

domain controller   A computer that authenticates the domain logons and maintains a Windows Server 2003 domain's Active Directory, which stores all information and relationships about users, groups, policies, computers, and resources.

domain functionality level   Windows Server 2003 domains can be in four functional levels, and those levels impact what type of groups are possible, the type of replication supported, and other features.

Domain Name Service (DNS) A naming system used to translate hostnames to IP addresses and to locate resources on a TCP/IP-based network.

driver signing All drivers from Microsoft and approved vendors are signed. A signed driver is one whose integrity is verified by Microsoft and digitally approved for installation. Windows Server 2003 can be configured to refuse to install any unsigned drivers.

dynamic disk A dynamic disk is divided into volumes instead of partitions. A clean install of Windows Server 2003 will create a basic disk, and any additional disks can be added as basic or dynamic disks. After the initial installation, the basic disk can be converted to a dynamic disk. Dynamic disks cannot be accessed by DOS.

E

Effective Permissions A tool that looks at a user's permissions and the permissions of the groups of which the user is a member to calculate the effective permissions for an object in Active Directory.

Emergency Repair Disk (ERD) A disk that can be used to repair a failed system; it is no longer available in Windows Server 2003.

Encrypting File System (EFS) A file system supported by Windows Server 2003 that provides the encryption of data stored on NTFS volumes.

event ID A field in every Event Log entry that can be used to identify the event type. This ID number can be used to aid in troubleshooting server problems.

Event Viewer A utility built in to Windows Server 2003 that is used to view and manage the various logs of Windows Server 2003.

extended partition Can be created only on a basic disk, and you can create a theoretically unlimited number of logical drives inside that partition.

F

FAT A file system originally developed for use with DOS. FAT does not include support for security or enhanced partition features such as compression.

FAT32 First introduced with Windows 95 OEM Service Release 2 (OSR2), FAT32 includes support for larger partitions, up to 32GB in Windows Server 2003.

fault tolerant Describes a system that's able to keep operating, even when a component has failed.

File Groups Defines the files that should or should not be blocked, and any exclusions to the blocking.

File Screen Allows you to prevent users from saving blocked file types to your servers. Similar to quotas, you can configure file screening to either block users from saving certain types of files, let them save them and notify you that they were saved, or a combination of both.

file screen exception A file screen that is used to override the screening for a folder and its subfolders.

file share   A folder that is visible to other computers over the network. Access to the share is controlled by share permissions.

File Signature Verification   A tool that inspects the files in a location you specify and tells you whether they are unsigned.

folder redirection   Allows the administrator to redirect the folders that are part of the user profile to a file share, typically on a server. When this user data is stored on a server, the user can access it from any workstation that user logs on to.

G–H

Gpresult   A command-line tool that allows you to display the Group Policy settings and the Resultant Set of Policy (RSoP) for a computer or user.

group policies   Used to manage computers, users, and resources. Group Policies can be assigned at the domain, OU, or site level.

group policy filtering   Works by applying permissions on the GPO so that it can be used only by certain users, computers, or groups. For a Group Policy to be applied to an object, that object must have at least Read permissions for the GPO.

group policy inheritance   Group Policy in Windows 2003 works according to the hierarchy of site → domain → OU, or *SDOU* for short. The Active Directory objects lower in the hierarchy inherit the settings from those higher in the hierarchy.

Group Policy Management Console (GPMC)   A GUI-based MMC that allows you to manage your GPOs in a more intuitive manner.

Group Policy Object   Applied by creating an object that contains the settings that control the users and computers access to network and machine resources. This *Group Policy Object* (GPO) is created from templates that are stored on the workstation or server.

hard limit   In disk quotas, when a hard limit is reached, a warning is issued, and the user is no longer allowed to save files.

Hardware Compatibility List (HCL)   A list of hardware devices supported by Windows. A version of the HCL is found on the Windows Server 2003 distribution CD, but a website version is updated regularly at www.microsoft.com/hwdq/hcl/.

Hardware Troubleshooter   An online aid used to help diagnose problems with device drivers and hardware.

I–K

incremental backup   Used to back up only the files and folders that have been created or modified since the last normal or incremental backup. It reads the archive bit to determine which files need to be backed up. It then changes the archive bit of these backed-up files so that the next time the backup program is run, these files will not be backed up again unless they are changed.

input/output (I/O) port   An I/O port is a channel through which data is transferred between a device and the CPU. It acts like an area of memory that can be read from and written to by the device and the CPU.

instance   The terminology used to refer to multiple occurrences of the same type of object, such as in a multiprocessor server, in System Monitor. A separate instance exists for each processor.

Internet Information Services (IIS)   A full-featured web-hosting platform for building web pages through true distributed, dynamic websites.

interrupt request (IRQ)   An IRQ line is a hardware channel line over which a device can interrupt the CPU for service. Some devices can share an IRQ line; others must have a dedicated IRQ.

L

Last Known Good Configuration   A startup option that allows you to restore the system to the state it was in at the time of the last logon.

LDAP   LDAP stands for *Lightweight Directory Access Protocol* and is an industry-standard protocol for accessing directories and the primary access control protocol for Active Directory.

LDAP Data Interchange Format (LDIF)   A definition of how data can be exchanged between LDAP-based directories.

Ldifde   Ldifde is short for *LDIF Directory Exchange*. The ldifde utility can be used to import, export, modify, and delete records in an LDAP-based directory.

Licensing   A Windows Server 2003 utility used to configure and manage the license of Windows Server 2003 and installed applications.

load balancing   This feature allows you to setup a group of servers running identical applications. All of the servers share a virtual address, so the user will be connected to any server that's available. If a server is removed from the load-balanced group, either for maintenance or because of a failure, the incoming connections are rebalanced over the remaining servers in the group.

Local Policies   Local Computer Policies are used to control the security of the local computer. The policies that will affect the local computer and its users are stored in the `\%systemroot%\system32\GroupPolicy` folder.

Local Users and Groups   The MMC snap-in used to create and manage local users and groups on workstations and member servers.

M–N

managed computer   A computer that is managed by the administrator through restrictive profiles and Group Policies.

Master Boot Record (MBR)   Contains a pointer to the location of the active partition on the hard drive, as well as the code needed to begin the startup process.

member server   Any server that is a member of a domain that is not a domain controller.

MMC   The Microsoft Management Console (MMC) is the de facto tool for administering anything and everything in Windows Server 2003. The MMC itself does none of the administration; it is simply a shell into which administration tools called *snap-ins* can be added, modified, and removed.

Microsoft Update   Used to keep your Windows system and selected components up-to-date by connecting to the Microsoft Update website over the Internet and automatically downloading and installing security fixes, critical updates, and new drivers.

mirrored volume   A fault-tolerant disk configuration in which data is written to two hard disks, rather than one, so that if one disk fails, the data remains accessible.

nested group   When a group is a member of another group. Nested groups are allowed only at the Windows 2000 native and the Windows Server 2003 domain functionality levels.

NT File System (NTFS)   The preferred file system of Windows 2003, NTFS supports file-level security, encryption, compression, auditing, and more.

network attached printer   A printer that is not physically attached to a print server. Usually connected to the network via an Ethernet interface.

O

OnNow Device Power Management   The intent of the OnNow Device Power Management initiative is to allow users to start their computers by simply touching any key on the computer's keyboard.

Organizational Unit (OU)   A container in Active Directory that can be used to hold users, groups, and resources. Group Policy is assigned via OUs.

P–Q

partition   Allows you to subdivide your physical disk into separate logical units of storage.

performance   The measurement of how efficiently a system runs.

permissions   Used to control access, and the type of access granted, to a resource.

Plug and Play   A technology that allows an operating system to recognize a device, install the correct driver, and enable the device automatically.

policy   A component that automatically configures user settings.

primary partition   Can be used to store a boot record so that you can boot your server from that partition. A hard disk can be configured with one or more (up to four) primary partitions. Primary partitions are used only on basic disks.

print device   The piece of hardware that most people refer to as a *printer*.

print driver   The software that enables the operating system to communicate with the printing device. The role of the print driver is to accept commands from the operating system and translate them into commands that the print device will understand.

print filters   Can be used to group printers according to various criteria so that they can be found and managed easily.

Print Management Console A print console, first introduced in release R2, that allows you to manage all printers in your organization from a single console.

print queue The contents of the spool file. Users have the ability to view the print queue by using the Print Manager applet.

print server Manages the printer driver settings for all printers connected to it.

print spooler Also known as the *spool file*, the print spooler is a service on the print server that manages the data to be printed. This service also contains the print data and the print device–specific commands needed to format the printed output.

Printer Pool A form of load balancing in that two or more print devices are represented by a single printer. When a print device finishes a print job, it receives the next job in the queue. You never have multiple jobs waiting for a specific printer while another printer is idle.

printer priority Used to set the default importance of the print jobs in the queue. Priority can be set from 1 to 99. The job assigned the higher numerical number is printed first.

quota The amount of disk space allotted to a user. It can be defined in any increment from kilobytes to terabytes. Quotas can be applied to either new or existing volumes or folders.

quota limit Quota limits can be either Hard or Soft. A hard quota will prevent the user from saving any more files. A soft quota will warn users, but will let them continue to save files. The soft quotas are typically used for space monitoring purposes.

quota template Similar to a group policy for quotas. After it is configured, it can be applied to multiple machines.

R

RAID-0 RAID-0 volumes write data anywhere from 2 to 32 physical disks in 64KB sequential stripes. The first stripe is written to the first disk, the second stripe is written to the second disk, and so forth. RAID-0 provides no fault tolerance. The advantage provided by RAID-0 lies in the overall disk I/O performance increase of the computer as the total disk I/O is split among all the disks in the volume.

RAID-1 RAID-1, also known as a *mirrored volume*, provides fault-tolerant data storage using two physical disks. Data is written simultaneously to each physical disk so that both contain identical information. If one of the drives in a mirrored volume fails, the system will continue to run using the other volume. The total volume capacity will be equal to that provided by one of the physical disks.

RAID-5 RAID-5 volumes are similar to striped volumes in that they use multiple disks, in this case from 3 to 32 physical disks of the same size. The total volume capacity will be equal to that provided by the number of physical disks minus one. Both data and parity information are written sequentially across each physical disk. For example, if you create a volume using four 1GB disks, your usable storage would be 3GB because 1GB is devoted to storing the parity information. The parity information from the set is used to rebuild the set should one disk fail, thus providing fault tolerance. RAID-5 volumes in Windows Server 2003 cannot sustain the loss of more than one disk in the set while still providing fault tolerance.

Recovery Console A command-line control system used in system recovery in the event of a failure of a core system component or driver. Through the Recovery Console, you can use simple commands to restore the operating system to a functional state.

recovery key Used to recover the contents of an encrypted file or folder when a user's private key is lost or corrupted.

Remote Assistance You can use Remote Assistance to grant a remote user the ability to observe your desktop as you are working. You can exchange messages via a chat session, or you can talk to each other if you both have the required sound cards and microphones. You can even grant a remote user the ability to take over your desktop to make changes and run programs.

remote control The process of taking control of a user session or console on a remote computer.

Remote Desktop for Administration With Windows Server 2003 Terminal Services in Remote Desktop for Administration mode, you are allowed two concurrent sessions, plus a console session to the Windows server. These sessions can be used to remotely access any programs or data on the server.

Remote Desktop Protocol (RDP) This protocol provides communication between the server running Terminal Services and the RDP client software. RDP runs only on TCP/IP.

Remote Installation Services (RIS) RIS can be used to automate the installation of Windows 2000 or later operating systems.

resource settings The mechanism by which a device can communicate with other hardware or the operating system.

Restricted Groups A feature that allows an administrator to control the membership of the local groups on workstations and member servers. The administrator is able to control the membership in the group by specifying the members of the group in the GPO. Any additional members that may have been added to the group are removed during the group policy refresh.

S

Safe Mode A startup option that starts Windows Server 2003 with the basic drivers for the mouse, video, monitor, mass storage, and keyboard.

SDOU Group Policy inheritance in Windows 2003 works according to the hierarchy of site → domain → OU, or *SDOU*.

Secure Sockets Layer (SSL) SSL is used with HTTP to encrypt all traffic between the browser and the web server.

Security Configuration and Analysis A tool that compares the security settings of a computer to those of a template, shows the results, and resolves any discrepancies that were revealed by the analysis. The tool allows you to perform comparisons with either the standard templates, or custom templates that you have created.

security descriptor The access-control information that is assigned to every object.

Security log   The log in Event Viewer that contains events relating to security and auditing.

Session Directory   A service that creates a database on a server that contains a record of the current sessions being hosted by a load-balanced cluster of Windows Server 2003 Terminal Servers. This database indexes the sessions by username instead of IP address. The username is used to look up the location of a disconnected session when the user is trying to log on to the Terminal Services server again. After it is determined which server is hosting the session that the user was disconnected from, his or her logon is routed to that server.

simple volume   The equivalent of a partition on a basic disk.

soft limit   In disk quotas, when a soft limit is reached, a warning is issued, but the user is still allowed to save files.

Software Update Service (SUS)   SUS is a service installed on an internal Windows 2000 or Windows Server 2003 server that can download all critical updates as they are posted to Windows Update. The client computers and servers can be configured through Group Policy or the Registry to contact the internal SUS server for updates, instead of going out over the Internet to the Microsoft servers. SUS is basically an internal version of the Windows Update service, with the exception that the network administrator has the option to control which updates get downloaded from Microsoft and which ones get installed on the computers in the environment. Microsoft is withdrawing all support on December 6, 2006. SUS has been replaced by Windows Server Update Services (WSUS).

spanned volume   A spanned volume takes various amounts of disk space from 2 to 32 physical disks to create one large volume. Spanned volumes provide no fault tolerance; they can be more prone to failure than other types of volumes because if any one disk should fail, the entire set is lost. The advantage of a spanned volume is that you can quickly add more storage space.

standalone server   A server that is not a member of a domain. It can be the only machine used, or it can be part of a Workgroup to provide distributed storage of files and printers.

striped volume   A striped volume writes data to 2 to 32 physical disks in 64KB sequential stripes. The first stripe is written to the first disk, the second stripe is written to the second disk, and so forth. Striped volumes, also known as *RAID-0*, provide no fault tolerance. The advantage provided by using a striped volume lies in the overall disk I/O performance increase of the computer because the total disk I/O is split among all the disks in the volume.

System File Checker   The System File Checker (`SFC.EXE`) is used to verify that the protected system files have not been overwritten.

System Monitor   Used to track the performance of your Windows Server 2003 server.

system partition   On an Intel-based system, the system partition contains the `BOOT.INI`, `NTDETECT.COM`, and `NTLDR` files. These files tell the server how to start the operating system. The system partition is also known as the *active partition*.

system state   A collection of data that contains the operating system configuration of the server.

T

Terminal Services   Windows Server 2003 includes Terminal Services, which allows thin clients to be employed as network clients. Terminal Services grants remote access to applications and offers limitation controls over application access.

Transmission Control Protocol/Internet Protocol (TCP/IP)   The most popular protocol suite in use today, TCP/IP was originally based on the network protocols developed by the Department of Defense. TCP/IP is the protocol used on the Internet.

trigger   An event used to generate an alert.

U

uninterruptible power supply (UPS)   A device used to protect computers and other electronic equipment from power loss, surges, spikes, and brownouts. A UPS uses batteries to ensure that a device can continue operating briefly during a power loss.

user profile   The file where the settings for a user's work environment are. This file is automatically created the first time a user logs on to a computer running any version of Windows, and any changes to the environment (Favorites, Start menu items, icons, colors, My Documents, local settings) are saved when the user logs off. The profile is reloaded when the user logs on again.

user rights   The actions that the user of a particular account is permitted to perform on a system.

user template   A preconfigured account that is saved with various characteristics. This account is copied whenever another user account with the same characteristics needs to be created.

V–Z

virtual private network (VPN)   An extension of a network that can be accessed securely through a public network such as the Internet.

Web Service Extensions   The EXE and DLL files required for the specific function that is enabled. For example, for Active Server Pages to be used, the `asp.dll` file must be enabled. To get a list of the files required for each Web Service Extension, in the IIS Manager MMC, highlight the desired extension and click the Properties button.

Windows File Protection (WFP)   WFP runs in the background and is alerted whenever a file in a protected folder is changed. It determines whether the new version of the file is signed. If it isn't, Windows File Protection automatically rolls back the file to the version kept in the `%systemroot%\system32\dllcache` folder.

Windows Internet Naming Service (WINS)   A service that dynamically maps IP addresses to NetBIOS computer names used by Microsoft operating systems other than Windows Server 2003.

Windows Server 2003 Readiness Analyzer   A utility that can be run on a server to check the software and hardware components for compatibility with Windows Server 2003.

Windows Server Update Services (WSUS)
WSUS is a service installed on an internal Windows 2000 or Windows Server 2003 server that can download all critical updates as they are posted to Microsoft Update. The client computers and servers can be configured through Group Policy or the Registry to contact the internal WSUS server for updates, instead of going out over the Internet to the Microsoft servers. WSUS is basically an internal version of the Microsoft Update service, with the exception that the network administrator has the option to control which updates get downloaded from Microsoft and which ones get installed on the computers in the environment. WSUS is a replacement for the discontinued Software Update Service (SUS).

Windows Update   A Microsoft website (http://windowsupdate.microsoft.com/) that provides an automated source of operating system fixes, security patches, and updated drivers. Mostly superseded by Microsoft Update.

Index

E

H

M

N

How can we make this index more useful? Email us at indexes@quepublishing.com

Q

U

UNC (Universal Naming Convention) paths, 107

uninstalling hardware device drivers, 681-682

universal groups, 130-133

Universal Naming Convention (UNC) paths, 96

Unix Printing service, 276

Update Quotas Derived from Template dialog box, 575

Update Sequence Number (USN), 801

updating

Active Directory, 74

device drivers, 657-658

disk quotas, 575

software

Microsoft Update, 826

WSUS, 827-833, 836-844

SUS (Software Update Service)

synchronizing, 846

update approval, 847

WSUS (Windows Server Software Update Services), fast facts, 876

upgrading hardware device drivers, troubleshooting, 679-682

URLs (Uniform Resource Locators), Event Logs, 709

Use Automatic Settings check box, 668, 678

user accounts, 61-62

adding to groups

ADUC console, 145-146

automation, 146-147

addresses, 75

assigning, 61

automation, 82

command-line tools, 82

dsadd command-line tools, 82-86

dsget command-line tools, 86-88

dsmod command-line tools, 88

dsmove command-line tool, 89-90

dsquery command-line tool, 88-89

dsrm command-line tool, 90

importing/exporting, 91

Net User command-line tool, 86

connections, 79

creating, 61

ADUC, 71-72

dsadd command-line tool, 82, 84-86

customizing, 88

deleting, 90

disabling, 73

domain, 65, 70-73. *See also* domain controllers

domain controller built-in, 70

environment, 78

groups, 126

automation, 149-150

creating with ADUC console, 138-141

default, 134-137

distribution, 129

domain functional levels, 127-128

domain local, 131

domain membership, 148-149

forest functional levels, 128-129

global, 132

local, 131

membership, 144-145

nesting, 131

policies, 76

scope, 129-130, 142-143

security, 129

sequence, 133-134

system, 137-138

types, 129

universal, 132-133

users, adding, 151-152

home folders, 76

local, 62-64

local computers, 147

logons, 75

moving, 89-90

multiple, 107

X - Y - Z

EXAM✓CRAM

MCSE titles from Exam Cram

Prepare for the MCSE, MCSA, and other Microsoft Certifications with Exam Cram

Exam Cram has the resources you are looking for to prepare for your MCSE certification. These proven and popular Exam Cram series match the different learning needs of different certification candidates, providing expert authors, proven practice tools, and valuable learning and exam readiness feedback. Look to Exam Cram for

MCSE Titles

ISBN	TITLE
0-7897-3617-9	MCSA/MCSE 70-290 Exam Cram
0-7897-3648-9	MCSA/MCSE 70-290 Exam Prep
0-7897-3618-7	MCSA/MCSE 70-291 Exam Cram
0-7897-3649-7	MCSA/MCSE 70-291 Exam Prep
0-7897-3619-5	MCSE 70-293 Exam Cram
0-7897-3650-0	MCSE 70-293 Exam Prep
0-7897-3620-9	MCSE 70-294 Exam Cram
0-7897-3651-9	MCSE 70-294 Exam Prep
0-7897-3360-9	MCSA/MCSE 70-270 Exam Cram
0-7897-3363-3	MCSA/MCSE 70-270 Exam Prep

EXAM✓CRAM

QUICK Exam Crams provide strong foundational knowledge review, test-taking tips, exam practice, and readiness feedback. Exam Crams provide you with a succinct way to hone your knowledge for test day to ensure you maximize your score.

EXAM✓PREP

COMPREHENSIVE
Exam Preps are the whole package. You get in-depth tutorial learning on the test topics, practice testing on both individual test sections as well as simulating the complete exam, test-taking strategies, and feedback on areas requiring further preparation.

Visit www.examcram.com for more information on these and other Exam Cram products.

BOOK IS SAFARI ENABLED

CLUDES FREE 45-DAY ACCESS TO THE ONLINE EDITION

The Safari® Enabled icon on the cover of your favorite technology book means the book is available through Safari Bookshelf. When you buy this book, you get free access to the online edition for 45 days.

Safari Bookshelf is an electronic reference library that lets you easily search thousands of technical books, find code samples, download chapters, and access technical information whenever and wherever you need it.

TO GAIN 45-DAY SAFARI ENABLED ACCESS TO THIS BOOK:

- Go to **www.examcram.com/safarienabled**

- Complete the brief registration form

- Enter the coupon code found in the front of this book on the "Copyright" page

If you have difficulty registering on Safari Bookshelf or accessing the online edition, please e-mail customer-service@safaribooksonline.com.